Wanda Smith
91 Concord Ave
White Plains,
N.Y. 10606

-0169

28, 1988

IDMS/R SYSTEMS

DESK REFERENCE

IDMS/R SYSTEMS
DESK REFERENCE

SRS Network, Inc.
330 7th Ave., NY, NY 10001-5010

Robert W. Husband
Terence J. McHenry
Judith C. Wooten

Judith Christison Wooten, Editor
Linda Taylor, Ph.D., Associate Editor

A Wiley-Interscience Publication
JOHN WILEY & SONS
New York   Chichester   Brisbane   Toronto   Singapore

Library of Congress Cataloging in Publication Data

Husband, Robert W.
  IDMS/R systems desk reference

  Bibliography:p.
  1. IDMS/R (Computer system) I. McHenry, Terence J.
II. Wooten, Judith Christison. III. Taylor, Linda L.
IV. SRS Network, Inc. (New York, N.Y.) V. Title.
QA76.9.D3H876 1987   005.4'3   87-10696
ISBN 0-471-85236-8

Printed in the United States of America

10 9 8 7 6 5 4 3 2

To the memory of Robert W. Husband Sr.

Preface

Problem: Your site has just acquired IDMS/R® (Integrated Database Management System/Relational) and you need to know how to perform the various tasks required for a viable and efficient system. In the beginning everything is unfamiliar, and, as is usual in most data processing environments, users clamor for everything to be done immediately. Although Cullinet® software has traditionally been easy to use and Cullinet offers excellent training and support, the first few weeks of IDMS/R use can be confusing in terms of organizing your approach to the problem.

If you are the person responsible for implementing and supporting IDMS/R, just trying to figure out where to start can be discouraging. There is no shortage of Cullinet manuals and courses, covering detail after detail. The sheer number of manuals (more than one hundred) and courses (dozens) is part of the problem. Where do you start? Which books will tell you what you need to know to perform a certain task? When will you find the time to attend all those courses?

Solution: In the *IDMS/R Systems Desk Reference* we provide a step-by-step guide to implementing a new IDMS/R environment from installation through generation of multiple systems. If your site already has IDMS/R, this book will help you understand what has been done to establish your system and how to improve it. It is especially valuable if you are new to the job or new to IDMS/R.

During the preparation of this book, we concentrated on the system implementation and support functions of IDMS/R. The main topics covered are:

- Choosing Central Version or local mode operating environment for batch program execution,
- Selecting security facilities appropriate for the installation,
- Implementing backup and recovery procedures,
- Creating separate test and production systems, each tailored to different processing requirements,
- Maintaining the systems,

®IDMS/R is a registered trademark of Cullinet Software, Inc.
®Cullinet is a registered trademark of Cullinet Software, Inc.

•Trouble shooting system problems, and

•Tuning the systems to achieve maximum performance.

Database and application design decisions are not the main thrust of this book. Only those aspects of database and application design relating to security, backup, recovery, maintenance, and performance tuning are discussed.

The book is aimed primarily at persons managing an IDMS/R database(s) or its system support functions for the first time. This audience includes Database Administrators (DBA's), Data Communications Administrators (DCA's), and Data Administrators (DA's) who have no previous exposure to IDMS/R and those at installations which have just acquired IDMS/R. However, most portions of the book are suitable for anyone working with IDMS/R. Upper-level management personnel and consultants working with installations which have recently acquired IDMS/R, or who are considering it, will also benefit from the information contained in the text.

This manual in not intended as a comprehensive treatment of IDMS/R. It is meant to serve as a source of readily accessible, usable information for the DBA about to confront an unfamiliar situation. The guidelines suggested are based on practical experience with a wide variety of clients. These suggestions represent a single approach; alternative methods may be equally effective.

Heretofore, information contained in this book was scattered throughout the many Cullinet manuals for IDMS/R or could be obtained only through experience, and was rarely distilled into a single conceptual and functional framework. The impetus for this book was the realization that most clients suffer in similar problem areas. As consultants we were asked repeatedly about topics with which clients were unfamiliar or topics such as security which crossover Cullinet's product lines (most of Cullinet's classes and technical manuals are organized by product line). In addition, we noticed great demand throughout our client base for practical implementation suggestions as well as for information on the pros and cons of various system features and alternative system support strategies. The effort to write a book that would help meet these needs began at SRS Network, Inc., of New York. We at SRS came to realize the value of a single book addressing the entire dynamics of IDMS/R system implementation and support functions. The personnel of SRS has drawn on their wealth of practical experience with IDMS/R in a wide variety of settings to produce a text in response to known areas of need in the user community.

Throughout this book you will see references to Release 10 of IDMS/R and Release 5.7 of IDMS. Most system support functions have remained unchanged from one release to the other. However, some of the Release 10 features alter the ways in which system support functions are implemented. When such is the case, both the Release 5.7 and Release 10 methods will be discussed as an aid to those still using Release 5.7 and as a guide to those changing from Release 5.7 to Release 10. Because IDMS/R continues to evolve, you may wish to obtain current Cullinet manuals to check for any recent changes.

Bob Husband
Judy Wooten
Terry McHenry

Acknowledgments

In any major endeavor there are always many people involved whose counsel and effort were instrumental in getting the project off the ground. While there are too many people to thank individually, we particularly want to extend our gratitude to Amy Isaacs and Gerald Foley Jr. of SRS for their expert help in verification of the detailed technical points covered in the book. Amy Isaacs provided valuable advice and suggestions while reviewing Chapters 2, 4, 12, and 13. Gerald Foley Jr. contributed information on maintaining databases and provided excellent suggestions while reviewing chapters 3 and 11. We want to thank Tom Gougherty for contributing information on multiple dictionaries and reviewing chapters of the book. We extend our thanks to Thomson McKinnon Securities Inc. of New York City for generously sharing their naming standards, used as samples in Chapter 4.

We also want to thank Linda Taylor, Ph.D., for her many hours of superb editing. Linda Taylor was responsible for minimizing "computerese" and ensuring consistency of form.

Lastly, we want to thank the partners of SRS, Cliff Samara and Tom Sheridan. Their financial and moral support during difficult development periods made this book possible.

Contents

List of Figures

List of Tables

IDMS/R SYSTEMS

DESK REFERENCE

Introduction to IDMS/R System Implementation and Support

1.1 THE IDMS/R SYSTEM IMPLEMENTATION AND SUPPORT PROBLEM

Your organization has chosen IDMS/R (Integrated Database Management System/Relational), a product of Cullinet Software, Inc., to manage its data resources. IDMS/R is a powerful tool which requires sophisticated implementation and support to achieve maximum system performance. The job of implementing and supporting IDMS/R can be very confusing to personnel at new installations and to new personnel at existing sites. Several steps are required in the correct sequence to create test and production systems. Once systems are operational, statistics should be monitored and parameter choices fine tuned to improve efficiency. Changes to databases, programs, and systems need to be incorporated smoothly into the environment.

If you are the person responsible for implementing a new IDMS/R environment, you are faced with many complex and vital tasks which, it seems, must be finished yesterday. Where to start? What must be done to create an IDMS/R Database/Data Communications (DB/DC) system? What parameter values are appropriate for test and production systems? Which manuals contain information relevant to each implementation step?

If your organization already has IDMS/R Release 10, or earlier versions of IDMS® (Release 5.7 or earlier), you are faced with the tasks of maintaining and improving the environment. How can maintenance of the system be facilitated? Which statistics point out trouble areas in system performance? What techniques can improve system performance? Where can you find help quickly when you need it?

1.2   THE DESK REFERENCE SOLUTION

This *IDMS/R Systems Desk Reference* provides a step by step guide to implementing a new IDMS/R environment from installation through generation of test and production DB/DC systems. For sites where IDMS/R has been in use for some time, the *IDMS/R Systems Desk Reference* is a valuable guide to understanding and improving your systems.

This book is not intended as a comprehensive treatment of IDMS/R. It is meant to serve as a source of readily accessible, useful information for the DBA about to confront an unfamiliar situation. The guidelines we suggest are based on practical experience at a wide variety of client sites and provide insights into how other sites have fulfilled needs that may exist at your site. These suggestions represent only a few approaches; alternative methods may be equally effective. What we offer in this book is guidance, rather than 'gospel' or the absolute and sole solution to all problems. Because we cannot anticipate the precise problems or requirements of your site, the advice and recommendations contained herein should not be taken verbatim, but must be tailored to your installation's unique processing environment.

In this book we concentrate on the implementation and support functions of IDMS/R systems. An overview is provided on each topic, critical areas are highlighted, and specific recommendations are offered for setting up efficient, maintainable systems. No attempt is made to be exhaustive in every detail; there are dozens of technical manuals which do that. Suggestions for further reading are inserted throughout and summarized at the end of each chapter.

Aspects of application and database design relating to security, backup, recovery, maintenance, and performance tuning are discussed. The primary focus of this book, however, is not logical and physical database design. Database design is so broad a topic that it deserves an entire volume.

The main thrust of this book is implementation of IDMS/R systems. This book is organized by subject, in contrast to existing technical manuals which are organized by product. Technical manuals present information from a particular product's point of view; to learn about security, one would have to read the manuals on each of the products. This book presents information by implementation subject; to learn about security, read one chapter which describes the security facilities of all major products and how they interrelate.

1.3 INTRODUCTION TO SYSTEM IMPLEMENTA-TION AND SUPPORT FUNCTIONS

An IDMS/R installation is a complex highly interrelated environment which requires sophisticated support. Some understanding of the environment is necessary to make informed system implementation decisions. Figure 1-1 illustrates the IDMS/R multiple system environment.

The IDMS/R environment has a minimum of two systems, test and production; often more systems are in concurrent use. The production system manages the processing of operational production data, whereas the test system is used for development of new databases and applications. Systems may reside on the same or different CPU's. Each system has one or more dictionaries, one or more databases, and many online and batch applications. Data Dictionaries (DD's) contain definitions of database structures, system configurations, and application documentation. Databases (DB's)

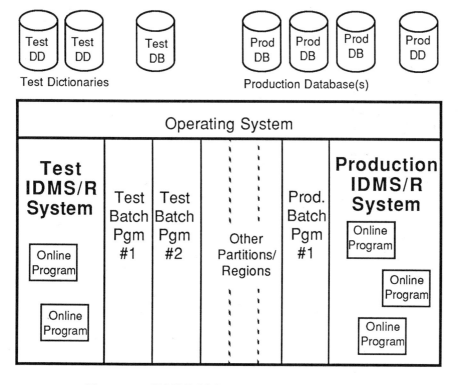

Figure 1-1 IDMS/R Multiple Systems Environment

contain the organization's operating and testing data. Online and batch programs may access database records concurrently.

Because creating a system involves choosing values for a large number of parameters, there is an almost infinite variety of ways a given system could be configured. The challenge is to achieve the best possible performance and still provide the protection and control necessary for valuable production databases and dictionaries. Several different tasks have to be accomplished, many of them all at once. A partial list includes:

- Establishing standards,
- Installing IDMS/R with appropriate parameter selection,
- Creating test systems at intervals,
- Creating production systems,
- Securing the systems,
- Providing backup and recovery procedures,
- Setting up procedures for program execution,
- Setting up procedures for migration of programs/systems from test to production,
- Handling changes to the environment,
- Monitoring database system statistics,
- Tuning the systems, and
- Trouble shooting system problems.

1.4 THE STRUCTURE OF THE BOOK AND A RECOMMENDED READING STRATEGY

A certain degree of familiarity is required to understand the steps of implementing a stable, efficient, and secure environment with multiple IDMS/R systems. Ideally, you could press this book against your forehead and instantly absorb the overall picture. Then on reading the specific details of installation, system generation, and tuning, you would understand how it all fits together. We have organized this book in two sections because it is impossible to instantly absorb its contents. Section One covers important considerations that impact every step of implementing multiple IDMS/R systems. Section Two covers the specific details of implementing and supporting IDMS/R.

Section One contains information on several important concepts and topics that one should consider before creating any systems. Figure 1-2 summarizes the topics covered in Section One. The need for multiple DB/DC systems and their use in the development cycle is examined. The role of the Integrated Data Dictionary and the uses for

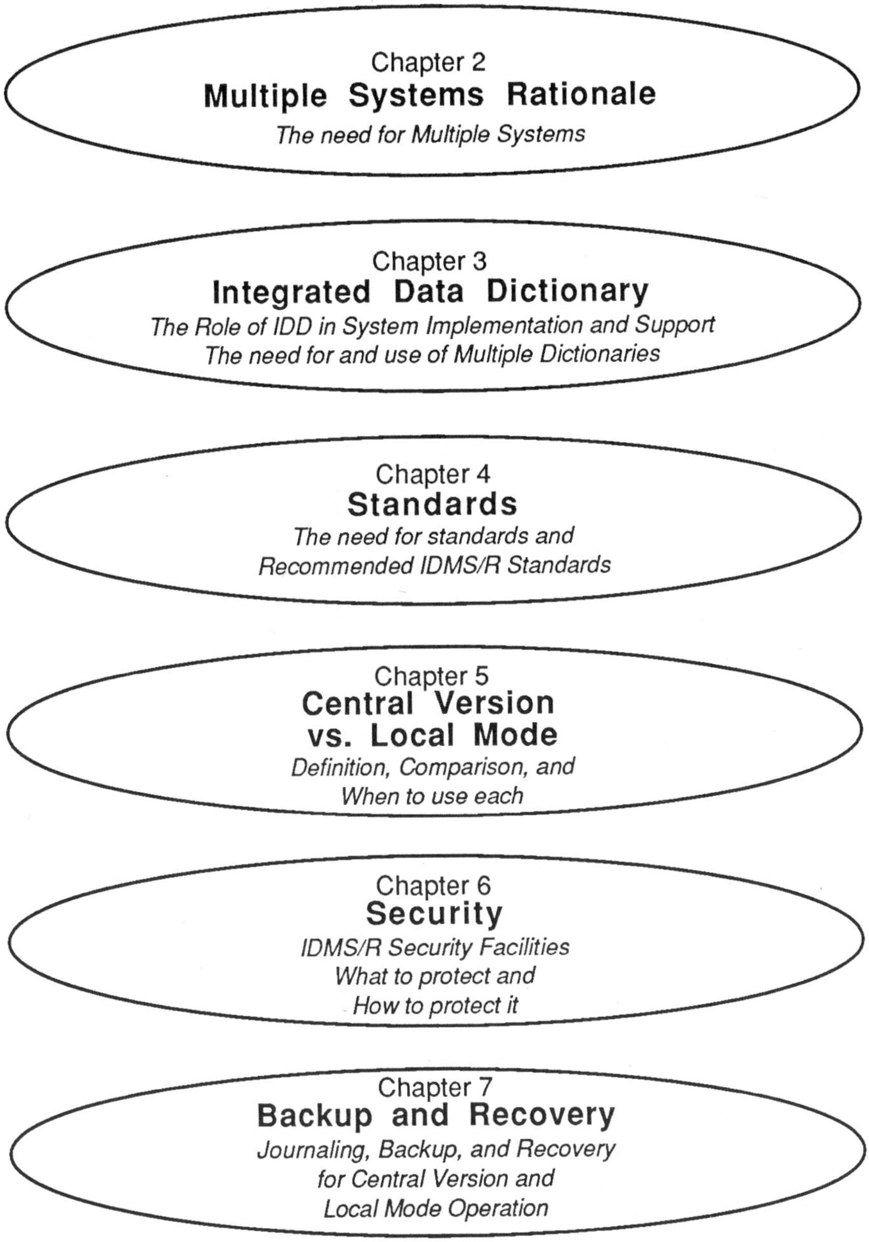

Chapter 2
Multiple Systems Rationale
The need for Multiple Systems

Chapter 3
Integrated Data Dictionary
The Role of IDD in System Implementation and Support
The need for and use of Multiple Dictionaries

Chapter 4
Standards
The need for standards and
Recommended IDMS/R Standards

Chapter 5
Central Version
vs. Local Mode
Definition, Comparison, and
When to use each

Chapter 6
Security
IDMS/R Security Facilities
What to protect and
How to protect it

Chapter 7
Backup and Recovery
Journaling, Backup, and Recovery
for Central Version and
Local Mode Operation

Figure 1-2 Section One Topics

multiple dictionaries are discussed. The need for standards and some recommended standards for use with IDMS/R are presented. The two different modes of operation for IDMS/R, Central Version and local mode, are defined and compared. The general topic of security and the security facilities available in IDMS/R are detailed next. Finally, backup and recovery options for both Central Version and local mode operation are discussed.

On your first reading of Section One, we recommend concentrating on the overall concepts and skimming the implementation details. Rather than split up information on a given topic, each is covered in depth when presented in Section One. As these topics reappear in Section Two, you will be referred back to the appropriate chapter for background information relevant to the implementation recommendations.

In Section Two, the implementation and support of multiple IDMS/R systems are examined in a logical progression, beginning with installation of IDMS/R software and ending with performance tuning. Figure 1-3 outlines the steps involved. First, installation of IDMS/R is described. Test system creation is then covered, including recommendations for parameter values. Next, the special concerns and problems of production systems are addressed. Types of maintenance and how to ease the maintenance burden are discussed. Finally, techniques for trouble shooting IDMS/R problems and tuning the environment are covered.

Appendix A contains sample listings referenced throughout the book. IDMS/R acronyms and abbreviations, a glossary of IDMS/R terms, and an index appear at the end of the book.

1.5   WHAT IS AN IDMS/R SYSTEM?

When we discuss an IDMS/R system we are referring to a system capable of handling multiple concurrent database access from both online and batch programs. The general term for this kind of system is a Database/Data Communications (DB/DC) system. In the IDMS/R world, there are two main types of DB/DC systems:

- CV/DC systems (Central Version/Data Communications), and
- CV/UCF systems (Central Version/Universal Communications Facility).

The first part of each system name, Central Version, means that there will be one central Database Management program (IDMS-CV) managing concurrent database access from several programs. Both

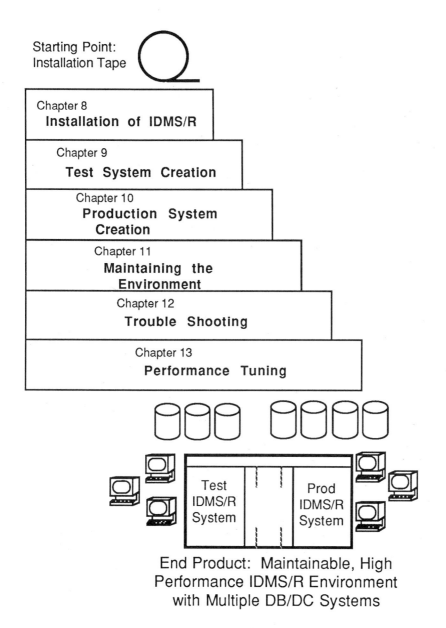

Figure 1-3 Steps to Implement and Support Multiple IDMS/R Systems

kinds of systems use the Central Version of IDMS/R database management logic. The second part of each name identifies how data communications are handled in the system. The difference between a CV/DC system and a CV/UCF system lies in the handling of online terminals. In a CV/DC system (Figure 1-4), IDMS-DC is the tele-processing (TP) monitor managing and communicating directly with the online terminals. When some other TP monitor, CICS for example, manages the online terminals (Figure 1-5), the Universal Communications Facility is used to pass input and output messages between the external TP monitor and IDMS/R CV.

1.6   HOW MANY IDMS/R SYSTEMS ARE IMPLEMENTED?

IDMS/R installations implement several IDMS/R systems. Four systems often used during application development are: Test, Quality Assurance, Production, and Production Maintenance. New applications and databases are developed on a test IDMS/R system. Some shops require that a new application be turned over to a separate group for quality assurance or user acceptance testing before putting it into production use; quality assurance groups often employ a separate system for their testing activities. Occasionally, production programs need emergency fixes. A separate production maintenance system is useful for testing emergency fixes. These and some additional IDMS/R systems are described in Chapter 2.

1.7   WHAT IS THE IDMS/R PRODUCT LINE?

Cullinet's integrated line of database and data communications software products are powerful tools for the management and manipulation of databases. Both system and application software are available. We are concerned here with system software, serving general system functions or application-development functions. Table 1-1 contains a listing of the major system software products and their primary orientation. These products work together to provide integrated database/data communications systems. A brief description of the major products follows.

IDMS/R
Integrated Database Management System/Relational manages all access to both network and relational databases. It is a powerful, high performance database management system (DBMS) capable of processing high volume, complex applications in both batch and online

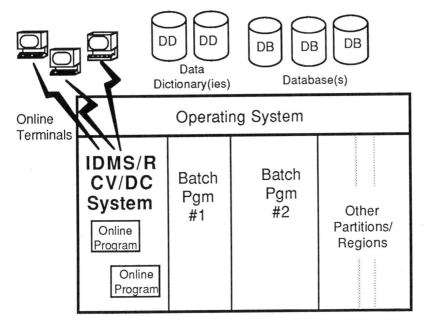

Figure 1-4 IDMS/R-CV/DC System

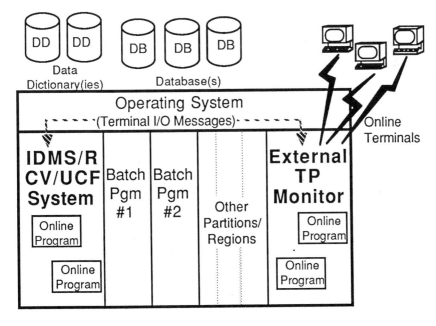

Figure 1-5 IDMS/R-CV/UCF System

Table 1-1 Major IDMS/R System Software Products

System-Related Products	Application Development-Related Products
IDMS/R®	GOLDENGATE®
IDMS®-DC/UCF	ASF
IDD®	ADS/O®
IDMS/R Performance Monitor	OLM
ICMS®	OLQ®
	OLE®
	CULPRIT®

®IDMS/R, IDMS, GOLDENGATE, ADS/O, IDD, ICMS, OLQ, OLE, and CULPRIT are registered trademarks of Cullinet Software, Inc.

environments. It has excellent backup and recovery capabilities. IDMS/R may be run as a Central Version (CV) or in local mode (LM).

- *IDMS-CV*
  IDMS-CV (Central Version) is the facility which controls concurrent access to the databases, and allows multithreading of both update and retrieval tasks. CV can process online and batch database access requests concurrently. Abend detection, security facilities, and recovery are all provided by CV.
- *IDMS Local Mode*
  IDMS local mode provides dedicated service for a single batch program's access to the database. A program executing in local mode may perform any mixture of database retrieval and update requests.

IDMS-DC or UCF
The data communications function is handled by either IDMS-DC or the Universal Communications Facility. Both products allow online application programs to execute in the same partition/region as IDMS-CV, thus saving the overhead of interpartition/region communication for each database access request. Refer to Figures 1-4 and 1-5 for illustrations of the two data communications alternatives.

- *IDMS-DC*
  IDMS-DC (Integrated Database Management System-Data Communications) is the teleprocessing (TP) monitor available from Cullinet. The TP logic is incorporated with the database logic to provide efficient online access to the database.

•*UCF*
The Universal Communications Facility makes it possible for
users to access the database from terminals attached to teleprocessing monitors other than IDMS-DC and still have online application programs running in the IDMS partition/region.
Interpartition/region communication overhead occurs once per
terminal I/O for ADS/O and DC programs.   Interpartition/
region communication overhead occurs twice per database call
for native TP online programs.

IDD
The Integrated Data Dictionary is a combination of the database
structure which defines Cullinet's data dictionary (DD) and the software which manipulates it.   The DD is the central storage area for
definitions of the database and data communications environment.
The IDD is an active data dictionary; system software automatically
captures much of the information required to define and document the
data processing environment.   Other data is entered manually via
online or batch IDD compilers.
Information stored in the dictionary is available to all IDMS
software products.   Integration of the different products is achieved
through their common use of the DD.   For example, record and element definitions can be stored once on the data dictionary and then
used by all the products.

IDMS/R Performance Monitor
The IDMS/R Performance Monitor offers a wealth of valuable system
and application tuning information.   It provides several reports
analyzing CPU and memory utilization, database requests versus
I/O's, and program/dialog processing.   The Performance Monitor's
online facilities permit selective monitoring of programs and
dialogs.

ICMS
The Information Center Management System is the mainframe software used to control microcomputer access to IDMS/R databases.   It
communicates with Goldengate software in microcomputers.

GOLDENGATE
Goldengate is a set of microcomputer software designed to accept information from IDMS database records on a mainframe source by
connecting with the Information Center Management System.

ASF
Based solely on user designated fields, the Automatic System Facility automatically generates schema, subschema, and record definitions as well as online transactions to load and maintain relational records. The generated online transactions are ADS/O dialogs and may be modified using ADS/O facilities.

ADS/O
The Application Development System/OnLine is a fourth generation programming language allowing rapid development of online programs (known as "dialogs"). Development typically takes place online; however, ADSOBGEN permits development in batch. Many teleprocessing and database functions are handled automatically by the ADS/O run time system. As a result, creating ADS/O dialogs is more easily learned than either CICS or IDMS-DC programming, making it possible for programmers to generate code sooner and, in many cases, faster.

OLM
OnLine Mapping allows interactive specification of TP screen layouts known as maps. The programmer "paints" the screen layout on an online terminal. Edit criteria for the input data and translation tables also can be specified. Maps are used by DC programs and ADS/O dialogs.

OLQ
OnLine Query enables programmers and end users to display information from IDMS/R databases and dictionaries. Multiple records may be retrieved with a single command and displayed in report format on a CRT or printer.

In Release 10, there is a menu mode of operation, making OLQ easier for end users. In Release 5.7, users needed to know database structure and program-like database access syntax to use OLQ. It was primarily a programmer's debugging tool, for which it was and still is invaluable. Although OLQ 5.7 did not lend itself readily to queries by end users, predefined inquiries could be stored in the DD and executed by end users.

OLE
OnLine English permits the use of unstructured, English-like statements for retrieval of database records. It is a good decision support tool for *ad hoc* management inquiries. However, exercise caution when allowing the use of OLE with production databases; it is easy to

generate a request that will consume a tremendous amount of resources and slow down normal production processing.

CULPRIT

CULPRIT is a report generator used for easy retrieval of database and/or conventional file information. CULPRIT provides automatic report formatting, sorting, and totalling. A special subset of prewritten CULPRIT programs, the Dictionary/Directory Reporter (DDR), is dedicated to reporting on information stored in the Data Dictionary.

1.8 INSTALLED COMPONENTS OF THE IDMS/R ENVIRONMENT

The installed components of the IDMS/R environment are the file architecture and programs which make up the products. File architecture is the logical structure for several kinds of files, namely database, data dictionary, journal, and log files. Database files contain a site's data and the logical relationships of one record to another. Data dictionary files contain database definitions, DB/DC system configurations, and other information about the data processing environment. Contained in the journal files are records of data updates for use in backing up and recovering the databases. Log files contain an ongoing record of activity in the user's system.

Three basic categories of programs will also be installed, namely compilers, utilities, and run time programs. The compilers are listed below in Table 1-2. They are used to define, maintain, and document components of the DB/DC system. Each compiler has a component to which it is dedicated. By running these programs, additional information will be stored in the data dictionary; in many instances, object code modules will be created as well. Utilities listed in Table 1-3 are special purpose programs which deal with database modification, backup, recovery, and documentation.

Run time programs do the processing most people associate with the products. These are the programs executed to perform the primary functions of each product. For example, IDMS-CV run time programs access user databases and data dictionaries and serve as the interface between user application programs and user databases. IDMS-CV run time programs include database management logic, database I/O logic, and multiple program access logic.

Table 1-2 IDMS/R Compilers and Generators

Database-Related	Program-Related	System-Related
Schema Compiler	Mapping Compiler	DDDL Compiler
Subschema Compiler	DML Processor	System Gen. Compiler
DMCL Compiler	ADS/A Generator	
	ADS/G Generator	

Table 1-3 IDMS/R Utilities

Database Utilities	Backup & Recovery Utilities	Reporting Utilities
IDMSINIT	IDMSAJNL	IDMSRPTS
IDMSPFIX	IDMSJFIX	RHDCPRLG
IDMSXPAG	IDMSDUMP	IDMSDBAN
IDMSLDEL	IDMSRSTR	RHDCTJIN
IDMSUNLD	IDMSRBCK	
IDMSDBLU	IDMSRFWD	
IDMSPCON	RHDCFIXK	
IDMSRSTU		
IDMSCALC		
IDMSDIRL		
IDMSRADM		
IDMSRNWK		
IDMSRSTC		
IDMSTABX		
IDMSIXAM		
IDMSIXUD		
IDMSTBLU		

1.9 SITE-DEVELOPED COMPONENTS OF THE IDMS/R ENVIRONMENT

After IDMS is installed, each site will develop the following:

- System configurations,
- Database definitions, and
- Application programs.

1.9.1   System Configurations

Configurations for database/data communications (DB/DC) systems will be defined by running the system generation compiler. Input to the system generation compiler is a set of parameters which describe the new system. The system generation parameters specify the number and type of online terminals, maximum number of concurrent tasks, task codes for online functions, and other values to tailor the new system. The system generation compiler populates the data dictionary with extensive user-defined, system-specific information. System creation, maintenance, and tuning are the primary thrusts of Section Two.

1.9.2   Database Definitions

A database is defined using three compilers:

- •Schema compiler,
- •Device Media Control Language (DMCL) compiler, and
- •Subschema compiler.

Schema Compiler: Initially, a new database is defined and named in a schema. Source database definitions are stored in the data dictionary when the schema is compiled. The schema defines record layouts, record placement, and relationships between records. Data elements are grouped into records. Relationships between records are maintained as sets. Record types are grouped into logical areas. One area contains all occurrences of one or more record types.

DMCL Compiler: The relationships between logical database areas and physical database files are defined for run time programs through the Device Media Control Language (DMCL). In addition, the DMCL defines journals and the size and number of input/output buffers. IDMS-CV uses a global DMCL containing information about all areas in the databases to which the CV has access. IDMS local mode uses a DMCL which contains information about only one database. At least one DMCL per database is required to allow database access in local mode. After running this compiler, source information is stored in the data dictionary and a DMCL load module is stored in either a load library (OS system) or a core image library (DOS system).

Subschema Compiler: Subschemas define the applications programs' ability to access the new database. Each set of application access restrictions requires compiling a separate subschema — at least one subschema for each database. Running the subschema compiler stores subschema source definitions in the data dictionary and creates a subschema load module which is stored in the data dictionary. The load module is then accessed from the load area of the data dictionary (or punched from the dictionary, link edited to a load library or core image library, and accessed from the library).

1.9.3   User Applications

User application programs are developed using Cullinet's system and application development products. Batch and online programs will be coded by users to access and modify records in the new database. Batch programs may be either CULPRIT programs, or Data Manipulation Language (DML) programs coded in COBOL, PL/I, Assembler, or Fortran. CULPRIT programs can only retrieve database records, whereas DML programs can retrieve or modify database records. Both DML and Culprit programs may update and/or retrieve relational tables. Online programs may be DC programs, ADS/O dialogs, or, in the case of external TP systems, programs containing DML statements written in a format appropriate for that TP monitor. Batch and online programs are compiled or generated to copy in database record layouts and to document the program's access to the database in the data dictionary.

1.10   CONCLUSION

The job of implementing and supporting IDMS/R can be confusing to new personnel because it involves many different functions. The functions include configuring, maintaining, and tuning both test and production IDMS/R systems, as well as providing security, backup, and recovery for databases and applications. The *IDMS/R Systems Desk Reference* offers guidelines for these and other functions to help readers attain their IDMS/R goals.

In the introduction, we discussed some background information:

- Each site implements at least two IDMS/R systems, namely Test and Production.
- An IDMS/R system handles database and data communications support for user applications, allowing online and batch programs to access the database(s) concurrently.
- The IDMS/R systems often used in an application-development cycle include: a test system, a quality assurance or acceptance test system, a production system, and a production maintenance system.

- The major IDMS/R products serving system or application-development functions are: IDMS/R, IDMS-DC/UCF, IDD, IDMS/R Performance Monitor, ICMS, Goldengate, ASF, ADS/O, OLM, OLQ, OLE, and Culprit.
- The installed components of the IDMS/R environment are the files and programs which make up the products. These files and programs are tools for the development of site-specific database application systems.
- The site-developed components of the IDMS/R environment are IDMS/R systems, databases, and applications.

This book concentrates on IDMS/R system implementation and support functions. Section One contains basic information on several topics which are vital to understanding the system implementation and support steps covered in Section Two.

Section 1

TOPICS RELEVANT TO ALL IMPLEMENTATION STEPS

Multiple IDMS/R Systems Rationale

IDMS/R installations usually implement multiple IDMS/R systems. Each system consumes resources such as main storage, CPU cycles, disk storage, maintenance personnel hours, and so forth. Therefore, users may want to limit the number of IDMS/R CV-DC/UCF systems active simultaneously.

In this chapter, we will cover:

- Systems frequently used in a development environment,
- Other systems which may be required,
- How many systems are required, and
- Migration considerations.

2.1 SYSTEMS FREQUENTLY USED IN A DEVELOPMENT ENVIRONMENT

The need for a Test Central Version for application development and a Production CV for production processing is readily apparent. What may not be as obvious are the reasons and situations that will call for additional CV's. A detailed look at a typical large scale systems development environment may help explain some uses of multiple systems. Figure 2-1 illustrates the four systems often used during application development: Test, Quality Assurance, Production, and Production Maintenance. Development and processing of IDMS/R applications do not end with a Test CV and a Production CV; attention must be paid to the requirements of systems testing, quality assurance, and production maintenance as well. Each of these phases in an application's life cycle may require its own CV and dictionary.

New applications and databases are developed on a Test IDMS/R system. Unit testing and systems testing of an application can be carried out on the same CV, or two separate CV's may be utilized. Before putting a new application into production use, some shops require

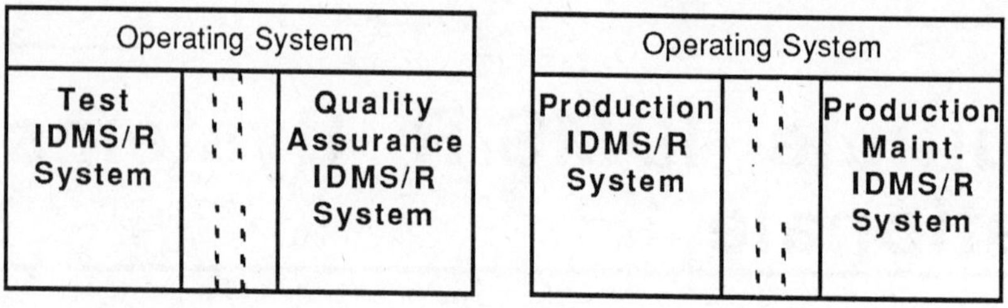

Operating System		
Test IDMS/R System		Quality Assurance IDMS/R System

Operating System		
Production IDMS/R System		Production Maint. IDMS/R System

Figure 2-1 Systems Used in the Development Cycle

that it be turned over to a separate group for quality assurance or user acceptance testing. Quality assurance groups often employ a separate CV for their testing purposes. When all parties are satisfied that the new application is reliable, it is moved into production. Occasionally, production programs need emergency fixes; a separate production maintenance system is useful for testing the fixes. A closer look at these systems and their use in a development cycle follows.

2.1.1   Test System

It is generally accepted that a separate system for development of applications and databases is imperative. A separate test system insulates the production system from abends, slowdowns, and/or data corruption which may be caused by the processing of new programs. The steps required for creation of a test system and suggested parameter values for it are provided in Chapter 9.

Processing in a test system consists primarily of executing application development tools, i.e., compilers and generators. Online IDD, Online Mapping, and the ADS application and dialog generators process frequently. Test databases tend to be comparatively small and accessed infrequently; test dictionaries tend to be fairly large and accessed frequently.

The number of databases used in a test system will vary. For small to medium development projects, one test database shared by the developers may be adequate. If the new development effort is extensive, with many small teams of programmers working on portions of the total project, it may be advisable to segregate testing by providing multiple 'unit-test' databases so that each programming team can run tests independently.

Multiple unit-test databases provide the means to segregate testing. Each unit-test database is created by compiling a separate schema. There will be one unit-test schema for each programming unit-test database. Each unit-test schema is identical except for having unique page groups (under Release 10) or unique page ranges (under Release 5.7) for each area. When any single unit-test schema is changed, all others must be changed as well. Each programming team is usually responsible for repopulating their test databases and modifying test data. Typically, test databases are reinitialized and reloaded when possible, otherwise each unit-test database must be restructured to reflect the schema change.

After each test, the unit-test copy should be restored to pre-run conditions. This method provides a controlled unit-test environment; the original database remains unchanged. Any changes in program output and database contents result from changes in a single program. When testing is complete at the unit-test level, emphasis shifts to system or integration testing.

The goal of system testing is ensuring that all parts of the application, known to work separately, function correctly as an integrated system. A system-test schema defines a separate database used during system testing. A single Central Version (CV) is probably adequate for both unit and system testing. Both unit-test databases and the system-test database can be accessed using the DBNAME facility with no conflict between the databases. A single primary or secondary dictionary is usually sufficient to contain the records, elements, schemas, and subschemas of both the unit-test and system-test databases. If schemas are developed on a secondary dictionary, the area and file portion of the schemas must be repeated on the primary dictionary to allow it to be copied into the global DMCL (Figure 2-2).

Unit-test databases are also helpful when more than one application is under rapid development and the applications share some of each other's data. If the shared data is undergoing frequent structural or value changes, having both multiple unit-test databases and multiple data dictionaries makes maintenance easier to implement and understand. For example, the Securities database is not connected physically to the Trading database (Figure 2-3), but the *data* and the *definitions* of both databases must be synchronized. If, during development, there is only one copy of each database and a change is made to Trading data which necessitates either a database reload or restructure (e.g., adding a new set and record type), Securities testing must also be suspended temporarily. However, if separate unit-test databases and data dictionaries are implemented (Figure 2-4), one application's data value and definition changes need not impact the other application. Structural changes caused by one application may be implemented by the other when convenient rather than immediately.

The multiple dictionary approach, when teamed with multiple test databases, allows identical names to be used across all environments (e.g., schema and subschema names), thus making recompiles

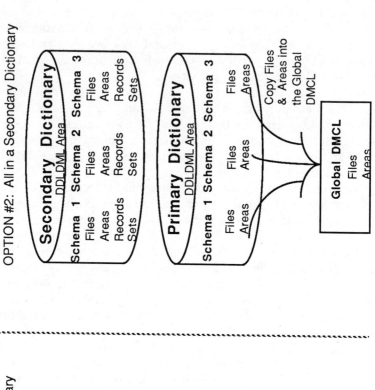

Figure 2-2 Defining Unit-Test Schemas in a Primary or a Single Secondary Dictionary

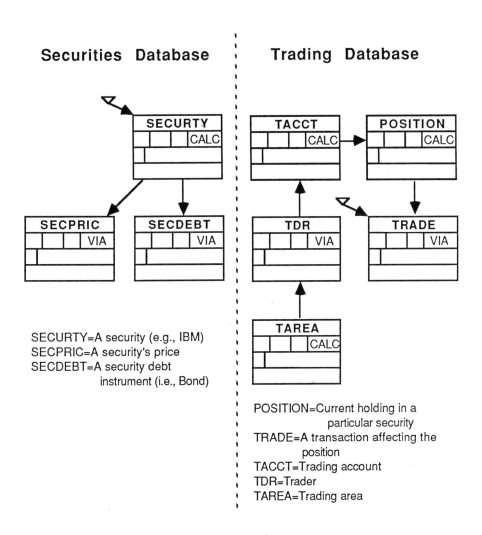

Figure 2-3 Synchronized Databases. SECURITY and POSITION must be synchronized for testing purposes, i.e., the security must exist before a trade can take place.

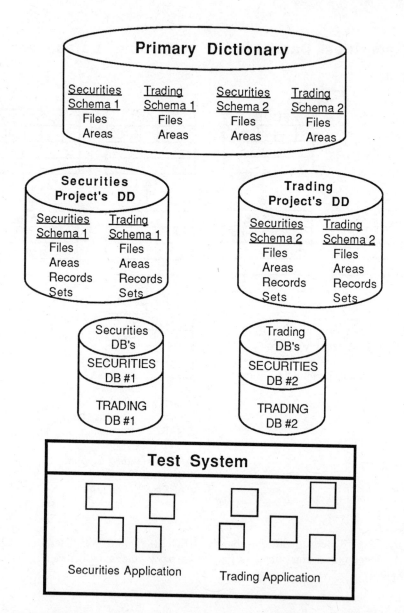

Figure 2-4 Synchronization and Multiple Dictionaries. Both the securities and trading development teams require synchronized databases. Multiple dictionaries, when used with multiple unit-test databases, allow both teams to implement and test changes independently.

unnecessary when moving a program from one environment to another. The price paid for this approach is the additional effort required to coordinate different definitions and data values across the dictionaries.

2.1.2   Quality Assurance or Acceptance Test System

Testing requirements often lead the DBA staff to create an intermediate system for testing applications between the initial testing phase and the final production phase. This intermediate system is usually used for quality assurance and/or acceptance testing. The terms quality assurance testing and acceptance testing mean different things at different sites. We use the term quality assurance testing when referring to testing carried out by a separate DP group to ensure that the new application or program meets site standards for reliability and performance. We use the term acceptance testing when referring to testing carried out by the user group to ensure that the new application satisfies user requirements for functionality and ease of use. One intermediate testing system may be used for both quality assurance and acceptance testing.

Auditors often require that quality assurance/acceptance testing be conducted by a separate group in an environment isolated from other testing. There are several reasons for using a separate system when an application is ready for quality assurance or acceptance testing, including:

- Enhancing security in the testing environment,
- Creating a more stable testing environment, and
- Mirroring the true production environment.

Enhancing security in the testing environment: In many shops, the test system is precisely that — a system available for all types of testing. As such, it is often relatively unsecured, leaving test data and application code available for retrieval and modification by anyone who knows how to do so. Because there is so little security at this level, programmers and users on a test system may adopt a cavalier attitude toward program changes. Although minimal security facilitates rapid development, a more ordered and secured framework is necessary to ensure that changes are made to the correct module once the initial testing phases are complete. Therefore, a second test central version is used to create a more highly secured environment in which only certain users are allowed to signon, change code, and recompile programs.

Creating A More Stable Testing Environment: In a busy development environment, many programs, databases, and system definitions are in a state of flux. Programming teams will be testing new programs and dialogs. The DBA may be testing changes to the sysgen, compiling schemas, or applying software maintenance to the test system. Some testing could occasionally bring down CV or result in severe system slowdowns.

A more stable test environment is recommended once users begin acceptance testing and in-depth testing or training on a new application. Otherwise, end users could develop a negative opinion of a new application's performance because a relatively untested program from another application is looping or bringing the system down. False negative impressions can be avoided by creating an intermediate system used for testing only those applications which have already passed the initial testing phase.

Mirroring the Production System: Prior to putting a major new application into production, the Quality Assurance system can be used to estimate the impact of the new application on current production processing. Activity has to be controlled to simulate the production environment with the addition of the new application. This type of testing can be carried out only on a separate CV; the test system usually has other development activity occurring which would interfere with the simulation. The additional system load caused by the new application may force the DBA staff to modify several sysgen parameters, for example increasing storage in both the storage and program pools (see the Test System chapter for further details on these pools). Pools and other components of the sysgen may require tuning and retesting to maintain performance standards.

When an application is ready for quality assurance testing it is brought into the quality assurance system. Bringing an application into quality assurance involves copying the application structures and components from the test dictionary to the Quality Assurance dictionary; this procedure is often called "migration". Migration is relatively easy for the first application – an operating system copy utility will suffice if the dictionaries are the same size and have the same page ranges (e.g., in OS shops perform an IEBGENER of the file containing the DDLDML area of the dictionary and DDLDCLOD plus any libraries). Subsequent applications, though, must have the means available to migrate only selected IDD entities from dictionary to dictionary. In addition, a migration procedure will be needed when migrating applications from quality assurance to production. To automate the migration process, either write or buy a dictionary migration utility (refer to Chapter 3 for details).

Quality assurance testing will often uncover bugs missed by unit and system testing. During quality assurance testing, further development (i.e., subsequent phases of a project) may be continuing in the test environment. A key maxim in phased implementation of applications is eliminating bugs on the quality assurance version, unless the problems are so severe that the entire application fails quality assurance testing and must be returned to development for a complete overhaul. Development work on the application usually has proceeded beyond the point at which it was turned over to the quality assurance group. Correcting the bugs on the test version and migrating the application again may be impossible without incorporating changes that development has made since the original turnover. It is likely that such changes are not ready to be put through the quality assurance process.

Corrections made to the quality assurance version of the application must be incorporated in the development version, however. Procedures should be established for communicating and implementing these corrections to the development database and application modules. The development effort required to accomplish integrating quality assurance corrections into the current development version should be included in initial project estimates. Integrating quality assurance corrections involves reverse migration, or moving an application (or selected portions of an application) from quality assurance back to the unit-test environment. Because other development for phased implementation may already be going on, either different version numbers or multiple dictionaries must be used. Different version numbers for entities are established with the DCUF TEST facility (only available under OS), which sets a version number at a terminal for all dialogs, maps, programs and subschemas executed. As an alternative, a secondary dictionary can be established for reverse migration, containing definitions of applications identical to those in the quality assurance dictionary, as illustrated in Figure 2-5.

After the quality assurance group has completed testing a new application, it is ready to be put into production. Going into production means another migration, into another Central Version.

2.1.3 Production System

Each IDMS/R installation defines at least one production system. The production system processes the applications which maintain the relevant data for an organization. A separate production system facilitates protecting production applications from modification or misuse. Occasionally, several production systems are defined. See Section 2.2.1 below for more information on multiple production systems.

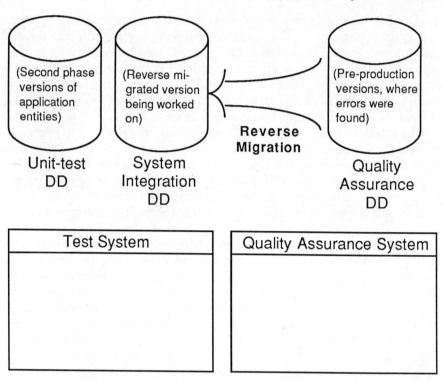

Figure 2-5 Reverse Migration and Multiple Dictionaries

Putting an application into production is not difficult for the initial application because it is simply a minor variation of the earlier migration process. Subsequent applications, or project phases that expand on existing database structure, are more involved because existing production data must be preserved. The existing database may require restructuring, or unloading and reloading when the new application is moved into production use.

A large number and variety of application transactions access vast databases in a production environment. Security, backup, and recovery of database and data dictionary contents are of primary importance, determining many of the changes to sysgen parameters from the test system to the production system. Chapter 10 describes creating a production system and offers guidelines for choosing parameter values.

2.1.4 Production Maintenance System

There always seems to be some bug that escapes extermination and burrows into a production program. When a production program needs emergency corrections, a separate Production Maintenance system is useful. Solving the problem may require recreating a production problem from a particular day's view of the files/databases. To recreate a problem of this nature, the data must be isolated from all other testing activity. The Test system may have other testing going on and may not have the proper copies of the modules to do the test. The Quality Assurance system also may be rejected for the same reasons. Testing against the actual production database is frowned upon by auditing departments.

The solution to isolating the data from all other activity lies in creating a special Production Maintenance system (Figure 2-6). It is active only when needed rather than on a daily basis. Its database structure is identical to production and contents of the database are extracted from production. A production maintenance system provides a separate yet accurate testing ground for emergency corrections.

Obviously, the feasibility of creating an exact copy of the production database for production maintenance is dependent on the size of the database involved. It may not be feasible to allocate a testing database the same size as the production database to find a bug in a load program accessing 800,000 records. In some instances, the production maintenance database may be a scaled-down copy of the production database. For these reasons, a program which extracts data selectively should be planned and coded for each application where the size of the database makes duplicate copies unfeasible.

New software releases can also be tested using the production maintenance CV, providing there are no structural dictionary changes in the release. If there are structural changes to the dictionary, the new release must be tested on a separate system.

2.2 WHAT OTHER SYSTEMS MAY BE REQUIRED?

The most common IDMS/R systems are those used in the development cycle. However, other systems may be necessary. Occasionally, more than one production system is required. One last reason for multiple systems is a change in Cullinet releases. A summary of the uses and characteristics of IDMS/R systems used in the development cycle and the additional systems discussed below is contained in Table 2-1.

Production Maintenance Databases

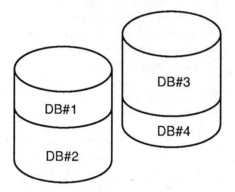

DB#3

DB#1

DB#4

DB#2

Production Maintenance Dictionary(ies)

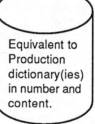

Equivalent to Production dictionary(ies) in number and content.

P.M. databases are often smaller copies of production databases, containing a representative sampling of data extracted from production.

Production Maintenance System

Production Program

Figure 2-6 Production Maintenance Environment

Table 2-1 Summary of IDMS/R Systems and Their Uses

System	Uses	Characteristics
Test	Application and database development	Small databases, large dictionaries. Typical processing: compiles and generations, with infrequent database access for program tests.
Quality Assurance	Quality assurance and end user testing of new applications	System-defined equivalent to production with the addition of the new application.
Production	Processing production applications	Large databases, medium dictionaries. Processing many application transactions accessing large databases; little dictionary access.
Production Maintenance	Testing emergency fixes to production programs; testing minor system software modifications	System definition identical to production system. Databases are copies of production databases but loaded with a smaller number of records extracted from production.
Additional Production	Processing production applications. Very large systems split into two systems. High visibility or vital systems which require isolation	Large databases, appropriate security and backup procedures
New Release Testing	Systems used to test major software changes, such as new releases	Equivalent to existing systems, but with new software

2.2.1   Multiple Production Systems

There are situations when multiple production systems should be considered. These include:

- Very large systems when operating system limitations on the amount of virtual storage available to any given partition or memory space restrict system performance, and
- High visibility and/or vital applications where contention for resources must be reduced to a minimum.

Very Large Systems: As new applications are added to the Test or Production environment, a heavier load is placed on the finite resources of the CV. Eventually, more main storage will be required to maintain an acceptable level of system performance, as illustrated in Figure 2-7. Many operating systems have a limitation on the maximum amount of virtual storage which can be allocated to a single partition or region (i.e., DOS/VSE, OS/VS1, and MVS non-XA shops). Once the maximum is exceeded there are two options, either accept limitations and attempt to reschedule activity accordingly, or expand to a second system and move some of the activity to that environment.

When creating a second system, ideally one should move entire applications and all their activity to the second CV. Although two CV's can retrieve data concurrently from the same database, both cannot hold the database for update. Synchronization between one CV updating a database while a second CV is retrieving against the same database is not automatically maintained without Cullinet's Distributed Database System (DDS) software. Applications and their databases that must communicate with each other should be moved to the same CV (unless DDS has been installed). Dividing system activity along both application and user responsibility lines reduces confusion for the terminal user. If each user's processing takes place entirely on one system, users will not have to keep track of where their data and applications reside.

High Visibility and/or Vital Applications: Another reason for multiple production systems is isolating a high visibility and/or vital application that requires high performance. On rare occasions, a company will create a separate system to insure that such an application experiences minimal contention within IDMS/R (e.g., for buffers, storage, or program loading). This approach, however, increases overall resource consumption because it creates two large, non-swappable (MVS), systems competing for real memory and CPU

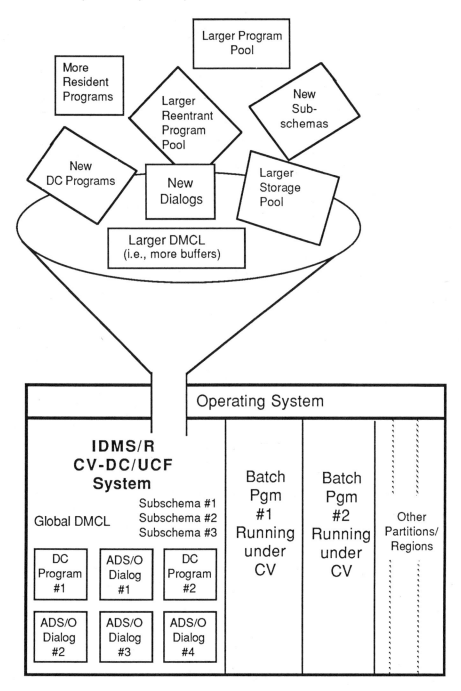

Figure 2-7 Growth May Cause Multiple Production Systems

cycles with one another and with other software processing at the same time. The resources consumed by a separate IDMS/R system include not only virtual and real memory, but also the disk space required for a separate set of dictionaries, journal files and libraries.

A small number of ASF users have relegated ASF (Automatic System Facility) work to its own Central Version because the resources consumed by extensive ASF usage, and accompanying ICMS data downloading activity, can cause performance degradations for other production work. If ASF is to be used heavily in your environment, Cullinet should be contacted for suggestions on CV configuration.

2.2.2   Additional Systems when Changing IDMS/R Releases

When a new release of IDMS/R is installed, there will usually be several additional systems required during the changeover period. For example, changing from a Release 5.7 to a Release 10 environment will necessitate at least two distinct systems while the new release is tested for compatibility with existing applications. Conceivably, all of the following systems could be in use simultaneously:

Test 5.7	Quality Assurance 5.7	Production 5.7
Test 10	Quality Assurance 10	Production 10

This extreme might occur if some applications require features of the new release but users are reluctant to run old applications under the new release. In any event, when a shop upgrades to a new release, converting existing applications to the new release is a primary goal.

2.3   HOW MANY SYSTEMS ARE NECESSARY?

Every installation is unique and not all systems are appropriate for each installation. Depending on the size of an installation and the amount of development and production processing occurring, different systems are appropriate. Generally, three or four systems are used in the development cycle. Other systems are occasionally necessary due to production considerations and new releases of IDMS/R.

If the shop is small, three systems may be adequate: test, production, and a combined quality assurance/production maintenance system. Sometimes quality assurance and production maintenance requirements can be satisfied with one system. The quality assurance environment usually mirrors production conditions with the addition of the new application(s) under testing. It is designed not only to facilitate user program testing, but also to evaluate the new application's impact on production system efficiency. If the quality assurance system has not been modified to accommodate another new application, testing a production fix on the quality assurance system would be quite possible. Additional systems to test new releases may be required for short periods of time.

If the shop is very large, all of the systems discussed above may be appropriate. Even if all the systems are defined, they are not necessarily all in use concurrently. Test and production systems are in use regularly. Quality assurance and production maintenance systems are up when necessary. Extra systems for new release testing also are up as needed. Additional production systems may be appropriate if a shop has one of the conditions discussed earlier, namely a very large amount of production processing or an application that requires isolation from other applications.

2.4   MIGRATION CONSIDERATIONS

Having multiple systems adds to the complexity of implementing and supporting IDMS/R, because components of the DB/DC environment are regularly migrated from system to system. When applications have been developed and/or modified, application components must be migrated from one system to another. Migration involves copying library and dictionary entities, and recompiling/regenerating maps, dialogs, etc. on the target system. A procedure should be developed for migrating application components.

Many non-IDMS/R shops establish a quality assurance control group to migrate programs from one system to another, e.g., from the test library to the quality assurance library where controlled testing and access can occur. In the IDMS/R world the need for a control group remains, however, the group's job is both easier and more difficult than in a non-database environment. It is easier because dictionary documentation shows the interdependencies of the application's components. It is more difficult because the entity to be migrated is often composed of many components. For example, an ADS/O dialog is composed of modules, tables, records, elements, and a map. When one component changes, all components affected by the change must also be migrated and, if appropriate, recompiled or regenerated.

The quality assurance control group is usually responsible for migrating application-related entities, such as programs, dialogs, applications, maps, and so forth. The DBA group is usually responsible for migrating database- and system-related entities.

There are two considerations when migrating applications or portions of applications from one system to another:

- Physically migrating the application's components, and
- Making system changes to permit access to the migrated application and to maintain system performance at an acceptable level.

2.4.1 Physical Migration of an Application's Components

Migration of an application's components consists of copying the new or changed entities to the target system. All the application's database, programs, dialogs, and other related entities must be migrated.

The new or modified database definition must be copied to the target system. If a "global" schema is used at your installation, i.e., one which contains all application database areas, the global schema must be modified and new/affected subschemas recompiled. In addition, the global DMCL must be updated. Chapters 10 and 11 contain information on copying databases and maintaining global schemas.

Many application components are stored in the data dictionary, e.g., dialogs, maps, records, tables, elements, and so forth. Dictionary information is migrated by copying source entities from one dictionary to another, followed by recompiling or regenerating maps, tables, ADS/O applications, and ADS/O dialogs to create load modules. Refer to Chapter 3 for further details on migration of dictionary entities.

Other application components are stored in load/core image libraries, e.g., IDMS-DC programs, batch DML programs, and online CICS/DML programs. Source and object modules for IDMS-DC programs, batch DML programs, and online CICS/DML programs are migrated using operating system utilities (e.g., IEBCOPY for OS installations). The appropriate modules are copied from one library to another.

2.4.2 Making System Changes

Several system generation changes may be required to permit access to the new/modified application and to maintain acceptable system performance. System generation statements are discussed in Chapters 9 and 10. TASK and PROGRAM statements must be added to the target system to permit access to online IDMS-DC programs. If REGISTRATION is specified on the SYSTEM statement in the sysgen, IDMS PROGRAM statements must be added to the sysgen for each batch DML program and each CICS/DML program. If security classes are employed in the target system, the sysgen USER statements must be modified for the new security classes (security classes and other security considerations are discussed in Chapter 6).

Other changes may be necessary to maintain system performance at an acceptable level. For example, MAXTASKS and MAXERUS may need to be increased if the new or changed application increases the load on the system. Chapters 10 and 13 cover performance considerations and relevant statistics.

2.5   CONCLUSION

Several systems are implemented at each installation. The systems often used in development are: Test, Quality Assurance, Production and Production Maintenance. Other systems required less often are: additional production systems and systems to test new releases of software.

Depending on the size of an installation and the kinds of processing being done, an appropriate number of systems is determined. Because each system consumes many resources (main storage, disk storage, CPU cycles, etc.) an unlimited number of systems is impractical. The number of systems an installation requires can occasionally be reduced by combining Quality Assurance and Production Maintenance systems, or Production Maintenance and new release testing systems. Whatever the final determination for number of systems, each system will be defined separately and will have its own dictionary(ies) and other supporting files.

A system can have one or more data dictionaries. Multiple dictionaries are often used in conjunction with multiple systems. In some instances, multiple data dictionaries on a single system can provide an alternative to multiple systems. The role of the Integrated Data Dictionary and the uses for multiple data dictionaries are the topics of the next chapter.

Suggestions for further reading on Multiple IDMS/R Systems environments:

The following Cullinet Manuals
   For Release 10 sites:
      1) System Generation Guide (Generating multiple systems)
      2) System Operations Guide (Bringing up systems and monitoring system performance)

3) IDMS/R Database Operations (Multiple databases and data dictionaries)
4) DDL Reference Guide (Defining databases)

For Release 5.7 sites:
1) System Generation Guide (Generating multiple systems)
2) IDMS-CV/DC System Operations (Multiple databases and data dictionaries, bringing up systems and monitoring system performance)
3) DB Design and Definition Guide (Defining databases)

3

The Integrated Data Dictionary

IDMS/R is a dictionary-driven system. The Integrated Data Dictionary (IDD) is the focal point for all software related to IDMS/R. IDMS/R will not run without a Data Dictionary. It is vitally important because all components of a database and data communications environment are defined by information stored in the database known as the Data Dictionary (DD). Information stored in the DD supports all the functions of IDMS/R from database access to online application design. Once defined and stored in the centrally located DD, information is universally available to all system components accessing it.

In addition, the Integrated Data Dictionary can be a powerful tool for controlling, organizing, and managing corporate data resources. It is a tool which Data Dictionary Administrators, Database Administrators, Data Administrators, and other systems personnel may use to manage and document the data processing environment.

In this chapter, we will discuss:

- IDD components,
- Installation and population of a DD and DB in a fictitious corporation which has just acquired IDMS/R,
- Dynamic interrelationships between the IDD and other system software products,
- Required uses of the IDD,
- Specific examples of optional uses of the IDD,
- Ways the IDD may be tailored to site-specific needs,
- An overview of multiple dictionaries,
- Uses of secondary dictionaries,
- How many dictionaries should be implemented, and
- Creating a new secondary dictionary.

3.1   IDD COMPONENTS

The IDD is composed of database and software components, as illustrated in Figure 3-1. The database component, known as the Data Dictionary (DD), is the storage site for information pertaining to the data processing environment. The major software components are the Data Dictionary Definition Language Compiler (DDDL Compiler) and the Dictionary/Directory Reporter (DDR).

3.1.1   The Data Dictionary

The Data Dictionary is the central repository for information on processing environments, databases, users, programs, and so on. Information on the processing environment may be, for example, IDMS/R system configurations including descriptions of the terminals, lines, and tasks specific to each system. Information on databases includes records, sets, areas, and subschemas. Stored information for programs consists of entry points, modules included,

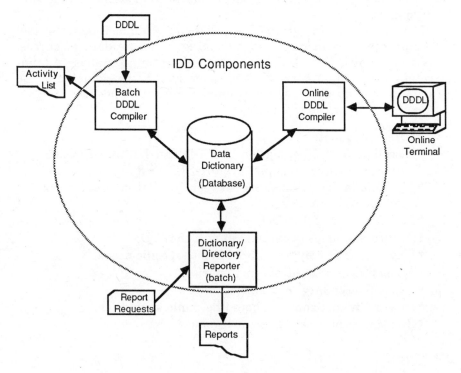

Figure 3-1 IDD Components

files opened, and database records used. When the "programs" are dialogs, subschemas, or maps stored information may also include load modules.

The basic logical unit of storage in the DD is the entity. Any named component of the data processing environment about which information is stored in the DD is called an entity. A list of the pre-defined entity types is contained in Table 3-1. The basic physical unit of storage is the record. An entity and its relationships to other entities are defined in an IDMS/R network database structure using multiple records and sets.

The dictionary network database is defined by the schema IDMSNTWK, which is loaded into the dictionary during installation of IDMS/R. The network database may be composed of up to eight areas (six in Release 5.7). Table 3-2 contains a list of area names and their uses.

Five of the dictionary areas have the same use in Release 10 and Release 5.7. The DDLDML area contains the data usually thought of as the DD information, namely entity descriptions and relationships. The DDLDCLOD area contains load modules created by the compilers and generators, such as maps created by OLM, subschemas created by the subschema compiler, tables created by the DDDL compiler, and dialog load modules created by the ADS/O generator. The DDLDCMSG area contains predefined system messages and site-defined messages used by ADS/O dialogs and DC programs. The DDLDCLOG area is an optional area used to store IDMS/R system log information, only if logging to the DD is chosen during system generation (see Chapter 9, Test System Creation, for a discussion of logging alternatives). The DDLDCTLF area is another optional area; it is used to store transaction logging information if transaction logging is enabled during system generation.

The remaining areas are used for scratch and/or queue record storage. Scratch and queue records serve various application needs when temporary data storage or sequential data storage is desired. Scratch records are maintained only for the duration of a single execution of the IDMS/R system. Queue records are maintained until they are deleted by a program or until a retention period, specified at queue creation, expires. DC programs and ADS/O dialogs can store, retrieve and/or delete scratch and queue records. In Release 5.7, both scratch and queue records are stored in the DDLDCRUN area. In Release 10, the single DDLDCRUN area still can be used for storage of scratch and queue records; however, it may be replaced by two separate areas, the DDLDCSCR and the DDLDCQUE areas. The DDLDCSCR area is used in Release 10 systems for storage of Scratch records; the DDLDCQUE area is used for storage of Queue records.

Table 3-1 Entity Types and How They are Established in the IDD

Basic Entities	Teleprocessing Entities	Other Entities	Schema Entities
USER[1]	MESSAGE[2]	CLASS[2]	SCHEMA[8]
SYSTEM[1]	PANEL[3](SCREEN)*	ATTRIBUTE[2]	SUBSCHEMA[9]
FILE[2]	MAP[3]	LOAD MODULE[4]	DMCL[10]
ELEMENT[5]	TASK[1]	User-Defined[2]	
RECORD[5](REPORT, TRANSACTION)*	QUEUE[1]		
PROGRAM[6]	TABLE[2]		
ENTRY POINT[6]	DESTINATION[1]		
MODULE[7](PROCESS, QFILE, TABLE)*	LINE[1]		
	PHYSICAL TERMINAL[1]		
	LOGICAL TERMINAL[1]		

[1] Established by the DDDL compiler and IDMS-DB/DC SYSGEN compiler.

[2] Established by the DDDL compiler.

[3] Established by the DDDL compiler and IDMS-DC/UCF mapping compiler.

[4] Established by the DDDL compiler, SUBSCHEMA compiler, ADS/O generator, and IDMS-DC/UCF mapping compiler.

[5] Established by the DDDL compiler and SCHEMA compiler.

[6] Established by the DDDL compiler, DML processor, SUBSCHEMA compiler, IDMS-DB/DC SYSGEN compiler, IDMS-DC/UCF mapping compiler, and ADS/O generator.

[7] Established by the DDDL compiler and INTERACT (QFILES can be updated from OLQ under Release 10).

[8] Established by the SCHEMA compiler.

[9] Established by the SUBSCHEMA compiler.

[10] Established by the DMCL compiler.

* Alternate names for an entity type are listed in parentheses.

Table 3-2 Dictionary Areas

DD Area Name	Contains	Used In Release
DDLDML	Entity descriptions	10 and 5.7
DDLDCLOD	Load modules	10 and 5.7
DDLDCMSG	Run time messages	10 and 5.7
DDLDCLOG	Run time log information	10 and 5.7
DDLDCTLF	Transaction Logging records	10 and 5.7
DDLDCRUN	Scratch and Queue records	10 and 5.7
DDLDCSCR	Scratch records	10
DDLDCQUE	Queue records	10

As of this writing, the DDLDCRUN area is still used in Release 10 as well as 5.7, unless the DDLDCQUE area is defined as an 'extent' area; Cullinet currently recommends using DDLDCRUN.

3.1.2   The Data Dictionary Definition Language (DDDL) Compiler

The DDDL Compiler is the primary tool for adding, maintaining, and deleting information stored in the DD. Entities, and the records which define them, are established in the DD by specific software components, the compilers (Figure 3-2). The DDDL compiler is dedicated solely to the DD and may populate, delete, and maintain all entity types. Other compilers have specialized functions, populating only specific entities in the DD.

The sample DDDL syntax shown below adds a new element (the DD name for a field) to the DD.

```
ADD ELEMENT NAME IS CUST-NAME
    ELEMENT DESCRIPTION IS 'CUSTOMER NAME'
    PICTURE IS X(30) USAGE IS DISPLAY.
```

The DDDL compiler can be used as a batch program or as an online task in an IDMS/R system; identical data dictionary definition language is used in either situation. Under Release 10 a full screen menu version of online IDD is available for users unfamiliar with DDDL syntax.

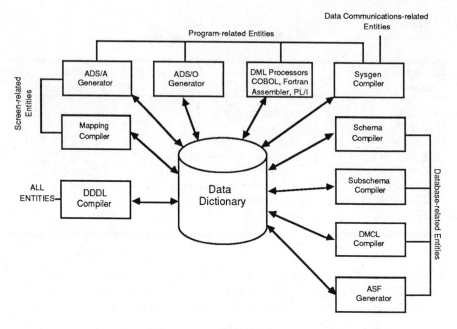

Figure 3-2 IDD Populators

3.1.3   The Dictionary/Directory Reporter (DDR)

Using the IDD results in the integration of entity documentation with
entity definition. As compilers are used to create system configurations, database definitions, and so on, associated entities are added to
the DD. The Dictionary/Directory Reporter (DDR) documents information stored in the DD through a wide variety of reports.

The function of the DDR is documentation. Documentation is
generated by DDR CULPRIT report modules stored in the DD during
installation of IDMS/R. The DDR provides reports on definitions,
descriptions, and interrelationships of data elements, reports,
records, programs, systems, etc.

The four major kinds of reports are detail, KEY, summary, and
cross-reference reports. Detail, KEY, and summary reports are
available for most dictionary entity types. Detail reports list all information for each occurrence of the entity type. KEY reports, like
detail reports, list all information about an entity, but only for the
particular entity occurrences named in the KEY statement(s).
Summary reports list a small amount of information about each occurrence of an entity type, for example an element summary report
lists the name, version number, and a short description of each element. Summary reports may be used to gather the keys necessary to
run KEY reports. Cross-reference reports provide information relat-

ing one entity to another. For example, the element/program cross-reference report relates elements to the programs which use them.

3.2 INSTALLATION AND POPULATION OF AN IDD

We will now consider the Spy Products, Inc. (SPI) site, a fictitious corporation specializing in the manufacture and distribution of covert operations equipment. SPI has just acquired IDMS/R; the tapes have been delivered – including source and object level modules for all the products SPI has ordered. During installation of IDMS/R, the DD is defined to the system and sparsely populated with its own schema, IDMSNTWK, and predefined entity/record types. Information on the physical configuration of the IDMS-DC/UCF environment is stored in the DD by running the system generation compiler during installation. At this stage, the DD contains mainly teleprocessing entity occurrences and Cullinet installation information (DDR report modules, protocols, etc.).

The DBA/DDA, Ms. Ima Plant, now begins active supervision of the Data Dictionary. She knows that a predefined USER entity ('CULL DBA') with the password 'DBAPASS' has been stored in the DD by the installation process. This user has carte blanche authority. Therefore, to prevent an unknown person who may be familiar with IDMS/R from tampering with the system at some future date, Ms. Plant may elect to change this entity immediately. She may do this by 1) changing the password, 2) changing the name and the password, or 3) adding another USER entity with global authority and deleting the 'CULL DBA' USER entity.

When the DD is established during installation, security is off at all levels. Security for dictionary entities is requested by setting the dictionary options. To set dictionary options for SPI, Ms. Plant uses the following DDDL statement:

```
SET OPTIONS FOR DICTIONARY
    SECURITY FOR IDMS IS ON
    SECURITY FOR IDMS-DC IS ON
    SECURITY FOR IDD IS ON
    SECURITY FOR IDD SIGNON IS ON
    SECURITY FOR ADS IS ON
    SECURITY FOR OLQ IS ON
    SECURITY FOR CULPRIT IS ON
    SECURITY FOR CLASS AND ATTRIBUTE IS ON.
```

For complete security information see Chapter 6, which contains a full discussion of dictionary security facilities.

If dictionary security facilities are in use, people working with dictionary entities must have USER id's, passwords, and authorities defined in the DD. Ms. Plant adds individual USER id's to the DD, along with their passwords and appropriate authorities, by entering statements similar to this:

```
ADD USER SMILEY
    PASSWORD IS 'INTREPID'
    IDD SIGNON ALLOWED
    AUTHORITY IS IDMS
    AUTHORITY IS CLASS AND ATTRIBUTE.
```

Thus, the DD is populated with USER entity occurrence(s).

Next, SPI begins development of its first application. Wisely, a simple, straightforward application with a fair amount of visibility has been chosen for SPI's first brush with IDMS/R — a customer/order database for use in the upcoming clearance sale on trench coats. To begin, SPI must analyze and normalize the data elements, group them into records, design the database, and define it with a schema, subschemas, and a DMCL. These processes add several entity occurrences to the DD, including elements, records, schema, subschema and DMCL source information, as well as subschema load modules. Database areas are defined and named along with the DB files to which they relate as part of the schema definition process.

All processes discussed so far have been populating the DD. Now, Ms. Plant and her staff allocate DB files using operating system utilities, and initialize them using the IDMSINIT utility. Ms. Plant also codes a batch DML program or an online application to load the database. After the program is written, it goes through either a DML compile (batch, CICS, or IDMS-DC program) or an ADS/O generation (ADS/O dialog). This populates the DD with information about the program. Running the program will populate the database. All new programs to access SPI's database will also go through a DML compile or ADS/O generation, populating the DD in turn with their program information.

SPI now has a DD populated with database, data communications, user, and program information. Their database has been loaded with initial data. Ms. Plant realizes that as the Data Dictionary is increasingly populated with information, it becomes a valuable data resource unto itself. As she does for all SPI databases, Ms. Plant institutes a regular backup protocol, namely a nightly backup of the dictionary using the IDMSDUMP utility. As the SPI databases and DD increase in size, the backup regimen may be changed to use a different utility, such as FDR® (Fast Dump Restore) for OS sites, to

---

®FDR is a registered trademark of Innovation Data Processing, Inc.

backup the DD more rapidly. Any file utility supporting BDAM or VSAM access methods may be used, see Chapter 7, Backup and Recovery, for details.

3.3 THE IDD AND OTHER SOFTWARE PRODUCTS

Now the "I" part of IDD begins – integration. Reciprocal interaction between the system software products and the IDD constitutes integration. Table 3-3 describes how various Cullinet software products use information stored in the DD and how they are, in turn, used by the three parts of the IDD, namely the DDDL compiler, the DDR, and the DD. In all cases, pertinent information stored in the DD can be maintained by the DDDL compiler and reported on by the DDR.

Table 3-3 Interdependencies between Other Products and the IDD

Product	Uses DD <--and-->	IDD Uses Product
IDMS/R	DD to store DB schemas (e.g., elements, records, sets,areas, and DB file information) and subschemas (e.g., access information).	IDMS/R to access the DD (a database) for the DDDL compiler and DDR.
IDMS-DC/UCF	DD to store SYSGEN and USER access information.	IDMS-DC/UCF to access DD online by the DDDL compiler.
CULPRIT	DD to control access to CULPRIT, conventional files, and subschemas at the USER level; and to supply copies of DB records.	CULPRIT to report on the DD for the DDR.
OLQ	DD to control access to OLQ, QFILES, and subschemas at the USER level; and to supply copies of DB records and subschema structure in response to SHOW or HELP commands.	
OLE	DD to control access to OLE and subschemas; and to supply copies of DB records.	

- (continued on next page) -

Table 3-3 Interdependencies between Other Products and the IDD (continued)

Product	Uses DD <--and-->	IDD Uses Product
OLM	DD to store source and object definitions of maps and panels. For each screen definition,OLM creates a PROGRAM, MAP, and PANEL entity, linking all records to the PROGRAM entity. When a map is used, the run time system accesses the DD for the map load modules, as well as any edit and code table load modules required.	
ADS/O	DD to store dialog load modules, also to supply copies of work records and DB records for run time use. ADS/O creates a PROGRAM entity and links the process source MODULEs to this PROGRAM.	
DML Programs (Online or Batch)	DD to supply copies of DB records, source code modules, and IDMS protocols during DML compiles. During initial compiles, the DML processor stores a PROGRAM entity and program statistics in the DD; during subsequent compiles of the same program, the DML processor simply updates the statistics.	
ASF/ICMS	DD to store catalog information in the DDLDML area, including user, group, folder, and access data. DD to store r-schema records and related information.	

3.4 REQUIRED USES OF THE IDD

Because IDMS/R is a dictionary-driven system there are required uses of the IDD at all installations, regardless of customized IDD applications created. IDMS/R will not run without a DD. The DD is the focal point for communications between system software products. Database definitions, system configurations, and some application information (for example, QFILES, maps, and ADS/O dialogs) must be stored in the DD. The database definition and system generation procedures populate the dictionary with many of the required entities. The description of these processes for SPI (Section 3.2) illustrates how population of the DD with required entities occurs.

3.5 ELECTIVE PROCEDURES: OPTIONAL USES OF THE IDD

Other information about DB and DC environments optionally may be defined and stored in the DD. It is possible to use the DD to store any information pertaining to a site's data processing environment, including manual and automated systems. The advantages of making extensive use of the DD are its central location, ease of maintenance (using the DDDL compiler), and reports available from the DDR.

The IDD can be used as a powerful tool for four major tasks:

- Controlling data redundancy,
- Predicting the impact of application changes,
- Designing databases, and
- Documenting the data processing environment.

Other common uses of the DD include storage of the following information: JCL (Job Control Language), screen layouts, report layouts, report distribution lists, and source document descriptions.

3.5.1 Controlling Data Redundancy

The IDD can be especially useful in controlling data redundancy if used in conjunction with standard naming conventions during the analysis phase of database design. Data redundancy control can be accomplished only if 'new' data elements are compared with the existing data elements and records during data analysis to determine which of the new elements are identical to those already on the IDD. Naming conventions help ensure that identical elements have the same name on the dictionary and links them together.

For example, many records may contain zipcode information, but the zipcode element ZIPCODE should be added to the DD only once. Synonyms and record prefixing/suffixing can be used to generate unique data names for each use of the ZIPCODE element and to link together all uses of the ZIPCODE element. The ZIPCODE element is added to the dictionary with the following DDDL statement:

```
ADD ELEMENT NAME IS ZIPCODE
    PICTURE 9(5) USAGE IS DISPLAY.
```

By using either record prefixing or record suffixing, the ZIPCODE element can be included in several records and have a unique name in each record. For example:

```
ADD RECORD NAME IS CUSTOMER
    RECORD NAME SYNONYM CUSTOMER PREFIX CU-.
        RECORD ELEMENT CUST-NUM.
        RECORD ELEMENT NAME
        RECORD ELEMENT PHONE.
        RECORD ELEMENT LINE1-ADDR.
        RECORD ELEMENT LINE2-ADDR.
        RECORD ELEMENT CITY.
        RECORD ELEMENT STATE.
        RECORD ELEMENT ZIPCODE.

ADD RECORD NAME IS VENDOR
    RECORD NAME SYNONYM VENDOR PREFIX VN-.
        RECORD ELEMENT VENDOR-NUM.
        RECORD ELEMENT NAME.
        RECORD ELEMENT PHONE.
        RECORD ELEMENT LINE1-ADDR.
        RECORD ELEMENT LINE2-ADDR.
        RECORD ELEMENT CITY.
        RECORD ELEMENT STATE.
        RECORD ELEMENT ZIPCODE.
```

Prefixes and suffixes apply to the record elements and subordinate elements, not to the record name. The record CUSTOMER contains the ZIPCODE element to which programs will refer using the name CU-ZIPCODE. The record VENDOR also contains the ZIPCODE element, but it will be referred to as VN-ZIPCODE.

If a record contains more than one zipcode, such as an order record with both bill-to and ship-to addresses, the additional zipcode(s) should be given record element synonyms to create unique field names for program reference. For example:

```
ADD RECORD NAME IS ORDR
    RECORD NAME SYNONYM ORDR PREFIX OR-.
    RECORD ELEMENT ORD-NUM.
        .
        .
        .
    RECORD ELEMENT ZIPCODE.
        .
        .
        .
    RECORD ELEMENT ZIPCODE
    ELEMENT SYNONYM SHIP-ZIPCODE.
```

The ORDR record contains two zipcodes, referenced by the names OR-ZIPCODE and OR-SHIP-ZIPCODE. Defining synonyms may seem like a lot of extra work, but it greatly increases the usefulness of DDR reports. An online display of the ZIPCODE element or an element report will show all the entities using it, including records, maps, and programs.

DDR reports and online IDD displays take on their greatest meaning when the same element names are used repeatedly to refer to the same thing. Without careful data analysis and uniform naming conventions, it is possible to duplicate the same problems of redundancy and confusion which existed before IDMS/R was installed. In other words, a site might end up with 20 different databases containing redundant data and no means of relating them to one another.

3.5.2 Predicting the Impact of Application Changes

The IDD can be used to predict the impact of application changes. If suggestions for controlling redundancy outlined in the previous section have been implemented, determining the scope of the maintenance effort will be relatively easy. The DDR cross-reference reports can track programs which use a particular element or record and document how the programs use them.

For example, records containing a ZIPCODE element can be cross-referenced with the programs in which they occur. When the ZIPCODE element was first defined, the assumption was made that zipcodes were 5 digits long. However, problems will arise when the 9-digit zipcode becomes standard. Although there are several methods for determining how widespread the 5-digit ZIPCODE problem may be, a straight forward approach uses the cross-reference information available from DDR reports. The element/program cross-reference report can identify all programs containing records with the ZIPCODE element. The element report will identify all records and maps containing the ZIPCODE element.

3.5.3 Designing Databases

During the database design process, the IDD can serve as a central repository for information germane to the design process. Typically, DB design involves meetings and discussions with many individual and departmental users concerning data involved, work flows, and business functions that affect the data. Information collected during interviews, including element names, synonyms, work flows, departments, documents, reports, etc., may be stored on the DD and linked together to produce DDR reports documenting how the data is used.

For example, 'CUSTOMER ACCOUNT' could be added as an ELEMENT entity. It could be connected to a SYSTEM entity called 'CAS', Customer Accounting System, and to a USER entity called 'BOB NELSON', the person interviewed. The 'BOB NELSON' USER entity could in turn be connected to a CLASS entity called 'USER DEPARTMENT' and an ATTRIBUTE entity of 'CREDIT'. During the interview, Bob Nelson may have mentioned that the customer account number appears on customer bills and on the Customer Activity List report. We might add a CLASS entity called 'DOCUMENTS' with an ATTRIBUTE entity of 'BILL'. We might also add a REPORT entity occurrence called 'CUSTOMER ACTIVITY LIST' and then link the 'CUSTOMER ACCOUNT' ELEMENT entity to the new ATTRIBUTE and REPORT. Thereafter, if an ELEMENT report was run, we would see that ELEMENT 'CUSTOMER ACCOUNT' is used in a REPORT called 'CUSTOMER ACTIVITY LIST' and in a 'DOCUMENT' called 'BILL' and, further, that information regarding the element came from USER 'BOB NELSON' in the 'USER DEPARTMENT' called 'CREDIT'. (See Section 3.6 for more information on using CLASS and ATTRIBUTE entities to tailor the IDD to site needs.)

The advantage of using the IDD to document the database design process is that a permanent record of documentation will be established. The IDD documentation, unlike written or printed paper documentation, cannot be lost or misplaced. Because it is online, documentation stored in the DD is easily changed and more likely to be kept up-to-date by subsequent analysts. Additionally, the central location of the IDD facilitates communication between analysts working on different portions of a large system, aiding in the elimination of data redundancy.

3.5.4   Documenting the Data Processing Environment

To make the dictionary's information more comprehensive and
meaningful, an installation may choose to document non-IDMS
applications using the IDD.   Documenting non-IDMS applications
usually is accomplished manually by adding to the DD non-IDMS
file and record layouts used by existing applications.   Those records
and files may then be associated with the programs using them.
Although adding information about non-IDMS applications to the DD
may be very time consuming, it could yield substantial benefits in the
future.   Having non-IDMS applications documented in the DD should
ease maintenance.   Also, as these systems get older and are replaced,
the data analysis portion of database design should be much easier
because older systems' data elements will already be documented in
the DD.

The cost in personnel hours to document all non-IDMS applications in the DD could be staggering.   It may be advisable to undertake
a study comparing the relative benefits and costs before beginning
such a project.

Many companies, in an effort to get some degree of documentation
of non-IDMS systems although unwilling to devote the time necessary
to document everything, adopt a middle of the road approach.   They
compile all existing programs through the DML processor to update
the dictionary with program, file, and record entities, and put existing copy library information into the IDD using the DDDL compiler.
If record copy members are added to the DD as records, the ADD
RECORD NAME IS *rec-name* clause must be inserted in the copy
member data.   If the COBOL compiler verbs SKIP or EJECT are present in the copy member data, the DDDL compiler will treat them as
syntax errors.   To avoid those errors, either remove SKIP and EJECT
statements or add the records to the DD as MODULE entity types.

Using the DML processor to document existing applications requires relatively little time to implement and at least captures some
information.   However, remember the old adage of "Garbage in,
Garbage out".   The record and element names in older systems might
not follow current naming conventions, resulting in a large amount
of data redundancy.   Non-IDMS information can be stored in a
secondary dictionary so that dictionaries containing current
database elements, the result of careful analysis and which adhere to
naming conventions, are not cluttered with the records and elements
of older systems.   As older systems are replaced, or as time permits,
the definitions in the secondary dictionary may be merged with those
in the primary DD.

A supplementary Cullinet product, the Dictionary Loader, generates DDDL syntax from program source code to populate the DD with

records and elements; it is an alternative method for documenting non-IDMS programs. It may be used to document programs containing records not stored in copy libraries. The Dictionary Loader also provides reports showing how elements are used in the PROCEDURE DIVISION of the programs (updated, moved, etc.).

3.6 CUSTOMIZING AN IDD

The contents of an IDD may be customized for site-specific requirements by defining:

- New types of entities,
- New descriptors for entities,
- User-defined comments, and
- User-defined nests.

Defining new entity types and new descriptors for entities is accomplished using CLASS and ATTRIBUTE entities. DDR CLASS and ATTRIBUTE reports may be used to report on new entity types and to list entities sorted by new descriptors. User-defined comment information and user-defined nest information appears on standard DDR reports for the affected entity.

3.6.1 Defining New Types of Entities

Cullinet supplies predefined entity types which must be included in the DD population; however, users also may create and define their own entity types. For example, the IDD may be used to create the entity type VENDOR for defining DP equipment and supply sources. The new entity type can be related to any other entity type. New entity types are defined using the CLASS and ATTRIBUTE entities provided with the IDD. A user may establish the entity type PROJECT and define its relationships to USERs and PROGRAMs. The DD can then be used to monitor project activity. The DDDL statements used at SPI to implement this are:

```
ADD CLASS PROJECT
    CLASS TYPE IS ENTITY
    ATTRIBUTES MANUAL PLURAL
    COMMENT 'THIS NEW ENTITY IS USED TO RELATE PROJECTS TO'
        -'USERS, PROGRAMS, AND OTHER ENTITIES'.

ADD PROJECT OVERLORD
    COMMENT 'DISTRIBUTION OF MERCHANDISE IN RESTRICTED '
        -'TRADE ZONES'.
```

```
MODIFY USER ABL
    PROJECT OVERLORD.
```

3.6.2 Defining New Descriptors for Entities

New descriptors may be defined for any entity. 'JOB TITLE', for example, may be added in the DD and associated with USER entities. At SPI, Ms. Plant entered the following DDDL statements:

```
ADD CLASS 'JOB TITLE'
    CLASS TYPE IS CLASS
    ATTRIBUTE MANUAL SINGULAR
    COMMENT 'THIS CLASS ASSOCIATES JOB TITLE WITH USERS'.

ADD ATTRIBUTE COURIER
    WITHIN 'JOB TITLE'.

MODIFY USER ABL
    'JOB TITLE' COURIER.
```

New descriptors defined using CLASS and ATTRIBUTE syntax are global. They may be associated with any entity type in the DD.

New descriptors defined using CLASS and ATTRIBUTE syntax can be a powerful tool for grouping otherwise unrelated entities for report or utility purposes. For example, all entities scheduled to migrate to the quality assurance dictionary might be grouped together by relating each to the same attribute.

3.6.3 User-Defined Comments

Comments are used to describe most entity types and document the entity occurrence more fully. Comments may be one or more lines of text, with each line containing up to 80 characters. IDD allows comments to be stored under any of several predefined headings, such as COMMENTS, DEFINITIONS, and REMARKS. Site-specific comment headings may be created to store comments under more informative headings. For example, a comment heading RESTART may be added to the IDD and used when storing restart documentation for the PROGRAM entity type. Whenever these comments are displayed on DDR reports they will be preceded by the label RESTART. The following DDDL syntax defines the new comment heading:

```
MODIFY ENTITY TYPE PROGRAM
    USER DEFINED COMMENT IS RESTART.
```

The new comment heading, also known as a comment key, may now be used as follows:

```
MODIFY PROGRAM XYZ001
     RESTART 'THIS PROGRAM ACCESSES RESTART RECORD '
          - 'RRXYZ001 TO DETERMINE THE POINT AT WHICH'
          - 'PROCESSING SHOULD RESUME.'.
MODIFY PROGRAM XYZ002
     RESTART 'THIS PROGRAM"S RESTART LOGIC '
          - 'CONSISTS OF .....'.
```

Comment keys are not global, they pertain only to the modified entity type.

3.6.4   User-Defined Nests

Relating one entity to another entity is one of the IDD's most powerful facilities. The IDD supports 'nesting' for most major entity types. Nesting means establishing a relationship between one occurrence of an entity type and another occurrence of the same entity type, relating one program to another program for example. Predefined nested relationships include:

```
ELEMENT -> SUBORDINATE ELEMENT
FILE -> RELATED FILE
PROGRAM -> PROGRAM CALLED
SYSTEM -> WITHIN SYSTEM
USER -> WITHIN USER
```

New types of nested relationships may be established by creating "Relational Keys". A relational key is the word or words that will be used to relate one occurrence of an entity to another. For example, a relational key 'REPORTS TO' may be created to document a USER's manager, another USER occurrence on the DD. The following DDDL syntax creates the 'REPORTS TO' relational key:

```
MODIFY ENTITY TYPE USER
     USER DEFINED NEST IS 'REPORTS TO'.
```

Now a nest can be established using the new relational key as follows:

```
MODIFY USER JOEPROGRAMMER
     'REPORTS TO' BIGBOSS.
```

Relational keys, like comment keys, are not global; they pertain only to the modified entity type.

3.7   AN OVERVIEW OF MULTIPLE DICTIONARIES

The primary dictionary in an IDMS/R environment is composed of
up to seven areas, up to six under Release 5.7. Each area has a unique
purpose, as described in Table 3-2. The system-related areas
DDLDCMSG, DDLDCLOG, DDLDCRUN (optionally replaced by
DDLDCSCR and DDLDCQUE under Release 10), and DDLDCTLF (if
used) are present in only the primary data dictionary. The areas
containing application-related information, the DDLDML area and
the DDLDCLOD area, can be duplicated to create secondary data dictionaries. The DDLDML area contains all source descriptions of
dictionary entities. The DDLDCLOD area contains load modules.
Under Release 10, multiple DDLDML and DDLDCLOD areas can be
set up; under Release 5.7 only the DDLDML area may be duplicated.
Figure 3-3 illustrates primary and secondary dictionary areas.

Each system (e.g., test, quality assurance, production, etc.) has its
own dictionary or dictionaries. A single dictionary system has only
a primary data dictionary. A multiple dictionary system has a primary data dictionary and one or more secondary data dictionaries.

Operating in a single dictionary environment offers several advantages. Entities with duplicate names are automatically rejected
by IDD upon entry. Using one dictionary simplifies the review process necessary to control and enforce standards because the element
report lists all elements. In addition, it is easier to maintain a single
dictionary than multiple dictionaries, thereby decreasing the time
required to make the latest versions of modules and other entities
available to all users.

Multiple dictionaries offer increased security because they permit
centralized control of system-level information and decentralized
control of user systems and data. When several companies exist
within one corporation, using multiple dictionaries permits each
company to establish and enforce its own standards; multiple
dictionaries provide security which can be maintained easily. Users
can be permitted access only to information in one dictionary, thereby
securing dictionary information at the dictionary level (and at the
entity type level within that DD) rather than at the entity occurrence
level.

Multiple dictionaries, one for each major project, also offer flexibility because programmers and managers do not have to wait for a
centralized DBA group to add elements, work/map records, modules,
and other non-DB entities to the DD. This is not to say that standards
adherence is being delayed or ignored in secondary dictionaries;
programmers should follow standards on all data dictionaries.
However, with multiple data dictionaries, programmers may be

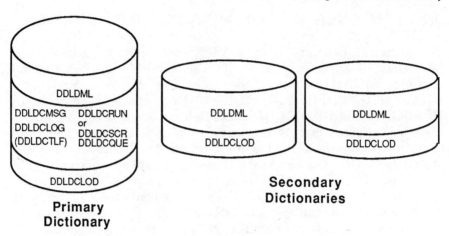

Figure 3-3 Primary versus Secondary Dictionary Areas

allowed to complete the initial testing phase without having to go through the DBA group. Programs should be reviewed after initial testing to verify that standards have been followed. If nonstandard names are found in applications, programmers should be required to go back and rename program components correctly.

3.8   USES OF SECONDARY DICTIONARIES

Secondary dictionaries can be used:

- As an alternative to multiple systems,
- To isolate and secure data descriptions,
- As dedicated project development environments,
- To facilitate phased implementation of projects, and
- To improve performance by reducing contention for dictionary resources.

3.8.1   An Alternative to Multiple Systems

Chapter 2 examined the types of systems implemented at most IDMS/R sites. Each system requires significant resources. When available resources limit the number of systems, multiple dictionaries can serve as an alternative to additional systems because they require less memory and CPU resources. Multiple systems provide better isolation than multiple DD's, which is useful for performance testing and prevention of system crashes. For example, system testing carried out on the test system using multiple DD's cannot show the affects of a new application on production processing as clearly as when system testing is carried out on a separate quality assurance system.

Production processing is usually run on a separate system because protection of the production environment is crucial to businesses dependent on data processing for normal business activities. In those rare instances when production and test processing are run under the same CV/DC system, protecting the production environment is the single most important reason for creating multiple DD's. Although destruction of test data or system definitions for projects under development is a major problem and can be a major disaster for a development team, clearly it is not as serious as the destruction of all production data. The DD contains the description and source code for many parts of the production system. Schemas, records, and dialogs may be isolated and protected in a separate production dictionary once they are developed and tested.

3.8.2   Isolation and Security for Data Descriptions

In the modern business climate, inadvertent destruction of data and data definitions is as disruptive as any other form of corporate resource loss.   Segregation of data definitions using multiple dictionaries allows for safe program testing by separate departments, agencies, and/or projects.   For example, in a service bureau environment when there are not enough resources for separate systems for each major client, separate dictionaries may be used to isolate and secure client data. Otherwise, with all client data in one DD, each entity would have to be secured with the INCLUDE USER *user-id* REGISTERED FOR *permitted-accesses*. Chapter 6, on security, details dictionary security facilities and considerations.

3.8.3   Providing a Dedicated Development Environment

A secondary dictionary can provide a dedicated development environment for application projects. Allocating separate dictionaries for major projects provides security, flexibility, and responsiveness to project needs. Separate dictionaries are essential to implementing a project in phases when each phase is developed on a common system.

Secondary dictionaries offer flexibility. Dictionary standards may be adopted which best apply to each project and which conform logically with the project's goals and objectives. Data descriptions may be placed in one secondary dictionary without conflicting with entries in other dictionaries (i.e., the same entity names may be used).

By fine tuning a dictionary to the needs of a project, responses to requests for service can be handled more efficiently. For example, applications personnel using a secondary dictionary could be given unlimited use of classes and attributes, facilitating listing of pertinent entities. A class of 'SYSTEM ID' could be defined with an attribute of 'CSA.' The 'CSA' attribute then could be included on all modules, records, elements, and maps belonging to CSA, making it a snap to list all entities related to the CSA system by issuing a 'DISPLAY ATTRIBUTE CSA' command. Another example of using classes and attributes might be defining a 'CHANGE AUTHORIZATION' class with an attribute of 'BOBH' which would be linked into all items involved in changes, i.e., maps, dialogs, modules, records. In general, unlimited use of IDD facilities such as CLASS and ATTRIBUTE definition is not permitted if only a primary dictionary is in use.

Reporting from the dictionary can become a localized function for each project with its own dictionary. Localization simplifies dictionary access and use by the project teams. For example, with secondary dictionaries an element report shows only those elements on that dictionary, i.e., one project's elements, whereas running the same report run when only one IDD is in use will show every project's elements.

Implementing secondary IDD's insures that only a portion of the shop is down if a dictionary DDLDML area becomes full. Only the project group whose dictionary is full need wait while the expand page utility or the unload/reload utilities are run, other project groups working with different dictionaries are unaffected.

3.8.4   Phased Implementation of Projects

Multiple dictionaries are essential when implementing projects in phases, if all phases are under development on the same system (i.e., there is no separate quality assurance system). A dictionary may be allocated for each phase of a project. As systems or subsystems are completed and tested they may be moved from one dictionary to the next for integration or further testing. Changes to modules and entity descriptions can be tested with less disruption to ongoing processing. One phase can be in system testing on the primary DD, while changes for the next phase are being worked on in a secondary DD. Phased implementation using multiple dictionaries permits different phases of the database definition to undergo testing concurrently even though the same names are used in each phase. Further, security can be tailored as appropriate for each phase.

Two levels of dictionaries are commonly used for phased implementation on a single system, namely, development and quality assurance. The development dictionary is controlled and administered by the development team for their specific needs. Access to this dictionary is generally available to all members of the development team having proper authority. Additions and modifications are usually allowed within the standards and conventions set for the dictionary.

The quality assurance dictionary is used during testing which verifies that individual parts of a system work together in an integrated environment. Additions to the QA dictionary are allowed for system turnover and testing. Development personnel are generally not permitted to modify entities in this dictionary.

After the project passes quality assurance testing, the entities are migrated to the production dictionary, which is usually associated with a *separate* system. The production dictionary is stringently controlled to guarantee the integrity of the production system.

Multiple systems or multiple versions of entities on one dictionary may be used as an alternative to multiple dictionaries in phased implementation. When the resources for a separate system are available, multiple systems are often used in conjunction with or as an alternative to multiple dictionaries during phased implementation of projects.

Using a distinct version number for each phase's dictionary entities along with the DCUF TEST facility (not available to DOS sites) permits one to set a specific version for programs and/or dialogs to be tested at a specific terminal. For phased implementation using DCUF TEST, separate versions of all changed modules must be set up and the DCUF TEST command issued. The separate version would be used only on the terminal where the DCUF TEST command was issued. When using the DCUF facility, IDMS-DC programmers must link the new versions of their programs into a separate load library. The DDNAME referencing the separate load library corresponds to the version number set at the terminal through the DCUF TEST command. For example, if version 2 was specified in the DCUF TEST command, a load library must be established and referenced in the system startup JCL with the DDNAME CDMSL002.

3.8.5 Performance Advantages Through Decreased Contention

Dictionaries are used heavily during development. Having multiple dictionaries rather than a single primary dictionary can improve performance by reducing contention, especially for those shops doing a large amount of Online Mapping and/or ADS/O development. The performance advantage achieved through implementing multiple dictionaries is mostly the result of reducing both the number of locks held and the incidence of deadlocking. Improved performance is even more noticeable when schema and sysgen changes are occurring along with application development.

Load area contention problems caused by very large dictionary load modules (e.g., load modules overflowing to several pages and slowing response) can be minimized or restricted with multiple secondary load areas. If, for example, Project 1 has a separate dictionary then even if its dialogs are extremely large, occupying 30 pages of load area on the average, the large load modules can impact only Project 1. Similarly, disk contention could be decreased by assigning each secondary dictionary to a separate pack.

3.9 HOW MANY DICTIONARIES SHOULD BE IMPLEMENTED?

A different number of dictionaries are implemented depending on the system with which the dictionary is associated. Initially, either a single or multiple dictionary environment is chosen for each system. If a multiple dictionary environment is selected the next decision is how many dictionaries to implement. The users of and purposes for each dictionary must be determined, i.e. one for each department or team or individual.

Although many organizations have no qualms about unrestricted use of secondary dictionaries on the test system, the control of production information is usually handled in a more centralized manner. There is often only one production dictionary. We will examine considerations for choosing number of dictionaries on the systems commonly used in the development cycle.

3.9.1 Test System's Dictionaries

At one end of the spectrum, each development team may have its own separate dictionary with total freedom of development; only database records and elements are entered by the DBA group. The opposite end of the spectrum is extremely tight control of all development under a single development dictionary, with the DBA group being responsible for all IDD entities, including ADS/O work records and elements, classes and attributes and so forth. Many alternatives lie between these two extremes.

Dictionaries may be allocated along organizational lines, giving each division, section, or department a separate dictionary for development. This is a 'natural' break point which provides an established framework for control and organization. Alternatively, secondary dictionaries may be allocated along the lines of application development. Each new major development project may have a separate dictionary established for the life of that project. Control and integration of dictionaries along either organizational or project lines is only as good as the management of the organization or project they serve.

One of the benefits of dictionary usage is increased control over data descriptions. Therefore, it is logical to require any implementation of secondary dictionaries to be controlled and organized. In many shops, tools such as a data dictionary are acquired by management to help control the environment and are promptly bypassed to allow development to continue in the usual pattern. For example, each group or each programmer can be allotted their own dictionary, thereby circumventing controls and allowing them total freedom. Total freedom is undesirable because it often results in nonstandard and/or redundant data descriptions. This is why it is extremely helpful to establish dictionaries along existing organizational or major project group lines. The built-in control provided by a framework already in place is very helpful where enforcement of standards and procedures is involved. In large installations, allocating DD's along organizational lines usually results in each subsidiary or division having their own dictionary, while in smaller installations, the allocation of dictionaries might be along section or department or major project lines.

It is important to remember that dictionaries provide centralized control of both the development and production environment. A multiple dictionary environment should allow flexibility, but still function within and not as a means to bypass system control. Allocating secondary dictionaries along existing organization lines, or at least only for major development efforts, assures a certain degree of control. Standards and usage which conform to the existing structure of control will be adhered to more easily.

3.9.2 Quality Assurance (QA) System's Dictionary

The quality assurance environment should mirror production with the addition of the new application. Therefore, the QA dictionary configuration should be the same as the production dictionary configuration.

3.9.3 Production System's Dictionary

The production system generally has only a single primary IDD. The requirements which lead to implementing multiple dictionaries in test systems, such as several applications requiring element and record definitions quickly, naming conflicts, security considerations, and phased implementation of projects, are no longer requirements in a production system. New element and record definitions should not be developed on the production dictionary. Naming conflicts should have been resolved during acceptance or QA testing and security can be handled through a separate QA group responsible for all migrations of definitions and modules from one system to another. Phased implementation of projects, where each phase is under development on the same system, is not a requirement of production systems. Clearly, these requirements are not applicable in the production environment. The benefits of a single dictionary environment, namely easier maintenance and control of dictionary entities, outweigh the benefits of a multiple dictionary environment for production systems.

3.9.4   Production Maintenance System's Dictionary

The production maintenance system's DD configuration should be identical to the production system's dictionary configuration. The only difference between the dictionaries would be area page ranges or page groups, and the files to which the areas map.

3.10   IMPLEMENTING A NEW SECONDARY DICTIONARY

There are several considerations when implementing a new secondary dictionary. These considerations include:

- •Advance planning,
- •Choosing the contents of the secondary dictionary,
- •Creating the new secondary dictionary,
- •Establishing procedures for accessing the secondary dictionary, and,
- •Establishing migration procedures.

3.10.1   Advance Planning for Secondary DD Implementation

Once the questions have been settled concerning how many dictionaries to install, it is time to plan the implementation of secondary dictionaries. The important point to keep in mind is that secondary dictionaries provide a great deal of flexibility but they still must be controlled. It is not sufficient for the DBA/DDA to provide an unlimited number of secondary dictionaries and declare that the users are now responsible for their use and control. The use of dictionaries may be decentralized but the control and responsibility for all dictionaries is ultimately that of the DBA/DDA. Proper planning and installation of secondary DD's are crucial steps to avoid problems in secondary DD use.

When planning implementation of a new secondary dictionary, the following steps should be taken into consideration:

- Creating standards and procedures for dictionary usage, and
- Establishing a solid migration plan.

Creating Standards and Procedures for Dictionary Usage: Standards must be created for entity names and descriptions as well as procedures for using various products with the secondary dictionary. Standards are detailed in Chapter 4. Section 3.10.4 covers considerations and procedures for using many Cullinet products with secondary dictionaries.

Establishing a Migration Plan: It may seem premature to discuss a migration plan for secondary dictionaries before establishing them, however it is critical to have such a plan as early as possible. It is not sufficient only to add information to the secondary dictionary, access to and extraction of that data are crucial also. Section 3.10.5 examines dictionary migration considerations.

3.10.2   What Goes in Each Secondary Dictionary?

Two choices must be made regarding dictionary contents. These choices are:

- How many areas should be created?
- Which Cullinet-supplied entities, source and load module, should be stored on the secondary DD as well as on the primary DD?

How many areas should be created? Creating a new DDLDML area means that a new secondary dictionary has been created. Under Release 5.7, only the DDLDML area may be duplicated. Under Release 10, a new DDLDCLOD area optionally may be created in addition to the DDLDML area for each secondary dictionary.

When all load modules are stored in primary load area, load module names must be unique throughout the system. Therefore, phased implementation would require different names for equivalent load modules which are in different stages of development (or, under OS, DCUF TEST and different version numbers may be used), negating many of the advantages of multiple dictionaries. For

Release 10 sites, we recommend setting up a secondary load area for each new secondary dictionary. We feel that secondary load areas are an improvement over DCUF TEST in facilitating phased implementation of a project, as well as providing performance advantages.

Production systems generally have only a primary dictionary. However, if packaged software is implemented, such as Cullinet's General Ledger application, it is often convenient to implement a secondary DDLDML area for the package but not a secondary load area. This eliminates naming conflicts for database definitions yet keeps user access simple. With only one DDLDCLOD area, a user never has to signon to any special DD to run application dialogs and programs, making the secondary dictionary transparent to the users.

Which Cullinet-supplied entities should be stored on the secondary DD? All Cullinet-supplied dictionary entities (i.e., DDR report source; dictionary schema, subschema, and DMCL source; protocols; and sysgen include modules) must be stored on the primary DD. All these entities can be repeated on each secondary dictionary. Some information must be repeated on each secondary DD, namely, ADS/O global records and DML program protocols. However, maintaining the rest only on the primary dictionary saves both disk space and maintenance effort.

The trade off between repeating all Cullinet-supplied entities versus repeating only the required entities comes down to ease of dictionary use by the applications staff versus how much duplication of information (and resulting maintenance) is tolerable. Our recommendation is that, wherever possible, maintain Cullinet-supplied entities only on the primary DD and use DICTNAME and DBNAME parameters to access the appropriate information when running the Cullinet compilers. This strategy will necessitate creating tailored procedures for each secondary DD (Section 3.10.4). There may be some confusion at first, but most organizations consider temporary confusion preferable to maintaining redundant information.

3.10.3 Creating a New Secondary Dictionary

An overview of creating a new secondary dictionary is presented in Figure 3-4. First, page ranges for the new DDLDML area and, optionally, the new DDLDCLOD area, are chosen. Next, the new area(s) are created and populated. Finally, the updates required for CV access to the new secondary dictionary are made.

Step 1, Assign Page Ranges for New Dictionary Area(s): Assign new page ranges for the new DDLDML area and DDLDCLOD area (Release 10) in the same fashion as for any new database. It is

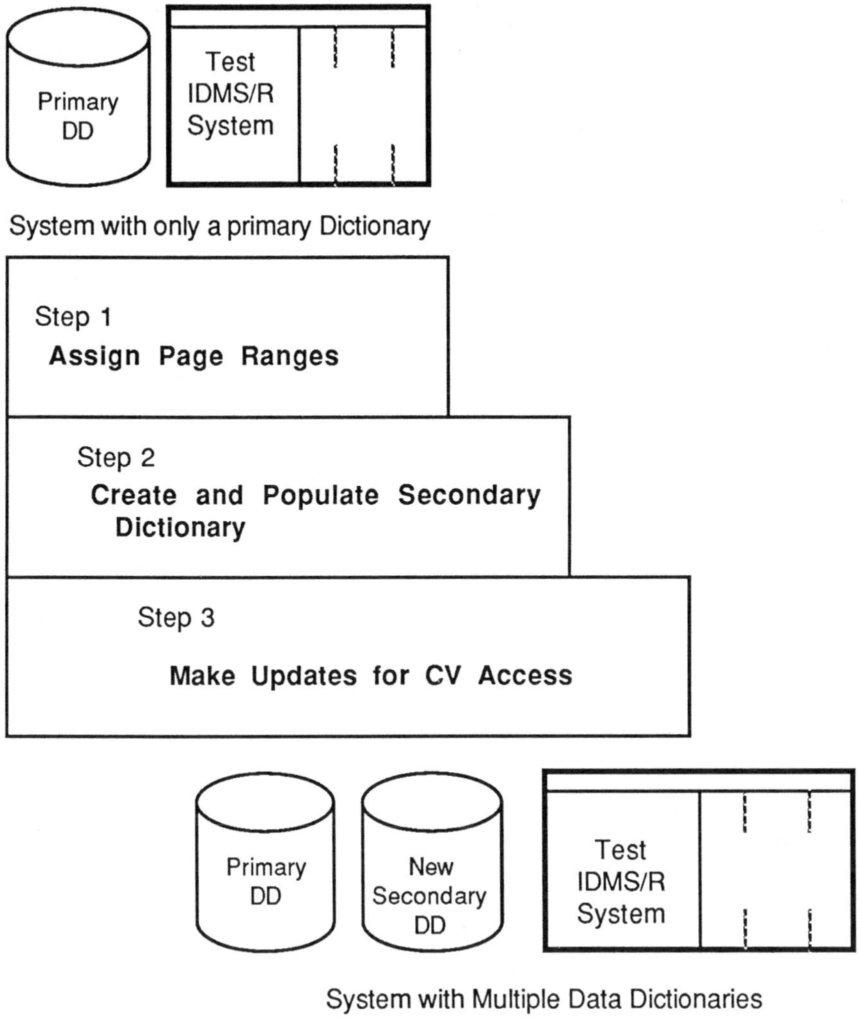
Primary
DD
Test
IDMS/R
System
System with only a primary Dictionary
Step 1
Assign Page Ranges
Step 2
Create and Populate Secondary Dictionary
Step 3
Make Updates for CV Access
Primary
DD
New
Secondary
DD
Test
IDMS/R
System
System with Multiple Data Dictionaries

Figure 3-4 Overview of Steps to Implement a New Secondary Dictionary

generally a good idea to restrict all database and dictionary page ranges on all CV's to unique ranges. When unique page ranges are not possible due to extremely large databases, attempt to restrict dictionary pages to unique ranges. If this guideline is followed, secondary dictionaries can reside on any CV without conflicting with other dictionaries or databases.

Step 2, Create and Populate the New Secondary Dictionary: Creating and populating the new secondary dictionary involves several steps. These steps are illustrated in Figure 3-5. Appendix A contains a sample OS jobstream, named 'CREATE EDUDICT' which

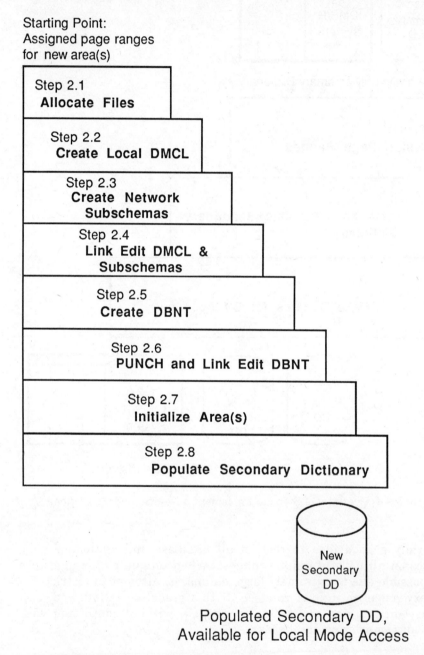

Starting Point:
Assigned page ranges
for new area(s)

Step 2.1
Allocate Files

Step 2.2
Create Local DMCL

Step 2.3
Create Network Subschemas

Step 2.4
Link Edit DMCL & Subschemas

Step 2.5
Create DBNT

Step 2.6
PUNCH and Link Edit DBNT

Step 2.7
Initialize Area(s)

Step 2.8
Populate Secondary Dictionary

New
Secondary
DD

Populated Secondary DD,
Available for Local Mode Access

Figure 3-5 Steps to Create and Populate a New Secondary Dictionary

builds a secondary DD under Release 10. The sample job creates both a new DDLDML area and a new DDLDCLOD area.

Step 2.1, Allocate Files: Allocate the new datasets for the files to which the new dictionary areas will map. While size is dependent on anticipated use and growth, we recommend starting with 25 cylinders on a 3380 disk drive for the DDLDML area and 10-15 cylinders for the DDLDCLOD area. The DDLDML area can be blocked on 4K boundaries whereas the DDLDCLOD area should have larger pages if ADS/O development is anticipated (perhaps 15,476 on a 3380).

Step 2.2, Create Local DMCL: Create a new DMCL containing the new page ranges assignments and the block mapping for the new files created in previous steps. This DMCL will be used to run the following secondary dictionary installation steps. Subsequently, this DMCL will be used for local mode access (refer to Chapter 5 for a discussion of local mode operations).

Step 2.3, Create Network Subschemas: Separate subschemas must be created for each secondary dictionary using the IDMSRNWK utility. The primary dictionary's subschemas are created during installation of IDMS/R. A similar generation must be performed for the group of subschemas needed for each secondary dictionary. The IDMSRNWK utility is run with a unique subschema name and a unique page range specified for each secondary dictionary being created.

The easiest solution is to create only one network subschema, *xxxxNWKA* (where *xxxx* is a unique acronym identifying the secondary dictionary), and to map all network subschemas to *xxxxNWKA* through a DBNT. The *xxxxNWKA* subschema contains everything needed at run time by most of the compilers, except the ASF compiler, which requires *xxxxNWKA, xxxxNWKX,* and *xxxxNWKS* subschemas.

Step 2.4, Link Edit DMCL and Subschemas: The local DMCL and network subschemas created previously must be link edited into the load or core image library referenced in subsequent steps.

Step 2.5 Create Database Name Table (DBNT): The next step to implementing a new secondary dictionary is establishing a DBNAME table. The DBNT translates each primary dictionary subschema name to the appropriate subschema name for the secondary dictionary. DBNT's are created using the sysgen compiler and provide a method of swapping page ranges/groups at run time. The access of secondary dictionaries by batch jobs run in local mode can be accomplished by using the PUNCH facility of the IDD to produce a load library/core image library module version of the DBNAME table.

Using the SYSGEN compiler, create a Database Name Table mapping each network subschema to the corresponding secondary dictionary subschema created in step 2.3 above. If *xxxxNWKA* was the only subschema created, the DBNT should map all network subschemas to *xxxxNWKA*, thus reducing the maintenance of multiple DD's because only one subschema need be maintained. Further, there will be less program loading because all subschema requests from any compiler become requests for the *xxxxNWKA* subschema. To improve performance, make the *xxxxNWKA* subschema resident. A DBNT for local mode use can be created by modifying a demo system, SYSTEM 90 in this example.

```
MOD SYSTEM 90.
    ADD DBNAME ABCDDICT
        SUBSCHEMA IDMS???? MAPS TO ABCDNWKA.
```

The subschema ABCDNWKA will be loaded and used at run time whenever the ABCDDICT database name table is invoked. ABCDNWKA contains area page ranges/groups unique to its secondary dictionary and corresponding to its discrete data sets.

Step 2.6, PUNCH and Link Edit DBNT: Run the IDD compiler, IDMSDDDL, to PUNCH the DBNT, by specifying PUNCH LOAD MODULE IDMSDBTB VERSION n where n is the system version number identifying the system modified in step 2.5. The IDMSDBTB load module contains all DBNAMEs associated with the specified system. Link edit the punched table into the load or core image library referenced in subsequent steps. The DBNT may now be used for local mode dictionary access.

Step 2.7, Initialize Area(s): Initialize the new DD area or areas using the IDMSINIT utility and the local DMCL created in step 2.2.

Step 2.8 Populate Secondary dictionary: Populate the secondary DD either by running all the install steps from JJOB3 of the Cullinet installation jobstream (if you want the secondary DD to contain its own copies of the DDR report source, IDMSNWKA subschema source, and sysgen modules) or by running only selected steps of the installation jobstream as shown in the sample jobstream 'CREATE EDUDICT' in Appendix A. To minimize redundant information, DDR report source and as many Cullinet entities as possible should exist only on the primary DD. However, several DD components must be established in each secondary dictionary regardless of what decision on DDR report source is made, i.e., protocols for DML compiles, ADS/O global records, and ADS/O status definition records. The Cullinet-supplied modules: DLODDEFS, DLODPROT, and ADSRECDS contain the bare minimum of information for the secondary dictionary DDLDML area. DLODDEFS contains standard classes and attributes, e.g., 'ELEMENT DESIGNATOR' and LANGUAGE. DLODPROT contains module source for call translation and several versions of the subschema control block. ADSRECDS contains the layout of the ADS/O status definition records. If ADS/O will be used, also run IDMSDDDL to put the RHDCEVBY load module in each secondary dictionary load area. The RHDCEVBY table is required for Release 10 ADS/O extended functions.

During each maintenance reinstallation, the reinstall job stream should be reviewed to determine whether any additional entities or load modules are required in secondary dictionaries. If so, the secondary DD creation procedure should be modified accordingly.

Step 3, Make Updates for CV Access: After the secondary dictionary areas have been created and populated with the required Cullinet-supplied entities, several updates must be made so that the online IDMS/R system can access the secondary dictionary. Figure 3-6 illustrates the steps involved.

Step 3.1, Update Global Schema: The file and area descriptions for the primary dictionary are contained in the CDMSNTWK schema in the IDMS/R source library. Although new area and file descriptions for secondary dictionaries can be included in the CDMSNTWK schema, we highly recommend creating a new schema or updating the global application schema to contain information for secondary dictionaries. An inadvertent error while modifying CDMSNTWK could be disastrous because IDMS/R can function only with proper area descriptions for the primary dictionary.

Step 3.2, Update Global DMCL: The global DMCL used by the online system must be updated to include descriptions of the new areas. The buffer pools used during access to the new dictionary must be specified as well, either by identifying an existing buffer pool for the new area(s) to share or by creating a new buffer pool.

Step 3.3, Modify SYSTEM for new DBNT: For CV access, a database name table mapping primary network subschemas to secondary network subschemas is added to the CV system generation. The DBNT is identical to that created in step 2.5, but now the system being modified is the current CV system rather than a demo system.

Step 3.4, Update Startup JCL: Update the execution JCL for the IDMS-CV-DC/UCF system to include the new datasets.

Step 3.5, Bring up System: The next time the system is brought up, the new secondary dictionary is available for online access. See Section 3.10.4 for procedures for accessing secondary dictionaries from various products.

Step 3.6, Update USER Entities: The users who will be working with the must have a USER entity defined on the Primary DD, allowing them authority to signon to the online system. In addition, USERs must be defined in the new dictionary, specifying their authorities when working in the new dictionary. Under Release 10, user profiles should be updated to specify a CLIST which automates signon to the new secondary dictionary. Assuming that the user's

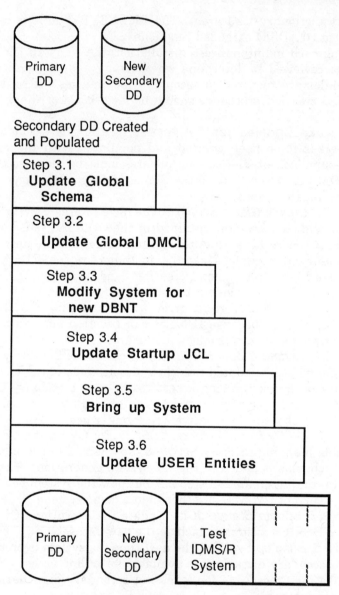

Figure 3-6 Updates for CV Access to a New Secondary Dictionary

profile in the primary DD identifies a CLIST which includes the DCUF SET DICTNAME command to switch processing to the secondary DD, all authorities should be specified on the secondary DD. See Section 3.10.4 for further details.

3.10.4   Procedures for Accessing Secondary Dictionaries

Access to a secondary dictionary is provided by specifying the correct DICTNAME and DBNAME parameter at execution time. These parameters identify database name tables which in turn identify databases, either primary or secondary dictionaries in this case. When we say DICTNAME=ABCDDICT, the DBNT corresponding to ABCDDICT swaps subschema names at run time:

```
ADD DBNAME ABCDDICT
    SUBSCHEMA IDMSNWKA MAPS TO ABCDNWKA.
```

The subschema ABCDNWKA will be loaded and used at run time for our application. The subschema contains area page ranges/groups unique to its dictionary and corresponding to its unique data sets.

The DICTNAME parameter, used by itself, identifies the dictionary where Cullinet compilers/generators can find the Cullinet-supplied entities needed for the task at hand (DDR report source, subschema source, network subschema load modules, etc.). The DICTNAME parameter also indicates where the object of the run resides. If both DICTNAME and DBNAME are specified, the DICTNAME parameter indicates to the software where Cullinet-supplied entities are to be found and the DBNAME parameter identifies the target dictionary where the object of the run resides. For example, to run DDR reports against a secondary dictionary when DREPORT source is stored only on the primary dictionary, specify a DICTNAME parameter value equal to the primary DD name and a DBNAME parameter value equal to the secondary dictionary name, e.g.,

```
DATABASE DICTNAME=primary-DD-name DBNAME=ABCDDICT
DREPORT=009
```

Protocols are the only exception to DICTNAME indicating to the compilers where Cullinet-supplied entities are to be found. Program compiles will fail if the program's subschema resides in a secondary dictionary and the protocol resides in the primary DD. Because application subschemas commonly reside on secondary dictionaries, we recommend that protocols be repeated on each secondary dictionary.

Using Cullinet Products with Secondary Dictionaries: Some special procedures should be developed to automate dictionary identification when using various Cullinet products. Assuming that the minimum Cullinet-supplied entities are repeated on secondary dictionaries, DICTNAME and DBNAME parameters must be supplied when using various products.

DICTNAME specification can be automated at Release 10 sites and will apply to an entire online session. The USER entity for each user working with the new secondary dictionary should be modified to include a signon profile CLIST (see Figure 3-7). When the user signs on to the online system, the signon automatically invokes the CLIST which issues the command:

DCUF SET DICTNAME=*secondary-DD-name*

This command switches the entire online session to the secondary DD. Under releases of IDMS prior to 10, the CLIST facility does not exist and users must be relied upon to specify the proper DICTNAME when using each of the software compilers and generators.

To run DDR reports, code the DATABASE card to read:

DATABASE DICTNAME=*primary-DD-name* DBNAME=*secondary-DD-name*

For OLQ to access a secondary dictionary's sets, the following signon statement should be entered:

SIGNON DICTNAME=*pri-DD-name* DBNAME=*sec-DD-name* SS=IDMSNWKA

If there are multiple dictionary load areas (Release 10) and an IDMS-DC program's map and subschema are stored in a secondary load area, a DCUF SET DICTNAME=*secondary-DD-name* command must be issued prior to execution of that DC program. Otherwise, a '4633' error status will result, indicating that the system is unable to load the map or table. The DC program will be loaded from a load or core image library. For batch or CICS programs, subschemas developed on a secondary dictionary must be duplicated on the primary load area, or be punched and link edited to a load or core image library (LL/CIL), or code the BIND RUN-UNIT DICTNAME *secondary-DD-name* statement in the program. When choosing between those options, keep in mind that the subschema must be punched and link edited to an LL/CIL to be available for local mode use.

3.10.5   Migrations of Dictionary Entities

Migration of dictionary entities can be an extremely time consuming and involved procedure. As of this writing, Cullinet does not offer any automated procedures for migration of entities from one dictionary to another. The problem can be approached entity-by-entity, identifying each component to be transferred, and then manually coding the JCL job streams and the input parameters to the compilers.

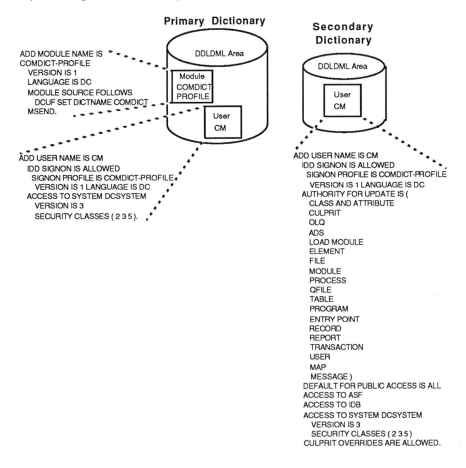

Primary Dictionary

Secondary Dictionary

ADD MODULE NAME IS
COMDICT-PROFILE
    VERSION IS 1
    LANGUAGE IS DC
    MODULE SOURCE FOLLOWS
        DCUF SET DICTNAME COMDICT
    MSEND.

ADD USER NAME IS CM
    IDD SIGNON IS ALLOWED
        SIGNON PROFILE IS COMDICT-PROFILE
        VERSION IS 1 LANGUAGE IS DC
    ACCESS TO SYSTEM DCSYSTEM
        VERSION IS 3
    SECURITY CLASSES (2 3 5).

ADD USER NAME IS CM
    IDD SIGNON IS ALLOWED
        SIGNON PROFILE IS COMDICT-PROFILE
        VERSION IS 1 LANGUAGE IS DC
    AUTHORITY FOR UPDATE IS (
        CLASS AND ATTRIBUTE
        CULPRIT
        OLQ
        ADS
        LOAD MODULE
        ELEMENT
        FILE
        MODULE
        PROCESS
        QFILE
        TABLE
        PROGRAM
        ENTRY POINT
        RECORD
        REPORT
        TRANSACTION
        USER
        MAP
        MESSAGE)
    DEFAULT FOR PUBLIC ACCESS IS ALL
    ACCESS TO ASF
    ACCESS TO IDB
    ACCESS TO SYSTEM DCSYSTEM
        VERSION IS 3
    SECURITY CLASSES (2 3 5)
    CULPRIT OVERRIDES ARE ALLOWED.

Figure 3-7 User Signon Profiles

In a busy development environment, manual migrationprocedures often become a full time job for several employees.

Alternatively, an automated migration procedure can be developed in-house or purchased from third party software vendors. The automated procedure should extract entities from one IDD and add or update the entities in the target IDD. Several vendors, including the authors of this book, offer utilities to generate syntax for input to the various Cullinet compilers, permitting migration to be completed with minimal manual involvement. If personnel are available, creating in-house migration utility programs might be considered as an alternative to purchasing a migration utility.

Any migration program, purchased or developed, should meet the following criteria:

- The method for identifying entities to be migrated should be simple.
- An audit trail of entities which have been migrated should be readily available.
- All related entities should be migrated concurrently when a changed entity is migrated.

Identifying entities to be migrated: Entities to be migrated are often identified using CLASS and ATTRIBUTES. They may also be identified using a SYSTEM entity and migrating all entities associated with that system entity.

Audit Trail: The ideal way to track those entities which have been migrated is to link each one to a unique CLASS-ATTRIBUTE structure, thus enabling an IDD report or display to show both when and how many times an entity has been migrated.

Automatically migrating related entities: The ideal migration utility will determine all maps, dialogs, schemas, and subschemas affected by the change and will not only migrate but also recompile all affected entities. On a map record change, for example, migrating and recompiling related entities would entail migrating the map record and regenerating the associated dialog or recompiling the DC program as well as recompiling the map on the target dictionary. Table 3-4 contains a sample list of the related entities to be migrated along with the specified entity.

Overview of Writing an In-house Migration Utility: A migration utility for specific site requirements can be written in-house. The main idea behind all migration utilities is that a starting point must be provided, usually the name of a changed entity. Starting points include names of dialogs, maps, records, modules, schema, and subschemas which have changed and should be migrated. One method of providing a starting point is defining a class/attribute structure and requiring the applications group to link the changed entities to that class/attribute. Using a class/attribute construct leaves a permanent audit trail in the dictionary of how many times and when entities were migrated. For example,

```
ADD CLASS MIGRDATE.
ADD ATTRIBUTE 031887R1
      WITHIN CLASS MIGRDATE.
MOD MODULE ABCD-UTIL-RP
      MIGRDATE IS 031887R1.
MOD RECORD DBD002A-WK
      MIGRDATE IS 031887R1.
```

Table 3-4 Migration of Related Entities

Name Supplied	Main Entity Type	Related Entities Transferred
Dialog name	PROGRAM	MODULEs LOAD MODULEs MAPs RECORDs (database, work, and map) GROUP and SUBORDINATE ELEMENTS
Map name	MAP	RECORDs (used in MAP) GROUP and SUBORDINATE ELEMENTS
Module name	MODULE	All dialog LOAD MODULES in which this MODULE is used
Record name	RECORD	GROUP and SUBORDINATE ELEMENTS
Table name	MODULE	LOAD MODULEs

The migration program should then bind a retrieval run unit to the desired sending dictionary (subschema IDMSNWKA using a BIND DBNAME=DICTNAME where appropriate). Then the program should issue an OBTAIN CALC of the attribute name provided to this migration run, e.g., 031887R1 (where 'R1' indicates the first migration run of the day). After verifying that the attribute is associated with a class of MIGRDATE, the appropriate dictionary sets must be walked and PUNCH *entity-name* syntax card images must be written to output data sets. The output data sets will be used later as input to Cullinet compilers.

A migration program must walk sets on the DD to identify all components of the entity to be transferred, e.g., dialogs, maps, or records. Information needed to code programs accessing a dictionary database is contained in the IDMSDDDL Network Reference Guide (i.e., record names, set names, elements names, area names, and their uses). A sample migration program is included in Appendix A. The sample migration program is specific to one site's requirements and is presented solely as a model for those interested in writing their own migration programs.

3.11   CONCLUSION

In this chapter we discussed:

- The components of the Integrated Data Dictionary: the Data Dictionary, the Data Dictionary Definition Language Compiler, and the Dictionary/Directory Reporter;
- The population of a Data Dictionary and database at SPI, a fictitious corporation which has just acquired IDMS;
- The function of the IDD as a central repository of information, serving to integrate the system software products;
- The required uses of the IDD for storage of system configurations, database definitions, maps, and ADS/O dialogs;
- Making optional use of the IDD: to minimize data redundancy, to predict the impact of application change, to aid in the database design process, and to store and report on information documenting non-IDMS applications as well as IDMS applications;
- How the IDD may be tailored to site-specific needs by creating new entity types, new descriptors for entities, user-defined comments, and user-defined nests;
- The uses of secondary data dictionaries: as an alternative to multiple systems, to isolate and secure entities, to provide a dedicated project development environment, and to facilitate phased project implementation; and
- How to implement a new secondary dictionary.

In conclusion, we would like to stress again the importance of the IDD within an IDMS/R system. It is the focal point for communication between system software products. Because of the IDD's importance, standards for dictionary entity names should be implemented early on.

Suggestions for further reading on Data Dictionaries:

The following Cullinet manuals
    For Release 10 installations:
        1) IDD DDDL Reference (DDDL syntax)
        2) IDD User's Guide (Overview of IDD, security, multiple DD's)
        3) IDD Network Reference (Dictionary database structure)
        4) DDR User's Guide (Report formats, how to customize reports)

5) The Integrated Installation Guide (DD area descriptions)
6) IDMS/R Database Operations (Multiple DD's)

For Release 5.7 installations:
1) IDD DDDL Reference (DDDL syntax)
2) IDD User's Guide (Overview of IDD, security, multiple DD's)
3) IDD Network Reference (Dictionary database structure)
4) DDR User's Guide (Report formats, how to customize reports)
5) The Integrated Installation Guide (DD area descriptions, multiple DD's)

4

Standards

Standards are part of everyday life. Standards help ensure product uniformity for both producers and consumers. For example, there are standards of measurement for such items as clothing, shoes, plumbing supplies, and electrical supplies. If every shoe manufacturer adopted a different sizing standard, shopping for a pair of shoes would be very confusing.

In the data processing environment standards are a way of life also. There are standard programming languages, standard data communications protocols, and standard file organizations among others. For example, COBOL is a standard language assuring portability of software across different types of hardware. Most organizations establish standard naming conventions for data processing entities. Standards facilitate communication among data processing staff and help eliminate redundant data. Data processing consistency is achieved by such standards.

Most organizations rely on the DBA/DDA groups to provide standards, guidelines, and procedures in many areas. Detailing all possible standards, guidelines, and procedures is beyond the scope of this book because it would entail another volume. Instead, our primary aims are to provide an overview of the types of standards, guidelines, and procedures commonly established, followed by detailed coverage of standard naming conventions.

In this chapter we will cover:

- Areas for standards, guidelines, and procedures,
- Naming standards overview, and
- Sample naming standards.

4.1 AREAS FOR STANDARDS, GUIDELINES, AND PROCEDURES

The degree to which standards, guidelines, and procedures are implemented varies from one organization to another. One shop may have only naming standards, while another may have two volumes of detailed standards, guidelines, and procedures covering naming standards, programming, logical database design, physical database design, JCL, and so forth. Some of the factors influencing the degree of standardization adopted by an organization include the size of the data processing environment, skill level and turnover rate of data processing staff, the mix of users on the system, and management's philosophy regarding centralized management of data resources. Larger organizations tend to have more requisite procedures and accompanying documentation than do smaller organizations. Standards, guidelines, and procedures must be tailored to each site's environment and needs.

Most organizations rely on the DBA/DDA groups to develop standards, guidelines, and procedures in many areas. Some of these areas are touched upon in this book, information on others can be obtained from third party software companies, Cullinet, the IDMS Users Association, and other user sites. Standards, guidelines, and procedures obtained from outside sources, however, will require some degree of customization.

4.1.1   Standards and Guidelines

Standards are the conventions an installation chooses to follow, often related to the naming of entities. Guidelines are recommendations for product usage agreed upon by members of an organization. Table 4-1 lists standards and guidelines typically developed for the IDMS/R environment.

Table 4-1 Standards and Guidelines

Standards	Guidelines
Naming entities	Product Usage
Dictionary entity templates	Programming
Screen and report design	Database design
Documentation	Security

Naming Standards: Naming standards are covered in detail in Sections 4.2 and 4.3. Standardized naming conventions help identify and reduce data redundancy and simplify maintenance. In addition, having and using a naming convention facilitates one programmer understanding and maintaining another programmer's code.

Data Dictionary Entity Templates: Data Dictionary usage is often subject to standards. Without standards, the dictionary tends toward chaos. The problems of non-dictionary environments develop in which each program and programmer operates in a separate and often redundant universe. The DDA or DBA usually chooses the descriptive clauses which will be required for each type of dictionary entity. The entity name clause is system-required information, other clauses may be site-required.

Dictionary entries can be reviewed manually using online IDD or batch DDR reports. Alternatively, a program can be written to review IDMSDDDL input automatically prior to update of the dictionary (refer to discussion in Section 4.2.2).

Screen and Report Design: Standards might also be established for screen and report design. Often standard header information is required in both reports and screen displays. Header information may include date, time, name of screen or report, organization name, and screen or report title. Screen design standards may designate the placement of error message field(s). Terminal identifiers might also be displayed on the screen.

Documentation Standards: Because the data dictionary is used heavily during development, DDR reports automatically provide documentation for much of the environment. In addition, ADSORPTS provide dialog documentation. Standards might be set up to outline the non-IDD information required to document each stage of database and application development, such as a flow-of-control diagram for an online application. For example, program documentation standards might specify that a flowchart, a description of processing, a HIPO (Hierarchical Input Processing Output) chart, lists of error messages, end-user procedures, and recovery procedures were required documentation.

Product Usage Guidelines: The DBA group often develops guidelines for using each IDMS/R component. Recommended uses of each product, as well as who is allowed to use the product, should be part of the guidelines. These guidelines might include some of the information provided in this text, in addition to information learned through testing each product prior to its usage by applications development personnel. Some examples of guidelines which might be developed include: establishing proper usage of QFILEs under OLQ, the advantages and disadvantages of using QFILEs versus developing an application under ADS/O, the pros and cons of an ASF application versus an ADS/O application developed using a network database, and the relative merits of using OLM automatic editing versus program/dialog editing.

IDMS/R Programming Guidelines: It is recommended that programming guidelines be established for each programming mode, e.g., ADS/O, batch DML, IDMS-DC, CICS/IDMS, ADS-Batch, and Culprit. Programming guidelines range from nonexistent, to simple guidelines for IDMS/R statements, to detailed standards for every phase of program design, specification, and coding. Standards for the maximum size allowed for dialogs and DC programs are often adopted to promote efficient use of main storage. Standards for batch DML programs, IDMS-DC programs, ADS/O dialogs, and CULPRIT report parameters should be considered as well.

Programming guidelines might include documenting peculiarities for each programming mode, as well as recommendations for uses of other software products in conjunction with IDMS/R (e.g., Intertest with CICS/IDMS programs and optimizers with COBOL-IDMS programs).

For batch DML programs, standards might specify whether or not AUTOSTATUS error handling is required. A standard could be instituted requiring programs to issue ACCEPT DB-STATISTICS INTO IDMS-STATISTICS just prior to issuing FINISH to collect statistics on database processing. Batch programs which update a LARGE number of records should be coded to issue COMMITs at intervals and contain restart logic (see discussion in Section 7.3.1)

For ADS/O dialogs and applications, standards for error handling and the use of AUTOSTATUS might be considered. Guidelines for the maximum number of levels in a dialog thread as well as the maximum size of a dialog might be established. We suggest limiting the number of dialog levels to three and keeping dialogs small, under 40K. Use of PROTECTED or EXCLUSIVE usage modes on READY statements by online dialogs and programs should be strongly discouraged, perhaps prohibited, because these usage modes lock out other access to records in the area.

Logical and Physical Database Design Guidelines: Detailed coverage of logical and physical database design guidelines is beyond the scope of this text. Several Cullinet manuals and courses cover database design considerations. Many books have been written about generic database design concepts.

Many shops establish guidelines for each aspect of database design, e.g., record, set, area, file guidelines. As an example, consider the guidelines which might be established for set definition. For each set defined, several decisions must be made, including 1) determining the pointers which will be maintained, 2) determining the order of member records in the set, and 3) choosing set membership options. Taking the example one step further, let's examine the first decision more closely.

Set pointers are part of owner and member record prefixes, therefore, having fewer pointers makes for smaller records. IDMS/R requires 'NEXT' pointers on every set. 'PRIOR' and 'OWNER' pointers are optional. Although specifying only NEXT pointers for a set saves disk storage, it is not recommended unless the member records are stored 'VIA' the owner record and do not participate in other set relationships.

Lack of PRIOR pointers increases the overhead of erase and disconnect operations and can result in logically deleted records. Logically deleted records are those which have been erased but, due to lack of PRIOR pointers in some of its set relationships, IDMS/R cannot easily modify the set to remove the record physically. Logically deleted records can be identified and physically deleted using batch utilities. Lack of OWNER pointers increases the overhead of accessing the owner record directly after accessing a member record. As a general guideline, we suggest choosing NEXT, PRIOR, and OWNER pointers unless the sets are very small, the member records are never (or infrequently) erased/disconnected, and the member records do not participate in many other set relationships.

This example barely scratches the surface of guidelines for database design. Further information on IDMS/R database design specifics can be found in the IDMS/R Database Operations manual and the DDL Reference Guide (Release 10) or the IDMS Database Design and Definition Guide (Release 5.7).

Security Guidelines: Standard security guidelines might be established. For example, a security class may be assigned to each task and program/dialog, and a list of security classes assigned to each user. Only users with the matching security class in their list can execute a secured task, program, or dialog. The DBA may be involved in establishing a hierachy of security class values. A hierarchy of security class values eases the overhead of maintaining myriad security class values. The DBA, DDA, or a security officer might establish prototype USER definitions for 'DBA', 'DDA', 'PROJ MNGR', 'ANALYST', and 'PGMR' in the test system, and prototypes for different user areas in production systems. Standard dictionary security can include specifying PUBLIC ACCESS ALLOWED FOR NONE and identifying the users REGISTERED FOR UPDATE of entities. These and many other security considerations are detailed in Chapter 6.

4.1.2   Procedures

Procedures are the proscribed steps which should be followed to accomplish customary tasks. Documented procedures are essential to smooth operations in an IDMS/R installation. DBA, systems, and operations personnel must coordinate activities during crucial recovery situations. Coordination and smooth recovery are facilitated when there are formalized procedures for handling day to day operations.

Documented procedures may be appropriate for several groups of data processing personnel, including operations personnel, DBA staff, and applications developers. Table 4-2 lists some procedures which the DBA/DDA group may be responsible for creating.

Table 4-2 Procedures by Group

Operations Group	DBA/DDA Group	Applications Group
CV startup (9)*	Logical and physical database design	Signing on, using, and signing off online products (IDD, OLM, ADSA, ADSG, OLQ)
CV shutdown (12)		
Journal archiving (7)	Maintenance (11)	
Log archiving (9, 12)	Turnover of programs for production (13)	Compiling and linking programs (3, 5)
Recovery (7, 12)		
Backup (7)	Migration of DD entities (3)	Testing, unit and system (2)
	Performance tuning (13)	
	Trouble shooting (12)	
	Running utilities and DDR reports (3, 5)	

*Numbers in parentheses identify chapters containing relevant information

Operations procedures: The DBA group is usually responsible for developing procedures for running the Central Version systems, archiving journal files and the CV log, and documenting job dependencies for CV being up or down. Procedures for backup and recovery of databases and data dictionaries must be developed. When developing backup procedures, several considerations come into play, e.g., whether or not the database is up 24 hours a day, the frequency of backups, the length of time backups should be maintained, etc. Chapter 7 details IDMS/R backup and recovery considerations.

DBA procedures: The DBA/DDA group develops several procedures for its own use. In addition to guidelines for database design, many organizations implement a procedure of reviews at different stages of the logical and physical design process. Several procedures may be developed for common maintenance situations, for example, a procedure to decompile and delete maps to allow changes to map records. Chapter 11 is dedicated to examining common maintenance situations.

A procedure for handling the turnover of applications from test into quality assurance or acceptance testing should be instituted to allow proper system planning. For example, frequency-of-use estimates and CREPORT050 should be part of the documentation turned over to the DBA group. Dictionary report CREPORT050 reports on dictionary load modules, displaying load module names, types (dialog, table, subschema, or map), and, most importantly, load module sizes. IDMS STATISTICS printout (recommended for all test programs) and area usage modes should be reviewed at turnover to see how many records are locked during program processing. These reviews circumvent performance problems with batch programs which update an extremely large number of records.

Migration of entities from one dictionary to another entails either a manual procedure or an automated procedure. Details on migration procedures may be found in Chapter 3.

Performance tuning and trouble shooting procedures may be established. Regular monitoring of statistical reports should be set up. Chapters 12 and 13 examine performance tuning and trouble shooting considerations.

Running utilities and DDR reports will require customized JCL and control cards if multiple DD's are in use or if local mode is used in retrieval utility runs (such as DDR jobstreams, IDMSDDDL, RHDCMAP1, RHDCMPUT, IDMSRPTS, IDMSDBAN, ADSOBGEN, ADSORPTS, etc.). Standard JCL procedures might be developed to minimize user confusion.

Applications procedures: The DBA/DDA group should be involved in creating procedures for the applications development group. Detailed procedures for signing on, using, and signing off the online development tools (i.e., IDD, OLM, ADSA, ADSG, and OLQ) should be developed along with product usage guidelines. If multiple dictionaries are in use, CLISTs to automate secondary dictionary signon are recommended (details in 3.10.3).

Procedures and documentation for compiling and linking different types of programs should be developed. For example, the modules IDMS and IDMSCANC must be included in batch DML program links, whereas the module IDMSCINT must be included in links of CICS Command Level DML programs.

The DBA/DDA group may help develop procedures for unit testing and system testing new applications. Statistics gathered during system testing are crucial to planning system changes for efficient production implementation of the new application.

4.2 NAMING STANDARDS OVERVIEW

The primary focus of this chapter is naming standards. At a minimum, standardized naming conventions should be established and adhered to religiously. Standardized naming conventions help identify and reduce data redundancy and allow maintenance changes to be identified more easily. In addition, having and using a naming standard facilitates one programmer understanding and maintaining another programmer's code. Compare the following lines of code designed to move information from a record field to a work field:

```
    MOVE AR-CUST-NAME TO WK-CUST-NAME.
versus
    MOVE Z TO Y.
```

Both lines of code meet COBOL language requirements, but the first line is much easier to understand and needs no "mind reading" to decipher.

For each type of name, there are restrictions imposed by software for determining which names are valid. Within these restraints, most DBA's select standards to which entity names must comply. Naming standards may be chosen for many entities. These entities include data elements, records, areas, sets, schemas, subschemas, DMCL's, maps, panels, programs, dialogs, work records, processes, QFILEs, scratch and queue records, and so forth. Words used in names are often abbreviated owing to limitations placed on the name length. Many sites maintain a list of approved abbreviations, agreeing on a single abbreviation for each word and thereby reducing the possibility of redundant data on the dictionary.

Abbreviations frequently represent the greatest arena of contention in attempts to implement naming standards. Perhaps the most important step in developing naming conventions is to make certain that standard abbreviations are established, circulated to the applications group, and adopted as soon as possible. It is always advisable to involve end users in the search for solid, agreed-upon abbreviations.

Other important considerations concerning implementation of naming standards include:

- Integration of IDMS/R naming standards with existing standards

- Implementation of and adherence to standard naming conventions
- Solutions to common problem areas

4.2.1 Integration of IDMS/R Naming Standards with Existing Standards

Most data processing organizations have naming standards in place before IDMS/R is implemented. Assuming that the standards are working and the staff is using them, standards established for the IDMS/R environment should follow overall DP standards as closely as possible.

Standards chosen for the IDMS/R environment may differ from existing standards because databases are centralized resources. Previously, data often was thought of as being "owned" by an application or program, and names of records and elements may have been prefixed by an application identifier. In a database environment data is usually considered a common resource available to multiple applications. Therefore, database record and element names should be application independent.

4.2.2 Implementation of and Adherence to Standard Naming Conventions

Standard naming conventions must be used consistently to be effective. Standards are implemented most easily with the compliance of the applications staff. They are enforced most effectively, however, by having a method of detecting noncompliance. These exceptions can be identified either before or after entities are added to the dictionary.

Encouraging the Compliance of the Applications Staff: Sometimes personnel rebel against standards, perhaps feeling that their creativity is being stifled. A combination of education, review, and rewards may be employed to encourage the use of standards. The staff should be educated about benefits returned when standards are followed. If a programmer must work on another programmer's code, the task will be much easier if common standards have been followed. Programs should be reviewed to ensure that they adhere to standards. Reviews may be done manually or a program can be written to automate the process. Staff adherence to standards can be encouraged by rewarding a project team that implements a well-documented system which meets standards.

Detecting Noncompliance: Entities added to the dictionary should be reviewed to ensure that naming standards have been followed and that standard information has been provided for each new entity. In shops where all entities are added to the DD exclusively by a Dictionary Administration group, compliance can be monitored by visually scanning the forms made out by the applications group prior to entering the entities. In shops where diverse groups add entities to the DD, templates can be prepared on a text editor or on the DD to serve as examples of required information. When using manual methods such as visual scans or templates, mistakes can infiltrate the DD.

An automated method of monitoring compliance provides more effective protection of the data dictionary. Two automated methods are:

- Syntax checking programs and
- IDD User Exits.

Syntax Checking Programs: Syntax checking programs monitor information already in the IDD to determine if it complies with site standards. These programs can be written by dictionary administration staff to run against the dictionary directly or against files created by extracted information from the DD. The DDDL Network Reference Guide and the dictionary data structure diagram provide the set, record, and element names needed to code programs accessing the data dictionary.

For example, a syntax checking program to monitor uniform completeness of element definitions might check for adherence to the following standards:

1) Is there a DESCRIPTION and a DEFINITION for this element?
2) Are there any differences between the element's picture/usage and the picture/usage of the element when included in records (i.e., the RECORD-ELEMENT's picture and/or usage)?
3) Is the element's name an appropriate length (element names may be limited to a site-standard maximum length to allow room for prefixing the element's name when it is included in records)?
4) Are all other site-required descriptors present, e.g.,
a) Has the user department or manager primarily responsible for maintaining the element been identified?
b) Has a system acronym been specified, identifying the system(s) to which the element is related (either linked to a

SYSTEM entity or to a CLASS/ATTRIBUTE defined for the same purpose)?

c) Have all appropriate CLASS and ATTRIBUTE clauses been specified?

IDD User Exits: Coding IDD user exits is the only means of trapping incorrect or incomplete information *before* it is stored in the IDD. IDD user exits can prohibit the addition of entities which do not comply with naming standards and/or which have incomplete descriptions (such as elements lacking a DEFINITION, DESCRIPTION, or other site-required descriptors). Refer to the DDDL Reference Guide for details on coding IDD user exits.

4.2.3   Solutions to Common Problem Areas

Existing systems and packaged software are two common problem areas encountered when implementing standards. Retrofitting standards in existing production systems is probably not worth the cost. If a system is being converted to IDMS/R, rigid adherence to standards might be waived if doing so greatly reduces the cost of conversion. However, if the conversion involves functionally changing the system and rewriting code, that's a different story. From a standards point of view, the rewritten program is a new program and it should, therefore, follow standards.

If packaged software is purchased which is intended to interface with IDMS/R, a decision must be made about standards for the new package. There are three alternatives, namely 1) implementing the package as is, 2) forcing adherence to site standards by requiring the vendor or site staff to rewrite the code to standard, or 3) making a distinction between internal and external components of the package and requiring only external components to meet standards.

Making a distinction between the internal/external components of packaged software generally provides the most practical solution. Internal components are those parts of a package with little or no impact on the external environment, for example, program code or the names of elements. Internal components form the major portion of the package and follow the vendor's standards. For practical reasons, do not require these internal components to meet site standards. External components are those parts of the package which interface outside of the package, including JCL, file names, subschemas, and so forth. External components should conform to site standards.

4.3 SAMPLE NAMING STANDARDS

Ideally, naming standards for the database and data communications environment should be adopted prior to extensive use of IDMS/R. It may seem difficult to determine shop standards in advance. However, if databases and applications are developed before standards are agreed upon, the dreaded tasks of reeducating staff and modifying programs will have to be undertaken. Idiosyncratic names and redundant data elements are difficult to identify and eliminate once established in databases and programs.

The sample naming conventions shown in this section were provided by a user site and are specific to that site's requirements. These standards may be used as a model upon which to build your own standards, but must be tailored to meet the needs and existing standards of your installation. Other examples of naming standards may be obtained from Cullinet, the IDMS Users Association, other IDMS/R installations, and from third party software vendors.

We will discuss the sample naming standards grouped by type of entity, namely:

- Schema-related entities,
- Application-related entities, and
- System-related entities.

4.3.1 Naming Schema-Related Entities

Schema-related entities include schemas, subschemas, DMCL's, elements, database records, sets, areas, and files. Sample naming conventions for schema-related entities are summarized in Table 4-3. Further discussion of element, record, and set naming alternatives follows.

Element Naming: Although the IDD element names can be up to 32 characters long, COBOL limits user-defined data names to 30 characters. Many organizations choose to limit element names to an even fewer characters to reserve space for prefixing the element name with the record name or a portion thereof. Prefixing provides several benefits, namely, creating unique element names when the same element is used in several records, minimizing redundancy, and easing maintenance (discussed in Sections 3.5.1 and 3.5.2).

The name format for an element as shown in Table 4-3 is (qualifier(s))-(category). The maximum length of an element name is limited to 22 characters, allowing the element name to be prefixed by a 7-character record name and a hyphen, and still satisfy COBOL

Table 4-3 Sample Naming Standards For Schema-Related Entities

Entity	Max. # of Characters	Sample Format[1]	Legend/Example[2]
Schema	8	sSCHaann	Example: TSCHCH01
Subschema	8	sSUBaann	Example: PSUBCH20
DMCL	8	sDMCaann	Example: PDMCGL01
Element	32	(qualifier(s))-(category)[3] Limit to 22 characters to leave room for record prefix	(qualifier(s))=one or more words indicating the unique characteristics of an element within a category (category)=generic data category, the class of data to which an element belongs Examples: SRT-ADR BRNCH-ACCT-KEY
Record	16	m(7)[4]	Examples: ACCOUNT, BRANCH
Set	16	(owner)-(member) or (owner)-m(7)[5] or (record subject relationship)[5] or (index key)-IX[5]	(owner)=owner record name (member)=member record name Examples: CUST-ACCOUNT CUST-ASSETS CUST-NAME-IX
Area	16	m(11)-AREA	Example: CUST-AREA
File	16	m(11)-FILE	Example: CUST-FILE

[1]Substitute for lower case letters as described in Legend/Example column, use upper case letters and hyphens as shown.
[2]s=system identifier: T for test, P for production, Q for quality assurance
aa=two-character application code or GL for Global or SY for system-wide
nn=unique numeric identifier assigned by DBA
m(number)=meaningful mnemonic up to 'number' characters long which makes the name unique
[3]Refer to discussion of element naming standards for further details
[4]Refer to discussion of record naming standards for further details
[5]Refer to discussion of set naming standards for further details

naming restrictions. For (qualifier(s)), substitute one or more words, separated by hyphens, that indicate the unique characteristics of an element within a generic data category. All words should be taken from a list of site-standard data qualifier abbreviations (examples in Table 4-4). For (category), substitute one word identifying the generic class of data to which the element belongs. This word should be taken from a list of standard generic data category abbreviations (examples in Table 4-5).

Table 4-4 Sample Standard Data Qualifier Abbreviations

Abbrev.	Word(s)	Abbrev.	Word(s)
ACCPT	ACCEPT,ACCEPTANCE	CC	✳CENTURY
ACCT	ACCOUNT	CCYYDDD	✳CENTURY/YEAR/DAY
ACQRD	ACQUIRED	CCYYMMDD	✳CENTURY/YEAR/MONTH/DAY
ACRUD	ACCRUED	CDE	✳CODE
ACRUL	ACCRUAL	CENTS	CENTS
ACTV	ACTIVE	CERT	CERTIFIED,CERTIFICATE
ACTVY	ACTIVITY	CHAR	CHARACTER
ADDED	ADDED	CHILD	CHILDREN
ADDL	ADDITIONAL	CHK	CHECK
ADJ	ADJUST, ADJUSTMENT	CHKNG	CHECKING
ADMIN	ADMINISTRATION	CHNG	CHANGE
ADR	✳ADDRESS	CHRG	CHARGE
ADV	ADVICE	CITZN	CITIZEN
ADVSR	ADVISOR	CLASS	CLASSIFICATION
AE	ACCOUNT-EXECUTIVE	CLEAR	CLEARING
AFFRM	AFFIRM, AFFIRMATION	CLERCL	CLERICAL
AGNCY	AGENCY	CLIEN	CLIENT
AGNST	AGAINST	CLNDR	CALENDAR
AGRMT	AGREEMENT	CLOTH	CLOTHING
AGT	AGENT	CLSD	CLOSED
ALL	ALL	CLSE	CLOSE
ALLOC	ALLOCATION	CMDTY	COMMODITY
ALT	ALTERNATE	CMPLT	COMPLETE
AMSE	AMERICAN STOCK EXCHANGE	CMPNY	COMPANY
AMT	✳AMOUNT	CMPUT	COMPUTE,COMPUTED
ANNL	ANNUAL	CNCES	CONCESSION
APPL	APPLICATION	CNCL	CANCEL
APPLD	APPLIED	CND	✳CONDITION
APPRC	APPRECIATION	CNFDTL	CONFIDENTIAL
APPRVD	APPROVED	CNFRM	CONFIRM
APPRVL	APPROVAL	CNFRMD	CONFIRMED
AREA	AREA	CNT	✳COUNT
ASSN	ASSOCIATION	CNTL	CONTROL
ATL	ATLANTIC (REGION)	CNTCT	CONTACT
ATTY	ATTORNEY	CNTRCT	CONTRACT
AUTH	AUTHORIZED	CNTRY	COUNTRY
AUTO	AUTOMATIC	CNTY	COUNTY
AVAIL	AVAILABLE	COLEG	COLLEGE
AVG	AVERAGE	COLLAT	COLLATERAL
BAL	BALANCE	COMM	COMMISSION
BASIS	BASIS	COMPNS	COMPENSATION
BDGE	BADGE	COND	CONDITION
BEG	BEGIN	CONTRB	CONTRIBUTE, CONTRIBUTION
BEGIN	BEGIN, BEGINNING	CORCT	CORRECT
BENEF	BENEFIT	COST	COST
BILL	BILL	COVER	COVER
BKGND	BACKGROUND	CPN	COUPON
BLK	BLOCK	CREAT	CREATE, CREATION
BNFCY	BENEFICIARY	CRED	CREDIT
BOUGHT	BOUGHT	CRNCY	CURRENCY
BUY	BUY	CTR	COUNTER
BRCKT	BRACKET	CURNCY	CURRENCY
BRDCST	BROADCAST	CURR	CURRENT
BRNCH	BRANCH	CUSIP	CUSIP
BRKR	BROKER	CUST	CUSTOMER
BUSN	BUSINESS	CUSTOD	CUSTODIAN
CALC	CALCULATE, CALCULATE	CYTROL	CYTROL
CALL	CALL	DATA	DATA
CAPTL	CAPITAL	DAY	DAY
CASH	CASH	DBASE	DATABASE

- (continued on next page) -

*Abbreviation identifies a Generic Data Category also included in Table 4-5

Table 4-4 Sample Standard Data Qualifier Abbreviations (continued)

Abbrev.	Word(s)	Abbrev.	Word(s)
DBNTR	DEBENTURE	FMLY	FAMILY
DD	*DAY	FOOD	FOOD
DDD	*DAY	FORMAT	FORMAT
DEB	DEBIT	FORGN	FOREIGN
DECI	DECIMAL	FRAC	FRACTION, FRACTIONAL
DEGR	DEGREE	FREQ	FREQUENCY
DENIED	DENIED	FULLY	FULLY
DEPOS	DEPOSIT	FUNC	FUNCTION
DES	*DESCRIPTION	FUND	FUND
DESK	DESK	FUT	FUTURES
DEST	DESTINATION	GDG	GENERATION DATA GROUP
DFT	DEFAULT	GENRL	GENERAL
DIFF	DIFFERENCE	GO	GO
DIG	DIGIT	GOV	GOVERNMENT
DISB	DISBURSEMENT	GOVT	GOVERNMENT
DISC	DISCOUNT	GR	GROWTH
DISCL	DISCLOSE, DISCLOSURE	GRAD	GRADUATE
DISP	DISPOSITION	GROSS	GROSS
DIST	DISTRICT	GROW	GROWTH
DISTRB	DISTIBUTE, DISTRIBUTION	GRP	*GROUP
DIVND	DIVIDEND	GTC	GOOD-TILL-CANCELED
DIVRCD	DIVORCED	GUAR	GUARANTEE
DIVSN	DIVISION	HDR	HEADER
DLV	DELIVER	HH	*HOUR
DMSTIC	DOMESTIC	HHMM	*HOUR/MINUTE
DO	DO	HHMMSS	*HOUR/MINUTE/SECONDS
DOC	DOCUMENT	HHMMSSSS	*HOUR/MINUTE/SECONDS
DOLR	DOLLAR	HI	HIGH
DPNDCY	DEPENDENCY	HIST	HISTORY
DPNDT	DEPENDENT	HLDAY	HOLIDAY
DSCNRY	DISCRETIONARY	HLDNGS	HOLDINGS
DSN	DATASET NAME	HOLD	HOLD
DSPLY	DISPLAY	HOU	HOUSING
DSTRCT	DISTRICT	HRCT	HAIRCUT
DTC	DEPOSITORY TRUST COMPANY	HSHLD	HOUSEHOLD
DT	DATE	HUSB	HUSBAND
DTE	DATE	IBIS	INTER BRANCH INFORMATION
DUE	DUE		SYSTEM
DUPL	DUPLICATE	ID	IDENTIFICATION
DVP	DELIVERED AGAINST PAYMENT	IMAGE	IMAGE
EDUC	EDUCATION	IN	IN
ELIG	ELIGIBLE	INACT	INACTIVE
EMPLYE	EMPLOYEE	INC	INCORPORATED
EMPLYR	EMPLOYER	INCL	INCLUDE
END	END	INCOM	INCOME
ENT	ENTRY	INCMPL	INCOMPLETE
ENTERT	ENTERTAINMENT	INCR	INCREASE, INCREMENT
ENTRD	ENTERED	IND	*INDICATOR
EQ	EQUAL	INDIV	INDIVIDUAL
EQTY	EQUITY	INDUS	INDUSTRY
ERR	ERROR	INDX	INDEX
ESTAT	ESTATE	INFO	INFORMATION
ESTBL	ESTABLISH	INHRT	INHERITANCE
ESTIM	ESTIMATE	INIT	INITIAL
EXCEP	EXCEPTION	INPTY	INTERESTED PARTY
EXCH	EXCHANGE	INSRT	INSERT
EXCTR	EXECUTOR	INSTI	INSTITUTION
EXCTV	EXECUTIVE	INSTIT	INSTITUTION
EXEC	EXECUTE, EXECUTION	INSTRC	INSTRUCTION
EXMPT	EXEMPT	INSTRM	INSTRUMENT
EXPCT	EXPECTED	INSUR	INSURANCE
EXPER	EXPERIENCE	INT	INTEREST
EXPIR	EXPIRE, EXPIRATION	INTNTL	INTERNATIONAL
EXPAND	EXPAND	INV	INVENTORY
EXPNS	EXPENDITURE, EXPENSE	INVST	INVESTMENT, INVESTOR
EXT	EXTENT, EXTENSION	IRA	IRA
FED	FEDERAL	ISS	ISSUE
FEE	FEE	IX	INDEX
FGN	FOREIGN	JRNL	JOURNAL
FIGRD	FIGURED	KEEP	KEEP,KEEPING
FIGRM	FIGURATION	KEY	*KEY
FINAN	FINANCE	LANG	LANGUAGE
FINCL	FINANCIAL	LDGR	LEDGER
FINS	FINANCIAL INSTITUTE	LEAP	LEAP
	NUMBERING SYSTEM	LGL	LEGAL
FIRM	FIRM	LGND	LEGEND
FIXINC	FIXED INCOME (REGION)	LIAB	LIABILITY
FLA	FLORIDA (REGION)	LIC	LICENSE

- (continued on next page) -

*Abbreviation identifies a Generic Data Category also included in Table 4-5

Table 4-4 Sample Standard Data Qualifier Abbreviations (continued)

Abbrev.	Word(s)	Abbrev.	Word(s)
LIFINSUR	LIFE INSURANCE	ORIG	ORIGINAL
LIMIT	LIMIT, LIMITED	OTC	OVER-THE-COUNTER
LIQ	LIQUID, LIQUIDITY	OTH	OTHER
LISTD	LISTED	OUT	OUT
LNGTH	LENGTH	OVRDU	OVERDUE
LO	LOW	OVRID	OVERRIDE
LOC	LOCATION	PARM	PARAMETER
LONG	LONG	PARTL	PARTIAL
LOSS	LOSS	PCT	*PERCENT, PERCENTAGE
LVL	LEVEL	PEND	PENDING
MAJOR	MAJOR	PENS	PENSION
MAIL	MAILING	PERF	PERFORMANCE
MARK	MARK	PERM	PERMANENT
MARR	MARRIED	PERS	PERSON, PERSONAL
MARTL	MARITAL	PGM	PROGRAM
MAST	MASTER	PHONE	PHONE
MATCH	MATCH	PL	PROFIT/LOSS
MATRL	MATERIAL	PLCY	POLICY
MATUR	MATURITY	PLUS	PLUS
MAX	MAXIMUM	POINT	POINT
MBR	MEMBER, MEMBERSHIP	POSN	POSITION
MEMO	MEMO	POSTGE	POSTAGE
MFUND	MONEY FUND	PRE	PRE
MGMT	MANAGEMENT	PREF	PREFERRRED
MGR	MANAGER	PREFIG	PREFIGURED
MIC	MICROFILM	PREM	PREMIUM
MID	MIDDLE	PREV	PREVIOUS
MIDWST	MIDWEST (REGION)	PRFRNC	PREFERENCE
MIN	MINIMUM	PRFT	PROFIT
MINOR	MINOR	PRFX	PREFIX
MISC	MISCELLANEOUS	PRICE	PRICE
MKR	MAKER	PRIM	PRIMARY
MKT	MARKET	PRIME	PRIME
MKTBL	MARKETABLE	PRIN	PRINCIPAL
MM	*MONTH,MINUTE	PROC	PROCEDURE
MMDDYY	*MONTH/DAY/YEAR	PROCES	PROCESS
MMDDYYYY	*MONTH/DAY/YEAR	PROD	PRODUCT, PRODUCTION
MNEM	MNEMONIC	PROJ	PROJECT
MNY	MONEY	PROP	PROPERTY
MODE	MODE	PROSP	PROSPECT, PROSPECTIVE
MONY	MONEY	PROVSN	PROVISION
MOVEMT	MOVEMENT	PRPCTS	PRPCTS
MRGN	MARGIN	PRTNR	PARTNER, PARTNERSHIP
MTD	MONTH-TO-DATE	PRTY	PRIORITY
MTGE	MORTGAGE	PS	PURCHASE AND SALES
MTH	MONTH	PURCH	PURCHASE
MTUR	MATURE, MATURITY	PURG	PURGE
MULTI	MULTIPLE	PURP	PURPOSE
MUNI	MUNICIPAL	PUT	PUT
MUT	MUTUAL	PVT	PRIVATE
NAM	*NAME	PWR	POWER
NASD	NATIONAL ASSOCIATION OF SECURITIES DEALERS	PYMT	PAYMENT
		PYMTS	PAYMENTS
NC	NORTH CENTRAL (REGION)	PYOUT	PAYOUT
NE	NORTHEAST (REGION)	QTR	QUARTER
NEG	NEGOTIABLE	QTRYL	QUARTERLY
NET	NET	QTY	*QUANTITY
NEXT	NEXT	QUAL	QUALITY
NO	NO	RATE	RATE
NONE	NONE	RCPT	RECEIPT
NONNEG	NON-NEGOTIABLE	RCV	RECEIVE
NORM	NORMAL	RCVD	RECEIVED
NOT	NOT	REA	REASON
NUM	*NUMBER	REAS	REASON
NY	NEW YORK (REGION)	REBIL	REBILL
NYSE	NEW YORK STOCK EXCHANGE	REC	RECORD
OA	OPTION AGREEMENT	REDEF	REDEFINE
OBJ	OBJECT, OBJECTIVE	REDUC	REDUCTION, REDUCE
OCCP	OCCUPATION	REFND	REFUND,REFUNDED
OF	OF	REFRL	REFERRAL
OFF	OFF	REFRNC	REFERENCE
OFFC	OFFICE	REGIS	REGISTER, REGISTRATION
OFFCR	OFFICER	REGLR	REGULAR
OFRG	OFFERING	REGN	REGION
ON	ON	REGUL	REGULATE, REGULATION
OPEN	OPEN, OPENING	REJCT	REJECT
OPER	OPERATION, OPERATOR	RELAT	RELATIONSHIP
OPT	OPTION, OPTIONAL	REMIT	REMIT
ORD	ORDINARY	REP	REPRESENTATIVE
ORDR	ORDER		

-------------------- (continued on next page) --------------------

*Abbreviation identifies a Generic Data Category also included in Table 4-5

Table 4-4 Sample Standard Data Qualifier Abbreviations (continued)

Abbrev.	Word(s)	Abbrev.	Word(s)
REPO	REPURCHASE AGREEMENT	SUBSCR	SUBSCRIPTION
REQ	REQUEST	SUFFX	SUFFIX
REQMT	REQUIREMENT	SUMM	SUMMARY
RES	RESIDENT	SUPLM	SUPPLEMENT, SUPPLEMENTAL
RESDNC	RESIDENCE, RESIDENCY	SUPRT	SUPPORT
RESP	RESPONSE	SW	SOUTH WESTERN
RESTRT	RESTART	SYM	*SYMBOL
RETIR	RETIRED, RETIREMENT	SYS	SYSTEM
RETRN	RETURN	TANG	TANGIBLE
REVLV	REVOLVING	TAPE	TAPE
RGHT	RIGHT	TAX	TAX, TAXABLE
RL	REAL	TBL	TABLE
RLESTE	REAL ESTATE	TCKLR	TICKLER
RLZD	REALIZED	TEMP	TEMPORARY
RNGE	RANGE	TERM	TERMINAL
RNVST	REINVEST	TESCTL	TES CONTROL NAME
RNVT	REINVEST	TIME	TIME
RPT	REPORT	TITL	TITLE
RSK	RISK	TKR	TICKER
RSLT	RESULT	TKT	TICKET
RSPBLT	RESPONSIBILITY	TO	TO
RSRCH	RESEARCH	TODAY	TODAY
RSTRCT	RESTRICTION	TOMRRW	TOMORROW
RUN	RUN	TOT	TOTAL
SAFE	SAFE	TRAN	TRANSACTION
SALE	SALE	TRAV	TRAVEL
SALES	SALES	TRD	TRADE
SALRY	SALARY, SALARIED	TRDNG	TRADING
SAV	SAVINGS	TRDR	TRADER
SC	SALES CREDIT	TRDT	TRADE DATE
SCHED	SCHEDULE	TRLR	TRAILER
SEC	SECURITY, SECURITIES & EXCHANGE COMMISSION	TRNEE	TRAINEE
		TRNSF	TRANSFER
SECND	SECOND, SECONDARY	TRUST	TRUST
SECUR	SECURITY	TX	TAX
SECURD	SECURED	TYPE	TYPE
SEGRE	SEGREGATION	UNIT	UNIT
SELL	SELL	UNRLZD	UNREALIZED
SEQ	SEQUENCE	UNSECD	UNSECURED
SER	SERIAL	UPDT	UPDATE
SERV	SERVICE	UTLTY	UTILITY
SETT	SETTLEMENT	VAL	VALUE
SETTLD	SETTLED	VALDTE	VALIDATE
SFEKP	SAFEKEEPING	VALID	VALID
SHLT	SHELTER	VAR	VARIABLE
SHLTR	SHELTER	VEND	VENDOR
SHLTRD	SHELTERED	VEST	VESTED
SHORT	SHORT	VOL	VOLUME
SHR	SHARE	VP	VICE-PRESIDENT
SHRT	SHORT	VRNC	VARIANCE
SINGL	SINGLE	WASH	WASH ACCOUNT
SIZE	SIZE	WAY	WAY
SOLD	SOLD	WCENT	WEST CENTRAL (REGION)
SOM	SECURITY ORDER MATCH	WEEK	WEEK
SOW	SECURITIES OVER THE WIRE	WHEN	WHEN
SPCL	SPECIAL	WHNDIS	WHEN DISTRIBUTED
SPECUL	SPECULATION	WHNISS	WHEN-ISSUED
SPOU	SPOUSE	WIDOW	WIDOWED,WIDOW,WIDOWER
SPRD	SPREAD	WILL	WILL
SPRVSR	SUPERVISOR, SUPERVISORY	WIRE	WIRE
SRCE	SOURCE	WITH	WITH
SRCHG	SURCHARGE	WORK	WORK
SS	*SOCIAL-SECURITY,SECONDS	WRKNG	WORKING
STAT	STATUS	WRNT	WARRANT
STATE	STATE	WRTH	WORTH
STATN	STATION	WTHDBL	WITHDRAWABLE
STD	STANDARD	WTHDWL	WITHDRAWAL
STDT	SETTLEMENT DATE	WK	*WEEK
STK	STOCK	WWW	*WEEK
STMT	STATEMENT	XPND	EXPAND
STNDIN	STANDING INSTRUCTIONS	YEAR	YEAR
STNDNG	STANDING	YIELD	YIELD
STOP	STOP	YR	YEAR
STR	STREET	YSTRDY	YESTERDAY
STRTUP	STARTUP	YTD	YEAR-TO-DATE
STRGY	STRATEGY	YY	*YEAR
STRIKE	STRIKE	YYDDD	*YEAR/JULIAN DAY
SUBJCT	SUBJECT	YYMMDD	*YEAR/MONTH/DAY
		YYYYMMDD	*YEAR/MONTH/DAY

*Abbreviation identifies a Generic Data Category also included in Table 4-5

Table 4-5 Sample Generic Data Categories

Category*	Abbr.	Description	Example
Address	ADR	Part of an address	STR-ADR
Amount	AMT	Monetary amount	ESTIM-PROP-VAL-AMT
Code	CDE	An occurrence within a predefined table of values	CUST-RPT-FREQ-CDE
Condition	CND	An 88-level condition to an indicator, usually 'Y' and 'N'	CUST-HOME-ADR-YES-CND
Count	CNT	Numeric value arrived at by counting occurrences	MTH-OTC-TRAN-CNT
Description	DES	Free-form description	CRED-REFRNC-DES
Group	GRP	Group element defined for programming purposes	INVST-PRFRNC-GRP
Time	HHMM HHMMSS HHMMSSSS	Time, use appropriate category depending on the format	CREAT-HHMMSSSS
Indicator	IND	An indicator having two possible values	EMPLYE-ACCT-IND
Key	KEY	Group element defined as a key field	BRNCH-ACCT-KEY
Name	NAM	Proper noun by which an entity is commonly known	OWED-LOAN-INSTIT-NAM
Number	NUM	An identifying number, it need not be numeric	AGT-BANK-FINS-NUM
Percentage	PCT	A numeric value expressed as a percentage	TOP-TAX-BRCKT-PCT
Quantity	QTY	A non-monetary numeric quantity	MTH-AVG-BUY-SHR-QTY
Symbol	SYM	An identifying symbol	TCKR-SYM

- - - - - - - - - - - - - - - - - - - (continued on next page) - - - - - - - - - - - - - - - - - - -

Table 4-5 Sample Generic Data Categories (continued)

Category*	Abbr.	Description	Example
Date		A date, use appropriate Format:	
	CCYYMMDD	century/year/month/day	
	YYYYMMDD	year/month/day	
	YYMMDD	year/month/day	INSTRM-MATUR-
	MMDDYY	month/day/year	YYMMDD
	YYDDD	Julian date format	
	YY	year (only)	
	MM	month (only)	
	DD	day (only)	

*Also known as "designator"

Alternatively, some organizations use the format (subject)-(identifier(s)) and do not include category information, often called the element's "designator", as part of the name. Instead, the element's designator, an abbreviation for the class or category of data (e.g., IND, QTY, AMT) is included in the data dictionary by entering a separate clause. For example,

```
ADD ELEMENT EMPLYE-SSN
    'ELEMENT DESIGNATOR' IS NUM
    DEF 'NUMBER USED TO UNIQUELY IDENTIFY AN EMPLOYEE'.
```

where EMPLYE is the subject, SSN is the identifier, and NUM is the "category", "designator", or "class" of data. Using a separate clause to enter designator/category information allows DDR reports to list elements grouped by designator/category, which is useful for identifying redundant data elements. The same type of report is available when the category is part of the name, if the category is also added to the DD as a separate clause, e.g.,

```
ADD BRNCH-NUM
    CATEGORY IS NUM
    DEF 'NUMBER USED TO IDENTIFY A BRANCH UNIQUELY'.
```

Record Names: Schema record names are restricted to 16 characters. Some DBA's choose to limit record names to seven characters as shown in Table 4-3. This limitation allows many set names, also restricted to 16 characters, to be created by appending the member record name to the owner record name. For example, a set between CUST records and ACCOUNT records could be named CUST-ACCOUNT.

Alternatively, longer record names can be allowed and set names can be composed from portions of record names. An example of a longer format is 'aaannn-m(9)' (where aaa=application code, nnn=the 3 low-order digits of schema record identifier, and m(9)=mnemonic describing record contents), the prefix portion of the name 'aaannn-' provides a unique record identifier which may be used in constructing set names. For example, a set between EMS040-DEPT records and EMS070-EMPLOYEE records would be named EMS040-EMS070.

Set Names: Set names can be up to 16 characters long and generally follow a different naming format depending on the type of set. Table 4-3 shows four sample formats for set names.

The first format, (owner)-(member), is used for single-member sets (i.e., sets with only one *type* of member record). The set name is constructed from the owner record type's name, hyphen, and the member record type's name. This is the most common variety of set, illustrated in Figure 4-1.

The second format, (owner)-(member records category), is used for multi-member sets (i.e., sets with more than one type of member record). The set name is constructed from the owner record type's name, hyphen, and a mnemonic prompt categorizing the member record types. A sample multi-member set is shown in Figure 4-2.

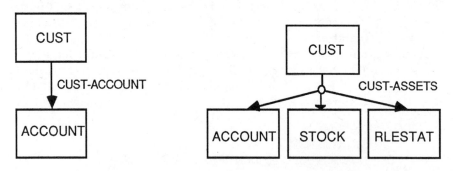

Figure 4-1 Single-Member Set   **Figure 4-2** Multi-Member Set

The third format, (record subject relationship), is used when more than one set relationship exists between two record types. Each set is named with one or more meaningful words describing the relationship between record subjects. An example of this type of set is shown in Figure 4-3.

The fourth format, (index key descriptor)-IX, is used to name system-owned indexed sets. For (index key descriptor), substitute one or more meaningful words identifying the key element(s). The fourth set format is illustrated in Figure 4-4.

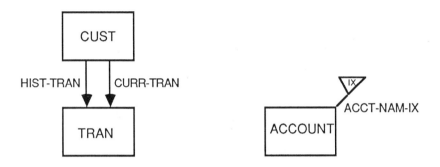

Figure 4-3 Multiple Sets Between   **Figure 4-4** System-Owned Index
      Two Record Types   Set

4.3.2   Naming Application-Related Entities

Table 4-6 contains a list of sample naming conventions for entities used during application development. Most of the sample formats start with 'aaCm(5)', where 'aa' identifies the application, 'C' is a constant identifying the entity type, and m(5) is a mnemonic prompt uniquely identifying one occurrence of an entity type. Related entities of different types should be identified with the same mnemonic. For example, dialog CPDADCUS's map should be named CPMADCUS, its premap process should be named CPDADCUS-PM, and its response processes should be named CPDADCUS-RP-m(20).

4.3.3   Naming System-Related Entities

Sample naming conventions for some system-related entities are contained in Table 4-7. These standards could be extended to include CLASS and ATTRIBUTE, REPORT, QFILE, TASK, AND SYSTEM names.

Table 4-6 Sample Naming Standards for Application-Related Entities

Entity	Max. # of Characters	Sample Format[1]	Legend/Example[2]
Program (Non-ADS/O)	8	aapm(5)	p=type of program: B for Batch or O for Online Example: CPBCUSRP
Table	8	aaTtm(4)	t=type of table: C for code table E for edit table Example: GLTCSTAT
Map	8	aaMm(5)	Example: CPMADCUS
Application	8	aaAm(5)	Example: CPACUSPR
Function	8	aaFm(5)	Example: CPFADCUS
Dialog	8	aaDm(5)	Example: CPDADCUS
Premap process	32	(dialog)-PM(-ma)	(dialog)=dialog name (-ma) is optional for premap processes Example: CPDADCUS-PM
Response process	32	(dialog)-RP(-ma)	(dialog)=dialog name (-ma) often includes the key which initiates the process Examples: CPDADCUS-RP-ADD-CUS CPDADCUS-RP-ENTR-EDIT
Global work record	32	aaWK-GLOBAL(-ma)	Example: CPWK-GLOBAL
Map work record	32	aaMR(-ma)	Example: CPMR-ADD-CUS
Dialog work record	32	aaWK(-ma)	Example: CPWK-CUS-SAVE

[1]Substitute for lower case letters as described in Legend/Example column, use upper case letters and hyphens as shown.

[2]aa=two-character application code, GL for Global or SY for system-wide; m(number)=meaningful mnemonic up to 'number' characters long which makes the name unique; (-ma)=a concatenation of meaningful acronyms separated by hyphens, or the constant 'GLOBAL'

Table 4-7 Sample Naming Standards for System-Related Entities

Entity	Restrictions	Sample Format[1]	Legend/Example[2]
Libraries	Site-specific	sssss.ccc.lllllll	sssss=type of system TIDMS,PIDMS, etc. ccc=type of library e.g., SYS, DBA, PGM lllllll=type of library (loadlib, srclib, cilib, etc.) Examples: OS DD statement TIDMS.SYS.LOADLIB DOS DLBL statement 'PIDMS.DBA.CILIB'
Message	6 digit number 900001-999999	nnnnnn	nnnnnn=number assigned by DBA
Queue	16 Char.	aaQm(5)nn	Same substitutions as for creating dialog or program, plus a sequence number, if needed
Scratch	16 Char.	aaSm(5)nn	Same substitutions as for creating dialog or program, plus a sequence number, if needed
User	32 Char. but most sites use only 8	ggiiinnn	gg=identifies group of users iii=initials of user nnn=tie breaker number

[1]Substitute for lower case letters as described in Legend/Example column, use upper case letters and hyphens as shown.
[2]aa=two-character application code, GL for Global or SY for system-wide; m(number)=meaningful mnemonic up to 'number' characters long which makes the name unique; nn=sequence number to make the QUEUE or SCRATCH name unique if there is more than one created by the dialog/program

4.4   CONCLUSION

Standards and procedures should be an integral part of advanced planning strategy and developed early in the implementation of IDMS/R. Choosing naming standards prior to designing databases and coding programs is essential to prevent proliferation of redundant data in databases and data dictionaries.

This chapter provided an overview of the types of standards, guidelines, and procedures developed at IDMS/R sites, as well as sample naming standards. The remainder of our text contains information helpful in developing standards and procedures tailored to the requirements of your installation.

Suggestions for further reading on Standards:

The following Cullinet manuals
    For Release 10 installations:
        1) IDD DDDL Reference (IDD user exits)
        2) IDD Network Reference (Syntax checking programs)
        3) IDD User's Guide (Setting up the DD)
        4) Course notes to DB302 - IDD Implementation and Control (Administering the DD and Standards)

    For Release 5.7 installations:
        1) IDD DDDL Reference (IDD user exits)
        2) IDD Network Reference (Syntax checking programs)
        3) IDD User's Guide (Setting up the DD)

5

Central Version versus Local Mode

IDMS/R offers two environments for running batch programs: Central Version (CV) and local mode. CV operation is a multi-threaded environment that handles multiple concurrent run units. Local mode operation is a single threaded processing method in which each run unit operates in a discrete universe, isolated from other IDMS/R programs. In this chapter we will discuss:

- Differences between Central Version and local mode processing,
- Situations mandating either CV or local mode,
- Situations when local mode is preferable, and
- A comparison of CV and local mode in two common processing situations.

5.1 DIFFERENCES BETWEEN CENTRAL VERSION AND LOCAL MODE PROCESSING

Briefly, the main difference between running a batch program in local mode rather than under CV is processing time; CV is slower. However, the automatic recovery features of CV are sacrificed for increased speed in local mode. A comparison of the salient features of local mode versus CV appears in Table 5-1 and is followed by detailed explanation below.

5.1.1 Locking

Locking at the area and record levels protects records in the database from concurrent update by more than one run unit. Area locks protect areas against concurrent update by multiple CV's and/or local mode run units. In each area of the database there are Space Management Pages (SMP's, Figure 5-1); area locks are maintained on the first

Table 5-1 Comparison of CV and Local Mode

CV	Local Mode
1. Area & Record locks	1. Area locks ONLY
2. 20-50% slower than local mode	2. 20-50% faster than CV
3. Automatic recovery using disk journals	3. Manual recovery using journal/dump tape or disk
4. Shared copies of DBMS, DBIO, global DMCL, subschemas, & buffer pools	4. Separate copies of DBMS, DBIO, DMCL, subschema, & buffer pool

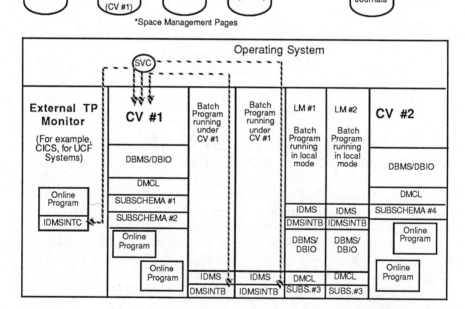

*Space Management Pages

Figure 5-1 An Overview of Central Version versus Local Mode. SMP's contain area lock indicators. Areas 1 & 2 are locked by CV #1, Area 3 by LM #1, and Area 4 by CV #2. If LM #2, just starting up, requires update access to any area, it will abend because all areas are currently locked. The batch programs executing under CV #1 communicate with it through an SVC issued by the batch interface program IDMSINTB. Native TP programs, i.e., online programs executing under an external TP monitor (such as CICS) in UCF systems, which issue database requests to CV #1 communicate through SVCs issued by the appropriate interface program (IDMSINTC for CICS).

SMP. When each CV and/or local mode update program starts up, it immediately checks for previous locks in the area(s) to be updated. If none are found, the CV or local mode update program sets its own lock on the area(s). Processing may then continue normally. However, if a local mode run unit attempts to READY an area with USAGE-MODE UPDATE which has a previously set lock, it will abend (error status 0966). It cannot be rerun until that lock is removed. Area locks set by a local mode application are removed at normal completion of a run unit with a FINISH. If the local mode update program should abend, the locks are removed and the database is recovered by running the IDMSRBCK utility. Area locks set by a CV are removed either by a normal shutdown of the CV, or by varying the area(s) offline. If a CV encounters a locked area at startup time, it sends a message to the console and the CV log identifying the locked area and continues processing without using that area.

Record locks protect individual records from concurrent update by multiple run units. Record locks are never maintained for local mode run units because there is only one program accessing the area for update at any given point in time.

Record locks protect records in the database against concurrent update by run units operating under the same CV. These locks are kept in main storage tables; one for each concurrently operating run unit. Each table contains the DBKEYs of the records locked by a run unit. CV maintains two types of record locks – shared and exclusive. A shared lock on a record allows other run units to retrieve the record; if no more than one run unit has a shared lock on a record, it may request to upgrade the lock to an exclusive lock and update the record. An exclusive record lock prohibits other run units from either retrieving or updating the exclusively locked record.

Record locks may be established implicitly or explicitly. Implicit locks are those which CV sets automatically. Explicit locks are requested by the run unit. CV automatically maintains implicit shared locks on all "current" records for each run unit. Current records are the most recently accessed record of each record type, each set type, and each area included in the run unit's subschema (see Programmer's Reference Guide for details on currency). CV automatically sets an implicit exclusive lock on a record that has been updated (prefix and/or data portion), preventing other run units from retrieving or updating the record until such time as the lock is removed. Run units may request locks explicitly with the KEEP/KEEP EXCLUSIVE clause on the FIND or OBTAIN statement. Specifying KEEP requests an explicit shared lock be maintained on a record. Specifying KEEP EXCLUSIVE requests an explicit exclusive lock be maintained on a record.

All locks are removed when a run unit issues a FINISH, ROLLBACK, or COMMIT ALL request to CV, or when the run unit abends and is automatically rolled back by CV. A COMMIT statement releases only exclusive and explicit record locks, implicit shared record locks remain. (See Programmer's Reference Guide for a complete discussion of locks.)

CV maintains another table in main storage for the DBKEYs of records concurrently locked by more than one run unit. This table is used to resolve "deadlock" situations. A deadlock occurs when two (or more) run units each request, implicitly or explicitly, a lock on a record on which the other run unit already has an exclusive lock. For example (Figure 5-2), if run unit #1 updates record A and run unit #2 updates record B, each run unit has an implicit exclusive lock on the updated record. A deadlock will occur if run unit #1 attempts to access record B and run unit #2 attempts to access record A. CV recognizes these deadlock situations and aborts the run unit completing the deadlock, run unit #2 in the example with an 'nn29' ERROR-STATUS.

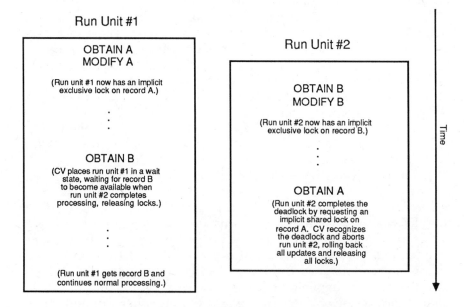

Figure 5-2 Sample Deadlock Situation

5.1.2   Processing Speed

Batch program processing speed is 20-50% more rapid in local mode than under CV for two main reasons: in local mode there is no CV overhead and no SVC's. CV overhead may be thought of as the complex logic necessary to control record locking and multiple concurrent run units within each CV. These run units compete for processing time within the CV because only one run unit may process at a given time until a wait, I/O pending for example, is encountered. CV controls processing priorities for the run units it contains. CV communicates with individual batch programs and online tasks in separate partitions through a supervisor call (SVC). SVC's are used to communicate between regions/partitions and to transfer chunks of data, called packets, from the IDMS/R region to the application region and vice versa (Figure 5-1).

In local mode there is only one run unit, no competition, and therefore, all processing time is devoted to a single run unit. Local mode issues no SVC's, contains no code devoted to setting and upgrading record locks, and is therefore faster.

CV's and local modes executing under a common operating system may be assigned priorities to facilitate throughput. In other words, in the hypothetical situation illustrated in Figure 5-1, the CV's may be assigned a higher priority than the local mode(s), giving the CV's preferential access to processing time in the mainframe. However, because local mode has no complex CV logic and no run unit competition within its partition/region, it could issue I/O's faster than CV; therefore, the local mode may execute more rapidly despite its lower priority. If CV and local mode are sharing a direct access storage device (DASD), local mode may receive a disproportionate share of access to the shared device because it issues I/O's more rapidly. Shared DASD(s) may slow the operation of both CV and local mode due to head and channel contention.

5.1.3 Recovery

The automatic recovery features of IDMS/R are in effect only under CV operation (discussed in Chapter 7). No automatic recovery measures are inherent in local mode. At startup time, CV disk journal files are dedicated for writing before and after images of every record each run unit updates. These images are used to restore automatically the before images to the database, dynamically backing out all updates, in the event of a run unit abend or system failure. CV automatic recovery rolls back one run unit without affecting any other run unit(s) operating concurrently. The exclusive record locks CV places on every record updated by a run unit make this possible (see above).

No automatic recovery mechanism operates within local mode. Manual intervention is always necessary when a local mode update program abends. Users may journal to tape (usually named by the SYSJRNL DD or SYS009 DLBL statements). In the event of an abend, the IDMSRBCK utility is run using the journal tape as input. Alternatively, a small database being processed in local mode may be backed up with the IDMSDUMP utility and the journals dummied or ignored. In the event of an abend in this situation, the IDMSRSTR utility is run to recover the database. This procedure is not recommended for larger databases because it is very time consuming.

5.1.4 Storage Requirements

CV requires only a single copy of DBMS, DBIO, DMCL, and subschemas for all run units under its "umbrella". Simultaneous requests for the same subschema result in one copy of that module being loaded and used. Buffers are allocated from pools in the DMCL which are shared between run units within the CV. In local mode nothing is shared. System software (e.g., DBMS, DBIO, DMCL) must be loaded into each region/partition (Figure 5-1). The DMCL named in the subschema will be used in local mode, therefore, care should be exercised in selecting an appropriate number of buffers. If there are five local mode programs starting up simultaneously, there must be separate copies of each module loaded into each of the five regions/partitions. By extension, local mode partitions/regions must be large enough to contain these copies; large partitions/regions may cause increased system paging and degraded performance.

5.2 SITUATIONS MANDATING EITHER CV OR LOCAL MODE

There are situations in which CV or local mode must be utilized. These situations are summarized in Table 5-2.

Table 5-2 Situations Requiring CV versus Local Mode

CV Required	Local Mode Required
All online programs.	IDMSDBLU
Any batch program requiring	IDMSUNLD
update access to areas	IDMSRSTU
that also must be available	IDMSPCON
to online programs.	RHDCPRLG
IDMSRADM	

5.3 SITUATIONS IN WHICH LOCAL MODE IS PREFERABLE

In situations other than the above, either the CV or local mode environment may be used. In most cases CV is the preferred environment. However, in the following instances we recommend the use of local mode:

- Most batch retrieval programs;
- Initial database loads;
- Applications requiring a static database; and
- Contingent or 'small window' processing.

5.3.1 Batch Retrieval Programs

Batch retrieval programs which access a large number of records can process more rapidly in local mode than under CV. Retrieval programs will run without incurring the usual disadvantages of locking out CV from areas in use and loss of automatic IDMS/R recovery capabilities, because programs which only retrieve do not update any records.

Local mode retrieval programs occasionally may perceive a broken chain where none exists if the area is concurrently being updated by a CV or another local mode program. For example, if another program running under CV or in local mode is in the middle of updating a set, perhaps storing a new member record just after the owner record in set order, and the owner and member records reside on different pages of the database, there is a very small period of time between when the first updated page and the second updated page is written back to the database. If a local mode retrieval program is retrieving records using that same set relationship and accesses the updated owner record followed by attempting to access the new member record (updated in the other CV or LM buffers and shortly to be written to the database), the local mode retrieval program will abend with an error status indicating broken chains on the database.

Don't panic, it only appears to be a broken chain and is not an actual broken chain. If the local mode program abends due to a perceived broken chain, it is an example of a rare timing problem and rerunning the program usually solves the problem.

5.3.2 Initial Database Loads

During an initial database load, local mode is preferred for three main reasons. First, until the initial load is complete, no other run units should have access to those areas of the database. Local mode uses area level locks which will provide this type of protection. Second, an initial load normally involves a large number of records; the load will be accomplished more quickly using local mode. Third, the automatic recovery of CV is superfluous during initial load. If the load program abends, the database is simply reinitialized and the program rerun.

5.3.3 Applications Requiring a Static Database

An area may be secured by an area lock if it is imperative that it remain static, i.e., immune to update, while the batch program processes. Although an area can be locked under CV by using the PROTECTED or EXCLUSIVE options of the READY statement, the relative speed of local mode processing minimizes the amount of time the area is unavailable to other run units. The single drawback of using local mode in this situation is the sacrifice of CV automatic recovery facilities.

5.3.4 Contingent or "Small Window" Processing

In a situation where processing of several run units is contingent upon the rapid completion of a single critical run unit, the critical run unit should be processed in local mode. Although this processing order could be accomplished under CV, the execution of the critical run unit, and therefore of all subsequent run units, will be much slower. By extension, when it is vital to process a run unit in the smallest "window" of time, local mode is the preferred environment.

5.4 COMPARISON OF CV AND LOCAL MODE IN TWO COMMON PROCESSING SITUATIONS

In some cases, CV and local mode are both viable environments. For example, DML program compiles and batch application programs designed to update a large number of records may be executed in either CV or local mode. Inherent in each environment are specific benefits and drawbacks. We will review these two cases and compare the consequences of running them under CV versus local mode.

5.4.1 DML Compiles

Batch, IDMS-DC, and Native TP application programs use data manipulation language (DML) statements to request database services. Programs using DML statements are processed initially by the appropriate host language DML processor (IDMSDMLx). The DML processor converts DML statements to host language statements, copies in record layouts, and updates the IDD with statistical and cross-reference information about the program. The DML Processor step is followed by the compile and linkage editing steps. Native TP programs, such as CICS Command Level programs, may require an additional step translating TP requests into the host language. These steps constitute a DML program compile.

DML program compiles may be run under CV or local mode. For programs in the early stages of testing, compiles are frequent and the captured statistical information is largely the same each time. When doing early compiles under CV, heavy SVC overhead is incurred — mainly for the copy function. Alternatively, early compiles may be run in local mode with *RETRIEVAL as the first statement in the program to suppress all writes to the IDD. At a later point in time, the program should be compiled under CV without the *RETRIEVAL statement, to document in the IDD statistical cross-reference information about the program. This approach minimizes SVC overhead and speeds compiles.

5.4.2 Batch Programs which Update a Large Number of Records

When running batch programs under CV which update a large number of records, two storage-related problems may occur: excessively large record lock tables in main storage and filling the disk storage on the journal files. If the number of records locked exceeds the RULOCKS sysgen parameter, additional storage is allocated from the storage pool to accommodate the extra large lock table. Further, if a request is made to upgrade the status of a lock from shared to exclusive, CV performs a linear search on the run unit's lock table to change the status for that DBKEY entry. Therefore, as the number of records locked increases, so does processing time for each lock upgrade request.

It is necessary to store before and after images of updated records on the journal file to satisfy the requirements of the automatic recovery facility of CV. As the journal files become full, the IDMSAJNL utility must be run to offload and condense the journal. After the condense phase, before images of records updated by run units still active remain in the journal — reducing space available for ongoing journaling. This situation may deplete all space allocated to journals when processing very large batch update programs. When all disk journals are filled to capacity the system stops.

There are three possible routes around both the journal space and large internal lock table problems: run the program in local mode;

use COMMITs to create checkpoints on the journal and run the program under CV; or, rewrite the program as several smaller programs. A fourth possible route, solving only the large internal lock table problem, is to run the program under CV with USAGE-MODE PROTECTED UPDATE

Running the program in local mode alleviates the main storage problem because it places no record level locks. The disk journal storage problem may be solved either by journaling to tape or by backing up the database and dummying the journals. Disadvantages of running the program in local mode are locking out update access by other run units and loss of automatic recovery.

Checkpoints will be written to the journal file and record locks released at intervals by coding COMMITs at specific points in the batch program. COMMIT ALL releases all record locks. COMMIT releases only exclusive record and explicit record locks; implicit shared locks remain. Releasing locks at intervals reduces the size of the lock table and the number of before images maintained on the journal file. If the program abends, automatic recovery will rollback to only the most recent COMMIT checkpoint, rather than to the beginning of the run unit (Chapter 7 discusses COMMITs and restart records).

Alternatively, a single large program may be written as several smaller programs. Each of these smaller run units has correspondingly smaller space and time requirements. However, running this particular group of programs concurrently may still result in disk journal storage shortages, much the same as running the original large, single program.

Running the program under CV with USAGE-MODE PROTECTED UPDATE places an area lock on all areas being updated. Therefore, the problem of an overly large lock table in the storage pool will not exist because CV will not maintain record locks. This route, however, will not solve the journal space problem. All before images must be maintained on the journal files until the program FINISHs or COMMITs.

5.5   CONCLUSION

In summary, there are two primary processing environments for batch programs – Central Version and local mode. Figure 5-1 illustrates how CV and local mode relate to each other under a common operating system. Users may elect to process batch programs in either CV or local mode, except in the situations listed in Table 5-2. Almost without exception, CV is the preferred environment for updating because of the automatic recovery features incorporated in it. When rapid processing becomes more important than having automatic recovery capabilities, local mode may be the environment of choice.

Suggestions for further reading on Central Version and local mode environments:

The following Cullinet Manuals
  For Release 10 sites:
    1) IDMS/R Database Operations (Overview of CV and Local Mode, record and area locks, recovery)
    2) IDMS Programmer's Reference Guide (record and area locks, currency, DML compiles, COMMIT statement)
    3) System Operations Guide (Communication between CV and batch programs, specifying CV or Local Mode for program execution)

  For Release 5.7 sites:
    1) IDMS Programmer's Reference Guide for the following languages: COBOL, FORTRAN, ASSEMBLER, and PL/I (record and area locks, currency, DML compiles, COMMIT statement)
    2) IDMS-CV/DC System Operations (Communication between CV and batch programs, specifying CV or Local Mode for program execution)

6

Security

Why security? The information stored in databases and data dictionaries is vital to successful operation in today's business world. Like other vital corporate assets, data requires protection against loss and theft. Loss may result from unauthorized persons accessing a database or data dictionary. Accidental or intentional misuse of these two resources can cause serious problems, such as the loss of deposit records or account histories. Outright theft of data or applications is invariably damaging to corporate operations. Security is therefore a must. But, the questions arise of 1) what should be secured and 2) how can specific items be protected with the minimum of overhead and downtime? The levels at which security measures are to be activated and how stringent these measures will be is, at best, a subjective decision. Excessive security is very expensive to maintain. A well-planned security strategy will yield adequate protection with minimal maintenance expense.

In this chapter we will discuss the security facilities of IDMS/R. Whenever possible these features should be used in conjunction with preexisting security measures such as operating system security, security software packages, and on-site physical security. We will examine:

- System components and security planning.
- The security facilities inherent in IDMS/R and the resources they are designed to protect. We will also discuss site-specific security applications.
- Securing system components.
- Security requirements of the test and production environments and how they differ.

6.1   SYSTEM COMPONENTS AND SECURITY PLANNING

Although security planning should be tailored to each organization, there are several system components (Figure 6-1) which should be

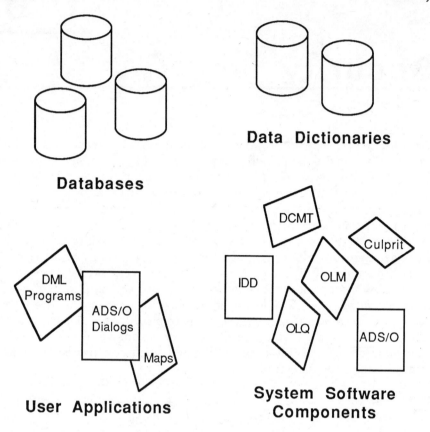

Figure 6-1 What to Secure

considered at the beginning of any security strategy. We suggest securing the following:

- Databases
- Data Dictionaries
- User Applications
- IDMS/R System Software Components.

Table 6-1 contains summary of security considerations for these system components.

6.1.1 Databases

A universal concern is the protection of databases. Their contents need to be protected from unauthorized access and unauthorized or

Table 6-1 The Four Components of the DB Environment and Their Security
Considerations

System Component	Security Considerations
Databases	Protect DB records and definitions (schemas, subschemas, and DMCL's) from unauthorized alteration and/or access.
Data Dictionaries	Protect entity occurrences from unauthorized alteration and/or access, limit access to security facilities initiated using the IDD.
User Applications	Protect programs and dialogs from unauthorized use or alteration, thereby restricting who may alter DB record occurrences.
IDMS/R Software Components	Restrict use of components (e.g., IDD, ADS/O, OLM, OLQ, etc.) and limit DB's and DD's accessed with these components

accidental alteration. The schema, subschema(s), and DMCL(s) also
require protection because they define each database.

6.1.2   Data Dictionaries

The database and data communications environment is defined by
entities stored in data dictionaries. These entities require protection
from unauthorized access or alteration. In addition, the IDD is instrumental in securing several system components, therefore access
to the security facilities of the IDD should be restricted.

6.1.3   User Applications

User applications may access or alter the contents of DB's and DD's;
therefore usage of these applications must be restricted to authorized
personnel. Several kinds of programs can be part of an application,
e.g., ADS/O applications and dialogs, batch DML programs, DC pro-

grams, Culprit report programs, and so on. Access restrictions may
be specified at the individual program level.

6.1.4 IDMS/R System Software Components

IDMS/R system software components that should be secured include
the following:

    IDD, ADS/O, OLM, OLQ, Culprit, ASF, ICMS, System Tasks.

It is important to secure system software components because they are
powerful tools. ADS/O, ASF, OLM, and IDD are used in the development of user applications. OLQ and Culprit provide online and batch
access to database and data dictionary record occurrences. ICMS
allows users to access the DB using microcomputers. System tasks
permit users to monitor and modify the status of the IDMS/R run time
system. A brief description of the main system tasks is provided
below as a guide in determining the security measures appropriate for
each.

System Tasks Overview: We are concerned here only with the following system tasks – DCUF, OPER, DCMT, SEND, and CLIST.
Further information about these and other system task codes may be
found in the System Operations Guide.

    DCUF is usually available to the general programming staff.
It allows online users to issue several commands, including SET
DICTNAME, SHOW USERS, TEST, and USERTRACE. SET
DICTNAME, a Release 10 function, allows users to specify a default
dictionary when secondary dictionaries are in use. This eliminates
the need to make a separate signon to the appropriate DD during each
use of a different software component. The DCUF SHOW USER
command displays all users currently signed on. TEST allows the
programmer to alter the version numbers of programs and dialogs
executed at his/her terminal. DCUF TEST facilitates testing a new
version of a program while the master version is still executed by
other users. USERTRACE allows the programmer to turn on a
terminal wrap around trace facility which may be used when
debugging DC programs.

    The OPER task code is usually secured because it allows a termi-
nal user to monitor system activity as well as to cancel an active task.
Authority to issue the OPER task code is often limited to the DBA and
systems programming staffs, for use as a tool to monitor system
resource utilization. Unlike the DCMT task, different forms of the
OPER task cannot be secured independently.

    The DCMT (DC Master Terminal) task code is an extremely
powerful task capable of aiding or harming a system. It can be used to

monitor system activity, display and modify main storage contents, enable or disable terminals, and many other system functions. It is usually secured, even though programmers may need to use some of the DCMT functions in the test system. Fortunately, IDMS/R has discrete security for the different versions of the DCMT command (Section 6.2.2).

The SEND task allows messages to be sent to a terminal, user, or groups thereof. It may be useful to the operations staff for sending out general information messages. SEND rarely requires securing.

The CLIST task (Release 10 only) is used to name a module on the DD which contains a list of replies to the "ENTER NEXT TASK CODE" prompt, i.e., tasks. User signon profiles (another Release 10 feature) are CLISTs. They may be used to issue the DCUF SET DICT-NAME command in a multiple dictionary environment. Then programmers assigned to a secondary dictionary would automatically be working in the proper dictionary. The amount of security desired usually depends on the kind of commands contained in the CLIST module. In general, CLIST modules on the IDD might be secured to prevent users from changing their normal signon profiles.

6.2   IDMS/R SECURITY FACILITIES

We will now discuss the security facilities available in IDMS/R to secure the critical system components: the databases, data dictionaries, user applications, and system software components. The relationship between the security facilities and the components they protect may be described in database terms as many-to-many. One facility may be used to protect several components; one component may be protected by several different facilities. We will look at this relationship from both sides. In this section the security facilities are described in detail, grouped by when and where each security facility is initiated. This will be followed by a section summarizing how these facilities are used to secure databases, data dictionaries, user applications, and IDMS/R system software components.

Table 6-2 contains an overview of IDMS/R security facilities. One facility is enabled during installation, several are initiated during system creation, others when a database is defined, several in the IDD, and some during user application definition.

6.2.1   Installation Time Security Specifications

Culprit is the only part of the system where security is affected by choices made during the initial installation of IDMS/R. If the

Table 6-2 IDMS/R Security Facilities: A Summary

When/Where Facility Specified	Which Facility
Installation	CULL-SECURE parameter
System Creation	Security class; Including/excluding task codes; UNDEFINED PROGRAM COUNT; REGISTRATION; and #CTABGEN macro
Database Definition	Subschema record views; Subschema verb restriction; Subschema AUTHORIZATION; Subschema Logical Record Facility; and Database procedures
IDD	SET OPTIONS FOR DICTIONARY; USER AUTHORITY(IES)/ACCESS(es); Entity USER registration/PUBLIC ACCESS (Release 10), USER RESPONSIBLE FOR DEFINITION (prior releases); Culprit/OLQ ACCESS TO SUBSCHEMA; and IDD AUTHORIZATION
Application Definition	Security class; Application logic; ADS/A Security

organization wants to secure Culprit using the dictionary security facilities described in Section 6.2.4 below, the installation parameter CULL-SECURE YES must be specified. If CULL-SECURE NO was specified, or is in effect by default, Culprit must be reinstalled before any of the dictionary security facilities may be used with it.

6.2.2 Security Facilities Defined During System Creation

Several security measures may be built in when a new IDMS/R system is created. Such security measures apply only to executions of that particular DB/DC system, and therefore should be tailored to the needs of the individual system.

Four facilities are defined by parameters input to the system generation (sysgen) compiler. A fifth security facility is implemented by assembling and linking the #CTABGEN macro. These facilities are:

- Security classes may be specified to limit execution of online tasks and programs to only those users with appropriate security clearance.
- Execution of specific online tasks and programs can be prohibited by excluding unwanted tasks and programs from the sysgen.

- The value of the UNDEFINED PROGRAM COUNT sysgen parameter determines whether dynamic definition of programs is allowed.
- Program registration may be selected to limit database and data dictionary access to only those programs included in the sysgen.
- The DCMT (DC Master Terminal) system task code may be secured at several different levels using the #CTABGEN macro.

System Creation Security Facility – Security Classes: Security classes are one of the major IDMS/R security facilities. They may be used to secure any online component, including both user applications and system software components. Security classes may be specified for tasks, programs, dialogs and users in the sysgen. Additionally, security classes may be specified for dialogs through the ADSA application generator.

A security class is a number between 0 and 255. One security class may be assigned to each task or program. Only users having that same security class in their list of security classes may execute the task or program. The default security class for tasks and programs is zero, which means anyone may access the task or program. User security classes are not carried in a downward progression; someone assigned security class of 10 would not be allowed access to every task with security classes of 1 through 9. This is an exact match only system.

Advance planning is important when implementing security classes for a new application. Separate security classes for each function within an application can lead to extensive maintenance of the user security class lists. For a further discussion of security class hierarchies refer to Section 6.3.3 under Limiting Use of Application Programs and Dialogs to Authorized Users.

System Creation Security Facility – Excluding Tasks and Programs: Undesirable online tasks and programs can be excluded from the sysgen. For example, the ADSA and ADSG tasks, used to create or modify online applications, might be excluded from the sysgen of a production system. Exclusion is only part of the concerted effort necessary to prevent the execution of unauthorized tasks and programs. It may be used in conjunction with prevention of dynamic program definition, limitations on the powerful DCMT system task code, and program registration.

System Creation Security Facility – Preventing Dynamic Program Definition: The UNDEFINED PROGRAM COUNT sysgen parameter determines whether dynamic definition is allowed for dialogs, DC programs, subschemas, maps, and tables. Dynamic program definition means informing the system about a new dialog or subschema which was not included in the sysgen. It can take place automatically, when a new dialog is generated, or manually using the DCMT command:

DCMT VARY DYNAMIC PROGRAM *program-name program-attributes*

Dynamic program definition is necessary in a test system to allow testing of newly developed applications without requiring an immediate regeneration of the test system.

System Creation Security Facility – REGISTRATION: If REGISTRATION is specified in the sysgen, only programs identified in the sysgen with IDMS PROGRAM statements will be allowed to access databases and data dictionaries. This security is often called 'program registration', and is the only method which can prevent unauthorized access to highly secured database information by batch programs or other external run units (e.g., CICS programs issuing IDMS/R calls).

Note, however, that this facility is not fail-safe protection. It will not prevent programs running in local mode from accessing the DB. Also, any program may be given the same name as a program registered in the sysgen and the system will not prevent its execution.

If an unauthorized program attempts to access the DB, IDMS CV will abort the run unit with the '1469' ERROR-STATUS code. The '1469' code can be confusing because it is also used to indicate that CV is not up or that one of several timeout errors occurred.

Program registration requires advance knowledge of all programs which will access the DB's and DD's for either update or retrieval purposes, a difficult requirement for a test system. All user programs must be included in the sysgen, as must all Cullinet compilers (the System Generation Guide contains a chart of all Cullinet programs to be included in the sysgen).

System Creation Security Facility – Securing the DCMT System Task Code with the #CTABGEN Macro: The DCMT task code should be highly secured. However, many different system functions are possible using the DCMT task code, e.g., displaying statistics or memory, varying the contents of system control tables and changing sysgen parameter values for the remainder of the system execution. Some of these functions, such as the VARY DYNAMIC PROGRAM command to define a new program to the system, are useful to programmers in the test system. Other functions, such as altering the contents of control tables, are much too powerful for release to the general programming staff.

An overall security class can be specified for the DCMT task code on the sysgen TASK statement. In addition, discrete security is available for the different types of the DCMT commands. One #CTABGEN macro may be coded during system creation. This macro allows specification of separate security classes for the different DCMT commands. In general, all VARY commands should be secured through the generic security class option of the #CTABGEN macro, except DCMT VARY PROGRAM *program-name* NEW COPY. The DCMT display commands would be adequately protected by securing the DCMT task itself.

The #CTABGEN macro is assembled and link edited with the DCMT security program, RHDCMT00. The resulting load module is stored in the load library or core image library used by the run time IDMS/R system. At any time in the life of the system, security for DCMT commands may be changed by coding a different #CTABGEN macro and following the above steps to replace the load module in the library used by the run time system.

6.2.3   Security Facilities Defined during Database Definition

Five decisions made during database definition affect the security and integrity of the database. Four choices are made at the subschema level and one at the schema level. They are:

- Subschemas may be designed to permit or prevent access to all occurrences of specific elements within a database record with use of a view-id.
- Protection against specific types of DB alteration may be achieved by subschema verb restriction.
- Logical Record Facility may be used to limit both the data values and the path of data access.
- Subschema authorization may be turned on to limit the programs which can be compiled using a specific subschema.
- At the schema level, database procedures (special purpose user programs) may be identified to execute when a particular area or record is accessed using specific verbs.

DB Definition Security Facility – Subschema View-Id: The view-id is a group of record elements (in any given order) within a subschema that does not necessarily include all elements in the physical data record on the actual database. For example, an employee record in a personnel database might include an element for salary information. The salary element would be included in the subschema view used by payroll programs, but not in the subschema view used by general programs. This type of security is effective only against all occurrences of an element on the database. Securing specific occurrences of an element on the database must be handled through Logical Record Facility, application logic, or database procedures.

DB Definition Security Facility – Subschema Verb Restriction: Verb restriction within a subschema can prevent dangerous verbs (e.g., ERASE) from being issued by programs using that particular subschema. Verb restriction might also be used to restrict a USAGE MODE of PROTECTED or EXCLUSIVE UPDATE in the subschemas of online programs and dialogs.

DB Definition Security Facility – Subschemas with Logical Records: The Logical Record Facility (LRF) is a major tool with utmost flexibility for controlling data access. In contrast to sub-schema view id's, LRF provides a method for handling data value security, i.e., limiting access to records based on the value of elements within the records. LRF also provides a method for limiting access to sensitive relationships within the DB.

A logical record may be composed of all or portions of several database records. When LRF is used, code is placed in a subschema defining the components of the logical record and paths for logical record retrieval and/or update. Only access and update anticipated by the logical record designer and provided for in the subschema code will be allowed to proceed. Because it is outside the program, this type of security cannot be overridden by the programmer.

DB Definition Security Facility – Subschema AUTHORIZATION: AUTHORIZATION ON can be specified in a subschema to limit the programs which may be compiled against that specific subschema. It requires a good deal of maintenance because programs must be added to the dictionary manually prior to the compilation, naming the subschema to be used with:

ADD PROGRAM *program-name* INCLUDE SUBSCHEMA *subschema-name.*

In addition, if subschema authorization is ON, each user must be authorized to access the individual subschema for use with Culprit and OLQ. Specifically, when signon security has been turned on for Culprit and OLQ, each user must be granted access to all subschemas which the user might employ. When signon security has been turned off, users need access to only those subschemas with AUTHORIZATION ON.

Note, however, that when a schema change is required, if the schema is deleted, all subschemas associated with that schema are also deleted along with their authorization relationship with users. Hence, a schema DELETE and ADD forces reentering the authorized subschema(s) for each user. Modifying schemas is permitted under Release 10 so the old DELETE and ADD syndrome is unnecessary. Modifying schemas preserves user and authorized subschema relationships.

DB Definition Security Facility – Schema Database Procedures: Security may also be incorporated through use of database procedures. Database procedures are user-written programs identified to execute when named areas or records are accessed using specific verbs. DB procedures are specified in the schema definition of a database and apply to all database access, regardless of subschema. Procedures provide extremely effective security because they are invoked at an high level which programmers and users cannot bypass.

IDMS/R database commands within a procedure are not allowed because they could cause currency problems for the calling program.

There are many possible uses for DB procedures. DB procedures, like LRF, may be used for examination of specific element values within subschema records to allow or disallow a verb based on that element value. This contrasts with view-id's which can restrict only total access to a given element. DB procedures, unlike LRF, apply to all database access, regardless of subschema.

Data encryption is another way of using a database procedure to provide strict security. A DB procedure could encrypt all data when it is entered into the database and then provide a decryption step prior to its display to users. This method would protect sensitive database and data dictionary files from access by programs unrelated to IDMS/R and therefore, not covered by IDMS/R security, e.g., operating system utilities. However, due to the extra overhead involved and the corresponding increases in response time, data encryption is often unacceptable in a heavy online transaction environment.

6.2.4 Security Facilities Defined Through the IDD

There are many different security facilities initiated through the Integrated Data Dictionary. The IDD may be used as a facility to

provide security for itself and other parts of the IDMS/R system. IDD security facilities include:

- • Product signon security,
- • Password security,

•Entity type security,
•Individual entity occurrence security,
•IDD AUTHORIZATION, and
•Culprit/OLQ ACCESS TO SUBSCHEMA clauses.

IDD Security Facility – Product Signon Security: IDD product signon security is one of the major security facilities of IDMS/R. If signon security has been turned on for a product, the user must signon with a valid user id and password, and must have authority or access to the product before being allowed to use it. Use of all major software products may be limited through security specifications in the dictionary. For example:

```
SET OPTIONS FOR DICTIONARY
    SECURITY FOR IDD SIGNON IS ON
    SECURITY FOR ADS IS ON
    SECURITY FOR CULPRIT IS ON
    SECURITY FOR OLQ IS ON
    ....
```

Each user is then granted access to these software components through individual ACCESS and AUTHORITY clauses on the USER entity record in the data dictionary. For example:

```
ADD USER JAV
    ACCESS TO ASF
    ACCESS TO IDB
    AUTHORITY IS ADS
    AUTHORITY IS OLQ
    ....
```

Keep in mind that this security only requires the user to signon for that product; except for IDD usage, once the signon has been processed, anything can be done. IDD usage is further secured by securing entity types and occurrences (details later in this section).

IDD Security Facility – Password Security: Password is a key IDD security facility. Other than a USER with the global AUTHORITY FOR UPDATE IS ALL, only users granted AUTHORITY FOR UPDATE IS PASSWORD are authorized to change other user's passwords. Individual users may be allowed to change their own password by specifying the INDIVIDUAL PASSWORD SECURITY OVERRIDE ON clause to the SET OPTIONS FOR DICTIONARY statement.

IDD Security Facility – Entity Type Security: The dictionary may be secured further by limiting the types of entities a user is authorized to access and/or alter. This security is activated with the statement:

```
SET OPTIONS FOR DICTIONARY
    SECURITY FOR IDMS IS ON
    SECURITY FOR IDMS-DC IS ON
    SECURITY FOR IDD IS ON
    SECURITY FOR CLASS AND ATTRIBUTE IS ON.
```

Corresponding authorities are granted on a user-by-user basis with the AUTHORITY IS clause on the USER statement, e.g.:

```
ADD USER ABC
    IDD SIGNON ALLOWED
    AUTHORITY IS IDD
    AUTHORITY IS CLASS AND ATTRIBUTE.
```

User ABC is authorized to work with basic entity types (IDD authority) and to define extended DDDL syntax (CLASS AND ATTRIBUTE authority).

Authorization for users to access entities in the DD is provided at the entity type level under Release 10. A user may be allowed access to ELEMENTs, RECORDs, MODULEs, TABLEs and MAPs but not MESSAGEs or FILEs, for example. Moreover, access can be limited to display only, or update privileges may be allowed. Within update privileges, differentiation can be made between ADDs, MODIFYs and DELETEs.

IDD Security Facility – Protection of an Individual Entity Occurrence: A major difference between Release 5.7 and Release 10 security is the degree of protection available for DD entities. Under Release 5.7 of IDMS, individual occurrences of entities can be secured by specifying the USER RESPONSIBLE FOR DEFINITION clause when the entity is defined or modified, e.g.:

```
ADD ELEMENT element-name
    INCLUDE USER user-name
    RESPONSIBLE FOR DEFINITION.
```

This will allow only the user(s) specified to access this element for display, update, or deletion. The responsible users may modify the element as necessary to allow new users access to the entity.

Under Release 10, the RESPONSIBLE FOR DEFINITION clause has been replaced with the REGISTERED FOR and PUBLIC ACCESS clauses which allow much more flexibility in securing specific occurrences of entities. Users may be registered only for display, or registered for modify and add but not delete. For example,

```
MODIFY ELEMENT SALARY
    INCLUDE USER MAC REGISTERED FOR ALL
    INCLUDE USER DAV REGISTERED FOR UPDATE
    PUBLIC ACCESS IS ALLOWED FOR DISPLAY.
```

Both user MAC and user DAV may display, modify or delete the element SALARY. User MAC may also specify new REGISTERED FOR and PUBLIC ACCESS clauses for this element. All other users (except those with the global AUTHORITY FOR UPDATE IS ALL) may only display the element definition for SALARY. The DDDL Reference Guide may be checked for details.

Entity occurrence protection provides low-level protection which may be desirable for breaking out one project's work from that of another. However, the amount of maintenance required for this protection often outweighs its advantages. Secondary dictionaries provide an alternative method for isolating the work of different projects.

IDD Security Facility – AUTHORIZATION: The authorization clause of the SET OPTIONS statement is useful for limiting the programs which may be compiled using the DD. If AUTHORIZATION ON is specified, all programs must have a program entity defined by the DBA staff in the DD prior to the compile taking place. If a program entity has not been added prior to compilation a '1469' ERROR-STATUS results. This feature is difficult to work with because of the maintenance involved and most users shy away from it, especially in the test environment.

IDD Security Facility – Culprit/OLQ ACCESS TO SUBSCHEMA clauses: If subschema authorization is on (Section 6.2.3), access to the database(s) using Culprit and OLQ is further limited by specifying the ACCESS TO SUBSCHEMA clause on the USER statement, naming each subschema available to a given user. Specifically, when signon security has been turned on for Culprit and OLQ, each user must be granted access to all subschemas which might be employed. When signon security has been turned off, users require access to only those subschemas with AUTHORIZATION ON.

6.2.5 Security Facilities Defined in User Applications

Additional security measures, appropriate for an individual application, can be coded in the programs and dialogs of the application.

ADS/O applications built with the ADSA application generator may take advantage of some extra security facilities. Each of these topics is discussed further below.

User Application Security Facility – Dialog and Program Code:
Programs and dialogs may request the following information for an individual execution of the program or dialog from the IDMS/R run time system:

user id   terminal id   task code   date   time.

Use of the program or dialog can be limited to select users on specific terminals. Security also may be enhanced by requiring passwords or undocumented commands before display or update of sensitive database records.

User Application Security Facility – ADSA Security Facilities:
There are some additional security features available to applications built with the ADSA application generator. Using the ADSA security screen, the application designer specifies the security class for the application as a whole, whether menus are to be "security tailored", and whether or not a signon is required prior to use of the application.

To facilitate security violation handling, security classes for ADS applications should be specified through the ADSA generator rather than directly through the sysgen (discussed in Section 6.3.3). One security class can be specified for signing on to the application and additional security classes specified for individual functions.

If security tailored menus are chosen, displays of menu screens will be tailored to the operator's security level. Only the responses valid for that operator will be shown on the menu screen. Security tailored menus help eliminate accidental security violations.

Signon should be required when implementing stringent security for online applications. This is accomplished by identifying one menu screen containing fields for operator entry of user id and password as the signon menu for the application. The signon function may be the system function SIGNON and the signon menu automatically defined by ADSA. Alternatively, the signon procedure can be customized by coding a dialog to perform application-specific security checks in addition to linking to the DC/UCF program RHDCSNON, a Cullinet-supplied module which performs user id and password checking.

6.3   SECURING SYSTEM COMPONENTS

We will now discuss how IDMS/R security facilities may be used to secure databases, data dictionaries, user applications, and system software components. Securing an individual component frequently involves use of several security facilities. Table 6-3 contains a summary of how system components may be secured.

6.3.1   Securing Databases

There are two different considerations when securing databases. They are:

- Protecting database records from unauthorized access and alteration, and
- Protecting the definitions of databases.

Protecting database records from unauthorized access and alteration: Database records are protected primarily by securing the user applications and system software components which access and alter DB records (Sections 6.3.3 and 6.3.4). In addition, subschema access restrictions and DB procedures may be used to limit the functions allowed programs and system software components. DB records can be further secured by using security systems outside of IDMS/R to limit access to DB files by non-IDMS programs.

For extremely sensitive databases, consider using DB procedures to encrypt and decrypt database records. These procedures can render such databases meaningless to non-IDMS programs. A word of caution about encryption...the overhead of encryption/decryption may slow down response time enough to make this method unacceptable for systems with many online transactions.

Protecting the definitions of databases: Database definitions, (schemas, subschemas, and DMCL's) can be secured using a combination of IDD security facilities. For any dictionary containing DB definitions that should be secured, specify as part of the SET OPTIONS FOR DICTIONARY statement:

SECURITY FOR IDMS IS ON.

The IDD will then limit access to DB definitions to only those users who have AUTHORITY IS IDMS. Under Release 10, permissible access may be limited further by specifying AUTHORITY FOR DISPLAY IS IDMS, which limits those users to display access only, an easy-to-implement security approach.

Table 6-3 Securing System Components: A Summary

System Component	How Secured
Databases:	
Record Occurrences	Secure user applications and system components which access/alter record occurrences, use DB procedures and subschemas access restrictions
DB Definition	IDD options, user authorities, and user registration/public access specifications
Data Dictionaries:	
Entity Occurrences	IDD options, user authorities, and user registration/public access specifications
Access to Security Facilities	Limit the number of users with AUTHORITY IS ALL or AUTHORITY IS PASSWORD
User Applications:	
Programs/Dialogs	Security class, program registration, IDD options, user authorities, user registration & public access specifications, undefined program count, application logic
System Software Components:	
IDD	IDD options, user authorities, user registration/public access specifications (Release 10), RESPONSIBLE FOR DEFINITION clause (prior releases)
ADS/O	Security class, IDD options
ASF	Security class, IDD options
ICMS	Security class, IDD options
OLM	Security class, IDD options
OLQ	IDD options, access to subschema, access to QFILE
Culprit	Installation parameter CULL-SECURE, IDD options, access to subschema
System Tasks	Security class, #CTABGEN macro

Individual schemas and subschemas can be further secured by user registration and public access specifications (under Release 10). For example:

```
MODIFY SCHEMA TESTDB01
    INCLUDE USER ABC REGISTERED FOR ALL
    INCLUDE USER DEF REGISTERED FOR UPDATE
    PUBLIC ACCESS IS ALLOWED FOR NONE.
```

Unregistered users cannot access the schema definition in any manner. Both user ABC and user DEF may display, modify, or delete the schema. In addition, user ABC may specify new registration and public access statements.

6.3.2   Securing Data Dictionaries

There are two important aspects of securing data dictionaries. They are:

- Protecting the entity occurrences in the DD from unauthorized access/alteration, and
- Limiting access to the security facilities of the IDD.

Protecting the entity occurrences in the DD from unauthorized access and/or alteration: The contents of a DD (entity occurrences) are protected by a combination of dictionary options, user authorities, and user registration/public access specifications. Password protection for DD contents is initiated using the SET OPTIONS FOR DICTIONARY statement and specifying which groups of entities should be secured (Section 6.2.4). Individual USERs are authorized to access and/or alter specific types of entities by allowing IDD SIGNON and including authorization for access and/or alteration of specific types of entities. Individual entity occurrences can be further secured by specifying particular users who are registered to update or display the entity and by limiting other users to no access or merely display access.

Limiting access to the security facilities of the IDD. The security facilities of the IDD are also used to protect other components of the IDMS/R environment (Section 6.2.4). It is important to limit the number of users with authority to manipulate the IDD security facilities. Only those users with AUTHORITY FOR UPDATE IS ALL can issue SET OPTIONS FOR DICTIONARY statements. Only users with AUTHORITY IS ALL or AUTHORITY FOR UPDATE IS PASSWORD can establish or modify passwords and authorities for other users. Only a few key users, most likely DBA's or DDA's, should be allowed these authorities.

Another Release 10 security aid is the ability to code IDD user exits. This allows users to trap any syntax input to the IDMSDDDL compiler and impose more stringent control on who may enter information into the dictionary. In addition, the statements can be edited to insure that they adhere to site dictionary standards.

In situations that demand a high level of dictionary security against unauthorized access or alteration, multiple dictionaries work well. With widespread use of the IDD by programmers, as required by ADS/O and OLM, implementing security for individual entity occurrences (e.g., modules, records, elements, maps) becomes a major maintenance problem. Largely unsecured secondary dictionaries can be extremely useful in this regard when combined with a well-secured primary test dictionary. A certain amount of redundancy will be absorbed here to gain the advantage of day-to-day dictionary use with a minimum of maintenance. A migration plan is required to move information easily from one dictionary to another, e.g., from a secondary dictionary to the primary dictionary. The migration process can be automated by coding a migration utility (Section 3.10.5) or by purchasing a migration utility such as the one available from the authors of this book or other vendors.

6.3.3   Securing User Applications

It is extremely important to secure application programs and dialogs because their main function is to access and alter database records. By securing user applications we are actually securing the databases.

In the realm of securing user applications there are three concerns, listed here in order of importance.

- Limiting use of application programs and dialogs to authorized users,
- Securing the application programs and dialogs themselves from unauthorized access and/or alteration, and
- Prohibiting unauthorized programs from accessing and/or altering databases or data dictionaries.

Limiting Use of Application Programs and Dialogs to Authorized Users: The main method used to limit use of application program/dialogs is security class designations made during the sysgen or during ADSA application definition. A second method lies in the logic of each individual application. For example, programs could require secondary passwords for highly secured functions or limit use of the program to only specified terminals (Section 6.2.5).

Security requirements should be determined during the design phase of applications development and the appropriate mixture of security facilities for the application selected. Any security logic that will be incorporated in the programs and dialogs of the application must be chosen at this time.

If security classes are used, the application design should require users to signon with a valid user identification and password prior to allowing any database access. Security classes may be assigned to ADS/O dialogs either through the sysgen or the ADSA application generator. Using the ADSA application generator is recommended because a security violation leaves the ADS run time program in control. An appropriate error message is issued and the user may continue processing within the application. If security classes are assigned through the sysgen, a security violation causes the task to be aborted and the user to be thrown out of ADS altogether. As discussed earlier (Section 6.2.5), ADSA also allows for enforced signon menus and security-tailored menus.

The application's functions and modules should be organized into a security hierarchy as part of the design effort. A security hierarchy can be developed by designating certain functions as relatively highly secured, unsecured, or anywhere in between. For example, a security class of 0 for a menu dialog/program indicates anyone may access it, a security class of 5 might be used for dialogs/programs which may be accessed by a wide range of users, and a security class of 10 might be applied to a highly restricted dialog/program. Figure 6-2 shows a sample security class hierarchy where the security levels are tied to the type of database access involved.

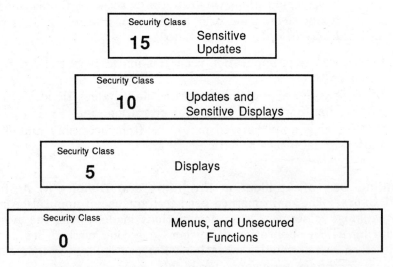

Figure 6-2 Sample Security Class Hierarchy

Dialogs/programs which simply display database information would have a security class of 5, while dialogs/programs which update database records would have a security class of 10. However, there are always exceptions to any hierarchy. Dialogs/programs which display records containing security-sensitive information might warrant a security class of 10, and those which update highly-secured records might require a security class of 15.

The security hierarchy should be viewed globally rather than on an individual application basis. Users frequently work with several different applications, and therefore require security clearance for each application. For example, if user ABC works with two application systems, user ABC's security class list must contain the security classes for programs, dialogs, and tasks in both systems.

Maintenance of user security class lists becomes a major effort if each application, or worse yet, each program, has a different security class. Whenever possible, the security requirements of a new application should be incorporated with those of existing applications to minimize maintenance overhead.

Each application should use a different security hierarchy only when it is necessary to limit users to a single application in a system with multiple applications. e.g.,

Application 1: Customer Order

TASK COMENU	SECURITY CLASS = 0
TASK ORDDISP	SECURITY CLASS = 5
TASK CUSTDISP	SECURITY CLASS = 5
TASK ORDUPDT	SECURITY CLASS = 10

Application 2: Inventory

TASK INVMENU	SECURITY CLASS = 0
TASK STKONHND	SECURITY CLASS = 6
TASK PRODDISP	SECURITY CLASS = 6
TASK PRODUPDT	SECURITY CLASS = 12

For user ABC to work with both applications for display and update of database records, user ABC must have the following security class list:

SECURITY CLASS = (5 6 10 12)

Users limited to the customer order application would have a security class list containing only 5 and 10; users limited to the inventory application would have a security class list containing only 6 and 12.

Securing Application Programs and Dialogs from Unauthorized Alteration: Securing programs and dialogs from alteration by unauthorized personnel is especially important in a production environment (versus a test environment). It is relatively easy to secure programs by putting password security on the source and object libraries where those programs reside. Prohibiting alteration of run time attributes and/or bringing in new copies of programs and dialogs may be accomplished by securing those particular functions of the DCMT task (using the #CTABGEN macro) and/or securing the DCMT task itself (using security classes).

Problems may occur, however, when use of application development software such as ADSG, OLM, IDD, etc., is permitted in production systems. It then becomes necessary to take measures to prevent new dialogs, tables, or maps from being generated, and to prevent changes to existing dialogs, tables, or maps. One possible measure is securing the task codes of the application development software using security classes. If securing the task codes is not sufficient security because several users will be allowed access to them, another layer of protection may be necessary. A second measure for preventing new unauthorized dialogs from being run against production databases is including all production programs and dialogs in the sysgen and specifying (0,0) for the UNDEFINED PROGRAM COUNT sysgen parameter (Chapter 9 describes this parameter).

Specifying (0,0) for UNDEFINED PROGRAM COUNT prohibits generation of new programs, dialogs, subschemas, or maps by the application development software. In addition, it prevents creation of new load modules (presumably altered) for existing dialogs, maps, etc., unless the user attempting the change has two security class clearances. The user's security class list must contain the security class required to execute the application development software and the security class required to execute the dialog, map, etc., that the user is attempting to change. For example, to change an existing dialog and generate a new load module, the user's security class list must contain the security class for the ADSG task code and the security class required to execute that specific dialog. For both the ADSG generator and the OLM generator, any unauthorized attempt to regenerate an existing dialog or map results in a DC021005 error message and a task abend. An unauthorized user attempting a change to a dialog will experience an immediate abend. The OLM compiler allows users to make modifications updating the DD but aborts any unauthorized attempt to create a modified load module. This method does not protect against changes made to process code or mapping code on the IDD but it does prevent those changes from generating load modules and thereby affecting the run time system.

Prohibiting Unauthorized Programs from Accessing and/or Altering Databases or Data Dictionaries: Protection in the production environment from execution of unauthorized dialogs and programs is easily maintained by putting all programs in the sysgen, prohibiting dynamic program definition by setting UNDEFINED PROGRAM COUNT to (0,0), and restricting use of the DCMT VARY DYNAMIC PROGRAM command through #CTABGEN macro specifications. Only online TASKs and PROGRAMs included in the sysgen would then be able to access the DB's and DD's, thereby forcing all programs, dialogs, maps, tables, and subschemas to be funnelled through the DBA staff. Although this method requires coordination and maintenance, it provides the security necessary to prevent execution of a new program, dialog, or subschema.

Further protection can be achieved by specifying AUTHORIZA-TION IS ON at the IDD and subschema levels and REGISTRATION in the sysgen (Section 6.2). Sysgen program registration limits DB and DD access to only those programs included in the sysgen with IDMS PROGRAM statements. REGISTRATION is the only means of preventing an unauthorized batch program from accessing the DB through Central Version; however, as discussed earlier, it is not a fail-safe protection.

6.3.4   Securing System Software Components

Initially, authorization to use system software components should be restricted because they are tools for development and monitoring of databases, IDD(s), or user applications. Subsequently, use of these tools should be restricted to prevent unauthorized or accidental alteration of production applications, databases, and IDD's.

Some security aspects are common among the software components. All the online components (online IDD, ADS/O, IDB, ASF, OLM, OLQ, and the system tasks) may be secured with appropriate SECURITY CLASS specifications on their TASK codes during sysgen. Authorized users would require matching security class specifications during the sysgen. All software components except for system tasks are further secured through dictionary product signon security.

Additional security measures for OLQ and Culprit: For OLQ and Culprit, individual users can be limited to certain views of the database by permitting them to have access to only specific subschemas. QFILEs are OLQ command sequences which generate reports. QFILEs are stored in the DD. Users may be granted access to specific QFILEs and not to others.

Securing DCMT functions: As discussed in Section 6.2.2, the DCMT task code can be secured with different security classes for different functions. This is done with the #CTABGEN macro, which can associate each DCMT function or group of functions with the appropriate security class. In general, all VARY commands should be secured through the generic security class option on the #CTABGEN macro. The VARY DYNAMIC PROGRAM command to create entries in the DC program definition table for new programs may be an exception. Most of the DCMT display commands would be adequately protected by the security class of the DCMT task itself. If the user has clearance to execute DCMT, most of the displays commands should be allowed.

Securing CLIST modules: CLIST modules on the DD should be secured to prevent users from changing their normal signon profiles. CLIST modules may be secured by specifying the INCLUDE USER *user-name* REGISTERED FOR ALL and PUBLIC ACCESS IS ALLOWED FOR NONE clauses. Task CLIST does not check IDD module security. If a user can execute the CLIST task (which must be allowed to implement signon profiles), the user can execute any CLIST module. However, the IDMS/R DC/UCF system performs normal security checking on each task within the CLIST.

6.4 TEST SYSTEM VERSUS PRODUCTION SYSTEM SECURITY MEASURES

Security can be tailored to individual system needs using the facilities described above. The measures required for protection of the Test System are different from those required for the Production System. Table 6-4 summarizes possible differences between security measures chosen for these two systems. Of course, these recommendations must be tailored to each site's special security requirements.

In the test system security classes often are used to secure only the system task codes OPER and DCMT (DCMT DISPLAY commands and some DCMT VARY commands may be allowed). In addition, some sites use security classes to limit access to application development system software such as ADSA, ADSG, OLM, and IDD; all other tasks, programs and dialogs have the default security class of zero.

Security classes are much more likely to be used in a production system. They are one of the major IDMS/R security facilities. Each end user must have a user id included in the sysgen with appropriate security classes for the kinds of functions for which he or she is authorized.

The system software components used for development of applications and databases, e.g., ADSG, ADSA, OLM, and IDD, are often excluded from the sysgen of production systems. Exclusion,

Table 6-4 Security Differences Between Test and Production

Security Facility	Test System	Production System
System Creation:		
Security Classes	Used for OPER and DCMT tasks only	Used Heavily
REGISTRATION	Not used	Sometimes used
UNDEFINED PROGRAM COUNT	Greater than zero	(0,0) for systems requiring heavy security
DCMT availability	Many authorized users	Very few authorized users
ADSG, OLM, IDD, OLQ	Present, many authorized users	If present, very restricted
Database Definition:		
Database Procedures	Used as Necessary	Used as Necessary
Subschema Record Views	Occasionally Used	Occasionally Used
Subschema Verb	Occasionally Used Restriction	Occasionally Used
LRF	Used frequently	Used frequently
AUTHORIZATION	OFF	OFF
IDD:		
AUTHORIZATION	OFF	OFF
Security OPTIONS	Loosely secured	Tightly secured
Culprit & OLQ Access to subschema/QFILE	Not used	Used occasionally

combined with prevention of dynamic program definition by setting
UNDEFINED PROGRAM COUNT to zero, restricting use of the
DCMT VARY DYNAMIC PROGRAM command, and password protecting libraries effectively eliminates the possibility of new or modified programs/dialogs executing in the system.

Registration and Authorization, at the sysgen, DD, and subschema levels, are rarely used in test systems due to the maintenance
involved. Sysgen authorization might be considered in production
systems.

6.5   CONCLUSION

Security should be considered for the major components of the IDMS/R environment. These components are databases, data dictionaries, user applications, and system software. IDMS/R has several facilities which may be used to protect these components. Security classes and product signon security are two of the most commonly used facilities. Security chosen for a test system is generally much less stringent than the security chosen for a production system.

It must be remembered, however, that it is almost impossible to protect one's databases and data dictionaries from any person sufficiently dedicated and intelligent who is bent on breaching security measures. The only surefire way to protect a company against total loss is the creation of a full set of backup tapes on a regular basis; tapes kept in a safe place, locked in the trunk of your car or stashed beneath the mattress. In the following chapter, we will discuss the ways and means of backing up and recovering data.

Suggestions for further reading on security:

The following Cullinet Manuals
   For Release 10 sites:
      1) Integrated Installation Guide (Culprit security)
      2) System Generation Guide (Sysgen security facilities, security classes, program registration, etc.)
      3) System Operations Guide (#CTABGEN macro and system task codes)
      4) IDD DDDL Reference (IDD security facilities)
      5) IDMS/R Database Operations (database security)
      6) DDL Reference Guide (subschema and schema syntax, DB procedures)
      7) ADS/O User's Guide (Securing dialogs and applications)
      8) ADS/O Reference Guide (ADSA security)
      9) Culprit Reference Guide (PROFILE and DATABASE cards)

   For Release 5.7 sites:
      1) Integrated Installation Guide (Culprit security)
      2) System Generation Guide (Sysgen security)
      3) System Operations Guide (#CTABGEN macro and system task codes)
      4) IDD DDDL Reference (IDD security facilities)

5) IDMS Database Design and Definition Guide (DB definition security facilities, schema and subschema syntax, DB procedures)
6) ADS/O User's Guide (Securing dialogs and applications)
7) ADS/O Reference Guide (ADSA security)
8) Culprit Reference Guide (PROFILE and DATABASE cards)

7

Backup and Recovery

Backup and recovery of the database are similar to security and protection of the database. The difference is that we are now concerned with insuring the integrity of the database by protecting it from problems like program failures, hardware/software problems, etc., rather than protecting it from problems like accidental alteration or unauthorized access. The three main topics we will discuss in this chapter are:

- Journaling,
- Backup, and
- Recovery.

Each of these is an integral part of protecting a database.

Database integrity is very much like insurance – you may pay a costly premium with no deductible and, as a result, be protected against any eventuality. Conversely, you may pay a very small premium with a high deductible figure and cover personally most losses incurred. IDMS/R provides its users with a full range of 'insurance coverage'. Each installation determines how great an overhead premium is desirable and affordable in comparison to the protection it provides in return. For example, a heavy premium is paid by double journaling, running everything under CV, maintaining 30 backup copies of the database and archive journal files, maintaining an online transaction image area, and turning on record locking for SHARED RETRIEVAL and PROTECTED UPDATE modes. With this 'coverage' data integrity is nearly 100% assured, but there is a lot of administrative work required to control all those backups. IDMS/R is going to do a great deal of extra work writing additional journal and online transaction images, and maintaining lock tables for report programs. On the other hand, IDMS/R may be run with journaling turned off. A system will 'fly' very rapidly without the overhead of journaling. However, data integrity problems are definitely being incurred. If problems occur, restore from the last backup and reprocess all 'lost' transactions, or simply turn off the area in-use indicators (refer to Chapter 5, area locks) and repair any

broken chains with IDMSPFIX. With such minimal coverage users
will become well acquainted with the IDMSPFIX utility.

Most users prefer middle-of-the-road coverage, i.e., the database
is taken down at night and backed up to tape, standard CV journaling
and record locking are used, and a week's worth of archive journal
tapes are maintained. If problems occur which cannot be solved by the
recovery measures discussed in the following sections, it may be reasonable to reinitialize the journals, unlock the areas, and fix any
broken chains which may have occurred. Such decisions about backup and recovery are dependent upon data sensitivity and manpower
available for recovery. It is important to maintain the level of data
integrity on a par with performance requirements.

7.1   JOURNALING

Journals constitute a record of what happens to a given database.
Because journals are used for backup and recovery, IDMS/R requires
that they be defined. Journaling applies to both the CV and local mode
uses of IDMS/R. In both modes, IDMS/R journals by putting a before
and after image of every record updated into a journal buffer. Note
than an update to a record will cause two journal images to be placed
in the buffer, although it does not necessarily translate into two I/O's
to the journal file. A journal buffer is written to the journal file when
the buffer fills, a run unit COMMITs or terminates, or a database
page must be written back to the database. This approach gives a
tremendous amount of data integrity with a minimum of I/O overhead.

At the cost of additional I/O overhead, a double set of journals may
be maintained, thereby creating a backup copy of the journals to be
used if a journal file I/O error occurred (such as a head crash).
IDMS/R provides an exit (IDMSDPLX) at the time journal buffers are
written to the journal file, permitting the contents of the journal buffer
to be written to a 'mirror' journal file. This is known as double journaling.

7.1.1   Basic Journaling Options

There are three basic options for journaling in IDMS/R. They are:

- Journaling to disk,
- Journaling to tape, and
- Dummying the journals.

Journaling to Disk: Most users journal to disk under CV because this enables the automatic recovery and warmstart features of IDMS/R. In the DMCL at least two disk journal files and one archive tape file should be defined. We recommend at least three disk journal files be established. The normal journaling to disk procedure also involves archiving to tape to clear disk journal files as they become full. Archiving procedures will be discussed later in this chapter, after journaling to tape and dummying journals are explained.

Journaling to Tape: The second option is journaling directly to tape. Under this method the automatic recovery and warmstart capabilities of IDMS/R CV are disabled. A failing run unit will cause CV to vary the affected area(s) offline. To recover in this environment, run IDMSRBCK (the manual rollback utility) using the CV tape journal as input. The only practical application of this option is in an environment where there is a severe disk shortage, and therefore, no space available for disk journals, or where a partition is unavailable for disk journal offloads. We do not recommend journaling to tape unless one of these specific problems arises.

Dummying or Ignoring the Journals: The third and final option is dummying or ignoring the journals. Journals may be defined as disks and then ignored (DOS) or dummied (OS). This eliminates the I/O overhead of journaling at the cost of disabling the warmstart and online recovery capabilities of IDMS/R. A run unit abort will lead to CV crashing or the affected area(s) being forced offline. This option yields the ultimate in speed along with the greatest sacrifice in database recovery capability. The only time this option should be used is when running an update program in local mode with backups of all areas taken just prior to the run. If the local mode program abends, recovery will not be handled automatically. All areas must be restored using the backups made prior to the run.

7.1.2 Archiving Disk Journal Files

When the common option of journaling to disk is chosen, the disk journal files must be archived when they become full. Archiving is a two-step procedure. First, the archiving utility IDMSAJNL writes all before and after images to a backup file (usually a tape). Second, IDMSAJNL condenses the disk journal file, i.e., after images for all run units and before images for completed run units are deleted from the disk journal file. Before images of active run units are maintained on the disk journal file because they are required for automatic recovery (in the event of abnormal run unit termination) and/or warmstart (in the event of operating system or CV failure). These images are condensed onto the beginning of the journal segment. If there are no active run units on the journal being archived, the condense phase is skipped.

It is critical that archiving be initiated before all disk journals become full. If all disk journals are full IDMS/R repeatedly issues the message DISK JOURNAL IS FULL and ceases any further processing until IDMSAJNL, the archiving utility, has been run. Archiving journal files can be started automatically by creating a WTOEXIT module to intercept the DISK JOURNAL IS FULL message issued by CV and to submit the archive job to an internal reader (OS) or a power reader (DOS). Sample code for this exit program is supplied on the installation tape. Customized code may be obtained from users who operate in similar environments.

7.1.3 Choosing the Number and Size of Disk Journal Files

Most users define three journal files. Some prefer to begin archiving immediately after the first file has filled because this method gives them a 'safety zone' of one empty journal file. Alternatively, others prefer to archive when two journals have filled because IDMSAJNL will select the oldest full journal for offloading into the tape journal file. In all probability, the information archived on the first full journal is from terminated run units only, i.e., run units no longer processing. When a journal contains no before and after images from currently active run units, the condense phase is skipped. When electing to run without the safety zone of an ever-empty journal file, each file must be large enough so that the last journal does not fill before the first is archived.

Size of the journals depends mainly upon the environment. Ideally, journals should be large enough that the IDMSAJNL job is not running constantly, yet small enough that the journals are offloaded in a timely fashion. In a normal production environment, running IDMSAJNL each hour is not excessive, but each site must determine its own requirements. An important consideration in determining the size of a journal file is the fact that until journal entries are offloaded to tape they are not available for use by manual recovery procedures. In addition, disk journal files are subject to the same possibility of disk crashes as any other file. Multiple-reel archive files should be avoided for ease in tape handling. Therefore, individual disk journal files should contain no more data than will fit on a single reel of tape.

Blocksize of Disk Journal Files: The appropriate blocksize of disk journal files is determined largely by the type of processing in each installation. If there are small records on the database and most processing consists of online updates, small journal blocksize is appropriate. On the other hand, if there are large database records, if processing consists mainly of large batch update jobs, or if there are many areas under CV control, then large journal blocksize is preferable.

The IDMSAJNL utility provides statistics helpful in determining journal blocksize, e.g., percent filled on each block archived. If these statistics indicate that most of the blocks archived were nearly empty, decreased blocksize should be considered. Alternatively, if almost all blocks archived were more than 90% filled, increased blocksize should be considered. When beginning, many shops define three disk journals of 6,000 quarter-track blocks (1/8 track blocks on 3380 disks) and subsequently tune these choices based on usage history.

The Archive Tape Journal File: The archive file should be blocked as close to 32K as possible to minimize tape I/O's during the offload process, assuming that sufficient main storage is available to contain the archive tape buffers and the DMCL module.

Journal Buffering Considerations: In Release 10, multiple journal buffers can and should be set up in the DMCL. Multiple journal buffers allow the journal to be a multithreaded resource, especially valuable in heavy batch update situations. If multiple batch or batch and online activity are taking place concurrently (very often the case in test systems, especially when accessing the dictionary), run units will not have to wait for buffer availability when the journal page is full and ready to be written back to the database. As a starting recommendation, define a pool of 5 pages, with a page size blocked appropriately for the device and to a multiple of 4K. Tune these values based on usage statistics.

7.2 BACKUP

Backing up a database refers to creating tape copies (or, in rare cases, disk copies) of database files and/or areas. Backup tapes, in combination with all archive journals created after the backup copies were made, are used to recover the database, (Section 7.3.2). Because the DD is also an important database it also should be backed up regularly. Specific suggestions for when and how to create backup files follow.

7.2.1   When Should Backups be Made?

It is important that backups be created on a regular basis. Timing for
creation of routine backup files is at the discretion of each user, however it may be most convenient to create backups each night after CV
is brought down. If CV must remain up while backups are created,
then vary the area(s) offline, backup the area(s), and vary the area(s)
online upon backup completion. Backups should also be created prior
to running any of the IDMS/R database modification utilities, e.g.,
IDMSRSTU, IDMSXPAG, IDMSDBLU. If programs are run under
local mode without journaling, backups should be made before program execution. We suggest keeping a week's archive journal and
database backup files on hand for recovery purposes.

7.2.2   Backup Procedures

Before beginning backup procedures in most shops the system is
brought down and all disk journal files are archived. Both full and
partially full journals files must be archived using the IDMSAJNL
utility. At sites where IDMS/R runs on a 24-hour schedule, database
areas may be backed up while the system is up. Details for this procedure are contained in Section 7.2.3, Backup Considerations for 24-
Hour Databases.

There are several methods which may be used to copy a database.
One is the Cullinet-supplied IDMSDUMP utility. It has the advantage
of producing database utilization statistics which are not readily
available from any other source, e.g., how full each area is and how
much space each record type occupies. In addition, IDMSDUMP allows the user to backup selected areas on a DASD which contains
multiple database areas. It has the disadvantage of running
relatively slowly. A popular second method for producing backup
tapes is a disk management utility, such as FDR at OS sites.
Database files are either BDAM or VSAM files (the choice is made
during installation of IDMS/R, see Chapter 8). Any disk management utility which supports the access method chosen during installation may be used. These utilities generally run much faster than
IDMSDUMP but do not produce utilization statistics. We recommend
the use of such a utility for nightly backups. IDMSDUMP (with a
REPORTS=ONLY option) or the Release 10 database analysis utility
IDMSDBAN should be run at regular intervals to monitor database
space utilization, perhaps once every one to two weeks.

It is possible to run multiple backups concurrently if there is a
need to minimize downtime while making backups. In other words,
if there are five initiators (partitions) and tape drives available, it is
possible to run backups of five disk packs simultaneously. All but the

largest databases can be backed up in under one hour using this approach.

7.2.3   Backup Considerations for 24-Hour Databases

When 24-hour update and retrieval access is required for a database, it may not be possible to backup the database nightly. If the choice is made not to backup nightly, realize that the time required to recover from a disk crash may be unacceptably long. In the event of a disk crash, the database would have to be restored from the most recent backup, probably from the previous weekend, and then rolled forward using several day's journal tapes. Assuming the problem is analyzed quickly and the journal tapes located rapidly, database recovery would probably take at least an hour and a half. Most installations prefer to bring down the system temporarily and backup all databases nightly, thus simplifying recovery processing. Management of the previous night's backup tape is much easier than management of multiple journal tapes accumulated over several days.

During database design, 24-hour uptime requirements should be taken into consideration. Data which always must be accessible could be assigned to an area separate from related data for which 24-hour uptime is not required, thus reducing the number of database areas posing special backup considerations.

To backup a database area while the system remains up requires that the database area be unavailable for update while the backup is taking place. It is still possible to retrieve information from the area, but not to update it. The DCMT VARY AREA *area-name* OFFLINE command tells CV that the areas is unavailable for update or retrieval access and flushes the journal buffers (discussed in 7.3.1, Mixed Mode Processing). This may be followed by a DCMT VARY AREA *area-name* RETRIEVAL command, permitting retrieval access while the backup is taking place.

There are two possible methods to achieve nightly database backups with very little sacrifice in database uptime. The first method involves determining a period of relative inactivity and backing up the database at that time. The second method requires coding a data collection system for use while the database is being backed up.

If a period of relative inactivity can be determined for the database, it may be worthwhile to sacrifice update access for the period of time required to backup the database areas. Retrieval access is still possible. This method involves varying the areas offline to flush the journal buffers, then varying the areas to retrieval, backing up the database areas, and finishing by varying the areas online when the

backups have been completed. This method allows only retrieval jobs
to access the database while the backup is taking place.

Another alternative is designing a data collection function which
uses retrieval against the database while the backups are taking
place. The mode could be determined by a system flag. While the
backups are taking place the data collection system stores records in a
separate data collection area. Upon backup completion, the stored input triggers a program to run in the background and update of the actual database areas. This method is sometime called "shadow post-
ing".

7.3   RECOVERY PLANNING AND PROCEDURES

The recovery of database integrity falls into two main concerns –
Recovery Planning and Recovery Procedures. The goal of recovery
is to restore database integrity following either hardware or software
failure, e.g., disk error or run unit abend in either CV or local mode.
Careful recovery planning enhances smooth, rapid restoration of the
database if and when problems do occur. We will discuss recovery in
CV and local mode briefly, and how recovery planning may be tailored to both online and batch programs. Three examples of specific
problems and recovery procedures suited to them will be presented.

Automatic recovery is inherent in CV; automatic rollback in the
event of run unit(s) abend and warmstart following a system failure.
The disk journal file is used in both recovery processes. When a run
unit abends, CV employs the journaled before images of updated
records to rollback dynamically all updates made by the run unit. CV
automatic recovery rolls back one run unit without affecting other run
unit(s) operating concurrently. When CV is restarted following a
system failure, warmstart processing begins. CV reads the journal
file to determine which run units were active at the time of the system
failure. It then rolls back each active run unit and writes an abort
checkpoint on the journal file for each of those run units.

No automatic recovery features are inherent in local mode. Run
unit abend and system failure are roughly equivalent in this environment because only one run unit operates in local mode. There are
two alternatives for recovery from local mode program abends.
Either the database may be backed up prior to program execution and
restored if the program abends, or all updates may be journaled and
the IDMSRBCK utility run after an abend.

7.3.1   Recovery Planning

Recovery planning should be incorporated in the design phase of application development for both online and batch programs. We will discuss some recovery planning considerations for online programs, batch programs, and mixed CV and local mode access to database areas.

Online Programs: Most online applications, because they are run only under CV, are covered adequately by the automatic recovery facilities inherent in CV. If online recovery requirements are more stringent, automatic facilities may be enhanced by the additional establishment of a transaction image area in the database. After the image area is set up, all online transactions are reformatted and written to it. In the event of a disk journal failure the database is restored from the last backup (discussion below). The transaction images are then processed by a batch update program. Using this procedure, only the transactions actually in progress at the time of the journal crash need to be reentered online. The primary advantage of this approach is that it creates a solid audit trail of all transactions processed in the online environment. It should be noted, however, that updates of the transaction image area itself also will be journaled.

Batch Programs: The standard recovery facilities of CV and/or local mode are sufficient for most batch programs. Advance recovery planning is especially important for batch programs which update a large number of records because they can pose time consuming recovery problems. In other words, in the event of a large-update batch program abend, a lot of time is spent in rolling back many updates and then redoing them all when the program is rerun. If the program is run under CV, two additional problems may arise, i.e., excessively large record lock tables and filling all disk journal space.

These problems may be circumvented at the planning stage by designing the program to issue COMMIT or COMMIT ALL statements at specific intervals in the program and to use a 'restart record' on the database for processing control (Figure 7-1). The COMMIT or COMMIT ALL statement causes a checkpoint to be written in the journal file, thus dividing the run unit into several recovery units. Prior to each COMMIT/COMMIT ALL, the program updates the restart record with hallmarks for where to resume processing in the event of an abend before the next checkpoint is written. Hallmarks may be DBKEYs of records in the database or sequential record numbers of transaction input (on tape). In the event of an abend, the COMMIT/COMMIT ALL checkpoints in the journal determine how far back to roll the updates to the database. The restart record determines where the program will resume processing. When processing under CV, automatic rollback operates on the recovery unit level instead of rolling back the entire run unit. In local mode, run IDMSRBCK specifying RESTORE=INFLIGHT to rollback the recovery unit or RESTORE=YES to rollback the entire run unit.

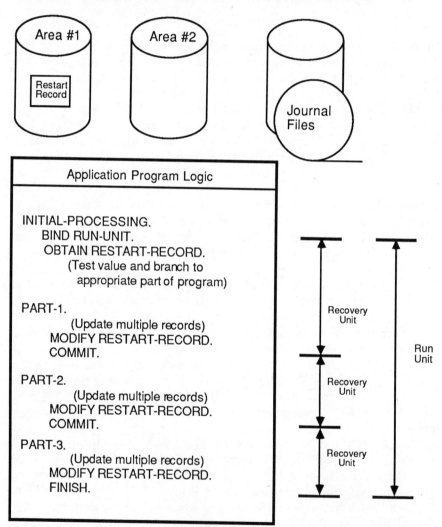

Figure 7-1 Overview of Restart Logic in A Batch Program Which Updates Many Records

Mixed Mode Processing: One situation that causes more database integrity problems than any other is mixing CV and local mode processing. IDMS/R allows only one local program or CV to have update access to any given area at a time. Some users seek to "have their cake and eat it too" by trying to run a local mode update with CV still allowed to access the area. Frequently users will vary the area to retrieval mode for the CV, run the update, and then vary the area back online. IDMS/R does not flush the database buffers with a DCMT VARY AREA *area-name* RETRIEVAL command. Therefore, when CV buffers are written back to the database they will overlay the local mode updated contents of the database with old data. This almost invariably causes broken chains. When local mode update programs must be run, first vary the areas OFFLINE to CV, followed by varying the areas to retrieval mode if concurrent CV access is required. The problem of CV not flushing journal buffers on a DCMT VARY *area-name* RETRIEVAL command is known to Cullinet. As of this writing it is in the process of being resolved; check with your Cullinet representative for the status of this maintenance.

7.3.2   Recovery Procedures

Recovery procedures involve journal files and the backup copy of the database. The generalized procedures discussed below are always feasible, but may not be the most efficient recovery procedures in a particular situation. Examples of specific recovery methods are provided in Chapter 12 (Trouble Shooting).

Three recovery problems are discussed below:

- Run unit abend,
- System failure, and
- Disk error.

Run Unit Abend: Run unit abend is perhaps the most frequently encountered problem. The automatic recovery features of IDMS/R come into play when running under CV with disk journaling. A message appears nearly everywhere (in the log, on the console, on the screen, etc.) indicating that automatic rollback is in progress and describing the error. Manual recovery in this situation involves only fixing the problem in the program that caused the initial abend and then rerunning the program. When journaling directly to tape, or running in local mode, none of the automatic recovery features of IDMS/R will operate. The program's changes to the database must be rolled back manually by running the IDMSRBCK utility. Again, the problem program should be fixed and rerun. If a run unit abend occurs while in local mode, with journaling dummied or ignored, recovery is more complex. A backup of all database areas accessed by the local mode program should be created <u>immediately prior</u> to running the program. In the event of an abend, restore the database using the newly-created backup. The last step is fixing and rerunning the problem program.

System Failure: System failure is a higher order problem. A system failure occurs when either CV or local mode comes down prior to normal shutdown. When running CV with journaling to disk, the automatic recovery features of IDMS/R commence when the system is brought back up. Console messages will appear indicating the initiation of recovery procedures. The warmstart facility of CV will automatically rollback recovery units active at the time of the system failure. These programs will have to be restarted manually; programs containing COMMIT statements must also contain restart logic (discussed above). In local mode or under CV with journaling to tape, recovery is no longer automatic. Recovery procedures are the same as those described for local mode and CV with journaling to tape in the run unit abend discussion. Recovery measures for running in local mode with no journaling are also the same as those described for run unit abend.

Disk errors: Disk errors can occur on any type of file. The reaction of IDMS/R to the error and the user's recovery procedures depend upon whether the error occurred on a database file or a journal file.

Disk error on a database file: When an I/O error occurs during a read operation to a database file, IDMS/R issues a console message (ERROR-STATUS '3010') and continues normal processing. When an I/O error occurs during a write operation to a database file, IDMS/R issues a console message (ERROR-STATUS '0376'), varies the offending area offline, and continues processing without the area. The following recovery procedures are necessary for write errors and advisable for read errors:

1) Shutdown CV. If CV shutdown normally, continue with steps 2 through 5 below to recover the database. Note that CV may abend during shutdown processing when it attempts to close the offending file, in which case, continue with steps 2 through 4, alternate step 5, step 6, and step 7 to recover the database.
2) Archive all the journal files.
3) Fix or replace the disk device.
4) Restore the affected database file using the most recent backup.

If CV shutdown normally, step 5 completes recovery.

5) Then run the roll forward utility (IDMSRFWD) using all archive journal files created since the backup. Specify PROCESS=FILE, RESTORE=YES, and the affected file's name.

If CV shutdown abended there may have been some run units which did not finish processing. Alternate step 5 through step 7 are necessary to avoid applying the incomplete run units' partial updates to the database area.

Alternate 5) Run IDMSJFIX, the journal fix utility, against the archive journal file active when CV shutdown failed. IDMSJFIX writes "ABRT" checkpoints for the incomplete run units and prints a report identifying the most recent "level 0 quiesce point" and all incomplete run units. A level 0 quiesce point is a time when the only active run unit terminates (i.e., no other run units are processing). The most recent level 0 quiesce point would identify a time before any of the incomplete run units had started processing.

6) Run IDMSRFWD only up to the most recent level 0 quiesce point, thereby avoiding incomplete run units' partial updates to the database area. Use all archive journal files created since the backup. Specify the affected file's name and RESTORE=YES,DATE=level-0-quiesce-date,TIME=level-0-quiesce-time.

7) In the final step rerun the run units which had started up after the most recent level 0 quiesce point (identified by the IDMSJFIX report).

Disk error on the active disk journal file: When there is an error on the active disk journal file, IDMS/R will come down. As a first attempt, restart IDMS/R in hopes that the warmstart facility will be able to recover with no further manual intervention. If this fails, all database areas must be restored using the following recovery procedures:

1) Archive all the journal files. If IDMSAJNL abends due to a disk error while archiving the offending journal file, also run the IDMSJFIX utility to 'fix' the archive tape (by writing "ABRT" checkpoints for all inflight run units).

2) Fix or replace the disk device.

3) Restore all database files using the most recent backup.

4) Run the roll forward utility (IDMSRFWD) using all archive journal files created since the backup, specifying PROCESS=TOTAL and RESTORE=YES.

5) Run IDMSRBCK to rollback all active run units, specifying RESTORE=INFLIGHT.

6) Reinitialize the new journal file.

7) In the final step, bring up IDMS/R and rerun all run units that were active at the time of the disk error.

Recovery is more rapid if double journals were created. Simply change the JCL to identify the alternate disk journal file and restart IDMS/R.

Disk error on an inactive disk journal file. If the disk journal error occurs on an inactive journal file, while archiving the journal for example, use the following recovery procedures:

1) Shutdown CV.

2) Backup all database areas. The newly-created backups eliminate the need for data from the "bad" disk journal file.

3) Fix or replace the disk device.

4) Initialize all journal files using the IDMSINIT utility.

5) Bring CV back up.

7.4   CONCLUSION

Information contained in a user's database and DD are as important to a corporation's success as the dollars stored in corporate cash accounts. Accordingly, they require similar protection from loss. Comprehensive protection planning, tailored to each user's needs, is vital to the successful implementation of protection measures. Database and data dictionary integrity is achieved through journaling, backup, and recovery procedures. The extent to which each is implemented results in specific costs and benefits to the user.

Suggestions for further reading on Journaling, Backup, and Recovery:

The following Cullinet manuals
     For Release 10 sites:
          1) IDMS/R Database Operations (Backup and recovery overview)

    2) IDMS-CV/DC System Operations (CV and local mode environments, WTOEXIT and IDMSDPLX exits)

    3) DB/DC Utilities Guide (Journaling, backup, and recovery utilities)

For Release 5.7 sites:

    1) IDMS-DB/DC Operations (Backup and recovery overview, CV and local mode environments, WTOEXIT and IDMSDPLX exits)

    2) DB/DC Utilities Guide (Journaling, backup, and recovery utilities)

Section Two

IMPLEMENTATION AND SUPPORT OF THE IDMS/R ENVIRONMENT

8

Installation of IDMS/R

Installation of IDMS/R software is the first step of implementing a new IDMS/R environment. The building blocks of future DB/DC systems are created during installation. The system software (run time programs, compilers, and utilities) and examples of what each organization must develop to create a functioning DB/DC system (sample DB/DC system configurations, sample databases, as well as sample batch and online applications) are installed.

In this chapter we will cover:

- Prerequisites for installation of IDMS/R at a site,
- Installation procedures, and
- An overview of work yet to be accomplished once installation procedures have been completed.

8.1 INSTALLATION PLANNING: IDMS/R PREREQUISITES

The installation process takes approximately two to three days. In most cases the Cullinet installer discusses the installation process in a pre-installation meeting. The purpose of this meeting is ensuring that the system and personnel resources required for the installation are readied (i.e., DASD, core, SVC, CPU time, Systems Programming support, tapes, printers, initiators). Effective communication between installer and site personnel is the key to smooth installation. Advance planning and coordination with operations personnel is especially important because an Initial Program Load (IPL) of the operating system to install the SVC is required at OS sites before the CV can be brought up; DOS has a dynamic SVC utility so an IPL is unnecessary. Control tables, and perhaps a few programs, must be modified and assembled if CICS or another external TP monitor is used in the shop. The CICS system also must be cycled (i.e., brought down and up) to include the modified definitions in the system. Most shops do not permit an IPL or TP monitor shutdown during the day, which may extend an installation schedule.

Adequacy of user preparation and system throughput can expedite or delay installation time.

The Cullinet product line has been designed to run on IBM® or IBM compatible mainframe hardware and software, e.g.,

Computers: IBM 360/370, 30xx, 43xx, or compatibles.

Terminals: 327x or compatibles.

Operating systems: OS MFT, OS MVT, OS/VS1, OS/VS2(SVS) or OS/VS2(MVS or MVS/XA), DOS/VS, DOS/VSE, DOS/VSE SP 1.3, or VM/CMS

Spooling systems: HASP, JES1, JES2, or JES3

Memory and disk storage requirements of IDMS/R vary with the components selected and with the type of applications that will run under IDMS/R. Frequently, IDMS/R, CV, DC or UCF, ADS/O, OLM, OLQ, IDD, and Culprit are purchased and installed together. The typical 'package purchase' requires three to four megabytes of memory; approximately one third thereof should consist of real memory. ASF is part of the package under Release 10, increasing memory requirements to approximately four megabytes. However, memory requirements vary with the number of terminals on the system and efficiency of applications design.

Ideally, approximately 500 megabytes of disk storage space should be available for allocation to software libraries, data dictionary files, and recovery journal files. If disk storage space is limited, it is possible to operate with considerably less space by specifying smaller dictionary and journal files. However, there are some potential problems inherent in allocation of insufficient space, specifically running out of space in the DD during development of initial databases and having frequent journal archiving runs. These considerations must be weighed carefully against the cost of increasing disk storage capacity.

8.2 INSTALLATION PROCEDURES

Installation of IDMS/R is a logical progression of ordered steps. Our discussion follows the steps of installation pictured in Figure 8-1.

The first and second steps consist of selecting of installation parameters and running the installation program CDMSIJMP. IJMP (an abbreviation of CDMSIJMP) produces a large stream of JCL

®IBM is a registered trademark of International Business Machines Corporation.

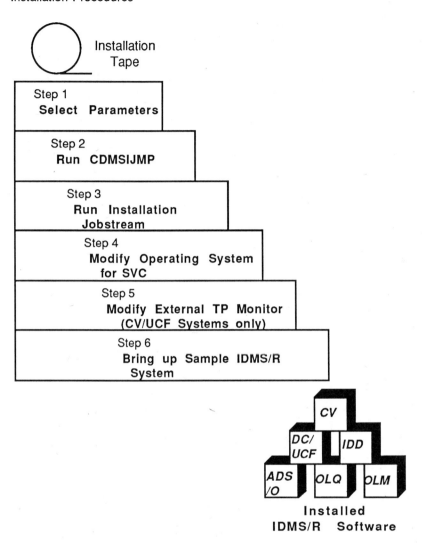

Figure 8-1 Installation Steps

which, when run, actually performs the installation (beginning with step 3 in Figure 8-1). After the installation jobstream is run, the operating system must be modified to include the SVC necessary for communications between IDMS/R and application programs executing in a different partition/region than IDMS/R. At this time modifications must also be made to any external TP monitors, such as CICS, that will be used with IDMS/R. Lastly the sample IDMS/R Central Version system is brought up.

8.2.1   Step 1: Selecting Parameters

The Cullinet installer, working in conjunction with the DBA and systems programmer, codes parameters which are the input to the installation program (CDMSIJMP). These parameters tell IJMP which products to install and what devices to use; they customize network subschemas and DMCL's, set up the dictionary(s) and libraries, and perform password checking, so that only authorized programs are installed.

Most of the parameters are self-explanatory or have only one valid value for each installation, for example OPSYS the parameter which names the operating system in use at the installation site. We concentrate on those parameters where alternative choices are available, and where the choice made affects overall system performance.

IDMS/R supports both BDAM and VSAM access methods for IDMS/R database and data dictionary files. As a general rule, the BDAM access method should be chosen, unless the disk devices used have fixed block architecture (FBA), i.e., 3310 and 3370 FBA devices. The VSAM access method is required for compatibility with the FBA disk devices. For other disk devices, choosing BDAM increases the efficiency of DB file accesses and reduces the size of the partition/region required to run IDMS/R.

The size of each dictionary area is another parameter specified during the installation. There are six areas in the primary dictionary and one area (Release 5.7) or a choice of one or two areas (Release 10) in each secondary dictionary (Chapter 3). Initially, the Cullinet installer chooses page ranges and page sizes for dictionary areas based on the products installed and the disk devices utilized. User's should monitor the dictionary area usage statistics closely following installation. Run either the IDMSDUMP or IDMSDBAN utility immediately after installation to obtain baseline information concerning dictionary usage. These two utilities report the amount of space used during installation. After installation and testing, we recommend running these utilities on a regular basis to monitor the space utilization as database and application development continues. For example, after three months reports may show that the DDLDML area has increased from a base level of 15% utilization to a current level of 30% utilization. If these figures represent only one tenth of the development work scheduled, soon either the dictionary area must be expanded (details in Chapter 11) or a secondary dictionary must be established (discussed in Chapter 3).

When allocating library space, special care should be exercised to insure adequate space for the libraries used in the installation. The appropriate amount of space is calculated based on the products being installed. Unless there is a severe disk space shortage use Cullinet's estimates of the space required. Insufficient library space can derail installation and possibly delay the entire process by hours.

If an organization is installing CULPRIT and plans to use the dictionary security features at any time in the future, the following parameter must be selected:

CULL-SECURE YES.

The default is NO security which disables dictionary validation of user id, password, and subschema authorization.

8.2.2 Step 2: Running CDMSIJMP

At this point in the installation progression, parameters have been carefully selected and the CDMSIJMP utility is ready to run. Running CDMSIJMP is a link-and-go procedure. The installation tape contains the installation program and a mixture of source and object level code for the products being installed. Initially, the CDMSIJMP program is selected off the installation tape and link edited. Then it executes, validating parameters and disclosing typographical or omission errors with specific error messages. A job stream (JCL) is created after errors are corrected and the CDMSIJMP utility has run successfully. Running the resulting job stream installs IDMS/R.

8.2.3 Step 3: Running the Installation Job Stream

The output from running the IJMP program is a large stream of JCL which, when run, performs the actual installation. The installation is, by default, done as five jobs, usually referred to as "JJOB1", "JJOB2", "JJOB3", "JJOB4", and "JJOB5".

JJOB1 allocates libraries and BDAM/VSAM database datasets (discussion of BDAM/VSAM alternative in Section 8.2.1). JJOB1 executes very quickly.

JJOB2 populates the new libraries. It consists of three phases. The first populates the OBJECT/RELO library; the second populates the SOURCE library; the third link edits the products and populates the LOAD/CORE IMAGE library. Dictionary subschemas are added to the load library during the last phase. This job usually runs in one to three hours.

JJOB3 initializes dictionary areas and populates the dictionary. JJOB3 takes a few hours to run, so creating the optional backup tapes may be advisable.

JJOB4 installs and runs demonstrations of the products. The demonstration information is stored in a secondary dictionary named TSTDICT by default. The demonstrations, while not necessary to the installation, are important because they provide a test of the newly installed system. Product demonstrations also supply sample JCL to initiate various types of system activities, among these are utilities, compilers, CULPRIT, and DDR. This JCL may be saved and modified by the user for the site's permanent use. Finally, running the demonstrations provides a small database which is ideally suited to on-site training courses.

JJOB5 creates the final backup of the newly-installed environment. At DOS sites, library DSERVs also run in JJOB5.

At the end of the installation (JJOB5) the user has:

- Populated Source, Object/Relo, and Load/Core Image Libraries;
- Populated dictionaries;
- Sample JCL;
- One to three backup tapes (optional); and,
- A small mountain of paper.

The Source library contains source statements for the DMCL, sysgen samples, and multiple macros. The Object or Relo library contains link edit control cards and the object code for system modules. The load or core image library contains all product software (run time programs, compilers, and utilities), and several dictionary subschemas, named IDMSNWKx, where 'x' has a different value for each subschema. One of the run time programs is the operating system dependent routine. It contains all logic that is operating system-specific and is part of the startup routine for every DB/DC system.

The dictionaries contain several schemas (for IDMSNTWK dictionary and IDMS/R employee skills demonstration databases), source code for Data Dictionary Reports, all system messages, and all online product maps.

8.2.4 Step 4: Modifying Operating Systems for SVC

IDMS/R accomplishes interpartition communications and storage protection via a Supervisor Call (SVC). The Cullinet-supplied SVC must be placed in the operating system. It is linked with the operating system nucleus (OS), necessitating a shutdown and startup of the operating system. The SVC may be assembled with the supervisor (DOS) or installed dynamically (DOS) using the IDMSESVC utility. An IPL of the operating system is not required if the SVC is installed dynamically (DOS).

8.2.5   Step 5: Establishing Communications with External TP Monitor (CV/UCF Systems Only)

When an external TP monitor manages the online network, several macros must be coded and some changes made to the TP monitor. This allows the organization to use the online system software (OLQ, OLM, Online IDD, etc.), ADS/O dialogs, and DC programs from terminals attached to the TP monitor.

Several UCF macros are required to define the front-end and back-end communications configuration. These macros are typically coded once during installation of IDMS/R and later included in each DB/DC system created (the back-end with IDMS/R and the front-end with the TP monitor, see System Operations Guide for details pertinent to each TP monitor).

There are specific modifications which must be made to each TP monitor to be used with IDMS/R. These changes are covered in detail in the Integrated Installation Guide and the System Operations Guide. For example, if CICS is the external TP monitor there are PPT, PCT, and optional PLT modifications that are made as part of the installation. These modifications facilitate communication between CICS and IDMS/R. They require some table reassemblies and a CICS shutdown and startup.

8.2.6   Step 6: Bringing Up a Sample IDMS/R System

The Cullinet installer creates a sample IDMS/R system for the user. Either a CV/DC or CV/UCF system is created. The presence of an external TP monitor determines which type of system is generated; CV/UCF is required when an external TP monitor manages the online terminals. The sample system is generally used only for a few days. It should be viewed primarily as a nonspecialized teaching vehicle for the users. The sample system will be entirely redesigned (Test System Creation, Chapter 9) because it is not tailored to the user's environment.

The sample system includes a SYSTEM generated by the system generation compiler, a DMCL, and a #DCPARM macro. The sample DMCL describes only the dictionary and sample database areas. Like the sample SYSTEM, the DMCL will later be expanded and tailored to include the site's databases as these are developed. Finally, a sample #DCPARM macro is assembled from the installation, identifying the sample SYSTEM and DMCL.

The startup routine loads the DMCL and accesses the data dictionary for the SYSTEM information using the #DCPARM information. The IDMS/R partition/region is configured based on the SYSTEM information. The status of the system from the last shutdown is taken from the journal files, and automatic recovery or warmstart is performed, if necessary. The database files are opened at this time. The sample system is then ready to process online and batch program requests for database access; however, only the dictionary and sample databases exist.

8.3 IMPLEMENTATION WORK TO BE STARTED NOW THAT IDMS/R HAS BEEN INSTALLED

Installation of IDMS/R software provides the tools for creating IDMS/R environments tailored to the needs of each organization. Development of IDMS/R systems, databases, and applications specific to the processing requirements of each site may now begin. The sample systems, databases, and applications created during the installation may be used as templates during subsequent development.

8.4   CONCLUSION

Installation of IDMS/R software provides the building blocks for creation of DB/DC systems tailored to the needs of each organization. Sample systems, databases, and applications are included in the installation.

Installation takes two to three days. It involves coding parameters for the installation program and running the installation job stream. Finally, the operating system SVC is installed and changes are made to any external TP monitors that will be used with IDMS/R. Demonstrations of the sample systems, databases, and applications should be run to ensure that the software has been installed properly.

Development of systems, databases, and applications specific to the processing requirements of each site may now begin. In the next chapter we will examine creation of a DB/DC system designed for development work.

Suggestions for further reading on Installation of IDMS/R:

The following Cullinet Manuals
> For Release 10 sites:
>> 1) Integrated Installation Guide (Installation procedures, parameters)
>> 2) IDMS-CV/DC System Operations Guide (SVC, external TP monitors, UCF macros)

For Release 5.7 sites:
  1) Integrated Installation Guide (Installation procedures, parameters)
  2) IDMS-DB/DC System Operations (SVC, external TP monitors, UCF macros)

9

Test System Creation

This chapter is about the creation of an IDMS/R test system, where development of new databases and applications will take place. Many of the considerations presented in this chapter apply to all IDMS/R systems.

In this chapter we will cover:

- What is an IDMS/R system?
- Why is the test system important?
- Components of the test system,
- Steps in creating the test system, and
- Causes and frequency of test system regeneration.

Primary system components, the system generation and the global DMCL, will be examined with emphasis on choices related to system performance.

9.1 WHAT IS AN IDMS/R SYSTEM?

An IDMS/R system is a system capable of handling multiple concurrent database accesses from online and batch programs. The generic term is a Database/Data Communications (DB/DC) system. There are several different types of IDMS/R DB/DC systems. The two types most frequently used are CV-DC systems (Central Version-Data Communications) and CV-UCF systems (Central Version-Universal Communications Facility). The only difference between a CV-DC system and a CV-UCF system lies in the handling of online terminals. In a CV-DC system (Figure 9-1), IDMS-DC is the teleprocessing (TP) monitor managing and communicating directly with the online terminals. When another TP monitor manages the online terminals (CICS for example) the Universal Communications Facility (UCF) is used to pass input and output messages between the external TP monitor and IDMS/R CV (Figure 9-2). Some less frequently encountered systems include: 1) IDMS/R CV-DC & UCF systems and 2) Distributed Database Systems. In the former IDMS-DC manages some

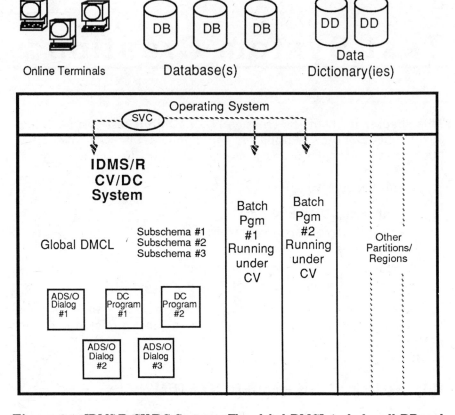

Figure 9-1 IDMS/R CV/DC System. The global DMCL includes all DB and DD areas to which the CV/DC system has access. Subschemas may be shared by concurrently processing programs and dialogs. Batch programs incur SVC overhead twice for each IDMS/R access statement. There is no SVC overhead for online programs.

terminals, while an external TP monitor manages others, and in the later, multiple IDMS/R systems, on the same or different CPU's, communicate with each other. We will limit our discussions to the two most common systems, IDMS/R CV-DC systems and IDMS/R CV-UCF systems.

There are usually several systems running concurrently at each installation, e.g., test, production, and so on. Each system is tailored to different processing requirements.

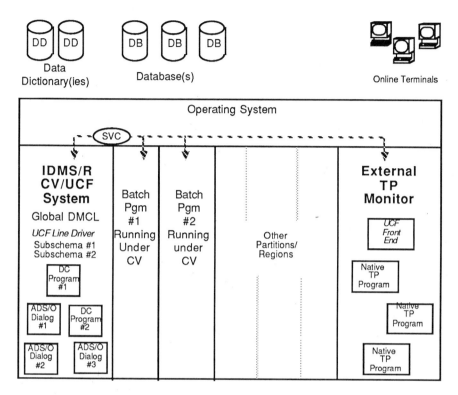

Figure 9-2 IDMS/R-CV/UCF System. The online terminals are managed by an external TP monitor. Both native TP programs and IDMS/R applications (ADS/O, DC, or online IDMS/R software components) may be executed from these terminals. The online programs executing under the TP monitor are 'native' TP programs coded in whatever language is appropriate for that monitor. Native TP programs can access IDMS/R databases if they are coded with embedded IDMS/R Data Manipulation Language (DML) statements. There will be SVC communications overhead for each DML statement. The online programs executing under IDMS/R may be either ADS/O dialogs or DC programs. There will be communications overhead when terminal input and output messages are passed between the TP monitor and IDMS/R.

9.2 THE TEST SYSTEM: WHY IS IT SO IMPORTANT?

Development of new IDMS/R databases and applications takes place in the test system. Therefore, it is extremely valuable to the entire IDMS/R shop. Most installations have a backlog of applications to

develop and give high priority to rapid development of new databases
and applications. Rapid development is possible only if the test system provides a productive work environment. In addition, the
primary exposure the applications development staff has with
IDMS/R is through the test system; its performance reflects on the
people who represent local IDMS/R knowledge. Because of the test
system's importance and prominence, it must exhibit the following
qualities shortly after the initial installation of IDMS/R: 1) stability,
2) appropriate security, and 3) high performance.

A database/data communications (DB/DC) system that rarely
crashes, and which has excellent recovery facilities when it does
crash, creates a stable development environment. A secure environment is important, especially during the first few days of
relatively inexperienced use of IDMS/R. Appropriate security options
should be selected to protect the users from accidentally hurting
themselves, e.g., by deleting a schema, while at the same time allowing them to experiment in the test system without a stifling amount of
restriction (Chapter 6). A high performance DB/DC system with fast
response time provides a more productive work environment for programmers and other users. Careful planning when creating the
components of the test system helps achieve the desired test system
qualities.

9.3   COMPONENTS OF THE TEST SYSTEM

There are several components in a test system. The same components are also used to create other types of systems, e.g., a production
system. The components of *any* IDMS/R CV-DC/UCF system are:

- The operating system-dependent routine,
- A #DCPARM macro,
- A 'SYSTEM' generated using the system generation com-
  piler, and
- A global DMCL.

For CV-UCF systems there is an additional component involved, the
UCF Macros.

There is one operating system-dependent routine at each site. It is
assembled and link edited during the installation process and contains all the operating system-specific logic of IDMS/R. It works in
conjunction with the module created by the #DCPARM macro to configure the run time system.

A separate #DCPARM macro is assembled for each different
IDMS/R CV-DC/UCF system (test, production, quality assurance,
etc.). This macro identifies the system defined using the system

generation compiler and stored on the DD. In addition, it names the global DMCL to be used by the system. Another parameter of the macro controls whether or not the console operator may enter modifications to the system number and/or options at system startup.

Each new system is defined primarily through the system generation compiler. Many statements and parameters are coded to determine the functionality of the new system, customize storage and error handling, and identify online operators, tasks, and programs. These parameters are input to the system generation compiler, RHDCSGEN, in Release 10. Prior to Release 10, this was a two-stage procedure involving the two system generation compilers RHDCSGN1 and RHDCSGN2. The compiler(s) validate the input parameters and, if all is well, store the SYSTEM definition in the DD. Each separate system must have a unique combination of system number and Central Version number.

A global DMCL must be established to identify all DB and DD areas available to the newly-created CV-DC/UCF system. Area definitions are copied into the global DMCL from the schemas stored in the primary Data Dictionary. CV uses area definitions at run time to relate DBKEYs (database keys) to the physical blocks on the database files where the desired records reside. Buffering and journaling considerations are also defined in the DMCL.

Several UCF macros are coded during installation of IDMS/R, creating the front-end and back-end programs to handle communications between IDMS CV and the external TP monitor. These programs rarely change from system to system, e.g., from test to production.

In summary, the operating system-dependent routine and the UCF communications programs are created during installation of IDMS/R and do not change from one system to another. The other components are what make each system unique (test, production, etc.). The three components that must be created to define a new system are 1) the system generation, 2) the global DMCL, and 3) the #DCPARM macro. These components are discussed in detail below.

9.4 SYSTEM CREATION: STEPS IN CREATING A TEST SYSTEM

The steps to create a new system are the same for a CV-DC system and a CV-UCF system (Figure 9-3); however, some of the parameter values specified in the system generation (sysgen) are different for UCF systems. These differences are covered in Sections 9.6 and 9.7.

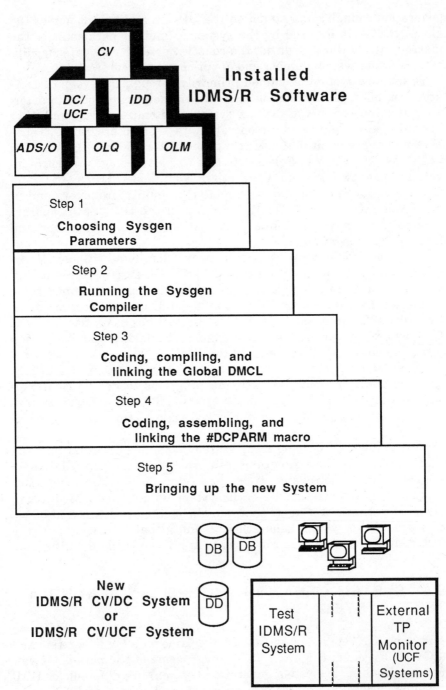

Figure 9-3 Steps to Create an IDMS/R CV/DC or CV/UCF System

IDMS/R software must be installed before any system can be created. After installation, the first steps are choosing appropriate sysgen parameters and running the sysgen compiler. Next the global DMCL is coded and compiled. Then, the #DCPARM macro is coded, specifying the newly-created system and global DMCL, and assembled. Finally, the new system is brought up. Each step in the progression is covered below, with emphasis on the choices affecting system performance.

9.5   STEP 1:   CHOOSING SYSTEM GENERATION PARAMETERS

After a brief overview of system generation statements, we will discuss those sysgen parameters that directly affect performance and those that have hidden costs or effects. Parameters are discussed from a practical point of view, and we will suggest recommended test system values for specific situations. These recommended values are only a starting point, and should be adapted to your environment as it changes through time. Information on these and other sysgen parameters may be found in the System Generation Guide.

9.5.1   System Generation Overview

Each new system is defined primarily by statements input to the system generation compiler. The results of running a sysgen compile are records stored on the DD; these records define the characteristics of a run time IDMS/R system. Several different statements are used to define the new system. Appendix A contains a sample listing of system generation statements for a test system.

The *SYSTEM* statement defines general system characteristics, including maximum number of concurrent tasks, sizes of internal tables and storage pools, and available error detection/debugging facilities. Parameters of the SYSTEM statement have a major effect on the system's performance and capabilities. A large portion of this chapter concentrates on choosing appropriate values for SYSTEM statement parameters.

PROGRAM statements identify online programs, dialogs, maps, tables, and subschemas. One PROGRAM statement should be coded for each such entity in existence at sysgen time. Entities developed between sysgens must be defined dynamically during each system execution until they are included in the next system generation.

TASK statements identify task codes used to initiate online processing in the DC/UCF system. Each task code is associated with a program. Optional TASK parameters include the security class and the priority assigned to each task, as well as overrides to a few system-wide timeout specifications. Several program and task statements are required to support the online portions of IDMS/R system software such as ADS/O, Online IDD, ASF, OLQ, and OLM.

USER statements identify each user of the online system. Most of the parameters on this statement relate to security, e.g., password and security class list, and to the processing priority for the user.

The *IDMS PROGRAM* statement is used to register programs for database access, if program registration has been chosen. Program registration is a security facility used to limit the programs allowed access to databases through CV (Chapter 6). In addition, the *IDMS AREA* and *IDMS BUFFER* statements may be used to override database area and buffer specifications made in the global DMCL.

The *DBNAME* statement identifies DB's and DD's accessed by the CV. It is used when implementing multiple dictionaries or when there are multiple versions of the same database on the system (e.g., test and acceptance test versions of a user database available under the same CV).

LINE, PTERM, and *LTERM* statements define the teleprocessing network. LINE statements define telecommunication line characteristics such as the kind of line (VTAM, UCF, and so on) and the status of the line at system startup. PTERM statements define physical terminal characteristics; LTERM statements define logical terminal identifiers and print class designations.

DESTINATION statements define groups of users, physical terminals and logical terminals, or any mixture thereof, to which output may be routed. A message can be defined on the dictionary in association with a particular destination to facilitate sending repetitive messages to large groups of users.

QUEUE statements are used to name the TASK which begins processing when the queue's threshold has been exceeded. The THRESHOLD parameter of the queue statement specifies the number of queue records which initiates task processing.

The *ADSO, OLM, OLQ,* and *KEYS* statements customize the use of the online portions of IDMS/R system software. Some Release 10 parameters on the ADSO statement significantly affect main storage consumption because they allow resources saved between terminal output and input messages to be stored on disk rather than in main storage.

Together, these statements define a CV-DC/UCF system. The SYSTEM statement parameter choices are covered in Section 9.6. Important considerations for some of the other statements are discussed in Section 9.7. Statements are submitted to the sysgen compiler for validation and generation after they have been coded (Section 9.8).

9.6 SYSTEM STATEMENT CONSIDERATIONS

First we will examine choices made in the SYSTEM statement.
Figure 9-4 is a sample listing of a SYSTEM statement and its parameters. There is one SYSTEM statement for each CV-DC/UCF system,
with many parameters which affect system efficiency.

```
ADD SYSTEM 2
    ABEND STORAGE IS 200
    ABRU NOSNAP
    NOBLDL
    CHKUSER TASKS IS 4
    CUSHION IS 80
    CVNUMBER IS 1
    DPE COUNT IS 500
  NODUMP
    EXTERNAL WAIT IS 600
    GEN ID IS IDMSDC0
    INACTIVE INTERVAL IS 180
    INTERNAL WAIT IS 600
  NOJOURNAL RETRIEVAL
LIMITS FOR ONLINE ARE ENABLED
LIMITS FOR EXTERNAL ARE ENABLED
    STORAGE LIMIT FOR ONLINE TASKS IS 64
    LOCK LIMIT FOR ONLINE TASKS IS 500
    CALL LIMIT FOR ONLINE TASKS IS   200
    DBIO LIMIT FOR ONLINE   TASKS IS 100
    LOCK LIMIT FOR EXTERNAL TASKS IS 10000
    CALL LIMIT FOR EXTERNAL TASKS IS 100000
    DBIO LIMIT FOR EXTERNAL TASKS IS 50000
    LOG DATABASE
    MAX ERUS IS 23
    MAX TASKS IS 13
    NEW COPY IS AUTOMATIC
    OPERATING SYSTEM IS MVS
    PREEMPTION THRESHOLD IS NO
    PROGRAM POOL IS 100
  NOPROTECT
    RCE COUNT IS 1500
    REENTRANT POOL IS   600
  NOREGISTRATION
    RESOURCE TIMEOUT INTERVAL   600 PROGRAM RHDCBYE
    RETRIEVAL NOLOCK
    RLE COUNT IS 1400
    RULOCKS 120
    RUNAWAY INTERVAL IS 120
    RUNUNITS FOR
        QUEUE          5
        MSGDICT        1
        SIGNON/DEST    1
        EXTENT         2
        LOADER         2
    RUPRTY IS 100
    SCRATCH/QUEUE JOURNAL BEFORE
    STACKSIZE IS 750
    STATISTICS NOLINE TASK COLLECT NOUSER NOT
    STORAGE POOL IS 800
    SVC IS 253
    SYSCTL IS SYSCTL
    SYSLOCK IS 2500
    SYSTRACE OFF
    TICKER INTERVAL IS 1
    TRANSACTION LOG OFF
    UNDEFINED PROGRAM COUNT IS (58,29)
    UPDATE NOLOCK
    USERTRACE ON ENTRIES 300
    WARMSTRT.
```

Figure 9-4 Sample SYSTEM Statement for a CV-UCF System

For ease of explanation, we have grouped the parameters into the following categories:

- System Identification
- Major System Functionality and Internal Tables
- Storage Pool
- Program Loading Considerations
- Timeout and Abend Detection
- Resource Limitations
- Locking
- Journaling
- Debugging
- System Log File Alternatives

Table 9-1 lists the parameters covered in each category (information concerning these and other parameters may be found in the System Generation Guide). We will examine the major decisions to be made in each category and offer recommendations for parameter values appropriate for a test system.

9.6.1   System Identification

There are two numbers used to identify an IDMS/R system, system version number and CVNUMBER. The system version number and the CVNUMBER are used at different times. The system version number differentiates one system definition from another stored in the same dictionary, whereas CVNUMBER differentiates one run time system from another on the same machine.

System Version Number
The system version number is specified at the beginning of the SYSTEM statement, just following the word SYSTEM. e.g.,

    ADD SYSTEM *system-version-number...*

The system version number identifies a system definition stored in a data dictionary. The number may be between 1 and 9999 and must be unique for the dictionary on which the definition is stored. As of this writing, system version number must also be unique among systems executing on the same physical machine.

We suggest selecting a range of system numbers for each different type of system to reduce confusion for the operations staff. For example, 1 through 9 might be used to identify test system definitions, 10 through 90 for quality assurance systems, and 100 through 900 for production systems.

Table 9-1 Categories of SYSTEM Statement Parameters

Category	Section	Parameters
System Identification	9.6.1	system-version-number CVNUMBER
Major System Functionality and Internal Tables	9.6.2	MAXIMUM ERUS MAXIMUM TASKS DPE COUNT RCE COUNT RLE COUNT STACKSIZE
Storage Pool	9.6.3	STORAGE POOL CUSHION CWA
Program Loading	9.6.4	UNDEFINED PROGRAM COUNT BLDL/NOBLDL REENTRANT POOL PROGRAM POOL
Timeout and Abend Detection	9.6.5	RESOURCE TIMEOUT INTERVAL RUNAWAY INTERVAL INACTIVE INTERVAL EXTERNAL WAIT INTERNAL WAIT CHKUSER TASKS
Resource Limitations	9.6.6	STORAGE LIMIT LOCK LIMIT CALL LIMIT DBIO LIMIT
Locking	9.6.7	RETRIEVAL NOLOCK/LOCK UPDATE NOLOCK/LOCK RULOCKS SYSLOCKS
Journaling	9.6.8	JOURNAL RETRIEVAL/ NORETRIEVAL RUNUNITS FOR QUEUE, MSGDICT, SIGNON, and LOADER
Debugging	9.6.9	ABRU NOSNAP/SNAP USERTRACE SYSTRACE
System Log File Alternatives	9.6.10	LOG DATABASE/FILE1 FILE2

CVNUMBER

Each run time system must have a unique CVNUMBER, distinct from all other systems running on the same CPU. The CVNUMBER is used by the SVC (Supervisor Call routine installed into the operating system during installation of IDMS/R) to identify the appropriate CV to pass data to. The general range of valid values is from 1 to 255. However, the chosen value must be unique among all CV's executing on the same CPU, and it may not be greater than the value of MAXCVNO specified during SVC assembly (details on MAXCVNO and SVC assembly may be found in the System Operations manual for the release of IDMS in use at your site).

9.6.2 Major System Functionality and Internal Tables

MAXIMUM ERUS and MAXIMUM TASKS are two parameters with a major effect on system functionality. These parameters control the number of external and internal tasks that can process concurrently. In this section we also discuss the parameters which determine the size of some important internal tables, the resource control table and the stack.

MAXIMUM ERUS

This parameter determines the maximum number of external run units that may be active concurrently. External run units include batch DML programs and for systems with an external TP monitor, UCF tasks and native TP programs which access IDMS/R databases.

The appropriate value for MAXIMUM ERUS depends on expected system activity levels and on whether or not an external TP monitor is in use. To calculate the value needed, start by adding one for each batch program that will be processing concurrently under the CV. If creating a CV-UCF system, add one for each UCF terminal that will be executing a task concurrently in IDMS/R, and one for each concurrent native TP program with DML statements.

If MAXIMUM ERUS specification is too small additional run units abend with ERROR-STATUS values of '1473' until an active external run unit completes processing and the number of concurrently processing run units falls below MAXIMUM ERUS.

MAXIMUM TASKS

This parameter determines the allowable number of concurrent internal units of work. Internal run units include ADS/O dialogs, DC programs, database procedures, and system tasks. The value specified depends on system activity. Allocate one for each concurrently active online terminal and background task.

Background tasks are DC programs that are ATTACHed by other DC programs to perform functions asynchronously to terminal processing. For example, recording audit trail information might be handled as a background task. The DC program which updates the database could attach the task which stores audit trail information just before sending the output message back to the online terminal. The audit task processing would take place in the background and therefore would not delay response to the terminal operator. Refer to IDMS-DB/DC DML Reference (Release 10) or IDMS-DC Programmer's Reference Guide (Release 5.7) for ATTACH verb information.

If the maximum number of tasks are already processing, any additional tasks are placed in a wait state until the number of concurrently processing tasks falls below MAX TASKS. The system statistics printed at shutdown contain a count of the number of times the maximum tasks condition occurred. This statistic should be monitored to aid tuning this parameter based on system history. Online tasks will occasionally wait to begin processing if MAX TASKS is too small. It is better to err on the large side, but not too large because some storage allocations are based on the MAX TASKS and MAX ERUS values (discussed in Section 9.6.3).

RCE, RLE, and DPE COUNTs

These parameters determine the total number of entries in a system table of control blocks that represent IDMS/R resources. The resources represented include programs, storage, run unit lock tables, abend storage, variable portions of the subschema tables, and more. RCE COUNT is the number of Resource Control Elements in the system, RLE COUNT is the number of Resource Link Elements in the system, and DPE COUNT is the number of Deadlock Prevention Elements. The RCE, RLE, and DPE entries are used to represent all resources currently held in the system. Because running out of entries can be a drastic problem, initial estimates for the number of entries needed should be set relatively high and usage should be monitored regularly.

No secondary allocations are made under Release 5.7. The system abends if all entries are used up. Initial values of 400 for RCE COUNT, 400 for RLE COUNT, and 120 for DPE COUNT have proven reliable. The highwater mark for system use of these entries may be seen in the log following shutdown. To view the current limits and allocations a DCMT DISPLAY MEMORY command may be issued to call up this information (display the system RCA header, the display is in hexadecimal and the number of RLE's and RCE's in use can be found at hex offset X'2C' and X'2E' respectively – see DSECT Reference Guide, RCADS information).

These values are not quite as critical under Release 10, because they are used as thresholds. The system adds a pad to the amount specified. If the threshold is exceeded, only the task causing the threshold to be exceeded is aborted; the rest of the system continues processing. The initial values recommended above should be increased to 800 for RCE, 1000 for RLE , and 500 for DPE if ASF or the menu version of OLQ is in use. The commands DCMT DISPLAY STATISTICS SYSTEM or OPER W CRIT may be used to display current limits and allocations.

For both releases of IDMS, the high water marks for these control blocks may be viewed through the DCMT DISPLAY STATISTICS SYSTEM command. Alternatively, they may be checked on the DC log following system shutdown.

Frequently, OLQ activity consumes a large number of RCE's and RLE's. Further, if buffer pool size changes are made, remember that buffers are resources and require an RCE and RLE for each pool page. Therefore, add one to the RCE and RLE counts for each additional page.

STACKSIZE

This parameter determines the number of entries in the register save area of the system. The register save area is used to establish and store linkage information for all system programs, user exits, and IDMS-DC assembly language programs.

Stack size should be large, under Release 5.7, because the system could crash if it is exceeded. A secondary allocation can be borrowed from abend storage, but if this is exceeded an abend occurs. Abend storage is a separate portion of the region reserved for setting up and writing dump information; its size is determined by the ABEND STORAGE parameter of the SYSTEM statement.

Stack size is used as a threshold, under Release 10, so size specification is not quite as critical.

The number of entries used in the stack varies with system activity; 750 entries has proven to be a reliable initial figure. This value should be tuned based on system statistics. Issue the DCMT DISPLAY STATISTICS SYSTEM command to monitor how high the stack got at any point in the life of the system. If it is apparent that the number of entries used is approaching the total stack size, increase the stack size during the next test system generation. Under Release 10, system histograms can be modified to show how often the stack reached each depth during the run.

9.6.3   Storage Pool Considerations

The STORAGE POOL parameter has a direct impact on processing efficiency within the system. The primary storage pool is used for a variety of system and application functions; sufficient storage allocation is crucial for efficient system processing. All storage needed by IDMS/R for system functions is allocated from the storage pool, for example signing on a run unit and allocating storage for subschema currency tables. In addition, IDMS-DC application programs issuing storage requests are allocated storage from the storage pool. These and other uses are summarized in Table 9-2.

Table 9-2 Storage Pool Uses

Category	Uses
System-Related	Subschema Currency Tables
	DMCL I/O Buffers*
	System Lock Table (SYSLOCKS parameter)*
	Map Request Blocks
	SPF work areas (if using the Sequential Processing Facility)
	Packet Data Movement Buffers (non-MVS systems)
	Secondary storage allocations for run unit lock tables (RULOCKS parameter)*
	Secondary storage allocations for extra entries in Program Definition Table (UNDEFINED PROGRAM COUNT parameter)
	Storage used to save information between conversations for online system software (e.g., OLM, online IDD, online subschema compiler, ADS/O Generator software, etc.)
Applications-Related	WORKING STORAGE for DC COBOL Programs
	Storage for DC Program GET STORAGE requests
	Storage used to save information between conversations for ADS/O Dialogs (e.g., variable portion of dialog, record buffers, and currency restoration table)

*Additional space is automatically added to the specified STORAGE POOL parameter for these uses. The STORAGE POOL parameter value must be large enough to accommodate all other uses.

The CUSHION parameter specifies the portion of the pool to be used as a safety margin to prevent the pool from becoming totally depleted. The CWA parameter defines an area of common storage in the storage pool, shared by all DC application programs. Detailed considerations for these parameters follow.

STORAGE POOL

The STORAGE POOL parameter determines the size of the primary storage pool, the only storage pool available prior to Release 10. It is known as storage pool 0 under Release 10; additional storage pools may be defined using the STORAGE POOL and XA STORAGE POOL statements (for MVS-XA systems only). Multiple storage pools allow greater flexibility in storage management (performance tuning details in Chapter 13).

Allocate 500K to the storage pool as a minimum. When additional storage is available, this amount should be increased to 800K in the initial test system. The value should be tuned in later sysgens based on system statistics. Calculations should use MAXIMUM ERUS and MAXIMUM TASKS parameter values to estimate worst-case storage needs. This evaluation changes constantly as new applications and users are brought onto the system.

CUSHION

This parameter defines a 'safety cushion' of reserved storage in the primary storage pool. Available space in the storage pool is critically important to normal system processing. The value assigned here is used as a strategic reserve within the system. A SHORT ON STORAGE condition occurs if the total amount of available storage in the primary storage pool falls below the cushion amount. All new activity within the system is suspended. Only tasks and run units that are already active may continue processing, dipping into the cushion reserve as needed. When the total amount of available storage is once again greater than the size of the cushion, normal requests for initiation of new run units and tasks will be processed.

During a short on storage condition, if the active tasks request enough additional storage so that even the cushion is exceeded, the system goes into a "WAIT" state. Usually the IDMS/R job must be cancelled by the operator and warmstarted.

System statistics provide an account of the number of times the short on storage condition occurred during the run. A high count indicates that either the storage pool is too small or the cushion is too large. These statistics are written to the log at system shutdown and are visible during the run using a DCMT DISPLAY STATISTICS SYSTEM command.

We recommend always specifying a CUSHION value because it defaults to zero. Processing with no safety cushion increases the probability of a system failure from lack of storage pool space. A typical value for the cushion is 10% of storage pool size. This allowance usually provides sufficient storage for active tasks and run units to continue processing. Additionally, the short on storage statistic provides a warning of increased storage pool usage when processing with a cushion.

CWA

The CWA (Common Work Area) parameter defines the size of a section of shared kept storage with a storage ID of 'CWA'. This storage is allocated at startup, and remains allocated for the duration of the run. It may be used as a scratch pad area for commonly-addressable application values and indicators. The CWA is accessed only by IDMS-DC application programs. System software does not use it. ADS/O dialogs cannot access it because the language contains no storage allocation commands. The parameter should be allowed to default to zero unless DC program use of the CWA is planned.

9.6.4   Program Loading Considerations

Several parameters of the SYSTEM statement affect the function of program loading and the pools into which programs are loaded. The UNDEFINED PROGRAM COUNT parameter determines if loading of new or modified programs is allowed. The BLDL parameter specifies when library directory load information is to be collected. Two pools of storage are available for loading of programs, dialogs, subschemas, and tables. The REENTRANT POOL parameter controls the size of a pool of storage used to load system programs and any fully reentrant user programs. The PROGRAM POOL parameter defines the size of a pool used to load nonreentrant and quasi-reentrant programs.

UNDEFINED PROGRAM COUNT

This parameter determines whether dynamic definition of dialogs, IDMS-DC programs, maps, tables, and subschemas is allowed in the system. Dynamic definition means defining to the system characteristics of dialogs, DC programs, maps, tables, and subschemas that were not included in the sysgen, or which have been modified since the system was brought up. Refer to the Security chapter, Section 6.3.3, for a discussion of dynamic definition security implications.

Most dynamic definition takes place automatically, handled by the ADS/O, IDD, OLM, and subschema compiler software. The DCMT VARY DYNAMIC PROGRAM command is used for manual dynamic definition, necessary for DC programs. Dynamic definitions last only for the duration of a single execution of the system and must be repeated during subsequent system executions. Dynamic definition suffices for programs that are used intermittently. However, if a new program will be used frequently it should be included in the next sysgen of the test system.

Two numbers may be specified for UNDEFINED PROGRAM COUNT. The first number defines the number of extra entries in the primary Program Definition Table. The second number determines the size of secondary tables created as the need arises if the Program Definition Table fills. Each program, map, table, subschema, and dialog defined during the sysgen with a PROGRAM statement has a permanent entry in the table, and there are UNDEFINED PROGRAM COUNT number of extra entries in the table. These entries, called null PDE's (Program Definition Elements), facilitate the dynamic definition of new and modified subschemas, tables, dialogs, and maps. In systems where frequent ADS/O and OLM development is occurring, create sufficient null PDE's for all maps and dialogs generated, regenerated or executed during the run. In a test system, where new development is occurring constantly, it is important to allow the programming staff enough entries to create and test new programs, dialogs, and maps. It is absolutely crucial to provide sufficient allocation with ADS/O and OLM. UNDEFINED PROGRAM COUNT defaults to zero, disabling ADS/O, OLM, and subschema development for new applications.

If the second number is omitted or set to zero, no secondary tables are created. In that case, no further dynamic definition is allowed when the primary Program Definition Table becomes full. The size of the secondary allocation is also important because it is a noncontiguous request for space. The initial allocation is taken out of its own portion of the startup region, but secondary allocations come out of the storage pool. Several more secondary allocations may be required if the secondary initial allocation is too small. Secondary tables are long term storage (i.e., lasting for the remainder of the run) and tend to fragment the storage pool, diminishing overall system performance.

In Release 10, 23 PDE's fit on a 4K frame; therefore, primary and secondary allocations should be specified as multiples of 23 to minimize storage pool fragmentation. The values chosen for primary and secondary allocation depend on system activity and on the number of programs defined in the sysgen, however, an initial value of (69,46) is reasonable.

BLDL/NOBLDL

This parameter determines when library directory information on programs, database procedures, etc., is collected. Once collected, directory information is stored in a buffer for the remainder of the run. Saving directory information facilitates rapid loading of programs.

The default value of BLDL tells the system to collect directory information at startup for all programs included in the sysgen. Specifying NOBLDL means that directory information is collected for each program the first time it is loaded. NOBLDL reduces the length of time it takes the system to start up, and impacts response time for only the first load of each program. Choosing NOBLDL is especially valuable for systems where rapid recovery from system failure is mandatory.

Program Pools

There are two types of program pools, the basic program pool and the reentrant program pool. All nonresident programs, dialogs, maps, tables, and subschemas (fixed portion of the table) are loaded as needed into either pool. Resident programs, dialogs, maps, tables and subschemas are loaded into a separate portion of the IDMS/R region at startup and remain there for the duration of the run.

The PROGRAM POOL parameter specifies the size of the program pool and is a required parameter. The REENTRANT POOL parameter determines the size of the reentrant program pool and is an optional parameter. All system and user nonresident programs, tables, etc., are loaded into the program pool if only a program pool is defined in the sysgen. If both parameters are specified, all reentrant modules are loaded into the reentrant pool, with the remainder loaded into the program pool. All tables, maps, dialogs, subschemas, and system software programs are reentrant and are loaded into the reentrant pool, along with any user programs and database procedures that are reentrant. Nonreentrant user DC programs (DC COBOL programs are only quasi-reentrant) and database procedures are always loaded into the program pool.

Although the REENTRANT POOL parameter is optional, we strongly recommend that it be specified to make more efficient use of main storage resources. The reentrant pool is allocated in 512-byte storage portions, as opposed to the program pool which is allocated in 4K pages. Therefore, the reentrant pool is far less fragmented than the program pool. For example, a 6K program would occupy two pages, or 8K, in the program pool. In the reentrant pool, the same program would occupy only 6K. IDMS/R manages the reentrant pool with far less wasted storage because of its smaller pages. Main storage is conserved by defining a reentrant pool in addition to the program pool because most programs, tables, dialogs, etc., are reentrant.

REENTRANT POOL: All system programs are loaded into this pool, as well as all dialogs, maps, tables, and subschemas, and any user code that is truly reentrant. Only nonreentrant DC programs and database procedures are loaded into the regular program pool. Therefore, the reentrant pool must be large enough to handle most of the program load. We suggest beginning with 800K here for Release 10, 600K for earlier releases. These values assume that some heavily-used Cullinet modules have been made resident; see Table 10-3 (Chapter 10) for a listing of the modules.

PROGRAM POOL: If a reentrant pool has been defined, only nonreentrant DC application programs and database procedures are loaded into the program pool. Hence, the program pool should be one fourth or less the size of the reentrant pool. Usually 64K is enough, unless heavy DC program or database procedure use is common. In that case, 500K should be sufficient.

9.6.5   Timeout and Abend Detection Parameters

There are several parameters for setting timeout intervals which affect users, internal and external run units. RESOURCE TIMEOUT INTERVAL may be used to limit the amount of time a terminal operator can take between receiving an output message and entering the next input message. Loop detection, abend detection, and how long a run unit may wait for a system resource are controlled by four parameters. RUNAWAY INTERVAL and INACTIVE INTERVAL are used to control internal run units, while INTERNAL WAIT and EXTERNAL WAIT are used for external run units.

The CHKUSER TASKS facility permits rapid detection of batch run unit abends. It is available for OS systems only.

RESOURCE TIMEOUT INTERVAL

RESOURCE TIMEOUT INTERVAL limits the amount of time an operator may be logged on to an IDMS-DC or UCF terminal without executing a task. RESOURCE TIMEOUT INTERVAL affects pseudo-conversational applications because there is no task executing during the wait for operator input. If the operator remains inactive beyond the timeout interval, a default system program (RHDCBYE) processes to release all DB/DC resources owned by the terminal, such as long-term storage and KEEP LONGTERM record locks. The operator must sign on to IDMS-DC and restart the transaction to resume work. Alternatively, a user program can be specified along with this parameter to allow specialized processing, such as sending a message to the terminal to warn the operator of impending task termination.

If a RESOURCE TIMEOUT INTERVAL is not specified, it defaults to forever, disabling the timeout facility. As a rule, it should be set fairly low in a test system, because long-term storage and locks acquired for a given operator could be held for an inappropriate amount of time, leading to greater competition for resources and a general slowdown of the system. A reasonable initial figure here would be 600 seconds.

The timeout interval can be overridden on the sysgen TASK statement for specific tasks where operators often take a long time to enter the next screen. The Online Mapping task is an excellent example. Designing and typing the layout of a complex screen often takes a long time. Specify the RESOURCE TIMEOUT INTERVAL parameter as 1200 seconds or longer on the sysgen TASK statement for OLM.

RUNAWAY INTERVAL

RUNAWAY INTERVAL is how long IDMS-DC waits between requests for service from a task before abending the task. RUNAWAY INTERVAL is used to detect programs that have gained exclusive control of the system, perhaps due to looping. Runaway tasks can be expensive, especially if they go undetected for long periods of time.

RUNAWAY INTERVAL applies to only internal run units, i.e., dialogs, DC programs, database procedures, and system tasks. External run unit monitoring is controlled by INTERNAL WAIT and EXTERNAL WAIT parameters, discussed below.

RUNAWAY INTERVAL causes the abend of any internal run unit that processes longer than the specified amount of time before issuing a wait. Set the RUNAWAY INTERVAL with care because it can cause the abend of a program that is not looping, just doing a large amount of processing. A reasonable starting value would be 120 seconds.

Online IDD is sometimes encountered as a runaway task when processing a time-consuming request such as adding a record with many elements. When Online IDD processes such a request, it invokes the system programs IDMSDBMS and IDMSDBIO as it stores new records on the DD. While these programs are performing the necessary I/O's, the IDD task is still "active". Although no loop is involved, IDD will be active a long time and might be abended as a runaway. If this problem is encountered, either increase the RUNAWAY INTERVAL, or perform such time-consuming DD activity using batch IDD, rather than Online IDD.

INACTIVE INTERVAL

INACTIVE INTERVAL determines how long an internal task, for example, an ADS/O dialog or a DC program, may wait for a system resource before 'timing out' and abending. System resources such as record locks, I/O buffers, and storage are covered by this parameter.

Internal tasks that wait longer than the INACTIVE INTERVAL are rolled back, and a DC001003 abend message is sent to the associated terminal.

Sixty seconds is a good initial value for this parameter. Examine the system statistics to pinpoint the causes of resource contention if timeout abend messages are encountered frequently.

EXTERNAL WAIT

The time specified here functions like RUNAWAY INTERVAL, but, applies only to external run units. External run units include batch programs and external TP monitor programs containing embedded DML statements (CICS Command Level Programs for example). EXTERNAL WAIT is the amount of time allowed between calls to IDMS/R. If more than the allotted EXTERNAL WAIT time has passed since the last time that IDMS/R has been called by the external run unit, IDMS/R assumes that the run unit has abended. IDMS/R aborts the run unit and rolls back any updates that it made.

Choosing the appropriate value for External Wait hinges on the following considerations:

- Will there be a mix of batch and TP external run units,
- How much swapping is taking place (in MVS systems), and
- What kind of processing taking place between calls to IDMS/R?

When there is a mix of batch and TP external run units, it is very difficult to choose an appropriate value. The kinds of processing involved and the relative timing are very different. Typically, a much shorter EXTERNAL WAIT is appropriate for TP programs as compared to batch programs. For these mixed situations, a compromise EXTERNAL WAIT of somewhere between 60 and 90 seconds would be suitable. Refer to the discussion of CHKUSER TASKS at the end of this section for an alternative solution to this dilemma at OS sites.

If batch programs are the only type of external run unit, a longer value, such as 300 seconds, would be better. For MVS systems, factor in the amount of virtual to real storage "swapping" that is occurring. If a program is swapped out of main storage, it would be a long time between calls to IDMS/R. Swapped programs could easily exceed the EXTERNAL WAIT period, but not because of an abend. Choose a longer EXTERNAL WAIT, e.g., 600 seconds, if storage is at a premium and swapping is a likely occurrence.

Also consider the kind of processing that takes place between calls to IDMS/R. A longer wait may be appropriate if detailed calculations and/or several non-database I/O's are common.

Inappropriate programming practices may lead to EXTERNAL WAIT abends. For example, if a program issues BIND and READY statements to initiate database processing and then opens a tape file requiring a tape mount, the run unit easily could time out. All non-database activities that may involve waiting should take place either before the run unit is initiated or after it has FINISHed.

EXTERNAL WAIT can be overridden for specific programs using the IDMS PROGRAM statement in the sysgen.

INTERNAL WAIT

INTERNAL WAIT is how long an external run unit is allowed to wait for an internal system resource (e.g., a record lock or a buffer) before timing out. A short waiting period of 60 to 90 seconds is usually reasonable. A longer waiting period may be required if any external run units use PROTECTED or EXCLUSIVE usage modes (usually inappropriate) on the READY statements.

This parameter can be overridden for specific programs using the IDMS PROGRAM sysgen statement.

CHKUSER TASKS

The CHKUSER TASKS facility, only available in OS systems, permits rapid detection of batch external run unit abends. The number of CHKUSER TASKS chosen limits the number of batch external run units which may process concurrently; therefore, specify a number for CHKUSER TASKS equal to the maximum expected number of batch DML programs and Culprit programs processing concurrently under the IDMS/R system. Additional batch run units will abend with a '0069' ERROR-STATUS code if the number specified is too small.

The dilemma of choosing an appropriate value for EXTERNAL WAIT in systems with a mixture of batch and TP external run units can be solved in OS systems by specifying the CHKUSER TASKS parameter of the SYSTEM statement. Abend situations are detected and cleared up long before EXTERNAL WAIT comes into play if CHKUSER TASKS are in use. Therefore, the value of EXTERNAL WAIT may be chosen with only TP external run units in mind, e.g., 30 seconds.

9.6.6 Limiting Resource Consumption (Release 10 only)

Limits may be placed on storage, locks, database calls, database I/O requests, and CPU seconds allotted to each internal and external run unit under Release 10. As of this writing, lock limits do not trap the sum of shared plus exclusive locks held, making lock limits almost useless. Task collection statistics must be turned on if LIMITS are used. See the sample sysgen for statistics syntax examples.

Global limits may be set for the entire system, with override capabilities for exception cases. Overrides are specified on the TASK statement for ADS/O and IDMS-DC programs, and the IDMS PROGRAM statement for batch and CICS programs. Global limits allow the DBA to define other parameters in the sysgen, such as STORAGE POOL, for the normal environment and to handle the exception cases individually, rather than define the system always to handle the worst cases.

The global limits set with applications in mind also apply to batch and online system software, such as the schema compiler and the sysgen compiler. These compilers, although infrequently used, often exceed consumption limits reasonable for application programs. Therefore, override the global limits for these compilers by including IDMS PROGRAM and TASK statements in the sysgen.

Reasonable limits for most applications might be:

```
STORAGE LIMIT FOR ONLINE TASKS IS 64
CALL LIMIT FOR ONLINE TASKS IS 200
DBIO LIMIT FOR ONLINE TASKS IS 100
CALL LIMIT FOR EXTERNAL TASKS IS 100000
DBIO LIMIT FOR EXTERNAL TASKS IS 50000
```

These limits assume that override statements for the Cullinet tasks have also been included in the sysgen. The following statements are samples showing overrides for the schema and sysgen compilers.

```
IDMS PROGRAM IDMSCHEM                    (Batch Schema Compiler)
    DBIO LIMITS OFF
    LOCK LIMITS OFF
    STORAGE LIMITS OFF
    CALLS LIMITS OFF.

TASK SCHEMA                             (Online Schema Compiler)
    DBIO LIMITS OFF
    LOCK LIMITS OFF
    STORAGE LIMITS OFF
    CALLS LIMITS OFF.

IDMS PROGRAM RHDCSGEN                    (Batch Sysgen Compiler)
    DBIO LIMITS OFF
    LOCK LIMITS OFF
    STORAGE LIMITS OFF
    CALLS LIMITS OFF.

TASK SYSGEN                             (Online Sysgen Compiler)
    DBIO LIMITS OFF
    LOCK LIMITS OFF
    STORAGE LIMITS OFF
    CALLS LIMITS OFF.
```

If limits are exceeded frequently, use one of the following techniques during every execution of the system until the limits are raised in the next sysgen. Either turn off limits globally with a DCMT VARY LIMITS DISABLE command, or change the limits to something more reasonable for each individual task, e.g.,

```
DCMT VARY TASK SNON
    STORAGE LIMIT 100.

DCMT VARY IDMS PROGRAM DBD000N
    CALL LIMIT 200000.
```

9.6.7 Locking

Four parameters affect record locking in the system. RETRIEVAL NOLOCK and UPDATE NOLOCK (defaults) specify that record locks should not be maintained for run units READYing areas in RETRIEVAL and PROTECTED UPDATE usage modes. These values are recommended because they reduce locking overhead in the system; however, they also allow a retrieval run unit to access records that another run unit is in the midst of updating. If this is invalid for all your applications, specify RETRIEVAL LOCK and UPDATE LOCK.

Two other parameters, RULOCKS and SYSLOCKS, determine the size of internal tables used to maintain locks. The values recommended assume NOLOCK was specified for retrieval and protected update run units. Choose correspondingly larger values if LOCK was specified.

RULOCKS

RULOCKS determines the number of entries in the primary lock table for each run unit. Each entry in this table is 8 bytes long and holds some status information and the DBKEY (database key) of a record locked by the run unit. At startup, enough storage pool space is allocated for one primary lock table for each possible concurrent run unit, as defined by the MAXIMUM ERUS parameter. This storage is added automatically by the sysgen compiler to the storage pool size specified in the sysgen. Additional space is allocated from the storage pool if a run unit locks more records than RULOCKS, forming a secondary lock table. Each additional allocation is twice the size of the previous allocation. Thus, if RULOCKS=100 and a run unit exceeds that, 200 more are allocated, then 400, 800, and so on.

It is important that the value for this parameter be realistic. Making secondary allocations from the storage pool may be an expensive proposition, because it potentially slows down subsequent storage management requests and locking requests. A good starting number is 120. Remember, IDMS/R implicitly locks many records as run units process. Refer to IDMS/R Database Operations (Release 10) or IDMS Database Design and Definition Guide (Release 5.7) for further details on locking.

Do not allow this parameter to default. The default value is zero, which disables record level locking and causes only area level locking to be in effect. Chapter 5, on CV and local mode, contains more information on area and record level locking.

SYSLOCKS
The SYSLOCKS parameter determines the number of entries in the system lock table. The system lock table contains the DBKEYs of all concurrently locked records. It is used in conjunction with a hashing table to identify deadlock situations. A good value for this parameter is 2,500 for a test system. Each entry in this table is 12 bytes long. The required storage is added automatically to the size of the storage pool and is allocated at startup time.

9.6.8   Journaling

JOURNAL RETRIEVAL/NORETRIEVAL and RUNUNITS FOR QUEUE/SCRATCH/etc., impact the amount of journaling taking place. Specifying values different from the default values reduces journaling overhead.

JOURNAL RETRIEVAL/NORETRIEVAL
This parameter determines whether "start" and "end" of retrieval run unit processing are journaled. The default value, RETRIEVAL, increases the overhead of journaling and provides little in return. If JOURNAL RETRIEVAL is specified, the journal reports (JREPORTS) can provide statistical information, such as number of calls and I/O's, for retrieval run units as well as update run units.

We recommend specifying NORETRIEVAL for most test system sysgens. JOURNAL RETRIEVAL might be considered in the sysgen for a production system, either to provide the additional statistical information or to gather chargeback information.

RUNUNITS FOR QUEUE
MSGDICT
SIGNON/DEST (Release 10)
LOADER
EXTENT (Release 10)
These parameters set up run units which are initiated at system startup time. The run units issue BIND RUN UNIT and READY *dd-area-*

name statements upon initiation and remain open until system shutdown. These run units, named RHDCRUAL or IDMSXTAL depending on the area, perform specific 'housekeeping' functions for application and system software programs. The system passes control to one of these run units when a program requires access to certain areas of the dictionary, e.g., to access scratch records, queue records, or dictionary messages. Because these run units already have issued BIND RUN UNIT and READY statements, access to the dictionary area is faster, requiring only DML access statement(s) such as OBTAIN.

Appropriate allocation of run units increases the efficiency of several types of dictionary access and minimizes journaling overhead for these functions. If there are too few of these run units, some dictionary accesses will be slowed because new run units are started if all existing ones are busy satisfying other requests. These new run units must be dispatched, issue BINDs, READYs, access statements and a FINISH; which takes more time than the access statements alone and also increases journaling overhead.

A good initial figure for single dictionary test systems is three run units each for scratch and message, and two for signon and loader. Each run unit occupies approximately 4K of main storage.

The values may be allowed to default to 1 for each type of run unit for multiple dictionary test systems. As of this writing, secondary dictionary access does not make use of the run units initiated at start up. Separate run units are created as needed, issuing BINDs, READYs, access statements and a FINISH.

These figures should be reviewed as system activity increases, especially if Online Query and Online IDD usage is heavy. Check the IDMSAJNL report to see if there is a disproportionate number of journal blocks in the 0 to 10% range, indicating that more run units may be necessary (see Chapter 7 discussion of this report for alternative meanings).

9.6.9   Debugging Considerations

Three parameters determine the availability of debugging information for solving application and system problems. They are ABRU, USERTRACE, and SYSTRACE.

ABRU NOSNAP
The ABRU (aborted run unit) sysgen parameter controls the writing of formatted snap dumps to the log for external run unit ABRU-type abends. An external run unit is defined as a run unit executing in a partition or region separate from IDMS/R. External run units include only batch programs and online programs executing under an

external TP monitor such as CICS. An ABRU abend occurs when an external run unit receives an unexpected non-zero ERROR-STATUS, due to a time out for example, when it regains control from IDMS/R and branches to the IDMS-STATUS routine to abort processing.

Choosing the NOSNAP value for the ABRU sysgen parameter suppresses the formatted dump of the external run unit's IDMS/R storage areas. If not suppressed, snap dumps tend to fill up the log. If LOG DATABASE (Section 9.6.10) was chosen, it can cause extra runs of the Log Archiving utility.

These formatted snap dumps provide information of interest only to programmers acquainted with IDMS/R internals. Most information needed by programmers can be obtained from the subschema control block or the statistics block, both of which are available without taking a snap dump. Therefore, we recommend specifying NOSNAP.

The following technique prepares users for a problem which requires information from IDMS/R storage areas. Generate a second test system for debugging purposes, specifying ABRU SNAP but otherwise identical to the actual test system. When such a problem arises, swap systems, and recreate the problem. Swap systems by shutting down the test system and specify the debugging system number in the startup JCL when it is brought back up again.

USERTRACE

The USERTRACE parameter controls the facility which traces IDMS/R DB/DC requests made by user programs. The trace facility is useful only for IDMS-DC programs and not for ADS/O dialogs because there is only one program, the ADS run time control program, executing within the ADS system. The USERTRACE facility should be turned OFF at sites where there are no IDMS-DC programs in use.

The trace facility should be turned on and an appropriate number of entries specified at sites where DC programs are in use. The number of entries specified determines the size of the main storage trace table. The main storage trace table is used to store information about each IDMS/R DB/DC request made by application programs running on a specific terminal. When the table is full, the next IDMS/R request is traced starting at the beginning at the table and overlaying previous information. The table must to be large enough to supply adequate debugging information. A good beginning number of trace entries is 100.

The USERTRACE facility is controlled by user commands. DB/DC requests are not traced until a DCUF USERTRACE ON command is issued from an online terminal. Then, only activity at that terminal is traced. The DCUF USERTRACE OFF command turns off the trace. The DCUF USERTRACE LIST command displays the entries from the trace table.

SYSTRACE

If enabled, this parameter creates excessive overhead in the test system. When the SYSTRACE is ON the number of 64-byte entries in the system trace table must be specified. Storage is allocated during startup for the system trace table. The DB/DC requests of every system module, and the register contents at the time of the request, are continually traced. The overhead of tracing all activity in the system is higher than one might expect. A single DB/DC request from a user module may generate several DB/DC calls from system modules, all of which are traced. In addition, trace table contents are written to the log whenever snap dumps are taken, making snap dumps voluminous. The log area tends to become full more often and more executions of the log archiving utility may be required.

The system trace is useful for debugging system problems, not application problems. It is difficult to decipher and typically used only by Cullinet personnel to resolve system problems. The user trace facility described earlier is the preferred tool for providing application trace information. Additionally, under Release 10, the Online Debugger provides valuable application debugging information.

We recommend that the system trace be specified as OFF in the sysgen because the resulting trace information is not worth its overhead on a daily basis. Generate a second system with the SYSTRACE turned on, but otherwise identical to the actual test system, to be prepared in the event of a system problem. While investigating a system problem with Cullinet, swap systems (specify the debugging system number in the startup JCL) and attempt to recreate the problem.

9.6.10 Selecting the System Log File Alternative

The IDMS/R log may be written either to the log area of the dictionary (LOG DATABASE) or to one or more sequential files (LOG FILE1 ddname1/fileid1 FILE2 ddname2/fileid2). Logging to the DD is preferable in most instances; however, both alternatives have advantages and drawbacks. The appropriate choice depends on your environment.

The overriding advantage of logging to the the DD is that the system statistics can be printed. These statistics supply important tuning information, and can be printed easily only if the log is written to the DD. Cullinet supplies a batch print log utility, RHDCPRLG, and an online print log task (OLP) to decipher and print log information. These utilities work only if the log is written to the database. Task statistics and system histogram information are only available if LOG DATABASE is chosen.

An additional advantage when logging to the database applies to users running ADS/Online or DC programs. The system writes a snap dump to the log if an ADS/O or DC program aborts. Snap dumps show all storage allocated to a run unit by IDMS-DC and are useful in debugging. Logging to the database allows the user to run the print log utility, RHDCPRLG, which can print snap dumps from the log based on a date/time stamp or a logical terminal ID. The snap dumps may be examined online using the OLP task under Release 10.

The main drawback of logging to the DD is that the system goes into a wait state if the log area is exhausted. The system continues to wait until the situation is cleared by running the archive/print log utility, RHDCPRLG. The system attempts to prevent this from happening by keeping the console operator informed about the status of the log area of the DD. The message DCLOG IS $nn\%$ FULL is sent to the console at startup time. An updated message is issued every time the available free space halves. These messages must be carefully monitored because the system can come to a grinding halt for lack of write space for log information.

There are two techniques which reduce the likelihood of using all available log area in the DD. We suggest both of the following techniques be implemented:

- Archive the log after each system shutdown as a standard procedure, and
- Automate the monitoring of DCLOG $nn\%$ FULL console messages.

It should be standard procedure to run the archiving utility following each system shutdown when logging to the DD. The log area of the DD is large enough to hold two or three full system dumps (if the default installation size is used). This is generally adequate to log a single run of the system without the log becoming full. Therefore, the log area will rarely become full if the it is archived following each execution of the system. Installations executing IDMS/R around the clock should schedule log archiving during a period of low system activity (similar to the periods chosen for backups).

Monitoring console messages can be automated using the same sample exit included on the installation tape to archive the journals automatically. The WTOEXIT can also intercept the DCLOG console messages. The WTOEXIT can automatically initiate the RHDCPRLG utility to archive the log when the log has reached a predetermined capacity threshold, i.e., when it is nn percentage filled. Include an IDMS AREA statement in the sysgen for area DDLDCLOG to override the area status to RETRIEVAL and to permit the log to be offloaded while the system is active.

The advantage of logging to sequential files is the assurance that the system never goes into a total wait state due to lack of log file space. Any number of log files may be defined, normally two are sufficient. IDMS/R automatically switches to the alternate file and continues processing when one log file becomes full. A message is written to the operator's console indicating that one of the files is full and requires printing. The WTOEXIT mentioned earlier may be used to initiate a job to archive/print the log automatically using operating system utilities (IEBGENER or DITTO). When the alternate file is full, IDMS/R switches back to the original file, reopens it, and starts writing new log records over whatever information the file already contains. Ideally, the job to print or archive the log has been run in the meantime.

A minor variation of logging to multiple sequential log files is specifying a single log file and assigning it to a printer. The disadvantages of logging to a printer rather than to sequential files are the inability to print the log while the system is still up and the inability to browse through the log dataset with a text editor.

The major drawback of logging to sequential files or to a printer is the loss of valuable tuning and debugging information. The on-line and batch print log utilities will work only when logging to the DD, so system statistics, task statistics, and histograms are lost. This drawback often leads users to choose logging to the database instead.

9.7 CONSIDERATIONS FOR OTHER SYSTEM GENERATION STATEMENTS

Some other sysgen statements are covered here. Use of the DBNAME statement when implementing multiple DD's and/or DB's, overriding parameters with the IDMS statement, UCF line considerations, and conserving main storage when using ADS/O are discussed below. Information on the remaining sysgen statements may be found in the System Generation Guide.

9.7.1 DBNAME Statement

The DBNAME statement identifies DD's and DB's to the CV. It must be used when implementing multiple dictionaries or when multiple versions of the same database may be accessed under one CV (e.g., test and quality assurance versions).

In most test environments, it is a sound precaution to establish a two-dictionary system initially. Multiple dictionaries afford the freedom to develop applications without having to go through the DBA/DDA every time a new work record element is needed in a dialog. A secondary dictionary is a working tool open to modifications which might damage the main dictionary. It also allows users to 'get their feet wet' experimenting with the software and yet still retaining the integrity of the main dictionary. Users incur the responsibility of maintaining standards for entity definitions on a daily basis, leaving the DBA/DDA free to check definitions which are submitted for inclusion in the main dictionary. The second dictionary requires much less security than the main dictionary because it is a working tool, open to testing. The main dictionary would be protected by more stringent security and is the place where sysgens and schemas might reside.

Implementing a two-dictionary system is accomplished by using a database name table (DBNT). The DBNAME statement creates the DBNT. See Chapter 6 for security suggestions and Chapter 3 for details on the procedure to set up multiple DD's.

9.7.2   IDMS Statement Considerations

There are three different kinds of IDMS statements: IDMS AREA, IDMS BUFFER, and IDMS PROGRAM. These statements are used to override specifications made elsewhere during system creation. IDMS AREA statements are used to override the default usage mode for database areas. IDMS BUFFER statements override the number of buffers assigned to a buffer pool in the global DMCL. IDMS PROGRAM statements have two functions, to override some system-wide values for a particular program and to register the program for database access.

IDMS AREA Statement

The status of all areas included in the global DMCL defaults to UPDATE, unless overridden in the sysgen with an IDMS AREA statement specifying a different usage mode (Section 9.9). If logging to the DD, include an IDMS AREA for the DDLDCLOG area of the dictionary, specifying RETRIEVAL. Also include IDMS AREA statements for any areas that are retrieval only or are offline to the CV (i.e., areas that will be available for update by other CV or Local Mode systems).

IDMS BUFFER Statement

IDMS BUFFER statements may be used to reduce the number of buffer pages specified in the buffer pools defined in the Global DMCL (Section 9.9). The only way to increase the number of buffer pages is to recompile the DMCL.

IDMS PROGRAM Statement

IDMS PROGRAM statements may be used to override INTERNAL WAIT and EXTERNAL WAIT timeout values for individual external programs. Overriding system-wide values is useful when there is a mix of batch and TP external run units. The system-wide values could be set with online TP run units in mind and overridden for each batch program. This method is suitable for a small number of programs, but becomes very cumbersome as the number increases.

If REGISTRATION was specified on the SYSTEM statement, all programs must be registered with the system or they will not be allowed access to databases. Programs are registered by including an IDMS PROGRAM statement for each valid program. The System Generation Guide contains a complete list of the Cullinet programs which also must be included. Program registration is not recommended for test systems because it generates extra work when maintaining sysgens, and does not provide fail-safe protection. See Chapter 6 for security details.

9.7.3   UCF Line Considerations

Specify only one UCF LINE when creating a CV-UCF system. All UCF terminals should be added to that line. Also, remember to add one to the value of MAX ERUS for each UCF terminal concurrently executing a task.

9.7.4   ADSO Statement Considerations

The ADSO statement may be used to conserve main storage in the Storage Pool. The default statement specification causes the ADS run time system to save dialog control and record information in the storage pool across a pseudo-converse, or the time when the dialog is not processing while waiting for the next input message from the terminal operator. Specifically, the currency restoration tables, the ADS variable dialog block (the variable portions of dialogs), and all record buffers are saved between conversations for each dialog 'active' in the application thread (i.e., all LINKed to or INVOKEd dialogs). If the terminal operator is slow to enter the next input message, these resources may occupy a significant portion of the storage pool for a long period of time.

A storage consumption threshold may be set using the FAST MODE THRESHOLD parameter of the ADSO statement in conjunction with RESOURCES ARE FIXED, FAST MODE THRESHOLD IS 10000 for example. When dialog resources exceed the threshold amount they are saved on disk rather than in main storage. Specifying a threshold permits most tasks to execute as rapidly as possible (i.e., resources are saved in main storage rather than on disk, thus reducing response time by saving I/O's), only the tasks which consume storage in excess of the threshold amount are slowed down.

In addition, dialog resources may be specified as relocatable under Release 10, using the RESOURCES ARE RELOCATABLE clause of the ADSO statement. When resources are relocatable, dialog resources initially are stored in the storage pool. However, when the storage pool is almost full IDMS-DC/UCF may relocate dialog resources to the Scratch area of the DD, thereby freeing space in the storage pool for use by other tasks. Resources are restored to the storage pool when the dialog resumes processing.

Only the threshold technique is available under Release 5.7. Record buffers are the only resources that qualify for disk storage. All other resources (i.e., currency restoration table and ADS variable dialog block) are saved in the storage pool.

Forcing some or all of the ADS/O dialog resources to disk allows users to specify a smaller storage pool and thereby conserve main storage. In the test system such flexibility could be extremely important, especially if storage is limited.

9.8   STEP 2:   RUNNING THE SYSTEM GENERATION COMPILER

Once all decisions have been made regarding parameters, the sysgen statements are submitted to the system generation compiler for validation and generation of the new system. System generation can be done online or in batch under Release 10. All parameters are input to the compiler, RHDCSGEN, for validation. After correcting any typing errors, the parameters are resubmitted with GENERATE as the last statement. The compiler then stores the new SYSTEM definition in the Data Dictionary.

System generation can be done only as a batch job under earlier releases. In addition, it is a two-step process using the two system generation compilers, RHDCSGN1 and RHDCSGN2.

Chapter 11, Maintaining the Environment, contains valuable information on running the sysgen compiler and smoothly handling changes to the system. Briefly, when changing anything in the sysgen the safest approach is to MODIFY a backup copy of the system under a different system number in the dictionary and generate it. The generation can be done online for very small modifications such as adding terminals or modifying some of the SYSTEM statement parameters. This approach leaves the current system intact as a backup in case the changes do not work out as planned (to drop back to the old system, simply bring up the system using a #DCPARM module specifying the old system number or for OS systems simply change the PARM=system-number in the JCL).

If a new system is planned or major modifications must be made to an existing system, the best approach is to DELETE and re-ADD the system. Under Release 10, always punch the current system definition from the data dictionary using the sysgen compiler before deleting an existing system. The punched output consists of 80-column card-image system source statements. Save the punched output in a library to use as a backup. Use a copy of the punched output as the base for the planned system modifications, making the changes and using the changed source code when ADDing the system to the DD. The Release 10 sysgen compiler syntax to punch a system definition from the DD is:

PUNCH ALL SYSTEM *system-version-number.*

9.9 STEP 3: CODING AND COMPILING THE GLOBAL DMCL

An IDMS/R CV-DC/UCF system uses only one DMCL (Device Media Control Language). It is called a global DMCL because it typically contains information about areas from several databases (i.e., schemas). The startup routine loads the global DMCL named in the #DCPARM macro.

Only the global DMCL is loaded during the run of Central Version, even if a run unit's subschema specifies a different DMCL name. Under CV, the subschema DMCL specification is ignored (the subschema DMCL specification controls which DMCL is used when programs run in Local Mode). The page range information specified in the global DMCL is compared to that specified in each run unit's subschema as an edit to catch errors in compatibility between the DMCL and Subschema.

The global DMCL has three functions:

* It identifies which database areas will be available at run time.
* It determines the number and size of the I/O buffer pools.
* It specifies the number and size of the journal files for backup and recovery of the system.

Performance considerations for each function are covered below. A sample DMCL may be found in Appendix A. DMCL syntax is covered in the IDMS/R DDL Reference (Release 10) or the IDMS Database Design and Definition Guide (Release 5.7).

9.9.1   DMCL Database Area Considerations

DMCL area information is used to locate database records at run time. Records are located by translating the DBKEY (IDMS/R's internal record identifier) to the actual block in the particular database file which contains the desired record. Database and data dictionary area definitions are copied into the global DMCL from the schemas where the areas were defined. In addition, the buffer pool to be used when accessing records in each area is specified.

All areas included in the DMCL have the default usage mode of UPDATE. The UPDATE usage mode causes CV to put a lock on the areas during startup processing to prevent concurrent update by another IDMS/R CV or Local Mode. Use the sysgen IDMS AREA statement (Section 9.7.2) if a different initial usage mode (e.g., RETRIEVAL or OFFLINE) is desired. Subsequently, DCMT VARY AREA commands may be used to change area usage modes while the system is executing.

9.9.2   DMCL I/O Buffer Pool Considerations

The buffer section of the DMCL names buffer pools, specifies the number of pages in each pool, and specifies the size of each page. The actual number of buffer pages in each pool is determined by a combination of the DMCL specifications and any IDMS BUFFER override statements included in the sysgen. The override may specify only a number less than or equal to the number of buffer pages assigned in the global DMCL. Buffers may be decreased either by recompiling the DMCL or by including an override statement in the next sysgen. Buffer allocations may be increased only by recompiling the DMCL.

The buffer section of the DMCL defines the number and size of buffers used for I/O to user databases and data dictionaries. Journal file buffering is also defined in the DMCL in Release 10.

Buffering Considerations for User Databases: Often, in the course of developing and bringing new database areas into production, users ask that a new buffer pool be created for exclusive use by their application. The object is to provide quick response time by preventing another application's buffer requests from competing with their application's request. If buffer performance problems arise they can be alleviated by assigning more pages to existing pools or by creating new buffer pools. However, three important questions must be considered:

1) How much main storage is available to devote exclusively to IDMS/R buffers?
2) How much concurrent activity is occurring among applications sharing each buffer pool?
3) How much CV overhead is incurred to manage many pages within a single buffer pool and/or many buffer pools?

Buffer storage is allocated when the DMCL is loaded at startup and is devoted exclusively to database buffering. If too many buffers are specified in the DMCL, the extra buffers are unused storage. Clearly, the database administrator should try to consolidate buffer pages and pools to some degree. Consolidation allows IDMS/R to manage the buffer resources, whereas creating a separate pool for each area restricts pool management. The consolidation technique works on two major principles:

1) Consolidate areas that have similar page sizes, and
2) Consolidate areas that have different timing requirements.

All buffers in a buffer pool are the same size and must be large enough to accommodate the largest page size of areas that share the pool. Therefore, consolidate only areas with similar page sizes into "global" pools to minimize wasted storage. For example, there might be a 4K page pool, an 8K page pool and so on. Global pools are generally appropriate for test systems, whereas individual pools might be considered for some production situations.

Database areas that are not accessed concurrently under normal circumstances can be grouped together with little impact on area processing. For example, batch and online areas can often be combined because online areas are accessed during the day whereas batch is generally run at night when there is little or no online activity.

As a guideline, the number of pages within a single buffer pool should not exceed 40. Beyond this level, performance declines because managing so many buffer pages starts to take its toll internally (i.e., more CPU cycles are used managing the pool). It may be wiser to accept a somewhat longer waiting time for buffer space on the few occasions when system activity is at its heaviest to minimize overhead for most normal activity.

Buffering Considerations For Data Dictionary Areas: In the test environment 30-40 buffers should be assigned to the DDLDML area and 15-20 buffers to the DDLDCRUN area. IDMS/R system components make extremely heavy use of these areas during application and database development.

Buffering Considerations For Journal Files: Multiple journal buffers can and should be established under Release 10. They allow the journal to be a multi-threaded resource, especially valuable in heavy concurrent update situations. Multiple batch, or batch and on-line updating, frequently occurs simultaneously in test systems, especially when accessing the dictionary. With multiple journal buffers, run units do not have to wait for buffer availability if the journal page is full and ready to be written back to the database. Initially, define a pool of 3 pages, with a page size blocked appropriately for the device and to a multiple of 4K. Subsequently, tune these choices based on usage statistics.

9.9.3   DMCL Journal File Considerations

The question of how many journals to assign in the global DMCL is often difficult to answer. In addition to how many files to assign, the number of blocks in each file and the size of each block also must be chosen. Detailed information on the considerations involved in these choices may be found in Chapter 7, Backup & Recovery.

No matter how many journals are selected, if all the journals become full and none has been offloaded, the entire system waits until this situation has been cleared. Offloading is accomplished by running the IDMSAJNL utility. Archiving full journals can be automated using a WTOEXIT. A sample WTOEXIT is included on the installation tape; this exit processes whenever a "JOURNAL FULL" message is written to the console and automatically starts a job to run the IDMSAJNL utility using the power reader queue (DOS) or the internal reader (OS).

Number of Journal Files: We recommend a minimum of three journal files be specified for any IDMS/R system. Three journals of 30 cylinders each on a 3380 device, or the equivalent on other devices, has proven to be a reliable starting figure for test systems.

Journal Block Size: Journal block length should be chosen by answering the question: "What is the nature of activity that is most prevalent on the CV?" Is most of the processing done in batch, or on-line, or some mix of the two? Unless journaling of retrieval run units is turned on in the sysgen, the relevant concern is the mix of update processing. If there is a high percentage of online updates, either to the dictionary or to user databases, choose a smaller blocksize (e.g., 3860 on a 3380 device). If, on the other hand, there is a higher percentage of batch updating, with the size of the records being updated relatively large, choose a block size large enough to prevent record images from spanning journal blocks. Spanning journal blocks increases journaling overhead. A final major consideration is choosing a blocksize that is efficient for each particular device type. For example, because the inter-block gap for 3380's is large (480 bytes) a large blocksize, such as 5492 or 7476, is most storage efficient.

9.10 STEP 4: CODING, ASSEMBLING, AND LINKING THE #DCPARM MACRO

A separate #DCPARM macro is assembled for each separate IDMS/R CV-DC/UCF system (Test, Production, Quality Assurance, etc.). During startup processing, the operating system-dependent routine uses information from #DCPARM macro to configure the run time system. The main functions of this macro are naming the global DMCL used by the CV-DC/UCF system and identifying the default system to be brought up. In an alternate startup method, discussed in Section 9.11.2, the default SYSTEM is overridden with a JCL parameter.

The PROMPT parameter of the macro controls whether or not the console operator is prompted at system startup for overrides to the system number specified in the #DCPARM macro and/or to several sysgen parameter values. Most installations specify NO for the PROMPT parameter, eliminating the necessity for daily operator intervention.

Linkage editing considerations vary depending on the operating system in use at the site. For OS sites, the #DCPARM macro is assembled, link edited, and included in the link edit of the operating system-dependent routine to create the startup routine for the new system. For DOS sites, the #DCPARM macro is assembled and link edited as a separate module, named RHDCPARM. The RHDCPARM module must be saved in the core image library named in the startup JCL for the new system. The RHDCPARM module is called and dynamically loaded during startup processing.

9.11 STEP 5: BRINGING UP THE NEW SYSTEM

The JCL to bring up the system executes the operating system-dependent routine. This routine is either linked with (at OS sites) or dynamically loads (at DOS sites) the module created by the #DCPARM macro. The operating system-dependent routine loads the startup routine. The startup routine loads the DMCL using the information specified in the #DCPARM macro. It looks in the data dictionary for the SYSTEM to be brought up, using the system number as the version number for the SYSTEM entity named 'DCSYSTEM' (for example, SYSTEM=2 parameter of the #DCPARM macro identifies DCSYSTEM VERSION 2 in the data dictionary). The default SYSTEM number, specified in the #DCPARM macro, can be overridden at run time (Section 9.11.2). The start up routine configures the IDMS/R environment based on the SYSTEM information found in the data dictionary. The status of the system from the last shutdown is read from the journal files and automatic recovery is performed if necessary. The database files are opened at this time and normal system processing of online and batch programs' requests begins.

Some JCL considerations and how to specify the SYSTEM being brought up follow.

9.11.1   JCL Considerations (OS)

There are two load libraries referenced in the JCL under OS, namely STEPLIB and CDMSLIB. STEPLIB identifies the library(ies) from which the operating system loads programs. STEPLIB contains IDMS/R system software, global DMCL, database procedures, and so forth. CDMSLIB identifies the library(ies) containing system software, database procedures, application programs, and modules not found in the load area of the dictionary (e.g., OLM compiler, DC programs, maps, ADS/O dialogs, tables, and subschemas), from which IDMS/R loads programs. CDMSLIB should have the same library concatenation order as STEPLIB with the addition of user load libraries, which need only be specified under CDMSLIB. For example, if new DC programs are linked into a separate load library, simply concatenate that load library with the others in CDMSLIB.

9.11.2   Alternative Methods to Identify the SYSTEM Being Brought Up

As many as 9,999 different systems can be maintained in the DD. The particular system used at run time is determined by one of the following methods:

1) A parameter on the execute card in the startup JCL, PARM='SYSTEM=*system-number*' for OS systems, or
2) Whatever was specified for the 'SYS=' parameter in the #DCPARM macro; or
3) The system number override keyed in by the console operator, if override of the system number was allowed in the #DCPARM macro.

The first method is the most convenient method for daily use. A PARM (for OS) on the execute card of the startup JCL identifies the system to be brought up.

To switch systems when using the second method above, maintain two different #DCPARM modules (as well as two different copies of the operating system dependent routine for OS systems) on different libraries, and either through changing the STEPLIB card (for OS) or changing the LIBDEF search chain (for DOS), swap #DCPARMs to identify different systems. This method is cumbersome and can lead to great confusion.

The third method, a console override, is also cumbersome because it requires operator intervention. Daily operator intervention might be acceptable if systems are changed frequently. However, in a more or less stable system, it is difficult to work with.

9.12   TEST SYSTEM CREATION REVISITED

Congratulations, you now have a test system!!! Sit back and relax for a while because it will probably be a week or two before the system must be regenerated. Now that the test system is up and running, development of user databases and applications begins. As new programs and tasks are defined, and database definitions are added or changed, corresponding changes must be made to the test system. Test systems are often changed on a weekly or biweekly basis in shops where heavy development is occurring. Chapter 11 examines techniques which ease the burden of constant test system regenerations.

9.13   CONCLUSION

The test system is extremely important to the entire IDMS/R installation. Rapid development of new databases and applications is possible only when the test system provides a stable, secure, and high performance work environment. These qualities result from prudent decisions made when creating the components of the test system.

The components of the test system are the operating system-dependent routine, the #DCPARM macro, a SYSTEM generated by the system generation compiler, a global DMCL and (for CV-UCF systems only) several UCF macros. The operating system-dependent routine and the UCF macros are created during installation of IDMS/R and need not be recreated for each new system. The three components which make each system unique are the #DCPARM macro, the SYSTEM, and the global DMCL.

First the system generation parameters are chosen and the SYSTEM is generated. Then the global DMCL is compiled. The #DCPARM macro is assembled, identifying the SYSTEM and global DMCL just created. When all components have been created, the system can be brought up. Database and application development may now begin.

The next chapter discusses the special considerations of production system creation. Techniques for maintaining, trouble shooting, and tuning systems may be found in Chapters 11, 12, and 13.

Suggestions for further reading on Test System Creation:

The following Cullinet manuals
   For Release 10 systems:
   1) System Generation (System generation parameters, system generation compiler)
   2) IDMS-CV/DC System Operations (#DCPARM macro, bringing up the new system, statistics, DCMT command)
   3) IDMS/R DDL Reference (Defining the global DMCL)

For Release 5.7 systems:
   1) IDMS-CV/DC System Generation (System generation parameters, system generation compiler)
   2) IDMS-DB/DC Operations Guide (#DCPARM macro, bringing up the new system, statistics, DCMT command)
   3) IDMS Database Design and Definition Guide (Defining the global DMCL)

10

Production System Creation

Implementation of production applications begins after development of pilot applications on the IDMS/R test system. Many users simply duplicate their test system and call it production. This practice can lead to serious performance problems. Differences between the processing characteristics of production and test systems generally lead to changes in the parameter values chosen during creation of a production system versus a test system. The specific values chosen depend on the applications already in production and on those about to be added to the production system.

Ideally, applications about to go into production are first transferred from the test system to an intermediate system, either a Quality Assurance (QA) system or an Acceptance Testing (AT) system. The QA/AT system should be a composite of existing production applications and the new applications. The reports and statistics gathered on the intermediate system during performance testing provide information to guide parameter choices during creation of the new or revised production system.

In this chapter we will discuss:

- Differences between production and test IDMS/R systems, and
- Steps to follow when creating a production system.

Recommendations for determining appropriate production system parameter values will be provided during discussion of production system creation steps.

10.1 DIFFERENCES BETWEEN PRODUCTION AND TEST SYSTEMS

The production environment differs from the test environment in many important ways. For example, major components of the IDMS/R environment, namely databases, data dictionaries, user applications, and system software, have different characteristics in a production system than in a test system. Performance, security, backup, and recovery are most crucial for production systems. Table 10-1 contains a summary of the differences commonly found between production and test systems. These differences set the production IDMS/R system apart from the test system in terms of configuration and operational procedures.

Table 10-1 Typical Characteristics of Production and Test Systems

What	Production	Test
Databases	Large	Small
Data Dictionaries	Single	Multiple
User Applications	Heavy volume	Light volume
Development Software	Rarely used	Often used
Performance & Stability	Primary importance	Moderate importance
Security	Stringent	Loose
Backup & Recovery	Primary importance	Moderate importance

10.1.1 Databases

An obvious difference between production and test databases is size. Production databases may be dramatically larger than test databases because test databases often contain only a representative sampling of the records on production databases.

In contrast to test databases, existing data must be preserved when production database structures are changed. Cullinet supplies a utility, IDMSRSTU, which handles the most frequently encountered structural changes, thus enabling the addition of fields, reordering of fields, and/or addition of pointers to records in databases. The IDMSRSTU utility makes it easy to implement structural changes while preserving existing data. The Schema Compare utility, IDMSRSTC, available in Release 10 only, helps eliminate restructure syntax errors; it analyzes the differences between an old schema and a new schema, automatically generating the restructure macros used by IDMSRSTU to perform the changes. It is possible to minimize use of any restructure utility by leaving some filler space in records that can be used later to contain new field definitions. Dummy pointers may be defined in records that are likely to be interface points for new applications by defining sets which are not used today, and redefining them when new sets are required later. In addition, multi-member sets may be used to implement new record types and relationships with existing owners.

Reorganizations are performed occasionally on production databases to improve performance. Reorganizations are accomplished using the utilities IDMSUNLD and IDMSDBLU for network databases, and the utility IDMSTBLU for relational tables and integrated indexes.

10.1.2   Data Dictionaries

Production systems usually have one Data Dictionary while test systems often have multiple data dictionaries. The common reasons for multiple DD's in test systems normally do not exist in production systems, i.e.,

- Naming convention conflicts between development groups,
- Several development projects urgently requiring new element and record definitions to meet development deadlines,
- Multiple phases of development, where one version of a system is in advanced testing on the primary DD, while minor program modifications are being coded and tested on a secondary DD, and
- Varying security requirements for dictionary entities.

Naming convention conflicts should have been resolved prior to putting the application into production, usually before or during QA/AT testing. There is no need for multiple dictionaries to facilitate rapid addition of elements or for testing of multiple development phases because development should not occur on a production system. Varying security requirements are no longer a problem in production because all production entities should be equally well secured. Often a separate group, perhaps QA personnel, is responsible for migration of definitions and modules from the test or QA/AT system's DD to the production DD, and other users are denied access to the production DD.

10.1.3   User Applications

The transaction mix that runs in production is not the same as that in the test environment. User applications may run hundreds of times per day in the production environment, with a great volume and variety of transactions against very large databases. In contrast, infrequent user application transactions take place against relatively small databases during testing.

It is important to monitor and restrict application READY US-AGE-MODEs, because of the high volume of user application transactions on a production system. The PROTECTED or EXCLUSIVE US-AGE-MODEs can cause waits and timeouts if used inappropriately because they generate area locks. Area locks prohibit update access (PROTECTED) or update and retrieval access (EXCLUSIVE) by other programs to all records in the named areas. The JREPORTS or on-line monitoring of individual run units in the QA/AT system may be used to determine if PROTECTED or EXCLUSIVE USAGE-MODE has been specified on the READY statements of programs and dialogs.

10.1.4   Application Development Software

Development software such as online IDD, online mapping, the ADS application and dialog generators, subschema and schema compilers, and online query rarely are run in a production environment. However, development software may run hundreds of times per day in a test environment. Development software task codes often are either omitted from production sysgens or heavily secured.

10.1.5   Performance and Stability Requirements

Performance and stability considerations are very important for production systems. Normal business operations may be impossible if a production system has slow response time or crashes. In contrast, the rest of the business can continue operating if a test system has slow response time or crashes, although it may be frustrating for developers on a tight schedule.

Monitoring statistics and reports on the QA/AT system helps determine parameter values for the initial production system. Production system statistics and reports should be monitored continually to identify existing or developing performance problems so they may be corrected quickly. In Chapter 13 we discuss some tools and techniques which have been used to improve performance at other installations.

10.1.6   Security Requirements

Security is often a primary concern for production systems and a minor concern for test systems. The intensified security usually required in a production environment is responsible for many of the changes made to IDMS/R system generation and operational procedures when a new application is put into production.

Securing the production environment involves deciding what needs securing from whom and why. Do you just want to protect your database from accidental access or update, or do you wish to actively frustrate deliberate unauthorized attempts to access or update the database? Some of the typical security changes made between test and production are shown in Table 6-4. Chapter 6 contains details on these and other security considerations.

10.1.7   Backup and Recovery Requirements

Backup and recovery are absolutely critical in a production system. Fully tested procedures for forward and backward recovery, as well as operations personnel thoroughly trained in these procedures, are required for smooth and timely recovery in the event of system or device failure. Database and journal files may be duplexed for extra protection. Most shops schedule a disaster recovery testing day when all recovery and coordination jobs are tested under a variety of conditions.

Backup and recovery jobs must be planned carefully, keeping in mind that different IDMS/R databases may have different 'exposure thresholds', i.e., there may be varying amounts of time between backups. Some databases may be too large and time consuming to backup on a daily basis, so backing up weekly becomes the rule with heavy reliance on the intervening journal tapes. Journal tapes must be synchronized with any volume or dataset backups made during the day which supersede prior journal offloads. Coordinating journal tapes and full backup tapes must be planned well in advance to ensure smooth recovery.

A single day's journal archive tapes can accumulate to many volumes if disk journal files are small or the number of updates is large. Therefore, it may be wise to create a job to merge multiple journal archive files into a single journal archive tape file containing an entire day's activity. Merging journal files ensures ease in tape handling. Similarly, for those shops which backup weekly and rely on daily journals to forward recover their databases, it may be expedient to create a second journal merge job to merge each daily activity journal file into a cumulative weekly journal file. Details on backup and recovery considerations may be found in Chapter 7.

10.2   CREATION OF A PRODUCTION SYSTEM

Some users duplicate their test system to use as a production system. This practice can cause serious performance problems because differences between production and test processing have not been taken into consideration.

A pilot application should go through Quality Assurance or Acceptance Testing on a separate IDMS/R system after its initial testing has been completed on the test system. A QA/AT system may be created by following the steps listed below for the creation of a production system. A best guess should be made for appropriate QA/AT system parameter values, realizing that these values can be tuned later based on statistics gathered during the system's processing.

Many statistics and reports on the pilot application should be gathered during extensive performance testing on a QA/AT system. Statistics and reports gathered during QA/AT system processing may be used as an aid in choosing production system parameter values when a production system is then created following the steps listed below.

The steps required to create a production system or any other additional system (a QA/AT system for example) are depicted in Figure 10-1. The assumed starting points are installed IDMS/R software and an operational test system. All the steps required to create a test system, as covered in the previous chapter, plus four additional steps, are necessary to create an additional system.

The four additional steps are: 1) creating separate software libraries, 2) creating a separate data dictionary, 3) creating separate databases, and 4) migration of applications (step 9 in Figure 10-1). The software libraries and the data dictionary(ies) created during installation of IDMS/R were used for the initial test system and no user databases or applications had been developed yet. Other systems require their own libraries, dictionary(ies), databases, and applications.

System creation steps 4 through 8 were covered in detail in Chapter 9, Test System Creation. In this chapter, the discussion on all steps concentrates on special considerations for production systems.

10.2.1   Step 1:   Creating Separate Software Libraries

Separate libraries for IDMS/R system software, user applications, and DBA modules, including database procedures, user exits, global DMCL's, local DMCL's, subschemas, and WTOEXIT should be maintained for the production system. A release of IDMS/R different from the release executing on the production system may be executing on the test or QA system. Also, different copies of WTOEXIT, DC user exits, or Database procedures may be used in the test system. Finally, separate libraries must be maintained if the test and production dictionaries are not identical in number, size, and page ranges because the network subschemas are different. Separate libraries can be created and modules copied from one library to another using operating system utilities.

10.2.2   Step 2:   Creating a Separate Data Dictionary

The single DD usually created for a production system should be at least as large as the primary DD on the QA/AT and test systems, because the production DD will eventually house all applications now

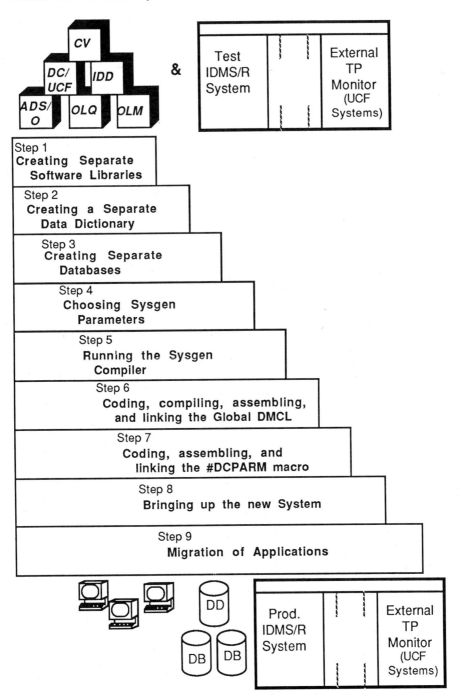

Figure 10-1 Steps to Create a Production System

under development. Movement of applications and recovery may be easier if the production DD areas have exactly the same page ranges and sizes as the QA/AT DD areas. For example, in the event of a production problem the production DD may be restored to the QA/AT or test DD, where problem investigation and resolution may take place quickly and easily.

Migration of the pilot application into production is relatively simple if production DD areas are equal in page ranges and page sizes to the QA/AT or test DD, as well as schema and subschema names being identical in all systems (Section 10.2.3). Allocate new files the same size as the QA/AT DD files using operating system utilities and then copy the contents of the QA/AT files to the new files, thus accomplishing the initial migration of application dictionary entities. Subsequent application migrations, or reinstallation of the system software due to software updates, requires use of migration utilities and Cullinet compilers. When using the technique of a production dictionary equal in size to the primary DD of QA and test systems, it may be preferable to remove demonstration information from the QA and production primary dictionaries and maintain all demonstration information left over from an initial installation on only a secondary test dictionary.

The alternative to defining a dictionary equal in size to the test primary DD is setting up and initializing a production DD with different page ranges and sizes. The new dictionary is created by modifying the standard installation job stream provided by Cullinet. This is accomplished by modifying the IJMP installation parameters (Chapter 8) and specifying dataset names, page sizes, and page ranges for the new DD areas. The installation steps required include only JJOB1, the last job stage from JJOB2, including the IDMSBASE assembly and creation of the network subschemas, and everything from JJOB3 except the ASF job stages, unless ASF is being set up in production. JJOB1 allocates all files, JJOB2 populates libraries, JJOB3 actually populates the primary dictionary. JJOB4 and JJOB5 are not necessary when creating a production data dictionary because these job steps merely install the demonstrations. Refer to Cullinet's Integrated Installation Guide for further information about these job stages.

10.2.3   Step 3: Creating Separate Databases

Separate databases must be created for the new system. Often production databases are much larger than test databases, so simply copying test database schemas, subschemas, and DMCL's is not a viable method of creating a production database. One method to create a production database with the same structure but different page ranges than the test database is:

1. Punching the test schema, modifying page sizes and ranges as necessary, identifying the production database files, and compiling it into the production DD for the new production schema.
2. Punching test subschemas and compiling them into the production DD.
3. Modifying the production global DMCL to include the production databases. Creating local DMCL's.
4. Allocating production DB files using operating system utilities.
5. Initializing production DB files using the IDMSINIT utility.
6. Loading the DB files using load programs or the utilities IDMSDBLU and IDMSTBLU.

A decision must be made on whether test and production schemas/subschemas are to have identical names. Separate subschema and schema names for test and production databases are difficult to maintain. Subschema and schema names are hard-coded in IDMS/R application programs and dialogs. Changing subschema and schema names between test and production forces changes to programs and dialogs when migrating from test to acceptance test to production. Changing subschema and schema names may force a recompile of programs and does force regeneration of dialogs during migration. Some sites prefer to opt for separate names for test and production databases and to recompile programs and regenerate dialogs as part of their migration procedures. Alternatively, identical names can be used for test and production databases; then programs need not be recompiled and dialogs need not be regenerated.

Database Name Tables (DBNT's) may be used to minimize the work involved in maintaining separate names for test and production databases because programs need not be recompiled. Batch programs, DC programs, and external TP monitor programs containing embedded DML statements (such as CICS-IDMS programs) can access either the test database or the production database by coding a single BIND RUN-UNIT DBNAME *dbnt-name* statement. The same dbnt-name identifies a different subschema on the test system than on the production system. The test system DBNT maps the program's subschema to the test database, whereas the production system DBNT maps the program's subschema to the production database. DBNT's may be used with ADS/O dialogs by setting the DBNAME using the DCUF task code or by typing DBNAME=dbnt-name when invoking the dialog. DD report information relating programs to subschemas will not reflect the subschemas actually used at run time if DBNT's are used frequently.

10.2.4 Step 4: Choosing System Generation Parameters

The parameter values chosen for production systems depends on information gathered in the QA/AT system or in the test system if a QA/AT system is not available. In addition, estimates of how often individual tasks and programs will be run in the production system is an important factor in choosing several parameter value. Some investigation of the following parameters is advisable prior to choosing production system values. The values suggested assume that ASF will not run in the production system. Appendix A contains sample system generation statements.

System Identification

Assigning different *CVNUMBERs* and *system version numbers* for test, QA/AT, and production systems helps eliminate confusion when multiple systems are executing concurrently. Both CVNUMBER and system version number are included in system messages sent to the CPU operator's console in Release 5.7, only the system number appears in Release 10 console messages. Consider adopting a documented policy of numbering, similar to the examples shown in Table 10-2, to make it clear which system one is dealing with. Two IDMS/R systems cannot be brought up on one CPU with the same CVNUMBER (or the same system version number, as of this writing) regardless of the numbering convention followed. The second CV will fail.

Table 10-2 System and CVNUMBER

System	System Version Numbers	CVNUMBER
Example 1:		
Test	1 to 9	0
QA/AT	10 to 19	1
Production	100 to 109	2
Example 2:		
Test	1, 10, 100, 1000	1
QA/AT	2, 20, 200, 2000	2
Production A	3, 30, 300, 3000	3
Production B	4, 40, 400, 4000	4

Major System Functionality and Internal Tables

MAXIMUM ERUS and *MAXIMUM TASKS* parameter values determine the number of run units and tasks which may process concurrently. MAXIMUM ERUS and MAXIMUM TASKS values should be based on expected system activity levels for external and internal units of work. If stress testing, or loading the system, was carried out on the QA/AT system, the system shutdown statistic "n TIMES AT MAX TASK" (Figure 10-2) may be checked to see if MAXIMUM TASKS should be increased from the QA/AT value. MAXIMUM ERUS should be increased from the QA/AT value if external run units abended during stress testing with '1473' ERROR-STATUS codes.

RCE/RLE/DPE COUNTs may be determined by taking into consideration the number of buffer pool pages in the new system and by examining average and/or maximum usage of RCE, RLE, and DPE entries in the QA/AT system. One RCE and RLE must be added to the total count for each buffer pool page. The average use of RCE entries may be calculated from information obtained using the OPER W LTERM command (Release 10 only). The OPER W LTERM command displays information about system resources used by online programs or dialogs executing for another terminal. The number of RCE entries used by individual programs and dialogs may be obtained by executing the OPER W LTERM command from one terminal while a user at another terminal executes each online program or dialog. OPER W LTERM can be used to determine lock usage, storage usage, and program sizes as well (Figure 10-3). Maximum RCE, RLE, and DPE usage statistics may be obtained from the QA/AT system by checking system shutdown statistics, Figure 10-2, "n MAX # DPES USED", "n OVER DPE THRESH" (Release 10), "n MAX # RLES USED", "n OVER RLE THRESH" (Release 10), "n MAX # RCES USED", "n OVER RLE THRESH" (Release 10).

The *STACKSIZE* parameter may be determined from stress testing the applications on the QA/AT system. The high water mark for number of stack entries used may be seen in the system shutdown statistic "n STK HI WATER MARK" (Figure 10-2) or using the DCMT DISPLAY STATISTICS SYSTEM command (Figure 10-4). Other useful statistics are also shown in Figure 10-4. If the high water mark is approaching STACKSIZE, the parameter value should be increased in the production system generation.

Storage Pool

The value chosen for the *STORAGE POOL* parameter is based on the maximum concurrent storage pool needs of production programs. The combined storage usages of all programs processing concurrently should be determined from statistics gathered on the QA/AT

```
IDMS-DB/DC      PRINT LOG UTILITY        IDMS-DB/DC IS A PROPRIETARY SOFTWARE PRODUCT      DATE            TIME    PAGE
C8509M          RELEASE 10.0                     LICENSED FROM CULLINET SOFTWARE           02/11/86 (86042)  193526    11

86042 19.34.46   IDMS DC260001 V2 SHUTDOWN COMMAND FROM LTE: UCFLT15 USER: DBBG1
86042 19.34.46   IDMS-DC IS BEING QUIESCED
86042 19.34.46   IDMS DC201002 V2 T1 IDMS CENTRAL VERSION 1 QUIESCING
86042 19.34.46   IDMS DC201007 V2 T1 IDMS CENTRAL VERSION 1 QUIESCED
86042 19.34.46   IDMS DC259001 V2 USER DBBG1 SIGNED OFF LTERM UCFLT15 AT 19:34:46.89 86.042
86042 19.34.47   IDMS DC089001 V2 TERMINAL LINE UCFLINE HAS BEEN CLOSED
86042 19.34.47   SYSTEM STATISTICS
```

0 PUT JOURNALS	2 PGMPOOL LOADS	0 PGMPOOL WAITS	28 PAGES IN PGMPOOL
130 GET QUEUES	73 PUT QUEUES	48 DELETE QUEUES	0 AUGSTART TASKS
1,214 GET SCRATCHES	779 PUT SCRATCHES	478 DELETE SCRATCHES	8,442 GET STORAGES
1,867 GET STORAGES	6,576 PASS 1 STG REQS	1,367 PASS 2 STG REQS	499 GETSTORAGES
773 SET TIME CANCELS	388 SET TIME REQS	.000 SET TIME POSTS	13 PASS 3 STG REQS
9,526 PAGES READ	340 TOTAL TIME WAITS	81,000 TIME IN USER MODE	2.15.6848 SET TIME SRTASKS
6 CALC RECS OFLOW	100 PAGES WRITTEN		TIME IN SYS MODE
63,587 RECORDS CURRENT	99 VIA RECS NO OFLOW	0 VIA RECS OFLOW	31 CALC RECS NO OFLOH
2 RUNAWY ABENDTD	77,079 DATA BASE REQS	0 FRAGMENTS STORED	102,630 RECORDS REQUESTED
104 TOTAL PGFREE REQS	104 TOTAL SYS TASKS	2 TOTAL TASKS ACTIVE	0 RECORDS RELOCATED
2,621 PAGES IN RRENTPOOL	0 PAGE RELEASE=0GFREED	124 SHORT ON STORAGE	345 TIMES AT MAX TASK
0 OVER RCE THRESH	0 OVER DPE THRESH	532 PAGES RELEASED	0 STK HI WATER MARK
55 MAX # DPES USED	0 COUNT OF PGFIX RQS	0 TOTAL PAGES PGFIXED	428 MAX # RCES USED
			0 OVER RLE THRESH

```
86042 19.34.47   HISTOGRAM OF TOTAL GET STORAGE SIZE
```

GETSTG SIZE	AMOUNT	GETSTG SIZE	AMOUNT	GETSTG SIZE	AMOUNT
LT NEXT ENTRY	6,987	6,000	57	10,000	119
14,000		18,000	52	26,000	
30,000	1	34,000		42,000	
46,000		50,000		54,000	657
62,000		66,000		70,000	
78,000		GT LAST ENTRY			

(AMOUNT 49)

```
86042 19.34.47   HISTOGRAM OF USER STORAGE SIZE
```

USR STG SIZE	AMOUNT	USR STG SIZE	AMOUNT	USR STG SIZE	AMOUNT
LT NEXT ENTRY	3,236	2,000	184	4,000	196
8,000		10,000	126	20,000	1
16,000		18,000	52	22,000	
24,000		26,000		28,000	
32,000		36,000		30,000	
40,000		GT LAST ENTRY		38,000	

```
86042 19.34.47   HISTOGRAM OF SCRATCH RECORD SIZES
```

SCRATCH SIZE	AMOUNT	SCRATCH SIZE	AMOUNT	SCRATCH SIZE	AMOUNT
LT NEXT ENTRY		200		300	
100		600		700	
900		1,000		GT LAST ENTRY	

```
86042 19.34.47   HISTOGRAM OF QUEUE RECORD SIZES
```

Figure 10-2 Sample Shutdown Statistics

IDMS-DB/DC   PRINT LOG UTILITY
CB509M   RELEASE 10.0

IDMS-DB/DC IS A PROPRIETARY SOFTWARE PRODUCT
LICENSED FROM CULLINET SOFTWARE

DATE 02/11/86 (86042)   TIME 193526   PAGE 12

QUEUE SIZE	AMOUNT	QUEUE SIZE	AMOUNT	QUEUE SIZE	AMOUNT
100	13	200	18	300	0
500	20	600	0	700	0
900	0	1,000	0		

LT NEXT ENTRY 400   GT LAST ENTRY

HISTOGRAM OF PROGRAM SIZES

PROGRAM SIZE	AMOUNT	PROGRAM SIZE	AMOUNT	PROGRAM SIZE	AMOUNT
4,000	528	8,000	244	12,000	240
20,000	36	24,000	53	28,000	168
36,000	30	40,000	11	44,000	0
52,000	30	56,000	0	60,000	0
68,000	0	72,000	0	76,000	0
84,000	0	88,000	0	92,000	0
100,000	0	104,000	0	108,000	0
116,000	0	120,000	0	124,000	0
132,000	0	136,000	0	140,000	0
148,000	0	152,000	0	156,000	0

GT LAST ENTRY 730   GT LAST ENTRY

HISTOGRAM OF RECORD SIZES WRITTEN TO JOURNAL

JRNL SIZE	AMOUNT	JRNL SIZE	AMOUNT	JRNL SIZE	AMOUNT
100	0	200	0	300	0
500	0	600	0	700	0
900	0	1,000	0		

LT NEXT ENTRY 400   GT LAST ENTRY

86042 19.34.47 STATISTICS FOR TASKCODE ADS   TIMES INVOKED: 6
86042 19.34.47 STATISTICS FOR TASKCODE ADS2   TIMES INVOKED: 67
86042 19.34.47 STATISTICS FOR TASKCODE BYE   TIMES INVOKED: 15
86042 19.34.47 STATISTICS FOR TASKCODE CLOD   TIMES INVOKED: 1
86042 19.34.47 STATISTICS FOR TASKCODE DCMT   TIMES INVOKED: 12
86042 19.34.47 STATISTICS FOR TASKCODE DCUF   TIMES INVOKED: 15
86042 19.34.47 STATISTICS FOR TASKCODE IDD   TIMES INVOKED: 38
86042 19.34.47 STATISTICS FOR TASKCODE OLQ   TIMES INVOKED: 24
86042 19.34.47 STATISTICS FOR TASKCODE QUED   TIMES INVOKED: 1
86042 19.34.47 STATISTICS FOR TASKCODE SCHEMA TIMES INVOKED: 14
86042 19.34.48 STATISTICS FOR TASKCODE SETTIME TIMES INVOKED: 27
86042 19.34.48 STATISTICS FOR TASKCODE SIGHOFF TIMES INVOKED: 1
86042 19.34.48 STATISTICS FOR TASKCODE SIGNON TIMES INVOKED: 15
86042 19.34.48 STATISTICS FOR PROGRAM ADSODBUG
   2 TIMES CALLED   2 TIMES LOADED   0 WAITED TO LOAD   0 TIMES PROG CHECK

Figure 10-2 Sample Shutdown Statistics (continued)

```
IDMS-DB/DC      PRINT LOG UTILITY        IDMS-DB/DC IS A PROPRIETARY SOFTWARE PRODUCT        DATE       TIME   PAGE
C8509M          RELEASE 10.0             LICENSED FROM CULLINET SOFTWARE                      02/11/86 (86042)  193526   13

86042 19.34.48  STATISTICS FOR PROGRAM ADSOGEN1
       0 TIMES CALLED              1 TIMES LOADED        0 WAITED TO LOAD        0 TIMES PROG CHECK
86042 19.34.48  STATISTICS FOR PROGRAM ADSOGEN2
       0 TIMES CALLED              1 TIMES LOADED        0 WAITED TO LOAD        0 TIMES PROG CHECK
86042 19.34.48  STATISTICS FOR PROGRAM ADSOMAIN
      73 TIMES CALLED              1 TIMES LOADED        0 WAITED TO LOAD        0 TIMES PROG CHECK
86042 19.34.48  STATISTICS FOR PROGRAM ADSOMBG1
       2 TIMES CALLED              2 TIMES LOADED        0 WAITED TO LOAD        0 TIMES PROG CHECK
86042 19.34.49  STATISTICS FOR PROGRAM ADSORUN1
       6 TIMES CALLED              2 TIMES LOADED        0 WAITED TO LOAD        0 TIMES PROG CHECK
86042 19.34.50  STATISTICS FOR PROGRAM CISDNHKA
      19 TIMES CALLED              1 TIMES LOADED        0 WAITED TO LOAD        0 TIMES PROG CHECK
86042 19.34.50  STATISTICS FOR PROGRAM COMDNHKA
      55 TIMES CALLED              1 TIMES LOADED        0 WAITED TO LOAD        0 TIMES PROG CHECK
86042 19.34.50  STATISTICS FOR PROGRAM DBADNHKA
       1 TIMES CALLED              1 TIMES LOADED        0 WAITED TO LOAD        0 TIMES PROG CHECK
86042 19.34.50  STATISTICS FOR PROGRAM DB000P
      14 TIMES CALLED              1 TIMES LOADED        0 WAITED TO LOAD        0 TIMES PROG CHECK
86042 19.34.50  STATISTICS FOR PROGRAM DB000P1
       1 TIMES CALLED              1 TIMES LOADED        0 WAITED TO LOAD        0 TIMES PROG CHECK
86042 19.34.50  STATISTICS FOR PROGRAM FTSDNHKA
       1 TIMES CALLED              1 TIMES LOADED        0 WAITED TO LOAD        0 TIMES PROG CHECK
86042 19.34.56  STATISTICS FOR PROGRAM IDDSCIDD
      25 TIMES CALLED              1 TIMES LOADED        0 WAITED TO LOAD        0 TIMES PROG CHECK
86042 19.34.56  STATISTICS FOR PROGRAM IDDSMAIN
      25 TIMES CALLED              1 TIMES LOADED        0 WAITED TO LOAD        0 TIMES PROG CHECK
86042 19.34.56  STATISTICS FOR PROGRAM IDDSMAP
      92 TIMES CALLED              1 TIMES LOADED        0 WAITED TO LOAD        0 TIMES PROG CHECK
86042 19.34.56  STATISTICS FOR PROGRAM IDDSMDBC
      19 TIMES CALLED              1 TIMES LOADED        0 WAITED TO LOAD        0 TIMES PROG CHECK
86042 19.34.56  STATISTICS FOR PROGRAM IDDSMELM
      16 TIMES CALLED              2 TIMES LOADED        0 WAITED TO LOAD        0 TIMES PROG CHECK
86042 19.34.56  STATISTICS FOR PROGRAM IDDSMERR
       9 TIMES CALLED              1 TIMES LOADED        0 WAITED TO LOAD        0 TIMES PROG CHECK
86042 19.34.56  STATISTICS FOR PROGRAM IDDSMGEN
      25 TIMES CALLED              1 TIMES LOADED        0 WAITED TO LOAD        0 TIMES PROG CHECK
```

Figure 10-2 Sample Shutdown Statistics (continued)

```
IDMS DB/DC V1          TASKS ACTIVE: 7              TIME: 14:06:49

  IDMS-DC RELEASE 10.0        LTERM RESOURCE USAGE DISPLAY

                                            PGM    DB       DB LOCKS
LTERM ID   USER ID  TASK CODE  TASK ID  STG SPACE  RUS  S/P/X NOTIFY RCES
BTAMLT02   CTH      OLM        641      30K 20K    0    10    0      22
BTAMLT01   DBA      OPER       637      5K  19K    0    0     0      7
CONSOLE             +IDLE+     0        OK  OK     0    0     0      0
BTAMLTFR            +IDLE+     0        OK  OK     0    0     0      0
```

Figure 10-3 Sample Output from the OPER WATCH LTERM Command

```
       DIS STA SYS
14:23:41.78 86/087 CURRENT TIME        00:00:00.00 TOT SYS TIME
09:43:54.41 86/087 STARTUP TIME        00:00:00.00 TOT USER TIME

TASKS:      801 PROCESSED         0 ABENDED          11 MAX TASKS
            192 SYSTEM            0 RUNAWAY           0 TIMES AT MAX

RUN/UNITS:  309 PROCESSED       297 NORM CMP          9 MAX CONC
              9 EXT PROC          9 EXT NORM          1 EXT CONC     3 MAX ERUS

DATABASE: 86457 CALLS        115343 PAGES RQST    145179 RECS REQUESTED
              0 BUFF WAIT      9092 PAGES READ     68134 RECS CUR R/U
           1684 PAGE WRIT        66 CALC NOFLO      2358 VIA NOFLO
                                  1 CALC OVFLO       637 VIA OVFLO
                                  7 FRAG STORD         0 RECS RELOC

JOURNAL:
PAGE        885   2 BUFF WAITS       0 USER PUTJRNL
                 0-10  18 11-20     10 31-40    16 41-50
DIST         29  51-60  27 61-70    19 81-90  1671 91-100
                 17 21-30  16 71-80

INTERNAL:
         RLES 496   RCES 369   DPES 45    STACK 417 HWM
              800        800        800        1000 SYSGEN THRESHOLD
PAGE 001 - NEXT PAGE:?   0         TIMES EXCEEDED

STORAGE:  16483 GETS       16272 FREES           0 TIMES SOS
              0 PGFIXS          0 PGFREES
              0 PAGES FXD       0 PAGES FREED     0 TIMES SOS
          12910 SCAN 1       3288 PGRLSES
           2562 SCAN 2       5752 PAGES RELSD
           1011 SCAN 3

PROGRAM:
NON-REENT     0 ACT LOADS       0 PAGES LOAD       0 WAIT/SPACE
REENT       176              4356                  0

SCRATCH:   3197 GETS        1715 PUTS            645 DELS
QUEUE:      395 GETS         149 PUTS            127 DELS

TIME:      3574 GETS        1030 POST              0 STARTED TASKS
              0 WAIT        1867 CANC              0 TASK AUTOST
```

Figure 10-4 Sample Output from the DCMT DISPLAY STATISTICS SYSTEM Command

system during system testing. The DCMT DIS ACT STORAGE command displays the high water mark for storage pool usage during that particular test (Figure 10-5) if system tests were run to determine storage usage. Make an estimate based on individual program averages and the expected mix of production processing if system test statistics are unavailable.

Data on storage pool usage per program or dialog may be obtained from transaction statistics (STORAGE HI-WATER MAR) on for the QA/AT system. Alternatively, storage use for individual ADS and IDMS-DC tasks may be obtained using the OPER W LTERM command under Release 10 (Figure 10-3). The amount of storage held

```
DIS ACT STO
        POOL NUMBER:            0
           LOCATION:        24-BIT
     CONTAINS TYPES:          ALL
           PAGE FIX:           NO
       SIZE OF POOL:        1016K
     SIZE OF CUSHION:         20K
CURRENT ALLOCATIONS:
        PAGES IN USE:        608K    60% OF POOL
           LONG TERM:        604K    99% OF PAGES IN USE
          SHORT TERM:          4K     1% OF PAGES IN USE
  HIGH WATER MARKS:
          PAGES USED:        768K    76% OF POOL
           LONG TERM:        724K    71% OF POOL
          SHORT TERM:         48K     5% OF POOL

          TIMES SOS:           0

     GETSTG REQUESTS:       15887
COMPLETED IN SCAN #1:       12440    78% OF REQUESTS
COMPLETED IN SCAN #2:        2483    16% OF REQUESTS
COMPLETED IN SCAN #3:         964     6% OF REQUESTS

    FREESTG REQUESTS:       15677
         PAGES FIXED:           0
       PGFIX REQUESTS:          0
         PAGES FREED:           0
      PGFREE REQUESTS:          0
      PAGES RELEASED:        5549
       PGRLSE REQUESTS:       3166
```

Figure 10-5 Sample Output from the DCMT DISPLAY ACTIVE STORAGE
Command

across a pseudo-converse can be obtained using the DCMT DISPLAY LTERM RESOURCES command. The average storage usage of an individual program, batch or online (ADS/O, IDMS-DC, or CICS), should be calculated based on the results of several tests.

The system shutdown statistic "n SHORT ON STORAGE" (Figure 10-2) indicates the number of times overall storage was insufficient during the system's processing. Check the log on the QA/AT system to determine the time periods when the SHORT ON STORAGE conditions occurred if the figure is greater than zero. Then consult task and transaction statistics to determine the storage usages of tasks processing during those time periods.

Program Loading Considerations

NOBLDL is recommended for production systems. Specifying NOBLDL expedites restart processing in the event of a system crash. See Chapter 9 for details.

Program Pools: Reentrant, regular, and resident program pool sizes may be determined based on program sizes and frequencies of use obtained during QA/AT testing. Load module sizes may be obtained from DDR reports and link edit maps. The DDR report CREPORT050 reports on IDMS/R load area modules (dialogs, tables, maps, and subschemas). Batch, CICS and IDMS-DC programs sizes may be obtained from their linkage editor maps. If a program has been loaded sometime during the execution of the QA/AT system, a DCMT DISPLAY PROGRAM *program-name* command also shows the size of the program. CREPORT050 should be included in an application turnover for all modules used in an application, as well as estimated frequency of use information.

Consult the system shutdown statistics (Figure 10-2) from the QA/AT system following system testing to determine how often a particular program was used during one system execution. The number of times a program has executed during a run of the QA/AT system to date may be obtained using the DCMT DISPLAY PROGRAM command online. The expected frequency of use of programs and dialogs in the production system can be estimated from testing in the QA/AT system. In addition, frequency of use estimates should be requested of the applications development group when any online or batch program is turned over for production implementation.

Which programs should be made resident: Only large, frequently-used dialogs, IDMS-DC programs, and DB procedures should be considered for residency in production systems. Virtually all Cullinet programs may be removed from the residency list in production systems, with the exception of ADSOMAIN and ADSOMENU when ADS/O dialogs are in use. Network subschemas may also be removed from the residency list, with the exception of IDMSNWKS which is used by RHDCRUAL run units. RHDCRUAL run units perform housekeeping functions for certain types of dictionary access (Chapter 9 discusses RUNUNITS FOR QUEUE/LOADER/etc.). The programs listed under OLQ in Table 10-3 might also be made resident if OLQ is used heavily in production.

Table 10-3 System Programs Suggested for Residency

Situation	Resident in a Test System	Resident in a Production System
Network Subschemas	IDMSNWKA	IDMSNWKS
OLQ Heavily Used	OLQSGCAN OLQSPARS OLQSDCAN IDMSOLQS IDMSNWKQ(*)	OLQSGCAN OLQSPARS OLQSDCAN IDMSOLQS IDMSNWKQ(*)
Record Compression and Decompression in Use	IDMSCOMP IDMSDCOM	IDMSCOMP IDMSDCOM
Online IDD in Use	IDMSDDDC IDDSMAIN IDDSMGEN IDDSCIDD IDDSMUTL	
Online Mapping Generator in Use	RHDCOMGP RHDCOMTC RHDCOMM1 IDMSNWKM(*)	
ADS/O in Use	ADSOGEN1 ADSOGEN2 ADSOMAIN ADSOMENU IDMSNWKO(*)	ADSOMAIN ADSOMENU(**)

*If network subschemas are not all mapped to IDMSNWKA.
**If the ADS run-time menu of dialogs is used.

Some installations include all programs in the sysgen and turn off *UNDEFINED PROGRAM COUNT* for security reasons. This technique is used to prevent database access by new or changed programs (Chapters 6 and 9 contain further details). The disadvantage of this method is that the Program Definition Table becomes enormous over time, potentially slowing the process of locating and setting up the next program to execute.

An alternative security technique to prevent database access by new or changed programs involves having all production programs migrated by a QA group and restricting access to Cullinet's application development software. Limiting access to the libraries and dictionaries which contain production programs and dialogs to only the QA group when coupled with restricting access to application development software, insures that nothing could be created or changed that has not been properly turned over to the QA group. When this technique is used, consider leaving out of the sysgen those dialogs, subschemas, maps, and tables that are used infrequently and specifying a small UNDEFINED PROGRAM COUNT, for example (23,23). The result would be a smaller Program Definition Table, permitting faster searches for programs which are used frequently. Maximum benefits are achieved when only frequently-used online programs, and subschemas used frequently by online applications in CICS-IDMS systems, are put in the sysgen.

Specifying a small UNDEFINED PROGRAM COUNT creates a pool of null Program Definition Elements (PDE's) which may be tapped by the infrequently-used programs left out of the sysgen. IDMS/R allocates PDE's automatically for dialogs, maps, subschemas, and tables not included in the sysgen if UNDEFINED PROGRAM COUNT has not been turned off. However, IDMS/R cannot allocate PDE's automatically for DC programs not included in the sysgen. DC programs not included in the sysgen must be defined manually by issuing DCMT VARY DYNAMIC PROGRAM *program-name* and DCMT VARY DYNAMIC TASK *task-code* commands during each run of the system in which they will be used.

IDMS/R uses a binary search in Release 10 to locate information on programs defined in the sysgen and a linear search is used to locate information on dynamically defined tasks and programs. Only linear searches are used in Release 5.7. Programs included in the sysgen should be ordered from the most frequently used to the least frequently used in a Release 5.7 system because of the different search techniques.

Twenty-three PDE entries fit on a single storage pool page without wasting or fragmenting space. Therefore the values chosen should be multiples of 23.

Timeout and Abend Detection Parameters
Timers in the production system usually are set approximately equal to their values in the test system, with the exceptions of *RESOURCE TIME OUT INTERVAL* and *RUNAWAY INTERVAL*. RESOURCE TIMEOUT INTERVAL should be either set extremely high or turned off. Terminal operators may take a very long time to enter data in production. If RESOURCE TIMEOUT INTERVAL is set too low,

IDMS/R aborts the task and the terminal operator is forced to sign on again and reenter all lost data. RESOURCE TIMEOUT INTERVAL may be overridden for individual programs, see Chapter 9 for details.

RUNAWAY INTERVAL should be set lower in the production system than in the test system because it is very important to trap looping dialogs or programs before other tasks have to wait long. Usually, 60 to 90 seconds is an appropriate value for RUNAWAY INTERVAL, depending on what QA/AT testing revealed. The system shutdown statistic "n RUNAWY TSKS ABRTD" (Figure 10-2) indicates the number of tasks that were aborted because the RUNAWAY INTERVAL timer expired before the task returned control to IDMS/R. If "n RUNAWY TSKS ABRTD" is greater than zero, consult the log to determine which programs were aborted and the time they "ran away".

Timers might be set artificially high in the test system if operating system performance is sluggish. IDMS/R checks timers from a wall clock perspective; if the operating system is sluggish, IDMS/R may not receive enough CPU cycles to do its processing, causing timers to expire without any real work being accomplished. If the production system runs on a mainframe separate from the test system, it would be valuable to investigate operating system conditions on the production machine before assigning values for the timers. Presumably, performance is better on the production machine, permitting timer values to be decreased.

The *CHKUSER TASKS* facility, available at OS sites only, allows the system to detect quickly batch DML program abends. Specify a number for CHKUSER TASKS equal to the maximum expected number of batch DML programs and Culprit programs processing concurrently under the production CV. Additional batch run units abend with a '0069' ERROR-STATUS code if too small a number is specified. The value of CHKUSER TASKS should be determined based on batch job scheduling estimates given by applications to operations at turnover time. Therefore, the DBA should receive a copy of batch run schedules as they pertain to IDMS/R jobs.

Limiting Resource Consumption (Release 10 only)

We recommend specifying *LIMITS FOR ONLINE/EXTERNAL TASKS* in production systems, with values chosen based on information from the QA/AT system. Resource consumption information for online tasks, IDMS-DC and ADS/O tasks, may be obtained from transaction statistics, OPER and DCMT task codes, or IDMS/R Performance Monitor reports and displays (also available only under Release 10). Resource consumption information for external tasks, both CICS and batch run units, may be obtained from JREPORTS and IDMS/R Performance Monitor reports and displays.

Although testing should have exposed most bugs, as well as revealing those programs with unusual resource requirements, it is still possible for problems to be uncovered in production that never appeared in testing. It is important to detect resource loop bugs quickly to prevent overall performance degradation due to lack of resources. Keep in mind, though, that often in testing phases only limited volume databases are being accessed as opposed to full-sized production databases. Resource limits should be extrapolated carefully for production systems, taking database size differences into account. Overrides may be specified in the sysgen for tasks and IDMS/R programs which have extreme resource requirements. In addition, limits for individual tasks and programs may be altered dynamically using DCMT commands.

One final note, CICS non-ADS shops may find it difficult to set reasonable limits for EXTERNAL run units because both batch and CICS run units are external run units. Limits appropriate for CICS programs probably are not appropriate for batch programs and vice versa. IDMS PROGRAM override statements may be necessary to overcome this problem. Refer to Chapter 9's discussion of limits for further details.

Locking

The values for *SYSLOCKS* and *RULOCKS* may be chosen based on statistical information from the QA/AT system. Lock use per application and over all may be obtained from transaction statistics or the JREPORTS on the QA/AT system as performance tests are done. The locks used by an individual program (ADS, batch, CICS, and IDMS-DC) may be obtained during program execution using the ACCEPT DB-STATISTICS FROM IDMS-STATISTICS statement. In addition, locks used by ADS dialogs and DC programs may be obtained online using the OPER W LTERM (Figure 10-3, Release 10 only) or using the DCMT DISPLAY RUN UNIT command (Figure 10-6). Locks used by batch DML programs and CICS-IDMS programs may be obtained online using the DCMT DISPLAY RUN UNIT command.

Journaling

Selecting *JOURNAL NORETRIEVAL* limits journaling to only update run units, minimizing journaling overhead. It is recommended unless chargeback information is required. *RUNUNITS FOR QUEUE/SCRATCH/etc.* may be set to one apiece unless heavy queue or scratch usage is foreseen. Three run units for queue and scratch should be adequate for heavy use.

```
    DIS RU 1002
IDMS DC200017 V1 T1   ---ID--   ORIG PROGRAM  SUBSCHEMA PRI STATUS
IDMS DC200019 V1 T1      1002 DBDC ADSOGEN1  IDMSNWKO 200 I H
IDMS DC200018 V1 T1   ------AREA------ MODE STATUS
IDMS DC200020 V1 T1   DDLDCLOD            SU    H..
IDMS DC200020 V1 T1   DDLDCMSG                  ...
IDMS DC200020 V1 T1   DDLDML              SU    H..
IDMS DC200021 V1 T1   PGS-READ:0     PGS-WRIT:0    PGS-RQSTD:1
IDMS DC200021 V1 T1   CALC-TARGT:0   CALC-OFLOW:0  VIA-TARGET:0
IDMS DC200021 V1 T1   VIA-OFLOW:0    LINS-RQSTD:1  RECS-CUR:0
IDMS DC200021 V1 T1   IDMS-CALLS:30  FRGS-STORD:0  RECS-RELOC:0
IDMS DC200021 V1 T1   RQSTD-LCKS:1   SHRD-HELD:1   EXCL-HELD:0
ENTER NEXT TASK CODE:
```

Figure 10-6 Sample Output from the DCMT DISPLAY RUN UNIT Command

Debugging Considerations
All the parameters affecting debugging facilities are usually turned off in production systems by specifying *ABRU NOSNAP, USERTRACE OFF*, and *SYSTRACE OFF*. Debugging facilities may be turned off to save storage and processing overhead in the production system. There should be no surprises in production.

Logging
We recommend specifying *LOG DATABASE* for production systems. Otherwise, valuable tuning statistics on the log are inaccessible.

ADSO Statement Parameters
The *ADSO* statement may be used to determine whether dialog resources are saved in the storage pool during a pseudo-converse, the time period between display of a map and the operator's subsequent response. We recommend saving all dialog resources in the storage pool, rather than forcing the resources to be saved on disk, to achieve the best possible response time for dialogs executing in the production system. Specifying FAST MODE THRESHOLD IS OFF as well as RESOURCES ARE FIXED clauses of the ADSO statement requests saving resources in the storage pool.

It may be necessary to specify FAST MODE THRESHOLD to force the larger-sized dialog resources to disk if main storage for the storage pool is extremely limited, thereby saving space in the storage pool. If FAST MODE THRESHOLD must be employed, an appropriate value may be chosen based on the average and worst cases of storage use revealed during testing on the QA/AT system. Programming corrections, such as application-specific work records or dialog-specific subschemas containing only the records necessary for a given function, can be made to ADS/O dialogs which consume large amounts of storage, bringing their storage consumption in line with site standards. Lowering the permissible number of dialog levels from ten (the default value) to three by specifying MAXIMUM LINKS IS 3 also helps conserve storage.

10.2.5   Step 5: Running the Sysgen Compiler

The system is initially generated by running the sysgen compiler in local mode to store the production system definition in the production DD. After the system is up and running any changes, e.g., to add new programs and tasks, may be accomplished by running the sysgen compiler (online or batch) under Central Version. As a rule, production system modifications are made during off hours, either after all online and batch processing is done for the day or on weekends.

10.2.6 Step 6: Coding, Compiling, Assembling, and Linking the Global DMCL

A separate global DMCL, with a name different than the test system's DMCL, should be maintained for the production system, for example TESTDMCL and PRODDMCL. A separate global DMCL must be defined for production because production databases are often a different size than test databases. The production global DMCL copies area information from production schemas.

Buffer pools required in the production environment often differ in size from those used in the test system. Production databases tend to be larger and accessed more frequently than test databases and therefore require larger buffer pools. Dictionaries tend to be accessed less frequently in a production than in a test system and no longer require the extra buffer pool pages allocated for the test system.

Buffer pool sizes for application databases may be determined based on performance testing in the Acceptance or QA testing phase of development. Statistics on file usage can be gathered through operating system utilities or by writing a DBIO exit to capture statistics during system testing. Alternatively, DB statistics information could be obtained by dialogs/programs issuing ACCEPT DB-STATISTICS FROM IDMS-STATISTICS statements or from transaction statistics or JREPORTS.

In the test system, 30-40 buffers should be assigned to the DDLDML area and 15-20 buffers to the DDLDCRUN area because the IDMS/R system components make extremely heavy use of these areas during testing. The DDLDML area is almost never accessed in a production system, with the exception of signing on users, and as a result no longer needs as many buffers. Six buffers are usually ample.

The DDLDCRUN, DDLDCQUE, and DDLDCSCR areas are used to save control information when dialog execution is suspended while the ADS/O run time system is operating in relocatable mode. In addition, these areas are used by ADS/O dialogs or IDMS-DC programs for storage of application-maintained scratch records, queue records, and pagable maps. If the ADS/O run time system is run in fixed mode and scratch records, queue records, and pagable maps are used infrequently, then these areas do not need as many buffers in production; six pages for each area should be adequate. Double these figures for the DDLDCQUE and DDLDCRUN areas if queues are heavily used.

Journaling for the production system is controlled by choices made in the global DMCL. Refer to Chapters 7 and 9 for details on choosing number and size of disk journal files.

10.2.7 Step 7: Coding, Assembling, and Linking the #DCPARM Macro

A separate #DCPARM macro is coded for the production system. #DCPARM parameter values may be identical to the test system's values, with the exception of the global DMCL name. The #DCPARM macro must be assembled and link edited into the production core image library for DOS shops and included in the operating system dependent routine for OS shops.

10.2.8 Step 8: Bringing up the New System

Separate names are recommended for the execution time IDMS/R jobs, for example IDMSTEST and IDMSPROD. Separate names help clarify which jobs are which when multiple systems are running concurrently. Assigning different CV numbers and system version numbers for test, QA/AT, and production systems also helps eliminate confusion. Different CV numbers are required if the systems are to execute concurrently on one CPU, otherwise the second CV will abend. In addition, we recommend that separate names be chosen for production and test system journal archive jobs, as well as log offload jobs. Table 10-4 lists some sample job names.

Table 10-4 Job Name Examples

Job Type	Production Job Name	Test Job Name
IDMS/R System Execution	IDMSPROD	IDMSTEST
Journal Archiving	DBPAJNL1	DBTAJNL1
Log Offloading	DBPPLOG1	DBTPLOG1

10.2.9 Step 9: Migration of Production Applications

Migration of online IDMS-DC programs from test to QA/AT to production is accomplished, in part, by including DC load modules in a load or core image library referenced in the execution JCL of the production system. It is also necessary to include PROGRAM and TASK statements in the production sysgen to complete the migration. Many installations have a separate group responsible for production load or core image libraries for security reasons, perhaps QA personnel.

Most migration of the pilot application is taken care of during the first three system creation steps. IDMS-DC programs are transferred by copying their load modules to the load or core image library accessed by the run time production system in step 1. ADS/O dialogs, maps used by dialogs or DC programs, work records, database records, and many other pilot application entities are transferred in step 2, if the production DD is created by copying the QA/AT dictionary. Migration of the pilot database is accomplished in step 3. The remainder of the migration takes place during the system generation when PROGRAM and TASK statements are included to identify online transactions.

Dictionary entities such as maps, dialogs, etc., must be copied from the QA/AT dictionary to the production dictionary if the production DD was created by modifying the installation job stream. Copying the entities may be accomplished by coding DDDL PUNCH statements and decompiling maps to generate DDDL syntax for each QA/AT entity to be moved, followed by adding the punched entities to the production DD and regenerating dialogs, maps, and tables. Alternatively, a migration utility, developed in-house (Chapter 3) or purchased, may be used to simplify the dictionary entity migration process.

Migration of applications is an ongoing process not limited to the pilot application. New applications must also be moved into the production system as they are developed. Operating system utilities may be used to copy source and load modules from the QA/AT libraries into the production libraries. The Cullinet compilers may be used to copy dictionary entities, namely maps, dialogs, modules, records, elements, tables, messages, load modules, schemas, subschemas, users, and so on from the QA/AT dictionary to the production dictionary.

10.3   CONCLUSION

In this chapter we discussed differences between production and test systems. Production and test systems differ in the characteristics of their databases, data dictionaries, user applications, and system development software. Performance, security, backup, and recovery requirements are more crucial in production systems. Table 10-1 contains a summary of differences between production and test systems.

We also covered the steps required to create a production system. Nine steps are necessary to create a production system. First, separate libraries are created for system, application, and DBA software. Second, a separate data dictionary for the production system is created. Separate databases for use by the production system also are created. System generation parameter values for the production system are chosen, usually based upon information gathered on a Quality Assurance or Acceptance Testing (QA/AT) system. Next the system generation compiler is run to store the new system definition in the production dictionary. The new production system is ready to bring up after a global DMCL and DCPARM module are created for production use. Finally, the new applications are moved into the production system.

Although a production system can be created directly from a test system, the application-oriented nature of the production system processing would cause this to be a poorly defined environment. As a general rule, production systems should be constructed based on data gathered through extensive testing on quality assurance or acceptance testing systems. The outputs from performance tests, namely JREPORTS, CREPORTS, transaction statistics, system shutdown statistics, online monitoring of specific activity using OPER and DCMT commands, and IDMS/R Performance Monitor constitute the inputs for determining production system parameter values. The technique of using QA/AT system statistics and reports to determine appropriate parameter values applies to creation of the initial production system and to major production system changes caused by implementation of new applications.

Suggestions for Further Reading on Production System Creation:

The following Cullinet manuals
   For Release 10 systems:
      1) System Generation Guide (System generation parameters, system generation compiler)
      2) System Operations Guide (#DCPARM macro, bringing up the new system, statistics, DCMT command)
      3) IDMS/R DDL Reference (creating separate databases, defining the global DMCL)
      4) IDMS/R Database Operations (creating a separate Data Dictionary)

   For Release 5.7 systems:
      1) System Generation Guide (System generation parameters, system generation compiler)
      2) DB/DC Operations Guide (#DCPARM macro, bringing up the new system, statistics, DCMT command)

3) IDMS Database Design and Definition Guide (creating separate databases, defining the global DMCL)
4) Integrated Installation Guide (creating a separate Data Dictionary)

11

Maintaining the Environment

In this chapter we will discuss maintaining systems and databases. Common system and database maintenance will be described, showing where changes made to one component affect other components in the environment. Alternative methods for performing maintenance will be discussed and their tradeoffs analyzed; general maintenance approaches will be recommended. Maintenance may be defined as any change to the IDMS/R environment which corrects problems or enhances existing capabilities. Our discussion of maintenance will range from adding a new record element to implementing the latest versions of Cullinet system software. We will cover:

- An overview of system maintenance,
- Maintaining system descriptions,
- Maintaining system software modules,
- An overview of database maintenance,
- Maintaining database descriptions, and
- Maintaining databases.

11.1 AN OVERVIEW OF SYSTEM MAINTENANCE

Maintenance of IDMS/R systems involves maintaining both system descriptions and Cullinet system software modules. Database/data communications administrators often change system description values to make adjustments better suited to the workload or to experiment with parameter values. Changes are made to system software modules to implement the latest versions or to correct software errors.

11.2 MAINTAINING SYSTEM DESCRIPTIONS

The description of a system is created during system generation and stored in a data dictionary. The startup routine uses the system description when configuring the system tables and loading the Cullinet software modules which comprise the run time system.

There are two major areas of concern for maintaining system descriptions:

- Maintaining system generation source statements, and
- Implementing changes to system generation parameter and statement values.

11.2.1   Maintaining System Generation Source

There are three alternative methods for storing system generation source statements. They are:

- PUNCHing system information from the DD when needed and not storing system generation source separately,
- Storing source statements in a source statement library, or
- Storing source statements in MODULEs on the DD and using the INCLUDE command to bring the module into a sysgen.

PUNCHing system information from the DD when needed and not storing system generation source separately: System generation source statements can be PUNCHed from the DD under Release 10 by issuing a single command, e.g., PUNCH ALL SYSTEM 9. In addition, any portion of a system can be PUNCHed (e.g., MOD SYSTEM 9. PUNCH ALL IDMS AREA AS SYNTAX.) PUNCHing source from the DD eliminates redundancy, and minimizes the confusion and mistakes caused by source modules in a library, or on the DD, whose descriptions do not match those in the dictionary.

However, a system PUNCHed from the DD is extremely large and unwieldy. A medium-sized PUNCHed CV system is approximately 20K to 30K lines of source because all clauses are PUNCHed on a separate line and none of the clauses default. Other disadvantages of PUNCHing source from the DD include the inability to separate and document parts of the source and the inability to document changes with comments.

System generation statements <u>cannot</u> be PUNCHed from the DD under Release 5.7. This limitation makes storage of system generation source on a source statement library or in a module on the DD the only alternatives for sites using Release 5.7.

Storing source statements in a source statement library: The advantages of storing system generation source statements on a source statement library are ease of use and backup considerations.

In addition, all system source can be seen in one place, without the 20,000 lines of syntax output from a PUNCH ALL SYSTEM *system-version-number* statement. It is relatively easy to create a new system that is similar to an existing system by copying the source and making a few changes, e.g., when creating a QA system with a separate CV and DD for the first time. Finally, storing the source statements on a source statement library provides a backup of the system. The backup is useful if anything untoward happens to the dictionary definition, e.g., DELETE SYSTEM 9., mistakenly run by a trainee DBA or programmer at sites where sysgen entities are not adequately secured.

The disadvantages of using a source statement library include synchronization problems, reduced security, and increased overhead for small changes. Quick and dirty changes might be made using a MODIFY SYSTEM statement on the IDD, without corresponding changes being made to the source statement library version of the system. The source statements may be less secure on a source statement library than on the DD because DD security facilities are unavailable. In addition, all system changes would be implemented by deleting and reading the entire system, thus greatly increasing the time it takes to implement small changes (deleting and readding a system definition ties up the DD for a minimum of 20-30 minutes).

Storing source statements in MODULEs on the DD and using the INCLUDE command to bring the module into a sysgen: Using IDD modules keeps the description on the DD and allows it to be secured appropriately using IDD security facilities (refer to Chapter 6 for details). Using the module approach is beneficial because information in IDD module(s) remains intact if the system is deleted. IDD modules are convenient when more than one person maintains the sysgen, e.g., one person and one module for each 1) IDMS AREA and BUFFER statements, 2) Network statements (LINEs, PTERMs, and LTERMs), 3) application statements (PROGRAMs and TASKs), and 4) USER statements.

Cullinet supplies several IDD modules containing sample product statements (e.g., the ADSO, ONLINE-QUERY, and ONLINE-MAPPING modules containing the associated statements). These modules are updated during demonstration and maintenance installations. If any site-specific changes are made directly to the Cullinet-supplied modules, those changes are lost the next time IDMS/R is reinstalled, during normal maintenance of Cullinet software and DD's for instance. Rather than modify the Cullinet-supplied modules, copy them to other modules with names unique to the site (specifying LANGUAGE IS SYSGEN), make changes to the copies, and include the copies in the sysgen. To change the default specification for the ADSO PRIMARY RECORD BUFFER clause on the ADSO statement, make a copy of the ADSO module, change the copy and include the copy in the sysgen, e.g.,

ADD SYSTEM 1.   ADD SYSTEM 1.
   INCLUDE *sitename*-ADSO.   versus   INCLUDE ADSO.

Similarly, site-specific line and terminal statements should be coded for each system rather than copying them from the sample systems, SYSTEM 90 or 99. If changes are made to SYSTEM 90 or SYSTEM 99, and IDMS/R is reinstalled, the reinstallation updates the sample systems and changes are lost. The statements can be stored in an IDD module.

Recommendations: Systems should be maintained on the DD for security and synchronization reasons. We recommend a combined approach, maintaining some sysgen source in IDD modules and PUNCHing the rest as needed. Using IDD modules for TASK, PROGRAM, and USER statements facilitates system maintenance.

All TASK and PROGRAM statements should be placed in IDD modules, using minimal syntax to keep the modules small (i.e., specifying only those clauses where values other than the default are needed). The modules can be secured using IDD security facilities. User programs and tasks can be kept in modules separate from those containing Cullinet-supplied tasks and programs (e.g., IDD and IDMSDDDL) to prevent accidental errors. Separate personnel can be assigned to maintain application modules as opposed to system modules if appropriate.

USER entity occurrences should be maintained on the DD using the DDDL compiler which permits full documentation. IDD security facilities can be used to restrict update privileges to authorized personnel. Adding users to the IDD and establishing USER-SYSTEM connections can be done by a security officer rather than the DCA/DBA. A separate IDD module, containing only user ID's and security classes, should be maintained to associate users with a system. The DCA/DBA can generate the system without any users (or perhaps the DCA/DBA USERs only) at security conscious installations. A security officer can then establish the USER-SYSTEM connection in a separate step (either SYSGEN MOD or IDD USER MOD) after the sysgen has been completed.

11.2.2 Implementing Changes to System Generation Statements

We recommend keeping two copies of each system in the dictionary for backup and ease of maintenance. The safest approach to sysgen maintenance is to make changes to the system which is not currently running, and swapping systems at the first opportunity. For example, assume that SYSTEM 1 and SYSTEM 2 are identical system descriptions stored on the DD (Figure 11-1). SYSTEM 1 is executing, therefore any changes should be made to SYSTEM 2 and the systems swapped at the earliest opportunity. SYSTEM 1 acts as a backup in the event of errors or problems with the modified system. Systems can be swapped by changing the value of PARM (for OS) in the startup JCL or by changing the SYSTEM=*system-version-number* in the DCPARM module, reassembling, and relinking it (for DOS). If these changes are successful, modify the old system later to bring it in line with the modified system.

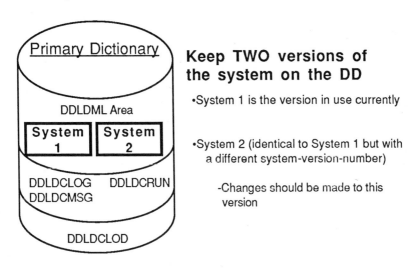

Figure 11-1 Current and Backup Systems on the DD

Alternatively, instead of maintaining two copies of the system on the DD, copy the source for the current system, change the copy, and rerun the sysgen, creating a new system identified by a new system number. Next, swap systems at the earliest opportunity. The disadvantage of this method is that even small changes take a long time to compile, because an entire system is being created.

Minor maintenance (i.e., not involving a tremendous amount of syntax) can be done online at Release 10 sites by modifying the alternate system and swapping systems at the earliest opportunity. For example, making changes to the SYSTEM statement parameter values, adding a database name table, and/or adding an IDMS AREA statement are easily handled online; the modification and regeneration take only seconds. Part or all of the modified system can be dis-

played using batch RHDCSGEN to provide documentation for the
revised system. Running CREPORT019 is the preferred method for
documenting PROGRAM changes, due to the extreme amount of
syntax shown when displaying all programs. The following sample
CULPRIT input parameters can be used to list only resident programs:

```
DATABASE DICTNAME=pridict DBNAME=pridict
PROFILE RELEASE=6 EX=E PARMLIB=STANDARD PE=5
CREPORT=019
SELECT SYS-041 WHEN SYS-VER-041 EQ system-version-number
SELECT PROG-051 WHEN RESIDENT-051 EQ 1
```

where *pridict* is the name of the DBNT which describes the primary
dictionary and *system-version-number* identifies the target system's
version number.

We recommend that large scale changes and new sysgens be
done in batch, after first punching the desired system to a library for
use as a prototype. For example, creating an alternate system with
debugging facilities by punching and modifying the existing system
(specifying a new version number and turning on the system trace)
and adding the alternate system is best done in batch. Adding a system takes a minimum of 20-30 minutes to run under Central Version
and causes significant slowdowns because of the locks generated.
The generation is faster if it is run in PROTECTED UPDATE mode.
However, this procedure locks out all other update access to the DD and
is generally considered unacceptable in a single dictionary environment.

A special procedure should be developed to punch an entire system
if the combined approach of maintaining system source described
earlier is employed (i.e., partially in IDD include modules and partially in the system definition itself). There is no syntax in the sysgen compiler to exclude entities as part of a PUNCH ALL SYSTEM *n*
statement. Therefore, statements similar to those shown in Figure
11-2 must be issued to punch system source without the expanded syntax of tasks and programs. The sysgen input shown above the dotted
line is common to all sites (Figure 11-2). Punch statements below the
dotted line may be required at some sites. The IDD modules named
CULL-TASKS and CULL-PROGRAMS must be created at the user
site by combining various installation source library members
(e.g., DLODIDDO). The punched output from RHDCSGEN and
IDMSDDDL provides everything in the sysgen, but with the TASKs,
PROGRAMs, and USERs in an abbreviated, manageable form.
Changes are then made to the punched data, followed by deleting and
readding the system. The System Activity Reports output from the

Step 1: RHDCSGEN input

```
PUNCH SYSTEM system-version-number.
    PUNCH ALL OLQ AS SYNTAX.
    PUNCH ALL OLM AS SYNTAX.
    PUNCH ALL ADSO AS SYNTAX.
    PUNCH ALL DBNAMES AS SYNTAX.
    PUNCH ALL LINES AS SYNTAX.
    PUNCH ALL PTERMS AS SYNTAX.
    PUNCH ALL LTERMS AS SYNTAX.
    PUNCH ALL KEYS AS SYNTAX.
- - - - -(optional statements below this line)- - - - - - - -
    PUNCH ALL IDMS BUFFERS AS SYNTAX.
    PUNCH ALL IDMS AREAS AS SYNTAX.
    PUNCH ALL IDMS PROGRAMS AS SYNTAX.
    PUNCH ALL DDS AS SYNTAX.
    PUNCH ALL DESTINATIONS AS SYNTAX.
    PUNCH ALL QUEUES AS SYNTAX.
    PUNCH ALL AUTOTASKS AS SYNTAX.
    PUNCH ALL STORAGE POOLS AS SYNTAX.
```

Step 2: IDMSDDDL input

```
PUNCH MODULE CULL-TASKS AS SYNTAX.
PUNCH MODULE CULL-PROGS AS SYNTAX.
PUNCH MODULE sitename-TASKS AS SYNTAX.
PUNCH MODULE sitename-PROGS AS SYNTAX.
PUNCH MODULE sitename-USERS AS SYNTAX.
....(additional punch statements for other site-specific modules)
```

Figure 11-2 Steps to PUNCH a System Definition

sysgen compiler yield complete documentation for the newly-added system.

It is acceptable to modify the current system while it is running, provided a backup of the current system exists on the DD (i.e., identical to the current system but with a different system version number). Errors can cause severe problems if there is no backup. Suppose the SVC number was accidently overtyped during a change to the SYSTEM statement increasing the size of the STORAGE POOL. When the revised system is brought up, it will abend due to the invalid SVC number. It would be impossible to modify the system under CV to correct the problem without a backup system on the DD; a local mode sysgen or a restore of the DD would be required to recover from the error. However, if there were a backup system on the DD, one could fall back on it and correct mistakes whenever convenient.

Rerunning the entire sysgen works better than modifying specific values in the DD for Release 5.7 sites, because there is no single dictionary report documenting an entire IDMS system. CREPORTS, the dictionary reports which list system-related information, provide piecemeal information about systems. The sysgen compiler reports (entitled SYSTEM ACTIVITY REPORTS) show all system parameters, programs, tasks, and terminals for newly added, or deleted and readded systems wrapped up in one neat listing. However, if a system is modified rather than deleted and readded, the sysgen reports list the modifications only. CREPORTS of a system may be run for a specific component of a system, e.g., the system statement or the programs included in a sysgen. The only way to acquire a full picture of the current system after modifying a system definition is to run all the CREPORTS. Because it is not possible to display or punch an entire system easily under Release 5.7, it is advantageous to delete and add systems so a full picture of the system can be seen in the system activity reports.

SYSTEM Statement Changes: Most modifications to a system involve changing parameter values on the SYSTEM statement. SYSTEM statement changes are easily done online, taking only seconds to perform. For example,

```
MOD SYSTEM 9
    RUNAWAY INTERVAL 120.
GENERATE.
```

The new parameters take effect the next time the system is brought up. Current SYSTEM statement parameter values may be displayed by running CREPORT011.

Changing or Adding TASKs and PROGRAMs: The method chosen for changing or adding TASKs and PROGRAMs depends upon whether or not dynamic definition of programs is allowed in the sysgen (see discussions of UNDEFINED PROGRAM COUNT in the Security and Test System chapters). The system automatically handles dynamic definitions of dialogs, maps, subschemas, and tables if dynamic definition of programs is allowed and sufficient UNDEFINED PROGRAM COUNT entries were allocated in the previous sysgen. Dynamic definition of DC program's TASK and PROGRAM entities is a manual function, accomplished by entering DCMT commands to change or add program/task characteristics between sysgens, e.g.,

```
DCMT VARY DYNAMIC PROGRAM new-program ...
DCMT VARY DYNAMIC TASK new-task ...
```

However, these DCMT commands are effective only for the current run of IDMS-DC and must be repeated each time the system is cycled.

A sysgen should be scheduled to add or change tasks/programs if dynamic definition of programs is prohibited. One method of maintaining task and program statements is adding the new task or program to a list of programs and tasks stored in the dictionary as module source. Next use the sysgen 'INCLUDE' statement to pull the list into the next sysgen. This method keeps all program and task statements in one place so they are displayed comprehensively on IDD reports. Simply rerun the sysgen (RHDCSGEN with a 'GENERATE', in Release 10) to implement the changes. Under Release 10, systems can be modified online to add tasks and programs to the sysgen. This method of adding tasks and programs, however, does not accommodate the comments and documentation that can be part of an included module, nor can one extract a subset of all programs. Application-specific INCLUDE modules allow one to PUNCH or DISPLAY only those tasks and programs of a given application.and are useful when migrating an application from one system to another, e.g.,

```
MOD SYSTEM 9.
INCLUDE MODULE application-name-programs.
```

Changing or Adding Terminals and Lines: If a BTAM line and/or terminal is being added, modify the system to include the new PTERM and LTERM statements, along with their device addresses. Consider whether or not the SYSTEM statement MAXIMUM TASKS parameter needs to be increased to handle the extra activity likely to be caused by the new terminal users. Also, include the JCL for the new devices in the execution deck.

If a VTAM line or terminal is being added, modify the system to include the new LINE, PTERM, and LTERM statements, remember the 'APPLICATION ID' parameter on the new LINE statement, and look at the MAXIMUM TASKS parameter to see if it needs to be increased for the new load on the system. Rerun the sysgen after the preceding steps have been completed.

If new terminals are being added to run in a UCF mode, add the terminal statements to the existing UCF line. Never create more than one UCF line. Also, check the MAXIMUM ERUS parameter to see if it needs to be increased to accommodate the new terminals; there should be one for each UCF terminal concurrently executing a task plus one for each batch external run unit executing concurrently. Finally, check to see that the appropriate front ends have been included in the host teleprocessing monitor (UCFTSO, UCFCICS, UCFCMS, etc.).

Terminal and line changes take effect the next time the system is brought up. Refer to the System Generation Guide for information on lines and terminals.

Changing or Adding Users: USERs can be added to the DD and linked to a system while the system is up by using the IDD syntax:

MODIFY USER *user-name* INCLUDE DCSYSTEM *nn.*

However, adding users in this manner can cause confusion later, especially if the sysgen source is stored in a library or in an IDD include module. The update must be made in two places or the new user will be lost the next time the system is deleted and readded.

A more straightforward approach to adding or changing users is to maintain an IDD module containing user ID's and security classes for all users of the system, so that the module can be INCLUDEd in the sysgen each time changes are made. This regime allows better control of USER maintenance. It is recommended that the module containing user source definitions be secured from unauthorized access and modification through appropriate USER REGISTRATION and PUBLIC ACCESS restrictions (under Release 5.7 include the USER RESPONSIBLE FOR DEFINITION clause for similar security). Modify the system with the updated module in place, e.g.,

```
MOD SYSTEM 9.
    INCLUDE MODULE sitename-users.
GENERATE.
```

User security classes can also be changed online. The user must sign off and sign back on again for the changes to take affect.

11.3   MAINTAINING CULLINET SYSTEM SOFTWARE MODULES

Changes are made to system software modules to implement new versions of the software or to fix software problems. Always backup the object libraries, or at least backup modules targeted for maintenance, before applying any type of object code maintenance. The importance of these backups cannot be overstated. A corrupted system module can cause disastrous problems, perhaps more severe than the problems the maintenance was designed to solve.

Cullinet supplies software maintenance in three ways, as illustrated in Figure 11-3. Cullinet software modules are maintained by replacing entire object modules or by applying PTF's (Program Temporary Fixes). Entire modules are replaced using the installation program CDMSIJMP and maintenance installation tapes. PTF's are applied (using operating system utilities) to solve system software problems between maintenance installations. PTF's may be applied from object code replacement tapes or from over-the-phone maintenance.

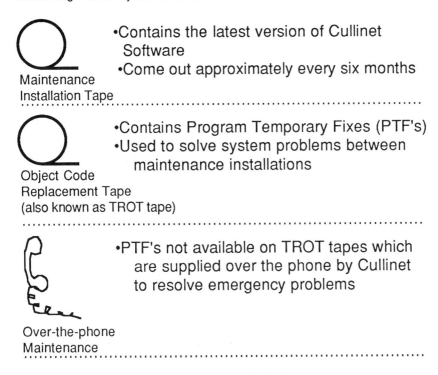

•Contains the latest version of Cullinet Software
•Come out approximately every six months

Maintenance
Installation Tape

•Contains Program Temporary Fixes (PTF's)
•Used to solve system problems between maintenance installations

Object Code
Replacement Tape
(also known as TROT tape)

•PTF's not available on TROT tapes which are supplied over the phone by Cullinet to resolve emergency problems

Over-the-phone
Maintenance

Figure 11-3 Maintenance of IDMS/R System Software

All selective maintenance (i.e., maintenance that does not replace the entire object module), whether from object code replacement tapes or taken over the phone from Cullinet, should be documented on the IDD or in a text edit library with the date the maintenance was applied, a description of the maintenance, the modules and CSECTs affected, and a reference to the PTF number. If the change solves a problem logged in Cullinet's TSIS (Technical Support Information System) system, also document the TSIS problem number.

11.3.1 Maintenance Installation Tapes

Maintenance installation tapes contain the latest version of all software modules, as well as all system messages, protocols, report source, and so forth. Entire libraries of Cullinet system software modules are replaced using JCL produced by running CDMSIJMP, the installation program. Typically, maintenance installations are done approximately every six months.

11.3.2   Object Code Replacement Tapes

Object code replacement tapes, also known as TROT (Technical Reports On Tape) tapes, are issued approximately every other month. They are used to resolve problems selectively rather than to replace object libraries completely. Included on the TROT tape are descriptions of each problem solved and the modules affected by the solution. If maintenance is being considered which would result in multiple PTF's applied to one module, try to postpone the maintenance until the next maintenance installation tape is available or it may be difficult to coordinate the changes. Consider a site experiencing four problems, the solution to Problem One requires a change to IDMSDDDL. The solutions to Problems Two, Three, and Four (perhaps from later tapes) also affect IDMSDDDL. If new trouble develops with IDMSDDDL after the fixes have been applied, it will be difficult to determine which PTF caused the new problem.

11.3.3   Over-the-Phone Maintenance

Cullinet technical support representatives may provide maintenance over the phone to solve emergency problems. A problem may appear which is too new to be included on a TROT tape. Descriptions of new problems are called in to Cullinet's TSIS system, where a solution is eventually logged for inclusion in future TROT tapes. Always ask the TSIS technician to send a listing of the PTF's by mail whenever PTF's are received over the phone. Special care should be taken to backup the modules involved because the solution may not have been fully tested at this point. Use extreme caution when applying the maintenance. Any abnormal consequences should be logged and reported to Cullinet. At the first sign of problems, restore the module from the backup and call Cullinet.

11.4   AN OVERVIEW OF DATABASE MAINTENANCE

All DBMS's share one common feature, the description of a database and the database itself are stored separately. However, the database description must match the corresponding database exactly because it is referenced at run time.

There are many database description components in the IDMS/R environment, as illustrated in Figure 11-4. The complete source description of a database resides in the dictionary's DDLDML area in schemas, subschemas, and DMCL's. DMCL and subschema load modules are used at run time. DMCL load modules are stored in load

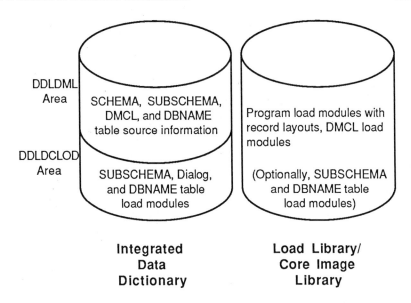

DDLDML
Area — SCHEMA, SUBSCHEMA, DMCL, and DBNAME table source information

Program load modules with record layouts, DMCL load modules

DDLDCLOD
Area — SUBSCHEMA, Dialog, and DBNAME table load modules

(Optionally, SUBSCHEMA and DBNAME table load modules)

Integrated Data Dictionary

Load Library/ Core Image Library

Figure 11-4 Components of Database Descriptions

libraries or core image libraries; subschema load modules are stored in a dictionary DDLDCLOD area (optionally in a load library or core image library). File and area descriptions are duplicated in global schemas and DMCL's. The record format descriptions compiled into program load modules also are part of the database description. Database name tables may be thought of as part of the database description because they control selection of the proper subschema at run time.

IDMS/R database and description changes are common and occur for several reasons (Figure 11-5). A database description might be changed to correct an oversight or error in its original design. Databases are not static, just as most applications are not static. The database design might be changed as part of overall system evolution in which new applications are added or existing applications enhanced. Databases experiencing storage growth must be expanded periodically to prevent them from becoming full. Databases are occasionally reorganized through an unload/reload procedure, thereby correcting physical storage problems and improving response time. A reorganization may or may not require a description change. Physical changes may also be made to optimize storage utilization following a DASD conversion.

The database description must be changed to match any structural changes made to the database. Similarly, if a change is made to the

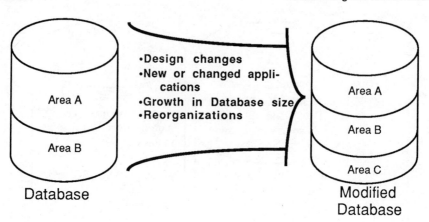

Figure 11-5 Reasons for Database Changes

description, the database must be processed by a reorganization procedure (typically a restructure, or an unload and reload of the areas) before any application access is made to that database. The DBA must ensure that database change and the database description change are done in tandem and that each correctly reflects the other (Figure 11-6).

We detail several common types of database description changes in the next section. Most description changes require the database to be restructured, or unloaded and reloaded, to incorporate changes. The tools used to restructure or unload and reload databases are examined in Section 11.6.

11.5 MAINTAINING DATABASE DESCRIPTIONS

Database descriptions are maintained using the DDL compilers (schema, subschema, and DMCL compilers) and the dictionary's DDDL compiler. Although the DDL compilers are used for maintaining most of the description, the DDDL compiler is recommended for record and element maintenance.

Release 10 and Release 5.7 are fundamentally different with regard to database description maintenance. Schemas can be modified without deleting and recompiling (i.e., without impacting) the entire schema and all subschemas under Release 10. The schema and IDD compilers in this release allow records to be changed without deleting and reading either the schema or schema records in question.

Schemas cannot be modified under Release 5.7. Any change to the schema is implemented by deleting and reading the entire

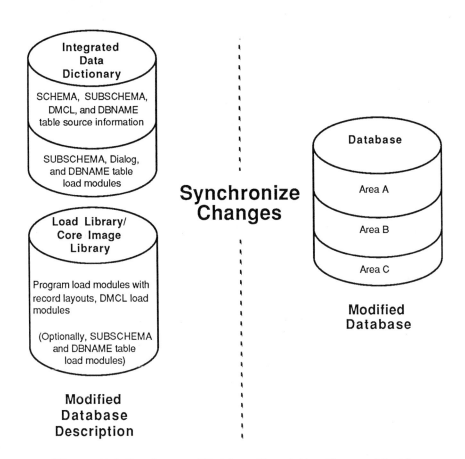

Figure 11-6 Database and Database Description Changes Must be
Synchronized

schema. A heavy price is paid for deleting and readding a schema.
All DMCL's and subschemas which were compiled referencing the
deleted schema are deleted automatically from the dictionary along
with the schema. Thus, implementing even a small change under
Release 5.7 is time consuming because the entire schema, all subschemas, and all related DMCL's must be recompiled. Further, some
security facilities are difficult to maintain because subschemas are
deleted during changes (e.g., subschema AUTHORIZATION,
PROGRAM REGISTRATION, and QFILE security).

We examine the following aspects of database description maintenance in detail:

- Maintaining database description source,
- Methods of including records in schemas,

- Global schema uses and practicality,
- Maintaining a global schema,
- Maintaining records,
- Maintaining sets,
- Maintaining areas,
- Maintaining files, and
- Maintaining buffers.

11.5.1   Maintaining Database Description Source

It is possible to issue a single PUNCH SCHEMA command, under Release 10, which causes all components and entities making up that schema to be punched. This makes it practical to maintain schema source solely on the DD, thereby eliminating redundancy and the potential problems caused when the source statement library version of the database description source does not match the DD version. Subschemas, like schemas, can be punched from the DD. DMCL source, however, cannot and must be maintained on a source statement library.

There is no command to extract schema source information from the dictionary under Release 5.7. Therefore, it is necessary to keep a copy of schema and DMCL source on a source statement library.

11.5.2   Methods of Including Records in Schemas

Another difference between Releases 10 and 5.7 is the way in which records are included in schemas. Records may be added to schemas by:

- Using the SHARE STRUCTURE clause (Release 10) or the COPY RECORD (Release 5.7) clause,
- Using the COPY ELEMENTS FROM RECORD (Release 10), or
- Hard-coding record definitions in the schema source.

Each of these methods has specific advantages and disadvantages as explained in the following paragraphs.

Using the SHARE STRUCTURE Clause (Release 10) or the COPY RECORD Clause (Release 5.7):   The SHARE STRUCTURE clause under Release 10, or the COPY RECORD clause under Release 5.7, references a previously created IDD record and causes the schema to share that record definition. Complete documentation is possible because the record is created using the IDD DDDL compiler. Two steps are required to include a record in a schema, first an IDD step to add the record and then a schema step identifying the record.

SHARE STRUCTURE locks the IDD record, preventing most changes to the record by the DDDL compiler. If the record is modified using the schema compiler directly, a new version of the record is generated by the schema compiler and the old version is not deleted, proliferating versions. However, under Release 10, records included in a schema using the SHARE STRUCTURE clause can be maintained by carefully adhering to the procedures outlined in Section 11.5.5, this method leaves only a single version of the record on the IDD.

Using the COPY ELEMENTS FROM RECORD clause: The COPY ELEMENTS FROM RECORD clause creates a copy of an existing IDD record labeled with the next higher version number. COPY ELEMENTS FROM RECORD allows complete documentation and, under Release 10, can be modified directly by the schema compiler. Multiple versions of the original IDD record are created as well and may cause synchronization problems if an element in the record must be changed. COPY ELEMENTS FROM RECORD allows change to either the schema-built record through the schema compiler or to the DDDL-built record through the DDDL compiler, providing the records have not been used in any maps.

Hard-coding record definitions in the schema source: Hard-coding record definitions in schemas is accomplished by coding the COBOL definitions in the schema source. Coding records in the schema under Release 10 does not allow for as complete documentation as IDD-built record definitions, but, unlike its counterpart under Release 5.7, the record can be modified through the schema compiler.

Hard-coding a record in schema source increases the overhead of deleting and readding a schema under Release 5.7. Coding records in the schema means that each record is deleted and readded by the schema compiler during any schema change. This procedure greatly increases the time required to compile the schema. If the record was defined separately through the DDDL compiler, its definition remains in the DD even if the schema is deleted. Defining records separately from schemas is highly desirable in Release 5.7 where a schema cannot be modified; if a change has to be made to a schema record, necessitating a schema deletion, other records need not be touched.

Recommendations: We recommend using the SHARE STRUCTURE method at Release 10 sites because of its documentational and synchronizational advantages. The procedures outlined in Section 11.5.5 show how to use the schema and IDD compilers to maintain schema-shared records. Thus a single version of a record can be maintained efficiently without deleting and readding either the schema or schema records in question. We recommend using the COPY RECORD method at Release 5.7 sites.

Under both releases, however, using schema records in maps still poses a problem. Once a record is used in a map, changes to the record by either the schema or DDDL compilers are prohibited until the maps are decompiled and deleted. Most shops either use SHARE STRUCTURE to include records in schemas and create different subsets of each record for use in DC maps, or they use COPY ELEMENTS FROM RECORD to include records in schemas and use the original record versions as mapping records. Both methods have the potential to require updating two versions of each record if a key element changes, i.e., one record for the schema and another for maps.

11.5.3   Global Schema Uses and Practicality

A 'global' schema is one which contains all application database areas. Dictionary and demonstration database areas should remain in the Cullinet-supplied schemas, IDMSNTWK, CDMSNTWK, and GLBLSCHM, separate from application areas to facilitate updating during maintenance installations. The alternative to a global application schema is multiple schemas, usually one for each application.

The advantage of a global schema becomes apparent when an application develops a need for data in another application's database (Figure 11-7). A subschema can include records, sets, and areas from only one schema. If two applications were developed under separate schemas, it is impossible to create a subschema containing data from both schemas. With a global schema, however, applications can share information easily. Any combination of records, sets, or areas (potentially crossing application boundaries) can be included in one subschema. One disadvantage of implementing a global schema is that it becomes difficult to identify everything affecting a particular application.

Creating a global schema is possible in both releases, although maintaining a global schema is practical only under Release 10. The schemas can be changed under Release 10 without deleting and recompiling the entire schema and all subschemas. Maintenance is faster than under Release 5.7 because only those portions of the schema which need to be changed are updated. This facility greatly streamlines the process of schema modification, making it practical to implement a centralized, global schema. The Release 10 schema

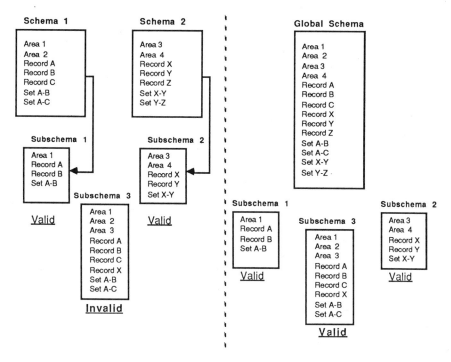

Figure 11-7 Sharing Data – Application Schemas versus a Global Schema

compiler allows implementation of a global schema with minimal end-user impact from new and/or changing definitions of records, sets, and areas. The global schema approach is recommended for Release 10 installations and for Release 5.7 installations which are planning to convert to Release 10. The global schema approach should be used whenever practical (it is not practical for purchased packages, for example).

A global schema is impractical under Release 5.7. All applications defined to a global schema must be down while changes are made because the entire schema must be deleted and then readded. A global schema would be deleted and readded constantly as new applications or changes to existing applications became necessary. Therefore, Release 5.7 sites generally create several schemas, one for each application, to reduce the impact of change on users and applications not requiring the change. The application approach is recommended for Release 5.7 environments with the proviso that applications which require subschemas with information from other applications be set up under a combined schema whenever possible.

11.5.4 Overview of Maintaining a Global Schema (Release 10)

For a global schema to be practical it must be possible to modify one application's portion of the schema without affecting other applications. Under Release 10, if there are no changes to any areas, files, records, or sets used in a subschema, processing with that subschema is unaffected (e.g., compiling and testing programs can continue normally), even if major modifications are being made to other portions of the global schema. In other words, applications not requiring the change are unaffected by it. Such insularity of applications is extremely important.

A change can impact the affected application(s) in several ways. Some changes force recompilation of programs that access the changed entity. Other changes are more transparent to the program, yet still require a subschema regeneration. Compiles are affected by the changes even when the changes are transparent to the program. For example, changing a record from fixed length to compressed may be necessary to improve disk storage utilization. Although the change is transparent to application code, program and dialog compiles to implement other changes will fail while the maintenance is occurring if the subschema contains the record being changed. Furthermore, testing cannot proceed until the area containing the record is restructured.

The critical questions concerning a proposed change are:

- Can programs and dialogs continue to execute during the change?
- Can compiles/generations for application development continue?
- Must any programs/dialogs be recompiled/regenerated?
- Must the database be changed to reflect the description change?
- Does the system have to be cycled to implement the change?

Can programs and dialogs continue to execute during the change? Programs and dialogs using subschemas unaffected by the change can continue to process normally; they are accessing areas unaffected by the change. Some changes, such as replacing FILLER in a record with new elements, affect the processing of only those programs which access the changed entity. If the changes force a restructure or an unload/reload of the database, the affected areas should be varied offline before the subschemas are regenerated. Subsequently, the schema and subschemas should be regenerated and the database changed prior to bringing the areas back online and permitting program access to resume.

Processing can continue until the affected subschemas are regenerated; all the old load modules of subschemas and dialogs continue to work as before. Existing subschema load modules are not replaced until the subschema is regenerated. Therefore, most existing applications can run while changes are being entered, as long as no subschema regenerations are done. Batch DML programs, ADS/O applications, and DC programs can be run while subschema source changes are being made but OLQ and Culprit cannot because they require unmodified subschema source. It may be practical to enter the changes while normal processing continues and to generate the subschemas at a convenient time depending on the processing mix at an installation.

Can compiles/generations for application development continue normally? Compiles referencing affected subschemas will not work while the schema and affected subschemas are being changed. Dialog generations will fail with the message SUBSCHEMA ERROR FLAG SET - MUST BE REGENERATED. Programs compiled through the DMLx preprocessors will receive an *UNKNOWN NAME message flagging the subschema name in the DB statement. When displayed, the schema in question will show a SCHEMA IN ERROR designation until the change is completed and a schema validation is done. Dialog generations and program DMLx compiles will work only after the affected subschemas have been regenerated. None of the subschemas associated with the error schema can be displayed, regardless of whether the change impacts them directly or not. Compiles of programs and generations of dialogs involving subschemas unaffected by the change will work.

Which programs/dialogs must be recompiled/regenerated? Programs and dialogs using subschemas affected by the change may need to be recompiled or regenerated. In general, programs and dialogs using the changed or added records, sets, or areas must be recompiled. However, if a record is changed to redefine FILLER, a recompilation is necessary only if the program references the new fields. If new fields are either added to the end of a record or inserted in the middle of the record, thereby increasing the size of the record, programs which do not reference the new fields need not be recompiled. Their subschema must be modified to add view id's or the ELEMENTS ARE clause to include only those elements that the programs use (in the order required to match the old version of the record). Programs referencing the new fields would require a new subschema which typically includes the entire record description, i.e., the schema view of the record.

All ADS/O dialogs that LINK or INVOKE other dialogs must have the same record length. If a higher or lower level dialog is regenerated to use the new fields, related dialogs must also be regenerated to match record buffer length even if the dialog does not use any of them (otherwise ADS/O dialog abends result due to record buffer sizes not matching).

Must the database be changed to reflect the description change? If the database must be changed, the affected areas is off-line for the duration of the change and program access to the area is prohibited. Most description changes require the database to be restructured, or unloaded and reloaded, to incorporate the changes. Database changes are detailed in Section 11.6.

Does the system have to be cycled to implement the change? The global DMCL must be modified when area and file description changes are made. Changes to the global DMCL take effect the next time the system is brought up. Therefore, area and file changes will briefly impact the processing of applications other than those requiring the change because the system must be cycled to implement the change.

11.5.5   Maintaining Schema Records

A record change is the most common change made to a schema. A change may be necessary due to new elements, redefinition of elements, or changes in the order of the elements. Answers to the critical questions above concerning common modifications to records in a global schema are summarized in Table 11-1. In preparing this table, we assumed that the schema was modified rather than deleted and readded to make the change. Therefore, Table 11-1 is relevant to only Release 10 sites. The purpose of this table is to give our readers an appreciation of the impact of different types of changes on end users and applications (i.e., will the application be down minutes, days, or hours?). Each question is answered in a table column. The effects of change on programs and dialogs using subschemas affected by the change is shown as well as the effect on the database and system. Remember, programs and dialogs using subschemas unaffected by the change continue to process normally, except when the change requires the system to be cycled.

Release 10 users can implement record changes by modifying the record definition rather than deleting and readding the record.

Table 11-1 Effects of Schema Record Modifications

CHANGE	IMPACT				
	Processing Halted	Compiles Halted	Recompiles Needed[1]	Data Change Needed	System Cycles
Add elements to FILLER	No[2]	No	Yes[2]	No[2]	No
Add new record elements	Yes	Yes	Yes[3]	Yes	No
Reorder or change length of record elements	Yes	Yes	Yes	Yes	No
Delete record elements	Yes	Yes	Yes	Yes	No
Add a new record	Yes	Yes	Yes	Yes	No
Delete a record	Yes	Yes	Yes	Yes	No
Change CALC or Index Keys	Yes	Yes	Yes[4]	Yes	No
Transfer a record from one area to another	Yes	Yes	Yes	Yes	No
From compressed to uncompressed, or vice versa	Yes	Yes	No	Yes	No
Change a record from fixed to variable length, or vice versa	Yes	Yes	Yes[5]	Yes	No
Change root/fragment size for a variable length record	Yes	Yes	No	Yes	No

[1]Yes in this column means recompile/regenerate any program/dialog which used to access the deleted entity or which requires access to the new or changed entity.

[2]Processing continues unless the new elements must be initialized, then processing is halted during the data change. Recompile only those programs requiring access to the new elements.

[3]Recompile all programs accessing the record, unless the new elements were added to the end of the record, then only recompile programs accessing the new elements.

[4]Change and recompile/regenerate only those programs/dialogs which access the record through the changed CALC or index key.

[5]Change and recompile/regenerate programs/dialogs which STORE the changed record.

Throughout this section, we are assuming that the SHARE STRUCTURE METHOD was used to include the record in the schema. The procedures we present detail how to maintain one version (VERSION-1) of the record and make changes to it as necessary.

Some record description changes can be implemented rapidly because they do not require any structural change to the database. These changes are:

- Redefining space originally defined as FILLER to use all or part of the space for new data elements.
- Making an elementary element into a group element and adding subordinate elements whose sum is equal in length to the original element.

Only programs and dialogs which access the new/subordinate elements must be recompiled.

Other record changes, such as adding or deleting elements (not using FILLER) or rearranging them, also can be implemented without deleting the record from the IDD, provided the special procedure outlined later in this section is followed. In addition, the database must be changed to reflect the modified structure by restructuring the area and all programs/dialogs which access the record must be re-compiled/regenerated to incorporate the changes.

Replacing FILLER with New Elements (Without Changing Overall Record Length): Any FILLER field (originally defined as 'FIL nnnn', where nnnn is a four-digit number specifying the length of the field) can easily be modified to include one or more additional record elements. The combined length of additional record elements may be less than or equal to the size of the FILLER. If the combined length is less than the size of the FILLER, another FILLER field is defined to make the overall lengths equal. Changes to FILLER may be made regardless of where the FILLER exists in the record, i.e., in the beginning, middle, and/or end of the record. New records whose field requirements are not fully known could be defined with large, interspersed FILLER fields during initial application development and the space subsequently modified when record fields are further defined.

To add new elements to an existing schema record using its FILLER, first display the record and note the line number of the FILLER. For example, suppose we need to redefine the FILLER at the end of the EMPLOYEE record, as illustrated in Figure 11-8. An abbreviated display of the EMPLOYEE record is shown below:

```
DISPLAY RECORD EMPLOYEE VERSION 1.            (input)

*+   ADD
*+   RECORD NAME IS EMPLOYEE VERSION IS 1.     (output)
*+            .
*+            .
*+            .
*+       RECORD ELEMENT IS 'FIL 0002' VERSION 1
*+       LINE IS 003200
*+       LEVEL NUMBER IS 02
```

```
*+        PICTURE IS X(8)
*+        USAGE IS DISPLAY
*+
```

In this example we replace the FILLER in the record (line number 003200) with a group element having two subordinate elements.

```
ADD ELEMENT BOBH-EMP-CODE1 PIC X USAGE DISPLAY.        (input)
ADD ELEMENT BOBH-EMP-CODE2 PIC X USAGE DISPLAY.
ADD ELEMENT BOBH-EMP-CODE
    SUBORDINATE ELEMENTS
        BOBH-EMP-CODE1
        BOBH-EMP-CODE2.
MODIFY RECORD EMPLOYEE VERSION 1.
    REPLACE RECORD ELEMENT BOBH-EMP-CODE LINE 3200.
```

The REPLACE subcommand is used in the first RECORD ELEMENT statement, specifying the line number of the old FILLER. If the FILLER is being replaced with multiple elements, subsequent RECORD ELEMENT statements (for additional elements or 'FIL nnnn' FILLERs) should not include the REPLACE subcommand and should be assigned new line numbers with values between the replaced line number and the next higher line number in the record.

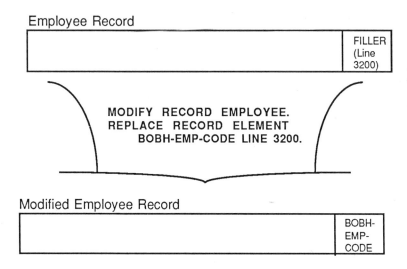

Figure 11-8 Replacing FILLER with an Element

The change is automatically shared by the schema and all subschemas because the SHARE STRUCTURE method was used to include this record in a schema. No subschema regenerations are required. Only programs and dialogs requiring access to the new elements(s) must be recompiled/regenerated.

Modifying an Element to Make It a Group with Subordinate Elements: Another uncomplicated change is modifying an element to make it a group with subordinate elements, thereby permitting program access to discrete portions of the original element. Consider the example of the element EMP-PHONE becoming a group composed of two subordinate elements, EMP-AREA-CODE and EMP-PHONE-LOCAL. Figure 11-9 shows the DDDL statements which implement the modification.

Employee Record

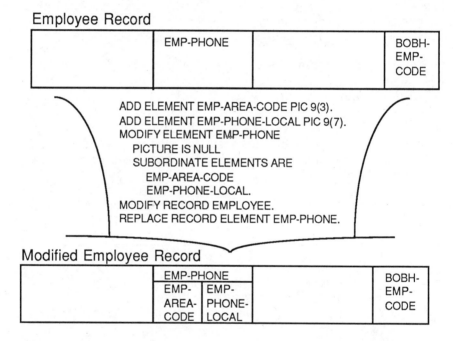

Figure 11-9 Changing an Element into a Group with Subordinate Elements

Programs and dialogs requiring the new breakdown need to be recompiled. No schema or subschema changes are necessary because those modules are sharing the structure of the changed record, simply validate the schema and regenerate all affected subschemas.

Remember not to exceed the length of the original element (EMP-PHONE) with the combined lengths of the subordinate elements (EMP-AREA-CODE and EMP-PHONE-LOCAL), otherwise the procedure under described Other Record Changes must be followed. Further, the original element name must be used as the group level element name. A variable length record's control field and any record's sort key field cannot be changed in this fashion.

Other Record Changes: A different technique is used when changing the order of elements in a record, redefining many portions of the record, inserting or deleting elements, or affecting any changes which cannot be handled by simply replacing FILLER fields. These kinds of changes require a restructure or an unload/reload of the database to implement the new structure.

The steps required to implement other record changes are illustrated in Figure 11-10. Assuming that the existing EMPLOYEE record and related subschemas are all VERSION 1 on the IDD, the following steps implement changes to the EMPLOYEE schema record.

Step 1: PUNCH the current version of the requisite subschema load module and link edit it to a LL/CIL. The old subschema is needed by the utility used to change the database to reflect the data description change. Some utilities also require the new subschema load module, so there must be a way to distinguish between the two load modules.

One method to distinguish between subschema load modules is to generate a separate subschema identical to an existing subschema but with a different name. Then PUNCH and link edit it to an LL/CIL (this subschema reflects the old definition). All subschemas are regenerated by issuing the REGENERATE ALL AFFECTED SUBSCHEMAS statement after the schema changes are made. Now a new subschema load module is PUNCHed and link edited to the same LL/CIL to be used by the restructure utility (this subschema reflects the new definition). Alternatively, PUNCH an existing subschema load module and link edit it into a different LL/CIL than is used by the new subschema load module. Specify different LL/CIL's in the JCL to distinguish between the modules. The old subschema load module should be deleted if the restructure appears to be correct.

Step 2: Create a new version of the employee record incorporating the changes using the online or batch DDDL compiler. For example,

DISPLAY RECORD EMPLOYEE VERSION 1 AS SYNTAX.   (Input)

ADD RECORD NAME IS EMPLOYEE VERSION 1.   (Output)

.
.
.

Employee Record

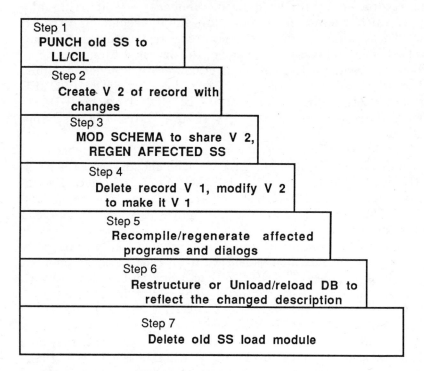

Modified Employee Record

Figure 11-10 Steps for Making Other Record Changes

Overtype the 1 with a 2, make all the changes, and end by entering the
definition of the new record, version 2.

ADD REC EMPLOYEE VERSION 2...

Step 3: Modify the schema to share the new record structure using
the online or batch schema compiler. This change is implemented by
entering the DDL syntax shown below.

MODIFY SCHEMA BOBHSCHM.
MOD REC EMPLOYEE
     SHARE STRUCTURE OF RECORD EMPLOYEE VERSION 2.
VALIDATE.
REGENERATE ALL AFFECTED SUBSCHEMAS AS LOAD MODULES.

Step 4: Use the online or batch IDD DDDL compiler to remove the old version of the record and make the new record VERSION 1.

DELETE REC EMPLOYEE V 1.
MODIFY REC EMPLOYEE V 2
     NEW VERSION IS 1.

The schema and affected subschemas automatically share this change. A display of the employee record now shows its version number as 1.

Step 5: Programs and dialogs accessing the employee record must be recompiled/regenerated to access the new definition. If there are any programs which do not require the new definition, the subschemas of those programs can be modified to include a view-id or the 'ELEMENTS ARE' clause listing the old view of the record. Modifying those subschemas makes it unnecessary to recompile programs which do not reference the new fields. However, if the number of programs is small, it may make more sense to recompile all programs referencing the changed record rather than creating specialized subschemas for new versus old views of the record. Consult the DDL Reference Guide for information on view-id's and the ELEMENTS ARE clause of the subschema compiler.

ADS/O dialogs require regeneration in most cases. A dialog must be regenerated if it uses the new fields, or links/invokes other dialogs that use the new fields, or is linked/invoked by a dialog which uses the new fields. Otherwise a record buffer length mismatch will occur, causing ADS/O dialog abends.

Step 6: Modify the database to reflect the description change. A restructure or an unload and reload of the area containing the customer record is required. The IDMSUNLD/IDMSDBLU utilities require both the old and new subschema. IDMSRSTU needs only the old subschema. If IDMSPCON is being run, then both the old and new subschemas are needed. These utilities use both an old subschema load module (created in step 1) and the new subschema load module (created in step 3) which must be punched and link edited to a LL/CIL. If a restructure or unload/reload must be performed, PUNCH the old IDD subschema load module and link edit it to a LL/CIL prior to this step. Refer to 11.6 for more information on database modification utilities.

Step 7: Delete the old subschema load module from the DD and LL/CIL.

Changing Records That Are Used In Maps: Schema records used in maps cannot be modified by the schema compiler until all maps using the record are deleted. As a general rule, mapping directly into schema records should be avoided because it delays schema modifications unnecessarily. Most shops generate one record as a schema buffer and one or more additional records, not necessarily including all elements from the schema record, to use with maps.

If schema records are mapped into directly, the schema compiler does not allow any changes to those records until the maps are deleted and the record is freed. Even minor changes to records used in maps, such as COBOL redefinitions or specifying a different value in an OCCURS clause, are prohibited by the schema compiler until the maps are deleted.

Prior to most map record modifications, any ADS/O or IDMS-DC maps which reference the record must be decompiled using the utility RHDCMPUT and, in some cases, deleted before the changes are made. The map must be deleted for changes other than adding new elements to the end of the record. However, a change to a map record element's (as opposed to the element's) PICTURE or USAGE can be accomplished without decompiling all maps associated with the record and only regeneration of the maps is necessary. PICTURE and USAGE changes, including changing the length of the field and therefore the overall record, are possible under both releases. Simply display the record as syntax, change ADD to MOD and type over the picture or usage to affect the change. Warning messages appear identifying all the maps to be regenerated.

Record changes that require all associated maps be decompiled, deleted, recompiled, and regenerated include adding new group levels to the record or inserting new elements in the middle of a record. To perform these and similar changes, consider using the sample procedure shown in Appendix A (programs marked Decompile Maps, Drop Dups) to automate the maps portion of the modification.

Other considerations: The element's PICTURE and USAGE clauses (as opposed to the record element's clauses) are not locked by either the schema compiler or the mapping compiler. Therefore, it is possible to modify an element's picture so that it differs from the way it appears in the record element. Similarly, the subordinate elements of a group can be modified. Such changes do not affect records until a rebuild occurs. If a record is rebuilt later to implement another change, the erroneously modified element replaces the record element. For example, some elements and a record were initially defined with these statements:

```
ADD ELEMENT SRS-NAME PIC X(10).
ADD ELEMENT SRS-ADDR PIC X(25).
```

```
ADD RECORD SRS-REC.
    REC EL SRS-NAME.
    REC EL SRS-ADDR.
```

Subsequently, the element SRS-NAME was modified by mistake:

```
MODIFY ELEMENT SRS-NAME PIC XX.
```

The record element SRS-NAME is unaffected by the change. However, suppose SRS-ADDR must be expanded to 30 characters. The following syntax is entered to make the change:

```
MOD EL SRS-ADDR  PIC X(30).
MOD REC SRS-REC.
REMOVE ALL.                    (or REBUILD RECORD ELEMENTS. Both
                               statements generate the same results)
REC EL SRS-NAME.
REC EL SRS-ADDR.
```

The resulting record is 32 characters long, having a two-character name field and a 30-character address field, and is not the expected 40character record.

A similar problem can be experienced with mapping records which were originally derived from elements used in the database. If the record's element is changed without corresponding changes being made to the element itself, unexpected results may occur when migrating the map record from one dictionary to another. Suppose the original elements and map record were defined as follows:

```
ADD ELEMENT SRS-NAME  PIC X(10) USAGE DISPLAY.
ADD ELEMENT SRS-ADDR  PIC X(25) USAGE DISPLAY.
ADD RECORD SRS-CUST.
    RECORD ELEMENT SRS-NAME.
    RECORD ELEMENT SRS-ADDR.
```

If the map record's SRS-NAME field is changed to PIC XX (using the technique described under Changing Records That Are Used In Maps), the 'real' element does not match the record's element. If the record is migrated to the Quality Assurance dictionary by PUNCHing it without picture overrides, the following syntax results:

```
PUNCH RECORD SRS-CUST
    WITHOUT PICTURE OVERRIDES AS SYNTAX.              (input)

ADD RECORD SRS-CUST.                                  (output)
    RECORD ELEMENT SRS-NAME.
    RECORD ELEMENT SRS-ADDR.
```

The original element definition is pulled in, PIC X(10), not the modified version. Therefore, if a mapping record element's picture or usage is modified, it is mandatory that the original element also be modified to reflect the change.

11.5.6   Maintaining Sets

Answers to the critical questions discussed in Section 11.5.4 for common modifications to sets are summarized in Table 11-2 . Because we assumed that the schema was modified rather than deleted and readded to make these change, Table 11-2 is relevant to only Release 10 sites. Most set changes require a corresponding change to the database.

Table 11-2 Effects of Schema Set Modifications

CHANGE	IMPACT				
	Processing Halted	Compiles Halted	Recompiles Needed[1]	Data Change Needed	System Cycles
Add new set/index/pointer positions (on an existing set)	Yes	Yes	Yes	Yes	No
Delete set, index, or pointer positions (on an existing set)	Yes	Yes	Yes	Yes	No
Change set order options, set membership options, or index sequence	No	Yes	No	No	No
Change sort sequence	Yes	Yes	No	Yes	No
Add new record type to multi-member set	No[2]	Yes	No	No[2]	No

[1]Yes in this column means recompile/regenerate any program/dialog which used to access the deleted entity or which requires access to the new or changed entity.

[2]If occurrences of the record need to be loaded, processing will be halted for the duration of the load (i.e., data change)

However, if dummy sets have been defined, adding a new set can be done without restructuring the area. Dummy sets are those sets defined in the schema but not used, and are designed simply to reserve space in record prefixes. Dummy sets can be defined for a record, but the record's designation as an owner or member of the dummy set must match its role in the subsequently-defined set or a restructure is required anyway.

For example, assume the records and sets illustrated in Figure 11-11 have been defined in the schema. Suppose only A and B represent real data records; records Y and Z are in the schema merely to reserve pointer space in A's prefix. Suppose further that new requirements subsequently lead to defining a new record C and a new set A-C (Figure 11-12). There is no problem with assigning the old A-Z pointer positions to the new A-C set because A is the OWNER record in both cases; only a schema modification is required and no data restructure is required. The schema changes required are deleting record Z, deleting set A-Z, adding record C, and adding set A-C using the same pointer positions as the old set A-Z.

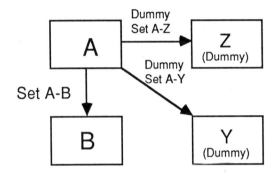

Figure 11-11 Schema with Dummy Sets

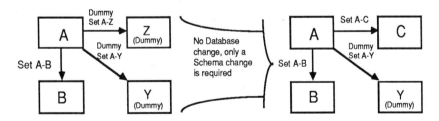

Figure 11-12 Adding a New Set by Replacing a Dummy Set – No Restructure Required

If, however, subsequent requirements lead to defining a new record, D, which is the *owner* of A in the new set D-A, trouble arises if the dummy A-Y pointer positions are used. Storing a new D would succeed but connecting an A record to a D record would fail. The connect would fail because the pointer on A, defined for the old A-Y set, was initialized to point to A (identifying a null set). The pointer

should be initialized to -1 (X'FFFFFFFF'), identifying an uncon-
nected member, to be valid for set D-A. Therefore, a restructure, or an
unload and reload, of the database is required to implement the new
set D-A (Figure 11-13).

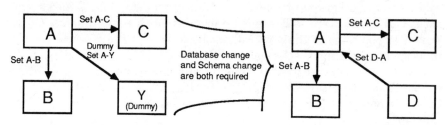

Figure 11-13 Adding a New Set – Restructure Required

Dummy pointers take up real space in the prefix of existing
records. In our original example A-Z and A-Y were dummy sets reserving space in A's prefix. If NEXT, PRIOR, and OWNER pointers
were specified for each set, 16 bytes have been reserved in the prefix of
each occurrence of record A, i.e., space for next and prior pointers for
each set, owner pointers exist only in the member record's prefix.
Thus, there is a tradeoff between wasting disk storage now and saving restructures of the database later. The size of the owner and
member records will increase if new sets are implemented using the
restructure utility, perhaps forcing some records to be relocated. An
unload and reload of the affected area is often scheduled soon after the
restructure to "clean up" relocated records. For very large databases,
it may be appropriate to reserve space with dummy pointers because a
restructure, possibly creating relocated records, might not be followed
by an unload/reload due to the size of the database.

When adding new sets that are not replacing dummy sets, be
careful about using the auto pointer option on the schema compiler
(Release 10). When the auto pointer option is used and schema sets
are punched (with the intention of deleting and adding the entire
schema or a portion of a schema), the pointers assigned for an existing set may be different when the sets are added back to the dictionary. Differences occur when new sets were added or the syntax is
moved around. If data on the database is not reloaded, '1111' abends
result (discussed in Chapter 12). We recommend using the auto
pointer option on the initial ADD of a schema and assigning pointers
manually on subsequent deletes and adds of sets, to ensure that pointers match existing pointers. Alternatively, the auto pointer option
may be used exclusively, provided the database is unloaded and
reloaded (or initialized, for test databases in the early stages of
development) after every schema set change.

Portions of the schema are likely to be deleted and added at intervals if a global schema is in use, i.e., portions that are related to the application being changed. The delete-and-add technique may be appropriate if massive changes are being made, i.e., adding ten new sets, changing the pointer options on all existing sets, changing four sets from sorted sets to sets with user-defined indexes, etc. Pointer mismatches tend to happen when quick and dirty modifications are made. Pointer mismatches also occur when Release 5.7 delete-and-add techniques continue to be used in a Release 10 environment. Time spent learning procedures for Release 10 is worthwhile in terms of the time saved by not having to correct errors arising from using old Release 5.7 procedures inappropriately.

11.5.7 Maintaining Areas

The effects of common types of area maintenance under Release 10 are summarized in Table 11-3. Implementing area changes requires a corresponding change to the global DMCL, which does not become effective until the next time the system is brought up. Therefore, area changes impact applications that do not require the change because the system must be cycled.

It is often convenient to create several schemas under Release 5.7, so that when a new area is needed a global schema need not be deleted and recompiled. This procedure eliminates compile time and down time for unaffected applications. Only the new area schema, the global DMCL, and relevant subschemas need to be recompiled.

Table 11-3 Effects of Schema Area Modifications

	IMPACT				
CHANGE	Processing Halted	Compiles Halted	Recompiles Needed[1]	Data Change Needed	System Cycles
Add new area	Yes	Yes	Yes	Yes	Yes
Change area page range/ page size	Yes	Yes	No	Yes	Yes
Delete area	No[2]	No	No	No	No[2]

[1]Yes in this column means recompile/regenerate any program/dialog which used to access the deleted entity or which requires access to the new or changed entity.

[2]There is no impact if the area is being deleted because it is not used (the global DMCL can be changed and the system can be cycled when it is convenient). However, if the area is being deleted because all of its records are being transferred to other areas, the value in each impact column becomes 'Yes'.

To add a new area to the database, include it in a site-specific schema rather than CDMSCHM or GLBLSCHM, Cullinet-supplied schemas which are created and updated during installation and re-installation procedures. Also include the new area in the global DMCL, local mode DMCL's, and in any subschemas that use it.

Area definitions must be stored in the primary dictionary so they can be included in the global DMCL and made available at run time. The application schema containing all the record, set, area, and file information may be developed on either the primary or a secondary dictionary, however area and file definitions must also be on the primary dictionary to be available for inclusion in the global DMCL (Figure 11-14).

The schema, the global DMCL, and only those subschemas that include the area must be recompiled to change an existing area. Unlike adding a new area, though, a change to the page range or the page size of an area requires some change to data already stored in the area. The database change is accomplished with either the utilities IDMSUNLD and IDMSDBLU, or the utility IDMSXPAG (Section 11.6). The SPACE MANAGEMENT INTERVAL (SMI) clause in all affected DMCL's must specify the original page size if the area's page size is changed with the IDMSXPAG utility; refer to the DDL Reference (Release 10) or the Database Design and Definition Guide (Release 5.7) for details.

Always check the sysgen when adding or changing areas to determine if any IDMS AREA statements must be added or modified. Rerun the sysgen compiler if IDMS AREA changes are required.

ADS/O dialogs whose subschemas have been affected must be regenerated following the elimination or renaming of an area. If the dialog is not regenerated after area names are changed or deleted, but the subschema is regenerated, the dialog abends with a message indicating that the area cannot be located. When ADS/O dialogs are generated a RAT (READY Area Table) is created containing literals for all the areas included in the dialog's subschema. All areas in the RAT are readied by default when the dialog issues its first DB request; the dialog abends if it has not been regenerated.

11.5.8 Maintaining Database Files

Table 11-4 contains a summary of the effects of common types of file maintenance under Release 10. Implementing file changes (like area changes) requires corresponding changes to the global DMCL. DMCL changes do not become effective until the next time the system is brought up. Therefore, file changes impact applications that do not require the change because the system must be cycled.

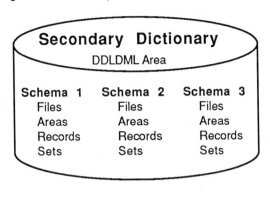

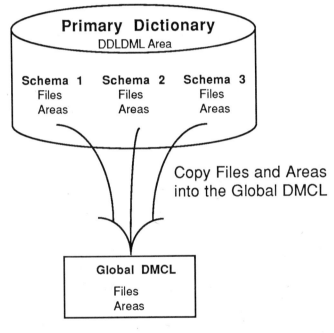

Copy Files and Areas
into the Global DMCL

Figure 11-14 Considerations for Schemas Developed on Secondary Dictionaries File names may be the same but area page ranges/groups must be unique among the schemas on the secondary dictionary. On the primary dictionary, file names must be unique and area page ranges/groups must be identical to those specified on the secondary dictionary

Corresponding area definitions must also be changed when adding, changing, or deleting files. It is best to assign a large area to multiple files, where each file can be assigned to a separate pack and moved around as needed to reduce contention.

Table 11-4 Effects of Schema File Modifications

CHANGE	Processing Halted	Compiles Halted	Recompiles Needed[1]	Data Change Needed	System Cycles
			IMPACT		
Add new file	Yes	Yes	No	Yes	Yes
Change which areas are assigned to a file	Yes	Yes	No	Yes	Yes
Change file's assignment name	No	Yes	No	No	Yes
Delete file	No[2]	No	No	No	No[2]

[1]Yes in this column means recompile/regenerate any program/dialog which used to access the deleted entity or which requires access to the new or changed entity.

[2]There is no impact if the file is being deleted because it is not used (the global DMCL can be changed and the system can be cycled when it is convenient). Otherwise, the impacts shown for 'Change which areas are assigned to a file' are applicable.

11.5.9   Adding or Changing Buffer Pools

Adding buffers or changing buffer pool assignments requires no database change. Simply change the global DMCL to include a particular area in a pool or add a new pool with its appropriate number of buffer pages. The global DMCL can be changed at any time; the change takes effect the next time the system is brought up. Areas with smaller page sizes can use buffer pools with equal or larger buffer sizes, but not vice versa. Also, check the sysgen for IDMS BUFFER override statements and rerun the sysgen compiler if any buffer override statements need changing.

Don't forget to add extra space to the overall partition/region size specified in the system's startup JCL for each additional pool page. Modify the 'REGION=' clause (OS) or the 'SIZE=' clause (DOS) as needed to ensure sufficient space at startup time.

11.6   MAINTAINING DATABASES

The database must often be changed when the database description is modified. In many test environments test data need not be preserved following a description change, thus allowing the database to be initialized and reloaded (the load procedure must be changed to include new or changed structures). Data must be preserved in all production environments and some test environments. Therefore, the database must be reorganized, restructured, unloaded/reloaded, etc., as appropriate following a change to the database description. A few changes can be made to a database description without requiring major database changes. Examples of such description changes are contained in the following paragraphs.

Intra-record modifications that do not change the length of the data portion of a record can be made easily. For example, changing a PIC 9(5) field to a PIC X(5) field does not require any database change. If FILLER was included in the record new fields can be added transparently and the FILLER reduced; at most, a numeric field initialization would be needed.

If dummy pointers were reserved in a record (i.e., sets defined but never used), some new sets and new record types can be included in the schema later without requiring a restructure. New member record types can be added to the description of a multi-member set without any database changes. Sets with a single type of member record can be changed to multi-member sets without database change.

Page reserves can be changed in the DMCL and become effective the next time the system is brought up. No database change is required.

With Release 10's integrated indexing, the number of entries per SR8 record can be increased or decreased without a database change. The SR8 record is the system record type which contains index entries.

An area's page range can be increased without an unload and reload of the area if it does not contain any CALC record types. A new file must be allocated and initialized with sufficient number of blocks to contain the new pages. The area definition in the schema (and affected DMCL's) must be modified to map the area to both the old and new files.

Most description changes, however, also require database changes. There are a variety of tools for database maintenance in the IDMS/R environment. Table 11-5 lists database maintenance tools.

11.6.1   Batch DML Programs

Custom batch DML programs may be coded and used to implement database changes. They provide additional capabilities and often execute faster than generalized utility programs. Typically, batch DML programs are written in COBOL, but they may also be written in assembly language, Fortran, or PL/I.

Table 11-5 Database Maintenance Tools

DB Maintenance Tool	Description
Batch DML programs	Custom-coded utilities
IDMSUNLD/IDMSDBLU	Unload/reload utilities
IDMSRSTU	Restructure utility
IDMSXPAG	Page expand utility
IDMSTBLU	Index maintenance utility (R. 10)
IDMSIXUD	Index Maintenance utility (R. 5.7)
Operating system utilities	General file utilities
Third party utilities	Miscellaneous

Batch COBOL DML programs can be used for initial database loads. The IDMS/R fastload utility, IDMSDBLU, requires a user-written format program of COBOL, non-DML code. The format program is usually as complicated as a standard COBOL DML load program, so the fastload utility provides no savings in human resources. However, the fastload utility loads a database faster than a COBOL DML program if there is a high degree of networking in the database structure (i.e., there are many set relationships between records with many junction records as opposed to hierarchies).

COBOL DML programs are often used to reinitialize fields or to make other intra-record changes that do not alter the length of the data portion of the record, adding and initializing a new field and reducing the amount of FILLER in the record for example. A COBOL DML program should be used instead of the restructure utility when there are different values to initialize dependent on other data in the record. The restructure utility can initialize a new field to only one value.

Custom COBOL unload and reload procedures are needed in instances where the IDMS/R unload/reload utilities will not work, for example, moving one record type to a different area without unloading the entire area. Moving records might be necessary when changing a VIA record type's area from the owner's area to a separate area. Custom procedures also are needed when changing a CALC record to a VIA record, a VIA record to a CALC record, or a one-to-many relationship to a many-to-many relationship. Under Release 10, customized procedures are useful for connecting selected records to a system or user defined integrated index. Under Release 5.7, customized procedures are required to rebuild or reorganize indexes.

Custom unload and reload procedures usually involve several custom COBOL DML programs and some standard DB utilities. For example, three custom programs and two utilities would be used to move all occurrences of a VIA record type from the owner's area to a separate area:

1) IDMSDUMP or a disk management utility to backup the database
2) A custom COBOL DML program to write a copy of all occurrences of the VIA record type to tape along with the owner record's key (DBKEY)
3) A second custom COBOL DML program issuing DML ERASE statements to erase the VIA record occurrences from the owner's area
4) IDMSINIT utility to initialize the new area
5) A third custom COBOL DML program to store the VIA record occurrences in the new area

Steps one through three use the old subschema and DMCL. Steps four and five require the new subschema and DMCL.

11.6.2   IDMSUNLD/IDMSDBLU Utilities

The IDMSUNLD and IDMSDBLU utilities unload one or more areas in a database to tape or disk and then reload the data into newly initialized areas. The reload program usually invokes a new subschema incorporating changes made to the database description. Frequently, major logical and physical changes are implemented with custom DML procedures as described above. Some changes possible with the unload/reload utilities include:

- Page range change
- Page size change (Used instead of IDMSXPAG only when other changes are implemented at same time as page size change)
- Locate a VIA record VIA a different owner
- Compress records
- Record location mode change (e.g., CALC to VIA)
- Record placement change from one area to another (unloading the whole area)

The most common change implemented through an unload/reload is an increase in the number of pages in an area, thereby expanding the area.

Unload/reload operations are done on occasion without a description change, i.e., the load subschema is the same as the unload subschema. This physical reorganization cures some problems with the database such as reducing record overflow, eliminating variable length record fragmentation, and eliminating relocated records.

Any logically deleted records must first be physically deleted by running the IDMSLDEL utility. A reorganization can be very helpful but it will not cure all storage problems, for example, it will not fix a physically corrupted database (see discussion of broken chains in Chapter 12).

11.6.3   IDMSRSTU Utility

The IDMSRSTU utility restructures a database to implement logical and physical database description changes. IDMSRSTU modifies the database in place by expanding, contracting, or rearranging records. The utility allows both data and prefix portions of records to be adjusted. Changes than can be implemented using the restructure utility include:

- Adding or deleting fields
- Initializing fields
- Changing the order of fields
- Adding or deleting sets
- Adding or deleting pointers for existing sets
- Compressing records

Changing the order of fields within a record can be done with IDMSRSTU, or a COBOL DML program. However, be cautious of changes which modify the control length of compressed records. The control length is the displacement into the record to the record's key field. If the restructure adds a field before a key field, and the key was not specified as CTRL (restructure syntax), IDMS/R will attempt to compress the key field and subsequent access to that record will fail.

Areas must be offline to CV during restructure. A backup of the areas should be taken prior to running the restructure utility because the areas are modified in place. Operation of the utility is controlled by a table created with assembly language macros. We recommend using the schema compare utility, IDMSRSTC (available only under Release 10), to help define the restructure input macros, thereby reducing the chances of a bad restructure. Run IDMSPFIX to dump several pages of the areas both before and after the restructure as an additional precaution. Next, manually verify that record structures match the new database description after the restructure operation.

Expand the page size or increase page range (by running IDMSXPAG, or IDMSUNLD and IDMSDBLU) prior to running the restructure if implementing the changes causes the amount of available free space per page to drop below 30% of page size. Expanding the area first reduces the likelihood of the restructure utility creating overflowed record fragments.

11.6.4   IDMSXPAG Utility

The IDMSXPAG utility is used to increase the page size of a database area without reorganizing the DB. IDMSXPAG provides the simplest and fastest method of expanding an area when it has become too full. The IDMSXPAG utility reads the old file and writes the information to a newly initialized file with a larger blocksize. The original page size must be specified on the SMI (Space Management Interval) clause of all DMCL's containing the area the first time the page size is increased using IDMSXPAG. Thereafter, the page size can be expanded any number of times without further changes to the SMI clause.

Whenever blocksize is increased (because page size was expanded), the total buffer pool size increases if the number of buffers remains the same. Therefore, a larger Central Version or fewer buffers for the area (which may increase I/O) is one disadvantage of increasing page size.

Page expands are often done after migration to new disk devices (e.g., from 3350 to 3380) to make more efficient use of disk space. For example, a half-track block on a 3350 is 9,440 bytes. Only four of these blocks can be placed on a 3380 track. However, quarter-track on a 3380 is 11,476 bytes long, therefore about 2K bytes are being wasted per block. Expanding the page size up to 11,476 bytes allows the disk space to be used more efficiently.

IDMSXPAG also can be used to create space when new VIA record types are added to an area. Running IDMSXPAG reduces the possibility of VIA record overflow by ensuring that there are no full pages.

A planned IDMSXPAG can be used in place of the DMCL's page reserve. Page reserve reduces the amount of space available for storing new records on a page. The reserved space normally is used for expansion of variable length records. Pages can be expanded when statistics indicate a need, rather than reserving space on each page for potential growth of variable length records.

IDMSXPAG is not a cure-all solution for space problems. A page can be expanded only up to track size or 32K, whichever is smaller.

11.6.5   IDMSTBLU Utility (Release 10) and IDMSIXUD Utility (Release 5.7)

The utility IDMSTBLU (Release 10) is used to maintain integrated indexes. It may be used to build, rebuild, or delete an index. Only record types defined with a system-owned index can be loaded with this utility. Records with user-defined indexes cannot be built or rebuilt using the IDMSTBLU utility, as of this writing. COBOL programs or the unload/reload utilities can be used to build or rebuild user-defined indexes, however they also unload and reload the data; currently there is no facility to handle just the indexes.

The IDMSTBLU utility allows indexes to be constructed in the following three manners:

1) To build a system-defined index initially, use parameters:
   SUBSCHEMA=*subschema-name*
   BUILD INDEX=*set-name*

2) To reorganize an existing index, use parameters:
   SUBSCHEMA=*subschema-name*
   REBUILD INDEX=*set-name*,FROM=INDEX

3) If the index structure itself is invalid due to recovery problems, use parameters:
   SUBSCHEMA=*subschema-name*
   REBUILD INDEX=*set-name*,FROM=MEMBERS

The third type of index rebuilding is needed if the index was restored from a backup copy but the data it points to was not restored appropriately. Rebuilding from the members in this instance would recreate each entry in the index based on the target record occurrence rather than on information already in the index.

SPF indexes are maintained using the IDMSIXUD utility and custom DML programs. DML programs must be used to rebuild SPF index structures.

11.6.6 Operating System Utilities

Operating system utilities are useful for block level changes, i.e., changes that do not alter the contents of blocks. Operating system utilities can be used to copy or move database files from one device to another, to provide multiple user databases, and/or to perform simple reorganizations. For example, operating system utilities (IDCAMS utility REPRO command with block count specified) can be used to divide an area previously stored in a single file into two files. Only a schema definition change would be necessary to add the additional file name and area breakdown.

11.6.7 Third Party Utilities

Several third party vendors offer IDMS/R-compatible utilities. For example, some vendors provide a database reorganization utility with functions similar to the Release 10 version of IDMSUNLD. The National IDMS Users Association keeps a library of software contributed by users; several database maintenance programs are available.

11.7   CONCLUSION

Changes to DB/DC systems are natural and frequent phenomena.
System module changes are implemented to install the current version of software or to correct software errors. System description
changes are made to add or change components of the sysgen or to
modify resource allocations. Changes are made to database descriptions because of evolving database design and sizing requirements.
When database descriptions change, database contents often must be
processed by a utility program to reflect the change.

The techniques described in this chapter aid users in successfully
managing the ever changing environment. If changes are implemented in a haphazard fashion, and some components affected by the
change are not modified as well, trouble can arise. In the next chapter
we examine common problems and their resolution.

Suggestions for further reading on Maintaining the Environment:

The following Cullinet Manuals
  For Release 10 sites:
    1) Integrated Data Dictionary DDDL Reference (Record and
        element syntax)
    2) IDMS/R Database Operations (Maintaining databases
        and data dictionaries, description of database utilities)
    3) IDMS/R DDL Reference (Schema, DMCL, and subschema
        syntax and compiler information, modifying database
        definitions)
    4) Cullinet System Software–System Generation (System
        generation parameters, running sysgen compiler, modi-
        fying systems)
    5) IDMS-DB/DC Utilities and Supplement for Release 10
        (Detailed instructions for running utilities)
    6) IDMS-DC/UCF Mapping Facility User's Guide (Decom-
        piling and recompiling maps)

  For Release 5.7 Sites:
    1) Integrated Data Dictionary DDDL Reference Guide
        (Record and element syntax)
    2) IDMS Database Design and Definition Guide (Schema,
        DMCL, and subschema syntax and compiler information,
        maintaining databases)
    3) IDMS-CV/DC System Generation (System generation pa-
        rameters, running sysgen compiler, modifying systems)

4) IDMS-DB/DC Utilities (Detailed instructions for running utilities)

5) IDMS-DC/UCF Mapping Facility User's Guide (Decompiling and recompiling maps)

12

Trouble Shooting

In this chapter we will discuss trouble shooting IDMS/R problems. Trouble shooting and performance tuning are closely related. A system experiencing performance problems may be only a few steps away from more serious trouble. We will cover problems causing system, program, or dialog abends, problems resulting in corrupted database or journal files, and problems which leave a system hanging and unable to perform further processing. Slowdowns arising from unexpected activity levels and varied processing requirements will be discussed as performance tuning considerations in Chapter 13. Backup and Recovery, Chapter 7, covered general procedures for recovering from broad categories of problems. Here, we will discuss specific problems and how to correct or recover from the problem in an expedient manner.

It is impossible to cover every conceivable problem, so this chapter will focus on common and/or serious problems. Only experience helps one detect and deal with more esoteric problems.

We will examine:

- Trouble shooting tools,
- A general approach to trouble shooting,
- An overview of common problems,
- Identifying and resolving common problems, and
- Information that should be relayed to Cullinet support personnel when in-house problem resolution fails.

12.1 TROUBLE SHOOTING TOOLS

We will discuss trouble shooting tools in two sections. The first section examines tools used to analyze and resolve system problems and the second describes tools for debugging application problems.

12.1.1 Tools for Trouble Shooting System Problems

Tools for trouble shooting system problems may be divided into two categories, namely tools used to analyze problems and tools used to resolve problems. Table 12-1 contains a list of trouble shooting tools. We concentrate on trouble shooting system problems. Specific examples of how to use the tools for trouble shooting system problems comprise the bulk of this chapter.

Table 12-1 Tools for Analysis and Resolution of System Problems

Tools for Problem Analysis	Tools for Problem Resolution

Error messages/codes displayed
   by the system
Cullinet's Error Messages and
   Codes manual
System Statistics
IDMS/R Performance Monitor
Task/transaction statistics
JREPORTs
Hard copies of system outputs
DCMT DISPLAY commands
OPER task
IDMS/R system log
Console log
Operating system display commands
IDMS/R system trace
Dumps
	IDMS/R utilities (IDMSRBCK,
	   IDMSRFWD, IDMSRSTR,
	   IDMSJFIX, IDMSINIT, etc.)
	IDMS/R compilers (schema, subschema,
	   DMCL, system generation)
	DCMT VARY commands

Analysis Tools: Often, the error message or code displayed by the system provides a clue to the nature of the problem if not identifying the problem immediately. Look up the meaning of the message or code in the Error Messages and Codes manual. Error messages and codes are usually displayed on the system console and/or the IDMS/R DC log.

A four-digit number identifies a problem encountered by a system program. System problems usually cause a snap dump of the system to be written to the log and may cause an abend, e.g., '3964' (refer to the Error Messages and Codes Manual for description).

A six-position code prefixed by the two-letter code 'DC' identifies a problem generated by an application program or by Cullinet's application development software (ADS, ADSG, ADSA, OLM, IDD, etc.). The six-position code can appear on the console, a specific terminal, the log, or all of the above. The message associated with the six-position code can be merely informational or may describe a severe problem. To display the associated message online and check its description, issue a DCMT DISPLAY MESSAGE *message-code* command or the IDD request DISPLAY MESSAGE *message-code*.

The ERROR-STATUS field of the subschema control block is used by the system to pass a return code to application programs or dialogs following each request for service. Abnormal ERROR-STATUS values usually identify an application problem. However, some abnormal ERROR-STATUS values are symptoms of system-wide problems. For example, a '0361' ERROR-STATUS is indicative of a broken chain in the database.

System statistics provide valuable information for problem analysis and should be examined regularly. System statistics for an entire run are written to the DC log at shutdown. The statistics collected thus far during a run can be displayed online by issuing a DCMT DISPLAY STATISTICS SYSTEM command. Many DBA's save the log printout containing the system statistics because it provides historical information on changing resource requirements; keeping on hand one or two month's log reports allows current statistics to be compared to those for the same day of the preceding month. The number of times short-on-storage, MAXTASKS, waits-on-storage, and waits-on-program-loads occur, as well as the high water mark of stack should be monitored carefully; these statistics may show critical resource shortages developing.

The IDMS/R Performance Monitor (Release 10) provides in-depth analysis of major IDMS/R performance issues, including CPU usage, wait and response times; memory usage; DB calls and I/O's; and ADS/O activity. The online functions of the Performance Monitor permit monitoring selected dialogs and programs. If a program or dialog is suspected of causing trouble, the Performance Monitor could be used to track the program/dialog during attempts to recreate the problem. Reports from task, transaction, and ADS/O dialog statistics, along with journal reports (called JREPORTs), provide historical information about dialog and program processing. Although these tools are primarily useful for performance tuning, they may provide helpful information during trouble shooting. Further details on the Performance Monitor, task and transaction statistics, and journal reports can be found in Chapter 13.

Saving hard copy outputs from system and database changes equips the DBA staff to deal with problems when they arise. Hard copy printouts often speed recovery procedures by providing a record of changes. Table 12-2 contains a list of hard copy reports which we recommend having on hand at all times.

Table 12-2 Trouble Shooting Tools – Reports to Keep On Hand

Subject	Report	Frequency of Printing Report
Installation or reinstallation	JJOB2 and any portions of JJOB3 that were run	Every new reinstall tape
Software Maint.	AMASPZAP or MAINT/ PDZAP output for all modules zapped, Listings of PTF's,and of affected modules	At the time maintenance is applied
Database	IDMSRPTS	Every Schema change
	IDMSDBAN, all reports	Weekly for each prod. database
	IDMSJRPT reports 2, 3, 4	Daily, or accumulate for a week and print
	IDMSUBSC to DIS-PLAY/PUNCH the subschema	Every subschema change
DC System	Activity Report or CREPORTs	Every sysgen change
	System shutdown statistics from the log	Daily
Global DMCL	IDMSDMCL Assembly output	Every global DMCL change
Applications	CREPORT 050 (for load module sizes), and transaction statistics for relevant modules	Every major new system implementation

DCMT DISPLAY commands are used frequently during problem analysis. Various commands display task, program, run unit, area, physical terminal, logical terminal, system statistics, main storage contents, and much more. The analysis sections of the problem descriptions provide several examples of using DCMT DISPLAY commands to analyze a problem. The OPER task can be used to monitor processing at a particular terminal or to keep an eye on critical system resources. OPER commands are often used along with DCMT DISPLAY commands during problem analysis.

The IDMS/R system log, also called the DC log, provides useful analysis information. As described earlier, error messages and codes usually are written to the IDMS/R system log. Task and system snap dumps, as well as system trace data, are written to the log.

The operating system console log also provides useful information. Error messages and codes are displayed on the console log as well as the IDMS/R log. Problems with the journal archiving utility or the print log utility are often documented only on the console log.

Operating system display commands can be used to display jobs currently executing and those awaiting execution. These commands are especially useful when the IDMS/R system is hanging, causing DCMT commands to be unavailable.

System trace data and system dumps provide information for analyzing complex problems. Detailed analysis of system traces and dumps is usually left to Cullinet support technicians or users well-versed in IDMS/R internals.

Resolution Tools: IDMS/R utilities, compilers, and DCMT VARY commands are the major tools used to resolve system problems. For example, if the system encounters an uninitialized journal block and crashes, the IDMSINIT utility must be run to initialize the journal file properly (details in Section 12.4.6).

One or more of the compilers is run when part of a database or system definition must be modified to resolve a problem. For example, if a system often experiences Short on Storage conditions, the value of STORAGE POOL and/or CUSHION parameters should be changed in the next system generation compile (as discussed in Section 12.7.1).

DCMT VARY commands can solve a variety of problems. Varying the physical terminal offline followed by varying it online may resolve the problem if UCF users are experiencing trouble accessing IDMS/R, for example (details in Section 12.8).

12.1.2   Debugging Tools for Application Problems

Several tools are available to the applications programmer for debugging application problems. These tools are listed in Table 12-3. Brief descriptions of application trouble shooting tools follow; details may be found in programmer's reference manuals for the various products.

The ERROR-STATUS field of the subschema control block is used by the system to pass a return code to application programs/dialogs following each request for service from IDMS/R. ERROR-STATUS is a four byte field that should not be confused with the four byte system abend codes discussed earlier. An abnormal ERROR-STATUS code is displayed on the console or terminal screen indicating that an application program or dialog has abended; the system is still up and processing. Abnormal ERROR-STATUS values are displayed by the

Table 12-3 Tools for Trouble Shooting Application Problems

Application-Related Trouble Shooting Tools
ERROR-STATUS field
DEBUG option of the PROTOCOL statement
Online Debugger
USERTRACE facility
SNAP dumps of application storage
Database access statistics

IDMS-STATUS routine during abort processing of batch run units. When an IDMS-DC program abends, the ERROR-STATUS value as well as the rest of the subschema control block is written to the DC log by the IDMS-STATUS routine. The ERROR-STATUS value for ADS/O dialogs abends is displayed at the terminal as part of the error message, DC173008 - APPLICATION ABORTED. BAD IDMS STATUS RETURNED; STATUS=xxxx, and a snap dump of the subschema control block is written to the DC log. The ERROR-STATUS code can be translated using charts in programmer's reference cards and manuals.

If DEBUG is specified as part of the PROTOCOL statement in a DML program (i.e., batch, CICS, or DC programs), the DML compiler identifies DML verbs with sequential numbers in the program listing and in the CALL to IDMS/R. If the program abends because of an unexpected non-zero ERROR-STATUS code, the DML sequence number identifies the DML verb which resulted in the error. PROTOCOL IS DEBUG does not apply to ADS/Online dialogs.

Cullinet's Online Debugger task (available only in Release 10 shops) is particularly useful for debugging IDMS-DC programs and ADS/O dialogs. Online Debugger allows the programmer to establish breakpoints at which execution of the program or dialog is to be halted. When processing is halted at a breakpoint, the programmer can display and/or alter memory contents and restart the program/dialog at the next or any other instruction.

USERTRACE is helpful for debugging DC programs. It keeps track of the program in control, the DML sequence number being executed, and register contents each time DB/DC services are requested by the program.

The SNAP verb causes the system to write a dump to the DC log of all storage and program areas associated with the issuing task. SNAP is available to DC programs and ADS/Online dialogs.

The ACCEPT DATABASE STATISTICS statement may be issued by application programs and ADS/O dialogs to capture the number of database I/O's incurred, database calls issued, and shared locks and exclusive locks placed during the run unit's processing. This information also can be displayed online while the program/dialog is executing by issuing the DCMT DISPLAY RUN UNIT command or using the OPER task.

12.2 A GENERAL APPROACH TO TROUBLE SHOOTING

The first step in trouble shooting is checking the system console messages and the IDMS/R log for either a four-digit number or a six-position code prefixed by 'DC'. Looking up the number or code in the Error Messages and Codes manual is a good starting point and often identifies the problem and recommended solution immediately. A description of the message associated with six-position error codes can be displayed online by issuing a DCMT DISPLAY MESSAGE *message-code* or the IDD request DISPLAY MESSAGE *message-code*.

The second step is printing the log and partition dumps, providing dumps exist (e.g., for problems resulting in system failure, such as a program check in a Cullinet-supplied module). Both the log dump and the partition dump should be printed because the problem's specifics often change during the time delay between Central Version's dumping of itself to the log and the operating system's dump of the partition/region. Analyze the PSW (Program Status Word) in the dump(s) to determine the type of program check and the address of the module which aborted. Next, find out if any maintenance has been applied to that module recently. In general, look for anything that has changed in the environment, e.g., a reinstallation, a sysgen or DMCL change, PTF's (Program Temporary Fixes) that have been applied, or modules that have been relinked. Look for changes in interfacing system software environments (e.g., a relink of the supervisor without the IDMS/R SVC, or a new release of CICS in a UCF-CICS environment) as well as in IDMS/R application and software environments. Also, refer to Cullinet's latest IDMS/R technical reports for any problems showing similar symptoms.

Often, trouble shooting does not lend itself to a simple series of steps. When the above approach fails to identify the problem, see if the symptoms match those of common system problems described in the next sections.

12.3   AN OVERVIEW OF COMMON PROBLEMS

Trouble may arise from a number of sources. Problems often occur
as a direct result of a change in systems, databases, or applications.
Unexpected activity levels at run time are another source of trouble.
Other problems are caused by system software bugs or hardware mal-
functions. Finally, application errors can corrupt database contents
(not in the sense of broken chains, but in terms of the data contents
being wrong, e.g., a member record connected to the wrong owner
occurrence because of incorrect currency). Table 12-4 categorizes
common problems by their causes.

Table 12-4 Causes of Common Problems

Cause	Specific Problem	Symptoms
Changes to the Environment	No application database areas defined in global DMCL	All programs/dialogs abending with '0966' ERROR-STATUS codes
	New database areas not defined in global DMCL	Programs/dialogs READYing new areas abending with '0966' ERROR-STATUS code
	New database areas defined in DMCL but not included in CV startup JCL	IDMS/R varying the areas offline during startup with '3003' or '3005' error message
	Global DMCL page range or page size does not match database	IDMS/R varying areas offline during startup with '3003' or '3005' error message, and programs receive '0966' ERROR-STATUS codes
	Improperly initialized database area	'3010' or '3011' DBIO error
	Improperly initialized journal file	System crashes during startup with '3005' error, or system crashes during run with '3010'/'3011' error
	Subschema page range does not match DMCL	Programs/dialogs abending 'nn71' ERROR-STATUS codes

- (continued on next page) -

Table 12-4 Causes of Common Problems (continued)

Cause	Specific Problem	Symptoms
Changes to the Environment	Length of prefix and/or data portion of DB record does not match length defined in subschema	'1111' error, and a system dump
	Subschema not found	Programs/dialogs abending with 'nn74' ERROR-STATUS
Unexpected Change in Activity Levels	Short on storage	System hangs (some activity continues)
	Too few UCF terminals defined	Users cannot make contact with IDMS/R through UCF
	Log full	System hangs (no activity continues)
	All journals full	System hangs (no activity continues)
System Software or Hardware Failures	Broken chain(s) on DB	Programs/dialogs abending with 'nn60', 'nn61', or 'nn71' ERROR-STATUS codes, and/or faulty processing results
	Bad journal block or inaccessible journal file	System will not come up or IDMSRBCK/IDMSRFWD utilities will not run
	Data check on DB or journal disk	Operating system messages written to the console
	Head crash on DB or journal disk	'3010'/'3011' error, and possibly a system crash (Journals errors only)
Faulty Application Updates	Logically corrupted database	Invalid data in a report or display
Improper Recovery	Broken chain(s) on DB	Programs/dialogs abending with 'nn60', 'nn61', or 'nn71' ERROR-STATUS codes, and/or faulty processing results

The following sections describe some specific problems and how to resolve them. Each section examines problems exhibiting a specific major symptom, for example several problems causing the system to 'hang' are discussed together. Table 12-5 contains a list of symptoms, possible problems exhibiting that symptom, and the section in which the problem is discussed. Each problem is discussed using a five part format. Figure 12-1 illustrates this format.

Table 12-5 Major Symptoms and Associated Problem Areas

Major Symptom	Associated Problem Area	Covered in Section
System will not come up	Insufficient memory	12.4.1
	Module not found	12.4.2
	Journals full	12.4.3
	Log full	12.4.4
	Bringing up a second CV with the same CVNUMBER or system version number as a CV already running	12.4.5
	Mismatch between disk journals and global DMCL	12.4.6
Database areas varied offline during startup	No JCL for area's files ('3005' error message)	12.5.1
	Areas previously locked ('3005' error message)	12.5.2
	DMCL and database page sizes do not match ('3005' error message)	12.5.3
	DMCL page ranges do not match database page ranges ('3003' error message)	12.5.4
System crashes during the run	Cause indicated by log or console messages	12.2
	Mismatch between disk journal and global DMCL	12.6.1
System hangs, unable to process further in some cases	Short on storage	12.7.1
	MAXTASKS reached	Ch. 13
	Runaway tasks	Ch. 13
	Run unit using PROTECTED or EXCLUSIVE USAGE-MODE	Ch. 13
	Run unit causing excessive I/O	Ch. 13
	Journals full	12.4.3
	Log full	12.4.4

- - - - - - - - - - - - - - - - - - - -(continued on next page)- - - - - - - - - - - - - - - - - - - -

Table 12-5 Major Symptoms and Associated Problem Areas (continued)

Major Symptom	Associated Problem Area	Covered in Section
CICS users unable to make contact with IDMS/R through UCF	CICS interface program not active	12.8.2
	Logic error in UCFCICS program	12.8.3
	Too few UCF terminals or MAXERUS defined in sysgen	12.8.4
	Transmission error	12.8.5
'1111' error	Length of prefix/data portion of DB record does not match length as defined in subschema	12.9.1
'3003'/'3005' error	Areas known to the global DMCL are unavailable, improperly initialized, or not present	12.5.1 through 12.5.4
'3010'/'3011' error	Data or equipment check	12.10.1
	Head crash on DB or journal disk	12.10.2
	Improperly initialized DB area	12.10.3
	DMCL and DB page ranges do not match	12.5.4
	Mismatch between disk journals and global DMCL	12.4.6
'3996' error	Broken chain(s) on DB	12.11.1
Programs/dialogs abending with 'nn60', 'nn61', or 'nn71' ERROR-STATUS	Broken Chain(s) on DB	12.11.1
Programs/dialogs abending with '0966' ERROR-STATUS code	Areas locked	12.5.2
	Wrong global DMCL used at run time	12.12.1
Programs/Dialogs abending with 'nn69' ERROR-STATUS code	Confusing array of problems	12.13
Programs/Dialogs abending with 'nn71' ERROR-STATUS code	Subschema and DB page ranges do not match	12.14.1
	Broken chain(s) on DB	12.11.1
Programs/Dialogs abending with 'nn74' ERROR-STATUS code	Subschema not found	12.15.1

- -(continued on next page)- -

Table 12-5 Major Symptoms and Associated Problem Areas (continued)

Major Symptom	Associated Problem Area	Covered in Section
Programs/Dialogs abending with 'nn75' ERROR-STATUS code	I/O error Improperly initialized area	12.10.2 12.10.3
Invalid data on report or display	Broken chain(s) on DB Faulty application updates	12.11.1 12.17.1
System hangs during shutdown	Tasks still executing	12.18.1
Utilities IDMSRFWD and IDMSRBCK abending	Journal sequence errors	12.19.1

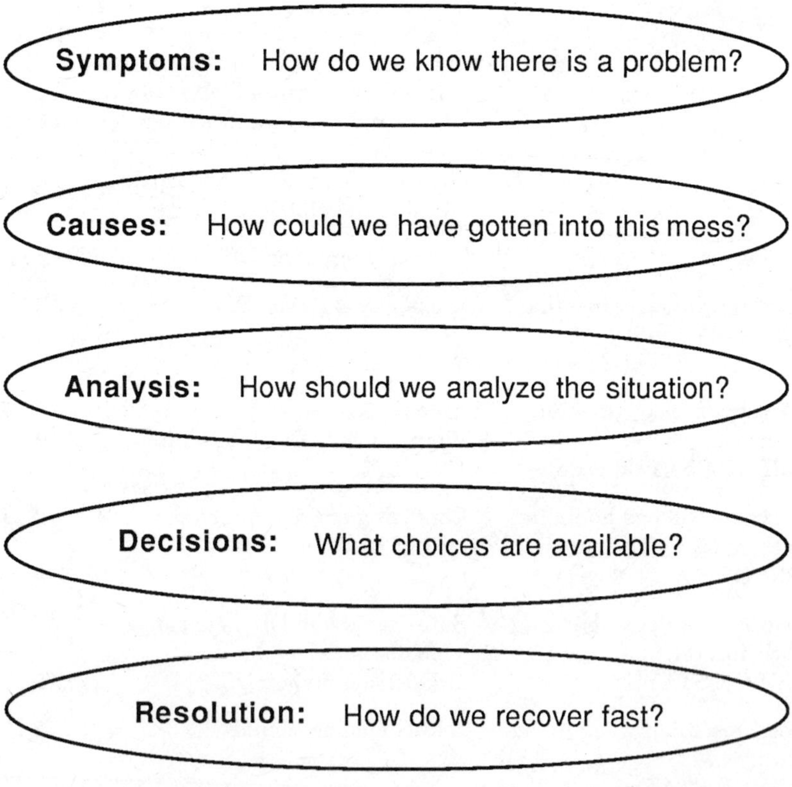

Symptoms: How do we know there is a problem?

Causes: How could we have gotten into this mess?

Analysis: How should we analyze the situation?

Decisions: What choices are available?

Resolution: How do we recover fast?

Figure 12-1 Format of Problem Descriptions

12.4 MAJOR SYMPTOM – THE SYSTEM WILL NOT COME UP

We will examine specific problems as they might occur in the sequence of a normal run, beginning with bringing up the system. If the system will not come up, the usual suspects include:

- Insufficient memory,
- Module not found,
- All disk journals are full,
- IDMS/R log is full,
- Trying to bring up two CV's with the same CVNUMBER or system version number on one physical machine, and
- Mismatch between the disk journals and the global DMCL.

12.4.1 Problem – Insufficient Memory

Symptoms: The system will not come up and aborts during start up processing with the abend code '3994'. The 80A system error code under OS indicates that insufficient memory caused the failure.

Causes: Typically, an insufficient memory problem is caused by making a change to the size of the storage pool, or one of the program pools in the sysgen, without making a corresponding change in the size partition/region specified in the startup JCL. Making a change in the global DMCL which increases the number of buffers or adds new buffer pools without increasing the partition's memory also can cause this problem. Insufficient memory problems can arise if native VSAM files have been added to an IDMS/R system because approximately 300K of extra memory is required for the VSAM access method routines.

Analysis: Determine which component of the system has changed recently and how much additional storage is required.

Decisions: None.

Resolution: Allocate additional memory to the partition/region and bring the system up.

12.4.2 Problem – Module Not Found

Symptoms: The system will not come up. The message '806-4' identifies the missing module under OS. Depending on which module is missing, CV message codes may identify the problem. Specifically, there is no message if the operating system-dependent routine is missing. Message '3981' is displayed if the global DMCL is missing. Message '2825' is displayed if the DCPARM module is not found (DOS only). Message '3982' is displayed if the DC system is not found in dictionary. Message '3997' is displayed if RHDCNTRY is not found.

Causes: The typical cause is either the startup routine name was changed, or the DCPARM module or global DMCL name was changed without a corresponding JCL change (remember, the global DMCL name is specified in the #DCPARM macro). Another possible cause is that the missing module may be in a new library not concatenated with the existing library list (OS) or not included in the LIBDEF search chain (DOS).

Further, the system will not come up if the RHDCNTRY module is missing, or if either RHDCNTRY or IDMSNWKI is improperly linked. RHDCNTRY is the system module that loads most of the partition/region during startup processing. RHDCNTRY uses subschema IDMSNWKI to bind to the dictionary locally, obtaining the dictionary SYS-041 record (CALC key = DCSYSTEM) for the system number being brought up (version number of SYS-041 record), before walking through the dictionary sets to locate all components of the system.

Analysis: None.

Decisions: None.

Resolution: Locate the missing module or correct the JCL/#DCPARM macro to specify the correct module name. Bring up the system.

12.4.3 Problem – All Journals Full

Symptoms: System will not come up or goes into a long wait state.

Causes: The system will go into a wait state if all disk journals are full when the system is brought up. If the system has been processing normally and all the journals become full, the system goes into a long wait state until one of the journals is offloaded and compressed.

The journal-full condition is probably caused by the archive journal job failing (due to JCL error, no initiator or partition available, or a problem with the WTOEXIT) or being cancelled by the operator. Alternatively, the journals may be full because a batch program up dated hundreds of thousands of records and never issued any

COMMITs; eventually, there will be no more room in any of the journals for more before images and after images.

Analysis: When all journals are full, it is impossible to get into the system to determine what is wrong, even through the master console. First, check the console log to see if any 'DC205002 - DISK JOURNAL IS FULL. WAITING FOR IDMSAJNL FOR *journal-name*' messages have been issued. If so, the problem has been identified. Next, check the jobs awaiting execution to see if any IDMSAJNL runs have been held, and check the console log to determine if IDMSAJNL runs aborted or were cancelled. Finally, use operating system display commands to check the batch jobs currently executing, looking for any that are known for updating excessive numbers of records.

Decisions: The system must be cancelled if the journal-full problem was caused by a batch program updating an inordinate number of records. Then a decision must be made either to restore the database from the most recent backup or to rollback all run units active (in flight) when the system was cancelled. The rollback will undoubtedly take a long time, but may be the best alternative if no backup has been taken recently.

Resolution: Running IDMSAJNL successfully and clearing one of the journals will resolve the problem if a journal archiving run has failed, been held, or cancelled. If the previous IDMSAJNL run failed or was cancelled, the input cards to the utility must be changed to specify a disk journal file name and a run type of RESTART (refer to the Utilities manual for details).

For journal-full conditions caused by a batch program updating an extremely large number of records, there may be nothing to compress in any of the journals (Figure 12-2). All before images of records updated by currently active run units must be maintained on the disk journals because they are required for automatic rollback. Cancel the system in this situation and either restore from a recent backup or rollback all those updates using the tapes output from IDMSAJNL. The disk journals must be reinitialized after they have been offloaded and before the system is brought back up.

Run the IDMSRSTR utility (or a disk management utility) to restore from the most recent backup if the choice is to restore the databases. Run IDMSAJNL to offload the outstanding journals to tape. Then run the utility IDMSJFIX on the journal tape to identify a level zero quiesce point just before the large update program began processing. A level zero quiesce point is a time when an ENDJ check

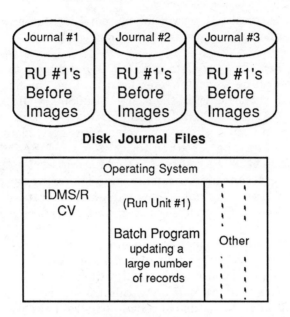

Figure 12-2 Journals Full Due to a Batch Program Updating Many Records

point was taken and no other run units were active (Figure 12-3). Run IDMSRFWD up to the level zero quiesce point for all areas by specifying the quiesce point DATE and TIME:

```
PROCESS=TOTAL,DMCL=dmcl-name
RESTORE=YES,DATE=quiesce-mm/dd/yy,TIME=quiesce-hhmmsshh
```

Initialize the journals by running the IDMSINIT utility and bring up the system. There may have been updates made by run units which started and completed processing between the level zero quiesce point and the time when the system was cancelled. If so, the run units can be identified from the IDMSJFIX report and rerun.

All journals must be archived first if the choice is to rollback the updates. Then IDMSJFIX must be run to write ABRT checkpoints for the run units active when the system was cancelled. Finally, IDMSRBCK can be run to rollback the updates, specifying RESTORE=INFLIGHT. Remember to initialize the journals before attempting to bring up the system.

We recommend COMMITs at intervals in the logic of programs which update a large number of records as a means to prevent future reoccurrences of this problem (refer to Section 7.3.1). Coding COMMITs in programs allows restart capability to be built into the

```
IDMSJFIX 10.00 C8509M  CULLINET SOFTWARE  - - LISTING OF MESSAGES - -  IDMS JOURNAL TAPE FIX      DATE 08/25/86      TIME 15402920      PAGE 1

DMCL=PCV1DMCL

LEVEL  1  BGIN  PROGRAM-ID  RHDCRUAL  DATE 08/25/86  TIME 06022081  RUN-UNIT ID  31159
LEVEL  1  COMT  PROGRAM-ID  RHDCRUAL  DATE 08/25/86  TIME 06025969  RUN-UNIT ID  31159

STATISTICS FOR  RHDCRUAL

   PAGES READ        1998     PAGES WRITTEN        1     PAGES REQUESTED      2058    CALC TARGET         0
   CALC OVERFLOW        0     VIA TARGET           0     VIA OVERFLOW            0    LINES REQUESTED     5
   RECS CURRENT        23     CALLS TO IDMS       31     FRAGMENTS STORED        0    RECS LOCATED        5
   LOCKS REQUESTED            SELECT LOCKS         2     UPDATE LOCKS            6                        0
   LEVEL  1  COMT  RHDCRUAL  DATE 08/25/86  TIME 07191480  RUN-UNIT ID  31159

STATISTICS FOR  RHDCRUAL

   PAGES READ           0     PAGES WRITTEN        0     PAGES REQUESTED         0    CALC TARGET         0
   CALC OVERFLOW        0     VIA TARGET           0     VIA OVERFLOW            0    LINES REQUESTED     0
   RECS CURRENT         0     CALLS TO IDMS        0     FRAGMENTS STORED        1    RECS LOCATED        0
   LOCKS REQUESTED      0     SELECT LOCKS               UPDATE LOCKS            0
   LEVEL  1  COMT  RHDCRUAL  DATE 08/25/86  TIME 07191507  RUN-UNIT ID  31159

STATISTICS FOR  RHDCRUAL

   PAGES READ           1     PAGES WRITTEN        0     PAGES REQUESTED         0    CALC TARGET         2
   CALC OVERFLOW        0     VIA TARGET           0     VIA OVERFLOW            0    LINES REQUESTED     0
   RECS CURRENT         0     CALLS TO IDMS        4     FRAGMENTS STORED        4    RECS LOCATED        0
   LOCKS REQUESTED      1     SELECT LOCKS               UPDATE LOCKS            0
   LEVEL  0  ENDJ  PROGRAM-ID  RHDCRUAL  DATE 08/25/86  TIME 07244690  RUN-UNIT ID  31159

STATISTICS FOR  RHDCRUAL

   PAGES READ           0     PAGES WRITTEN        0     PAGES REQUESTED         0    CALC TARGET         0
   CALC OVERFLOW        0     VIA TARGET           0     VIA OVERFLOW            0    LINES REQUESTED     0
   RECS CURRENT         0     CALLS TO IDMS        0     FRAGMENTS STORED        1    RECS LOCATED        0
   LOCKS REQUESTED      0     SELECT LOCKS               UPDATE LOCKS            0

   AREAS OPEN   PROG-ID      R/U ID    BEFORE   AFTER    USAGE MODE
   DDLDCRUN     RHDCRUAL     31159       10      10      SHARED UPDATE

   BLOCK COUNT   3   RECORD COUNT   35

   DATABASE IN QUIESCE AT END OF TAPE

   ACTIVE PROGRAMS AT END OF TAPE WERE:
   NONE

   DATA BASE MAY NOT NEED TO BE RECOVERED
```

Figure 12-3 Level Zero Quiesce Point

program and reduces the number of journal images and locks which must be maintained concurrently. IDMS STATISTICS, showing the number of records updated and the area usage modes, should be examined when new programs are turned over for production implementation to head off these problems before they occur. It may be appropriate to place limits on the number of calls and I/O's permitted internal tasks and external run units. Call and I/O limits can be turned on in the sysgen (at the time of this writing, lock limits do not trap the sum of shared plus exclusive locks held, making lock limits useless in this situation).

12.4.4 Problem – IDMS/R Log Full

Symptoms: The system will not come up or the system goes into a very long wait state until the log is offloaded. IDMS/R log status messages are appearing with increasing frequency on the console log and the last message shows almost no log space available. The IDMS/R system writes a log status message, DC050001 DCLOG IS nn% FULL, each time the amount of available log space halves. The status messages appear more frequently as the log fills.

Causes: Probable causes for the log area of the data dictionary, DDLDCLOG, becoming full are illustrated in Figure 12-4. The log can become full if the print log utility, RHDCPRLG, fails or is not initiated on a timely basis. The print log job may have failed due to JCL error, no space on output disk, or no initiator available. Another possible cause is a problem with the WTOEXIT program which traps the 'LOG nn% FULL' message and automatically initiates the print log program.

Repetitive system and/or task dumps tend to fill the log rapidly. There are many sources of dumps. Usually, a system dump is written to the log when a system program abends. A system dump is written to the DC log when the system receives a request to display messages with severity codes of 2, 4, or 8. In addition, the system abends on severity codes of 8 or 9. Severity codes and their meanings are listed in the DDDL Reference Guide under the MESSAGE entity. Any message's severity code can be changed to prevent unneeded dumps, or to correct a severity code mistakenly chosen for application messages (e.g., 8 or 9) and change it to a more appropriate value. In addition, any ADS/O dialog or IDMS-DC program can request a task snap dump, producing a dump much smaller than a full system dump, by displaying a message which was defined with a severity code of 1 or 3. External run units which abend cause snap dumps if ABRU SNAP was specified in the sysgen. If the system trace is turned on, each task

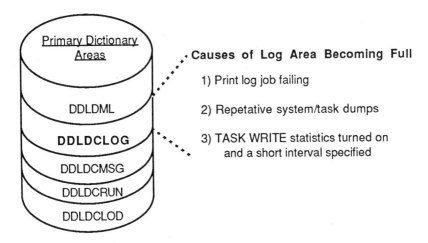

Figure 12-4 Causes of the Log Area Becoming Full

dump is much larger and takes more time to write out to the log than it would otherwise. The increased volume of log writes slows down the entire system in addition to increasing the likelihood of a log-full situation because all other activity must wait until the log writes are complete.

The log may become full if task write statistics are turned on with a short interval. Task write statistics are collected in main storage and written to the log at user-specified intervals. These statistics generate a tremendous volume of information which is written to the log, causing processing to slow down noticeably when the actual write is taking place. When the interval is short, the log is likely to fill up.

Analysis: When the log area of the dictionary is full, it is impossible to get into the system to determine what is wrong, even through the master console. Check the jobs awaiting execution to see if any print log utility (RHDCPRLG) runs have been held, and consult the operating system log to determine if RHDCPRLG runs have aborted or been cancelled. Also, examine the console messages to see if any tasks are abending repeatedly and causing dumps.

Decisions: none.

Resolution: Clear the log. An AREA-IN-USE lock will still be in effect for the DDLDCLOG area if the RHDCPRLG log job was cancelled or failed. Users often choose to write log output to sequential files, saving a week's worth of old logs. If there is insufficient space on the volume to which the sequential files are being written, the

RHCDPRLG run will abend and leave the area locked. The lock must be removed by running the IDMSPFIX utility program to unlock the DDLDCLOG area prior to rerunning the RHDCPRLG utility.

If the log is full because of repetitive system or task dumps, determine the cause of the dumps (start by looking at the console error messages) and put an end to them. For example, if a user executes OLQ with an old subschema whose pointers do not match the database, a DBIO '1111' error occurs and causes a system dump. Ask the user to stop executing OLQ with that subschema until the '1111' error is resolved. Also, issue a DCMT command to disable the subschema.

12.4.5 Problem – Trying To Bring Up Two CV's with the Same CVNUMBER or the Same System Version Number on One Machine

Symptoms: The system crashes during startup processing with a '3977' message number.

Causes: One problem that causes the system to crash during startup processing is trying to bring up two CV's with identical CVNUMBERs on the same physical machine. Every CV must have a unique CVNUMBER or the SVC routine catches it and aborts the second CV at startup time immediately after the WTOR is issued. Do not confuse CVNUMBER with system version number. The system version number can be any number from zero to 9999 and is used to differentiate one system definition from another in the same dictionary. The CVNUMBER, also specified in the sysgen, is used to differentiate one run time central version from another operating on the same physical machine. As of this writing, system version number must also be unique on one physical machine. As a general policy, it helps avoid confusion to specify the same number for both CVNUMBER and system version number, thereby identifying one unique system.

Analysis: Check the CVNUMBER and system version number specified for each system executing on the same physical machine in the hard copy system reports (always on hand as recommended in Section 12.1).

Decisions: None.

Resolution: Run a batch sysgen under local mode to change the CVNUMBER and/or system version number to a value unique to the physical machine. The value chosen for CVNUMBER must be within the limit specified by the MAXCVNO parameter at SVC assembly time. Consider adopting a documented standard of CVNUMBER values to prevent the problem from recurring.

12.4.6 Problem – Mismatch Between Disk Journal Blocksize and Global DMCL Specifications

Symptoms: The system abends during startup processing with a 'DC202010L 3005' error message indicating an error when opening a journal file. The text of the error message is shown in Figure 12-5.

Causes: Suspect a mismatch between the blocksize of the disk journal file and the page size specified in the global DMCL. A mismatch can occur if a DMCL other than the global DMCL was used to initialize the journal file.

Analysis: Compare the blocking factor of the journal file to the page size value specified in the global DMCL compile listing. Also, see which DMCL was used to initialize the journal file by checking the output from running IDMSINIT.

Decisions: None.

Resolution: Reallocate the journal files with the appropriate blocksize and initialize them using IDMSINIT and the global DMCL.

12.5 MAJOR SYMPTOM – DATABASE AREAS VARIED OFFLINE DURING STARTUP

IDMS/R varies database areas offline during startup processing if it detects a problem with the areas. Possible problems include:

- No JCL for DB area's file(s),
- The area has a previously-set lock on it,
- DMCL and database page sizes do not match, and
- DMCL and database page ranges do not match.

12.5.1 Problem – JCL for the Area's File is Missing

Symptoms: A 3005 -- ERROR LOCKING -- VARIED OFFLINE message appears on both the console and DC log, indicating an error when IDMS/R tried to open the associated file.

Causes: The most likely cause is a missing file assignment.

```
            J E S 2   J O B   L O G  --  S Y S T E M   S Y S A  --  N O D E   N 1

-------- JOB 4524  IEF097I        - USER       ASSIGNED
18.51.18 JOB 4524  ICH70001I        LAST ACCESS AT 18:50:06 ON MONDAY, AUGUST 18, 1986
18.51.18 JOB 4524  $HASP373          STARTED - INIT  7 - CLASS T - SYS SYSA
18.51.40 JOB 4524  +IDMS DC390009 V6 STARTING IDMS-CV/DC INITIALIZATION
18.51.40 JOB 4524  +IDMS DC202001L STARTING WARMSTART
18.51.40 JOB 4524  +IDMS DC202010L 3005 = DBIO STATUS  <---
18.51.40 JOB 4524  +IDMS DC391008 V6 WARMSTART FAILURE - IOSTATUS=0008
18.51.40 JOB 4524  IEA995I SYMPTOM DUMP OUTPUT
                   ABEND CODE  USER= 3962 TIME=18.51.39 SEQ=02558 CPU=0000 ASID=000D
                   PSW AT TIME OF ERROR  078D1000   00007038  ILC 2  INTC 0D
                     ACTIVE LOAD MODULE=IDMSDC6    ADDRESS=000062A8  OFFSET=00000D90
                     DATA AT PSW  00007032 - 00181610  0A0DE2C8  E4E3C4D5
                     GPR  0-3  80000000  80000F7A  00479F7A  0000900C
                     GPR  4-7  00002D00  50480B74  80470ED4  00010C14
                     GPR  8-11 00470ED4  00473880  00473388  00470CA8
                     GPR 12-15 00476A12  004738DC  60476A5C  00007002
                   END OF SYMPTOM DUMP
18.51.40 JOB 4524  IEF450I          IDMSSTRT - ABEND=S000 U3962 REASON=00000000
18.51.40 JOB 4524  $HASP395         ENDED



------ JES2 JOB STATISTICS ------



18 AUG 86 JOB EXECUTION DATE



    92 CARDS READ



   392 SYSOUT PRINT RECORDS



     0 SYSOUT PUNCH RECORDS



    20 SYSOUT SPOOL KBYTES



  0.37 MINUTES EXECUTION TIME
```

Figure 12-5 Sample Error Message Text (see arrow)

Analysis: Check the JCL to see if the associated file's DD or ASSGN information is present and correct.

Decisions: None.

Resolution: Make necessary JCL additions or changes, and bring the system down and up again.

12.5.2 Problem – Areas Locked

Symptoms: IDMS/R issues a message to the console and DC log if an area carries a previously-set lock and varies the offending area offline. The message 3005 ERROR LOCKING - VARIED OFFLINE identifies the problem.

Causes: An area can be locked for several reasons. An area is locked to prevent concurrent update if it is being updated by another CV or by a local mode batch program at the time of CV startup. Further, an area remains locked if a local mode update program abended and has not been recovered.

   Another possible cause for lock-up is a restore from a backup taken by non-IDMS utilities while CV was up and using the area (i.e., the area was locked). If that erroneous backup is used to restore the area, the area will appear to be in use when IDMS/R is brought back up. Attempts to vary the restored area online will fail.

Analysis: Use operating system commands to display a list of other jobs currently executing, looking for another CV or local mode IDMS/R which may be updating the area. Check the console log to see if any local mode update jobs abended and have not been recovered. Also, check with operations (or the appropriate department) to determine if the area has recently been restored, and if so, how and when the backup was taken.

Decisions: A choice may be made of restoring an area versus simply unlocking it if the locked area is not in use by another IDMS/R. An area should be restored if the problem is due to a local mode abend or cancellation. IDMSPFIX could be used to unlock an area if the problem is due to 1) a local mode update program not issuing a FINISH when all other processing completed normally or 2) a backup taken after CV was up but at a known time of no activity. However, IDMSDBAN Report 1A should be run to ensure that there are no broken chains before unlocking the area. Figure 12-6 shows only normal messages from Report 1A, indicating that there are no broken chains.

```
IDMSDBAN PHASE II - SET ANALYSIS                    REPORT 1A:  MESSAGES


599001 - PHASE II PROCESSING BEGUN
599803 - END PASS                                0
599801 - FROM-RECORDS WRITTEN TO SORT        66320
599802 - TO-RECORDS WRITTEN TO SORT          66320
599803 - END PASS                                1
599801 - FROM-RECORDS WRITTEN TO SORT        96579
599802 - TO-RECORDS WRITTEN TO SORT          46143
599805 - INDEX PATHS WRITTEN TO SORT          6764
599803 - END PASS                                2
599801 - FROM-RECORDS WRITTEN TO SORT        75052
299802 - TO-RECORDS WRITTEN TO SORT           6407
559805 - INDEX PATHS WRITTEN TO SORT         36564
595803 - END PASS                                3
599801 - FROM-RECORDS WRITTEN TO SORT         8820
599802 - TO-RECORDS WRITTEN TO SORT            965
599805 - INDEX PATHS WRITTEN TO SORT          4661
599803 - END PASS                                4
599801 - FROM-RECORDS WRITTEN TO SORT         4159
599802 - TO-RECORDS WRITTEN TO SORT            738
599803 - END PASS                                5
599801 - FROM-RECORDS WRITTEN TO SORT         4159
599802 - TO-RECORDS WRITTEN TO SORT            550
599803 - END PASS                                6
599801 - FROM-RECORDS WRITTEN TO SORT         4159
599802 - TO-RECORDS WRITTEN TO SORT            445
599803 - END PASS                                7
599801 - FROM-RECORDS WRITTEN TO SORT         4159
599802 - TO-RECORDS WRITTEN TO SORT            317
599803 - END PASS                                8
599801 - FROM-RECORDS WRITTEN TO SORT         4159
599802 - TO-RECORDS WRITTEN TO SORT            180
599803 - END PASS                                9
599801 - FROM-RECORDS WRITTEN TO SORT         4159
599802 - TO-RECORDS WRITTEN TO SORT              0




599002 - END OF IDMSDBAN - PHASE II
```

Figure 12-6 IDMSDBAN Report 1A Messages Indicating No Broken Chains

Resolution: If another CV or local mode IDMS/R has locked an area because of updates taking place currently, the area cannot be updated by this CV until the lock is removed by the other IDMS/R. Retrieval access can be enabled by issuing a DCMT VARY AREA *area-name* RETRIEVAL command. Issue a DCMT VARY AREA *area-name* ONLINE command to allow update access to the area when the conflicting update is complete and the lock has been removed.

　　If the area is locked because a local mode program abended, initiate appropriate recovery procedures, i.e., running IDMSRBCK if journaling was used or restoring the area from the backup made just prior to the local mode run.

12.5.3　Problem — Area and DMCL Page Sizes Do Not Match

Symptoms: An area is varied offline at startup time if there is a discrepancy between the DMCL's specification for an area's page size and the actual block or control interval size for the related file. A 3005 ERROR LOCKING -- VARIED OFFLINE message will be written to both the console and the DC log. Any attempts to VARY the area online will receive the same message written to the terminal. Application program accesses to the area will result in '0966' ERROR-STATUS return codes. A page size discrepancy will cause an '0370' ERROR-STATUS in local mode.

Causes: The source of the problem may be either a misassigned file, or an incorrect allocation of the file followed by initialization using a DMCL different than the global DMCL. Another likely cause of discrepancies is the IDMSXPAG utility being run against the area (to expand block size) without a corresponding change to the global DMCL.

Analysis: Verify the JCL assignment for files associated with the area(s) varied offline. Check the listing from initializing the area to see if the global DMCL was used. Check to see if the area's page size has just been expanded and whether or not the global DMCL had been modified to reflect the change.

Decisions: None.

Resolution: If a JCL assignment error was the cause of the problem, correct it. If the global DMCL does not match file blocksize, change it, and recompile it. Bring the system down and back up to implement the JCL or DMCL change.

12.5.4 Problem – DMCL and Database Page Ranges Do Not Match

Symptoms: IDMS/R issues a console message and varies the offending area(s) offline if area page ranges defined in the global DMCL do not reflect actual database page ranges; message 3003 -- ERROR LOCKING -- VARIED OFFLINE appears on both the console and DC log. The '3003' message appears when the block size and page size match but the first page in the area does not have the correct page number for this area. Programs attempting to access the area will receive an '0966' ERROR-STATUS code. A '0365' ERROR-STATUS is symptomatic of mismatched ranges in local mode.

Causes: This problem may have been caused by schema changes to database areas followed by reloads or reorganizations, without corresponding changes to and recompile of the global DMCL. Another likely cause is invalid JCL assignments where two files with the same blocksizes and page sizes are switched by mistake.

Analysis: To display the DMCL perceived database page range, issue a DCMT DISPLAY AREA *area-name* (where *area-name* is the problem area) and compare it to the latest schema compiled range in the IDMSRPTS listing. Verify the JCL for the files associated with the areas which were varied offline.

Decisions: None.

Resolution: Recompile the global DMCL if the problem was caused by schema changes to the area. Then, bring down the system and bring it back up. If the problem was caused by invalid JCL, make necessary changes and bring the system down and up again.

12.6 MAJOR SYMPTOM – THE SYSTEM CRASHES DURING THE RUN

If, after the system comes up successfully, it then comes down for unknown reasons, consult the console and IDMS/R log for error messages, numbers, or codes, following the general approach to trouble shooting outlined in Section 12.2. Try to bring the system back up in a warmstart mode. If the system seems to hang during warmstart processing, it is probably rolling back the updates of a large run unit and no action is necessary. Suspect a mismatch between the global DMCL and the disk journals if the system will not come back up.

12.6.1 Problem – Journal Block Range Does Not Match Global DMCL Specification

Symptoms: The system crashes with a DBIO '3010' or '3011' error message (i.e., an attempt to read or write from journal/database file has failed) and will not come back up after the crash.

Causes: Problems that arise when accessing journal files are usually caused by invalid journal blocks. An invalid journal block occurs when a journal file has a different block size (details in Section 12.4.6) or block range than that defined in the global DMCL. These problems are generally caused by initializing the journal file using a DMCL different than the global DMCL.

When looking for causes, suspect a change in the total number of blocks specified in the DMCL, without the journals being reallocated and/or reinitialized to reflect the increased number of blocks. A block range mismatch will cause an abend due to reading past the end of the file or accessing an unformatted block. Another possibility is a head crash on the pack containing the journal file. Follow the directions in Section 12.10.1 if access to all datasets on the device fails.

Analysis: If the system will not come back up after a '3010/'3011' abend, compare the number of blocks in the current journal file to the number specified in the global DMCL. The range of blocks defined in the file may be less than the range specified in the global DMCL, resulting in a read/write past the end of file and the system crashing (sample error message text if this problem occurs with BDAM journal files at an OS site appears in Figure 12-7). Alternatively, the new journals may have been initialized with a DMCL other than the global DMCL, and that DMCL contained the old, smaller block range. If the file was allocated with the appropriate space (i.e., equal to the range specified in the global DMCL), there are blocks in the file that are uninitialized. Uninitialized blocks cause DBIO errors when the unformatted block eventually is used by CV.

The database may need to be recovered if there were run units processing when the system crashed. Run the IDMSAJNL utility against the journal file which was active at the time of a crash (specify OFFLOAD=ONLY and the name of the journal file) to determine whether any run units were in flight. Next, run the IDMSJFIX utility against the tape output from IDMSAJNL and look at the checkpoint report output from IDMSJFIX to determine whether the database needs to be recovered.

Decisions: None.

```
J E S 2   J O B   L O G   --   S Y S T E M   S Y S A   --   N O D E   N 1

IEF097I  -  USER ACCESS ASSIGNED AT 17:08:12 ON MONDAY, AUGUST 18, 1986
$HASP001      LAST STARTED- INIT 17:08:12 - CLASS J - SYS SYSA
+IDMS DC200009L V9 STARTING WARMSTART - IDMS-CV/DC INITIALIZATION
+IDMS DC202001L V9 STARTING WARMSTART BYPASSED - IDMS INACTIVE
+IDMS DC390010 V6 LOADING NUCLEUS
+IDMS DC390015 V6 OPENING LINE UCFLINE
+IDMS DC390015 V6 OPENING LINE CONSOLE
+IDMS DC390005 V6 RHDCPARM FREESTG RELEASED:        4,200K
+IDMS DC390000 V6 REGION NEEDED TO START UP:        4,764K
+IDMS DC390000 V6 SYSTEM CONFIGURATION SIZE:        4,564K
+IDMS DC390000 V6 STORAGE RETURNED TO OPSYS:           32K
+IDMS DC390008 V6 TO ATTACHING DATABASE RESOURCE CONTROLLER
+IDMS REPLY 'IH' REQUEST TO IDMS DC
+IDMS DC201003 V6 IDMSDC IDENTIFY - IDMS TV6 VERSION 6 STARTED
+IDMS DC013003 V6 TO OPENING SYSTEM RUN UNITS
+IDMS DC013011 V6 TO OPENING QUEUE CLEANUP TASK
+IDMS DC013013 V6 TO DCLOG IS 43% FULL
+IDMS DC013005 V6 TO ATTACHING LOADAREA CLEANUP TASK
+IDMS DC007001 V6 TO ATTACHING DRIVER FOR LINE UCFLINE
+IDMS DC074100 V6 TO IDMS-CV/DC INITIALIZATION COMPLETE
+IDMS DC205 DMS 'VRT' V6 ? ENTER NEXT TASK CODE:
 IDMS DC205 DMS 'VRT' V6 ,*xx6,J2JRNL,*xxxx*, DISK JOURNAL IS FULL. SUBMIT IDMSAJNL FOR J1JRNL
 IDMS DC077007 DMS 'VRT' V9 T49 TASK:,START PROG-*xxx*, OUT OF EXTENT ,000000000000,BDAM
 IDMS DC077007 DMS 'VRT' V9 T49 TASK:,START PROG-*xxx*, FLUSHING JRNL-SEE,LOG CODE D002
+IDMS DC203003 DMS 'VRT' V9 T49 .J2JRNL,*xxDCMTC-**ABENDED WITH CODE ,000000000000,BDAM
+IDMS DC203003 DMS 'VRT' V9 T49 .DBIO J2JRNL STATUS = 3010; CODE D002
 IEA995I SYMPTOM DUMP OUTPUT
 ABEND CODE USER = 3996 TIME=17.38.39  SEQ=02464  CPU=0000  ASID=000D
 PSW AT TIME OF ERROR  078D1E00 00007038  ILC2 INTC 0D
 ACTIVE LOAD MODULE=IDMSDC6  ADDRESS=0062A8  OFFSET=00000D90
 DATA AT PSN  00007032  0018610 0A0E2C8 E4E3C4D5
 GPR 0--3  8000BECC8 00087238 000A496A AE085F08
 GPR 4--7  0000A5612 000BE78C 0002BA90 000BEBA8
 GPR 8-11  000029590 4E0A4AFE 00007002
 GPR 12-15 00007002
 IDMSSTRT - IDMSSTRT - ABEND=S000 U3996 REASON=00000000
 IEF450I ENDED
 $HASP395 IDMSSTRT ENDED
------ JES2 JOB STATISTICS ------
17.38.41 JOB 4387
17.38.42 JOB 4387
   18 AUG 86 JOB EXECUTION DATE
       92 CARDS READ
      415 SYSOUT PRINT RECORDS
        0 SYSOUT PUNCH RECORDS
```

Figure 12-7 Sample '3010' and '3011' Error Messages (see arrows)

Resolution: If analysis of IDMSJFIX output indicates that the database must be recovered, restore the database from the previous tape backup. Next, roll forward to the most recent quiesce point identified in the IDMSJFIX report (following the same general strategy as for resolving journal full situations). Reallocate and reinitialize the journals using the global DMCL. Bring the system back up.

12.7 MAJOR SYMPTOM – THE SYSTEM HANGS

When the system appears to 'hang' or is sluggish, suspect that one of the following situations has developed:

- Log or Journals full,
- Short on Storage,
- Run units causing excessive amounts of I/O,
- MAXTASKS,
- Runaway tasks,
- Inappropriate number of program loads,
- DB buffer pools too small,
- System snap dumps to the log,
- Transaction write statistics turned on with a very low interval specified,
- EXTERNAL WAIT specified at an inappropriate interval or turned off,
- Batch jobs running in PROTECTED or EXCLUSIVE UPDATE mode
- Update programs which update LARGE numbers of records without any COMMITs,
- Area sweeps for records that sparsely populate an area, especially from OLQ,
- IDMS/R running swappable (MVS consideration),
- IDMS/R running with a low priority and therefore getting too little of the CPU, or
- Frequent use of ASF.

The resolution depends on which problem is being experienced. Disable the program or transaction causing the problem or tolerate the dysfunction until the code is changed if the problem is application-related. If the problem is operating system-related, systems and operations personnel should be informed as soon as possible to change the characteristics of the CV job (e.g., changing the performance group or making the system nonswappable in an MVS environment), followed by bringing CV down and back up again with the new characteristics. A sysgen change may be necessary if the problem is

IDMS/R system-related, followed by bringing the old system down and the new system up.

Refer to Sections 12.4.3 and 12.4.4 for more information on resolving journal and log full situations. A discussion of the short on storage situation follows in Section 12.7.1. When the system hangs, it is usually due to a performance problem which has become critical. Refer to Chapter 13 for further discussion of the remaining causes.

12.7.1 Problem – Short on Storage (SOS)

Symptoms: The system hangs.

Causes: A short on storage situation occurs when the amount of free storage in the storage pool falls below the cushion amount (as defined in the sysgen). No new activity is allowed within the system once this condition occurs; only tasks and run units already dispatched are allowed to continue processing.

Unless abundant storage has been allocated to the storage pool, occasional short on storage conditions are to be expected and require no action. Typically, the dispatched tasks finish processing and release their storage, alleviating the storage problem. Normal processing resumes once the amount of available storage exceeds the cushion amount.

However, the system goes into a WAIT state if the dispatched tasks require further storage and all the cushion is consumed by existing activity. It is impossible to issue a DCMT DISPLAY STATISTICS SYSTEM to see if the storage pool is full because no new tasks can start up. It would then be impossible to shutdown the system gracefully; it must be cancelled by the operator.

A devastating short on storage condition can occur if an application program updates an excessive number of records, perhaps all records on the database, but does not issue COMMIT requests and is not running in PROTECTED or EXCLUSIVE usage mode. Hundreds of thousands of records are updated in this scenario, leading to many secondary allocations of run unit lock tables in the storage pool. Eventually the pool fills up and the system goes into a wait state (see 12.4.3, the journal full discussion, for other possible problems caused by excessive updates without COMMITs). This type of SOS is devastating because of the length of time it takes to recover (i.e., restore the database or rollback many updates).

Analysis: Use operating system commands to display a list of other jobs executing currently. Look for batch IDMS DML programs which are known to update large numbers of records.

If the system responds, use the OPER WATCH LTERM command to monitor online resource consumption. Issue a DCMT DISPLAY STATISTICS SYSTEM to determine the number of times the system has experienced short on storage conditions. DCMT DISPLAY RUN UNIT and DCMT DISPLAY RUN UNIT *rununit-id* commands can be used to check the number of database calls being issued by batch programs and other external run units.

Decisions: If one run unit updating many records caused the storage shortage, a choice must be made to restore the area and roll forward to just before the problem run unit started processing, or to allow normal warmstart to rollback the many updates. The restore may be the fastest method to get the system up quickly, but it is dependent on knowing that a run unit updating many records caused the problem.

Resolution: If it is a normal sporadic short on storage condition, just wait a while and the run units processing currently should finish and release their storage. This release of storage will alleviate the short-age and normal processing will resume. However, if the problem was caused by a run unit updating an excessive number of records, the system will not respond and usually must be cancelled. It may be possible to guess the identity of the problem run unit from operating system displays. If so, consider cancelling the batch job. The system will abort the run unit and rollback the updates after the batch job is cancelled. The rollback will take approximately one third to one half the time the program had been running before it was cancelled. The locks and the storage they occupied will be released as soon as the rollback has been completed, thereby resolving the SOS condition.

If the system must be cancelled, a normal warmstart recovers it. However, warmstart will take a very long time if the problem was caused by a batch program which updated an extremely large number of records. All the updates of the offending program must be rolled back, along with updates of other programs and dialogs active when the system was cancelled. No new system activity is possible until warmstart recovery has completed. Warmstart recovery will take approximately one third to one half the time the program had been running.

SOS is usually a sporadic condition that does not cause the system to crash or be cancelled. However, one should investigate to determine whether the pool is too small or a particular program is consuming extreme amounts of storage. Refer to Chapter 13 for information on tuning the storage pool.

12.8 MAJOR SYMPTOM – CICS USERS CANNOT MAKE CONTACT WITH IDMS/R

When CICS users cannot make contact with IDMS/R through UCF an ERROR-STATUS value or a four-character UCF error code may be displayed on the terminal screen. The meanings of UCF error codes are listed in Section 3 of the Error Messages and Codes manual (Release 10) and in the product authorizations sheets (Release 5.7). Alternatively, the meaning of the codes may be determined by browsing through the UCFCICS program source in the Cullinet software library.

First we will discuss some general UCF-CICS considerations. Next we will cover several reasons why CICS users might not be able to make contact with IDMS/R through UCF. The reasons include:

- CICS interface program, IDMSINTC, not started or not available,
- Logic error in the UCFCICS program,
- Too few UCF terminals or MAXERUS defined in the sysgen, and
- Transmission errors.

12.8.1 General CICS Considerations

There are several important points to keep in mind at UCF-CICS sites. First, the IDMSINTC and UCFCICS programs must be defined to CICS with the following table entries:

In the PPT:

```
DFHPPT TYPE=ENTRY,PROGRAM=IDMSINTC,
    PGMLANG=ASSEMBLER,RES=YES,RELOAD=NO
DFHPPT TYPE=ENTRY,PROGRAM=UCFCICS,
    PGMLANG=ASSEMBLER,RES=YES,RELOAD=NO
```

In the PCT:

```
DFHPCT TRANSID=DBDC,TWASIZE=408,TRANSEC=001,
    PROGRAM=UCFCICS,TYPE=ENTRY
```

In the PLT:

```
DFHPLT TYPE=ENTRY,PROGRAM=IDMSINTC
```

Second, be very cautious of TWASIZE changes for UCFCICS and of reassignment of the full word in the CICS CWA (into which IDMSINTC loads its own entry point address prior to any CICS-DML program processing or UCF session taking place). See the System Operations Guide for information on both UCFCICS and IDMSINTC.

An <u>erroneous</u> change to either TWASIZE (e.g., by Cullinet in a reinstallation without changing the PCT entry to reflect it) or the off-set of the full word in the CWA (a site-specified value) can result in CICS storage violations, program checks, and/or CICS terminals 'hanging up' when running the DBDC task code. Verify the value of TWASIZE in the product authorization sheets Cullinet sends along with the installation tape whenever the UCFCICS program is rein-stalled. Check with CICS systems programming to see if the CWA offset was mistakenly assigned twice. A storage overwrite is likely to occur if the full word which IDMSINTC uses in CWA is assigned by error to another program.

Third, never change the residency option in the PPT statements to 'NO'. The connection between UCFCICS and the back end terminals may be lost if UCFCICS and/or IDMSINTC is not resident in CICS, resulting in 'S012' UCFCICS abends and/or hung CICS terminals.

Fourth, UCFCICS must not be specified as reloadable to CICS. Session abends will occur intermittently if it is reloadable. Sessions 'in session' with IDMS/R get dropped (disconnected); symptoms of the problem include a UCFCICS message in upper left corner of the screen indicating abcnd and a dump written to the CICS log. Also, the user cannot reach IDMS/R and does not see the ENTER NEXT TASK CODE message.

12.8.2   Problem – CICS Interface Program Not Started

Symptoms: CICS DML programs abending with an ERROR-STATUS of 'nn68'.

Causes: IDMSINTC, the CICS interface program, was not started pri-or to attempted contact with UCF or was unavailable due to incorrect residency or reload options. Program IDMSINTC must execute prior to any UCF sessions taking place.

Analysis: None.

Decisions: None.

Resolution: Ensure that IDMSINTC processes before any CICS con-tact with UCF is attempted. Typically, this transaction is autostarted when the CICS memory space first comes up by providing a PLT entry, e.g.,

```
DFHPLT TYPE=ENTRY,PROGRAM=IDMSINTC
```

Alternatively, provide a PCT entry for transaction 'IDMS' which is associated with program IDMSINTC. Next enter 'IDMS' from any terminal prior to anyone else typing in 'DBDC' (if 'DBDC' is entered first, an 'nn68' ERROR-STATUS abend will result). The key board of the terminal used to enter 'IDMS' will lock up with no message; press the RESET key followed by pressing the CLEAR key to restore the terminal.

12.8.3   Problem – Logic Error in the UCFCICS Program

Symptoms: Logic errors usually result in 'S002', 'S004', 'S005', or 'S006' errors displayed at the terminal from UCFCICS. Other symptoms include 'S012' abends, hung terminals, and/or intermittent session abends.

Causes: Logic problems are usually caused by either memory space (CICS or IDMS/R) being shut down and brought up again immediately. The 'S002', 'S004', 'S005', or 'S006' error codes indicate that IDMS/R is treating the terminal session as a existing session that is still in progress, while UCFCICS is treating it is a brand new session (because CICS was brought down and up again immediately while CV was still up).
The connection between UCFCICS and the back end terminals may be lost if UCFCICS is not resident in CICS, resulting in S012 UCFCICS abends and/or hung CICS terminals. Session abends will occur intermittently if UCFCICS is reloadable. In additional, if CV is brought down and up again immediately and the terminal user has not pressed the ENTER key in the meantime, one of the 'S00x' messages will be returned because UCFCICS functions as though an existing session is resuming while CV treats it as a new session (e.g., 'S005', 'S006', 'S012').

Analysis: Check with operations personnel to see if either memory space has been cycled.

Decisions: None.

Resolution: The problem can be resolved most easily by bringing IDMS/R down and up again if several CICS/UCF terminal sessions were affected, provided cycling the system would not disrupt too many batch IDMS programs. Alternatively, if a small number of terminals were involved, or if some crucial batch IDMS programs cannot be interrupted, use the command DCMT VARY PTERM *physical-terminal-id* OFFLINE to vary each terminal experiencing problems offline. This should be followed by issuing the command DCMT

VARY PTERM *physical-terminal-id* ONLINE to vary each terminal back online again.

Check the value of RESOURCE TIMEOUT INTERVAL if this problem happens frequently. The resource timeout facility times terminal inactivity and abends terminal sessions if the threshold is exceeded.

12.8.4 Problem – Too Few UCF Terminals or MAXERUS Defined in the Sysgen

Symptoms: CICS or batch DML programs abending with an ERROR-STATUS of 'nn73'. New UCF sessions abending with 'S014' or 'E002'/'E003' messages returned to the terminal user.

Causes: Insufficient number of UCF terminals or MAXERUS defined in the sysgen.

Analysis: Issue a DCMT DIS PT command and see if all physical terminals are ACTIVE. If so, too few terminals are defined; new sessions are possible only if someone signs off. If additional terminal sessions abend with 'S014' UCF messages, not enough terminals have become available.

If attempts to signon a new terminal session fail repeatedly, but a DCMT DIS PT shows that some terminals are not active, the problem must be due to a lack of MAXERUS entries. Instruct users to keep trying when signons fail because eventually they will get in. A user assigned to a physical terminal may experience 'E002'/'E003' errors intermittently if there are insufficient MAXERUS entries because the entries are reusable and a user's task might be assigned one this time but not the next. Also, batch or CICS programs issuing calls to IDMS will abend intermittently with '1473' ERROR-STATUS codes.

Decisions: None.

Resolution: Find out if the increased use of UCF was caused by additional terminal groups for problems caused by too few terminals or MAXERUS defined in the sysgen. If new CICS terminals were added, corresponding increases should be made in the number of UCF terminals. In addition, consider increasing the number of MAXERUS if the additional terminals will add to the number of IDMS/R run units processing concurrently.

12.8.5   Problem – Transmission Errors

Symptoms: CICS users cannot make contact with IDMS/R. Usually, a 'PROG470' or 'PROG450' message appears in the lower left hand portion of the terminal, although not always. These messages are output by access method code and indicate a bad data stream.

Causes: This problem may be caused by a transmission error. Line and/or terminal problems can interfere with communication between UCFCICS and the back end system in IDMS/R. These types of messages also can be caused by binary fields in the data stream with no external picture defined.

Analysis: Use the DCMT command, DCMT V PTERM *pterm-id* TRACE ALL IO, to trace the I/O to determine if binary fields in the data stream are causing the problem.

Decisions: None.

Resolution: Use DCMT commands to vary the physical terminal offline and then online. This procedure should clear the problem, but the communications group at the site should be informed so the controller and terminal can be examined. Modify the map definition to specify an external picture for the erroneous field if binary fields in the data stream caused the transmission problem.

12.9   MAJOR SYMPTOM – '1111' ABENDS

'1111' abends indicate a mismatch between the database and a subschema. Specifically, prefix and/or data length as defined in the subschema does not reflect actual prefix size or data size as maintained in the database for a particular record.

12.9.1   Problem – Length of Prefix and/or Data Portion of Record in Database Does Not Match Lengths as Defined in Subschema

Symptoms: The '1111' abend code appears in various places. A '1111' error causes a dump of the entire system to be written to the log; the '1111' code appears just before the dump. The error message, PREVIOUS TASK ABENDED WITH 1111, will be displayed at the terminal when an OLQ, DC, or ADS/O task uses a mismatched subschema. On the DC log, the error message has the format, DC027007 TASK:ADS PROG:ADSOMAIN ABENDED WITH CODE 1111, followed by a system dump. Batch and CICS programs using a mismatched subschema receive '0300' ERROR-STATUS code and a system dump is written to the log.

The system waits until the dump is complete before any other processing can take place. Severe system problems result, therefore, if users repeatedly retry the transaction or if a batch job which accesses the problem record is rerun repeatedly. Extreme slowdowns in online processing are likely due to system dumps being written to the log, and the log may become full (Section 12.4.4).

Causes: A '1111' abend indicates that the length of the prefix and/or data portion of a record in the database does not match the corresponding lengths as defined in a subschema. The probable cause for the mismatch is a schema change (adding, deleting, or changing set definitions) without a corresponding reload or restructure of the data in the database. Another possible, although unlikely, cause of a '1111' abend is an I/O error. An I/O error is normally accompanied by a data check message on the console.

The '1111' abend indicates a problem with the length of the prefix or data portion of a DB record (usually the prefix portion), not necessarily with pointer positions. Suppose a mistake was made during a schema change and the value of existing pointer positions for the NEXT and PRIOR of the A-B set were switched with the NEXT and PRIOR positions of the A-C set. No '1111' abend will result. However, when a B record is accessed through the A-B set, an '0360' ERROR-STATUS results indicating broken chains (see discussion in Section 12.11.1)

Suppose, however, that a new physical set relationship is added to record types A and B without restructuring both A and B (or reinitializing and reloading the database). A '1111' abend will result whenever an occurrence of the A or B record types is accessed because the record's prefix is smaller than that defined in the schema. The length of each record's prefix is maintained in the line index entry of each record stored in the database. The '1111' abend therefore indicates a larger or smaller prefix than that specified in the subschema.

Analysis: Determine whether there is a mismatch between the schema definition and the actual database contents for the problem record. First, determine which set and/or record is involved by talking with the OLQ user or by checking the program ERROR RECORD and ERROR SET information. This information is displayed on the console for batch and CICS programs, and is also contained in the snap dump of the subschema control block written to the DC log for ADS and DC programs. The system dump can be analyzed for error record/set data if other sources are unavailable.

Scan for the 'VB50' eye-catcher when analyzing the dump to determine the cause of the situation. At offset X'110' past the eye-catcher is the full word containing the DBKEY of the record occurrence in question. A full word address is at offset X'114' from the eye-catcher; a literal identifying the error record's record type is at that address in the dump.

Now that the error record has been identified and its DBKEY is known, run the IDMSPFIX utility to dump the page containing the ERROR RECORD. Compare the pointers shown in the PFIX dump of the page to those defined in the schema. The problem lies in either a particular subschema that was not regenerated or a database that was not restructured/reorganized to reflect the new definition.

Decisions: The timing for the restructure must be scheduled if the problem is due to the database not being restructured. The choices are to vary the area offline for immediate restructure, to disable those programs which process the problem record(s) until a restructure can be scheduled, or to restore the old versions of subschemas until a restructure is done. The subschemas should be regenerated immediately if the problem is due to subschema(s) which have the old definition.

Resolution: Retrieval access resulting in a '1111' abend does not pose a difficult recovery problem. A restructure must be scheduled for '1111' abends caused by the database not being restructured after a schema change. The affected area(s) should be varied offline until the restructure has completed. Subschemas having the old definition of the database must be regenerated immediately if they are the source of the problem. The programs/dialogs using the subschemas should be disabled through DCMT commands until the regenerations are completed. After the regenerations, issue DCMT VARY NEW COPY commands for all affected subschemas.

If, however, STOREs of a bad record have been done, there is no easy solution to the problem because there are two different formats of the same record type in the database. If the problem is due to subschemas which have the old definition and data has been stored into the restructured database with the old definition, either 1) restore the DB from the last backup (i.e., prior to the restructure), regenerate the subschemas, and rerun all updates since that time, or 2) attempt to identify the run units which stored records with the old subschemas and delete the records with a program using the old subschema definition. The rollback utility could be used in this situation, but it would involve knowing which programs used the old subschemas and rolling back to a quiesce point prior to those programs being run. The subschemas should be regenerated following these steps and all valid updates should be rerun.

If the problem is due to lack of a restructure following schema and subschema changes and records have been stored by programs using the new subschemas, similar considerations apply i.e., either roll-back all updates to a level zero quiesce point before any of the bad stores or restore the database using a backup made prior to the schema changes and roll forward to a level zero quiesce point before any of the bad stores occurred. Finally, restructure the database and rerun all subsequent updates.

12.10 MAJOR SYMPTOM – '3010'/'3011' ERRORS OR DATA/EQUIPMENT CHECKS

Data checks and/or equipment checks are usually considered in-dicative of I/O related problems. IDMS '3010' and '3011' errors as well as application 'nn75' or 'nn76' ERROR-STATUS codes may also indicate I/O errors. The DBIO '3010' or '3011' error can be caused by:

- Sporadic data checks or equipment checks against a specific area,
- Constant failure when attempting to access to any file on a disk device,
- An improperly initialized database area, or
- An improperly initialized journal file (covered in Section 12.6.1).

12.10.1 Problem – Sporadic Data Checks or Equipment Checks during Access to a Specific Area

Symptoms: Data checks and equipment checks generate messages sent to the operator's console identifying the device and data set experiencing the problem. Contact your systems programming group for the specific messages identifying this problem at your site.

Causes: Data checks and equipment checks are usually caused by malfunction of the disk device.

Analysis: The systems programming group generally becomes in-volved in analyzing device problems. The disk pack must be taken offline so that the systems group can run utilities (such as ICKDSF in an MVS environment) to analyze the extent of the problem.

Decisions: The major decision is whether to take the pack offline (i.e., bring down the affected database area or areas) immediately for backup and analysis, or to wait until a more convenient time. One data check may be indicative of problems with other data sets or with the entire disk device. Investigation into the severity of the problem by the systems programming group should be scheduled as soon as possible although immediate backup of the device may not be necessary.

Resolution: Inform systems programming personnel of the data or equipment check, including the exact text of the message returned from the access method or the operating system message. Take the pack offline at the earliest opportunity so that the systems group can run utilities to analyze the extent of the problem.

The affected data sets should be restored from tape backups onto an alternate disk device (possibly restoring the entire pack if space permits) if analysis indicates that recovery is necessary. If duplexed files have been maintained, bring the system down and swap JCL to the duplexed files. Proceed to recover database areas or files as discussed in Section 12.10.2 if duplexed files are not available.

Further processing of CV may be impossible if a data check occurs on one of the disk journals. A DCMT VARY JOURNAL *active-journal-file* command should be issued immediately. If the VARY command is successful, set up an alternate journal file on a separate disk device and shut down CV at the first opportunity. Offload all journals and run IDMSINIT to reinitialize them. Then change the startup JCL to identify the alternate journal file and bring up IDMS/R.

If the VARY command fails (CV will probably abend if it cannot access the current journal block), shutdown CV immediately and try warmstart. Run IDMSAJNL against the current journal file to retrieve as much information as possible (use the OFFLOAD=ONLY and FILE=*current-journal-file-name* options) if the system will not come back up. Run the IDMSJFIX utility against the IDMSAJNL output tape after the IDMSAJNL utility completes processing the current journal file. The IDMSJFIX utility produces a checkpoint report and writes abort checkpoint for all incomplete run units. The safest course of action now is to restore the databases and roll forward using all archive tapes created since the last backup (including whatever was recovered from the active journal).

12.10.2   Problem – Constant Failure When Attempting to Access to Any File on a Disk Device (Head Crash)

Symptoms: There is no single message which indicates that a head crash has occurred. However, a head crash should be suspected if repeated attempts to access any file on a particular unit result in data check or equipment check messages. An IDMS '3010'/'3011' error or application and OLQ access failures with 'nn75' ERROR-STATUS codes can be supporting evidence of a head crash but should be investigated further if they are the only messages appearing. The system will most likely abend if a head crash occurrs on the active journal file. The system can continue processing if a head crash occurs on one or more databases.

Causes: Constant access failure can be due to logical or physical causes. Logical causes may be a restore being cancelled in the middle of the run or, under OS, the VTOC or system catalog being destroyed. A head crash is a physical cause.

Analysis: The head crash can be verified by systems programming personnel through messages and utilities that can be run to analyze the device. It can also be verified by trying to access a data set on the pack using a program other than IDMS/R (for example browsing data set information through TSO for MVS sites). A device malfunction has probably occurred if non-IDMS data sets, such as libraries or sequential files, reside on the pack and cannot be accessed either.

Decisions: A decision must be made to keep the system up or to bring it down during recovery processing for errors other than journal file errors. If the problem involves DB areas, those areas will be unavailable, although CV can remain up while recovery proceeds. If the problem is the dictionary, and IDMS-DC or ADS/O processing is occurring, users will be unable to sign on, programs will be unable to access queue or scratch records, and, if the dictionary load area was clobbered, dialog and subschema loads will fail. A dictionary head crash might force a shutdown of the system.

A head crash on the current journal file causes the system to crash. No decision is necessary.

Resolution: It is impossible to retrieve the current journal file data if the crash was on the pack containing the current journal file, therefore proceed with the instructions in the next paragraph. If the problem is not with a current journal, determine whether the next journal is on the bad pack. If the next journal is on the bad pack, allocate and initialize new journals, bring the system down and up with the new journals, and offload the old 'current' journal. If the next journal is not on the bad pack, vary the current journal offline and offload it to tape for roll forward processing. Specify a FILE parameter and OFFLOAD=ONLY as input to the IDMSAJNL utility during the offloading run.

All other full journals should be offloaded using the IDMSAJNL utility. Complete the journal tape by running IDMSJFIX to write abort checkpoints to the tape for incomplete run units (if any) and to obtain a report on checkpoints.

Next, restore all database areas on the affected pack. There are two options at this point, either run the roll forward utility to the end of the tape or run it to a time when no update activity was taking place against the affected areas. If roll forward is run to the end of the tape, it will automatically invoke roll back of inflight run units (provided abort checkpoints have been written to the tape by the IDMSJFIX utility). However, if there are only two or three run units at the beginning of the tape which update affected areas, the entire tape would be processed when only the beginning portion needed to be processed.

Alternatively, use the output from the IDMSJFIX report to identify a time when no run units were processing using areas from the pack. Normally, the time of a level zero quiesce point would be chosen if all database areas must be rolled forward, (i.e., a time when no update run units were active in CV). If, however, only specific areas or files are to be rolled forward, the checkpoint to which roll forward is run can be a quiesce point when there may be other run units active, providing those run units are processing against other areas or files than those which are being recovered. For example, refer to the sample IDMSJFIX listing shown in Figure 12-8. Suppose only the USRSESS-AREA, USR-AREA, AND USRTRAN-AREA require recovery. If so, roll forward could be run to DATE=12/04/86, TIME=16502752, which is not a level zero quiesce point.

Run IDMSRFWD up to a quiesce point when no run units were updating the affected areas. The following control card should be input to IDMSRFWD to roll forward only the files on the bad disk pack:

```
PROCESS=FILE,DMCL=dmcl-name
RESTORE=YES,DATE=mm/dd/yy,TIME=hhmmsshh
FILE=file-name-1
FILE=file-name-2
```

The DMCL specified must include all database files on the bad pack and each database file on the pack should be listed.

Restore all areas from the most recent backup and run IDMSRFWD to a level zero quiesce point if all database files need recovery. All database areas must be recovered if they are all on one

```
IDMS FIX 10.00 C850M  CULLINET SOFTWARE  --  LISTING OF MESSAGES - -     DATE 12/04/86     TIME 20:20:01     PAGE 1

DMCL=PCV1DMCL

LEVEL  1  BGIN   PROGRAM-ID  SSDSIGNO   DATE 12/04/86   TIME 10295036   RUN-UNIT ID   14
LEVEL  0  ENDJ   PROGRAM-ID  SSDSIGNO   DATE 12/04/86   TIME 10295122   RUN-UNIT ID   14

STATISTICS FOR SSDSIGNO

PAGES READ          2    PAGES WRITTEN          AFTER  2   PAGES REQUESTED        11   CALC TARGET          0
CALC OVERFLOW       0    VIA TARGET                    0   VIA OVERFLOW            0   LINES REQUESTED     11
RECS CURRENT        1    CALLS TO IDMS          12       0   FRAGMENTS STORED       6   RECS LOCATED         0
LOCKS REQUESTED     7    SELECT LOCKS           3        1   UPDATE LOCKS           6

                    R/U ID  14   BEFORE  2   AFTER  2   USAGE MODE
AREAS OPEN                       14         0          0          SHARED UPDATE
USRSESS-AREA  SSDSIGNO           14         0          0          SHARED RETRIEVAL
USR-AREA      SSDSIGNO           14         0          0          SHARED RETRIEVAL
TRAN-AREA     SSDSIGNO           14         0          0          SHARED RETRIEVAL
PASSWRD-AREA  SSDSIGNO           14         0          0          SHARED RETRIEVAL
IUSRSES-AREA  SSDSIGNO                      1          1          SHARED UPDATE

LEVEL  1  BGIN   PROGRAM-ID  SSDSIGNO   DATE 12/04/86   TIME 10301847   RUN-UNIT ID   15
LEVEL  0  ENDJ   PROGRAM-ID  SSDSIGNO   DATE 12/04/86   TIME 10301969   RUN-UNIT ID   15

STATISTICS FOR SSDSIGNO

PAGES READ          4    PAGES WRITTEN          BEFORE  2   AFTER  2   PAGES REQUESTED      34   CALC TARGET          1
CALC OVERFLOW       0    VIA TARGET                     0          0   VIA OVERFLOW          0   LINES REQUESTED     33
RECS CURRENT        7    CALLS TO IDMS          15       0          38  FRAGMENTS STORED      6   RECS LOCATED         0
LOCKS REQUESTED    19    SELECT LOCKS           15       1          3   UPDATE LOCKS

                    R/U ID  15   BEFORE  2   AFTER  2   USAGE MODE
AREAS OPEN                       15         0          0          SHARED UPDATE
USRSESS-AREA  SSDSIGNO           15         0          0          SHARED RETRIEVAL
USR-AREA      SSDSIGNO           15         0          0          SHARED RETRIEVAL
USRTRAN-AREA  SSDSIGNO           15         0          0          SHARED RETRIEVAL
TRAN-AREA     SSDSIGNO           15         0          0          SHARED RETRIEVAL
PASSWRD-AREA  SSDSIGNO                      1          1          SHARED UPDATE
IUSRSES-AREA  SSDSIGNO

LEVEL  1  BGIN   PROGRAM-ID  SSDSIGNO   DATE 12/04/86   TIME 10330180   RUN-UNIT ID   19
LEVEL  0  ENDJ   PROGRAM-ID  SSDSIGNO   DATE 12/04/86   TIME 10330313   RUN-UNIT ID   19

STATISTICS FOR SSDSIGNO

PAGES READ          1    PAGES WRITTEN          BEFORE  3   AFTER  2   PAGES REQUESTED      21   CALC TARGET          1
CALC OVERFLOW       0    VIA TARGET             19                  0   VIA OVERFLOW          0   LINES REQUESTED     20
RECS CURRENT        2    CALLS TO IDMS                             19  FRAGMENTS STORED      0   RECS LOCATED         0
LOCKS REQUESTED    16    SELECT LOCKS                             2   UPDATE LOCKS          8

                    R/U ID  19   BEFORE  3   AFTER  3   USAGE MODE
AREAS OPEN
USRSESS-AREA  SSDSIGNO                                             SHARED UPDATE
```

Figure 12-8 Sample Output from the IDMSJFIX Utility

```
. .IX 10.00 C8509M  CULLINET SOFTWARE  - - LISTING OF MESSAGES - -  IDMS JOURNAL TAPE FIX   DATE 12/04/86      TIME 20420601      PAGE 2

USR-AREA          SSDSIGN0   19    0   SHARED RETRIEVAL
USRTRAN-AREA      SSDSIGN0   19    0   SHARED RETRIEVAL
TRAN-AREA         SSDSIGN0   19    0   SHARED RETRIEVAL
PASSWRD-AREA      SSDSIGN0   19    0   SHARED RETRIEVAL
IUSRSES-AREA      SSDSIGN0   19    1   SHARED UPDATE

LEVEL 1 BGIN  PROGRAM-ID SSDSIGN0  DATE 12/04/86  TIME 10351120  RUN-UNIT ID   31
LEVEL 0 ENDJ  PROGRAM-ID SSDSIGN0  DATE 12/04/86  TIME 10351166  RUN-UNIT ID   31

STATISTICS FOR SSDSIGN0

PAGES READ        0    PAGES WRITTEN    0    PAGES REQUESTED    2    CALC TARGET       13
CALC OVERFLOW     0    VIA TARGET       0    VIA OVERFLOW       0    LINES REQUESTED    0
RECS CURRENT      1    CALLS TO IDMS    1    FRAGMENTS STORED  14    RECS LOCATED       6
LOCKS REQUESTED   9    SELECT LOCKS          UPDATE LOCKS       4

                                       BEFORE   AFTER   USAGE MODE
AREAS OPEN      PROG-ID    R/U ID  31
USRSES-AREA     SSDSIGN0   31        2       2   SHARED UPDATE
USR-AREA        SSDSIGN0   31        0       0   SHARED RETRIEVAL
USRTRAN-AREA    SSDSIGN0   31        0       0   SHARED RETRIEVAL
TRAN-AREA       SSDSIGN0   31        0       0   SHARED RETRIEVAL
PASSWRD-AREA    SSDSIGN0   31        0       0   SHARED RETRIEVAL
IUSRSES-AREA    SSDSIGN0   31        1       1   SHARED UPDATE

LEVEL 1 BGIN  PROGRAM-ID SSDSIGN0  DATE 12/04/86  TIME 10353036  RUN-UNIT ID   33
LEVEL 0 ENDJ  PROGRAM-ID SSDSIGN0  DATE 12/04/86  TIME 10353887  RUN-UNIT ID   33

STATISTICS FOR SSDSIGN0

PAGES READ        0    PAGES WRITTEN    0    PAGES REQUESTED    2    CALC TARGET       34
CALC OVERFLOW     0    VIA TARGET       0    VIA OVERFLOW       0    LINES REQUESTED    0
RECS CURRENT      7    CALLS TO IDMS         FRAGMENTS STORED  38    RECS LOCATED       6
LOCKS REQUESTED  19    SELECT LOCKS          UPDATE LOCKS       3

                                       BEFORE   AFTER   USAGE MODE
AREAS OPEN      PROG-ID    R/U ID  33
USRSES-AREA     SSDSIGN0   33        2       2   SHARED UPDATE
USR-AREA        SSDSIGN0   33        0       0   SHARED RETRIEVAL
USRTRAN-AREA    SSDSIGN0   33        0       0   SHARED RETRIEVAL
TRAN-AREA       SSDSIGN0   33        0       0   SHARED RETRIEVAL
PASSWRD-AREA    SSDSIGN0   33        0       0   SHARED RETRIEVAL
IUSRSES-AREA    SSDSIGN0   33        1       1   SHARED UPDATE

LEVEL 1 BGIN  PROGRAM-ID SSDSIGN0  DATE 12/04/86  TIME 10433538  RUN-UNIT ID   39
LEVEL 0 ENDJ  PROGRAM-ID SSDSIGN0  DATE 12/04/86  TIME 10433623  RUN-UNIT ID   39

STATISTICS FOR SSDSIGN0

PAGES READ        1    PAGES WRITTEN    1    PAGES REQUESTED    2    CALC TARGET       14
CALC OVERFLOW     0    VIA TARGET       0    VIA OVERFLOW       0    LINES REQUESTED    0
RECS CURRENT      1    CALLS TO IDMS         FRAGMENTS STORED  12    RECS LOCATED       0
```

Figure 12-8 Sample Output from the IDMSJFIX Utility (continued)

IDMSJFIX 10.00 C8509M   CULLINET SOFTWARE   -- LISTING OF   IDMS JOURNAL TAPE FIX --   MESSAGES --   DATE 12/04/86   TIME 20420601   PAGE 543

STATISTICS FOR   TEIUPDA1

PAGES READ	18	PAGES WRITTEN		PAGES REQUESTED	122	CALC TARGET	1
CALC OVERFLOW	0	VIA TARGET		VIA OVERFLOW	0	LINES REQUESTED	112
RECS CURRENT	8	CALLS TO IDMS		FRAGMENTS STORED	0	RECS LOCATED	0
LOCKS REQUESTED	1	SELECT LOCKS		UPDATE LOCKS	1		

AREAS OPEN	R/U ID	BEFORE	AFTER	USAGE MODE
DDLDCLOD	RHDCRUAL	3		
DDLDCRUN	RHDCRUAL	2		
TRDSRCE-AREA	TEIUPDA1	6694	60	SHARED UPDATE
PROCDTE-AREA	TEIUPDA1	6694	636	SHARED UPDATE
TRADE-AREA	TEIUPDA1	6694		SHARED UPDATE
STACTRD-AREA	TEIUPDA1	6694		UNKNOWN
TRDHIS-AREA	TEIUPDA1	6694		UNKNOWN
TRDHDR-AREA	TEIUPDA1	6694		UNKNOWN
TNACCT-AREA	TEIUPDA1	6694		UNKNOWN
BRKFIRM-AREA	TEIUPDA1	6694		UNKNOWN
IX-TES-MISC-AREA	TEIUPDA1	6694		UNKNOWN
IX-TRADE1-AREA	TEIUPDA1	6694		UNKNOWN
IX-TRADE2-AREA	TEIUPDA1	6694		UNKNOWN
IX-TRADE3-AREA	TEIUPDA1	6694		UNKNOWN
IX-TNACCT-AREA	TEIUPDA1	6694		UNKNOWN

LEVEL	3	BGIN	PROGRAM-ID	TEIUPDA1	DATE 12/04/86	TIME 16500394	RUN-UNIT ID	6698
LEVEL	2	ENDJ	PROGRAM-ID	TEIUPDA1	DATE 12/04/86	TIME 16500488	RUN-UNIT ID	6698

STATISTICS FOR   TEIUPDA1

PAGES READ	23	PAGES WRITTEN		PAGES REQUESTED	133	CALC TARGET	1
CALC OVERFLOW	0	VIA TARGET		VIA OVERFLOW	2	LINES REQUESTED	120
RECS CURRENT	8	CALLS TO IDMS		FRAGMENTS STORED	0	RECS LOCATED	0
LOCKS REQUESTED	1	SELECT LOCKS		UPDATE LOCKS	1		

AREAS OPEN	R/U ID	BEFORE	AFTER	USAGE MODE
DDLDCLOD	RHDCRUAL	3	60	SHARED UPDATE
DDLDCRUN	RHDCRUAL	2	636	SHARED UPDATE
TRDSRCE-AREA	TEIUPDA1	6698		SHARED UPDATE
PROCDTE-AREA	TEIUPDA1	6698		UNKNOWN
TRADE-AREA	TEIUPDA1	6698		UNKNOWN
STACTRD-AREA	TEIUPDA1	6698		UNKNOWN
TRDHIS-AREA	TEIUPDA1	6698		UNKNOWN
TRDHDR-AREA	TEIUPDA1	6698		UNKNOWN
TNACCT-AREA	TEIUPDA1	6698		UNKNOWN
BRKFIRM-AREA	TEIUPDA1	6698		UNKNOWN
IX-TES-MISC-AREA	TEIUPDA1	6698		UNKNOWN
IX-TRADE1-AREA	TEIUPDA1	6698		UNKNOWN
IX-TRADE2-AREA	TEIUPDA1	6698		UNKNOWN
IX-TRADE3-AREA	TEIUPDA1	6698		UNKNOWN

Figure 12-8 Sample Output from the IDMSJFIX Utility (continued)

```
IDMSJFIX 10.00 C8509M  CULLINET SOFTWARE  - - LISTING OF MESSAGES - -  IDMS JOURNAL TAPE FIX      DATE         TIME       PAGE
                                                                                                12/04/86     20420601    544

IX-TNACCT-AREA   TEIUPDA1      6698         10          10     UNKNOWN

LEVEL 3 BGIN   PROGRAM-ID SSDSIGNO   DATE 12/04/86   TIME 16502720   RUN-UNIT ID   6704
LEVEL 2 ENDJ   PROGRAM-ID SSDSIGNO   DATE 12/04/86   TIME 16502752   RUN-UNIT ID   6704

STATISTICS FOR SSDSIGNO

                    BEFORE   AFTER
PAGES READ            1        2      PAGES REQUESTED     16
CALC OVERFLOW         0        0      VIA OVERFLOW         0      CALC TARGET         0
RECS CURRENT          1       14      FRAGMENTS STORED     0      LINES REQUESTED    16
LOCKS REQUESTED      13        4      UPDATE LOCKS         8      RECS LOCATED        0

AREAS OPEN      PROG-ID   R/U ID    BEFORE   AFTER   USAGE MODE
DDLDCLOD        RHDCRUAL              60       60
DDLDCRUN        RHDCRUAL     3       636      636     SHARED UPDATE
USRSESS-AREA    SSDSIGNO   6704        3        3     SHARED UPDATE
USR-AREA        SSDSIGNO   6704        0        0     SHARED RETRIEVAL
USRTRAN-AREA    SSDSIGNO   6704        0        0     SHARED RETRIEVAL
TRAN-AREA       SSDSIGNO   6704        0        0     SHARED RETRIEVAL
PASSWRD-AREA    SSDSIGNO   6704        0        0     SHARED RETRIEVAL
IUSRSES-AREA    SSDSIGNO   6704        1        1     SHARED UPDATE

LEVEL 3 BGIN   PROGRAM-ID TEIUPDA1   DATE 12/04/86   TIME 16503871   RUN-UNIT ID   6709
LEVEL 2 ENDJ   PROGRAM-ID TEIUPDA1   DATE 12/04/86   TIME 16504152   RUN-UNIT ID   6709

STATISTICS FOR TEIUPDA1

                    BEFORE   AFTER
PAGES READ           26       22      PAGES REQUESTED    189
CALC OVERFLOW         0        0      VIA OVERFLOW         2      CALC TARGET         2
RECS CURRENT         13       48      FRAGMENTS STORED     0      LINES REQUESTED   170
LOCKS REQUESTED       1        1      UPDATE LOCKS         1      RECS LOCATED        0

AREAS OPEN         PROG-ID    R/U ID    BEFORE   AFTER   USAGE MODE
DDLDCLOD           RHDCRUAL              60       60
DDLDCRUN           RHDCRUAL     2       636      636     SHARED UPDATE
TRDSRCE-AREA       TEIUPDA1   6709        1        1     SHARED UPDATE
PROCDTE-AREA       TEIUPDA1   6709        1        1     SHARED UPDATE
TRADE-AREA         TEIUPDA1   6709       12       12     UNKNOWN
SIACTRD-AREA       TEIUPDA1   6709        1        0     UNKNOWN
TRDHIS-AREA        TEIUPDA1   6709        1        1     UNKNOWN
TRDHDR-AREA        TEIUPDA1   6709        5        5     UNKNOWN
TNACCT-AREA        TEIUPDA1   6709        5        5     UNKNOWN
BRKFIRM-AREA       TEIUPDA1   6709        0        0     UNKNOWN
IX-TES-MISC-AREA   TEIUPDA1   6709        0        0     UNKNOWN
IX-TRADE1-AREA     TEIUPDA1   6709        6        6     UNKNOWN
IX-TRADE2-AREA     TEIUPDA1   6709        1        1     UNKNOWN
IX-TRADE3-AREA     TEIUPDA1   6709        1        1     UNKNOWN
IX-TNACCT-AREA     TEIUPDA1   6709        6        6     UNKNOWN

LEVEL 3 BGIN   PROGRAM-ID TEIUPDA1   DATE 12/04/86   TIME 16504583   RUN-UNIT ID   6715
```

Figure 12-8 Sample Output from the IDMSJFIX Utility (continued)

```
IDMSJFIX 10.00 C8509M   CULLINET SOFTWARE  - - LISTING OF IDMS JOURNAL TAPE FIX MESSAGES - -          DATE        TIME       PAGE
                                                                                                      12/04/86    20420601   545

LEVEL  2  ENDJ  PROGRAM-ID  TEIUPDA1        DATE 12/04/86   TIME 16504667   RUN-UNIT ID   6715

STATISTICS FOR  TEIUPDA1

 PAGES READ         19      PAGES WRITTEN        16      PAGES REQUESTED      118      CALC TARGET        1
 CALC OVERFLOW       0      VIA TARGET            0      VIA OVERFLOW           2      LINES REQUESTED    0
 RECS CURRENT        8      CALLS TO IDMS        38      FRAGMENTS STORED       0      RECS LOCATED       3
 LOCKS REQUESTED     1      SELECT LOCKS          1      UPDATE LOCKS           1
```

AREAS OPEN	PROG-ID	R/U ID	BEFORE	AFTER	USAGE MODE
DDLDCLOD	RHDCRUAL	3	2	60	SHARED UPDATE
DDLDCRUN	RHDCRUAL	2	636	636	SHARED UPDATE
IRDSRCE-AREA	TEIUPDA1	6715	1	1	SHARED UPDATE
PROCDTE-AREA	TEIUPDA1	6715	1	1	UNKNOWN
TRADE-AREA	TEIUPDA1	6715	4	4	UNKNOWN
SIACTRD-AREA	TEIUPDA1	6715	0	0	UNKNOWN
IRDHIS-AREA	TEIUPDA1	6715	0	0	UNKNOWN
TRDHDR-AREA	TEIUPDA1	6715	0	0	UNKNOWN
TNACCT-AREA	TEIUPDA1	6715	5	5	UNKNOWN
BRKFIRM-AREA	TEIUPDA1	6715	0	0	UNKNOWN
IX-TES-MISC-AREA	TEIUPDA1	6715	4	4	UNKNOWN
IX-TRADE1-AREA	TEIUPDA1	6715	1	1	UNKNOWN
IX-TRADE2-AREA	TEIUPDA1	6715	1	1	UNKNOWN
IX-TRADE3-AREA	TEIUPDA1	6715	2	2	UNKNOWN
IX-TNACCT-AREA	TEIUPDA1	6715	2	2	UNKNOWN

```
LEVEL  3  BGIN  PROGRAM-ID  TEIUPDA1        DATE 12/04/86   TIME 16510212   RUN-UNIT ID   6722
LEVEL  2  ENDJ  PROGRAM-ID  TEIUPDA1        DATE 12/04/86   TIME 16510364   RUN-UNIT ID   6722

STATISTICS FOR  TEIUPDA1

 PAGES READ         26      PAGES WRITTEN        27      PAGES REQUESTED      206      CALC TARGET        2
 CALC OVERFLOW       0      VIA TARGET            1      VIA OVERFLOW           4      LINES REQUESTED  181
 RECS CURRENT       13      CALLS TO IDMS        48      FRAGMENTS STORED       0      RECS LOCATED       0
 LOCKS REQUESTED     1      SELECT LOCKS          1      UPDATE LOCKS           1
```

AREAS OPEN	PROG-ID	R/U ID	BEFORE	AFTER	USAGE MODE
DDLDCLOD	RHDCRUAL	3		60	SHARED UPDATE
DDLDCRUN	RHDCRUAL		636	636	SHARED UPDATE
TRDSRCE-AREA	TEIUPDA1	6722	1	1	SHARED UPDATE
PROCDTE-AREA	TEIUPDA1	6722	1	1	UNKNOWN
TRADE-AREA	TEIUPDA1	6722	12	12	UNKNOWN
SIACTRD-AREA	TEIUPDA1	6722	0	0	UNKNOWN
TRDHIS-AREA	TEIUPDA1	6722	1	1	UNKNOWN
TRDHDR-AREA	TEIUPDA1	6722	5	5	UNKNOWN
TNACCT-AREA	TEIUPDA1	6722	5	5	UNKNOWN
BRKFIRM-AREA	TEIUPDA1	6722	0	0	UNKNOWN
IX-TES-MISC-AREA	TEIUPDA1	6722	0	0	UNKNOWN
IX-TRADE1-AREA	TEIUPDA1	6722	14	14	UNKNOWN
IX-TRADE2-AREA	TEIUPDA1	6722	1	1	UNKNOWN

Figure 12-8 Sample Output from the IDMSJFIX Utility (continued)

```
IDMSJFIX 10.00 C8509M  CULLINET SOFTWARE  - - LISTING OF    IDMS JOURNAL TAPE FIX          DATE        TIME        PAGE
                                                            MESSAGES - -                    12/04/86    20420601    546

IX-TRADE3-AREA       TEIUPDA1       6722        1        1       UNKNOWN
IX-TNACCT-AREA       TEIUPDA1       6722        2        2       UNKNOWN

LEVEL  3  BGIN  PROGRAM-ID  TEIUPDA1  DATE 12/04/86   TIME 16512722  RUN-UNIT ID   6730

BLOCK COUNT   1273  RECORD COUNT   53381

LAST QUIESCENT POINT ON 12/04/86 AT 11022567

ACTIVE PROGRAMS AT END OF TAPE WERE:

LEVEL  2  ABRT  PROGRAM-ID  RHDCRUAL  DATE          TIME          RUN-UNIT ID   3

RHDCRUAL  MODE WAS  UPDATE
RHDCRUAL  MODE WAS  UPDATE

LEVEL  1  ABRT  PROGRAM-ID  RHDCRUAL  DATE          TIME          RUN-UNIT ID   2

RHDCRUAL  MODE WAS  UPDATE
RHDCRUAL  MODE WAS  UPDATE

LEVEL  0  ABRT  PROGRAM-ID  TEIUPDA1  DATE          TIME          RUN-UNIT ID   6730

TEIUPDA1  MODE WAS  UPDATE

DATA BASE RECOVERY NECESSARY  ↓
```

Figure 12-8 Sample Output from the IDMSJFIX Utility (continued)

pack or if there are set relationships between areas on the bad pack and other areas.

The abend code provides no indication of which area has suffered the I/O error on '3010' or '3011' abends. Try to contact the user groups involved (they should have received an 'nn75' ERROR-STATUS in ADS/OLQ or to batch jobs), and/or run IDMSDUMP against all areas. The IDMSDUMP utility displays each area's statistics as it is processing; the problem area can be determined from the abend of IDMSDUMP.

Proceed from here to determine whether the problem is actually a bad block or whether either of the two previously outlined situations has occurred (i.e., an uninitialized block or an attempt to read past the end of area), in which problems are the result of old/invalid DMCL page ranges.

12.10.3 Problem – Database Area Improperly Initialized

Symptoms: Intermittent '3010' and/or '3011' I/O errors occur during area accesses. Accesses to some pages are successful, whereas accesses to others are not. Application programs, dialogs, and/or OLQ abend intermittently with 'nn75' ERROR-STATUS codes.

Causes: It is likely that the area was initialized with a DMCL other than the global DMCL if accesses to some portions of an area are successful, but accesses to other portions result in I/O errors. There may be uninitialized pages in the area.

Analysis: Determine if the problem occurs only during access to the end of the DB area by running IDMSDUMP specifying the global DMCL, or by running IDMSPFIX to dump selected pages at the end of the area. Running either utility should disclose the nature of the problem. Next, check the IDMSINIT listing for this area to verify which DMCL was used during initialization. Suspect that the file was allocated with the correct number of blocks (i.e., equal to the page range specified in the global DMCL), but that a different DMCL or an old copy of the DMCL was used during area initialization, perhaps from the wrong library. Uninitialized blocks in the file will result if the DMCL used during initialization specifies a smaller number of blocks than that specified in the global DMCL.

Decisions: A decision must be made either to reorganize the area immediately or to change the schema, affected subschemas, and the global DMCL to match only the initialized portion of the area and reorganize at a more convenient time. The area must be reorganized immediately if CALC records have been stored in the area. Either choice can be made if only VIA and/or DIRECT records have been stored in the area. Processing with only the initialized portion may be adequate, depending on the amount of initialized space in the area, and the reorganization can be scheduled at a more convenient time.

Refer to the schema listing to see if any CALC records are targeted to the area. If so, determine whether any CALC records have been stored in the area yet by running IDMSDUMP and checking the number of occurrences of the CALC record types.

Resolution: An emergency reorganization must be scheduled immediately if some occurrences of CALC records have already been stored in the area. First run the IDMSUNLD utility using an old subschema with the initialized range only. Then run IDMSINIT using the current global DMCL to initialize all blocks in the file properly. Finally run IDMSDBLU using a new subschema with the appropriate range to reload the records into a properly initialized area. The IDCAMS utility may be run using the REPRO command to copy only the first 'n' blocks to a properly sized and initialized file as an alternative to the above procedure at OS sites.

The schema could be modified to make the area's range correspond with the initialized portion of the file if only VIA and/or DIRECT record types are involved, and the amount of space lost to uninitialized blocks does not cause an extreme shortage of free space. All affected subschemas and the global DMCL would require recompilation. Finally, the system must be cycled for the changed DMCL to take effect. Modifying the schema, affected subschemas, and the global DMCL allows the area to be brought back up quickly. However, a reorganization (and the reverse changes to the schema, affected subschemas, and the global DMCL) should be scheduled at the first available opportunity.

12.11 MAJOR SYMPTOM – PROGRAMS/DIALOGS ABENDING WITH 'nn60' OR 'nn61' ERROR-STATUS CODES

The 'nn60' and 'nn61' ERROR-STATUS codes are symptoms of broken chains on the database.

12.11.1 Problem – Broken Chain(s) on the Database

Symptoms: Programs/dialogs abending with 'nn60' or 'nn61' ERROR-STATUS codes. These ERROR-STATUS codes indicate a broken chain on the database. The 'nn71' ERROR-STATUS code sometimes indicates a broken chain (see Section 12.5 for other meanings of 'nn71' ERROR-STATUS). In addition, broken chains should be suspected if invalid data is noticed in reports or online displays (see Section 12.17 for other possible causes).

A broken chain is an IDMS/R set whose ring is <u>not</u> fully completed from one owner record occurrence through a group of members and, eventually, back to the original owner record occurrence. An intact set is illustrated in Figure 12-9.

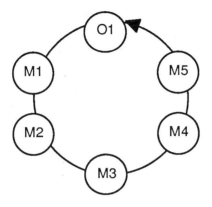

Figure 12-9 Intact Set Chain

There are three types of broken chains. In the first, the set chain points to the proper record type but wrong occurrence (Figure 12-10). The end-of-set condition is encountered when the program/dialog is positioned on O2 in walking this set from O1. Processing results are invalid although normal ERROR-STATUS values are received by the program/dialog.

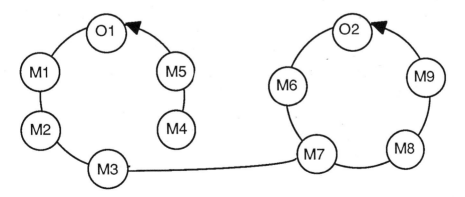

Figure 12-10 Type I Broken Chain

   The set chain points to an improper record type in the second type
of broken chain (Figure 12-11).   IDMS/R returns an 'nn60' ERROR-
STATUS when programs/dialogs processing the set whose owner is
O1 request the next record beyond M2.   Specifically, type II broken
chains result in 1) '0360' error status in batch/CICS programs,
2) DC173008 - APPLICATION ABORTED...STATUS=0360 message
plus the lines of ADS/O code that resulted in the error along with the
standard snap dump of the subschema control block for ADS/O
dialogs, and 3) DC095001 08 IDMS PROBLEM - DATABASE ERROR
STATUS=0360 message in OLQ.

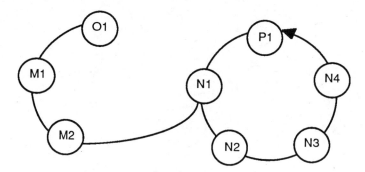

Figure 12-11 Type II Broken Chain

   The set chain points to a nonexistent record in the third type of
broken chain (Figure 12-12).   IDMS/R returns an 'nn61' ERROR-
STATUS when programs/dialogs walking this set from O1 request
the next record beyond M3.   Specifically, type III broken chains result
in 1) '0361' error status in batch/CICS programs, 2) DC173008 -
APPLICATION ABORTED ... STATUS=0361 message plus the lines

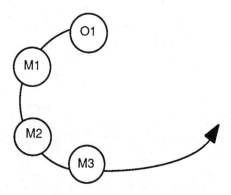

Figure 12-12 Type III Broken Chain

of code that resulted in the error plus the standard snap dump of the subschema control block for ADS/O dialogs, and 3) DC095001 08 IDMS PROBLEM - DATABASE ERROR STATUS=0361 message in OLQ.

An '0361' ERROR STATUS results when the page pointed to by M3 in our example is a valid page number in that it falls within a range known to the DMCL (not necessarily to the subschema) but IDMS cannot find a record with that line index number on that page. An '0371' error status results if the pointer points to a page number not known to the DMCL (i.e., outer space).

Type II and III broken chains are easily spotted because they cause program abends. Type I broken chains may go undetected for a long time, causing incorrect output but no processing errors. IDMSDBAN may be able to spot type I broken chains, especially if there are NEXT and PRIOR pointers on the set; it is unusual for both NEXT and PRIOR chains to be broken.

If the pointer points to a correct page and line index, but the information in the line index is incorrect (e.g., the offset to the beginning of the record being greater than page size) a system abend '3996' and a system dump results (ADS/O dialogs receive message DC204903). This last case is most likely caused by a non-IDMS program having over-written a portion of the DB file.

Causes: Broken chains can be caused by:

- Bad or incomplete manual recovery of a prior run against the database, followed by running the IDMSPFIX utility to remove the area-in-use lock,
- Running rollback selectively,
- Improper mixing CV and local mode access to an area,
- Running Local Mode updates without journaling, if the local mode job abends or is cancelled while in the act of updating the database and IDMSPFIX is run to remove the area-in-use lock, or
- The bad application of a PTF to a system module.

The major cause of broken chains occurs when two areas have a physical set relationship between them, and yet manual recovery has taken place for only one of the two areas. Don't laugh, improbable though this may sound, it happens frequently when areas are on separate files and one area is updated frequently whereas the other area is updated rarely. Operations personnel may not bother to restore both areas together in this situation or perhaps cannot restore both areas together because the areas were backed up at different times. It should be standard procedure to backup related areas together to avoid this problem.

Broken chains may occur when the IDMSRBCK utility is run selectively to rollback some rather than all run units. Suppose Run unit #1 updates and stores record type A's whereas Run unit #2 adds B's and C's to new A's. Assume that Program 1 runs normally, Program 2 runs normally, and CV comes down normally. If IDMSRBCK is run later to rollback only Program 1's run unit, the result is broken chains (Figure 12-13).

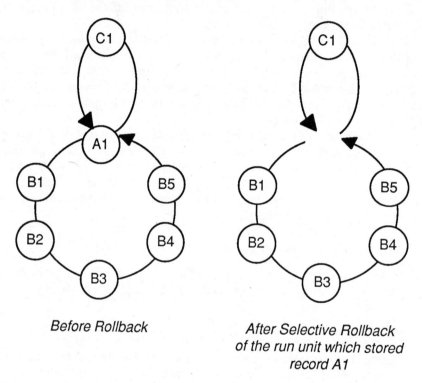

Before Rollback

After Selective Rollback
of the run unit which stored
record A1

Figure 12-13 Broken Chains Caused by Selective Rollback

Improper mixing of CV and local mode access to an area can cause database integrity problems. IDMS/R allows only one local mode program or Central Version update access to an area at a time. Some users want to run a local update, but allow CV access to the area as well, so they vary the area to retrieval mode for the CV, run the update, and then vary it back online. As of this writing, IDMS/R does not flush the database buffers with a vary retrieval command. Therefore, when CV's buffers do get written back to the database, they can overlay the local-mode-updated contents of the database with old data, almost invariably causing broken chains. <u>Always</u> vary the areas offline to CV before running a local mode update, thereby flushing the buffers. Varying the areas offline may be followed by varying the areas to retrieval mode to allow concurrent access by CV and the local mode update program.

Another possible cause of broken chains is running local mode updates without journaling. Look out for broken chains if a local mode job abends or is cancelled while in the process of updating the database and if IDMSPFIX is run to remove the area-in-use lock. The database area should be restored using the backup made just prior to the local mode run rather than running IDMSPFIX, (see Chapter 7, Backup and Recovery, for further details).

Analysis: It may be difficult to ascertain when and how the broken chain occurred unless there is a date/time stamp on the record which contains the bad pointer. Try to eliminate the obvious, e.g., a bad PTF (perhaps misapplied or taken over the phone incorrectly) or a bad recovery, by carefully going over all the old PTFs and consulting with operations personnel about all restores done recently. Follow this up with an emergency call to Cullinet to determine if any other sites have reported broken chains and under what conditions.

Run IDMSDBAN Report 1A to find out if the problem is widespread. Report 1A lists the DBKEYs of all sets that have broken chains, providing both the DBKEY of records with bad pointer and the pointer itself (next or prior). However, running IDMSDBAN for a large database may take a very long time.

Analyze the task dump for broken chain information. To identify quickly the set which has the broken chain causing the abend, analyze the dump from the run unit which encountered the broken chain. Follow these steps to locate the DBKEY of the record in the broken set which has an invalid pointer:

1. Print the task snap dump from the DC log.
2. Locate the run unit's currency tables in the dump by scanning the pages for the eye-catcher 'VB50' at X'8'. The currency tables are usually four or five pages into the dump.
3. Count X'C4' bytes from the 'VB50' eye-catcher. This full word contains the DBKEY of the record which is "current of run unit" (i.e., the last record accessed by the run unit). Usually, this is the DBKEY of the record whose prefix contains the 'bad' DBKEY pointer.
4. Count X'110' from the 'VB50' eye-catcher to find the full word containing the DBKEY which IDMS/R was using just prior to the dump. Normally, this is the 'bad' DBKEY which needs to be fixed. It should be different from the DBKEY found at X'C4' and probably is part of the prefix on the record whose DBKEY was found at X'C4'.

5. Count X'100' from the 'VB50' eye-catcher to find the DB trace table. The trace table lists the last eight calls to the DBMS and their results, enabling the analyst to determine which DBKEY is bad (the Next, Prior, or Owner pointer of the record whose address is at X'C4'.) The trace table is analyzed by matching each of the first eight bytes with the next eight bytes. The first byte is the least recently issued verb and the ninth byte its result. The second byte is the next issued verb and the tenth byte is its result, and so forth. The hexidecimal value of each of the first eight bytes must be converted to decimal and then translated using the IDMS call formats listed in the Programmer's Reference Guide. The results of the call also must be converted from hexidecimal to decimal and referenced to a list of ERROR-STATUS minor code values.

All the information necessary to find and correct the broken chain with IDMSPFIX has been collected after these steps have been completed. The DBKEY of the record containing the bad pointer is X'C4' after 'VB50'. The bad DBKEY is X'110' after 'VB50', and the DB trace table, which identifies the chain IDMS/R was following is X'100' after 'VB50'.

Decisions: A decision must be made either to fix broken chains using the IDMSPFIX utility or to recover the area(s) using backups and conceivably lose updates if local mode journaling was not done. Restoring the area(s) may be the only alternative if the number of broken chains is large.

Resolution: Unless it is known when and how the broken chain occurred, restoring from the last backup may or may not solve the problem (i.e., the broken chain might be in the backed up version as well). Running the rollback utility may or may not solve the problem for the same reason.

If there are only a few broken chains, determine from the IDMSDBAN report which record in each broken set contains the bad pointer and run IDMSPFIX to correct the record. IDMSPFIX may be run while CV is up by varying the areas offline. IDMSPFIX should not be run while the areas are online to CV because other run units may create or encounter broken chains while IDMSPFIX is processing.

Correcting the record is possible only if there is some data in the record to help identify its proper set occurrence, even then, the data could be corrupted also. The task dump can be used to find the break in the first broken set. IDMSDBAN, report 1A, should be run to identify the bad record in other sets.

Broken sets that have PRIOR or OWNER pointers in addition to NEXT pointers are much easier to recover than sets having only NEXT pointers. For example, a broken set can usually be walked in the prior direction and then PFIXed at the point where the break occurred if the set has prior pointers. If the set has only next and owner pointers and the 'next' chain is broken, one must sweep the database for the member record type and locate all members whose owner pointer is the owner record occurrence of the broken set. PFIX all member records to force them into a completed set with the owner record once all members have been located.

Many users have incorporated data elements in member records that identify owners of set relationships. Defining redundant fields in member records is not done as a standard merely to identify a broken chain's owner. However, if redundant data is being considered to improve performance, realize that carrying the owner's calc key can be useful for determining membership in broken chains.

ADS/Online can be helpful in tracking a broken chain, because it is much faster than executing a series of batch IDMSPFIX runs. Write a dialog to process the set in question one record at a time, displaying the current and next DBKEYs (also prior and owner pointers when available) until the break is discovered. Then run the IDMSPFIX utility to correct the 'bad' record. Alternatively, execute a series of batch PFIX runs to follow the bad set.

Finally, if the cause of the broken chain is unknown, do not assume that recovery or running IDMSPFIX has resolved the problem completely. The symptom may be cured, but not necessarily its cause. It may be only a matter of time until the original problem causes more broken chains. We recommend running IDMSDBAN Report 1A nightly on the problem database to catch the next broken chain promptly. Subsequent occurrences of broken chains often provide sufficient information to narrow down the cause and allow the situation to be recreated and corrected in the test system.

12.12 MAJOR SYMPTOM – PROGRAMS/DIALOGS ABENDING WITH '0966' ERROR-STATUS CODES

The '0966' ERROR-STATUS code returned from a READY statement indicates that the area is not available. Possible causes include:

- Wrong global DMCL used at run time
- Area varied offline during start up processing (Section 12.5)

12.12.1 Problem – Wrong Global DMCL Used at Run Time

Symptoms: Some or all application programs and dialogs are abending with '0966' error status codes when they attempt to READY application database areas, yet no messages indicating problems with IDMS/R have been written to the console or DC log. Areas being varied offline during startup with '3003' or '3005' error messages (Section 12.5) is another symptom.

Causes: When some or all application areas are missing from the global DMCL, the problem typically is caused by using the wrong DMCL at run time. Another common cause is a schema change to add new areas, without corresponding changes to the global DMCL.

The DMCL used at run time is named in the #DCPARM macro. The assembled DCPARM module is linked with (OS) or dynamically loaded by (DOS) the operating system-dependent routine. The wrong global DMCL might be used if the wrong DCPARM module was present in the object library during a relink of the operating system-dependent routine (OS), or an old DCPARM was picked up due to an incorrect LIBDEF SEARCH statement (DOS). For example, a sample DCPARM module is created during a reinstallation of Cullinet software, which names GLBLDMCL as the DMCL to be used at run time. GLBLDMCL includes standard Cullinet database areas (i.e., dictionary areas only) but not those areas created for user applications. Another reason to relink the operating system-dependent routine is to implement a change to WTOEXIT code or to a DCPARM parameter, e.g., FREESTG.

Analysis: Issue a DCMT DISPLAY AREAS command as a first step in analyzing the problem. If all application areas are missing, issue a DCMT DISPLAY MEMORY MAP command, which will show the name and address of the global DMCL. The problem has been identified if the name shown is not the normal DMCL name.

Issue a DCMT DISPLAY MEMORY MAP command if new application areas are the only areas missing. This command shows the name and address of the global DMCL. If the name is the same as expected, check the date-compiled and time-compiled fields in the DMCL by issuing a DCMT DISPLAY MEMORY *memory-address* command to display memory contents at the DMCL address.

Double check library concatenations and LIBDEF SEARCH statements in the startup JCL to determine if an incorrect version of the global DMCL is being picked up by mistake.

Decisions: none.

Resolution: Find out which object library contains the appropriate DCPARM module if all application areas are missing because GLBLDMCL was being used. Relink the operating system-dependent routine (OS) using a DCPARM module which names the correct DMCL. For DOS systems, either change the startup JCL to identify the object library which contains the appropriate DCPARM module or copy the module into the appropriate object library.

If new application areas are missing, find out if a new DMCL was compiled, including the new areas; if not, compile one. Reassemble the #DCPARM macro if the new DMCL has a different name than the old DMCL and, for OS sites, relink the operating system-dependent routine.

12.13   MAJOR SYMPTOM – PROGRAMS/DIALOGS ABENDING WITH 'nn69' ERROR-STATUS CODES

There are a confusing array of causes for the 'nn69' ERROR-STATUS. In general, it indicates that CV is not up or not available.

Symptoms: Programs and dialogs are abending with the error status 'nn69' (where nn varies depending on the request issued).

Causes: The 'nn69' error status code is a general catch-all status which has a variety of causes, including:

1. CV not coming up successfully,
2. A shutdown issued while active tasks or run units are still being serviced, once a shutdown has occurred no new users or programs are allowed to sign on to IDMS/R,
3. Timeouts such as exceeding external or internal waits for batch or CICS programs,
4. CV or a batch run unit being 'swapped out' for a long time (MVS consideration, see Chapter 13 for details).
5. Registration was turned on in the sysgen and an unregistered program attempted to access the database (refer to 6.2.2)
6. IDD AUTHORIZATION was turned on in SET OPTIONS statement and someone is attempting to compile an unknown program (refer to 6.2.4). Dialogs are also affected by IDD AUTHORIZATION, however the message DC187952 - REGISTRATION REQD. BUT NO PROG-051 is displayed rather than an '0069' ERROR-STATUS. The '0069' ERROR-STATUS pertains only to programs compiled with the DMLx pre-processors.

Analysis: Check with operations personnel to see if CV is up. Inquire if a shutdown request has been entered. Determine which request resulted in the 'nn69' ERROR-STATUS by examining the code displayed on the screen from an ADS/O abend, or the DML-SEQUENCE number from a batch or CICS program abend if the DEBUG option was specified in the PROTOCOL statement. Suspect a timeout or swap out (MVS) problem if the 'nn69' resulted from a request after the initial request (i.e., this is not the first call to IDMS/R).

Refer to the system reports to see if program registration is in effect. If so, check to see if the problem program was registered in the sysgen. Display the IDD options to see if AUTHORIZATION is ON if the '1469' occurred during a DMLx precompiler run. If so, check to see if the program has been added to the IDD.

Decisions: None.

Resolution: The resolution depends on the cause of the 'nn69' ERROR-STATUS. A resolution is suggested below for each of the causes, identified by the same number used above.

1. Check to see if CV is executing before running Batch or CICS or UCF programs. Some installations make use of the 'nn69' ERROR-STATUS to determine whether or not CV is up before running a program, e.g., to prevent backups from being run while CV is up, or to make certain CV is up and running prior to starting a crucial batch run. The first step of the job executes a program that attempts to bind a dictionary run unit under CV. If the bind is successful, the program issues a message, finishes, and ends. The cause can only be that CV has come down, is in the process of shutting down, or has never been brought up if the bind results in an 'nn69' ERROR-STATUS. Under OS, a return code could be set to control whether the next step of the job, i.e., the backup or the batch run, should proceed. Under DOS, a message could be sent telling the operator whether or not to start start the next job. While this is not a foolproof method of determining whether or not CV is up (CV could be swapped out in MVS shops), it is reliable in 99% of the cases.

2. Tighten control on those persons with security clearance to shutdown system. The #CTABGEN macro can be used to set a high security class for the DCMT SHUTDOWN command (Sections 6.2.2 and 6.3.4)

3. Investigate the program/dialog which experienced the 'nn69' abend to detect if something in its design could be causing the timeout. Also, see if CV or the external run unit was swapped out (MVS only) and that caused the timeout. Consider

increasing the value of the sysgen parameter which triggered the timeout, or overriding the time limit for the problem program/dialog.

4. Make CV non-swappable (refer to Chapter 13 for more details on MVS considerations). The number of initiators for batch run units could be reduced if storage contention and swapping is a problem.

5. Assuming the program should be allowed access to the database, DCMT commands may be used to register the DC program temporarily, i.e., for the duration of the run. For IDMS DML batch programs and CICS-IDMS programs, and as a permanent solution for DC programs, in the next sysgen, either turn off registration or register the missing programs.

6. Assuming it is permissible to compile the program, an authorized user should add a PROGRAM entity to the dictionary, thereby identifying the program/dialog and enabling compiles/generations. Alternatively, use the SET OPTIONS statement to turn off AUTHORIZATION. Inform the user to try the compile again after one of these solutions has been implemented.

12.14 MAJOR SYMPTOM – PROGRAMS/DIALOGS ABENDING WITH 'nn71' ERROR-STATUS CODES

The 'nn71' ERROR-STATUS code indicates either:

- Subschema and DMCL area page ranges do not match, or
- Broken chain on the database (covered in Section 12.11.1).

12.14.1 Problem – Subschema and DMCL Area Page Ranges Do Not Match

Symptoms: Dialogs and programs are abending with 'nn71' ERROR-STATUS codes.

Causes: Programs and dialogs will abend with an error status code of 'nn71' if page ranges defined in subschemas do not reflect actual page ranges as shown in the global DMCL (nn varies depending on the request issued by the program/dialog). IDMS-CV checks the page ranges at run time when a call affecting an area is received.

This mismatch problem is often caused by changing the database and global DMCL page ranges without making corresponding changes to all affected subschemas. This kind of error is most apt to occur when one person is responsible for implementing application changes (i.e., application schemas, local DMCL's, and subschemas) and another is responsible for implementing system changes (i.e., global DMCL changes, affecting everything running under that CV). The mismatch error may remain undetected for days if the subschema is not used often.

Another way this problem may occur is if the global DMCL is changed first, the system brought up, and then the subschema is changed. The 'nn71' abend is likely to occur if an old copy of the subschema remains in main storage because a DCMT VARY NEW COPY *subschema-name* command was not issued.

If the subschema was developed on a secondary load area and is to be used by external run units, e.g., batch or CICS programs, the load module must also be on the primary load area or the Load Library/Core Image library (LL/CIL), unless the initial CALL to IDMS identifies the secondary DD. The error may be caused by an old copy of the subschema load module present in either the primary load area or a LL/CIL.

Analysis: One method to double check the subschema's page range is to browse through the subschema load module if it resides in an LL/CIL. Turn on hexidecimal display and browse the module looking for the literal 'AC56' and the literal for the area's name. The page range follows the area name literal. Alternatively, if the subschema resides in a dictionary load area, browse the program/dialog dump in the log. Look for the literal 'IB50' followed by the subschema's name. Then use the same procedure as browsing the subschema load module.

Decisions: none.

Resolution: Recompile the offending subschema. Then issue a DCMT VARY NEW COPY *subschema-name* command. If the subschema was generated on a secondary dictionary and is used by external run units, either a) copy the load module to the primary load area, b) use IDMSDDDL to PUNCH the module and then link it to an LL/CIL, or c) change the program's code to identify explicitly the secondary dictionary.

12.15 MAJOR SYMPTOM – PROGRAMS/DIALOGS ABENDING WITH 'nn74' ERROR-STATUS CODES

The 'nn74' ERROR-STATUS code means that a dynamic load of a module failed. Usually, it indicates that IDMS/R was unable to locate a subschema load module.

12.15.1 Problem – Subschema Not Found

Symptoms: The symptoms of the subschema not found problem are programs abending with a '1474' ERROR-STATUS on the initial bind request and dialogs abending with 'nn74' ERROR-STATUS codes on the first call to IDMS/R.

Causes: 'nn74' abends occur when IDMS/R cannot find the run unit's subschema load module. This problem is most likely to occur when multiple dictionaries are in use and subschema load modules are stored in secondary dictionary load areas. Subschemas are not loaded from a secondary dictionary unless the calling program or dialog specifies the secondary dictionary name. The secondary dictionary name is specified either by:

1. A DCUF SET DICTNAME command being issued for the terminal (often as part of a signon profile) and thereafter affecting all DC programs, dialogs, and online system software executing for that terminal, or
2. A program explicitly identifying the secondary dictionary by including the DICTNAME parameter as part of the BIND RUN-UNIT call to IDMS/R.

External run units, e.g., batch and CICS DML programs, must use the second method.

When a secondary dictionary is not specified by the calling program, IDMS/R looks for the subschema in the primary dictionary's load area. IDMS/R next tries to load the subschema from an LL/CIL if the subschema is not found. If the subschema still is not found, the program or dialog will abend. An 'nn71' ERROR-STATUS may result if an old copy of the subschema is found (Section 12.14).

Analysis: Determine where the subschema load module resides. The dictionary syntax to display a subschema load module is:

DISPLAY LOAD MOD module-name.

Make sure the module is in the right library if it has been punched and link edited to an LL/CIL for use by local mode programs or external run units.

Decisions: None.

Resolution: Ensure that programs and dialogs specify the secondary dictionary name using one of the methods described above. Alternatively, move the subschema load module to the primary dictionary's load area or the load/core image library (PUNCH and link edit it).

12.16 MAJOR SYMPTOM – PROGRAMS/DIALOGS ABENDING WITH 'NN75' ERROR-STATUS CODES

The 'nn75' ERROR-STATUS code means that an I/O read error occurred. The I/O error can be caused by:

- Data/equipment checks or a head crash on the device containing the area's file (covered in Sections 12.10.1 and 12.10.2), or
- An improperly initialized area (covered in Section 12.10.3).

12.17 MAJOR SYMPTOM – INVALID DATA IN REPORTS OR ONLINE DISPLAYS

Invalid data can be a symptom of either a physically or logically corrupted database. Possible causes of invalid data include:

- 'Type I' broken chains on the database (i.e., a physically corrupted database, see discussion in 12.11.1)
- Improper updates by application programs/dialogs (i.e., a logically corrupted database)

12.17.1 Problem – Database Corrupted Logically By Improper Application Update

Symptoms: Invalid data is noticed in reports or online displays, invalid figures or the wrong date, for example. No other symptoms of the problem are apparent; the system continues processing normally.

Causes: Logical corruption occurs when invalid data is stored in some records but there is no physical damage to the database structure. A database can be corrupted logically by an incorrectly-coded application run with valid input data or by a correctly-coded application run with invalid input data. Presumably, an incorrectly-coded application run with valid input data would be discovered during testing. If the problem is uncovered during testing, restoring the test database would be sufficient recovery; concurrent run unit's updates probably need not be preserved. Recovery problems similar to those discussed below result if the problem is not uncovered until the program is running in production.

A correctly-coded application run with invalid input data poses a more serious recovery problem, especially if it was a batch program updating many records. For example, suppose a batch program which updates a securities database was run with the wrong input because the pricing service bureau provided yesterday's tape rather than today's. Not only must the invalid updates be rolled back or the database restored, but retrieval and update run units which ran after the bad update, perhaps basing decisions on faulty data, must also be considered. We examine this problem in two parts, assuming in the first that no other run units were updating the area(s) while the invalid updates took place and assuming in the second that other run units were updating the area(s) concurrently.

Simple Case: An Entire Batch Update Used An Improper Input File, No Other Run Units Updating the Area(s) Concurrently

Analysis: Check the program's input to determine how widespread the bad data problem is. Alternatively, if there is a date/time stamp in each DB record, perhaps it can be used to identify the affected data.

Decisions: The major decision is whether to restore the database area(s) from the most recent backup or to use the journal file and the IDMSRBCK utility to rollback the updates. The choice depends upon the size of the areas and how recently the backup was taken. The restore will probably be faster if the areas are small. The rollback operation may be faster if the areas are large, depending on how much of the area has been updated.

Resolution: We are assuming that the update was run under CV with a usage mode of PROTECTED or EXCLUSIVE UPDATE in this case. These usage modes prevent other run units from updating the areas concurrently. To simplify the problem further, assume that the error was discovered prior to other programs accessing the corrupted database.

Vary the affected areas offline to CV immediately to prevent other run unit's from accessing the corrupted areas until recovery processing is complete. Then, issue a DCMT VARY JOURNAL *active-journal-file* command to force an IDMSAJNL run, offloading the current disk journal, thereby ensuring that all journal images from the faulty run are offloaded to tape. Next, gather all journal tapes created during the update run (unless the volume of updates was tremendous only one tape is likely to be involved). Concatenate them as input to an IDMSJFIX run (IDMSJFIX accepts multiple input reels

and writes one output reel). IDMSJFIX produces a report of all run
units' checkpoints on the tape. Use the report to identify a level zero
quiesce point just before the faulty update started. Then, run
IDMSRBCK to rollback the faulty updates, specifying:

```
PROCESS=AREA,DMCL=dmcl-name
RESTORE=YES,DATE=mm/dd/yy,TIME=hhmmsshh
AREA=area-name-1
AREA=area-name-2
```

All affected areas (i.e., the corrupted areas as well as any areas
related by set relationships to the corrupted areas) should be rolled
back to the date and time of the BGIN checkpoint of the faulty batch
run. Finally, vary the areas back online to CV and rerun the batch
update using the correct input file.

Complex Case: An Entire Batch Update Used An Improper Input File; Other Run Units Updated the Area(s) Concurrently and Subsequently

Analysis: Offload all journals and run IDMSJFIX or the journal
reports to determine what other programs updated the affected areas.
Peruse the output, noting which areas were updated and by which programs.

Decisions: Same as the simple case, rollback the updates or restore
the database.

Resolution: Immediately vary the affected areas offline to CV to prevent other run unit's from accessing the corrupted areas until recovery processing is complete. Next, issue a DCMT VARY JOURNAL
active-journal-file command to force an IDMSAJNL run offloading
the current disk journal. Gather all journal tapes created during the
update run (probably only one tape) and concatenate them as input to
an IDMSJFIX run.
    We are assuming that other run units may have been updating the
area(s) concurrently in this complex case. Examine the report output
from IDMSJFIX to determine exactly what update processing tran-
spired during and after the faulty run unit's processing. The
IDMSJFIX report is easier to work with than either the roll forward or
roll back utility reports. Most sites journal only update run units (as
specified in the sysgen SYSTEM statement parameter NOJOURNAL
RETRIEVAL). Therefore, the report from IDMSJFIX will not identify retrieval run units. Any retrieval run units which processed during and/or after the faulty update may have produced erroneous
results. It will be difficult to determine the affects of the faulty updates

on retrieval run units unless a user-defined audit trail of retrieval processing has been maintained.

The rollback utility may be run only for the corrupted areas, as in the preceding simple case, if no other updates were run against the affected areas. Repeat the steps previously outlined and run IDMSRBCK to rollback the faulty updates specifying:

```
PROCESS=AREA,DMCL=dmcl-name
RESTORE=YES,DATE=mm/dd/yy,TIME=hhmmsshh
AREA=area-name-1
AREA=area-name-2
```

All affected areas should be rolled back to the date and time of the BGIN checkpoint of the faulty batch run. Finally, vary the areas back online to CV and rerun the batch update using the correct input file.

First rollback the areas to the level zero quiesce point at or just before the beginning of the batch run if other programs updated the corrupted areas during and/or after the faulty batch run. The rollback returns the database to a clean starting point.

Unfortunately, there is no quick fix for the rest of the problem. A simple run of IDMSRFWD to reapply the other run unit's updates will not work, because IDMSRFWD starts with the first image on the tape and forward recovers all updates to the area(s). Therefore, the updates of other run units must be extracted from the journal tape, otherwise the faulty updates would be reapplied along with the valid updates. Updates of specific run units can be extracted from the journal tape by using utility programs available from the IDMS Users Association or by coding an assembler language program in-house to perform the same function. The layouts of journal record types can be found in the Systems Operations Guide in the User Exits section (Release 10) or in the IDMS DB/DC Operations manual (Release 5.7).

The roll forward operation may not solve the problem even after the valid updates have been extracted from the journal tape because the before and after image of the entire record is journaled when any field in the data portion of the record is updated. It may be necessary to rerun the application programs rather than roll forward to recover, depending on which fields were updated by subsequent programs. Table 12-6 illustrates the problem. Rolling forward the online update puts the invalid data, BBBBB, back in the database along with the valid data, ZZZZZ, because the online program/dialog updated a different field than the batch program. There is no substitute for knowledge of each program's processing when choosing an appropriate method of recovery. If there is a high incidence of this kind of updates, the roll forward utility may be useless. Rerunning the batch update with proper input and rerunning the subsequent update transactions may be the only viable solution.

Table 12-6 Sample Record Contents Through a Series of Updates

Update Run	Date/Time	Contents of Data Record #1 After the Update
Prior to any updates	081386/110909	AAAAAYYYYYCCCCCDDDDD
Faulty batch run	081486/090108	AAAAABBBBBCCCCCDDDDD
Subsequent online update	081486/101004	AAAAABBBBBCCCCCZZZZZ
Roll back batch run	081486/111109	AAAAAYYYYYCCCCCDDDDD
Roll forward online update	081486/113018	AAAAABBBBBCCCCCZZZZZ

In addition, rolling back only the faulty update may cause broken chains if subsequent updates have been made which were dependent on the faulty update. If Run unit #1 has stored new occurrences of A and Run unit #2 has in turn stored new occurrences of B and C conccected to those new A's, broken chains will result (the owner pointer and the prior pointer on the first record and the next pointers on the last record in the sets A-B and A-C point to an A that no longer exists, causing an '0361' ERROR-STATUS). The faulty update and all subsequent updates dependent on the faulty update should be rolled back together.

12.18 MAJOR SYMPTOM – SYSTEM HANGS DURING SHUTDOWN

Problems encountered during system shutdown are usually related to tasks or run units still executing. IDMS/R allows a task to finish processing before coming down if shutdown is attempted while the task is running.

No new application tasks may start processing after a shutdown command has been entered. Once shutdown has been requested, DCMT and other system tasks cannot run. All terminals are shutdown, attempts to signon to UCF result in 'D902' messages and attempts to bind new run units result in 'nn69' ERROR-STATUSs. The only commands which will work are DB commands issued from the console (e.g., DISPLAY DATA BASE, DISPLAY RUN UNIT).

12.18.1 Problem – Tasks Still Executing

Symptoms: The system hangs during shutdown processing.

Causes: One cause of the system hanging during shutdown is UCF intermittent task codes being executed. Intermittent mode is when there are two sessions signed on concurrently at the same terminal, a CICS and a UCF terminal session. Intermittent mode allows the user to switch back and forth between CICS processing and UCF processing. Intermittent mode is accomplished by defining a transaction identifier in CICS and the same identifier as a task code in the IDMS/R sysgen (e.g., DBT1, specified as NOINPUT under IDMS/R). When DBT1 is typed in from CICS, the program in IDMS/R associated with the task code DBT1 will start automatically. The task code can invoke a dialog providing the program it invokes is ADSORUN1 and there is a dialog named DBT1. Control automatically passes back to CICS without the ENTER NEXT TASK CODE prompt ever being seen by the operator when the program/dialog terminates without naming a new task to be executed on the terminal or issuing a transfer or link command. The UCF terminal still is held and the user is not signed off as is the case with the BYE or SIGNOFF tasks. Intermittent mode is explained in the Systems Operations Guide (Release 10) or the IDMS-DC System Administrator's Guide (Release 5.7).

An undrained CICS/UCF printer is another cause of the system hanging during shutdown, because there are tasks associated with undrained printers. Central Version cannot come down while the print tasks are running. The print tasks do not terminate automatically when a SHUTDOWN command is issued; the printers must be drained and the print terminal varried offline to terminate the print tasks.

Analysis: If the shutdown has already been issued and the system is hanging, check for active run units from the operator's console and abort them if need be. The DCMT DISPLAY PTERM command can be issued to check for intermittent tasks prior to issuing a shut down request. The display will show a status of INSRV for terminals which are executing intermittent tasks. A DCMT DISPLAY PRINTERS command will show a status of INSRV for undrained printers.

Decisions: One may want to abort the run unit(s) if large batch update run units are executing. Be advised, however, that the rollback of the aborted run units may prolong system shutdown as well.

Resolution: If UCF intermittent task codes are being executed, the tasks must either be aborted or the physical terminal varied offline, which also aborts the task. Cancel the system if printers in a UCF/CICS environment are the cause of the problem. Cancelling the system will not cause harm because no other activity is possible.

A CLIST can be defined containing preliminary DCMT commands as well as the shutdown command to prevent the system hanging during shutdown. The responsible user or operator then invokes the CLIST rather than issuing only a shutdown command. Alternatively, the commands can be placed in a dataset for input to UCF batch jobs, to be run by operations personnel to shut the system down. The printers must be properly drained by issuance of DCMT VARY PRINTER ALL DRAIN, and their physical terminals varied offline before the system will shutdown successfully. Here is a sample CLIST:

```
DCMT VARY PRINTER ALL DRAIN
DCMT VARY LINE UCFLINE OFF
DCMT SHUTDOWN
```

12.19 MAJOR SYMPTOM – UTILITIES IDMSRBCK AND/OR IDMSRFWD ABENDING

When the utilities IDMSRBCK and/or IDMSRFWD abend it is usually due to journal sequence errors.

12.19.1 Problem – Journal Sequence Errors

Symptoms: The batch utilities IDMSRBCK and IDMSRFWD will not run. The message 'JOURNAL RECORD SEQUENCE ERROR' is displayed.

Causes: Journal sequence errors are usually caused by applying the archive journal tapes in some sequence other than the sequence in which they were created. Improper sequencing can occur when multiple journal tapes are set up in a generation data group (OS) to be merged together. If an unqualified request for the cataloged tapes is made, the tapes will be mounted in reverse of the order expected by the utilities.

Analysis: None.

Decisions: None.

Resolution: Specify all necessary archive journal tapes in the appropriate order, i.e., the order in which they were created, when running IDMSRFWD and IDMSRBCK. To be safe, always sort journal images by date and time stamp before applying them (see the IDMS utilities manual under IDMSRBCK or IDMSRFWD for information about sort exits). An alternative at OS sites is specifying the JCL disposition of MOD to piggyback journal images from multiple runs together on the same tape or disk. Ensure that the input tapes are mounted in the correct order if a standard job is run to merge all journal tapes created during a processing day into one tape.

12.20 INFORMATION THAT SHOULD BE SUPPLIED TO THE CULLINET SUPPORT TECHNICIAN WHEN IN-HOUSE PROBLEM RESOLUTION FAILS

Attempt to recreate a complex problem which withstands all efforts at resolution with SYSTRACE on in the sysgen (i.e., the SYSTEM statement) and print a dump before contacting Cullinet. The messages, dumps, and SYSTRACE must be relayed to the Cullinet support technician to solve the problem. Failure to have all the information at hand with the sequence of events set down in a clear, concise manner will delay problem resolution.

It is helpful to have both an operating system dump and a print log dump in instances where CV has crashed or must be cancelled. IDMS console messages are also appropriate, especially if the DC log output is lost. Lastly, ensure that all PTF's applied since the last installation tape can be identified quickly. Many users have adopted a standard of recording all PTF's in a text editor file or on the IDD for quick review. Cullinet provides the load module IDMSPTFS which is updated as part of each PTF application. A dump of this module provides a quick listing of all PTF's applied since the last installation.

12.21 CONCLUSION

When trouble arises, check the console and IDMS/R log first for identifying error messages and codes, following the general approach to trouble shooting outlined in Section 12.2. Next, compare the problem's symptoms to symptoms of common problems described in this chapter along with their resolution. Gather all pertinent materials and call the Cullinet support technician if attempts at in-house problem resolution fail.

Being prepared is the best defense against major problems. It is essential that output from system and utility runs be reviewed periodically for early warning signals of impending disaster. Monitoring system activity and making appropriate changes prior to actual trouble is the essence of performance tuning, discussed in Chapter 13.

Remember the old adage, "An ounce of prevention is worth a pound of cure!"

Suggestions for further reading on Trouble Shooting:

The following Cullinet materials
  For Release 10 sites:
   1) IDMS/R Database Operations (Overview of backup and recovery, description of database utilities)
   2) IDMS-CV/DC System Operations (DCMT commands, system startup, journal record layouts)
   3) Cullinet System Software – System Generation (System generation parameters)
   4) IDMS-DB/DC Utilities (Detailed instructions for running utilities)
   5) Cullinet System Software – Error Codes and Messages, Volumes I & II, (Explanations of console and log error numbers and codes)
   6) IDMS-DB/DC DSECT Reference (outlines structure of system tables and control blocks, e.g., DMCL)
   7) Class aids for IDMS for the DBA (DB54)
   8) Class aids for IDMS/R System Performance and Tuning (SP503)

  For Release 5.7 Sites:
   1) IDMS-DB/DC Operations (DCMT commands, system startup, overview of backup and recovery, layout of journal records)
   2) IDMS-CV/DC System Generation (System generation parameters)
   3) IDMS-DB/DC Utilities (Detailed instructions for running utilities)
   4) IDMS-DB/DC Error Codes and Messages (Explanations of console and log error numbers and codes)
   5) IDMS-DB/DC DSECT Reference (outlines structure of system tables and control blocks, e.g., DMCL)
   6) Class aids for IDMS for the DBA (DB54)

13

Performance Tuning

Problems covered under performance tuning differ from those covered under trouble shooting by degree. We will discuss problems causing system slowdowns under performance tuning whereas the problems discussed under trouble shooting usually cause system stoppages and/or program abends.

Problem areas in system performance often do not become apparent until the number of users on the system and the amount of work they generate becomes fairly large. Once this situation occurs, however, steps taken to improve system performance are vital to successful implementation of IDMS/R. Performance tuning is an ongoing function. As changes are made to a system and new transactions increase the load on it, system performance should be monitored to determine which changes should be made to improve performance.

In this chapter we will cover:

- An overview of performance problem areas,
- System-related performance issues,
- Application-related performance issues, and
- Sources of information relevant to performance tuning.

Performance tuning will be discussed in two categories, namely system-related and application-related performance issues, for ease of explanation. System-related issues are those bearing on IDMS/R systems in general and those affected by decisions made during system creation. Application-related performance issues are those caused by and/or affected by application design decisions (i.e., database or program/dialog design decisions). Application design decisions often affect overall system performance and vice versa.

13.1 AN OVERVIEW OF PERFORMANCE PROBLEM AREAS

Performance problem areas are those areas of system/application configuration and usage which have the potential to affect overall system performance. Our discussion concentrates on system-related

performance issues, although some important application-related
performance issues are also discussed.

The following tables outline conditions or situations which can
cause poor performance. Each table also provides information on the
detection and resolution of performance problems. Table 13-1 contains a list of system-related causes of poor system performance.
Application-related causes of poor system performance are outlined
in Table 13-2. The problems listed in these tables are covered in
greater detail in the following sections.

Table 13-1 System-Related Performance Problems

Problem	Impact	Detection[1]	Resolutions
SOS, (Short on Storage) conditions occur because the storage pool is too small or too frag- mented, or because the cushion is too large.	All new activity waits; existing dispatched tasks continue to execute using cushion space.	SS	Increase size of storage pool or decrease size of cushion. Under Release 10, specify storage limits.
Large programs loading into a program pool which is too small.	Terminal seems to be in a prolonged wait, other processing may seem sluggish	SS, L	Investigate programs to be loaded for size and frequency of use, Increase program pool size Make some programs resident. Discuss program size and coding techniques with applications development group. Increase the size of DD load area pages to make individual loads faster (e.g., 16-24K).
Inappropriate val- ues for SYSTEM parameters such as MAXTASKS, RUNAWAY INTER- VAL, and EXTERNAL WAIT	Short to potentially long waits	SS, L, D	Modify parameter values in next sysgen.

- - - - - - - - - - - - - - - - - - - -(continued on next page)- - - - - - - - - - - - - - - - - - - -

Table 13-1 System-Related Performance Problems (continued)

Problem	Impact	Detection[1]	Resolutions
Buffer pool too small	Short to potentially long waits, depending on nature of activity (batch or online).	D, O, SS	Increase size of buffer pool Combine pools for areas with similar page sizes.
Log waits, caused by DCMT WRITE STATS, system dumps, ABRU SNAP, and/or task write statistics with a low interval.	Short waits	D, O	Turn task write statistics off or increase the interval, Turn off ABRU SNAP Investigate cause of system dumps. Remove SNAP commands from programs/dialogs after the problem has been solved.
Poor operating system configuration	Short to long waits	O	Change operating system parameters describing the IDMS/R job.
Inappropriate DASD configuration	Short to long waits, increased vulnerability to data loss	O	Configure to minimize loss Balance access to channels volumes
Excessive CPU utilization	Short to long waits	O	Reduce number of buffers Reduce number of areas Arrange subschema records in order of access frequency Avoid using compression/ decompression routines Check for runaways and discuss with programmers Generate ADS/O dialogs with executable code Run batch retrievals locally (where possible) and at a lower priority than CV

[1]Codes: C=Console messages, D=DCMT command, J=Journal reports, L=Log messages or dumps, S=Sysgen parameter values, SS=System Statistics, O=Other (Jobs in system, observation, examination of program code, etc.)

Table 13-2 Application-Related Performance Problems

Problem	Impact	Detection[1]	Resolutions
Excessive storage pool consumption by individual dialogs or programs	Increased probability of SOS	T	Talk to applications development about reducing storage consumption. Under Release 10, set LIMITS for storage
ADS/O primary record buffer too large	Increased probability of SOS	T, S	Talk to applications development about limiting size of DB and work records used by main line dialogs
EXCLUSIVE or PROTECTED READY usage modes	Extremely long to short waits	J, D, O	Talk to applications development staff about usage modes. Change subschemas to prevent use of EXCLUSIVE or PROTECTED modes
Excessive number of record locks	Extremely long waits, potential for SOS condition	J, D, O	Talk to applications development staff about designing large-update programs to issue COMMITs. Consider running job locally
Inappropriate usage of Online Debugger	Increased probability of SOS and general system slowdowns	T, SS	Talk to applications development staff about limiting concurrent generations of dialogs with symbol tables
Poor DB design for application requirements	Intermittent excessive I/O and CPU utilization	J	Redesign the database and use the restructure utility to implement the changes. Talk to development team about requirements. Under Release 10, specify DBIO limits

[1]Codes: C=Console messages, D=DCMT command, J=Journal reports, L=Log messages or dumps, S=Sysgen parameters, SS=System Statistics, T=Transaction statistics, O=Other (Jobs in system, observation, examination of program code, etc.)

13.2 SYSTEM-RELATED PERFORMANCE ISSUES

In this section we will cover the performance issues presented in Table 13-1. Several aspects of system performance tuning are universally important. The advice and suggestions found in this section are based on our experience with IDMS/R in a wide variety of settings. Your site's individual requirements should be used to temper our suggestions.

13.2.1 Storage Pool Usage

One of the foremost performance considerations in a large teleprocessing and batch environment is achieving maximum benefit from the storage pool. The primary storage pool, defined by the STORAGE POOL parameter of the SYSTEM statement, is used for a variety of system and application functions. For example, signing on a run unit and allocating storage for subschema currency tables consumes space in the storage pool. ADS/O dialog's record buffers, currency tables, and the variable portion of the dialog usually are saved in the storage pool as well. Refer to Table 9-2 in the Test System Creation chapter for a summary of storage pool uses. Sufficient storage allocation for and efficient use of the storage pool is crucial to system throughput.

A Short On Storage (SOS) condition occurs when the amount of available space in the storage pool drops below the cushion amount, as discussed in Chapter 9 under the CUSHION parameter. While the system is short on storage, new tasks cannot begin processing. Tasks which have already begun are allowed to continue processing, dipping into the storage cushion as necessary. Normal processing resumes when the amount of free space once again exceeds the cushion amount.

The number of times an SOS condition occurred during the run is shown in the shutdown statistics and can be displayed online by issuing a DCMT DISPLAY STATISTICS SYSTEM command. If frequent SOS conditions occur either the pool is too small or the cushion is too large. One or both parameters should be modified in the next sysgen. There are other helpful statistics for determining the cause of the problem.

The system uses three types of scans to search for space to satisfy storage requests: SCAN-1 PASS, SCAN-2 PASS, and SCAN-3 PASS. Space in the pool is allocated in multiples of 64 bytes. Scans for long term storage start at the high address of the pool, scans for short term storage start from the low address of the pool, leaving the free space in the middle of the pool. The SCAN statistics indicate how fragmented the storage pool has become. Scan statistics may be viewed in the system statistical display, in the shutdown statistics, or in the DCMT DISPLAY ACTIVE STORAGE command output.

The system must do more work to search for available storage as the pool becomes more fragmented, causing the proportion of requests satisfied by SCAN-3 to increase. A high percentage of SCAN-3 allocations indicates that the storage pool is too small and/or too fragmented. If the SCAN-3 statistic is consistently greater than 30% of all storage requests, the situation should be investigated further by monitoring system activity.

Several tools are available for monitoring storage pool usage and pin pointing the cause(s) of storage problems. The commands DCMT DIS ACT STG, OPER W LTERM, and OPER W STORAGE can be used to display storage usage statistics online. The IDMS/R Performance Monitor, if available at your site, can provide a wealth of helpful information. The batch report of task statistics, Report #2, lists storage pool use broken down by task (Figure 13-1). Tasks identified as extreme storage consumers can be selected for detailed monitoring online. The online IDMS/R Performance Monitor displays a summary screen showing a list of executions of those monitored tasks. The details of specific executions can be selected and displayed. Further details on performance monitoring tools are covered later in this chapter.

One task may be consuming a tremendous amount of user kept storage (e.g., an ADS/O dialog with a tremendous number of records and/or levels). If so, redesigning the task may be the best solution. If, however, the increased storage consumption appears to be due to a rise in the number of users and activity on the system rather than excessive storage consumption for a few programs, the storage pool should be enlarged to handle increased demand.

Fragmentation: Long term fragmentation of the storage pool should be avoided because each storage request can be satisfied most easily with contiguous storage. To reduce long term fragmentation, make sure that the initial allocations for such parameters as UNDEFINED PROGRAM COUNT and RUN UNIT LOCKS are high enough to meet the worst case situation rather than accommodating just the average demand. Also, make the secondary allocation parameter for UNDEFINED PROGRAM COUNT fairly high to reduce the number of further secondary allocations made. Above all, continue monitoring system activity closely to spot new demand levels that warrant changing system parameters.

Multiple storage pools: Multiple storage pools can be allocated for different types of storage in Release 10 (i.e., shared, shared kept, user,

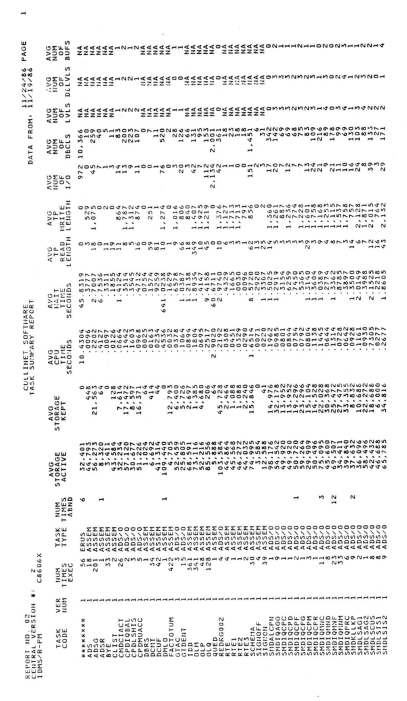

Figure 13-1 Sample Output from IDMS/R Performance Monitor Report 2

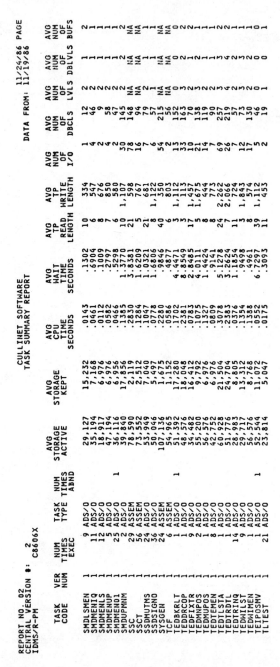

Figure 13-1 Sample Output from IDMS/R Performance Monitor Report 2
(continued)

user kept, database buffers, and terminal I/O buffers), affording better control over the amount of storage available for each type of usage. Multiple storage pools allow the DBA to tailor the environment so that storage may be allocated into several pools based on needs existing in the system, rather than having one huge pool. If shared storage is seldom used, little space is allocated for it. On the other hand, large demands for user kept storage (e.g., ADS/O storage) will not affect allocations for shared kept storage. Multiple storage pools localize the effects of fragmentation and may cut down on the incidence of fragmentation as well. A single primary pool is preferred if requirements for each type of storage usage cannot be determined or are largely mixed.

ADS/O Storage Usage: A major use of the storage pool is saving ADS/O dialog resources (records, currency information, variable dialog block, etc.) while a dialog is waiting for the operator to enter the next screen full of information. Saving some ADS/O dialog resources on disk, in the scratch area of the DD, allows users to specify a smaller storage pool and thereby conserve main storage. Realize, however, that storing resources in the scratch area of the DD adds I/O overhead to dialog processing. Also, access to the scratch area of the DD is single-threaded (see discussion of Scratch and Log later in this section). Because of these disadvantages, using the storage pool to save dialog resources is recommended in production systems. Specifications made in the ADSO statement during system generation determine where dialog resources are stored (refer to Chapter 9, under ADSO Statement Considerations, for details on the FAST MODE THRESHOLD and RESOURCES ARE RELOCATABLE features).

Benefits of Small, Specific Subschemas: The fixed portion of a subschema table is loaded into a program pool. The variable portion is allocated storage from the storage pool. The fixed portion is shared, but a separate copy of the variable portion is required for each concurrently processing run unit using the same subschema.

Creation of small, specific subschemas is an important method of conserving storage pool space because the variable portions of subschema tables can take up a large amount of storage per run unit. A single, large general-purpose subschema takes a great deal more time to load and occupies more storage than several small specific subschemas. The variable portion of a subschema table is at least 4K and can be much larger depending on the number of records, sets, areas, and logical records included in the subschema. The trade off here is less sharing of the fixed portion of subschema tables to achieve smaller variable portions.

In general, subschemas used by online tasks should include only the areas, sets, and records necessary for processing, leading to establishment of a separate small subschema for each different type of online request. Subschemas should also be small and fairly specific for external run units, containing only the areas, records, and sets necessary for that program or group of programs. Logical Record Facility (LRF) usage increases the size of both the fixed and variable portions of the subschema. Subschemas with LRF records should contain only the paths required for current processing, rather than all possible paths for all possible records.

The size of the variable portion of an existing subschema table may be determined by modifying the system statistics histogram to collect data on greater size variations (see the Operations Guide for information on modifying histograms). Execute a program using this subschema and issue DCMT commands to write system statistics to the log before and after execution. Then note the results under the 'system storage' histogram. The 'system storage' histogram shows the combined size of all subschema variable portions of concurrently processing tasks and run units. Make sure no other activity is going on, thereby isolating one subschema's storage consumption. DC and ADS/O non-subschema storage shows up as 'user' not 'system' storage in the histograms.

Another method for determining the size of the variable portion of an external run unit's subschema is checking storage consumption in the task statistics. External run units use storage pool space only for the variable portion of the subschema and lock tables (where applicable).

Limiting Storage Consumption: The Release 10 sysgen parameter STORAGE LIMITS provides a useful tool for managing the storage available to individual tasks. Storage thresholds can be set for internal and external requestors. Run units or tasks exceeding the limit either are aborted or an exit program can be invoked to perform site-specific processing. An exit program could write a message to the log noting the offending program's name. LIMITS on test systems are helpful for identifying programs which are storage gluttons, allowing changes to be effected prior to production implementation of the program/dialog.

Another method of limiting storage consumption is limiting the number of map detail pages which may be created during a pageable mapping session and stored in the storage pool. DBA's at sites where pageable maps are used should specify PAGING STORAGE IS storage-amount in the OLM statement during system generation (Release 10 only). This clause defines a threshold for the number of map detail records that may be generated during a pageable mapping session.

13.2.2   Program Loading Considerations

Loading programs is a time consuming activity for any monitor. Therefore, reducing the time it takes to load a module and reducing the total number of loads are important considerations.

Figure 13-2 provides an overview of program loading. Modules are loaded from a Load Library/Core Image Library (LL/CIL) or a

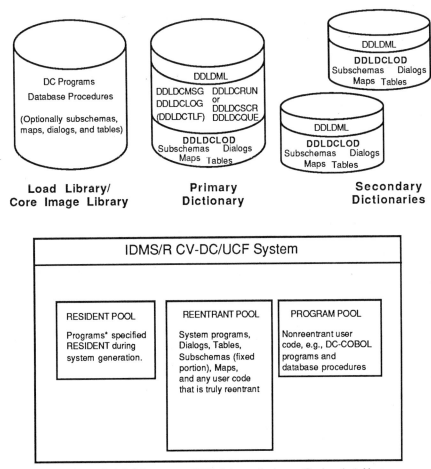

Figure 13-2 Program Loading Overview

dictionary load area. Modules are loaded into one of three areas of main storage: the resident pool, the reentrant pool, or the program pool.

In this section we will discuss:

- Load library/core image library considerations,
- DD load area considerations,
- Loading from a DD load area versus an LL/CIL,
- Program pools,
- Residency considerations,
- Reducing the number of loads of DD network subschemas,
- Sysgen program specifications, and
- DCUF TEST considerations.

Load Library/Core Image Library (LL/CIL) Considerations: DC programs, database procedures, and many Cullinet modules are loaded only from an LL/CIL. Subschemas, tables, maps, and dialogs are usually loaded from a dictionary load area but also may be loaded into main storage from either a DD load area or an LL/CIL (see discussion of tradeoffs under LL/CIL versus DD Load Area following DD Load Area Considerations).

An operating system load, i.e., loading a module from an LL/CIL, is a single-threaded operation causing other loads to wait. It can cause the entire memory space to wait (OS only) if a BLDL operation is necessary (see the System Generation guide or Chapter 9 for more information on when directory lists are built. Look under BLDL/NOBLDL parameter of SYSTEM statement). DC programs, database procedures, and/or Cullinet modules which are large and frequently used should be considered for residency to minimize the number LL/CIL load operations.

DD Load Area Considerations: Subschema, table, map, and dialog modules are usually loaded from a dictionary load area into main storage. Program loading performance can be directly dependent on the page size and page range of the DDLDCLOD area because many modules are loaded from the dictionary load area.

An IDD load module is composed of one 'LOADHDR-156' CALC record and as many variable length 'LOADTEXT-157' VIA records as are needed to store the entire load module (refer to the DD Network diagram and Network Reference Manual for details). Each LOADHDR record is 100 bytes long and contains information about the module as a whole. Each LOADTEXT record contains a 512-byte segment of the load module.

Ideally, the number of pages specified by the page range for the DDLDCLOD area for any dictionary should be equal to the estimated number of modules that will reside on that dictionary. Then IDMSCALC (the CALC algorithm) will, on the average, store each module on an empty page. An appropriate page size can be determined by setting up an extremely large dialog or LRF subschema to gauge the 'worst case', and then blocking the pages accordingly. Pages should be large, perhaps 12K to 24K, to fit the greatest number of LOADTEXT records on the page without wasting space. Sizes of existing load modules can be determined using Online IDD and the DISPLAY LOAD MOD *module-name* command or through the DCMT DIS PROGRAM *program-name* command or through CREPORT050 output.

Assume that a load area has been defined with a page size of only 3-4K, as an example of the problems caused by poor choices for page size and page range. The LOADTEXT VIA records of a large load module (32K to 40K, e.g., an ADS/O dialog with 1,600 lines of code or a subschema with logical record commands) would overflow from the page on which the LOADHDR was stored and fill nine or ten additional pages. Loading a program that large would require ten or eleven I/O's. As time goes on, each of these overflowed VIA records could precipitate CALC and VIA record overflow on other pages as well, considerably degrading system performance. By the same token, the CALC algorithm has far fewer pages over which to target a load module if an insufficient page range is selected; hence several load modules could target to the same page, creating further havoc.

Each secondary dictionary may contain its own load area in Release 10. Multiple load areas help reduce time spent searching for load modules and lessen the effects of load module overflow. This feature also segregates those load areas experiencing problems because of overflow, so one dictionary's problems do not affect any other dictionaries. However, as of this writing, secondary load areas do not use RHDCRUAL run units specified during sysgen, which reduces the efficiency of secondary DD loads somewhat (see discussion of RUN UNITS FOR SCRATCH, QUEUE, LOAD, etc., in Chapter 9 for details).

Size analysis of the current DD load area may be advisable if ADS/Online or LRF development is beginning or increasing. It will be necessary to increase the size of the load area to avoid extra I/O overhead during loads, due to overflow, because of the new or increasing potential for large load modules. The size of the DD load area may be increased by expanding the load area's page size or page range. Refer to Chapter 11 and to the Utilities manual for details on these operations.

Loading From a Dictionary Load Area Versus a Load Library/Core Image Library: Subschemas, tables, maps, and dialogs may be loaded into main storage from either a DD load area or an LL/CIL. DC programs, database procedures, and Cullinet software compilers (e.g., OLM, ADD, SCHEMA, ADSG, SSC, etc.) can be loaded only from an LL/CIL. A DC program's maps, tables, and subschema may be loaded from either. Which method is preferable when a choice exists, letting dialogs, maps, tables, and subschemas be loaded from the DD or moving all modules in a library?

Loading from a dictionary load area allows multi-threading of program loads and other IDMS/R processing. In contrast, loading from a library is single-threaded. Therefore, we strongly recommend accepting the default situation and loading all eligible modules from a dictionary load area (i.e., everything except DC programs and database procedures).

An exception to this rule might be made if the IDMS/R system processes only external run units, e.g., CICS and batch programs are the only run units executing. The amount of loading into the IDMS/R memory space is relatively low in this situation (only subschemas and, where applicable, database procedures) and libraries may be a viable alternative. Even then, loading subschemas from a library should be considered only if most subschemas are resident. Maintenance can be easier in shops like this if subschemas are loaded only from an LL/CIL, especially if extensive local mode batch processing is planned.

When running a batch program in local mode, the program's subschema must be PUNCHed from the DD load area and link edited into an LL/CIL prior to program execution. This requirement increases maintenance problems because there are now two versions of the subschema load module, the LL/CIL version and the load area version. The LL/CIL version is used only locally and the dictionary load area version is used only centrally (CV always attempts to use the load area version first). Some users delete the load area module, forcing the system to use the LL/CIL version for both CV and local modes, because of the potential for the versions being different.

In summary, we recommend that all eligible modules be loaded from the dictionary load area. Operating systems loads should be avoided.

Program Pools: There are three areas of main storage into which programs, dialogs, subschemas, tables, and maps may be loaded: storage allocated during startup processing, the reentrant pool, and the program pool. Resident programs are loaded into a separate portion of main storage during startup processing. Reentrant programs and all subschemas, dialogs, maps, and tables are loaded into the reentrant pool as they are needed. Nonreentrant, nonresident programs are loaded into the program pool (e.g., COBOL DC programs, which are quasi-reentrant, and nonreentrant database procedures). All nonresident programs are loaded into the program pool if no reentrant pool was allocated during the system generation. Refer to Chapter 9 for details on the program pools.

In contrast to an operating system, IDMS/R requires enough contiguous main storage to load the entire program before the program can execute. There is no operational equivalent to virtual system paging in IDMS/R's management of program pools. It becomes difficult to find contiguous core resources for extremely large programs in an active system. Therefore, it is important to keep programs modular and small in size. It is far easier to load four 20K modules when needed than it is to load a single 'monster' 80K program that uses only a small portion of the code at any one time.

Residency Considerations: Large, heavily-used modules should be made resident. Resident programs are loaded into a different portion of the region during startup processing and never overlaid. Response time for processing with a resident program never includes waiting for the program to be loaded (unless the program is marked 'NEW COPY' by DCMT command, then it is loaded into one of the two other pools). When deciding which programs, dialogs, subschemas, maps, and tables to make resident, consider not just system subschemas, like IDMSNWKA, but also heavily-used application modules, such as a driver dialog in an ADS/O application.

Table 10-3, in the Production System Creation chapter, contains a list of the system programs which should be considered for residency in test and production systems. For example, the ADSOGEN1 and ADSOGEN2 modules should be made resident in a test system if ADS/O is being used to develop new applications.

Several statistics are available to help determine which user modules are large and frequently accessed, and therefore should be considered for residency. The system statistics on the log printed at shutdown time, the DCMT DISPLAY PROGRAM command, and the DCMT DISPLAY ACTIVE REENTRANT PROGRAM command supply information relevant to program loading. The number of times a program is called versus the number of times it is loaded is important. If a program is loaded every time it is called, but is called infrequently, it is probably an acceptable situation. However, a program should be considered for residency if it is frequently called, loaded when it is called, and is also 'large'. A 'large' program is one which requires several I/O's to load the module. The definition of large varies with load area page size, being different if the page size is 24K as opposed to 4K. For example, a 40K program would be considered large if the load area page size was 8K, because five to six I/O's would be required per load.

Reducing the Number of Loads of DD Network Subschemas in Test Systems: Frequent dictionary access is normal in test systems and leads to frequent loads of DD network subschemas. Consider creating a database name table (DBNT), and mapping all network subschemas to IDMSNWKA to reduce the number of network subschema loads. IDMSNWKA has all IDD records, sets, and areas included within it. If all system software uses IDMSNWKA rather than IDMSNWKO (used by ADSG), IDMSNWKQ (used by OLQ), IDMSNWKC (used by CULPRIT), or IDMSNWKM (used by OLM), and IDMSNWKA is made resident, much of the time otherwise spent in loading these other subschemas can be saved. IDMSNWKA should be made resident because all online and batch IDMSDDDL compiler runs utilize it (especially if the database name table technique described above is being employed).

A disadvantage of this method is increased load on the storage pool. The variable portion of network subschema tables in the storage pool are significantly larger for IDMSNWKA than for any other network subschema. The variable portion of IDMSNWKA is about 36K in Release 5.7 and between 38 and 41K under Release 10. The size of IDMSNWKA variable portion was determined from the histograms and shutdown statistics shown in Figure 13-3.

In addition, users must specify the database name table to take advantage of this translation. Release 10 sites which map all network subschemas to IDMSNWKA can automate user specification of the DBNT by defining a signon profile for each user. The signon profile includes the DCUF command:

DCUF SET DICTNAME *dictionary-name*

where *dictionary-name* identifies the DBNT defined in the sysgen with the following statement:

ADD DBNAME *dictionary-name* SUBSCHEMA IDMSNWK? MAPS TO
    IDMSNWKA.

Release 10 sites with multiple dictionaries may use the same technique for each secondary dictionary, i.e., mapping all network subschemas to 'xxxxNWKA' (where xxxx identifies the secondary dictionary's subschemas) and including a signon profile that automatically invokes the secondary dictionary name at signon time.

IDMS-DB/DC IS A PROPRIETARY SOFTWARE PRODUCT
LICENSED FROM CULLINET SOFTWARE

IDMS-DB/DC   PRINT LOG UTILITY   DATE   TIME   PAGE
C8509M   RELEASE 10.0   07/17/86 (86198) 040902   13

```
     4 TASKS ABENDED            257 SYS TASKS ACTIVE          2 TOTAL TSKS ACTIVE         0 TIMES AT MAX TASK
     0 RUNAWY TSKS ABRTD          0 TOTAL SYS TASKS         430 SHORT ON STORAGE        382 SIK HI WATER MARK
     0 TOTAL PGFREE RQS           0 TOTAL PAGES PGFREED       0 RENTPOOL WAITS            0 OVER RLE THRESH
11,634 PAGES IN RENTPOOL         0 PAGE RELEASES           476 MAX # RLES USED         383 MAX # RCES USED
     0 OVER RCE THRESH            0 OVER DPE THRESH           0 TOTAL PAGES PGFIXED
    58 MAX # DPES USED            0 COUNT OF PGFIX RQS
```

HISTOGRAM OF TOTAL GET STORAGE SIZE

```
86198 04.07.17
GETSTG SIZE    AMOUNT   GETSTG SIZE    AMOUNT   GETSTG SIZE    AMOUNT   GETSTG SIZE    AMOUNT
               35,587                   3,462                    705                    774
LT NEXT ENTRY    104                       38                     18                      0
 2,000                   6,000                   6,000                  10,000
18,000             3    22,000             1    22,000             0    26,000             1
34,000             1    38,000             0    38,000             0    42,000             0
50,000             0    54,000             1    54,000             0    58,000             0
66,000             1    70,000             0    70,000             0    74,000             0
78,000             0                       3
GT LAST ENTRY
```

HISTOGRAM OF USER STORAGE SIZE

```
86198 04.07.18
USR STG SIZE   AMOUNT   USR STG SIZE   AMOUNT   USR STG SIZE   AMOUNT   USR STG SIZE   AMOUNT
               18,411                     577                  1,834                  1,834
LT NEXT ENTRY     39                       11                      5                      1
 8,000                   4,000                   4,000                   6,000
16,000             7    12,000            35    12,000             5    14,000             0
22,000             0    20,000             0    20,000             0    22,000             0
32,000             0    28,000             0    28,000             0    30,000             0
40,000             0    36,000             8    36,000             0    38,000             0
GT LAST ENTRY
```

HISTOGRAM OF SCRATCH RECORD SIZES

```
86198 04.07.18
SCRATCH SIZE   AMOUNT   SCRATCH SIZE   AMOUNT   SCRATCH SIZE   AMOUNT   SCRATCH SIZE   AMOUNT
                  725                      52                      3                     39
LT NEXT ENTRY    383                       10                      5                      1
  100                    200                     200                     300
  900              2    600                     600                     700                  852
                       1,000                   1,000            GT LAST ENTRY
```

HISTOGRAM OF QUEUE RECORD SIZES

```
86198 04.07.18
QUEUE SIZE     AMOUNT   QUEUE SIZE     AMOUNT   QUEUE SIZE     AMOUNT   QUEUE SIZE     AMOUNT
                    6                      87                     87                      0
LT NEXT ENTRY     93                       18                      0                      6
  400                    200                     200                     300
  800              0    500                     600                     700            GT LAST ENTRY
                        900            1,000
```

HISTOGRAM OF PROGRAM SIZES

```
86198 04.07.18
PROGRAM SIZE   AMOUNT   PROGRAM SIZE   AMOUNT   PROGRAM SIZE   AMOUNT   PROGRAM SIZE   AMOUNT
                4,418                   3,676                  1,826                    861
LT NEXT ENTRY    257                      412                    139                     43
16,000                   4,000                  24,000                  12,000                  950
32,000           135    20,000           488    40,000           430    28,000             0
48,000           103    36,000           147    56,000                  44,000             0
64,000                  52,000           996    72,000           616    60,000             0
96,000           663    68,000                  88,000                  76,000             0
112,000                 84,000                 104,000           120    92,000             0
128,000            8   100,000                 120,000                 108,000             0
144,000                116,000                 136,000                 124,000             0
160,000               132,000            24   152,000                 140,000             0
GT LAST ENTRY         148,000                                          156,000             0
```

HISTOGRAM OF RECORD SIZES WRITTEN TO JOURNAL

```
86198 04.07.18
JRNL SIZE      AMOUNT   JRNL SIZE      AMOUNT   JRNL SIZE      AMOUNT   JRNL SIZE      AMOUNT
```

Figure 13-3 Determining the Size of IDMSNWKA's Variable Portion

```
IDMS-DB/DC          PRINT LOG UTILITY           IDMS-DB/DC IS A PROPRIETARY SOFTWARE PRODUCT        07/17/86 DATE (86198)  TIME     PAGE
C8509M              RELEASE 10.0                   LICENSED FROM CULLINET SOFTWARE                                          040902     14

LT NEXT ENTRY          0       100       200       300
        400           0       500       600       700
        800           0       900     1,000    GT LAST ENTRY

86198 04.07.18  STATISTICS FOR TASKCODE ADS       TIMES INVOKED:          47
86198 04.07.18  STATISTICS FOR TASKCODE ADSG      TIMES INVOKED:           8
86198 04.07.18  STATISTICS FOR TASKCODE ADS2      TIMES INVOKED:         949
86198 04.07.18  STATISTICS FOR TASKCODE BYE       TIMES INVOKED:          19
86198 04.07.18  STATISTICS FOR TASKCODE CLOD      TIMES INVOKED:           1
86198 04.07.18  STATISTICS FOR TASKCODE DCMT      TIMES INVOKED:          75
86198 04.07.19  STATISTICS FOR TASKCODE IDD       TIMES INVOKED:          33
86198 04.07.19  STATISTICS FOR TASKCODE OLM       TIMES INVOKED:          14
86198 04.07.19  STATISTICS FOR TASKCODE OLQ       TIMES INVOKED:         103
86198 04.07.19  STATISTICS FOR TASKCODE QUED      TIMES INVOKED:           1
86198 04.07.19  STATISTICS FOR TASKCODE SIGNOFF   TIMES INVOKED:           1
86198 04.07.19  STATISTICS FOR TASKCODE SIGNON    TIMES INVOKED:          13
86198 04.07.19  STATISTICS FOR TASKCODE SSDSIGNO  TIMES INVOKED:           9

86198 04.07.20  STATISTICS FOR PROGRAM ADSA       9 TIMES CALLED    1 TIMES LOADED   0 WAITED TO LOAD   0 TIMES PROG CHECK
86198 04.07.20  STATISTICS FOR PROGRAM ADSERRMP   2 TIMES CALLED    1 TIMES LOADED   0 WAITED TO LOAD   0 TIMES PROG CHECK
86198 04.07.20  STATISTICS FOR PROGRAM ADSGMPDG  14 TIMES CALLED    1 TIMES LOADED   0 WAITED TO LOAD   0 TIMES PROG CHECK
86198 04.07.20  STATISTICS FOR PROGRAM ADSOAGMS   2 TIMES CALLED    1 TIMES LOADED   0 WAITED TO LOAD   0 TIMES PROG CHECK
86198 04.07.20  STATISTICS FOR PROGRAM ADSOAPFK   1 TIMES CALLED    1 TIMES LOADED   0 WAITED TO LOAD   0 TIMES PROG CHECK
86198 04.07.20  STATISTICS FOR PROGRAM ADSODBUG   3 TIMES CALLED    2 TIMES LOADED   0 WAITED TO LOAD   0 TIMES PROG CHECK
86198 04.07.21  STATISTICS FOR PROGRAM ADSOGEN1   8 TIMES CALLED    1 TIMES LOADED   0 WAITED TO LOAD   0 TIMES PROG CHECK
86198 04.07.21  STATISTICS FOR PROGRAM ADSOGEN2  24 TIMES CALLED    2 TIMES LOADED   0 WAITED TO LOAD   0 TIMES PROG CHECK
```

Figure 13-3 Determining the Size of IDMSNWKA's Variable Portion
(continued)

```
IDMS-DB/DC          PRINT LOG UTILITY                 IDMS-DB/DC IS A PROPRIETARY SOFTWARE PRODUCT      DATE       TIME   PAGE
C8509M              RELEASE 10.0                          LICENSED FROM CULLINET SOFTWARE            07/17/86 (86198)  040902   15

86198 04.07.21 STATISTICS FOR PROGRAM ADSOMAIN            1 TIMES LOADED     0 WAITED TO LOAD     0 TIMES PROG CHECK
             978 TIMES CALLED

86198 04.07.21 STATISTICS FOR PROGRAM ADSOMBG1           2 TIMES LOADED     0 WAITED TO LOAD     0 TIMES PROG CHECK
               3 TIMES CALLED

86198 04.07.21 STATISTICS FOR PROGRAM ADSOMENU           1 TIMES LOADED     0 WAITED TO LOAD     0 TIMES PROG CHECK
              58 TIMES CALLED

86198 04.07.21 STATISTICS FOR PROGRAM ADSOMPLD           1 TIMES LOADED     0 WAITED TO LOAD     0 TIMES PROG CHECK
               6 TIMES CALLED

86198 04.07.21 STATISTICS FOR PROGRAM ADSORUN1           3 TIMES LOADED     0 WAITED TO LOAD     0 TIMES PROG CHECK
              71 TIMES CALLED

86198 04.07.23 STATISTICS FOR PROGRAM ASFOOAKD           1 TIMES LOADED     0 WAITED TO LOAD     0 TIMES PROG CHECK
               4 TIMES CALLED

86198 04.07.23 STATISTICS FOR PROGRAM ASFOOAKM           1 TIMES LOADED     0 WAITED TO LOAD     0 TIMES PROG CHECK
               2 TIMES CALLED

86198 04.07.23 STATISTICS FOR PROGRAM DBIGTTRM          15 TIMES LOADED     0 WAITED TO LOAD     0 TIMES PROG CHECK
             157 TIMES CALLED

86198 04.07.23 STATISTICS FOR PROGRAM IDB                1 TIMES LOADED     0 WAITED TO LOAD     0 TIMES PROG CHECK
               2 TIMES CALLED

86198 04.07.35 STATISTICS FOR PROGRAM IDDSCIDD           1 TIMES LOADED     0 WAITED TO LOAD     0 TIMES PROG CHECK
              10 TIMES CALLED

86198 04.07.35 STATISTICS FOR PROGRAM IDDSMAIN           2 TIMES LOADED     0 WAITED TO LOAD     0 TIMES PROG CHECK
              10 TIMES CALLED

86198 04.07.35 STATISTICS FOR PROGRAM IDDSMAP            2 TIMES LOADED     0 WAITED TO LOAD     0 TIMES PROG CHECK
              60 TIMES CALLED

86193 04.07.35 STATISTICS FOR PROGRAM IDDSMDBC           2 TIMES LOADED     0 WAITED TO LOAD     0 TIMES PROG CHECK
               7 TIMES CALLED

86198 04.07.35 STATISTICS FOR PROGRAM IDDSMERR           2 TIMES LOADED     0 WAITED TO LOAD     0 TIMES PROG CHECK
               8 TIMES CALLED

86198 04.07.35 STATISTICS FOR PROGRAM IDDSMGEN           2 TIMES LOADED     0 WAITED TO LOAD     0 TIMES PROG CHECK
              10 TIMES CALLED

86198 04.07.35 STATISTICS FOR PROGRAM IDDSMREP           2 TIMES LOADED     0 WAITED TO LOAD     0 TIMES PROG CHECK
               7 TIMES CALLED

86198 04.07.35 STATISTICS FOR PROGRAM IDDSMSEC           2 TIMES LOADED     0 WAITED TO LOAD     0 TIMES PROG CHECK
               7 TIMES CALLED

86198 04.07.35 STATISTICS FOR PROGRAM IDDSMUTL           2 TIMES LOADED     0 WAITED TO LOAD     0 TIMES PROG CHECK
              10 TIMES CALLED
```

Figure 13-3 Determining the Size of IDMSNWKA's Variable Portion (continued)

```
IDMS-DB/DC        PRINT LOG UTILITY        IDMS-DB/DC IS A PROPRIETARY SOFTWARE PRODUCT       DATE       TIME    PAGE
C8509M            RELEASE 10.0             LICENSED FROM CULLINET SOFTWARE                  07/17/86 (86198)  040902    16

86198 04.07.35 STATISTICS FOR PROGRAM IDDSTDDL  1 TIMES LOADED     0 WAITED TO LOAD     0 TIMES PROG CHECK
      3 TIMES CALLED
86198 04.07.36 STATISTICS FOR PROGRAM IDDSTHLV  2 TIMES LOADED     0 WAITED TO LOAD     0 TIMES PROG CHECK
     10 TIMES CALLED
86198 04.07.36 STATISTICS FOR PROGRAM IDDSTMOD  1 TIMES LOADED     0 WAITED TO LOAD     0 TIMES PROG CHECK
      3 TIMES CALLED
86198 04.07.36 STATISTICS FOR PROGRAM IDDSTOPT  2 TIMES LOADED     0 WAITED TO LOAD     0 TIMES PROG CHECK
      7 TIMES CALLED
86198 04.07.36 STATISTICS FOR PROGRAM IDDSTPRG  1 TIMES LOADED     0 WAITED TO LOAD     0 TIMES PROG CHECK
      1 TIMES CALLED
86198 04.07.37 STATISTICS FOR PROGRAM IDMSCOMP  1 TIMES LOADED     0 WAITED TO LOAD     0 TIMES PROG CHECK
      1 TIMES CALLED
86198 04.07.37 STATISTICS FOR PROGRAM IDMSDCOM  1 TIMES LOADED     0 WAITED TO LOAD     0 TIMES PROG CHECK
      1 TIMES CALLED
86198 04.07.37 STATISTICS FOR PROGRAM IDMSDDDC  2 TIMES LOADED     0 WAITED TO LOAD     0 TIMES PROG CHECK
     33 TIMES CALLED
86198 04.07.37 STATISTICS FOR PROGRAM IDMSNWKA  1 TIMES LOADED     0 WAITED TO LOAD     0 TIMES PROG CHECK
     18 TIMES CALLED
86198 04.07.37 STATISTICS FOR PROGRAM IDMSNWKM  2 TIMES LOADED     0 WAITED TO LOAD     0 TIMES PROG CHECK
     12 TIMES CALLED
86198 04.07.38 STATISTICS FOR PROGRAM IDMSNWKO  3 TIMES LOADED     0 WAITED TO LOAD     0 TIMES PROG CHECK
     85 TIMES CALLED
86198 04.07.38 STATISTICS FOR PROGRAM IDMSNWKQ  4 TIMES LOADED     0 WAITED TO LOAD     0 TIMES PROG CHECK
     37 TIMES CALLED
86198 04.07.38 STATISTICS FOR PROGRAM IDMSNWKS  1 TIMES LOADED     0 WAITED TO LOAD     0 TIMES PROG CHECK
     25 TIMES CALLED
86198 04.07.38 STATISTICS FOR PROGRAM IDMSNWKX  1 TIMES LOADED     0 WAITED TO LOAD     0 TIMES PROG CHECK
      0 TIMES CALLED
86198 04.07.38 STATISTICS FOR PROGRAM IDMSOLQS  1 TIMES LOADED     0 WAITED TO LOAD     0 TIMES PROG CHECK
    103 TIMES CALLED
86198 04.07.38 STATISTICS FOR PROGRAM IDMSROAK  1 TIMES LOADED     0 WAITED TO LOAD     0 TIMES PROG CHECK
      1 TIMES CALLED
86198 04.07.38 STATISTICS FOR PROGRAM IDMSRUTL  1 TIMES LOADED     0 WAITED TO LOAD     0 TIMES PROG CHECK
      3 TIMES CALLED
86198 04.07.39 STATISTICS FOR PROGRAM OLQGRTHS  1 TIMES LOADED     0 WAITED TO LOAD     0 TIMES PROG CHECK
      0 TIMES CALLED
```

Figure 13-3 Determining the Size of IDMSNWKA's Variable Portion (continued)

For example,

> In the sysgen specify:
> ADD DBNAME FISDICT SUBSCHEMA ????NWK? MAPS TO FISDNWKA
> In the primary dictionary add:
> ADD MODULE FIS-SIGNON
>   LANGUAGE IS DC
>   MODULE SOURCE FOLLOW
>   DCUF SET DICTNAME FISDICT
>   MSEND.

For each user of the secondary dictionary, make the following modification to their user entity in the primary dictionary:

> MOD USER *user-name*
>   INCLUDE SIGNON PROFILE FIS-SIGNON
>   LANGUAGE IS DC.

Sysgen Program Specification Considerations: We recommend putting all production subschemas, programs, dialogs, and tables into the sysgen so they do not occupy undefined program slots in the program definition table. Test subschemas, programs, dialogs, and tables which are used daily should be included in the test system generation. Including all programs, dialogs, tables, and subschemas in the sysgen allows security classes to be established more easily.

It is advantageous to arrange all tasks and programs included in the sysgen in ascending order, based upon frequency of use, under Release 5.7. Task and program tables, like most tables in the system, are searched in linear sequence.

The Program Definition Table is sorted under Release 10, thus permitting binary search techniques and making the order of programs and dialogs in the sysgen unimportant. The binary search has been made more efficient through the addition of a look-aside buffer. Dynamically-defined dialogs/programs (defined by DCMT command or online compilers) are searched for in a linear fashion.

DCUF TEST Considerations (OS Only): Using the DCUF TEST function is not recommended because it causes a significant amount of overhead searching for both the desired version and version 1 in the load area and in the LL/CIL. The overhead is even worse when there are secondary load areas or multiple libraries are concatenated.

13.2.3 Considerations for Sysgen SYSTEM Statement Parameter Values

The values chosen for several SYSTEM statement parameters can affect system performance. Refer to Chapters 9 and 10 for further details. For example, the values chosen for MAX TASKS, RUNAWAY INTERVAL, and EXTERNAL WAIT can affect system performance.

All new activity must wait when the number of concurrently processing tasks equals the value chosen for MAX TASKS; only ongoing tasks continue to execute. Monitoring system statistics for the number of times at MAX TASKS facilitates noticing this problem before it becomes acute. Increase the number of MAX TASKS in SYSTEM statement during the next system generation to resolve this condition.

When a RUNAWAY condition occurs, typically caused by a DC program or DB procedure in exclusive control of the IDMS/R memory space, all activity waits while the runaway processes (i.e., loops) until RUNAWAY INTERVAL expires. Runaway programs cause short to potentially long waits, depending on the value of RUNAWAY INTERVAL. The runaway task can be identified from system statistics and log messages. Identify which task is causing the condition and correct the program to resolve the problem. Finally, reconsider the value of RUNAWAY INTERVAL. If runaways occur frequently, lower the value to 60-90 seconds until the problems are found and eliminated. Keeping the threshold too low can cause tasks like IDD, SYSGEN, and SCHEMA to abend as runaways.

Short to extremely long waits may result if EXTERNAL WAIT is turned off or set at 1800 or greater. These waits are caused by locks of aborted programs not being rolled back on a timely basis. The problem can be detected using DCMT commands and through operating system commands displaying the programs processing during the slowdown. Issue a DCMT DIS RU command to determine run unit identifiers. Then issue a DCMT DIS RU *rununit-id* command and monitor the output briefly to detect an aborted program which has not been rolled back. If the value in the 'number of DB calls' field does not change, the run unit has probably abended.

Decrease the value of EXT WAIT, especially for CICS programs, to ensure prompt detection of aborted programs. In addition, use the IDMSRELC (CICS) and CHKUSER (OS only) facilities for abend detection.

13.2.4 Buffering Considerations

IDMS/R database I/O efficiency is heavily dependent on adequate buffering. Several statistics are available for monitoring buffer usage. To determine how many buffers are enough or how many are being used, review the DCMT DISPLAY BUFFERS command output, the buffer wait count in the system shutdown statistics, and/or the DCMT DISPLAY STATISTICS SYSTEM output. Buffer utilization by individual run unit may be seen in JREPORTS 3 and 4, task statistics, and the ACCEPT DB-STATISTICS DML verb.

The statistics PAGES READ versus PAGES REQUESTED should be examined to determine how many requests actually resulted in physical reads or writes. Investigate the type of requests issued by the run unit if the ratio of PAGES READ to PAGES REQUESTED is greater than 30%. It is normal for the ratio to be high if the requests are primarily OBTAIN CALC statements. A low ratio is normal and a high ratio may indicate inadequate buffering if the access statements are a mixture of CALC and VIA retrieval.

Report 2 of the IDMS/R Performance Monitor reports the number of buffer pages used by individual tasks (Figure 13-1). It is useful for determining how many buffer pools and pages are required.

13.2.5 Scratch and Log Area Considerations

I/O to the scratch and log areas of the data dictionary is single-threaded under Release 10 and 5.7 (i.e., no other concurrent access to a scratch area or log area can ocurr). Minimize access to the scratch and log areas to enhance performance in a test environment, and certainly in a production environment. RELOCATABLE RESOURCES and FAST MODE THRESHOLD in the ADSO statement of the sysgen should be avoided, unless storage pool space is extremely limited, to minimize scratch area utilization .

Access to the log area may be minimized by eliminating extraneous dumps and log messages, i.e., those not examined during debugging. Dumps can be eliminated by specifying ABRU NOSNAP on the SYSTEM statement during system generation and by changing the severity level of messages on the data dictionary (see the DDDL Reference Guide under Messages for an explanation of severity codes). Also, ensure that SNAP commands have been removed from the code of DC programs and ADS/O dialogs prior to production implementation. If WRITE STATISTICS are turned on, ensure that the interval is such that statistics are written to the log only during periods of low activity, or at shutdown.

13.2.6 Operating System Considerations

MVS Considerations: All IDMS/R environments should be run non-swappable and assigned a performance group equal to CICS, if applicable, but below the terminal access method, as recommended by

Cullinet. Running non-swappable is important because IDMS/R issues many MVS waits (requests of MVS time management) which are considered long waits, making IDMS/R an excellent candidate for swapping. In addition, an IDMS/R region is large enough that, even when running at a high performance group, IDMS/R would inevitably be chosen to be swapped. Swapping increases the amount of operating system overhead which in turn affects overall MVS performance.

The frequency of MVS paging has a significant effect on performance in most shops. Therefore, it is important to look into making heavily-utilized IDMS/R components non-pageable using either MVS' storage fencing facility or the Release 10 PAGE FIX facility. Refer to MVS' Resource Monitoring Facility (RMF) manual for details on running non-swappable, storage fencing, and performance groups.

Consider putting the programs IDMSDBMS, IDMSDBIO, and RHDCNUCL in the MVS' LPA. Then one copy of these modules can be shared by concurrently executing IDMS/R CV's and local modes, thereby reducing the size of the IDMS/R working set. This technique is particularly useful when many IDMS/R systems are running concurrently and/or when a significant volume of local mode processing is planned.

Turning on the PAGE RELEASE parameter in the sysgen should be considered at MVS sites. PAGE RELEASE causes unused frames to be released back to the operating system in a more efficient manner, thus decreasing the size of the IDMS/R working set.

DOS/VSE Considerations: All DOS IDMS/R environments should assign a high partition priority (PRTY) to the Central Version partition. As is recommended by Cullinet, CV's priority should be made equal to CICS' and below that of the terminal access method.

Programs IDMSDBMS, IDMSDBIO, and RHDCNUCL might be loaded into the DOS SVA when many IDMS/R systems are running concurrently and/or when significant amounts of local mode processing are planned. Then one copy of these modules can be shared by concurrently executing IDMS CV's and Local Modes.

CMS/CV Considerations (Release 10 only): The CP command SET FAVORED should be used to give the CV virtual machine a high performance level. This parameter is expressed as a percentage. Refer to the IDMS/R Operations Under CMS/VM Guide for all CMS/CV performance considerations.

13.2.7   DASD Considerations

Efficient disk access is extremely important to successful database utilization. There are many reports available on channel and device contention for each operating system. Information about these reports can be found in the various performance products' manuals listed in Table 13-3. For example, the Komand® data acquisition statistical package gives exact EXCP counts for all data sets, including libraries, at MVS sites.

Table 13-3 Performance Products By Operating System

Operating System	Product	Manual Name
MVS	Omegamon	Omegamon Reference Manual, MVS version (Candle Corp.)
	Komand®	Komand Planning and Implementation Guide (Pace Applied Technology)
	RMF	Resource Measurement Facility (IBM)
VM	VMAP	VM Map
	SMART	VM Real Time Monitor
	JARS Reports	VM Real Time Monitor
DOS/VSE	PT	DOS/VSE PT (Performance Tool)

®Komand is a registered trademark of Pace Applied Technology

The configuration of system datasets should be chosen to minimize device and channel contention and to reduce the impact of device malfunction. It is especially important in test environments to minimize disk contention caused by frequent dictionary access. It is essential in production environments to keep the journals, load area, and library separate from the application databases.

Test systems typically have large amounts of I/O against the dictionary (DDLDML, DDLDCLOD, Scratch, and Queue areas), LL/CIL, and one or more journals. In contrast, there is relatively little I/O against the application DB's. Figure 13-4 shows a sample DASD configuration for a test system. This configuration is designed to minimize dictionary contention. If there are many secondary DD's, attempt to keep each dictionary's source and load areas on the same volume and to segregate them from other secondary dictionaries.

Very little access against the IDD is likely in production systems unless applications make heavy use of scratch or queue records, with

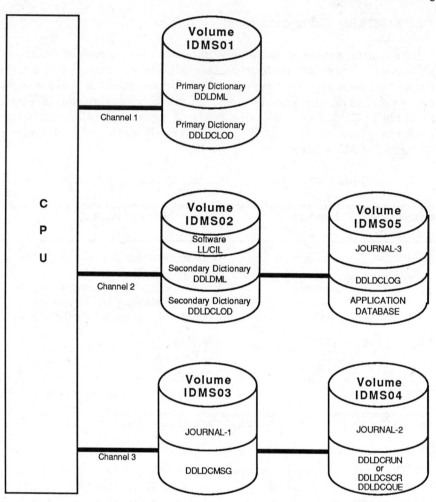

Figure 13-4 Sample Test System DASD Configuration

the exception of the load area. Therefore, most of the IDD can exist on one volume. Some I/O is probable against the LL/CIL for loading programs (e.g., ADSORUN1, ADSOMAIN, any DC COBOL or BAL programs), but the bulk of I/O will be against journals and application databases. Figure 13-5 shows a sample DASD configuration for a production system. A head crash will destroy both the data and the means to restore the data up to the point of the crash if the journals and the database are on the same pack (the most recent backup and the archived journals can partially restore the database, but not up to the point of the head crash). Separation of datasets onto different devices

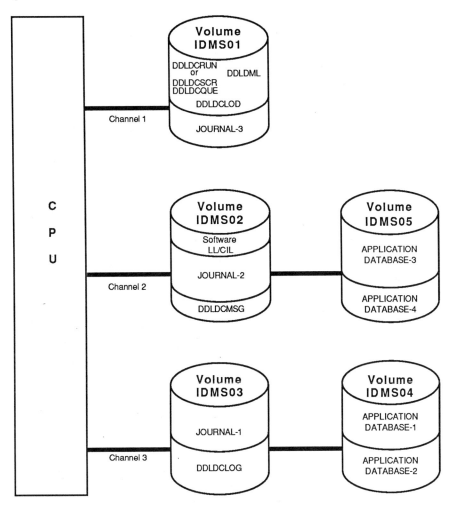

Figure 13-5 Sample Production System DASD Configuration

minimizes the damage caused by a head crash and speeds recovery. Separating the load area and libraries from the database minimizes head/channel contention. Minimizing contention is important because it speeds program loading, an expensive proposition for any monitor.

13.2.8 CPU Utilization

The system statistics USER MODE TIME and SYSTEM MODE TIME highlight CPU utilization. These statistics are captured individually by program with task/transaction/ADS statistics and by the OPER task. They are available from the IDMS/R Performance Monitor both in online review of monitored tasks and in report 2 printed in batch (Figure 13-1). Some changes can be made to reduce CPU demands from IDMS/R run units if excessive CPU utilization is a problem with IDMS/R processing. The following paragraphs suggest methods of reducing CPU utilization.

Keep the number of buffers and buffer pools to a minimum, especially in DMCL's used by programs running in local mode. Be reasonable here, because too few buffers will cause extra I/O and internal work to reread a page that has been overlaid.

Cut down the number of areas defined in application databases by consolidating areas. An estimated 30% of all IDMSDBIO processing revolves around searching the area chain in the global DMCL.

Use the PRIORITY feature in the subschema compiler to organize the records in most-frequently-accessed-records-first order. DB calls are matched by linear search of the subschema record chain.

The compression and decompression routines provided by Cullinet compress/decompress blanks, zeros, binary zeros, and repeating character strings. Consider using the Cullinet Users Group Association's routines instead of those provided by Cullinet for textual, or name and address information. The Users Group's routines compress/decompress only blanks, zeros, and binary zeros, and ignore repeating strings. They allow an installation to reap most of the benefits of compression without incurring as much CPU overhead.

Batch programs which issue a tremendous number of DB calls might best be run under local mode and at a lower priority than CV. By running them locally, the I/O requests do not have a priority as high as CV's requests, and the overall effect of the job can be more closely regulated. Running the program under local mode also eliminates the heavy SVC utilization incurred by running the program under CV. Lastly, consider using the Logical Record Facility (LRF), if available, to retrieve information from several records with a single call to IDMS/R.

Sites using ADS/O for online processing should consider linking to COBOL or Assembler language programs when long or complex calculations are required or when a high degree of table usage is envisioned (there is no indexing or search verb in ADS, only subscripting). Similarly, COBOL is preferable for routines that are used for batch as well as online processing. Another method of reducing CPU utilization is to generate dialogs to use executable code (Release 10).

Turning on task statistics, especially task write statistics, causes a significant amount of CPU overhead, as does storage protection. Consider defining alternate systems with those facilities enabled and bringing up these versions only as needed, rather than all the time, to reduce CPU utilization.

13.3 APPLICATION-RELATED PERFORMANCE ISSUES

An important point in achieving peak performance is an early review of any applications to be put into production. It is very difficult to "tune the system" to provide acceptable performance for a poorly designed online application or database. Specific suggestions for database and program efficiency require knowledge of the database and functions which comprise the application. There are general suggestions, however, which should be brought to the attention of applications development staffs.

These suggestions include:

* Reducing the amount of storage held by individual programs and dialogs,
* Keeping the ADS/O primary record buffer small,
* Choosing an appropriate READY USAGE MODE,
* Record locking considerations,
* Online Debugger usage, and
* Some database design considerations.

13.3.1 Reducing the Amount of Storage Held by Individual Programs/Dialogs

Storage pool usage is optimized by reducing the amount of storage needed by each application program, especially across the pseudo-converse. The primary concern for ADS/O usage is the manner in which dialogs give control to other dialogs, because that determines the amount of storage held across the pseudo-converse.

Storage consumption is increased when dialogs use the LINK or INVOKE command to initiate other dialogs which do mapping commands. The variable dialog storage and database currencies storage of the initiating dialog is preserved in memory for the entire length of time the initiated dialog is 'current' in the application thread (i.e., processing time plus all pseudo-converses). The number of times, or levels, of these commands allowed determines how much storage potentially can be held (MAX LINKS clause of the ADSO statement defines the maximum number of levels allowed). Developers therefore should design their systems to use the TRANSFER command, which does not save storage upon initiating the next dialog. The LINK NOSAVE verb can be used as a compromise, because it does not cause currencies to be saved, although variable dialog storage still is saved.

Determining the storage used by individual programs/dialogs is important when trying to tune application systems and overall performance. If activity and the amounts of storage requested seems too high, a review of the application may be necessary to suggest alternate methods of holding data (for example, using scratch and queue records for DC and ADS/O applications, and smaller subschemas with frequent use of COMMITs for batch programs and other external run units). FAST MODE THRESHOLD may have to be enabled for heavy ADS/O use despite the disadvantage of single-threaded access to the scratch area.

There is no facility under Release 5.7 for determining total storage usage by an active task; it can only be estimated. Release 10 users may turn on task/transaction statistics to determine storage usage by active tasks. These statistics show high water marks for storage use by dialogs, external run units, and DC programs. In addition, the OPER WATCH LTERM command shows storage pool usage per logical terminal when various tasks are in use.

The amount of storage held by a task across a pseudo-converse can be determined by issuing a DCMT DISPLAY LTERM *lterm-id* RESOURCES command. System histograms show cumulative information on how often large requests for storage are taking place.

13.3.2   Keeping the ADS/O Primary Record Buffer Small

The size of the primary record buffer for ADS/O dialogs is specified in the ADSO statement during system generation. The primary record buffer block (RBB) must be at least the size of the largest database record, logical record, or work record used in any main line ADS/O dialog (a main line dialog is one initiated by a task code or by user selection of the dialog from the ADS run time menu, low level dialogs are those initiated by LINK or INVOKE commands issued by other dialogs). In other words, if the size of the primary record buffer block is changed to accommodate one application which defines a work record or DB record 6K bytes long, all ADS/O dialogs receive a 6K primary record buffer in the storage pool even though they may only need 4K. The size of the primary record buffer cannot be overridden by dialogs which do not require the large amount of space. Therefore, application designers should be informed of the potential for excess storage pool consumption caused by large global record definitions and/or huge DB record buffers used in a main line dialog.

Dialogs requiring a larger buffer will abend if the value specified for the primary record buffer is too small. The message 'DC171027 Application Aborted. Buffer Pool too small to hold one record.' will be displayed on the terminal screen.

ADS/O secondary buffers are allocated only as needed. There-fore, one application's excessive buffer requirements do not affect another application.

13.3.3 Choosing Appropriate READY Usage Modes

As a rule of thumb, programs and dialogs should not specify EXCLUSIVE or PROTECTED usage modes when READYing database areas for access. These usages modes lock entire areas and can cause concurrently processing programs and dialogs to experi-ence waits and/or timeouts.

13.3.4 Locking Considerations

Programs and dialogs should be coded to minimize the number and duration of record locks. For example, batch programs which READY the database in UPDATE usage mode and update large num-bers of records should be coded to issue COMMITs at intervals to release the locked records. Refer to Section 7.3.1 for further details.

ADS/O dialogs and DC programs should issue KEEP LONGTERM NOTIFY commands rather than KEEP LONGTERM commands when application design requires knowledge of record changes across the pseudo-converse. KEEP LONGTERM places a lock on the record during a pseudo-converse, which may cause other run units to experience waits or timeouts. KEEP LONGTERM NOTIFY simply requests IDMS/R to monitor the record and to inform the issuing dialog/program of record changes (refer to the program-ming manuals for details on KEEP LONGTERM).

13.3.5 Online Debugger Usage

The Online Debugger software is an extremely useful and effective tool for debugging ADS/O dialogs and DC programs. To use the Online Debugger with a dialog, the dialog first must be generated to include symbol tables, required for interactive debugging. Performance problems can result because the ADS generator con-sumes large amounts of storage pool space while creating symbol tables during dialog generation. Depending on the size and complexity of the dialog, generating a dialog with symbol tables can consume anywhere from 200 to 300K during generation and can last up to 30 wall clock seconds. Short On Storage (SOS) conditions and system slowdowns often result if many dialogs with symbol tables are generated concurrently. This is particularly true when many and/or large records are involved. Applications groups must be made aware of these possibilities and should regulate the use of online generations for dialogs with symbol tables. A possible alternative to regulating concurrent generations would be regenerating the dialog in batch using the ADSOBGEN utility.

Ensure that symbol tables are not included when dialogs are migrated into production. Removing symbol tables, used only for debugging, dramatically reduces the size of the dialog.

13.3.6   Database Design Considerations

IDMS/R system considerations are the main thrust of this book, rather than database design considerations. Therefore, our coverage of database design considerations is brief. When a database has been poorly designed for application requirements, intermittent excessive I/O and CPU utilization can result.

For example, extreme amounts of I/O and CPU cycles may be consumed when there is a requirement for area sweep processing and multiple record types must be retrieved from the area. If this is the case, talk with the applications development staff to determine if there is a more efficient method to satisfy the requirement. Consider redesigning the database into more areas, or adding sets to facilitate the processing requirements.

Another example of poor design is sets without PRIOR or OWNER pointers, when there is an application requirement to ERASE or DISCONNECT member records. Consider redesigning the database and using the restructure utility to implement the changes if records are ERASEd or DISCONNECTed frequently.

Setting DBIO limits in the test system under Release 10 facilitates identifying problem programs. Under both releases, data from accepting IDMS STATISTICS can provide information on the number of database I/O's resulting from a program's processing.

13.4   SOURCES OF INFORMATION RELEVANT TO PERFORMANCE TUNING

Throughout the chapter, we have suggested monitoring various system statistics, but where can one find information needed to answer specific questions concerning performance tuning? Several reports and online tasks provide useful information on system and application-related performance issues. These reports and commands are categorized in Table 13-4.

Table 13-4 Performance Review Reports/Commands

System-Related	Application-Related
Shutdown Statistics	JREPORTS
System Statistics (DCMT)	ADSO statistics (Release 10 only)
Histograms	Task/transaction Statistics
OPER command	Performance Monitor (especially Report 2)
DCMT displays	ACCEPT DB-STATISTICS
CREPORTS	IDMSDUMP
IDMS/R Performance Monitor	IDMSDBAN (Release 10 only)
(Release 10)	IDMSRPTS

13.4.1   System-Related Sources

Shutdown system statistics and system statistics displayed dynamically using the DCMT task provide valuable tuning information. The histograms printed from the system log may be used to analyze storage and program pool utilization. The OPER and DCMT task codes allow online display of performance information.   The IDMS/R Performance Monitor provides a variety of useful information, including a load balancing report. CREPORTS may be used to extract current system definitions from the data dictionary.

Shutdown system statistics: The system shutdown statistics provide valuable system tuning information. For example, statistics on the maximum numbers of RCE's, RLE's, DPE's, and stack entries, when compared to values defined in the sysgen, may indicate that sysgen values should be modified. Number of times at MAX TASKS and number of Short on Storage conditions are also key statistics to monitor.

DCMT DISPLAY STATISTICS SYSTEM: This command allows online access to system statistics up to the current time in the run. The same information as is displayed in the shutdown system statistics is available online.

Histograms: System histograms are generally useful if they are modified to show large variation in storage allocations and program sizes. Modifying the system histograms means specifying the range for each collection bucket (e.g., 2-4K might be one collection bucket, causing the system to keep a running counter of the number of storage allocations where the amount of storage allocated was between 2K and

4K). Histogram output is shown in Figure 13-3 and Appendix A contains a sample histogram modification.

OPER task: The OPER task permits interactive evaluation of all activity in the system. However, it is a powerful command, permitting tasks to be cancelled for example, and expensive to run because it is conversational rather than pseudo-conversational. Unlike DCMT commands, different formats of the OPER task cannot be secured separately. Therefore, sites often limit use of the OPER command to the DBA group and/or the systems programming staff.

The OPER task is often used for performance evaluation and/or debugging when problems occur. In particular, the Release 10 command OPER WATCH LTERM is useful in determining program and storage pool usage per terminal. The OPER task displays size of storage allocations, number of locks held, and user id (if the user signed on) by terminal.

DCMT DISPLAY LTERM *lterm-id* RESOURCES: This command displays detailed information about one terminal's resources. It yields excellent information on long-term storage held across a pseudo-converse. However, the command works only if there is no other task being executed on the terminal being watched.

IDMS/R Performance Monitor: The IDMS/R Performance Monitor provides in-depth analysis of major IDMS/R performance issues, including CPU usage, wait and response times; memory usage; DB calls and I/O's; and ADS/O activity. Task COLLECT statistics must be turned on in the sysgen in order to use the Performance Monitor (task write statistics may be turned on but are not required or recommended, refer to Section 13.4.2).

The online facilities of the Performance Monitor allow selection and monitoring of tasks and dialogs/programs (further details on the application-related statistics of the Performance Monitor are covered in Section 13.4.2). The batch component of the Performance Monitor reports valuable system-related information as well as specific ADS/O statistics in a quick at-a-glance format for easy comparison of dialogs. It also contains a load balancing report showing peak times of activity as well as CPU and DASD utilization. Batch Report 2 (Figure 13-1), Report 4 (Figure 13-6), and Report 80 (Figure 13-7) are particularly useful.

CREPORTS: CREPORTS are dictionary reports which list system-related information, similar to information provided by the sysgen reports. The sysgen reports (output of RHDCSGEN for Release 10, and

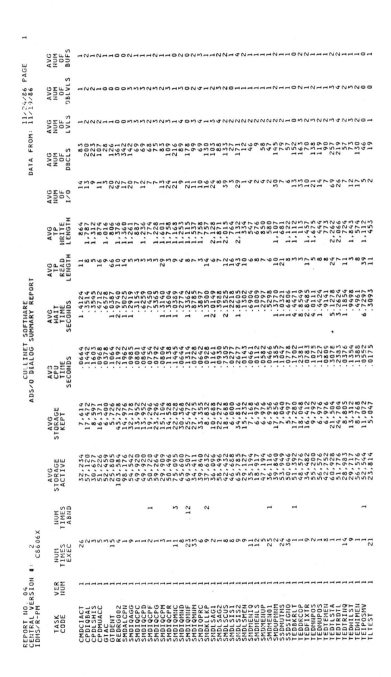

Figure 13-6 Sample Output from IDMS/R Performance Monitor, Report 4

REPORT NO. 80
CENTRAL VERSION#: 2
IDMS/R-PM   C8606X

CULLINET SOFTWARE
LOAD BALANCING REPORT

DATA FROM: 11/24/86 PAGE 2
           11/19/86

TIME	RESOURCE	VALUE	GRAPH
BATCH 06:00	TASKS	.0000	
	CPU	.0000	
	I/O	0	
ONLINE 06:00	TASKS	.0000	
	CPU	.0000	
	I/O	0	
BATCH 07:00	TASKS	.0000	
	CPU	.0000	
	I/O	0	
ONLINE 07:00	TASKS	29	T
	CPU	3.0362	
	I/O	2.144	IIII
BATCH 08:00	TASKS	11	
	CPU	55.7755	CCCCCCC
	I/O	6,160	IIIIIIIIIII
ONLINE 08:00	TASKS	118	TTTTTT
	CPU	8,8386	C
	I/O	1,389	II
BATCH 09:00	TASKS	6	
	CPU	65.0810	CCCCCCCCC
	I/O	7,641	IIIIIIIIIIII
ONLINE 09:00	TASKS	280	TTTTTTTTTTTTTTT
	CPU	24.0476	CCC
	I/O	5,812	IIIIIIIIIII
BATCH 10:00	TASKS	16	
	CPU	315.8997	CCCCCCCCCCCCCCCCCCCCCCCCCCCCCCCCCC
	I/O	23,263	IIIIIIIIIIIIIIIIIIIIIII
ONLINE 10:00	TASKS	413	TTTTTTTTTTTTTTTTTTTTT
	CPU	47.6004	CCCCCC
	I/O	6,551	IIIIIIIIIII
BATCH 11:00	TASKS	18	
	CPU	124.4628	CCCCCCCCCCCCCC
	I/O	15,129	IIIIIIIIIIIIIII
ONLINE 11:00	TASKS	724	TTTTTTTTTTTTTTTTTTTTTTTTTTTTTTTTTTTTTTTT
	CPU	75.6882	CCCCCCCCCC
	I/O	17,347	IIIIIIIIIIIIIIIIII

Figure 13-7 Sample Output from IDMS/R Performance Monitor, Report 80

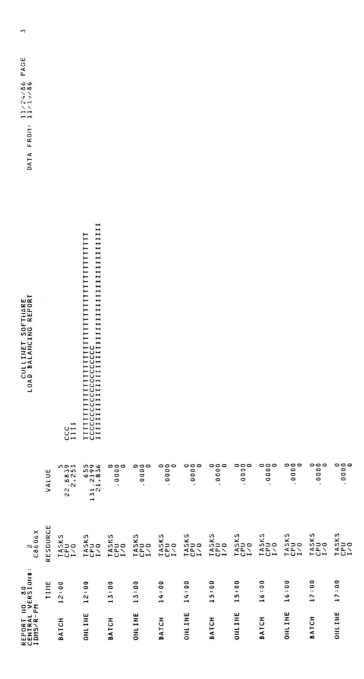

Figure 13-7 Sample Output from IDMS/R Performance Monitor, Report 80
(continued)

RHDCSGN1/RHDCSGN2 in prior releases), entitled SYSTEM
ACTIVITY REPORTS, provide complete information about a newly-
added system or a system which has been deleted and re-added. All
system parameters, programs, tasks, and terminals are included in
the sysgen reports, wrapped up in one neat listing. However, there is
no single CREPORT which shows a similar amount of information if
a system is modified rather than deleted and re-added. CREPORTs
of a sysgen may be run for a specific component of a system, e.g., the
system statement or the programs included in a sysgen. The only
way to get a full listing of the current system, after modifying its
definition, is to run all the CREPORTs.

Most modifications to a system revolve around changing parameter values on the SYSTEM statement. Current SYSTEM statement
parameter values may be displayed by running CREPORT011. Other
reports useful after common sysgen changes are CREPORT004,
which displays all programs included in the sysgen (this report can
be subselected to pull off only resident programs), and CREPORT009,
which lists all USERs. A complete list of CREPORTS may be found
in the appendix of the system generation guide for your release of
IDMS.

CREPORT019 lists program descriptions and may be used to list
all resident programs. The following Culprit parameters specify that
only resident programs should be listed:

```
DATABASE DICTNAME=PRIDICT DBNAME=PRIDICT
PROFILE RELEASE=6 EX=E PARMLIB=STANDARD PE=5
CREPORT=019
  SELECT SYS-041 WHEN SYS-VER-041 EQ system-version-number
  SELECT PROG-051 WHEN RESIDENT-051 EQ 1
```

Substitute the sysgen system number for *system-version-number*
above. Sample output from CREPORT019 is shown in Figure 13-8.

Dictionary report CREPORT050 (Figure 13-9) documents all dictionary load modules. It displays load module names, types (dialog,
table, subschema, or map), and, most importantly, load module sizes.
This report should be run monthly and compared with task and program usage statistics to identify unused load modules for removal
from the DD and to head off potential program pool problems caused by
usage of extremely large or frequently-used modules.

13.4.2 Application-Related Sources

We discuss sources of information for both program and database
performance tuning in this section. Several sources provide information on the impact of individual tasks, programs, and dialogs on

```
REPORT NO. 19                    IDMS-DC SOURCE REPORT   C8604M                          10/15/86 PAGE  1
CREPORT 019                      SYSTEM NAME: DCSYSTEM
                                 SYSTEM VERSION: 2
                                 PROGRAM DESCRIPTION

PROGRAM    TYPE        BUILDER ACTION VERSION

ADSOGEN1   PROGRAM     G              1    ISA-SIZE    ERROR       DUMP        SECURITY   LANGUAGE   SAVE     RESIDENT
                                           0           THRESHOLD   THRESHOLD   CLASS CODE ASSEMBLER  AREA     YES
                                                       5           0           0                     NO
                                           CONCURRENT  REUSABLE    REENTRANT   OVERLAYABLE DISABLED  PROTECT  NEW COPY
                                           YES         YES         REENTRANT   YES         NO        YES      NO

ADSOGEN2   PROGRAM     G              1    ISA-SIZE    ERROR       DUMP        SECURITY   LANGUAGE   SAVE     RESIDENT
                                           0           THRESHOLD   THRESHOLD   CLASS CODE ASSEMBLER  AREA     YES
                                                       5           0           0                     NO
                                           CONCURRENT  REUSABLE    REENTRANT   OVERLAYABLE DISABLED  PROTECT  NEW COPY
                                           YES         YES         REENTRANT   YES         NO        YES      NO

ADSOMAIN   PROGRAM     G              1    ISA-SIZE    ERROR       DUMP        SECURITY   LANGUAGE   SAVE     RESIDENT
                                           0           THRESHOLD   THRESHOLD   CLASS CODE ASSEMBLER  AREA     YES
                                                       5           0           0                     NO
                                           CONCURRENT  REUSABLE    REENTRANT   OVERLAYABLE DISABLED  PROTECT  NEW COPY
                                           YES         YES         REENTRANT   YES         NO        YES      NO

ADSOMENU   MAP         G              1    ISA-SIZE    ERROR       DUMP        SECURITY   LANGUAGE   SAVE     RESIDENT
                                           0           THRESHOLD   THRESHOLD   CLASS CODE ASSEMBLER  AREA     YES
                                                       5           0           0                     NO
                                           CONCURRENT  REUSABLE    REENTRANT   OVERLAYABLE DISABLED  PROTECT  NEW COPY
                                           YES         YES         REENTRANT   YES         NO        YES      NO

ADSORUN1   PROGRAM     G              1    ISA-SIZE    ERROR       DUMP        SECURITY   LANGUAGE   SAVE     RESIDENT
                                           0           THRESHOLD   THRESHOLD   CLASS CODE ASSEMBLER  AREA     YES
                                                       5           0           0                     NO
                                           CONCURRENT  REUSABLE    REENTRANT   OVERLAYABLE DISABLED  PROTECT  NEW COPY
                                           YES         YES         REENTRANT   YES         NO        YES      NO

CISDNHKA   SUBSCHEMA   G              1    ISA-SIZE    ERROR       DUMP        SECURITY   LANGUAGE   SAVE     RESIDENT
                                           0           THRESHOLD   THRESHOLD   CLASS CODE ASSEMBLER  AREA     YES
                                                       5           0           0                     NO
                                           CONCURRENT  REUSABLE    REENTRANT   OVERLAYABLE DISABLED  PROTECT  NEW COPY
                                           YES         YES         REENTRANT   YES         NO        YES      NO

COMDNHKA   SUBSCHEMA   G              1    ISA-SIZE    ERROR       DUMP        SECURITY   LANGUAGE   SAVE     RESIDENT
                                           0           THRESHOLD   THRESHOLD   CLASS CODE ASSEMBLER  AREA     YES
                                                       5           0           0                     NO
                                           CONCURRENT  REUSABLE    REENTRANT   OVERLAYABLE DISABLED  PROTECT  NEW COPY
                                           YES         YES         REENTRANT   YES         NO        YES      NO
```

Figure 13-8 Sample Output from CREPORT019, List of Resident Programs

```
REPORT NO. 19                              IDMS-DC SOURCE REPORT   C8604M          10/15/86 PAGE   2
CREPORT 019                                SYSTEM NAME:NEW.DCSYSTEM
                                           SYSTEM VERSION:DCSYSTEM2
PROGRAM   TYPE       BUILDER ACTION VERSION     PROGRAM DESCRIPTION

DB000P    PROGRAM           M          1    ISA-SIZE  ERROR      DUMP       SECURITY    OVERLAYABLE DISABLED PROTECT SAVE   RESIDENT
                                               0      THRESHOLD  THRESHOLD  CLASS CODE      YES        NO      YES   AREA     YES
                                                          5          5          0                                    YES
                                            CONCURRENT REUSABLE  REENTRANT  SECURITY    LANGUAGE    DISABLED PROTECT SAVE   NEW COPY
                                               NO        YES      QUASI     CLASS CODE   COBOL         NO      YES   AREA     NO

FTSDNHKA  SUBSCHEMA         G          1    ISA-SIZE  ERROR      DUMP       SECURITY    OVERLAYABLE DISABLED PROTECT SAVE   RESIDENT
                                               0      THRESHOLD  THRESHOLD  CLASS CODE      YES        NO      NO    AREA     YES
                                                          5          0          0                                    NO
                                            CONCURRENT REUSABLE  REENTRANT              LANGUAGE                             NEW COPY
                                               YES       YES     REENTRANT              ASSEMBLER                              NO

IDBCMCTL  PROGRAM           G          1    ISA-SIZE  ERROR      DUMP       SECURITY    OVERLAYABLE DISABLED PROTECT SAVE   RESIDENT
                                              512     THRESHOLD  THRESHOLD  CLASS CODE      YES        NO      NO    AREA     YES
                                                          5          0          0                                    NO
                                            CONCURRENT REUSABLE  REENTRANT              LANGUAGE                             NEW COPY
                                               YES       YES     REENTRANT              ASSEMBLER                              NO

IDBCMSRV  PROGRAM           G          1    ISA-SIZE  ERROR      DUMP       SECURITY    OVERLAYABLE DISABLED PROTECT SAVE   RESIDENT
                                               0      THRESHOLD  THRESHOLD  CLASS CODE      YES        NO      YES   AREA     YES
                                                          5          0          0                                    NO
                                            CONCURRENT REUSABLE  REENTRANT              LANGUAGE                             NEW COPY
                                               YES       YES     REENTRANT              ASSEMBLER                              NO

IDBCMXEC  PROGRAM           G          1    ISA-SIZE  ERROR      DUMP       SECURITY    OVERLAYABLE DISABLED PROTECT SAVE   RESIDENT
                                               0      THRESHOLD  THRESHOLD  CLASS CODE      YES        NO      YES   AREA     YES
                                                          5          0          0                                    NO
                                            CONCURRENT REUSABLE  REENTRANT              LANGUAGE                             NEW COPY
                                               YES       YES     REENTRANT              ASSEMBLER                              NO

IDBCMX34  PROGRAM           G          1    ISA-SIZE  ERROR      DUMP       SECURITY    OVERLAYABLE DISABLED PROTECT SAVE   RESIDENT
                                               0      THRESHOLD  THRESHOLD  CLASS CODE      YES        NO      YES   AREA     YES
                                                          5          0          0                                    NO
                                            CONCURRENT REUSABLE  REENTRANT              LANGUAGE                             NEW COPY
                                               YES       YES     REENTRANT              ASSEMBLER                              NO

IDBCMX35  PROGRAM           G          1    ISA-SIZE  ERROR      DUMP       SECURITY    OVERLAYABLE DISABLED PROTECT SAVE   RESIDENT
                                               0      THRESHOLD  THRESHOLD  CLASS CODE      YES        NO      YES   AREA     YES
                                                          5          0          0                                    NO
```

Figure 13-8 Sample Output from CREPORT019, List of Resident Programs (continued)

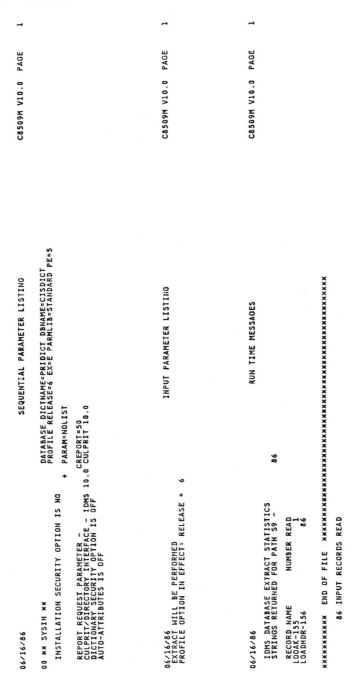

Figure 13-9 Sample Output from CREPORT050, Load Module Report

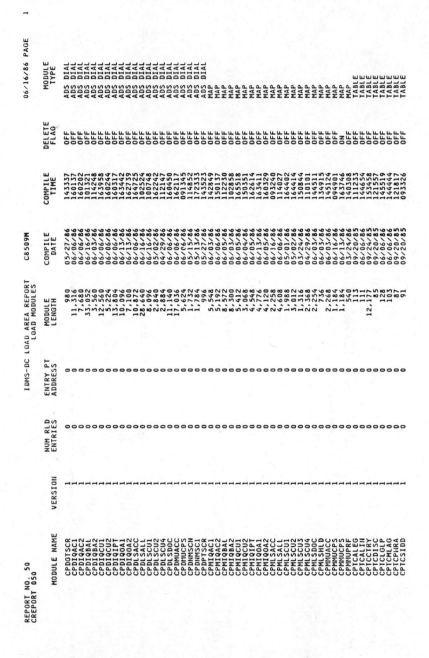

Figure 13-9 Sample Output from CREPORT050, Load Module Report
(continued)

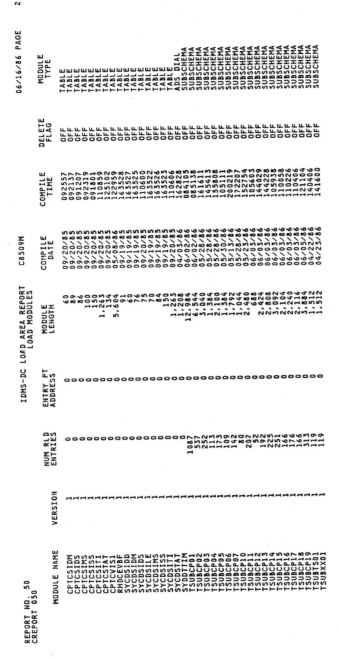

Figure 13-9 Sample Output from CREPORT050, Load Module Report
(continued)

the system. These sources include JREPORTS; task, transaction, and ADS/O statistics; the IDMS/R Performance Monitor; and ACCEPT DB-STATICTICS.

The major reports available for reviewing databases are provided by the IDMSDUMP and IDMSDBAN utilities. IDMSDBAN is available only at Release 10 sites. These utilities provide information on space utilization within a database. One or both of the utilities should be run on a regular basis to monitor production databases, perhaps weekly. ACCEPT DB-STATISTICS provides database usage statistics from individual program executions. IDMSRPTS reports current database schema and subschema information from the data dictionary.

Journal reports: The journal reports (also called JREPORTs) are a good source of information for evaluating run unit activity in production systems. These reports are run using archived journal tapes as input; therefore, journal reports do not cause degradation of run time system efficiency. It is recommended that journal reports be run daily in a production environment.

JREPORTs provide statistical information on all journaled run units. Only update run units appear in the journal reports unless JOURNAL RETRIEVAL was specified in the sysgen. Specifying JOURNAL RETRIEVAL causes additional run time I/O and is not recommended for production systems unless detailed chargeback information is required.

The JREPORTs provide database and program information. As of this writing, individual dialog statistics are unavailable through the journal reports because all dialog activity is logged to ADSOMAIN. The reports of primary interest are JREPORTs 2, 3, and 4.

JREPORT 2 provides detailed program statistics on locks, DB calls, records requested and made current, overflows, and fragments stored or returned (basically the same information is available from ACCEPT DB-STATISTICS). This information is useful in detecting problems with individual programs, database design, and/or database size. Programs performing excessive numbers of calls and/or holding excessive numbers of locks might be looping. A single run unit holding an excessive number of exclusive locks may cause concurrently-processing run units to experience waits. A large number of CALC overflows may suggest a database design flaw or indicate that IDMSDUMP should be run to determine if the database is becoming full. The IDMSDUMP reports shows the number of variable length record fragments which have been stored. Retrieval run units may take a long time to retrieve a relatively small number of variable length records if there are a large number of variable length record fragments. If this is the case, a purge job or a reorganization is in order to bring the fragments back together with the root of the record.

JREPORT 3 deals with I/O buffering statistics. It provides useful information for determining if DMCL buffer allocations need to be reviewed.

JREPORT 4 summarizes all the runs of an individual program and provides averages for each of the statistics. This report might be the first one checked in a production cycle, to see whether the other reports require close inspection. The IDMS Utilities Guide may be checked for details on individual statistics.

Task/Transaction/ADS Statistics: Task statistics provide information at the individual task level. They are enabled by SYSTEM statement parameters specified in the sysgen. There are three options when specifying task statistics in the system: 1) task collect statistics, 2) task write statistics, or 3) no task statistics. Statistics on individual tasks are accumulated in main storage when task collect statistics are enabled. Task statistics are collected in main storage and written to the DC log at specified intervals when task write statistics are enabled (the interval may be modified dynamically using DCMT commands). Several tools for monitoring and regulating performance are disabled if task statistics are not at least collected. Specifically, LIMITS cannot be specified, the IDMS/R Performance Monitor cannot be used, and both transaction and ADS statistics are unavailable without task statistics.

SREPORTs (statistics reports) summarize information collected when task collect statistics have been turned on. The SREPORTs are run against the archived output of the RHDCPRLG utility. Refer to the System Operations Guide for further information on SREPORTs.

Transaction statistics summarize information across tasks. Statistics for related tasks can be grouped together through use of the BIND TRANSACTION STATISTICS and END TRANSACTION STATISTICS DML commands (typically issued by DC programs, unavailable to external run units) if transaction statistics are on. Task collect or task write statistics must be enabled to use transaction statistics. Task and transaction statistics report identical information, but summarized and reported at different levels.

ADS/O statistics, also known as dialog statistics, report information specific to individual dialogs (record buffer size, number of levels, DB statistics, etc.). All dialog statistics are rolled together under task ADS and program ADSORUN1 when task statistics are on but ADS/O statistics are off, making it impossible to discern when a particular dialog processed or what it did. To use dialog statistics, both task and transaction statistics must be turned on. Sample sysgen SYSTEM and ADSO statements for enabling ADS/O statistics are shown in Figure 13-10.

A common symptom of declining performance is overall re-sponse times slowing down when a particular program or series of programs is running. The ADS/task/transaction statistics may be useful in determining which programs or dialogs are to blame. Task and transaction statistics are composed of two types of information, database statistics (the same information available to each program through the ACCEPT DB-STATISTICS DML statement) and data communication statistics showing storage, queue, and scratch uti-lization as well as programs called versus loaded. In addition, task/transaction statistics provide CPU timings on system time and user time (corresponding to service time and application execution times).

The database requests, overflow information, and pages read versus pages requested statistics are helpful in assessing a given transaction's processing, because they may provide evidence of a loop or poor programming practices. In addition, comparing the number of pages requested to the number of pages actually read to satisfy those requests provides valuable information for tuning buffers. The DC-related information is valuable for determining program load on the program pool. Programs which are frequently loaded and overlaid degrade overall system performance, especially if the programs are large. Scratch and Queue usage may indicate unusual amount of I/O in the same manner as database page reads. The amount of storage held by a task is included in information on storage pool utilization under Release 10, which could be useful in understanding SOS prob-lems or slowdowns caused by tasks requesting extreme amounts of storage. CPU times should be monitored, especially the user mode time, as an indication of ADS/O or IDMS-DC programming loops or poorly-written code.

We feel that the task/transaction statistics yield information too general in nature to warrant daily use. There is no breakdown of system mode time or system wait time – vital for determining where the response time problems are coming from (for example, how much time was spent waiting for the task to be set up, for a buffer, for storage, or for a lock to clear). These statistics can make the amount of paper in the log report voluminous when used on a daily basis and cause a degradation of the system by their use and an extreme degradation when they are written to the log. The preferred methods, at least for DB information, are using the ACCEPT DML verb in test systems by each program/dialog and monitoring the JREPORTs in produc-tion systems. Database statistics are captured automatically by the system for each run unit's processing, therefore, using the ACCEPT

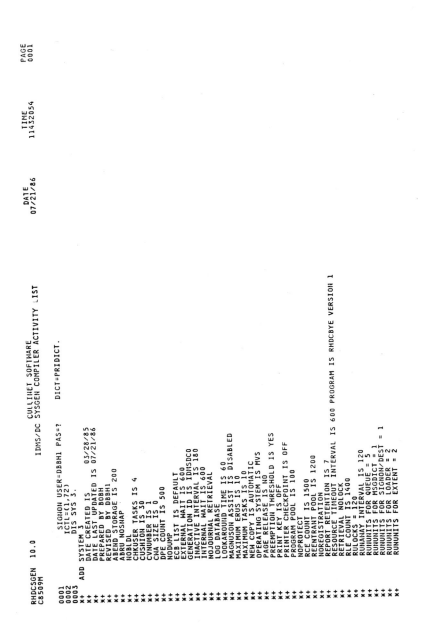

Figure 13-10 Sysgen Statements to Enable ADS/O Statistics

```
RHDCSGEN 10.0                        CULLINET SOFTWARE                DATE        TIME      PAGE
C8509M                    IDMS/DC SYSGEN COMPILER ACTIVITY LIST       07/21/86    11432054  0002

**   RUPRTY IS 100
**   QUEUE JOURNAL BEFORE
**   STACKSIZE IS 750
**   STATISTICS INTERVAL OFF NOLINE TASK WRITE HOUSER TRANSACTION
**   STORAGE KEY IS 9
**   STORAGE POOL IS 800
**   SVC IS 253
**   SYSCTL IS SYSCTL
**   SYSLOCKS IS 2500
**   SYSTRACE OFF
**   TICKER INTERVAL IS 1
**   TRANSACTION LOG IS OFF DDNAME IS CDMSTLF
**   UNDEFINED PROGRAM COUNT IS ( 58 29 ) FOR (ALL)
**   UPDATE NOLOCK
**   USERTRACE ON ENTRIES = 300
**   XA PROGRAM POOL IS 0
**   XA REENTRANT POOL IS 0
**   WARMSTRT
**   STORAGE LIMIT FOR ONLINE TASKS IS 64
**   LOCK LIMIT FOR ONLINE TASKS IS 500
**   LOCK LIMIT FOR EXTERNAL TASKS IS 10000
**   CALL LIMIT FOR ONLINE TASKS IS 200
**   CALL LIMIT FOR EXTERNAL TASKS IS 100000
**   DBIO LIMIT FOR ONLINE TASKS IS 100
**   DBIO LIMIT FOR EXTERNAL TASKS IS 50000
**   LIMITS FOR ONLINE ARE ENABLED
**   LIMITS FOR EXTERNAL ARE ENABLED

0004        DIS ADSO.
     ADD ADSO.
**   ADS1TASK IS ADS
**   ADS2TASK IS ADS2
**   ADS2CEF TASK IS ADS2T
**   ACTIVITY LOG IS YES
**   AUTOSTATUS IS YES OPTIONAL
**   COBOL MOVE IS NO
**   DIAGNOSTIC SCREEN IS YES
**   FAST MODE THRESHOLD IS OFF
**   MAXIMUM LINKS IS 10
**   MENU IS USER
**   NEWPAGE MAPOUT IS NO
**   PRIMARY POOL IS 4084
**   SECONDARY POOL IS 2036
**   RESOURCES ARE FIXED
**   DIALOG STATISTICS ON SELECTED CHECKPOINT INTERVAL IS 200
**   STATUS DEFINITION RECORD IS ADSO-STAT-DEF-REC OPTIONAL
```

Figure 13-10 Sysgen Statements to Enable ADS/O Statistics (continued)

Figure 13-10 Sysgen Statements to Enable ADS/O Statistics (continued)

statement does not cause system degradation. Using the IDMS/R Performance Monitor to selectively monitor problem programs and/or dialogs is recommended over using task and transaction write statistics because less overhead is incurred.

If statistics from the ACCEPT statement and the JREPORTs indicate performance problems but provide insufficient information, it may be helpful to enable task write statistics but write them to the log only at infrequent intervals or during low activity periods. We recommend setting up an alternate system with task and transaction write statistics selected in the sysgen. Bring up the alternate system and turn on the statistics only at times of the day when performance is known to be poor or irregular. In addition, DCMT commands may be used to set the interval at which the statistics are written to the log so that they are written at a period of low activity, e.g., once every two hours or at noon (or turn the interval off, causing the statistics to be written to the log only at shutdown). Thereby, the worst effects of the statistics, the log writes, are put off until an opportune time. The statistics overhead is incurred only when monitoring is necessary if the alternate system technique is used.

ADS statistics are quite useful, but it is best to run them only on a systems testing basis. ADS statistics can be turned on selectively as long as task and transaction statistics are being collected. In this fashion, task and transaction statistics could be collected (but not written to the log necessarily) and ADS statistics turned on when a particular dialog or new application is being tested. For example,

To turn on ADS statistics, issue the command:
    DCMT VARY ADSO STAT ON
Next, run the tests, followed by issuing the command
    DCMT VARY ADSO STAT OFF

The DCMT VARY ADSO STATISTICS CHECKPOINT INTERVAL *interval-value* command which determines when these statistics are written to the log. Statistics are written to the log at application termination if no ADSO checkpoint interval is set (refer to the System Generation Guide under 'Statistics' for details).

Collecting task/transaction/ADS statistics for dialogs and programs or using the performance monitor to collect similar information is recommended prior to any system going into QA testing and certainly prior to going production. Minimum efficiency standards should be set and measured against the transaction statistics output to head off problems.

IDMS/R Performance Monitor: Task COLLECT statistics must be turned on in the sysgen to use the IDMS/R Performance Monitor.

Task write statistics may be on as well but are not required or recommended.

The IDMS/R Performance Monitor's online facilities allow selection of tasks and dialogs/programs for which statistics are to be gathered. Statistics for the selected tasks, dialogs, and programs then can be reviewed online at any time during the run to see details on that entity. The statistics displayed, as of this writing, include exactly the same statistics as are available from task/transaction write statistics detailed reports. The advantage of using the performance monitor is that it allows one to select only those entities which require monitoring.

The Performance Monitor is the ideal tool for checking ADS/O and DC performance standards compliance. It would be the preferred method of gathering detailed statistics for a systems test prior to putting a new application into production. The online monitor can be helpful in monitoring programs or dialogs suspected of causing performance bottlenecks in the production environment.

The Performance Monitor is the preferred method of collecting all application-related statistical information because it requires only task collect statistics not task write statistics. We recommend using it heavily during system testing, periodically in production (possibly weekly), and frequently during development.

IDMSDUMP: IDMSDUMP is the utility which backs up databases, files, or areas. In addition, it provides overall information on how full the database has become. The statistic AREA UTILIZATION IS $nn\%$ should be monitored closely. Expanding the page range or the page size should be considered if an area is more than 70% full. When an area is more than 70% full, the search for free space during a MODIFY or STORE operation often involves one or two extra I/O's, as well as causing variable length record fragments and newly-stored records to overflow beyond the target page. The target page is the page on which the record would have been stored if there had been enough free space. Records which overflow beyond the target page also cause extra I/O's during subsequent update and retrieval operations.

The number of pages which are greater than 70% full is another pertinent statistic. The page space situation for the entire area may not be too bad on the average, but portions of the area may be full, causing overflows of records. For example, a set where the member records are stored VIA the owner record (i.e., member records are targeted for storage on the same page as the owner record when both records are stored in the same area) and some of the sets have far more members than originally estimated may be causing overflow. However, the IDMSDUMP report does not provide enough information to determine <u>why</u> some pages are overly full. Overly-full pages may be examined using IDMSPFIX to dump the page contents.

IDMSDBAN (Release 10 only): The IDMSDBAN utility is more useful than IDMSDUMP because it provides more detailed information on individual set lengths, including minimums, maximums, and averages (Figure 13-11). For example, IDMSDBAN reports the average number of members for a given set type and the total number of owner records and member records. This information may help determine why some pages are more than 70% full. In general, IDMSDBAN provides information useful for comparing estimated record volumes and set lengths to actual production volumes and lengths.

   Possible actions to be taken for occasional extra-long sets that cause overflow include adding sets to increase performance for transactions which must walk sets and/or storing via members in a separate area to avoid overflow in the owner's area. Making indexed sets of sorted sets that have become longer than originally anticipated would be the normal course of action.

IDMSRPTS: The IDMSRPTS utility provides detailed information about schemas and subschemas currently in use. If a programmer calls the DBA and asks, "Can you check what we have specified for the duplicates option on the Customer-Order set and on the Customer record type? My program is aborting with a '1205' ERROR-STATUS" (i.e., a STORE operation failed because it would create a duplicate). The easiest solution is to check the source statement library for the schema in question. However, the source statement library information may be out of date, so it is better to extract current database definitions from the IDD by running IDMSRPTS. IDMSRPTS displays complete schema and/or subschema information (including pointer positions, useful when looking at an IDMSPFIX dump of a database page). It also provides record layouts and displacements to each element within the record. IDMSRPTS should be run and filed for each schema created or modified.

ACCEPT DB-STATISTICS: The DML statement ACCEPT DB-STATISTICS INTO IDMS-STATISTICS may be coded in programs and dialogs to request statistics on database accesses made during the run unit's processing. It is often a standard procedure for programs and dialogs to ACCEPT statistics just prior to FINISHing database processing. The database requests, number of overflows, pages read versus pages requested, and number of locks held are some of the statistics available.

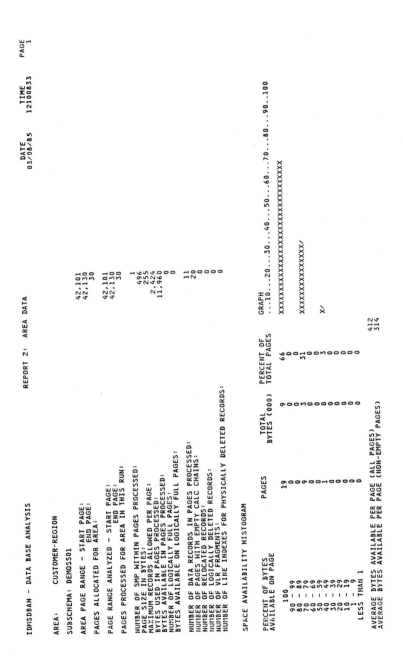

Figure 13-11 Sample Output From IDMSDBAN

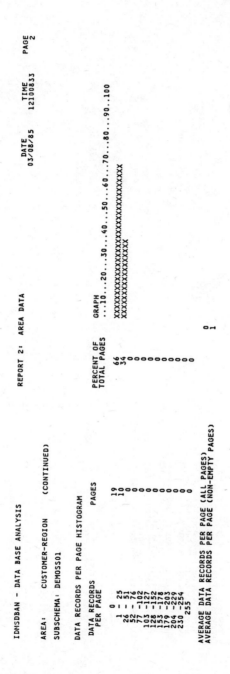

Figure 13-11 Sample Output From IDMSDBAN (continued)

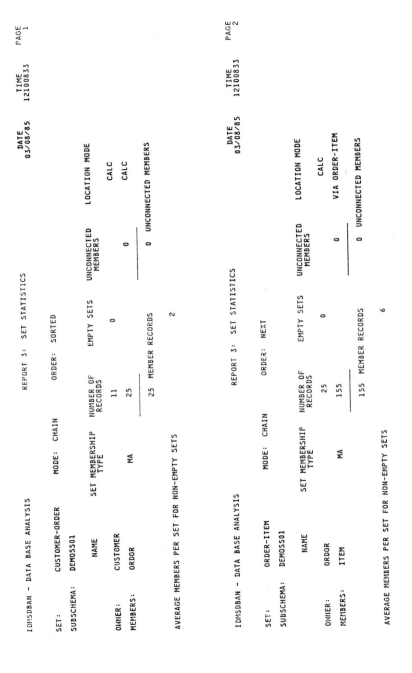

Figure 13-11 Sample Output From IDMSDBAN (continued)

```
IDMSDBAN - DATA BASE ANALYSIS          REPORT 4:  RECORD DATA              DATE        TIME       PAGE
                                                                        03/08/85    12100833       1

RECORD:    CUSTOMER        RECORD ID:  611        LOCATION MODE:  CALC

SUBSCHEMA:  DEMOSS01
AREA:       CUSTOMER-REGION
FLR/VLR:    FLR

DATA LENGTH:
RECORD LENGTH (DATA AND PREFIX):                                    104
                                                                   128

PAGE RANGE FOR RECORD IN AREA - START PAGE:                      42,101
                                 END PAGE:                       42,130
PAGES ALLOCATED FOR RECORD IN AREA:                                  30

PAGE RANGE ANALYZED - START PAGE:                                42,101
                        END PAGE:                                42,130
PAGES PROCESSED FOR RECORD IN AREA IN THIS RUN:                      30

NUMBER OF SMP WITHIN PAGES PROCESSED:                                 1
PAGE SIZE IN BYTES:                                                 496
BYTES USED FOR THIS RECORD TYPE IN PAGES PROCESSED:              1,496
BYTES AVAILABLE IN PAGES PROCESSED:                             11,960

NUMBER OF RECORDS OF THIS TYPE IN PAGES PROCESSED:                   11

NUMBER OF RELOCATED RECORDS:                                          0
NUMBER OF LOGICALLY DELETED RECORDS:                                  0

DATA RECORDS PER PAGE HISTOGRAM

DATA RECORDS                    PERCENT OF    GRAPH
 PER PAGE          PAGES        TOTAL PAGES   ...10...20...30...40...50...60...70...80...90...100

     0              19             66         XXXXXXXXXXXXXXXXXXXXXXXXXXXXXXXXXXXXXXXXXX
   1 -  25          10             34         XXXXXXXXXXXXXXXXXXXXX
  26 -  51           0              0
  52 -  76           0              0
  77 - 102           0              0
 103 - 127           0              0
 128 - 152           0              0
 153 - 178           0              0
 179 - 203           0              0
 204 - 229           0              0
 230 - 254           0              0
     255             0              0

AVERAGE DATA RECORDS PER PAGE (ALL PAGES)                             0
AVERAGE DATA RECORDS PER PAGE (PAGES WITH THIS RECORD TYPE)           1
```

Figure 13-11 Sample Output From IDMSDBAN (continued)

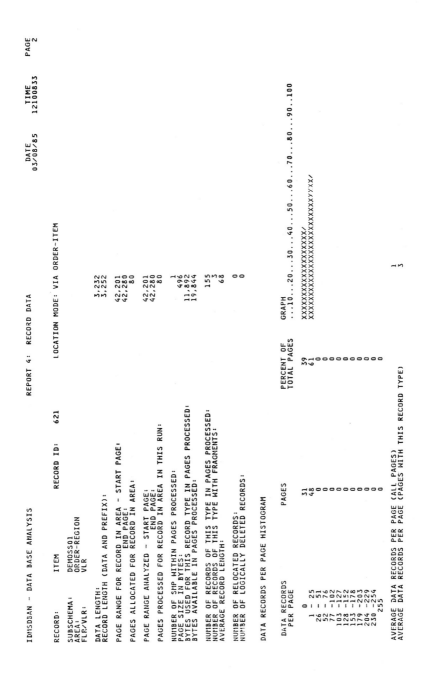

Figure 13-11 Sample Output From IDMSDBAN (continued)

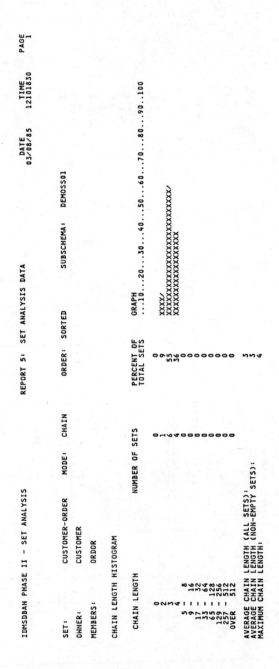

Figure 13-11 Sample Output From IDMSDBAN (continued)

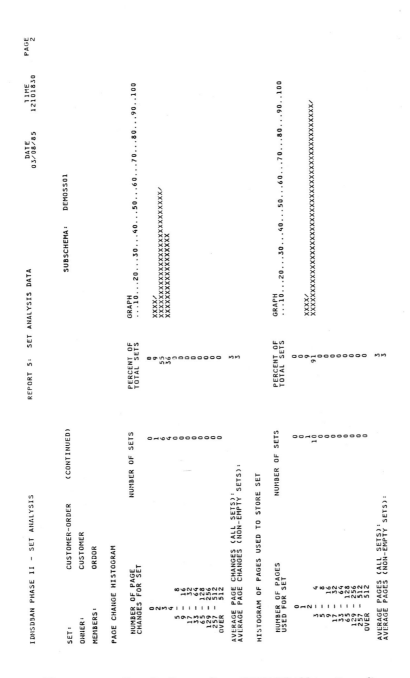

Figure 13-11 Sample Output From IDMSDBAN (continued)

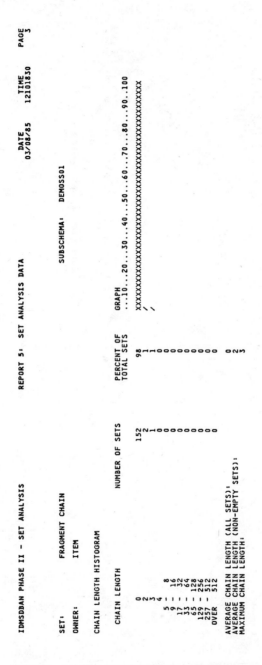

Figure 13-11 Sample Output From IDMSDBAN (continued)

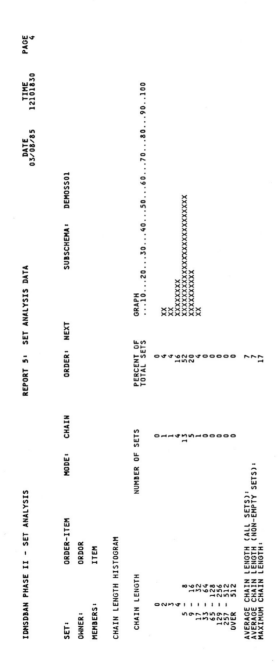

Figure 13-11 Sample Output From IDMSDBAN (continued)

13.5   CONCLUSION

Performance tuning is an ongoing, dynamic function. System performance should be monitored to determine the changes necessary to maintain optimal performance as applications evolve and new transactions increase the load.

Maximizing the efficiency of storage pool usage and program pool usage is of primary importance. Several reports and online tasks have been discussed which provide information useful during performance tuning. Early review of applications to be put into production is an important step in achieving peak performance.

Suggestions for further reading on Performance Tuning:

The following Cullinet Manuals
   For Release 10 sites:
      1) Cullinet System Software -- System Generation (Enabling statistics)
      2) IDMS-CV/DC Operations (Performance tools, i.e., OPER, DCMT, DCUF USER TRACE, Statistics, SREPORTs)
      3) IDMS/R Database Design (Database design considerations)
      4) IDMS/R DDL Reference (Integrated indexing)
      5) IDMS-DC/UCF Mapping Facility User's Guide (Pageable maps)
      6) IDMS/R Performance Monitor User's Guide (Performance tools, Performance Monitor)
      7) IDMS-DB/DC Utilities (Performance tools, i.e., IDMSDBAN, IDMSDUMP)
      8) Class aids for Internals of IDMS-DC/UCF (Storage pool and program loading considerations)
      9) Class aids for Database Design class (database design considerations)
      10) Class aids for IDMS-CV/DC Systems Performance and Tuning (Program loading, operating system and DASD considerations, disk pack layouts)

   For Release 5.7 sites:
      1) IDMS-CV/DC System Generation (Enabling statistics)
      2) IDMS-DB/DC Operations (Performance tools, i.e., OPER, DCMT, DCUF USER TRACE, Statistics, SREPORTs)
      3) IDMS Database Design and Definition Guide (Database design considerations)

4) IDMS-DC/UCF Mapping Facility User's Guide (Pageable maps)

5) IDMS-DB/DC Utilities (Performance tools, i.e., IDMSDUMP)

6) Class aids for Internals of IDMS-DC/UCF (Storage pool and program loading considerations)

7) Class aids for Database Design class (database design considerations)

8) Class aids for IDMS-CV/DC Systems Performance and Tuning (Program loading, operating system and DASD considerations, disk pack layouts)

Appendix A

Sample Listings

In the appendix, we will present the sample listings referenced in the text. These listings are provided as *examples* and must be tailored to your site's unique environment before use. The following sample listings are included:

- An OS jobstream to create and populate a secondary dictionary,
- A dictionary entity migration jobstream and program,
- Listings from creation of test and production systems,
- A procedure and programs to automate decompiling and recompiling maps, and
- A histogram modification.

A.1 A SAMPLE OS JOBSTREAM TO CREATE AND POPULATE A SECONDARY DICTIONARY

CREATE EDUDICT is a sample OS jobstream which creates and populates a new secondary dictionary (functions illustrated in Figure 3-5). CREATE EDUDICT builds a secondary DD under Release 10, creating both a new DDLDML area and a new DDLDCLOD area. If modifying this example for use with Release 5.7, remove all references to the DDLDCLOD area. This jobstream was taken from original installation JCL to set up the 'TSTDICT' secondary dictionary and modified to fit the new dictionary.

The following assumptions were made when this sample procedure was developed:

- Page ranges for the new DD must be assigned by the DBA prior to the run.
- DDR report source and as many Cullinet entities as possible will exist only on the primary DD. Several DD components must be established in each secondary dictionary regardless of decisions made regarding DDR report source (e.g., proto-

cols for DML compiles, ADS/O global records and ADS/O
status definition records).

- The job runs locally, therefore it creates a DBNT for its local
execution, by modifying a demo system (system 90 in this
example), punching, and link editing the DBNT load module to a load library for subsequent use.

After successful completion of this standard job, a DBNT must be
created for use in the CV/DC system. Schema and global DMCL compiles should then be set up and the startup routine JCL changed to include the new data sets.

```
//T80EDU JOB (IDMS,7784),'CREATE EDUDICT',CLASS=E,
//     MSGCLASS=X,NOTIFY=T80
//*    ***********************************************************
//*    ** THIS JOB BUILDS A NEW SECONDARY IDD FOR USE BY PROJECT
//*    **    GROUPS.  TO ADD A NEW IDD MERELY USE THE TSO/SPF GLOBAL
//*    **    CHANGE COMMAND TO CHANGE AN EXISTING ACRONYM, FOR EXAMPLE
//*    **    CIS, TO A NEW ACRONYM LIKE FTS.  ALL DBNAME TABLES AND
//*    **    NETWORK SS AND FILE NAMES WILL HAVE THE SAME PREFIX.  ALL
//*    **    ALLOCATIONS OF SECONDARY IDD'S WILL BE EXACTLY THE SAME,
//*    **    BUT REMEMBER - YOU MUST ALWAYS MANUALLY CHANGE THE
//*    **    PAGE RANGES FOR THE DICTDB AND DLODDB PORTIONS OF THE
//*    **    BASE DMCL ASSEMBLY AND THE NETWORK SS.  ADDITIONALLY, DON'T
//*    **    FORGET TO UPDATE THE GLOBAL DMCL AND SCHEMA IN ORDER TO
//*    **    MAKE THESE NEW AREAS AVAILABLE TO CV (CVODMCL AND CVOSCHM
//*    **    RESPECTIVELY), AND INCLUDE THE JCL IN THE START UP JCL.
//*    ***********************************************************
//*
//*          STEP ALLOC - TO ALLOCATE THE NEW DICTIONARY & LOAD AREAS
//*
//S1ALLOC EXEC PGM=IEFBR14
//EDUDICT   DD DSN=PIDMS.R10.EDUDICT,DISP=(,CATLG,DELETE),
//  UNIT=SYSDA,VOL=SER=IDMS01,
//  SPACE=(3156,3000),DCB=(RECFM=F,LRECL=3156,BLKSIZE=3156)
//EDUDLOD   DD DSN=PIDMS.R10.EDUDLOD,DISP=(,CATLG,DELETE),
//  UNIT=SYSDA,VOL=SER=IDMS01,
//  SPACE=(3156,3000),DCB=(RECFM=F,LRECL=3156,BLKSIZE=3156)
//*
//*  TO ASSEMBLE A NEW IDD "DMCL" FOR LOCAL MODE ACCESS
//*  TO THE DICTIONARY
//*
//S2BASE   EXEC PGM=IFOX00,PARM='DECK,NOLOAD,NORLD,NOXREF',
//           REGION=3000K
//SYSTERM   DD SYSOUT=*
//SYSPRINT  DD SYSOUT=*
//SYSLIB DD DSN=PIDMS.R10.SRCLIB,DISP=SHR
//  DD DSN=SYS1.MACLIB,DISP=SHR
//SYSUT1    DD DSN=&&WRKAWORK,UNIT=SYSDA,
//  VOL=SER=,SPACE=(CYL,(5,1))
//SYSUT2    DD DSN=&&WRKBWORK,UNIT=SYSDA,
//  VOL=SER=,SPACE=(CYL,(5,1))
//SYSUT3    DD DSN=&&WRKCWORK,UNIT=SYSDA,
//  VOL=SER=,SPACE=(CYL,(5,1))
//SYSPUNCH  DD DSN=PIDMS.R10.QBJLIB(EDUBASE),DISP=SHR
//SYSIN     DD *
         PRINT NOGEN
EDUBASE IDMSBASE LOPAGE=165001,HIPAGE=168000,              X
                MGLOPAG=25001,MGHIPAG=27000,               X
                LDLOPAG=169001,LDHIPAG=172000,             X
                DBMFILE=EDUDICT,PAGESZ=3156,               X
                DBMDEV=3380,                               X
                SMI=,                                      X
                LDFILE=EDUDLOD,LDPGSZ=3156,                X
                LDDEV=3380,                                X
                LDSMI=,                                    X
                MGFILE=DMSGDB,MGPGSZ=3860,                 X
                MGDEV=3380,                                X
                MGSMI=,                                    X
                JTFILE=SYSJRNL,                            X
                JTSIZE=8000,NOBUFF=006
                END
```

Figure A-1 Sample OS Jobstream to Create and Populate a Secondary
Dictionary

```
//*
//*   RUN IDMSRNWK FOR THE NETWORK SUBSCHEMA -IDMSNWKA
//*
//S3DNWKA EXEC PGM=IDMSRNWK,REGION=3000K
//STEPLIB   DD DSN=PIDMS.R10.LOADLIB,DISP=SHR
//SYSLST    DD SYSOUT=*
//SYSPCH    DD DSN=PIDMS.R10.OBJLIB(EDUDNWKA),DISP=SHR
//SYSIPT    DD *,DCB=BLKSIZE=8000
      SUBSCHEMA NAME IS EDUDNWKA
      DMCL NAME IS EDUBASE
      PAGE RANGE FOR DDLDML    IS 165001 THRU 168000
      PAGE RANGE FOR DDLDCMSG IS 25001 THRU 27000
      PAGE RANGE FOR DDLDCLOD IS 169001 THRU 172000
      PAGE RANGE FOR DDLDCLOG IS 20001 THRU 22000
      PAGE RANGE FOR DDLDCRUN IS 60001 THRU 62000
      PAGE RANGE FOR DDLDCSCR IS 35001 THRU 37000
      PAGE RANGE FOR DDLDCQUE IS 40001 THRU 42000
      OBJECT DECK FOLLOWS
//        DD DSN=PIDMS.R10.SRCLIB(IDMSNWKA),DISP=SHR
//*
//*   RUN IDMSRNWK FOR THE SUBSCHEMA -IDMSNWKS
//*
//S4DNWKS   EXEC PGM=IDMSRNWK,REGION=3000K
//STEPLIB   DD DSN=PIDMS.R10.LOADLIB,DISP=SHR
//SYSLST    DD SYSOUT=*
//SYSPCH    DD DSN=PIDMS.R10.OBJLIB(EDUDNWKS),DISP=SHR
//SYSIPT    DD *,DCB=BLKSIZE=8000
      SUBSCHEMA NAME IS EDUDNWKS
      DMCL NAME IS EDUBASE
      PAGE RANGE FOR DDLDML    IS 165001 THRU 168000
      PAGE RANGE FOR DDLDCMSG IS 25001 THRU 27000
      PAGE RANGE FOR DDLDCLOD IS 169001 THRU 172000
      PAGE RANGE FOR DDLDCLOG IS 20001 THRU 22000
      PAGE RANGE FOR DDLDCRUN IS 60001 THRU 62000
      PAGE RANGE FOR DDLDCSCR IS 35001 THRU 37000
      PAGE RANGE FOR DDLDCQUE IS 40001 THRU 42000
      OBJECT DECK FOLLOWS
//        DD DSN=PIDMS.R10.SRCLIB(IDMSNWKS),DISP=SHR
//*
//*       TO LINK THE DMCL AND NEW SUBSCHEMAS
//*
//S5LINK    EXEC PGM=IEWL,REGION=3000K,
//             PARM='LET,LIST,MAP,XREF,SIZE=(196608,65536),NCAL,RENT'
//SYSPRINT DD SYSOUT=*
//SYSUT1    DD DSN=&&WRKAWORK,UNIT=SYSDA,
//  VOL=SER=,SPACE=(CYL,(5,1))
//SYSLMOD   DD DSN=PIDMS.DBA.LOADLIB,DISP=SHR
//OBJLIB    DD DSN=PIDMS.R10.OBJLIB,DISP=SHR
//SYSLIN    DD *
 INCLUDE OBJLIB(EDUBASE)
 NAME    EDUBASE(R)
 INCLUDE OBJLIB(EDUDNWKA)
 INCLUDE OBJLIB(IDMSCOMP)
 INCLUDE OBJLIB(IDMSDCOM)
 ENTRY   EDUDNWKA
 NAME    EDUDNWKA(R) RENT
 INCLUDE OBJLIB(EDUDNWKS)
 INCLUDE OBJLIB(IDMSCOMP)
 INCLUDE OBJLIB(IDMSDCOM)
 ENTRY   EDUDNWKS
```

Figure A-1 Sample OS Jobstream to Create and Populate a Secondary
Dictionary (continued)

```
 NAME     EDUDNWKS(R) RENT
//*
//*           MODIFY A GARBAGE SYSTEM TO CREATE A DBNAME
//*           TABLE IN ORDER TO RUN THE REST OF THE STEPS LOCALLY
//*
//S6MODDBN EXEC PGM=RHDCSGEN,REGION=3000K
//STEPLIB DD DSN=PIDMS.R10.LOADLIB,DISP=SHR
//SYSLST   DD SYSOUT=*
//SYSUDUMP DD SYSOUT=*
//SYSCTL   DD DSN=PIDMS.CV0.SYSCTL,DISP=SHR
//SYSJRNL DD DUMMY
//SYSIPT   DD  *
      SIGNON USER=DBBH1 PAS=DBBH1.
      ICTL=(1,72)
 SYSTEM 90.
 ADD DBNAME EDUDICT
 SUBSCHEMA IDMSNWKS MAPS TO EDUDNWKS
 SUBSCHEMA IDMSNWK? MAPS TO EDUDNWKA.
 GENERATE.
//*
//*    PUNCH THE NEW IDMSDBTB WITH IDMSDDDL
//*
//S7PUNDBN EXEC PGM=IDMSDDDL,REGION=3000K
//STEPLIB DD DSN=PIDMS.R10.LOADLIB,DISP=SHR
//SYSLST   DD SYSOUT=*
//SYSCTL   DD DSN=PIDMS.CV0.SYSCTL,DISP=SHR
//SYSJRNL DD DUMMY
//SYSPCH   DD DSN=&&WRK1WORK,UNIT=SYSDA,DISP=(NEW,PASS),
//  VOL=SER=,DCB=BLKSIZE=80,SPACE=(CYL,(5,1))
//SYSIPT   DD *
      SIGNON USER=DBBH1 PAS=DBBH1.
      PUN LOAD MOD IDMSDBTB V 90.
//*
//*    LINK THE LOAD MODULE FOR THE DBNAME TABLE
//*
//S8LKDBN  EXEC PGM=IEWL,REGION=3000K,
//             PARM='LET,LIST,MAP,XREF,SIZE=(196608,65536),NCAL'
//SYSPRINT DD SYSOUT=*
//SYSUT1    DD DSN=&&WRKAWORK,UNIT=SYSDA,
//  VOL=SER=,SPACE=(CYL,(5,1))
//SYSLMOD  DD DSN=PIDMS.DBA.LOADLIB,DISP=SHR
//SYSLIN   DD DSN=&&WRK1WORK,DISP=(OLD,DELETE)
//          DD *
 ENTRY IDMSDBTB
 NAME IDMSDBTB(R)
//*
//*    STEP TO INITIALIZE THE NEW DICTIONARY
//*
//S9INIT    EXEC PGM=IDMSINIT,REGION=3000K
//STEPLIB DD DSN=PIDMS.DBA.LOADLIB,DISP=SHR
//          DD DSN=PIDMS.R10.LOADLIB,DISP=SHR
//SYSLST DD SYSOUT=*
//EDUDICT   DD DSN=PIDMS.R10.EDUDICT,DISP=SHR
//EDUDLOD   DD DSN=PIDMS.R10.EDUDLOD,DISP=SHR
//SYSIPT DD *
PROCESS=FILE,DMCL=EDUBASE
FILE=EDUDICT
FILE=EDUDLOD
//*
//*    STEP  TO PUT THE SYSTEM ATTRIBUTES IN THE NEW IDD
```

Figure A-1 Sample OS Jobstream to Create and Populate a Secondary
Dictionary (continued)

```
//*
//S10LATTR EXEC PGM=IDMSDDDL,REGION=3000K
//STEPLIB DD DSN=PIDMS.DBA.LOADLIB,DISP=SHR
//         DD DSN=PIDMS.R10.LOADLIB,DISP=SHR
//SYSLST   DD SYSOUT=*
//EDUDICT  DD DSN=PIDMS.R10.EDUDICT,DISP=SHR
//EDUDLOD  DD DSN=PIDMS.R10.EDUDLOD,DISP=SHR
//DMSGDB   DD DSN=PIDMS.R10.DMSGDB,DISP=SHR
//SYSJRNL DD DUMMY
//SYSIPT   DD  *,DCB=BLKSIZE=8000
 DBNAME = EDUDICT
        SET OPTIONS DEFAULT IS ON NO LIST INPUT 1 THRU 72.
// DD DSN=PIDMS.R10.SRCLIB(DLODDEFS),DISP=SHR
//*
//*     STEP  PUT THE SYSTEM PROTOCOLS IN THE NEW IDD
//*
//S11LPROT EXEC PGM=IDMSDDDL,REGION=3000K
//STEPLIB DD DSN=PIDMS.DBA.LOADLIB,DISP=SHR
//         DD DSN=PIDMS.R10.LOADLIB,DISP=SHR
//SYSLST   DD SYSOUT=*
//EDUDICT  DD DSN=PIDMS.R10.EDUDICT,DISP=SHR
//EDUDLOD  DD DSN=PIDMS.R10.EDUDLOD,DISP=SHR
//DMSGDB   DD DSN=PIDMS.R10.DMSGDB,DISP=SHR
//SYSJRNL DD DUMMY
//SYSIPT   DD  *,DCB=BLKSIZE=8000
 DBNAME = EDUDICT
        SET OPTIONS DEFAULT IS ON NO LIST INPUT 1 THRU 72.
// DD DSN=PIDMS.R10.SRCLIB(DLODPROT),DISP=SHR
//*
//*     STEP ADSRECDS - TO PUT THE ADS GLOBAL RECORD DEFS IN NEW IDD
//*
//S12LADS  EXEC PGM=IDMSDDDL,REGION=3000K
//STEPLIB DD DSN=PIDMS.DBA.LOADLIB,DISP=SHR
//         DD DSN=PIDMS.R10.LOADLIB,DISP=SHR
//SYSLST   DD SYSOUT=*
//EDUDICT  DD DSN=PIDMS.R10.EDUDICT,DISP=SHR
//EDUDLOD  DD DSN=PIDMS.R10.EDUDLOD,DISP=SHR
//DMSGDB   DD DSN=PIDMS.R10.DMSGDB,DISP=SHR
//SYSJRNL DD DUMMY
//SYSIPT   DD  *,DCB=BLKSIZE=8000
 DBNAME = EDUDICT
        SET OPTIONS DEFAULT IS ON NO LIST INPUT 1 THRU 72.
// DD DSN=PIDMS.R10.SRCLIB(ADSRECDS),DISP=SHR
//*
//*   THIS STEP ADDS THE FUNCTION TABLE FOR ADS(SUBSTRING,INDEX ETC)
//*
//S13FADS  EXEC PGM=IDMSDDDL,REGION=3000K
//STEPLIB DD DSN=PIDMS.DBA.LOADLIB,DISP=SHR
//         DD DSN=PIDMS.R10.LOADLIB,DISP=SHR
//SYSLST   DD SYSOUT=*
//EDUDICT  DD DSN=PIDMS.R10.EDUDICT,DISP=SHR
//EDUDLOD  DD DSN=PIDMS.R10.EDUDLOD,DISP=SHR
//DMSGDB   DD DSN=PIDMS.R10.DMSGDB,DISP=SHR
//SYSJRNL DD DUMMY
//SYSIPT   DD  *,DCB=BLKSIZE=8000
 DBNAME = EDUDICT
        SET OPTIONS DEFAULT IS ON NO LIST INPUT 1 THRU 72.
        ADD LOAD MOD RHDCEVBF TYPE IS TABLE
          OBJECT DECK FOLLOWS
// DD DSN=PIDMS.R10.SRCLIB(RHDCEVBF),DISP=SHR
//
//* ***************** JCL TO ELIMINATE THE IDD FOR RERUN *************
//ALLOC  EXEC PGM=IEFBR14
//EDUDICT  DD DSN=PIDMS.R10.EDUDICT,DISP=(OLD,DELETE)
//EDUDLOD  DD DSN=PIDMS.R10.EDUDLOD,DISP=(OLD,DELETE)
//* ***************************************************************
```

Figure A-1 Sample OS Jobstream to Create and Populate a Secondary
Dictionary (continued)

A.2 A SAMPLE JOBSTREAM AND PROGRAMS TO AUTOMATE MIGRATION OF DICTIONARY ENTITIES

Three listings are included in this section:

- A sample migration program (Figure A-2),
- The Working Storage and Procedure Division of a sample program to delete duplicate syntax from the migration program's output(Figure A-3), and
- A sample OS jobstream which runs the migration programs and Cullinet compilers to migrate selected entities (Figure A-4),

The migration program generates compiler syntax to transfer the named entity, as well as related entities, from one dictionary to another. The type of entity name supplied determines the related entities also migrated (Table 3-4).

The following assumptions were made when the sample migration program was designed:

- All entities to be migrated are linked with:
  CLASS=MIGRDATE
  ATTRIBUTE=date-of migration.
- One of the following entity names is provided as input to the program: dialog name, map name, module name, record name, or element name.
- The version number of all entities is always 1.
- Schemas, DMCL's, and subschemas are not transferred by this program.
- ADS/A applications are not transferred by this program.
- Relationships of entities to other CLASSES, ATTRIBUTES, and documentational items are not migrated.

```
00001        *RETRIEVAL
00002         IDENTIFICATION DIVISION.
00003         PROGRAM-ID.                    BOBHMIG9.
00004         REMARKS.                       THIS PROGRAM MIGRATES
00005                                        IDD ENTITIES FROM ONE DC SYS
00006                                        TO ANOTHER
00007                                        IT INCLUDES CODE FOR MIGRATING
00008                                        ALL DIALOGS THAT USE A GIVEN
00009                                        MODULE.
00010
00011         ENVIRONMENT DIVISION.
00012         INPUT-OUTPUT SECTION.
00013         FILE-CONTROL.
00014            SELECT PUNFILE ASSIGN UT-S-SYSPCH.
00015        *IDMS-CONTROL SECTION.
00016        *PROTOCOL.                      MODE IS BATCH DEBUG
00017        *                               IDMS-RECORDS MANUAL.

00019         DATA DIVISION.
00020        *SCHEMA SECTION.
00021        *DB  IDMSNWKA WITHIN IDMSNTWK.

00023         FILE SECTION.
00024         FD  PUNFILE
00025            RECORDING MODE F
00026            LABEL RECORDS ARE OMITTED
00027            RECORD CONTAINS 80 CHARACTERS.
00028         01  PUN-REC              PIC X(80).
00029         WORKING-STORAGE SECTION.
00030         01  MISCELLANEOUS-FIELDS.
00031            02  COUNTS.
00032               03  TOT-EL-GEN          PIC 9(6)      VALUE ZEROES.
00033               03  TOT-MAP-GEN         PIC 9(6)      VALUE ZEROES.
00034               03  TOT-REC-GEN         PIC 9(6)      VALUE ZEROES.
00035               03  TOT-MOD-GEN         PIC 9(6)      VALUE ZEROES.
00036               03  TOT-PGM-READ        PIC 9(6)      VALUE ZEROES.
00037               03  TOT-EL-READ         PIC 9(6)      VALUE ZERO.
00038               03  TOT-REC-READ        PIC 9(6)      VALUE ZERO.
00039               03  TOT-MOD-READ        PIC 9(6)      VALUE ZERO.
00040            02  END-OF-EL-SW           PIC 9         VALUE ZEROES.
00041            02  END-OF-REC-SW          PIC 9         VALUE ZEROES.
00042            02  END-OF-MOD-SW          PIC 9         VALUE ZEROES.
00043            02  END-OF-PGM-SW          PIC 9         VALUE ZEROES.
00044            02  END-OF-MAP-SW          PIC 9         VALUE ZEROES.
00045            02  SAVE-NEXT-DBKEY        PIC 9(8) COMP VALUE ZEROES.

00047         01  PUN-WORK-EL.
00048            05  PWE-SORT-KEY PIC X VALUE ZEROES.
00049            05  FILLER PIC X(8)  VALUE ' PUN EL '.
00050            05  PWE-INQ-NAM-058 PIC X(30) VALUE SPACES.
00051            05  FILLER              PIC XX VALUE 'V '.
00052            05  PWE-ELEM-VER-058 PIC 9(4) VALUE ZEROES.
00053            05  FILLER              PIC X(26)
00054                                    VALUE ' WITHO REC ATT SYN AS SYN.'.
00055            05  FILLER              PIC X(9) VALUE SPACES.
00056         01  PUN-WORK-DEL-MAP.
00057            05  FILLER PIC X VALUE '8'.
00058            05  FILLER PIC X(9)  VALUE ' DEL MAP '.
00059            05  PWDM-MAP-NAME-098 PIC X(8) VALUE SPACES.
00060            05  FILLER              PIC X VALUE SPACES.
00061            05  FILLER              PIC XXXX VALUE 'VER '.
00062            05  PWDM-MAP-VER-098 PIC 9(4) VALUE ZEROES.
00063            05  FILLER              PIC X  VALUE '.'.
00064            05  FILLER              PIC X(53) VALUE SPACES.
00065         01  PUN-WORK-DEL-PAN.
00066            05  FILLER PIC X VALUE '8'.
00067            05  FILLER PIC X(11) VALUE ' DEL PANEL '.
00068            05  PWDP-PAN-NAME-098 PIC X(8) VALUE SPACES.
00069            05  FILLER              PIC X(9)  VALUE '-OLMPANEL'.
00070            05  FILLER              PIC X VALUE SPACES.
00071            05  FILLER              PIC XXXX VALUE 'VER '.
00072            05  PWDP-PAN-VER-098 PIC 9(4) VALUE ZEROES.
00073            05  FILLER              PIC X  VALUE '.'.
00074            05  FILLER              PIC X(42) VALUE SPACES.
00075         01  PUN-WORK-DEL-REC.
00076            05  FILLER        PIC X VALUE '9'.
00077            05  FILLER PIC X(9)  VALUE ' DEL REC '.
00078            05  PWDR-SR-NAM-036    PIC X(8) VALUE SPACES.
00079            05  FILLER              PIC XX VALUE 'V '.
00080            05  PWDR-RCD-VERS-036 PIC 9(4) VALUE ZEROES.
00081            05  FILLER              PIC X  VALUE '.'.
00082            05  FILLER              PIC X(37) VALUE SPACES.
00083         01  PUN-WORK-REC.
00084            05  PWR-SORT-KEY  PIC X VALUE ZEROES.
00085            05  FILLER PIC X(9)  VALUE ' PUN REC '.
00086            05  PWR-SR-NAM-036     PIC X(30) VALUE SPACES.
00087            05  FILLER              PIC XX VALUE 'V '.
00088            05  PWR-RCD-VERS-036 PIC 9(4) VALUE ZEROES.
```

Figure A-2 Sample Migration Program

```
00089           05  FILLER          PIC X(32)
00090               VALUE ' AS SYN WITHOUT ATT DET HIS.'
00091           05  FILLER          PIC X(5) VALUE SPACES.
00092       01  PUN-WORK-PROG.
00093           05  PWP-SORT-KEY  PIC X VALUE '7'.
00094           05  FILLER PIC X(13)  VALUE ' PUN LOA MOD '.
00095           05  PWP-PROG-NAME-051 PIC X(30) VALUE SPACES.
00096           05  FILLER          PIC XX VALUE 'V '.
00097           05  PWP-PROG-VER-051 PIC 9(4) VALUE ZEROES.
00098           05  FILLER          PIC X(10)
00099               VALUE ' WITH SYN.'.
00100           05  FILLER          PIC X(20) VALUE SPACES.
00101       01  PUN-WORK-MOD.
00102           05  PWM-SORT-KEY  PIC X VALUE ZEROES.
00103           05  FILLER PIC X(9)  VALUE ' PUN MOD '.
00104           05  PWM-MOD-NAME-067 PIC X(30) VALUE SPACES.
00105           05  FILLER          PIC XX VALUE 'V '.
00106           05  PWM-MOD-VER-067 PIC 9(4) VALUE ZEROES.
00107           05  FILLER          PIC X(32)
00108               VALUE ' AS SYN WITHOUT ATT ALL COM TYP.'
00109           05  FILLER          PIC X(2) VALUE SPACES.
00110       01  PUN-WORK-TAB.
00111           05  PWT-SORT-KEY  PIC X VALUE ZEROES.
00112           05  FILLER PIC X(9)  VALUE ' PUN TAB '.
00113           05  PWT-MOD-NAME-067 PIC X(30) VALUE SPACES.
00114           05  FILLER          PIC XX VALUE 'V '.
00115           05  PWT-MOD-VER-067 PIC 9(4) VALUE ZEROES.
00116           05  FILLER          PIC X(32)
00117               VALUE ' AS SYN WITHOUT ATT ALL COM TYP.'
00118           05  FILLER          PIC X(2) VALUE SPACES.
00119       01  PUN-WORK-MAP-FILL.
00120           05  FILLER      PIC X VALUE 'A'.
00121           05  FILLER      PIC X(24) VALUE '  PROCESS=DECOMPILE
00122           05  FILLER      PIC X(56) VALUE SPACES.
00123       01  PUN-WORK-MAP.
00124           05  FILLER      PIC X VALUE 'B'.
00125           05  FILLER PIC X(3)  VALUE SPACES.
00126           05  FILLER  PIC X(4) VALUE 'MAP='
00127           05  PWM-MAP-NAME-098 PIC X(8) VALUE SPACES.
00128           05  FILLER          PIC X VALUE SPACES.
00129           05  FILLER          PIC XX VALUE 'V '.
00130           05  PWM-MAP-VER-098 PIC 9(4) VALUE ZEROES.
00131           05  FILLER          PIC X(59) VALUE SPACES.
00132       01  PUN-WORK-MAPSYN-FILL.
00133           05  FILLER      PIC X VALUE 'C'
00134           05  FILLER      PIC X(24) VALUE '  PROCESS=LOAD
00135           05  FILLER      PIC X(56) VALUE SPACES.
00136       01  PUN-WORK-MAPSYN.
00137           05  FILLER      PIC X VALUE 'E'.
00138           05  FILLER PIC X(3)  VALUE SPACES.
00139           05  FILLER  PIC X(4) VALUE 'MAP='
00140           05  PWMS-MAP-NAME-098 PIC X(8) VALUE SPACES.
00141           05  FILLER          PIC X VALUE SPACES.
00142           05  FILLER          PIC XX VALUE 'V '.
00143           05  PWMS-MAP-VER-098 PIC 9(4) VALUE ZEROES.
00144           05  FILLER          PIC X(59) VALUE SPACES.
00145       01  PUN-WORK-ADSBSYN.
00146           05  FILLER PIC X VALUE 'F'.
00147           05  FILLER PIC X(3)  VALUE SPACES.
00148           05  FILLER  PIC X(15)
00149               VALUE 'GEN LOAD DIAL=('.
00150           05  PWA-DIAL-NAME   PIC X(8) VALUE SPACES.
00151           05  FILLER          PIC XX VALUE ') '.
00152           05  FILLER          PIC XXXXX VALUE 'VER ('.
00153           05  PWA-DIAL-VER    PIC 9(4) VALUE ZEROES.
00154           05  FILLER          PIC XX VALUE ').'.
00155           05  FILLER          PIC X(43) VALUE SPACES.
00156       01  CARD-IMAGE.
00157           02  CI-DATA-IMAGE.
00158             03  CI-KEYFIELDS.
00159               04  FILLER              PIC X.
00160               04  CARD-DATE           PIC 999999 VALUE ZEROES.
00161               04  FILLER              PIC X.
00162               04  CARD-DICTNAME       PIC X(8)   VALUE SPACES.
00163             03  FILLER                PIC X(64).
00164       *   COPY IDMS SUBSCHEMA-CTRL.
                        :
00210       *   COPY IDMS SUBSCHEMA-NAMES.
                        :
00982       *   COPY IDMS ATTRIBUTE-093.
00983       01  ATTRIBUTE-093.
00984           02  ATTR-NAME-093       PIC X(40).
00985           02  DATE-LU-093         PIC X(8).
00986           02  DATE-CREATED-093    PIC X(8).
00987           02  PREP-BY-093         PIC X(8).
00988           02  REV-BY-093          PIC X(8).
00989           02  DEL-CODE-093        PIC X.
00990           02  FILLER              PIC X(0007).
```

Figure A-2 Sample Migration Program (continued)

```
00991     *     COPY IDMS PROG-051.
00992        01  PROG-051.
00993            02  PROG-NAME-051         PIC X(8).
00994            02  PROG-VER-051          PIC 9(4)
00995                                      USAGE COMP.
00996            02  BUILDER-051           PIC X.
00997                                  88  SCHEMA-BUILT-051 VALUE 'S'.
00998                                  88  DIR-BUILT-051 VALUE 'X'.
00999                                  88  SYSGEN-BUILT-051 VALUE 'G'.
01000                                  88  DML-BUILT-051 VALUE 'M'.
01001                                  88  SUBSCH-BUILT-051 VALUE 'V'.
01002                                  88  MAP-BUILT-051 VALUE 'C'.
01003                                  88  SYSGN2-BUILT-051 VALUE 'R'.
01004                                  88  DICT-BUILT-051 VALUE 'D'.
01005            02  ENTRY-051            PIC X.
01006            02  DESCR-051            PIC X(40).
01007            02  DATE-LU-051          PIC X(8).
01008            02  DATE-CREATED-051     PIC X(8).
01009            02  PREP-BY-051          PIC X(8).
01010            02  REV-BY-051           PIC X(8).
01011            02  PROG-DATE-051        PIC X(8).
01012            02  EST-LINES-051        PIC S9(8)
01013                                     USAGE COMP.
01014            02  ISA-SIZE-051         PIC S9(8)
01015                                     USAGE COMP.
01016            02  COUNT-051            PIC S9(4)
01017                                     USAGE COMP.
01018            02  FILLER               PIC X(0006).
01019            02  FILLER               PIC X(0004).
01020     *     COPY IDMS MAPATTR-123.
01021        01  MAPATTR-123.
01022            02  JCT-TEXT-123         PIC X(40).
01023     *     COPY IDMS MAPRCD-125.
01024        01  MAPRCD-125.
01025            02  MAP-INDEX-125        PIC S9(4)
01026                                     USAGE COMP.
01027            02  JCT-TEXT-125         PIC X(40).
01028            02  MAP-RECNAM-125       PIC X(32).
01029            02  RCD-VERS-125         PIC S9(4)
01030                                     USAGE COMP.
01031            02  FILLER               PIC X(0004).
01032     *     COPY IDMS MODLST-055.
01033        01  MODLST-055.
01034            02  JCT-TEXT-055         PIC X(40).
01035            02  BUILDER-055          PIC X.
01036                                  88  SCHEMA-BUILT-055 VALUE 'S'.
01037                                  88  DIR-BUILT-055 VALUE 'X'.
01038                                  88  SYSGEN-BUILT-055 VALUE 'G'.
01039                                  88  DML-BUILT-055 VALUE 'M'.
01040                                  88  SUBSCH-BUILT-055 VALUE 'V'.
01041                                  88  MAP-BUILT-055 VALUE 'C'.
01042                                  88  SYSGN2-BUILT-055 VALUE 'R'.
01043                                  88  DICT-BUILT-055 VALUE 'D'.
01044            02  FILLER               PIC X(0003).
01045            02  FILLER               PIC X(4).
01046     *     COPY IDMS RCDSYN-079.
01047        01  RCDSYN-079.
01048            02  RSYN-NAME-079        PIC X(32).
01049            02  RSYN-VER-079         PIC 9(4)
01050                                     USAGE COMP.
01051            02  BUILDER-079          PIC X.
01052                                  88  SCHEMA-BUILT-079 VALUE 'S'.
01053                                  88  DIR-BUILT-079 VALUE 'X'.
01054                                  88  SYSGEN-BUILT-079 VALUE 'G'.
01055                                  88  DML-BUILT-079 VALUE 'M'.
01056                                  88  SUBSCH-BUILT-079 VALUE 'V'.
01057                                  88  MAP-BUILT-079 VALUE 'C'.
01058                                  88  SYSGN2-BUILT-079 VALUE 'R'.
01059                                  88  DICT-BUILT-079 VALUE 'D'.
01060            02  PREFIX-IND-079       PIC X VALUE ' '.
01061                                  88  PREFIX-079 VALUE 'P'.
01062                                  88  SUFFIX-079 VALUE 'S'.
01063                                  88  NO-PREFIX-079 VALUE ' '.
01064            02  PREFIX-VAL-079       PIC X(10).
01065            02  VIEW-079             PIC X(32).
01066            02  FILLER               PIC X(0006).
01067            02  FILLER               PIC X(4).
01068     *     COPY IDMS RCDCOPY-063.
01069        01  RCDCOPY-063.
01070            02  JCT-TEXT-063         PIC X(40).
01071            02  FILLER               PIC X(0004).
01072            02  FILLER               PIC X(4).
01073     *     COPY IDMS MAP-098.
01074        01  MAP-098.
01075            02  MAP-NAME-098         PIC X(8).
01076            02  MAP-VER-098          PIC 9(4)
01077                                     USAGE COMP.
01078            02  BUILDER-098          PIC X.
01079                                  88  SCHEMA-BUILT-098 VALUE 'S'.
01080                                  88  DIR-BUILT-098 VALUE 'X'.
01081                                  88  SYSGEN-BUILT-098 VALUE 'G'.
01082                                  88  DML-BUILT-098 VALUE 'M'.
```

Figure A-2 Sample Migration Program (continued)

```
01083                                              88  SUBSCH-BUILT-098 VALUE 'V'.
01084                                              88  MAP-BUILT-098 VALUE 'C'.
01085                                              88  SYSGN2-BUILT-098 VALUE 'R'.
01086                                              88  DICT-BUILT-098 VALUE 'D'.
01087                   02  FILLER                     PIC X(0001).
01088                   02  MAP-FLDCNT-098             PIC S9(4)
01089                                                  USAGE COMP.
01090                   02  MAP-RCDCNT-098             PIC S9(4)
01091                                                  USAGE COMP.
01092                   02  MAP-DATE-098               PIC X(8).
01093                   02  MAP-TIME-098               PIC X(6).
01094                   02  MAP-ID-098                 PIC XX.
01095                   02  DESCR-098                  PIC X(40).
01096                   02  PREP-BY-098                PIC X(8).
01097                   02  REV-BY-098                 PIC X(8).
01098                   02  DATE-LU-098                PIC X(8).
01099                   02  DATE-CREATED-098           PIC X(8).
01100                   02  MAP-CURSOR-098             PIC X(32).
01101                   02  MAP-ORG-098                OCCURS 10.
01102                     03  FILLER                   PIC X(0001).
01103                     03  ORIGIN-ROW-098           PIC X.
01104                     03  ORIGIN-COLM-098          PIC X.
01105                   02  FILLER                     PIC X(0001).
01106                   02  MAP-ERR-ON1-098            PIC X.
01107                   02  MAP-ERR-ON2-098            PIC X.
01108                   02  MAP-ERR-ON3-098            PIC X.
01109                   02  MAP-ERR-OF1-098            PIC X.
01110                   02  MAP-ERR-OF2-098            PIC X.
01111                   02  MAP-ERR-OF3-098            PIC X.
01112                   02  MAP-COR-ON1-098            PIC X.
01113                   02  MAP-COR-ON2-098            PIC X.
01114                   02  MAP-COR-ON3-098            PIC X.
01115                   02  MAP-COR-OF1-098            PIC X.
01116                   02  MAP-COR-OF2-098            PIC X.
01117                   02  MAP-COR-OF3-098            PIC X.
01118                   02  FILLER                     PIC X(0001).
01119                   02  FILLER                     PIC X(0004).
01120          *        COPY IDMS PROGMAP-126.
01121          01  PROGMAP-126.
01122                   02  JCT-TEXT-126               PIC X(40).
01123                   02  FILLER                     PIC X(0004).
01124                   02  FILLER                     PIC X(4).
01125          *        COPY IDMS PROGATTR-065.
01126          01  PROGATTR-065.
01127                   02  JCT-TEXT-065               PIC X(40).
01128          *        COPY IDMS SDR-042.
01129          01  SDR-042.
01130                   02  SEQ-042                    PIC 9(6).
01131                   02  DR-LGTH-042                PIC S9(4)
01132                                                  USAGE COMP.
01133                   02  PIC-LGTH-042               PIC S9(4)
01134                                                  USAGE COMP.
01135                   02  DR-BOFF-042                PIC S9(4)
01136                                                  USAGE COMP.
01137                   02  DR-BLTH-042                PIC S9(4)
01138                                                  USAGE COMP.
01139                   02  USE-042                    PIC S9(4)
01140                                                  USAGE COMP.
01141                   02  SYNC-042                   PIC S9(4)
01142                                                  USAGE COMP.
01143                   02  OCC-042                    PIC S9(4)
01144                                                  USAGE COMP.
01145                   02  DR-LVL-042                 PIC 99.
01146                   02  OCC-LVL-042                PIC S9(4)
01147                                                  USAGE COMP.
01148                   02  RDF-LVL-042                PIC S9(4)
01149                                                  USAGE COMP.
01150                   02  DR-NAM-042                 PIC X(32).
01151                   02  PIC-042                    PIC X(32).
01152                   02  SIGN-042                   PIC X.
01153                   02  SEPARATE-042               PIC X.
01154                   02  ISEQ-042                   PIC X.
01155                                              88  ISEQ-ASC-042 VALUE 'A'.
01156                                              88  ISEQ-DES-042 VALUE 'D'.
01157                                              88  ISEQ-NONE-042 VALUE ' '.
01158                   02  BUILDER-042                PIC X.
01159                                              88  SCHEMA-BUILT-042 VALUE 'S'.
01160                                              88  DIR-BUILT-042 VALUE 'X'.
01161                                              88  SYSGEN-BUILT-042 VALUE 'G'.
01162                                              88  DML-BUILT-042 VALUE 'M'.
01163                                              88  SUBSCH-BUILT-042 VALUE 'V'.
01164                                              88  MAP-BUILT-042 VALUE 'C'.
01165                                              88  SYSGN2-BUILT-042 VALUE 'R'.
01166                                              88  DICT-BUILT-042 VALUE 'D'.
01167                   02  ELEM-JUST-042              PIC X.
01168                                              88  JUST-ON-042 VALUE 'J'.
01169                                              88  JUST-OFF-042 VALUE ' '.
01170                   02  ELEM-BONZ-042              PIC X.
01171                                              88  BONZ-ON-042 VALUE 'B'.
01172                                              88  BONZ-OFF-042 VALUE ' '.
01173                   02  ALT-PIC-TYPE-042           PIC S9(4)
01174                                                  USAGE COMP.
```

Figure A-2 Sample Migration Program (continued)

```
01175                   02  VAL-SW-042             PIC X.
01176                   02  SDR-FLAG-042           PIC X.
01177                   02  SCHM-SEQ-042           PIC S9(4)
01178                                              USAGE COMP.
01179                   02  DR-VLGTH-042           PIC S9(4)
01180                                              USAGE COMP.
01181                   02  DR-VBLTH-042           PIC S9(4)
01182                                              USAGE COMP.
01183                   02  DR-VBOFF-042           PIC S9(4)
01184                                              USAGE COMP.
01185                   02  FILLER                 PIC X(0008).
01186                   02  FILLER                 PIC X(4).
01187       *       COPY IDMS CLASS-092.
01188       01  CLASS-092.
01189                   02  CLASS-NAME-092         PIC X(20).
01190                   02  DATE-LU-092            PIC X(8).
01191                   02  DATE-CREATED-092       PIC X(8).
01192                   02  PREP-BY-092            PIC X(8).
01193                   02  REV-BY-092             PIC X(8).
01194                   02  AUTO-ATTR-092          PIC X.
01195                   02  SING-ATTR-092          PIC X.
01196                   02  DEL-CODE-092           PIC X.
01197                   02  ENTITY-092             PIC X.
01198                   02  FILLER                 PIC X(0004).
01199                   02  FILLER                 PIC X(4).
01200       *       COPY IDMS ELEMATTR-090.
01201       01  ELEMATTR-090.
01202                   02  JCT-TEXT-090           PIC X(40).
01203       *       COPY IDMS ELEMNEST-087.
01204       01  ELEMNEST-087.
01205                   02  NEST-CODE-087          PIC S9(8)
01206                                              USAGE COMP.
01207                   02  JCT-TEXT-087           PIC X(40).
01208                   02  EL-OCC-087             PIC S9(4)
01209                                              USAGE COMP.
01210                   02  FILLER                 PIC X(0006).
01211                   02  FILLER                 PIC X(4).
01212       *       COPY IDMS RCDATTR-081.
01213       01  RCDATTR-081.
01214                   02  JCT-TEXT-081           PIC X(40).
01215       *       COPY IDMS MODATTR-069.
01216       01  MODATTR-069.
01217                   02  JCT-TEXT-069           PIC X(40).
01218       *       COPY IDMS MODULE-067.
01219       01  MODULE-067.
01220                   02  MOD-NAME-067           PIC X(32).
01221                   02  MOD-VER-067            PIC S9(4)
01222                                              USAGE COMP.
01223                   02  DATE-LU-067            PIC X(8).
01224                   02  DESCR-067              PIC X(40).
01225                   02  BUILDER-067            PIC X.
01226                                          88  SCHEMA-BUILT-067 VALUE 'S'.
01227                                          88  DIR-BUILT-067 VALUE 'X'.
01228                                          88  SYSGEN-BUILT-067 VALUE 'G'.
01229                                          88  DML-BUILT-067 VALUE 'M'.
01230                                          88  SUBSCH-BUILT-067 VALUE 'V'.
01231                                          88  MAP-BUILT-067 VALUE 'C'.
01232                                          88  SYSGN2-BUILT-067 VALUE 'R'.
01233                                          88  DICT-BUILT-067 VALUE 'D'.
01234                   02  DATE-CREATED-067       PIC X(8).
01235                   02  PREP-BY-067            PIC X(8).
01236                   02  REV-BY-067             PIC X(8).
01237                   02  LANG-067               PIC X(40).
01238                   02  FILLER                 PIC X(0005).
01239       *       COPY IDMS INQ-058.
01240       01  INQ-058.
01241                   02  INQ-NAM-058            PIC X(32).
01242                   02  ELEM-VER-058           PIC 9(4)
01243                                              USAGE COMP.
01244                   02  DATE-LU-058            PIC X(8).
01245                   02  BUILDER-058            PIC X.
01246                                          88  SCHEMA-BUILT-058 VALUE 'S'.
01247                                          88  DIR-BUILT-058 VALUE 'X'.
01248                                          88  SYSGEN-BUILT-058 VALUE 'G'.
01249                                          88  DML-BUILT-058 VALUE 'M'.
01250                                          88  SUBSCH-BUILT-058 VALUE 'V'.
01251                                          88  MAP-BUILT-058 VALUE 'C'.
01252                                          88  SYSGN2-BUILT-058 VALUE 'R'.
01253                                          88  DICT-BUILT-058 VALUE 'D'.
01254                   02  DATE-CREATED-058       PIC X(8).
01255                   02  PREP-BY-058            PIC X(8).
01256                   02  REV-BY-058             PIC X(8).
01257                   02  DESC-058               PIC X(64).
01258                   02  VAL-SW-058             PIC X.
01259                   02  PIC-DEF-058            OCCURS 5.
01260                     03  ALT-PIC-TYPE-058     PIC S9(4)
01261                                              USAGE COMP.
01262                     03  ELEM-LGTH-058        PIC S9(4)
01263                                              USAGE COMP.
01264                     03  PIC-LGTH-058         PIC S9(4)
01265                                              USAGE COMP.
01266                     03  USE-058              PIC S9(4)
01267                                              USAGE COMP.
```

Figure A-2 Sample Migration Program (continued)

```
01268                03  ELEM-JUST-058            PIC X.
01269                                          88 JUST-ON-058 VALUE 'J'.
01270                                          88 JUST-OFF-058 VALUE ' '.
01271                03  ELEM-BONZ-058            PIC X.
01272                                          88 BONZ-ON-058 VALUE 'B'.
01273                                          88 BONZ-OFF-058 VALUE ' '.
01274                03  SIGN-058                 PIC X.
01275                03  SEPARATE-058             PIC X.
01276                03  PIC-058                  PIC X(32).
01277         *     COPY IDMS SR-036.
01278         01  SR-036.
01279             02  SR-NAM-036                  PIC X(32).
01280             02  OCCURS-036                  PIC S9(8)
01281                                             USAGE COMP.
01282             02  RCD-VERS-036                PIC S9(4)
01283                                             USAGE COMP.
01284             02  DLGTH-036                   PIC S9(4)
01285                                             USAGE COMP.
01286             02  BUILDER-036                 PIC X.
01287                                          88 SCHEMA-BUILT-036 VALUE 'S'.
01288                                          88 DIR-BUILT-036 VALUE 'X'.
01289                                          88 SYSGEN-BUILT-036 VALUE 'G'.
01290                                          88 DML-BUILT-036 VALUE 'M'.
01291                                          88 SUBSCH-BUILT-036 VALUE 'V'.
01292                                          88 MAP-BUILT-036 VALUE 'C'.
01293                                          88 SYSGN2-BUILT-036 VALUE 'R'.
01294                                          88 DICT-BUILT-036 VALUE 'D'.
01295             02  DESCR-036                   PIC X(40).
01296             02  DATE-LU-036                 PIC X(8).
01297             02  RECTYPE-036                 PIC X(16).
01298             02  FILLER                      PIC X(0001).
01299             02  ALT-PIC-TYPE-036            PIC S9(4)
01300                                             USAGE COMP.
01301             02  DATE-CREATED-036            PIC X(8).
01302             02  PREP-BY-036                 PIC X(8).
01303             02  REV-BY-036                  PIC X(8).
01304             02  ENT-TYPE-036                PIC X.
01305             02  FILLER                      PIC X(0003).


01307         PROCEDURE DIVISION.
01308         *    **************************************************************
01309         *    *  PROCEDURE DIVISION GENERAL STRATEGY:                     *
01310         *    *  1) READ DATE CARD TO DETERMINE WHERE TO BEGIN MIGRATION  *
01311         *    *  2) OBTAIN THE APPROPO ATTRIBUTE                          *
01312         *    *  3) FOLLOW THE SETS FOR THAT ENTITY TYPE                  *
01313         *    *  4) WRITE OUT THE APPROPO SYNTAX AND NAMES FOR THE ENTITY *
01314         *    *  5) CONTINUE UNTIL END OF ATTRIBUTE-ENTITY CHAIN          *
01315         *    *  OUTPUT RECORDS GO INTO ONE 80 BYTE FILE TO BE SORTED AND *
01316         *    *  LATER SEPERATED INTO INDIVIDUAL FILES AFTER DROPPING     *
01317         *    *  DUPLICATES.  THESE INDIVIDUAL FILES WILL BE INPUT TO     *
01318         *    *  THE VARIOUS COMPILERS WHICH ACTUALLY DO THE EXTRACTION   *
01319         *    *  AND UPDATING OF ENTITIES.                                *
01320         *    *  SORT TAGS FOR THE VARIOUS 80 BYTE RECORDS ARE SET UP AS  *
01321         *    *  FOLLOWS:                                                 *
01322         *    *  0-3 DESIGNATE THE ELEMENT ENTITY (THE ZERO,1,2 OR 3      *
01323         *    *      DEPENDING ON THE ELEMENTS RELATIONSHIP TO OTHER      *
01324         *    *      ELEMENTS IE: GROUP,SUBORDINATE, OR A GROUP OWNED     *
01325         *    *      BY ANOTHER GROUP                                     *
01326         *    *  4   DESIGNATE THE RECORD ENTITY                         *
01327         *    *  5   DESIGNATE THE MODULE ENTITY (SOURCE NOT LOAD)        *
01328         *    *  6   DESIGNATE THE TABLE  ENTITY                         *
01329         *    *  7   DESIGNATE THE LOAD   MOD ENTITY (NEEDED FOR DIALOG   *
01330         *    *      REGENERATION)                                        *
01331         *    *  8   DESIGNATE THE MAP    ENTITY                         *
01332         *    *  9   DESIGNATE THE RECORD ENTITY TO GENERATE DELETE SYN   *
01333         *    *  A   SETS UP A HEADER CARD FOR THE PUNCHING OF MAPS       *
01334         *    *  B   SETS UP CONTROL CARDS FOR THE PUNCHING OF MAPS       *
01335         *    *  C   SETS UP A HEADER CARD FOR THE LOADING OF MAPS        *
01336         *    *  D   SETS UP CONTROL CARDS FOR THE LOADING OF MAPS        *
01337         *    *  E   SETS UP CONTROL CARDS FOR THE GENERATING OF DIALOGS  *
01338         *    *  THE ONLY TRICKY LOGIC IN THIS PROGRAM INVOLVES THE       *
01339         *    *  GENERATING OF THE ELEMENT SYNTAX IN THE APPROPO          *
01340         *    *  SEQUENCE SUCH THAT WHEN IT HITS THE TARGET IDD ALL       *
01341         *    *  SUBORDINATES FOR EACH GROUP ARRIVE FIRST.  IF YOU        *
01342         *    *  FOLLOW THROUGH THE LOGIC AND LOOK AT THE IDD BACHMAN     *
01343         *    *  YOU SHOULD SEE WHY IT'S SET UP THE WAY IT IS.  THE RECORD*
01344         *    *  COUNTS DISPLAYED AT JOB END DO NOT TAKE DUPLICATES       *
01345         *    *  INTO CONSIDERATION - SORRY ABOUT THAT                    *
01346         *    **************************************************************
01347         0000-MAIN-LINE SECTION.
01348         0005-ML-START.
01349             OPEN OUTPUT PUNFILE.
01350             MOVE SPACES TO PUN-REC.
01351             ACCEPT CARD-IMAGE.
01352             IF CARD-DICTNAME = SPACES
01353         *        BIND RUN-UNIT                                       DMLC0001
01354                 MOVE 0001 TO DML-SEQUENCE
01355                 CALL 'IDMS' USING SUBSCHEMA-CTRL
```

Figure A-2 Sample Migration Program (continued)

```
01356                                   IDBMSCOM (59)
01357                                   SUBSCHEMA-CTRL
01358                                   SUBSCHEMA-SSNAME;
01359              ELSE
01360          *     BIND RUN-UNIT DBNAME CARD-DICTNAME.
01361                   MOVE 0002 TO DML-SEQUENCE                          DMLC0002
01362                   MOVE SPACES TO SSC-NODN
01363                   MOVE CARD-DICTNAME TO SSC-DBN
01364                   CALL 'IDMS' USING SUBSCHEMA-CTRL
01365                                   IDBMSCOM (59)
01366                                   SUBSCHEMA-CTRL
01367                                   SUBSCHEMA-SSNAME
01368                                   SUBSCHEMA-CTRL
01369                                   SSC-NODN.
01370              IF ERROR-STATUS = '0000'
01371                   NEXT SENTENCE
01372              ELSE DISPLAY 'INVALID DBNAME ON CARD' CARD-DICTNAME
01373                   PERFORM IDMS-STATUS.
01374          *     BIND ATTRIBUTE-093.
01375                   MOVE 0003 TO DML-SEQUENCE                          DMLC0003
01376                   CALL 'IDMS' USING SUBSCHEMA-CTRL
01377                                   IDBMSCOM (48)
01378                                   SR93
01379                                   ATTRIBUTE-093.
01380          *     BIND PROG-051.
01381                   MOVE 0004 TO DML-SEQUENCE                          DMLC0004
01382                   CALL 'IDMS' USING SUBSCHEMA-CTRL
01383                                   IDBMSCOM (48)
01384                                   SR51
01385                                   PROG-051.
01386          *     BIND MAPATTR-123.
01387                   MOVE 0005 TO DML-SEQUENCE                          DMLC0005
01388                   CALL 'IDMS' USING SUBSCHEMA-CTRL
01389                                   IDBMSCOM (48)
01390                                   SR123
01391                                   MAPATTR-123.
01392          *     BIND MAPRCD-125.
01393                   MOVE 0006 TO DML-SEQUENCE                          DMLC0006
01394                   CALL 'IDMS' USING SUBSCHEMA-CTRL
01395                                   IDBMSCOM (48)
01396                                   SR125
01397                                   MAPRCD-125.
01398          *     BIND MODLST-055.
01399                   MOVE 0007 TO DML-SEQUENCE                          DMLC0007
01400                   CALL 'IDMS' USING SUBSCHEMA-CTRL
01401                                   IDBMSCOM (48)
01402                                   SR55
01403                                   MODLST-055.
01404          *     BIND RCDSYN-079.
01405                   MOVE 0008 TO DML-SEQUENCE                          DMLC0008
01406                   CALL 'IDMS' USING SUBSCHEMA-CTRL
01407                                   IDBMSCOM (48)
01408                                   SR79
01409                                   RCDSYN-079.
01410          *     BIND RCDCOPY-063.
01411                   MOVE 0009 TO DML-SEQUENCE                          DMLC0009
01412                   CALL 'IDMS' USING SUBSCHEMA-CTRL
01413                                   IDBMSCOM (48)
01414                                   SR63
01415                                   RCDCOPY-063.
01416          *     BIND MAP-098.
01417                   MOVE 0010 TO DML-SEQUENCE                          DMLC0010
01418                   CALL 'IDMS' USING SUBSCHEMA-CTRL
01419                                   IDBMSCOM (48)
01420                                   SR98
01421                                   MAP-098.
01422          *     BIND PROGMAP-126.
01423                   MOVE 0011 TO DML-SEQUENCE                          DMLC0011
01424                   CALL 'IDMS' USING SUBSCHEMA-CTRL
01425                                   IDBMSCOM (48)
01426                                   SR126
01427                                   PROGMAP-126.
01428          *     BIND PROGATTR-065.
01429                   MOVE 0012 TO DML-SEQUENCE                          DMLC0012
01430                   CALL 'IDMS' USING SUBSCHEMA-CTRL
01431                                   IDBMSCOM (48)
01432                                   SR65
01433                                   PROGATTR-065.
01434          *     BIND SDR-042.
01435                   MOVE 0013 TO DML-SEQUENCE                          DMLC0013
01436                   CALL 'IDMS' USING SUBSCHEMA-CTRL
01437                                   IDBMSCOM (48)
01438                                   SR42
01439                                   SDR-042.
01440          *     BIND CLASS-092.
01441                   MOVE 0014 TO DML-SEQUENCE                          DMLC0014
01442                   CALL 'IDMS' USING SUBSCHEMA-CTRL
01443                                   IDBMSCOM (48)
01444                                   SR92
01445                                   CLASS-092.
01446          *     BIND ELEMATTR-090.
01447                   MOVE 0015 TO DML-SEQUENCE                          DMLC0015
```

Figure A-2 Sample Migration Program (continued)

```
01448                          CALL 'IDMS' USING SUBSCHEMA-CTRL
01449                                           IDBMSCOM (48)
01450                                           SR90
01451                                           ELEMATTR-090.
01452           *    BIND ELEMNEST-087.                                        DMLC0016
01453                          MOVE 0016 TO DML-SEQUENCE
01454                          CALL 'IDMS' USING SUBSCHEMA-CTRL
01455                                           IDBMSCOM (48)
01456                                           SR87
01457                                           ELEMNEST-087.
01458           *    BIND RCDATTR-081.                                         DMLC0017
01459                          MOVE 0017 TO DML-SEQUENCE
01460                          CALL 'IDMS' USING SUBSCHEMA-CTRL
01461                                           IDBMSCOM (48)
01462                                           SR81
01463                                           RCDATTR-081.
01464           *    BIND MODATTR-069.                                         DMLC0018
01465                          MOVE 0018 TO DML-SEQUENCE
01466                          CALL 'IDMS' USING SUBSCHEMA-CTRL
01467                                           IDBMSCOM (48)
01468                                           SR69
01469                                           MODATTR-069.
01470           *    BIND MODULE-067.                                          DMLC0019
01471                          MOVE 0019 TO DML-SEQUENCE
01472                          CALL 'IDMS' USING SUBSCHEMA-CTRL
01473                                           IDBMSCOM (48)
01474                                           SR67
01475                                           MODULE-067.
01476           *    BIND INQ-058.                                             DMLC0020
01477                          MOVE 0020 TO DML-SEQUENCE
01478                          CALL 'IDMS' USING SUBSCHEMA-CTRL
01479                                           IDBMSCOM (48)
01480                                           SR58
01481                                           INQ-058.
01482           *    BIND SR-036.                                              DMLC0021
01483                          MOVE 0021 TO DML-SEQUENCE
01484                          CALL 'IDMS' USING SUBSCHEMA-CTRL
01485                                           IDBMSCOM (48)
01486                                           SR36
01487                                           SR-036.
01488           *    READY DDLDML USAGE-MODE IS RETRIEVAL.                     DMLC0022
01489                          MOVE 0022 TO DML-SEQUENCE
01490                          CALL 'IDMS' USING SUBSCHEMA-CTRL
01491                                           IDBMSCOM (37)
01492                                           DDLDML.
01493               PERFORM IDMS-STATUS.
01494           0020-ML-LOOP.
01495               MOVE CARD-DATE TO ATTR-NAME-093.
01496           *    FIND CALC ATTRIBUTE-093.                                  DMLC0023
01497                          MOVE 0023 TO DML-SEQUENCE
01498                          CALL 'IDMS' USING SUBSCHEMA-CTRL
01499                                           IDBMSCOM (32)
01500                                           SR93.
01501               IF DB-REC-NOT-FOUND
01502                   DISPLAY 'INVALID DATE CARD ' CARD-DATE
01503           *         FINISH                                              DMLC0024
01504                          MOVE 0024 TO DML-SEQUENCE
01505                          CALL 'IDMS' USING SUBSCHEMA-CTRL
01506                                           IDBMSCOM (02);
01507                   MOVE '0069' TO RETURN-CODE
01508                   GOBACK
01509               ELSE
01510                   PERFORM IDMS-STATUS.
01511               WRITE PUN-REC FROM PUN-WORK-MAP-FILL.
01512               WRITE PUN-REC FROM PUN-WORK-MAPSYN-FILL.
01513               PERFORM 0400-READ-ATTR-PGM THRU 0499-EXIT
01514                   UNTIL END-OF-PGM-SW = 1.
01515               PERFORM 0450-READ-ATTR-MAP THRU 0459-EXIT
01516                   UNTIL END-OF-MAP-SW = 1.
01517               PERFORM 0500-READ-ATTR-EL THRU 0599-EXIT
01518                   UNTIL END-OF-EL-SW = 1.
01519               PERFORM 0600-READ-ATTR-REC THRU 0699-EXIT
01520                   UNTIL END-OF-REC-SW = 1.
01521               PERFORM 0700-READ-ATTR-MOD THRU 0799-EXIT
01522                   UNTIL END-OF-MOD-SW = 1.
01523           *    FINISH.                                                   DMLC0025
01524                          MOVE 0025 TO DML-SEQUENCE
01525                          CALL 'IDMS' USING SUBSCHEMA-CTRL
01526                                           IDBMSCOM (02).
01527               CLOSE PUNFILE.
01528               DISPLAY 'RUN SUCCESSFUL FOR MIGRDATE ' CARD-DATE.
01529               DISPLAY 'TOTAL PROGRAMS INVESTIGATED ' TOT-PGM-READ.
01530               DISPLAY 'TOTAL MAPS      GENERATED ' TOT-MAP-GEN.
01531               DISPLAY 'TOTAL RECORDS   GENERATED ' TOT-REC-GEN.
01532               DISPLAY 'TOTAL ELEMENTS  GENERATED ' TOT-EL-GEN.
01533               DISPLAY 'TOTAL MODULES   GENERATED ' TOT-MOD-GEN.
01534               DISPLAY 'TOTAL ELEMENTS  PUNCHED ' TOT-EL-READ.
01535               DISPLAY 'TOTAL RECORDS   PUNCHED ' TOT-REC-READ.
01536               DISPLAY 'TOTAL MODULES   PUNCHED ' TOT-MOD-READ.
01537               PERFORM 0030-COND-CODE-CHECK THRU 0039-EXIT.
01538               GOBACK.
```

Figure A-2 Sample Migration Program (continued)

```
01539        0030-COND-CODE-CHECK.
01540            IF TOT-MAP-GEN = ZEROES MOVE 0070 TO RETURN-CODE.
01541            IF TOT-PGM-READ = ZEROES
01542                IF TOT-MAP-GEN NOT = ZEROES
01543                    MOVE 0071 TO RETURN-CODE.
01544        0039-EXIT.    EXIT.
01545        0400-READ-ATTR-PGM.
01546            PERFORM 04AA-ATTR-PGM-LOOP THRU 04AA-EXIT
01547                UNTIL END-OF-PGM-SW = 1.
01548        0499-EXIT.
01549            EXIT.
01550        0450-READ-ATTR-MAP.
01551            PERFORM 04GG-ATTR-MAP-LOOP THRU 04GG-EXIT
01552                UNTIL END-OF-MAP-SW = 1.
01553        0459-EXIT.
01554            EXIT.
01555        04AA-ATTR-PGM-LOOP.
01556        *    FIND NEXT PROGATTR-065 WITHIN ATTR-JCT.
01557                    MOVE 0026 TO DML-SEQUENCE                    DMLC0026
01558                    CALL 'IDMS' USING SUBSCHEMA-CTRL
01559                                IDBMSCOM (10)
01560                                SR65
01561                                ATTR-JCT.
01562            IF DB-END-OF-SET
01563                MOVE 1 TO END-OF-PGM-SW
01564                GO TO 04AA-EXIT.
01565            PERFORM IDMS-STATUS.
01566        *    OBTAIN OWNER WITHIN PROG-PROGATTR.
01567                    MOVE 0027 TO DML-SEQUENCE                    DMLC0027
01568                    CALL 'IDMS' USING SUBSCHEMA-CTRL
01569                                IDBMSCOM (31)
01570                                PROG-PROGATTR
01571                                IDBMSCOM (43).
01572            MOVE PROG-NAME-051 TO PWP-PROG-NAME-051.
01573            MOVE PROG-VER-051 TO PWP-PROG-VER-051.
01574            MOVE PROG-NAME-051 TO PWA-DIAL-NAME.
01575            MOVE PROG-VER-051 TO PWA-DIAL-VER.
01576            WRITE PUN-REC FROM PUN-WORK-PROG.
01577            WRITE PUN-REC FROM PUN-WORK-ADSBSYN.
01578            ADD 1 TO                    TOT-PGM-READ.
01579            PERFORM 04BB-EVAL-PGM THRU 04BB-EXIT.
01580        04AA-EXIT.    EXIT.
01581        04BB-EVAL-PGM.
01582        04B1-FIND-MAP.
01583        *    FIND NEXT PROGMAP-126 WITHIN PROG-PROGMAP.
01584                    MOVE 0028 TO DML-SEQUENCE                    DMLC0028
01585                    CALL 'IDMS' USING SUBSCHEMA-CTRL
01586                                IDBMSCOM (10)
01587                                SR126
01588                                PROG-PROGMAP.
01589            IF DB-END-OF-SET
01590                GO TO 04B2-FIND-REC
01591                ELSE PERFORM IDMS-STATUS.
01592        *    OBTAIN OWNER WITHIN MAP-PROGMAP.
01593                    MOVE 0029 TO DML-SEQUENCE                    DMLC0029
01594                    CALL 'IDMS' USING SUBSCHEMA-CTRL
01595                                IDBMSCOM (31)
01596                                MAP-PROGMAP
01597                                IDBMSCOM (43).
01598            PERFORM 04CC-PUN-MAP THRU 04CC-EXIT.
01599        04B2-FIND-REC.
01600        *    FIND NEXT RCDCOPY-063 WITHIN PROG-RCDCOPY.
01601                    MOVE 0030 TO DML-SEQUENCE                    DMLC0030
01602                    CALL 'IDMS' USING SUBSCHEMA-CTRL
01603                                IDBMSCOM (10)
01604                                SR63
01605                                PROG-RCDCOPY.
01606            IF DB-END-OF-SET
01607                GO TO 04B3-FIND-MOD
01608                ELSE
01609                PERFORM IDMS-STATUS.
01610        *    FIND    OWNER WITHIN RCDSYN-RCDCOPY.
01611                    MOVE 0031 TO DML-SEQUENCE                    DMLC0031
01612                    CALL 'IDMS' USING SUBSCHEMA-CTRL
01613                                IDBMSCOM (31)
01614                                RCDSYN-RCDCOPY.
01615        *    OBTAIN OWNER WITHIN SR-RCDSYN.
01616                    MOVE 0032 TO DML-SEQUENCE                    DMLC0032
01617                    CALL 'IDMS' USING SUBSCHEMA-CTRL
01618                                IDBMSCOM (31)
01619                                SR-RCDSYN
01620                                IDBMSCOM (43).
01621            IF SR-NAM-036 = 'ADSO-STAT-DEF-REC'
01622                GO TO 04B2-FIND-REC.
01623            IF SCHEMA-BUILT-036
01624                GO TO 04B2-FIND-REC.
01625            ADD 1            TO TOT-REC-GEN.
01626            PERFORM 06BB-PUN-REC THRU 06BB-EXIT.
01627            MOVE ZEROES TO END-OF-EL-SW.
01628            PERFORM 06CC-REC-EL-LOOP THRU 06CC-EXIT
01629                UNTIL END-OF-EL-SW = 1.
01630            MOVE ZEROES TO END-OF-EL-SW.
01631            GO TO 04B2-FIND-REC.
01632        04B3-FIND-MOD.
01633        *    FIND NEXT MODLST-055 WITHIN PROG-MODLST.
```

Figure A-2 Sample Migration Program (continued)

```
01634                         MOVE 0033 TO DML-SEQUENCE              DMLC0033
01635                         CALL 'IDMS' USING SUBSCHEMA-CTRL
01636                                           IDBMSCOM (10)
01637                                           SR55
01638                                           PROG-MODLST.
01639              IF DB-END-OF-SET
01640                 GO TO 04BB-EXIT
01641              ELSE
01642                 PERFORM IDMS-STATUS.
01643          *    OBTAIN OWNER WITHIN MODULE-MODLST.
01644                         MOVE 0034 TO DML-SEQUENCE              DMLC0034
01645                         CALL 'IDMS' USING SUBSCHEMA-CTRL
01646                                           IDBMSCOM (31)
01647                                           MODULE-MODLST
01648                                           IDBMSCOM (43).
01649              ADD 1              TO TOT-MOD-GEN.
01650              PERFORM 07BB-PUN-MOD THRU 07BB-EXIT.
01651              GO TO 04B3-FIND-MOD.
01652          04BB-EXIT.     EXIT.
01653          04CC-PUN-MAP.
01654              MOVE MAP-NAME-098 TO PWMS-MAP-NAME-098.
01655              MOVE MAP-VER-098 TO PWMS-MAP-VER-098.
01656              WRITE PUN-REC FROM PUN-WORK-MAPSYN.
01657              MOVE MAP-NAME-098 TO PWM-MAP-NAME-098 PWP-PROG-NAME-051.
01658              MOVE MAP-VER-098 TO PWM-MAP-VER-098   PWP-PROG-VER-051.
01659              WRITE PUN-REC FROM PUN-WORK-MAP.
01660              WRITE PUN-REC FROM PUN-WORK-PROG.
01661              ADD 1 TO                          TOT-MAP-GEN.
01662              MOVE MAP-NAME-098 TO PWDM-MAP-NAME-098.
01663              MOVE MAP-VER-098 TO PWDM-MAP-VER-098.
01664              WRITE PUN-REC FROM PUN-WORK-DEL-MAP.
01665              MOVE MAP-NAME-098 TO PWDP-PAN-NAME-098.
01666              MOVE MAP-VER-098 TO PWDP-PAN-VER-098.
01667              WRITE PUN-REC FROM PUN-WORK-DEL-PAN.
01668          04CC-EXIT.     EXIT.
01669          04GG-ATTR-MAP-LOOP.
01670          *    FIND NEXT MAPATTR-123 WITHIN ATTR-JCT.
01671                         MOVE 0035 TO DML-SEQUENCE              DMLC0035
01672                         CALL 'IDMS' USING SUBSCHEMA-CTRL
01673                                           IDBMSCOM (10)
01674                                           SR123
01675                                           ATTR-JCT.
01676              IF DB-END-OF-SET
01677                 MOVE 1 TO END-OF-MAP-SW
01678                 GO TO 04GG-EXIT.
01679              PERFORM IDMS-STATUS.
01680          *    OBTAIN OWNER WITHIN MAP-MAPATTR.
01681                         MOVE 0036 TO DML-SEQUENCE              DMLC0036
01682                         CALL 'IDMS' USING SUBSCHEMA-CTRL
01683                                           IDBMSCOM (31)
01684                                           MAP-MAPATTR
01685                                           IDBMSCOM (43).
01686              PERFORM 04CC-PUN-MAP THRU 04CC-EXIT.
01687              MOVE ZEROES TO END-OF-REC-SW.
01688              PERFORM 04HH-PUN-MAP-REC THRU 04HH-EXIT
01689                 UNTIL END-OF-REC-SW = 1.
01690              MOVE ZEROES TO END-OF-REC-SW.
01691          04GG-EXIT.     EXIT.
01692          04HH-PUN-MAP-REC.
01693          *    FIND NEXT MAPRCD-125 WITHIN MAP-MAPRCD.
01694                         MOVE 0037 TO DML-SEQUENCE              DMLC0037
01695                         CALL 'IDMS' USING SUBSCHEMA-CTRL
01696                                           IDBMSCOM (10)
01697                                           SR125
01698                                           MAP-MAPRCD.
01699              IF DB-END-OF-SET
01700                 MOVE 1 TO END-OF-REC-SW
01701                 GO TO 04HH-EXIT.
01702          *    FIND OWNER WITHIN RCDSYN-MAPRCD.
01703                         MOVE 0038 TO DML-SEQUENCE              DMLC0038
01704                         CALL 'IDMS' USING SUBSCHEMA-CTRL
01705                                           IDBMSCOM (31)
01706                                           RCDSYN-MAPRCD.
01707          *    OBTAIN OWNER WITHIN SR-RCDSYN.
01708                         MOVE 0039 TO DML-SEQUENCE              DMLC0039
01709                         CALL 'IDMS' USING SUBSCHEMA-CTRL
01710                                           IDBMSCOM (31)
01711                                           SR-RCDSYN
01712                                           IDBMSCOM (43).
01713              IF SR-NAM-036 = 'ADSO-STAT-DEF-REC
01714                 GO TO 04HH-EXIT.
01715              IF SCHEMA-BUILT-036
01716                 GO TO 04HH-EXIT.
01717              PERFORM 06BB-PUN-REC THRU 06BB-EXIT.
01718              MOVE ZEROES TO END-OF-EL-SW.
01719              PERFORM 06CC-REC-EL-LOOP THRU 06CC-EXIT
01720                 UNTIL END-OF-EL-SW = 1.
01721              MOVE ZEROES TO END-OF-EL-SW.
01722          04HH-EXIT.     EXIT.
01723          0500-READ-ATTR-EL.
01724          *    FIND CURRENT ATTRIBUTE-093.
01725                         MOVE 0040 TO DML-SEQUENCE              DMLC0040
```

Figure A-2 Sample Migration Program (continued)

```
01726                          CALL 'IDMS' USING SUBSCHEMA-CTRL
01727                                            IDBMSCOM (07)
01728                                            SR93.
01729                    PERFORM IDMS-STATUS.

01731            0510-READ-CLASSATTR.
01732                PERFORM 05AA-ATTR-EL-LOOP THRU 05AA-EXIT
01733                    UNTIL END-OF-EL-SW = 1.
01734            0599-EXIT.
01735                EXIT.
01736            05AA-ATTR-EL-LOOP.
01737        *        FIND NEXT ELEMATTR-090 WITHIN ATTR-JCT.
01738                          MOVE 0041 TO DML-SEQUENCE                   DMLC0041
01739                          CALL 'IDMS' USING SUBSCHEMA-CTRL
01740                                            IDBMSCOM (10)
01741                                            SR90
01742                                            ATTR-JCT.
01743                    IF DB-END-OF-SET
01744                        MOVE 1 TO END-OF-EL-SW
01745                        GO TO 05AA-EXIT.
01746                    PERFORM IDMS-STATUS.
01747        *        OBTAIN OWNER WITHIN INQ-ELEMATTR.
01748                          MOVE 0042 TO DML-SEQUENCE                   DMLC0042
01749                          CALL 'IDMS' USING SUBSCHEMA-CTRL
01750                                            IDBMSCOM (31)
01751                                            INQ-ELEMATTR
01752                                            IDBMSCOM (43).
01753                    PERFORM 05BB-PUN-EL THRU 05BB-EXIT.
01754            05AA-EXIT.     EXIT.
01755            05BB-PUN-EL.
01756                    MOVE INQ-NAM-058 TO PWE-INQ-NAM-058.
01757                    MOVE ELEM-VER-058 TO PWE-ELEM-VER-058.
01758        *        FIND NEXT ELEMNEST-087 WITHIN ELEMNEST-EXPL.
01759                          MOVE 0043 TO DML-SEQUENCE                   DMLC0043
01760                          CALL 'IDMS' USING SUBSCHEMA-CTRL
01761                                            IDBMSCOM (10)
01762                                            SR87
01763                                            ELEMNEST-EXPL.
01764                    IF DB-END-OF-SET
01765                        MOVE 0 TO PWE-SORT-KEY
01766                    ELSE
01767                        PERFORM IDMS-STATUS
01768        *                FIND CURRENT INQ-058
01769                          MOVE 0044 TO DML-SEQUENCE                   DMLC0044
01770                          CALL 'IDMS' USING SUBSCHEMA-CTRL
01771                                            IDBMSCOM (07)
01772                                            SR58;
01773                        PERFORM IDMS-STATUS
01774        *                IF ELEMNEST-IMPL NOT EMPTY
01775                          MOVE 0045 TO DML-SEQUENCE                   DMLC0045
01776                          CALL 'IDMS' USING SUBSCHEMA-CTRL
01777                                            IDBMSCOM (65)
01778                                            ELEMNEST-IMPL;
01779                            IF ERROR-STATUS EQUAL TO '1601'
01780                        MOVE 1 TO PWE-SORT-KEY
01781        *                FIND CURRENT INQ-058
01782                          MOVE 0046 TO DML-SEQUENCE                   DMLC0046
01783                          CALL 'IDMS' USING SUBSCHEMA-CTRL
01784                                            IDBMSCOM (07)
01785                                            SR58;
01786                        PERFORM 05CC-EVAL-NEST THRU 05CC-EXIT
01787                    ELSE
01788                        MOVE 3 TO PWE-SORT-KEY.
01789                    WRITE PUN-REC FROM PUN-WORK-EL.
01790                    ADD 1 TO TOT-EL-READ.
01791            05BB-EXIT.     EXIT.


01793            05CC-EVAL-NEST.
01794        *        FIND NEXT ELEMNEST-087 WITHIN ELEMNEST-EXPL.
01795                          MOVE 0047 TO DML-SEQUENCE                   DMLC0047
01796                          CALL 'IDMS' USING SUBSCHEMA-CTRL
01797                                            IDBMSCOM (10)
01798                                            SR87
01799                                            ELEMNEST-EXPL.
01800                    IF DB-END-OF-SET
01801                        GO TO 05CC-EXIT.
01802        *        FIND OWNER WITHIN ELEMNEST-IMPL
01803                          MOVE 0048 TO DML-SEQUENCE                   DMLC0048
01804                          CALL 'IDMS' USING SUBSCHEMA-CTRL
01805                                            IDBMSCOM (31)
01806                                            ELEMNEST-IMPL;
01807        *        IF ELEMNEST-EXPL NOT EMPTY
01808                          MOVE 0049 TO DML-SEQUENCE                   DMLC0049
01809                          CALL 'IDMS' USING SUBSCHEMA-CTRL
01810                                            IDBMSCOM (65)
01811                                            ELEMNEST-EXPL;
01812                            IF ERROR-STATUS EQUAL TO '1601'
01813                        MOVE 2 TO PWE-SORT-KEY
01814                        GO TO 05CC-EXIT.
01815                    GO TO 05CC-EVAL-NEST.
01816            05CC-EXIT.     EXIT.
```

Figure A-2 Sample Migration Program (continued)

```
01817          0600-READ-ATTR-REC.
01818      *      FIND CURRENT ATTRIBUTE-093.
01819                   MOVE 0050 TO DML-SEQUENCE                    DMLC0050
01820                   CALL 'IDMS' USING SUBSCHEMA-CTRL
01821                       IDBMSCOM (07)
01822                       SR93.
01823              PERFORM IDMS-STATUS.
01824              PERFORM 06AA-ATTR-REC-LOOP THRU 06AA-EXIT
01825                  UNTIL END-OF-REC-SW = 1.
01826          0699-EXIT.
01827              EXIT.
01828          06AA-ATTR-REC-LOOP.
01829      *      FIND NEXT RCDATTR-081 WITHIN ATTR-JCT.
01830                   MOVE 0051 TO DML-SEQUENCE                    DMLC0051
01831                   CALL 'IDMS' USING SUBSCHEMA-CTRL
01832                       IDBMSCOM (10)
01833                       SR81
01834                       ATTR-JCT.
01835              IF DB-END-OF-SET
01836                  MOVE 1 TO END-OF-REC-SW
01837                  GO TO 06AA-EXIT
01838              ELSE
01839                  PERFORM IDMS-STATUS.
01840      *      OBTAIN OWNER WITHIN SR-RCDATTR.
01841                   MOVE 0052 TO DML-SEQUENCE                    DMLC0052
01842                   CALL 'IDMS' USING SUBSCHEMA-CTRL
01843                       IDBMSCOM (31)
01844                       SR-RCDATTR
01845                       IDBMSCOM (43).
01846              PERFORM IDMS-STATUS.
01847              PERFORM 06BB-PUN-REC    THRU 06BB-EXIT.
01848              MOVE ZEROES TO END-OF-EL-SW.
01849              PERFORM 06CC-REC-EL-LOOP THRU 06CC-EXIT
01850                  UNTIL END-OF-EL-SW = 1.
01851              MOVE ZEROES TO END-OF-EL-SW.
01852          06AA-EXIT.    EXIT.
01853          06BB-PUN-REC.
01854              MOVE 4 TO PWR-SORT-KEY.
01855              MOVE SR-NAM-036 TO PWR-SR-NAM-036.
01856              MOVE RCD-VERS-036 TO PWR-RCD-VERS-036.
01857              WRITE PUN-REC FROM PUN-WORK-REC.
01858              ADD 1 TO                              TOT-REC-READ.
01859              MOVE SR-NAM-036 TO PWDR-SR-NAM-036.
01860              MOVE RCD-VERS-036 TO PWDR-RCD-VERS-036.
01861              WRITE PUN-REC FROM PUN-WORK-DEL-REC.
01862          06BB-EXIT.    EXIT.
01863          06CC-REC-EL-LOOP.
01864      *      FIND PRIOR SDR-042 WITHIN SR-SDR.                  DMLC0053
01865                   MOVE 0053 TO DML-SEQUENCE
01866                   CALL 'IDMS' USING SUBSCHEMA-CTRL
01867                       IDBMSCOM (12)
01868                       SR42
01869                       SR-SDR.
01870              IF DB-END-OF-SET
01871                  MOVE 1 TO END-OF-EL-SW
01872                  GO TO 06CC-EXIT
01873              ELSE
01874                  PERFORM IDMS-STATUS.
01875      *      OBTAIN OWNER WITHIN INQ-SDR.                       DMLC0054
01876                   MOVE 0054 TO DML-SEQUENCE
01877                   CALL 'IDMS' USING SUBSCHEMA-CTRL
01878                       IDBMSCOM (31)
01879                       INQ-SDR
01880                       IDBMSCOM (43).
01881              PERFORM IDMS-STATUS.
01882              PERFORM 05BB-PUN-EL THRU 05BB-EXIT.
01883              ADD 1 TO TOT-EL-GEN.
01884          06CC-EXIT.    EXIT.
01885          0700-READ-ATTR-MOD.
01886      *      FIND CURRENT ATTRIBUTE-093.                        DMLC0055
01887                   MOVE 0055 TO DML-SEQUENCE
01888                   CALL 'IDMS' USING SUBSCHEMA-CTRL
01889                       IDBMSCOM (07)
01890                       SR93.
01891              PERFORM IDMS-STATUS.
01892              MOVE ZEROES TO END-OF-PGM-SW.
01893              PERFORM 07AA-ATTR-MOD-LOOP THRU 07AA-EXIT
01894                  UNTIL END-OF-MOD-SW = 1.
01895          0799-EXIT.    EXIT.
01896          07AA-ATTR-MOD-LOOP.
01897      *      FIND NEXT MODATTR-069 WITHIN ATTR-JCT.             DMLC0056
01898                   MOVE 0056 TO DML-SEQUENCE
01899                   CALL 'IDMS' USING SUBSCHEMA-CTRL
01900                       IDBMSCOM (10)
01901                       SR69
01902                       ATTR-JCT.
01903              IF DB-END-OF-SET
01904                  MOVE 1 TO END-OF-MOD-SW
01905                  GO TO 07AA-EXIT
01906              ELSE
01907                  PERFORM IDMS-STATUS.
01908      *      OBTAIN OWNER WITHIN MODULE-MODATTR.
```

Figure A-2 Sample Migration Program (continued)

```
01909                    MOVE 0057 TO DML-SEQUENCE
01910                    CALL 'IDMS' USING SUBSCHEMA-CTRL              DMLC0057
01911                              IDBMSCOM (31)
01912                              MODULE-MODATTR
01913                              IDBMSCOM (43).
01914            PERFORM IDMS-STATUS.
01915            IF LANG-067 = 'TABLE
01916               PERFORM 07CC-PUN-TAB THRU 07CC-EXIT
01917            ELSE
01918               PERFORM 07DD-EVAL-MOD THRU 07DD-EXIT
01919                  UNTIL END-OF-PGM-SW = 1
01920               MOVE ZEROES TO END-OF-PGM-SW
01921               PERFORM 07BB-PUN-MOD  THRU 07BB-EXIT.
01922       07AA-EXIT.    EXIT.
01923       07BB-PUN-MOD.
01924            MOVE 5 TO PWM-SORT-KEY.
01925            MOVE MOD-NAME-067 TO PWM-MOD-NAME-067.
01926            MOVE MOD-VER-067  TO PWM-MOD-VER-067.
01927            WRITE PUN-REC FROM PUN-WORK-MOD.
01928            ADD 1 TO                         TOT-MOD-READ.
01929       07BB-EXIT.    EXIT.
01930       07CC-PUN-TAB.
01931            MOVE 6 TO PWT-SORT-KEY.
01932            MOVE MOD-NAME-067 TO PWT-MOD-NAME-067 PWP-PROG-NAME-051.
01933            MOVE MOD-VER-067  TO PWT-MOD-VER-067 PWP-PROG-VER-051.
01934            WRITE PUN-REC FROM PUN-WORK-TAB.
01935            WRITE PUN-REC FROM PUN-WORK-PROG.
01936            ADD 1 TO                         TOT-MOD-READ.
01937       07CC-EXIT.    EXIT.
01938       07DD-EVAL-MOD.
01939     *    FIND NEXT MODLST-055 WITHIN MODULE-MODLST.
01940                    MOVE 0058 TO DML-SEQUENCE                     DMLC0058
01941                    CALL 'IDMS' USING SUBSCHEMA-CTRL
01942                              IDBMSCOM (10)
01943                              SR55
01944                              MODULE-MODLST.
01945            IF DB-END-OF-SET
01946               MOVE '1' TO END-OF-PGM-SW
01947               GO TO 07DD-EXIT.
01948            PERFORM IDMS-STATUS.
01949     *    OBTAIN OWNER WITHIN PROG-MODLST.
01950                    MOVE 0059 TO DML-SEQUENCE                     DMLC0059
01951                    CALL 'IDMS' USING SUBSCHEMA-CTRL
01952                              IDBMSCOM (31)
01953                              PROG-MODLST
01954                              IDBMSCOM (43).
01955            PERFORM IDMS-STATUS.
01956            MOVE PROG-NAME-051 TO PWP-PROG-NAME-051 PWA-DIAL-NAME.
01957            MOVE PROG-VER-051  TO PWP-PROG-VER-051 PWA-DIAL-VER.
01958            WRITE PUN-REC FROM PUN-WORK-PROG.
01959            WRITE PUN-REC FROM PUN-WORK-ADSBSYN.
01960            ADD 1 TO TOT-PGM-READ.
01961            GO TO 07DD-EVAL-MOD.
01962       07DD-EXIT.    EXIT.
01963     *COPY IDMS IDMS-STATUS.
01964     ***********************************************************************0063100
01965       IDMS-STATUS
01966     **********************************************************SECTION.0063200
                                                                              0063300
01967            IF DB-STATUS-OK GO TO ISABEX.                        0063400
01968            PERFORM IDMS-ABORT.                                  0063500
01969            DISPLAY '***************************'                0063600
01970                    ' ABORTING - ' PROGRAM-NAME                  0063700
01971                    ', ' ERROR-STATUS                            0063800
01972                    ', ' ERROR-RECORD                            0063900
01973                    ' **** RECOVER IDMS ****'                    0064000
01974                    UPON CONSOLE.                                0064100
01975            DISPLAY 'PROGRAM NAME ------ ' PROGRAM-NAME.         0064200
01976            DISPLAY 'ERROR STATUS ------ ' ERROR-STATUS.         0064300
01977            DISPLAY 'ERROR RECORD ------ ' ERROR-RECORD.         0064400
01978            DISPLAY 'ERROR SET -------- ' ERROR-SET.             0064500
01979            DISPLAY 'ERROR AREA -------- ' ERROR-AREA.           0064600
01980            DISPLAY 'LAST GOOD RECORD -- ' RECORD-NAME.          0064700
01981            DISPLAY 'LAST GOOD AREA ---- ' AREA-NAME.            0064800
01982            DISPLAY 'DML SEQUENCE--------' DML-SEQUENCE.         0064900
01983     *      ROLLBACK.
01984                    MOVE 0060 TO DML-SEQUENCE                     DMLC0060
01985                    CALL 'IDMS' USING SUBSCHEMA-CTRL
01986                              IDBMSCOM (67).
01987            CALL 'ABORT'.
01988       ISABEX. EXIT.                                             0065100
01989       IDMS-ABORT.                                               0065200
01990            EXIT.
```

Figure A-2 Sample Migration Program (continued)

```
00079    000850 WORKING-STORAGE SECTION.
00080    000920 01  PUN-WORK-PROG.
00081    000921     05  PWP-SORT-KEY  PIC X VALUE '7'.
00082    000922     05  FILLER PIC X(13) VALUE ' DIS LOA MOD '.
00083    000923     05  PWP-PROG-NAME-051 PIC X(30) VALUE SPACES.
00084    000924     05  FILLER        PIC XX VALUE 'V '.
00085    000925     05  PWP-PROG-VER-051 PIC 9(4) VALUE ZEROES.
00086    000926     05  FILLER        PIC X(15)
00087    000927         VALUE ' WITH HIST DET.'.
00088    000928     05  FILLER        PIC X(15) VALUE SPACES.
00089    001336 01  MISCELLANEOUS-FIELDS.
00090    001337     02  COUNTS.
00091    001338         03  TOT-REC-READ          PIC 9(6)    VALUE ZERO.
00092    001339         03  TOT-REC-WRITTEN       PIC 9(6)    VALUE ZERO.
00093    001340 01  PUN-WORK-REC.
00094    001341     05  PWR-SORT-ID           PIC X.
00095    001342     05  PWR-BUFF-REC          PIC X(79).
00096    001343 01  PUN-HOLD-REC.
00097    001344     05  PHR-SORT-ID           PIC X.
00098    001345     05  PHR-HOLD-REC.
00099    001346         10  FILLER                PIC X(13).
00100    001347         10  PHR-MOD-NAME          PIC X(30).
00101    001348         10  FILLER                PIC XX.
00102    001349         10  PHR-PROG-VER          PIC 9(4).
00103    001350         10  FILLER                PIC X(30).
00104    001351 01  PUN-WORK-REC-FILL.
00105    001352     05  FILLER      PIC 9 VALUE 4.
00106    001353     05  FILLER      PIC X(23) VALUE '
00107    001354     05  FILLER      PIC X(13) VALUE ' .
00108    001360     05  FILLER      PIC X(43) VALUE SPACES.


00110    001950 PROCEDURE DIVISION.
00111    002050 0000-MAIN-LINE SECTION.
00112    002060 0005-ML-START.
00113    002061     OPEN INPUT PUNFILE.
00114    002062     OPEN OUTPUT PUNNFILE.
00115    002063     OPEN OUTPUT LODFILE.
00116    002064     OPEN OUTPUT PRNTFILE.
00117    002065     OPEN OUTPUT MDELFILE.
00118    002066     OPEN OUTPUT RDELFILE.
00119    002067     OPEN OUTPUT RGENFILE.
00120    002068     OPEN OUTPUT MAPFILE.
00121    002069     OPEN OUTPUT MAPSYN.
00122    002070     OPEN OUTPUT ADSBSYN.
00123    002071 0010-READ-PUNFILE.
00124    002072     MOVE SPACES TO PUN-WORK-REC.
00125    002073     READ PUNFILE INTO PUN-WORK-REC
00126    002074         AT END
00127    002075         DISPLAY 'NO RECORDS INPUTTED'
00128    002076         GOBACK.
00129    002077     ADD 1 TO TOT-REC-READ.
00130    002078     MOVE PUN-WORK-REC TO PUN-HOLD-REC.
00131    002080     PERFORM 0100-READ-PUNFILE THRU 0199-EXIT
00132    002200 0100-READ-PUNFILE.
00133    002631     READ PUNFILE INTO PUN-WORK-REC
00134    002632         AT END
00135    002633         PERFORM 0200-WRITE-PUNREC THRU 0299-EXIT
00136    002634         DISPLAY 'SUCCESSFUL COMPLETION '
00137    002635         DISPLAY 'TOTAL RECORDS READ          ' TOT-REC-READ
00138    002636         DISPLAY 'TOTAL RECORDS WRITTEN       ' TOT-REC-WRITTEN
00139    002637         CLOSE PUNFILE  PUNNFILE
00140    002640               MDELFILE RDELFILE RGENFILE
00141    002641               MAPFILE  MAPSYN
00142    002642               ADSBSYN  LODFILE PRNTFILE
00143    002646         GOBACK.
00144    002647     ADD 1 TO TOT-REC-READ.
00145    002648     IF PUN-WORK-REC = PUN-HOLD-REC
00146    002650        GO TO 0100-READ-PUNFILE
00147    002660     ELSE
00148    002670        PERFORM 0200-WRITE-PUNREC THRU 0299-EXIT
00149    002671        MOVE PUN-WORK-REC TO PUN-HOLD-REC
00150    002680        GO TO 0100-READ-PUNFILE.
00151    002911 0199-EXIT.
00152    002912     EXIT.
00153    002920 0200-WRITE-PUNREC.
00154    002921     PERFORM 02AA-EVAL-SORTTAG THRU 02AA-EXIT.
00155    002924     ADD 1 TO TOT-REC-WRITTEN.
00156    002925     IF PHR-SORT-ID = 4
00157    002926        PERFORM 0300-PUN-REC-FILL-CARD THRU 0399-EXIT.
00158    002930 0299-EXIT.    EXIT.
00159    002931 02AA-EVAL-SORTTAG.
00160    002932     IF PHR-SORT-ID = 'A'
00161    002933        MOVE SPACES TO PHR-SORT-ID
00162    002934        WRITE MAP-REC FROM PUN-HOLD-REC
00163    002935        GO TO 02AA-EXIT.
00164    002936     IF PHR-SORT-ID = 'B'
00165    002937        MOVE SPACES TO PHR-SORT-ID
00166    002938        WRITE MAP-REC FROM PUN-HOLD-REC
00167    002939        GO TO 02AA-EXIT.
```

Figure A-3 A Program to Delete Duplicate Entities From Migration Program Output

```
00168  002940      IF PHR-SORT-ID = 'C'
00169  002941          MOVE SPACES TO PHR-SORT-ID
00170  002942          WRITE MAP-SYN FROM PUN-HOLD-REC
00171  002943          GO TO 02AA-EXIT.
00172  002944      IF PHR-SORT-ID = 'E'
00173  002945          MOVE SPACES TO PHR-SORT-ID
00174  002946          WRITE MAP-SYN FROM PUN-HOLD-REC
00175  002947          GO TO 02AA-EXIT.
00176  002948      IF PHR-SORT-ID = 'F'
00177  002949          MOVE SPACES TO PHR-SORT-ID
00178  002950          WRITE ADSB-SYN FROM PUN-HOLD-REC
00179  002951          GO TO 02AA-EXIT.
00180  002952      IF PHR-SORT-ID = '4'
00181  002953          MOVE SPACES TO PHR-SORT-ID
00182  002954          WRITE RGEN-REC FROM PUN-HOLD-REC
00183  002956          GO TO 02AA-EXIT.
00184  002957      IF PHR-SORT-ID = '7'
00185  002958          MOVE SPACES TO PHR-SORT-ID
00186  002959          WRITE LOD-REC FROM PUN-HOLD-REC
00187  002960          MOVE SPACES TO PRNT-REC
00188  002961          MOVE PHR-MOD-NAME TO PWP-PROG-NAME-051
00189  002962          MOVE PHR-PROG-VER TO PWP-PROG-VER-051
00190  002963          WRITE PRNT-REC FROM PUN-WORK-PROG
00191  002964          GO TO 02AA-EXIT.
00192  002965      IF PHR-SORT-ID = '8'
00193  002966          MOVE SPACES TO PHR-SORT-ID
00194  002967          WRITE MDEL-REC FROM PUN-HOLD-REC
00195  002968          GO TO 02AA-EXIT.
00196  002969      IF PHR-SORT-ID = '9'
00197  002970          MOVE SPACES TO PHR-SORT-ID
00198  002971          WRITE RDEL-REC FROM PUN-HOLD-REC
00199  002972          GO TO 02AA-EXIT.
00200  002973      WRITE PUNN-REC FROM PUN-HOLD-REC.
00201  002974  02AA-EXIT.      EXIT.
00202  002980  0300-PUN-REC-FILL-CARD.
00203  002990      WRITE PUNN-REC FROM PUN-WORK-REC-FILL.
00204  003100  0399-EXIT.      EXIT.
```

Figure A-3 A Program to Delete Duplicate Entities From Migration Program
Output (continued)

```
//N         JOB (SYSF        ,0000),
//          CLASS=S,MSGCLASS=3,
//DBMIGR    PROC REG=512K,
//          PGM1=DBMIGRUN,
//          PGM2=DBMIGDUP,
//          CULLIB=C8402,
//          STAGE=TEST,STAGE1=ACPT,
//          COBLIB='PP.SYS1.COBLIB',
//          MIGRLIB='NELSON.LCADLIB.LOAD',
//          SORTLIB='SM01.SORTLIB',
//          SOUT='*'
//*---------------------------------------------------------------*
//*                                                               *
//*             MIGRATION STANDARD ENTITES                        *
//*         (CV MUST BE UP BOTH FOR TEST AND ACPT)                *
//*                                                               *
//*---------------------------------------------------------------*
//*
//MIGRRUN   EXEC PGM=&PGM1,REGION=&REG
//STEPLIB   DD   DSN=&MIGRLIB,DISP=SHR
//          DD   DSN=IDMS.MGT.&STAGE.LOAD,DISP=SHR
//          DD   DSN=IDMS.&CULLIB..LOADLIB,DISP=SHR
//          DD   DSN=&COBLIB,DISP=SHR
//DICTDB    DD   DSN=IDMS.TEST.DICTDB,DISP=SHR
//DLODDB    DD   DSN=IDMS.TEST.DLODDB,DISP=SHR
//DMSGDB    DD   DSN=IDMS.TEST.DMSGDB,DISP=SHR
//J1JRNL    DD   DUMMY
//J2JRNL    DD   DUMMY
//J3JRNL    DD   DUMMY
//SYSJRNL   DD   DUMMY
//SYSOUT    DD   SYSOUT=*
//SYSLST    DD   SYSOUT=*
//SYSPCH    DD   DSN=&&IDDIPT,DISP=(,PASS),UNIT=SYSDA,
//          DCB=(RECFM=FB,LRECL=80,BLKSIZE=8000),
//          SPACE=(CYL,(12,1))
//SYSIN     DD   DUMMY
//*    ********************************************************
//*
//MIGRSORT  EXEC PGM=SORT,REGION=&REG,COND=(69,EQ)
//STEPLIB   DD   DSN=&SORTLIB,DISP=SHR
//SORTLIB   DD   DSN=&SORTLIB,DISP=SHR
//SYSOUT    DD   SYSOUT=*
//SYSPRINT  DD   SYSOUT=*
//SORTPRNT  DD   SYSOUT=*
//SORTMSG   DD   SYSOUT=*
//SORTWK01  DD   DSN=&&WRKAWORK,UNIT=POOL,
//          SPACE=(CYL,(5,1))
//SORTWK02  DD   DSN=&&WRKBWORK,UNIT=POOL,
//          SPACE=(CYL,(5,1))
//SORTWK03  DD   DSN=&&WRKCWORK,UNIT=POOL,
//          SPACE=(CYL,(5,1))
//SORTWK04  DD   DSN=&&WRKDWORK,UNIT=POOL,
//          SPACE=(CYL,(5,1))
//SORTIN    DD   DSN=&&IDDIPT,DISP=SHR
//SORTOUT   DD   DSN=&&IDDSRTD,DISP=(,PASS),UNIT=POOL,
//          DCB=(RECFM=FB,LRECL=80,BLKSIZE=8000),
//          SPACE=(CYL,(12,1))
//SYSIN     DD   DUMMY
//*    ********************************************************
//*
//MIGRDROP  EXEC PGM=&PGM2,REGION=&REG,COND=(69,EQ)
//STEPLIB   DD   DSN=&MIGRLIB,DISP=SHR
//          DD   DSN=&COBLIB,DISP=SHR
//SYSOUT    DD   SYSOUT=*
//SYSPCH    DD   DSN=&&IDDSRTD,DISP=SHR
//SYSPCHN   DD DSN=&&IDDMRG,DISP=(,PASS),UNIT=SYSDA,
//          DCB=(RECFM=FB,LRECL=80,BLKSIZE=8000),
//          SPACE=(CYL,(12,1))
//MDELPCH   DD   DSN=&&MDEL,DISP=(,PASS),UNIT=SYSDA,
//          DCB=(RECFM=FB,LRECL=80,BLKSIZE=8000),
//          SPACE=(CYL,(2,1))
//RDELPCH   DD   DSN=&&RDEL,DISP=(,PASS),UNIT=SYSDA,
//          DCB=(RECFM=FB,LRECL=80,BLKSIZE=8000),
//          SPACE=(CYL,(2,1))
//RGENPCH   DD   DSN=&&RGEN,DISP=(,PASS),UNIT=SYSDA,
//          DCB=(RECFM=FB,LRECL=80,BLKSIZE=8000),
//          SPACE=(CYL,(2,1))
//MAPSYN    DD   DSN=&&MAPSYN,DISP=(,PASS),UNIT=SYSDA,
//          DCB=(RECFM=FB,LRECL=80,BLKSIZE=8000),
//          SPACE=(CYL,(12,1))
//MAPPCH    DD   DSN=&&MAPPCH,DISP=(,PASS),UNIT=SYSDA,
//          DCB=(RECFM=FB,LRECL=80,BLKSIZE=8000),
//          SPACE=(CYL,(12,1))
//ADSBSYN   DD   DSN=&&ADSBPCH,DISP=(,PASS),UNIT=SYSDA,
//          DCB=(RECFM=FB,LRECL=80,BLKSIZE=8000),
//          SPACE=(CYL,(2,1))
//LODPCH    DD   DSN=&&LODPCH,DISP=(,PASS),UNIT=SYSDA,
//          DCB=(RECFM=FB,LRECL=80,BLKSIZE=8000),
//          SPACE=(CYL,(12,1))
//PRNTPCH   DD   DSN=&&PRNTPCH,DISP=(,PASS),UNIT=SYSDA,
//          DCB=(RECFM=FB,LRECL=80,BLKSIZE=8000),
//          SPACE=(CYL,(2,1))
```

Figure A-4 A Sample OS Jobstream to Migrate Entities from One Dictionary to Another

```
//*   ************************************************************
//*
//DDDL1    EXEC PGM=IDMSDDDL,REGION=&REG,COND=(69,EQ)
//STEPLIB  DD  DSN=IDMS.MGT.&STAGE.LOAD,DISP=SHR
//         DD  DSN=IDMS.&CULLIB..LOADLIB,DISP=SHR
//DICTDB   DD  DSN=IDMS.TEST.DICTDB,DISP=SHR
//DLODDB   DD  DSN=IDMS.TEST.DLODDB,DISP=SHR
//DMSGDB   DD  DSN=IDMS.TEST.DMSGDB,DISP=SHR
//J1JRNL   DD  DUMMY
//J2JRNL   DD  DUMMY
//J3JRNL   DD  DUMMY
//SYSJRNL  DD  DUMMY
//SYSLST   DD  DUMMY
//SYSPCH   DD  DSN=&&PCHFIL,DISP=(,PASS),UNIT=POOL,
//         DCB=(RECFM=FB,LRECL=80,BLKSIZE=8000),
//         SPACE=(CYL,(11,1))
//SYSIPT   DD
//         DD  DSN=&&IDDMRG,DISP=(OLD,PASS)
//*   ************************************************************
//*
//DDDL1B   EXEC PGM=IDMSDDDL,REGION=&REG,COND=(69,EQ)
//STEPLIB  DD  DSN=IDMS.MGT.&STAGE.LOAD,DISP=SHR
//         DD  DSN=IDMS.&CULLIB..LOADLIB,DISP=SHR
//DICTDB   DD  DSN=IDMS.TEST.DICTDB,DISP=SHR
//DLODDB   DD  DSN=IDMS.TEST.DLODDB,DISP=SHR
//DMSGDB   DD  DSN=IDMS.TEST.DMSGDB,DISP=SHR
//J1JRNL   DD  DUMMY
//J2JRNL   DD  DUMMY
//J3JRNL   DD  DUMMY
//SYSJRNL  DD  DUMMY
//SYSLST   DD  DUMMY
//SYSPCH   DD  DSN=&&PCHREC,DISP=(,PASS),UNIT=POOL,
//         DCB=(RECFM=FB,LRECL=80,BLKSIZE=8000),
//         SPACE=(CYL,(11,1))
//SYSIPT   DD
//         DD  DSN=&&RGEN,DISP=(OLD,PASS)
//*   ************************************************************
//*
//DDDL1LOD EXEC PGM=IDMSDDDL,REGION=&REG,COND=((71,EQ),(69,EQ))
//STEPLIB  DD  DSN=IDMS.MGT.&STAGE.LOAD,DISP=SHR
//         DD  DSN=IDMS.&CULLIB..LOADLIB,DISP=SHR
//DICTDB   DD  DSN=IDMS.TEST.DICTDB,DISP=SHR
//DLODDB   DD  DSN=IDMS.TEST.DLODDB,DISP=SHR
//DMSGDB   DD  DSN=IDMS.TEST.DMSGDB,DISP=SHR
//J1JRNL   DD  DUMMY
//J2JRNL   DD  DUMMY
//J3JRNL   DD  DUMMY
//SYSJRNL  DD  DUMMY
//SYSLST   DD  DUMMY
//SYSPCH   DD  DSN=&&PCHLOD,DISP=(,PASS),UNIT=POOL,
//         DCB=(RECFM=FB,LRECL=80,BLKSIZE=8000),
//         SPACE=(CYL,(11,1))
//SYSIPT   DD
//         DD  DSN=&&LODPCH,DISP=(OLD,PASS)
//*   ************************************************************
//*
//MPUTOUT  EXEC PGM=RHDCMPUT,REGION=&REG,COND=((70,EQ),(69,EQ))
//STEPLIB  DD  DSN=IDMS.MGT.&STAGE.LOAD,DISP=SHR
//         DD  DSN=IDMS.&CULLIB..LOADLIB,DISP=SHR
//SYSCTL   DD  DSN=IDMS.&STAGE..SYSCTL,DISP=SHR
//SYSLST   DD  DUMMY
//SYSPCH   DD  DSN=&&MPTPCH,DISP=(,PASS),UNIT=POOL,
//         DCB=(RECFM=FB,LRECL=80,BLKSIZE=8000),
//         SPACE=(CYL,(12,1))
//SYSIPT   DD  DSN=&&MAPPCH,DISP=(OLD,PASS)
//*   ************************************************************
//*
//MDEL1IN  EXEC PGM=RHDCMAP1,REGION=&REG,COND=((70,EQ),(69,EQ))
//STEPLIB  DD  DSN=IDMS.MGT.&STAGE1.LOAD,DISP=SHR
//         DD  DSN=IDMS.&CULLIB..LOADLIB,DISP=SHR
//SYSCTL   DD  DSN=IDMS.&STAGE1..SYSCTL,DISP=SHR
//SYSLST   DD  DUMMY
//SYSPCH   DD  DUMMY
//SYSIPT   DD  DSN=&&MDEL,DISP=SHR
//*   ************************************************************
//*
//DDDL2    EXEC PGM=IDMSDDDL,REGION=&REG,COND=(69,EQ)
//STEPLIB  DD  DSN=IDMS.MGT.&STAGE1.LOAD,DISP=SHR
//         DD  DSN=IDMS.&CULLIB..LOADLIB,DISP=SHR
//SYSCTL   DD  DSN=IDMS.&STAGE1..SYSCTL,DISP=SHR
//SYSLST   DD  DUMMY
//SYSPCH   DD  DUMMY
//SYSIPT   DD  DUMMY
//         DD  DSN=&&PCHFIL,DISP=SHR
//*   ************************************************************
//*
//DDDL2B   EXEC PGM=IDMSDDDL,REGION=&REG,COND=(69,EQ)
//STEPLIB  DD  DSN=IDMS.MGT.&STAGE1.LOAD,DISP=SHR
//         DD  DSN=IDMS.&CULLIB..LOADLIB,DISP=SHR
//SYSCTL   DD  DSN=IDMS.&STAGE1..SYSCTL,DISP=SHR
//SYSLST   DD  DUMMY
//SYSPCH   DD  DUMMY
```

Figure A-4 A Sample OS Jobstream to Migrate Entities from One Dictionary to Another (continued)

```
//SYSIPT    DD   DUMMY
//          DD   DSN=&&RDEL,DISP=SHR
//          DD   DSN=&&PCHREC,DISP=SHR
//*         xxxxxxxxxxxxxxxxxxxxxxxxxxxxxxxxxxxxxxxxxxxxxxxx
//*
//DDDL2LOD EXEC PGM=IDMSDDDL,REGION=&REG,COND=((71,EQ),(69,EQ))
//STEPLIB   DD   DSN=IDMS.MGT.&STAGE1.LOAD,DISP=SHR
//          DD   DSN=IDMS.&CULLIB..LOADLIB,DISP=SHR
//SYSCTL    DD   DSN=IDMS.&STAGE1..SYSCTL,DISP=SHR
//SYSLST    DD   DUMMY
//SYSPCH    DD   DUMMY
//SYSIPT    DD   DUMMY
//          DD   DSN=&&PCHLOD,DISP=SHR
//*         xxxxxxxxxxxxxxxxxxxxxxxxxxxxxxxxxxxxxxxxxxxxxxxxx
//*
//MAP1IN   EXEC PGM=RHDCMAP1,REGION=&REG,COND=((70,EQ),(69,EQ))
//STEPLIB   DD   DSN=IDMS.MGT.&STAGE1.LOAD,DISP=SHR
//          DD   DSN=IDMS.&CULLIB..LOADLIB,DISP=SHR
//SYSCTL    DD   DSN=IDMS.&STAGE1..SYSCTL,DISP=SHR
//SYSLST    DD   DUMMY
//SYSPCH    DD   DUMMY
//SYSIPT    DD   DSN=&&MPTPCH,DISP=SHR
//*         xxxxxxxxxxxxxxxxxxxxxxxxxxxxxxxxxxxxxxxxxxxxxxxxx
//*
//MPUTIN   EXEC PGM=RHDCMPUT,REGION=&REG,COND=((70,EQ),(69,EQ))
//STEPLIB   DD   DSN=IDMS.MGT.&STAGE1.LOAD,DISP=SHR
//          DD   DSN=IDMS.&CULLIB..LOADLIB,DISP=SHR
//SYSCTL    DD   DSN=IDMS.&STAGE1..SYSCTL,DISP=SHR
//SYSLST    DD   SYSOUT=&SOUT
//SYSPCH    DD   DUMMY
//SYSIPT    DD   DSN=&&MAPSYN,DISP=SHR
//*         xxxxxxxxxxxxxxxxxxxxxxxxxxxxxxxxxxxxxxxxxxxxxxxxx
//*
//ADSBGEN  EXEC PGM=ADSOBGEN,REGION=1000K,COND=((71,EQ),(69,EQ))
//STEPLIB   DD   DSN=IDMS.MGT.&STAGE1.LOAD,DISP=SHR
//          DD   DSN=IDMS.&CULLIB..LOADLIB,DISP=SHR
//SYSCTL    DD   DSN=IDMS.&STAGE1..SYSCTL,DISP=SHR
//SYSLST    DD   SYSOUT=&SOUT
//SYSPCH    DD   DUMMY
//SYSIPT    DD
//          DD   DSN=&&ADSBPCH,DISP=SHR
//*         xxxxxxxxxxxxxxxxxxxxxxxxxxxxxxxxxxxxxxxxxxxxxxxxx
//*
//PRNTLOD  EXEC PGM=IDMSDDDL,REGION=&REG,COND=((71,EQ),(69,EQ))
//STEPLIB   DD   DSN=IDMS.MGT.&STAGE1.LOAD,DISP=SHR
//          DD   DSN=IDMS.&CULLIB..LOADLIB,DISP=SHR
//DICTDB    DD   DSN=IDMS.ACPT.DICTDB,DISP=SHR
//DLODDB    DD   DSN=IDMS.ACPT.DLODDB,DISP=SHR
//DMSGDB    DD   DSN=IDMS.ACPT.DMSGDB,DISP=SHR
//J1JRNL    DD   DUMMY
//J2JRNL    DD   DUMMY
//SYSJRNL   DD   DUMMY
//SYSLST    DD   SYSOUT=&SOUT
//SYSPCH    DD   DUMMY
//SYSIPT    DD   DUMMY
//          DD   DSN=&&PRNTPCH,DISP=(OLD,PASS)
//*         xxxxxxxxxxxxxxxxxxxxxxxxxxxxxxxxxxxxxxxxxxxxxxxxx
//*
//*------------------------------------------------------------x
//  PEND
//*---------WARNING, WARNING, ANYONE RUNNING THIS JOB        ----
//*---------  THE LAST STEP, ADSOBGEN, INTERMITTANTLY SOC7'S. ----
//*---------  IT SEEMS TO BE ASSOCIATED WITH EITHER A MISSING ----
//*---------  SCHEMA OR SS ASSOCIATED WITH THE DIALOG GENERATED. ----
//*---------  ALWAYS DOUBLE CHECK WHEN MIGRATING THAT ALL SS ----
//*---------  HAVE BEEN SHIPPED OVER PROPERLY!!!!!!!!!!!!!!----
//DTEST1 EXEC  DBMIGR
//*DTEST1 EXEC  DBMIGR,COND.DDDL1=(99,NE),COND.DDDL1B=(99,NE),
//*            COND.DDDL1LOD=(99,NE),
//*            COND.MPUTOUT=(99,NE),
//*            COND.MDEL1IN=(99,NE),COND.DDDL2=(99,NE),
//*            COND.DDDL2B=(99,NE),
//*            COND.DDDL2LOD=(99,NE),
//*            COND.MAP1IN=(99,NE),COND.MPUTIN=(99,NE),
//*            COND.ADSBGEN=(99,NE),
//*            COND.PRNTLOD=(99,NE)
//MIGRRUN.SYSIN  DD *
R21005
//MIGRSORT.SYSIN  DD *
 SORT FIELDS=(1,46,CH,A),EQUALS
 END
//*
//DDDL1.SYSIPT  DD *
    SIGNON USER=DA-ADMN PAS=     USA RET.
    SET OPT FOR SES INP 3 THRU 80.
//DDDL1B.SYSIPT  DD *
    SIGNON USER=DA-ADMN PAS=     USA RET.
    SET OPT FOR SES INP 3 THRU 80.
//DDDL1LOD.SYSIPT  DD *
    SIGNON USER=DA-ADMN PAS=     USA RET.
    SET OPT FOR SES INP 3 THRU 80.
```

Figure A-4 A Sample OS Jobstream to Migrate Entities from One Dictionary to Another (continued)

```
//DDDL2.SYSIPT   DD *
        SIGNON USER=DA-ADMN PAS=        USA PRO UPD.
        SET OPT FOR SES INP 2 THRU 80 DEF IS ON.
//DDDL2B.SYSIPT   DD *
        SIGNON USER=DA-ADMN PAS=        USA PRO UPD.
        SET OPT FOR SES INP 2 THRU 80 DEF IS OFF.
//DDDL2LOD.SYSIPT   DD *
        SIGNON USER=DA-ADMN PAS=
        SET OPT FOR SES INP 2 THRU 80.
//ADSBGEN.SYSIPT   DD *
     ICTL=(1,72)
//      DD  DSN=&&ADSBPCH,DISP=SHR
//PRNTLOD.SYSIPT   DD *
        SIGNON USER=DA-ADMN PAS=      USA RET.
        SET OPT FOR SES INP 2 THRU 80.
//
```

Figure A-4 A Sample OS Jobstream to Migrate Entities from One Dictionary to
Another (continued)

A.3 SAMPLE LISTINGS FROM CREATION OF TEST AND PRODUCTION SYSTEMS

Sample listings are included from creation of test and production systems. These listings should be viewed only as examples because they are tailored to the processing requirements of one site. Table A-1 lists the processing characteristics of the test and production systems at that site.

Table A-1 Processing Characteristics at the Sample Site

Test System	Production System
No ASF	No ASF
Batch development	Batch processing
Some ADS/O development	Some ADS/O processing
OLQ used	OLQ not used

Three types of information are included for each system:

- System generation,
- Global DMCL, and
- #DCPARM information

Full system generation materials were not included because they are voluminous. Instead, two types of system generation information are included:

- Actual system generation syntax for the SYSTEM, ADSO, and OLM statements, and
- Output from a Culprit report listing the resident programs included in the sysgen.

Figures A-5 through A-8 are sample listings from creation of a test system. Figures A-9 through A-12 are sample listings from creation of a production system.

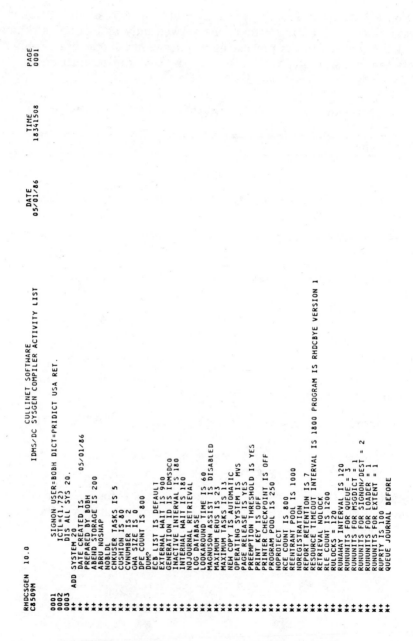

```
RHDCSGEN  10.0                    CULLINET SOFTWARE                          DATE        TIME        PAGE
C8509M                    IDMS/DC SYSGEN COMPILER ACTIVITY LIST            05/01/86    18341508     0001

0001           SIGNON USER=BOBH DICT=PRIDICT USA RET.
0002           ICTL=(1,72)
0003           DS ALL SYS 20.
     ADD SYSTEM 20
**        DATE CREATED IS.        05/01/86
**        PREPARED BY BOBH
**        ABEND STORAGE IS  200
**        ABRU NOSWAP
**        NOBLDL
**        CHKUSER TASKS IS  5
**        CUSHION IS 80
**        CVNUMBER IS 2
**        GWA SIZE IS 0
**        DPE COUNT IS 800
**        DUMP
**        ECB LIST IS DEFAULT
**        EXTERNAL WAIT IS 900
**        GENERATION ID IS IDMSDC0
**        INACTIVE INTERVAL IS 180
**        INTERNAL WAIT IS 180
**        NOJOURNAL RETRIEVAL
**        LOG DATABASE
**        LOOKAROUND TIME IS 60
**        MAGNUSON ASSIST IS DISABLED
**        MAXIMUM ERUS IS 23
**        MAXIMUM TASKS IS 13
**        NEW COPY IS AUTOMATIC
**        OPERATING SYSTEM IS MVS
**        PAGE RELEASE IS YES
**        PREEMPTION THRESHOLD IS YES
**        PRINT KEY IS OFF
**        PRINTER CHECKPOINT IS OFF
**        PROGRAM POOL IS 250
**        NOPROTECT
**        RCE COUNT IS 800
**        REENTRANT POOL IS 1000
**        NOREGISTRATION
**        REPORT RETENTION IS 7
**        RESOURCE TIMEOUT INTERVAL IS 1800 PROGRAM IS RHDCBYE VERSION 1
**        RETRIEVAL NOLOCK
**        RLE COUNT IS 1200
**        RULOCKS = 120
**        RUNAWAY INTERVAL IS 120
**        RUNUNITS FOR QUEUE = 3
**        RUNUNITS FOR MSGDICT = 1
**        RUNUNITS FOR SIGNON/DEST = 2
**        RUNUNITS FOR LOADER = 1
**        RUNUNITS FOR EXTENT = 1
**        RUPRTY IS 100
**        QUEUE JOURNAL BEFORE
```

Figure A-5 Test System Generation Statements

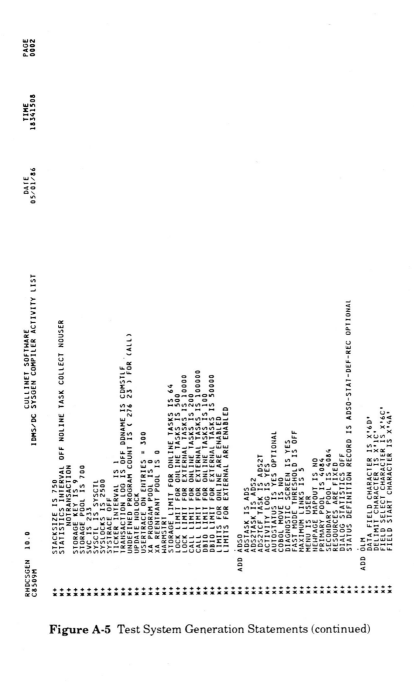

Figure A-5 Test System Generation Statements (continued)

```
RHDCSGEN  10.0        IDMS/DC  CULLINET SOFTWARE        DATE        TIME      PAGE
C8509M               SYSGEN COMPILER ACTIVITY LIST    05/01/86   18341508    0003

     **   TRANSLATE CHARACTER IS C'?'
     **   MODE IS STEP
     **   NEW COPY IS YES
     **   NUMERIC FIELD ORDER IS STANDARD
     **   NUMERIC DECIMAL-POINT IS PERIOD
     **   PAGE FORWARD PFKEY IS PF8
     **   PAGE BACKWARD PFKEY IS PF7
     **   PAGING STORAGE IS 20
     **   QUEUE RETENTION IS 60
```

```
RHDCSGEN  10.0        IDMS/DC  CULLINET SOFTWARE        DATE        TIME      PAGE
C8509M               SYSGEN COMPILER ACTIVITY LIST    05/01/86   18341508    0004

                    **  TRANSACTION SUMMARY  **

ENTITY              ADD  MODIFY  REPLACE  DELETE  DISPLAY
.......            ...  ......  .......  ......  .......
SYSTEM              0     0        0        0       1
IDMS AREA           0     0        0        0       1
IDMS BUFFER         0     0        0        0       1
IDMS PROGRAM        0     0        0        0       1
STORAGE POOL        0     0        0        0       1
XA STORAGE POOL     0     0        0        0       1
DDS                 0     0        0        0       1
DBNAME              0     0        0        0       1
AUTOTASK            0     0        0        0       1
KEYS                0     0        0        0       1
ADSO                0     0        0        0       1
OLQ                 0     0        0        0       1
OLM                 0     0        0        0       1
MAPTYPE             0     0        0        0       1
IDD                 0     0        0        0       1
LINE                0     0        0        0       1
PTERM               0     0        0        0       1
LTERM               0     0        0        0       1
DESTINATION         0     0        0        0       1
QUEUE               0     0        0        0       1
USER                0     0        0        0       1
DEFAULT PERM PROGRAM 0    0        0        0       1
DEFAULT TEMP PROGRAM 0    0        0        0       1
PROGRAM             0     0        0        0       1
TASK                0     0        0        0       1

NO ERRORS OR WARNINGS ISSUED FOR THIS COMPILE
```

Figure A-5 Test System Generation Statements (continued)

```
REPORT NO. 19                   IDMS-DC SOURCE REPORT  C8509M                                          04/14/86  PAGE  1
CREPORT 019                     SYSTEM NAME: DCSYSTEM
                                SYSTEM VERSION: 20
                                PROGRAM DESCRIPTION

PROGRAM    TYPE      BUILDER ACTION VERSION

ADSOGEN1   PROGRAM      G      U      1      ISA-SIZE     ERROR        DUMP         SECURITY
                                              0           THRESHOLD    THRESHOLD    CLASS CODE
                                                          0            0            0
                                             CONCURRENT   REUSABLE     REENTRANT    OVERLAYABLE  DISABLED  PROTECT  LANGUAGE   SAVE   RESIDENT  NEW COPY
                                              YES          YES          REENTRANT    YES          NO        YES      ASSEMBLER  AREA   YES       NO
                                                                                                                               NO

ADSOGEN2   PROGRAM      G      U      1      ISA-SIZE     ERROR        DUMP         SECURITY
                                              0           THRESHOLD    THRESHOLD    CLASS CODE
                                                          5            0            0
                                             CONCURRENT   REUSABLE     REENTRANT    OVERLAYABLE  DISABLED  PROTECT  LANGUAGE   SAVE   RESIDENT  NEW COPY
                                              YES          YES          REENTRANT    YES          NO        NO       ASSEMBLER  AREA   YES       NO
                                                                                                                               NO

ADSUMAIN   PROGRAM      G      U      1      ISA-SIZE     ERROR        DUMP         SECURITY
                                              0           THRESHOLD    THRESHOLD    CLASS CODE
                                                          5            0            0
                                             CONCURRENT   REUSABLE     REENTRANT    OVERLAYABLE  DISABLED  PROTECT  LANGUAGE   SAVE   RESIDENT  NEW COPY
                                              YES          YES          REENTRANT    YES          NO        YES      ASSEMBLER  AREA   YES       NO
                                                                                                                               NO

ADSOMENU   MAP          G      U      1      ISA-SIZE     ERROR        DUMP         SECURITY
                                              0           THRESHOLD    THRESHOLD    CLASS CODE
                                                          5            0            0
                                             CONCURRENT   REUSABLE     REENTRANT    OVERLAYABLE  DISABLED  PROTECT  LANGUAGE   SAVE   RESIDENT  NEW COPY
                                              YES          YES          REENTRANT    YES          NO        YES      ASSEMBLER  AREA   YES       NO
                                                                                                                               NO

ADSORUN1   PROGRAM      G      U      1      ISA-SIZE     ERROR        DUMP         SECURITY
                                              0           THRESHOLD    THRESHOLD    CLASS CODE
                                                          5            0            0
                                             CONCURRENT   REUSABLE     REENTRANT    OVERLAYABLE  DISABLED  PROTECT  LANGUAGE   SAVE   RESIDENT  NEW COPY
                                              YES          YES          REENTRANT    YES          NO        YES      ASSEMBLER  AREA   YES       NO
                                                                                                                               NO

IDDSCIDD   PROGRAM      G      U      1      ISA-SIZE     ERROR        DUMP         SECURITY
                                              0           THRESHOLD    THRESHOLD    CLASS CODE
                                                          5            0            0
                                             CONCURRENT   REUSABLE     REENTRANT    OVERLAYABLE  DISABLED  PROTECT  LANGUAGE   SAVE   RESIDENT  NEW COPY
                                              YES          YES          REENTRANT    YES          NO        NO       ASSEMBLER  AREA   YES       NO
                                                                                                                               NO

IDDSMAIN   PROGRAM      G      U      1      ISA-SIZE     ERROR        DUMP         SECURITY
                                              0           THRESHOLD    THRESHOLD    CLASS CODE
                                                          5            0            0
                                             CONCURRENT   REUSABLE     REENTRANT    OVERLAYABLE  DISABLED  PROTECT  LANGUAGE   SAVE   RESIDENT  NEW COPY
                                              YES          YES          REENTRANT    YES          NO        YES      ASSEMBLER  AREA   YES       NO
                                                                                                                               NO
```

Figure A-6 Test System Resident Programs

REPORT NO. 19
CREPORT 019

IDMS-DC SOURCE REPORT   C8509M
SYSTEM NAME: DN.DCSYSTEM
SYSTEM VERSION: 20
PROGRAM DESCRIPTION

04/14/86 PAGE 2

PROGRAM	TYPE	BUILDER	ACTION	VERSION
IDDSMAP	MAP	G	U	1
IDDSMOEN	PROGRAM	G	U	1
IDDSMUTL	PROGRAM	G	U	1
IDMSCOMP	PROGRAM	G	U	1
IDMSDCOM	PROGRAM	G	U	1
IDMSDDDC	PROGRAM	G	U	1
IDMSNHKA	SUBSCHEMA	X	U	1

For each program the following attributes are listed:

IDDSMAP:
ISA-SIZE	ERROR THRESHOLD	DUMP THRESHOLD	SECURITY CLASS CODE	LANGUAGE	SAVE AREA	RESIDENT
0	5	0	0	ASSEMBLER	NO	YES
CONCURRENT	REUSABLE	REENTRANT	OVERLAYABLE	DISABLED	PROTECT	NEW COPY
YES	YES	REENTRANT	YES		NO	NO

IDDSMOEN:
ISA-SIZE	ERROR THRESHOLD	DUMP THRESHOLD	SECURITY CLASS CODE	LANGUAGE	SAVE AREA	RESIDENT
0	5	0	0	ASSEMBLER	NO	YES
CONCURRENT	REUSABLE	REENTRANT	OVERLAYABLE	DISABLED	PROTECT	NEW COPY
YES	YES	REENTRANT	YES		NO	NO

IDDSMUTL:
ISA-SIZE	ERROR THRESHOLD	DUMP THRESHOLD	SECURITY CLASS CODE	LANGUAGE	SAVE AREA	RESIDENT
0	5	0	0	ASSEMBLER	NO	YES
CONCURRENT	REUSABLE	REENTRANT	OVERLAYABLE	DISABLED	PROTECT	NEW COPY
YES	YES	REENTRANT	YES		NO	NO

IDMSCOMP:
ISA-SIZE	ERROR THRESHOLD	DUMP THRESHOLD	SECURITY CLASS CODE	LANGUAGE	SAVE AREA	RESIDENT
0	5	0	0	ASSEMBLER	YES	YES
CONCURRENT	REUSABLE	REENTRANT	OVERLAYABLE	DISABLED	PROTECT	NEW COPY
YES	YES	REENTRANT	NO		NO	NO

IDMSDCOM:
ISA-SIZE	ERROR THRESHOLD	DUMP THRESHOLD	SECURITY CLASS CODE	LANGUAGE	SAVE AREA	RESIDENT
0	5	0	0	ASSEMBLER	YES	YES
CONCURRENT	REUSABLE	REENTRANT	OVERLAYABLE	DISABLED	PROTECT	NEW COPY
YES	YES	REENTRANT	NO		NO	NO

IDMSDDDC:
ISA-SIZE	ERROR THRESHOLD	DUMP THRESHOLD	SECURITY CLASS CODE	LANGUAGE	SAVE AREA	RESIDENT
0	5	0	0	ASSEMBLER	YES	YES
CONCURRENT	REUSABLE	REENTRANT	OVERLAYABLE	DISABLED	PROTECT	NEW COPY
YES	YES	REENTRANT	YES		NO	NO

IDMSNHKA:
ISA-SIZE	ERROR THRESHOLD	DUMP THRESHOLD	SECURITY CLASS CODE	LANGUAGE	SAVE AREA	RESIDENT
0	5	0	0	ASSEMBLER	NO	YES
CONCURRENT	REUSABLE	REENTRANT	OVERLAYABLE	DISABLED	PROTECT	NEW COPY
YES	YES	REENTRANT	YES		NO	NO

Figure A-6 Test System Resident Programs (continued)

```
REPORT NO. 19                    IDMS-DC SOURCE REPORT    C8509M              04/14/86 PAGE  5
CREPORT 019                      SYSTEM NAME: DCSYSTEM
                                 SYSTEM VERSION 20
                                 PROGRAM DESCRIPTION

PROGRAM    TYPE         BUILDER ACTION VERSION

IDMSNHKS   SUBSCHEMA       G       U      1

            ISA-SIZE      ERROR        DUMP         SECURITY
              0         THRESHOLD   THRESHOLD      CLASS CODE   OVERLAYABLE  LANGUAGE   DISABLED  SAVE     PROTECT  RESIDENT  NEW COPY
                            5       REENTRANT          0            YES     ASSEMBLER    NO      AREA       NO       YES        NO
            CONCURRENT   REUSABLE   REENTRANT                                                    NO
              YES          YES

IDMSOLQS   PROGRAM         G       U      1

            ISA-SIZE      ERROR        DUMP         SECURITY
              0         THRESHOLD   THRESHOLD      CLASS CODE   OVERLAYABLE  LANGUAGE   DISABLED  SAVE     PROTECT  RESIDENT  NEW COPY
                            5       REENTRANT          0            YES     ASSEMBLER    NO      AREA       NO       YES        NO
            CONCURRENT   REUSABLE   REENTRANT                                                    NO
              YES          YES

OLQSDCAN   PROGRAM         G       U      1

            ISA-SIZE      ERROR        DUMP         SECURITY
              0         THRESHOLD   THRESHOLD      CLASS CODE   OVERLAYABLE  LANGUAGE   DISABLED  SAVE     PROTECT  RESIDENT  NEW COPY
                            5       REENTRANT          0            YES     ASSEMBLER    NO      AREA       NO       YES        NO
            CONCURRENT   REUSABLE   REENTRANT                                                    NO
              YES          YES

OLQSGCAN   PROGRAM         G       U      1

            ISA-SIZE      ERROR        DUMP         SECURITY
              0         THRESHOLD   THRESHOLD      CLASS CODE   OVERLAYABLE  LANGUAGE   DISABLED  SAVE     PROTECT  RESIDENT  NEW COPY
                            5       REENTRANT          0            YES     ASSEMBLER    NO      AREA       NO       YES        NO
            CONCURRENT   REUSABLE   REENTRANT                                                    NO
              YES          YES

OLQSPARS   PROGRAM         G       U      1

            ISA-SIZE      ERROR        DUMP         SECURITY
              0         THRESHOLD   THRESHOLD      CLASS CODE   OVERLAYABLE  LANGUAGE   DISABLED  SAVE     PROTECT  RESIDENT  NEW COPY
                            5       REENTRANT          0            YES     ASSEMBLER    NO      AREA       NO       YES        NO
            CONCURRENT   REUSABLE   REENTRANT                                                    NO
              YES          YES

RHDCOMGP   PROGRAM         G       U      1

            ISA-SIZE      ERROR        DUMP         SECURITY
              0         THRESHOLD   THRESHOLD      CLASS CODE   OVERLAYABLE  LANGUAGE   DISABLED  SAVE     PROTECT  RESIDENT  NEW COPY
                            5       REENTRANT          0            YES     ASSEMBLER    NO      AREA       NO       YES        NO
            CONCURRENT   REUSABLE   REENTRANT                                                    NO
              YES          YES

RHDCOMM1   MAP             G       U      1

            ISA-SIZE      ERROR        DUMP         SECURITY
              0         THRESHOLD   THRESHOLD      CLASS CODE   OVERLAYABLE  LANGUAGE   DISABLED  SAVE     PROTECT  RESIDENT  NEW COPY
                            5       REENTRANT          0            YES     ASSEMBLER    NO      AREA       NO       YES        NO
            CONCURRENT   REUSABLE   REENTRANT                                                    NO
              YES          YES

RHDCOMTC   PROGRAM         G       U      1

            ISA-SIZE      ERROR        DUMP         SECURITY
              0         THRESHOLD   THRESHOLD      CLASS CODE   OVERLAYABLE  LANGUAGE   DISABLED  SAVE     PROTECT  RESIDENT  NEW COPY
                            5       REENTRANT          0            YES     ASSEMBLER    NO      AREA       YES      YES        NO
            CONCURRENT   REUSABLE   REENTRANT                                                    NO
              YES          YES
```

Figure A-6 Test System Resident Programs (continued)

```
DEVICE-MEDIA DESCRIPTION.                                           00000010
DEVICE-MEDIA NAME IS TESTDMCL SCHEMA NAME TESTCHEM VERSION 1.       00000020
                                                                   00000030
DATE.                                04/08/86.                      00000040
                                                                   00000070
BUFFER SECTION.                                                    00000080
                                                                   00000130
      BUFFER NAME IS DICT-BUFFER                                    00000090
         PAGE CONTAINS 3860 CHARACTERS                            00000150
         BUFFER CONTAINS 17 PAGES.                                00000120
                                                                   00000130
      BUFFER NAME IS LOAD-BUFFER                                   00000090
         PAGE CONTAINS 3860 CHARACTERS                            00000150
         BUFFER CONTAINS 10 PAGES.                                00000120
                                                                   00000130
      BUFFER NAME IS LOG-BUFFER                                    00000140
         PAGE CONTAINS 3860 CHARACTERS                            00000150
         BUFFER CONTAINS 3 PAGES.                                 00000170
                                                                   00000130
      BUFFER NAME IS SCRQUE-BUFFER                                 00000090
         PAGE CONTAINS 2004 CHARACTERS                            00000150
         BUFFER CONTAINS 10 PAGES.                                00000120
                                                                   00000130
      BUFFER NAME IS MSG-BUFFER                                    00000090
         PAGE CONTAINS 3860 CHARACTERS                            00000150
         BUFFER CONTAINS 3 PAGES.                                 00000120
                                                                   00000130
      BUFFER NAME IS IDMSR-BUFFER          .                       00000140
         PAGE CONTAINS 3860 CHARACTERS                            00000150
         BUFFER CONTAINS 3 PAGES.                                 00000170
                                                                   00000130
      BUFFER NAME IS GENERAL1-BUFFER                               00000090
         PAGE CONTAINS 4628 CHARACTERS                            00000100
         BUFFER CONTAINS 3 PAGES.                                 00000120

      BUFFER NAME IS DICTGL-BUFFER
         PAGE CONTAINS 3020 CHARACTERS
         BUFFER CONTAINS 7 PAGES.

      BUFFER NAME IS LODGL-BUFFER
         PAGE CONTAINS 4096 CHARACTERS
         BUFFER CONTAINS 6 PAGES.

      BUFFER NAME IS CGL-BUFFER
         PAGE CONTAINS 3020 CHARACTERS
         BUFFER CONTAINS 15 PAGES.

      JOURNAL BUFFER NAME JRNL-BUFF                                00000140
         PAGE CONTAINS 7476 CHARACTERS                            00000150
         BUFFER CONTAINS 3 PAGES.                                 00000170
                                                                   00000120
   AREA SECTION.                                                   00000190
*  DICTIONARY AREAS     ***********************************************00000260
      COPY DDLDML AREA BUFFER DICT-BUFFER                          00000280
         PAGE CONTAINS 3860 CHARACTERS.                           00000300
      COPY DDLDCMSG AREA BUFFER MSG-BUFFER                         00000310
         PAGE CONTAINS 3860 CHARACTERS.                           00000330
      COPY DDLDCLOD AREA BUFFER LOAD-BUFFER                        00000340
         PAGE CONTAINS 3860 CHARACTERS.                           00000360
```

Figure A-7 Test System Global DMCL

```
       COPY DDLDCQUE AREA BUFFER SCRQUE-BUFFER              00000370
          PAGE CONTAINS 2004 CHARACTERS.                    00000380
       COPY DDLDCRUN AREA BUFFER SCRQUE-BUFFER              00000370
          PAGE CONTAINS 2004 CHARACTERS.                    00000380
       COPY DDLDCSCR AREA BUFFER SCRQUE-BUFFER              00000390
          PAGE CONTAINS 2004 CHARACTERS.                    00000400
       COPY DDLDCLOG AREA BUFFER LOG-BUFFER                 00000410
          PAGE CONTAINS 3860 CHARACTERS.                    00000420
       COPY IDMSR-AREA AREA BUFFER IDMSR-BUFFER             00000590
          PAGE CONTAINS 3860 CHARACTERS.                    00000600
       COPY IDMSR-AREA2 AREA BUFFER GENERAL1-BUFFER         00000610
          PAGE CONTAINS 3860 CHARACTERS.                    00000620
       COPY ASF-DDLDML AREA BUFFER DICT1-BUFFER             00000630
          PAGE CONTAINS 3860 CHARACTERS.                    00000640
       COPY ASF-DDLDCLOD AREA BUFFER LOAD1-BUFFER           00000650
          PAGE CONTAINS 3860 CHARACTERS.                    00000660
*   GENERAL LEDGER                                          00000260
       COPY DDLDML AREA FROM SCHEMA NAME CGLGLOBL VERSION 1
          BUFFER IS DICTGL-BUFFER
          PAGE CONTAINS 3020 CHARACTERS
          ALIAS DDLDML-DICTGL.
       COPY DDLDCLOD AREA FROM SCHEMA NAME CGLGLOBL VERSION 1
          BUFFER IS LODGL-BUFFER
          PAGE CONTAINS 4096 CHARACTERS
          ALIAS DDLDCLOD-LODGL.
       COPY GLMDATA-AREA AREA FROM SCHEMA NAME CGLGLOBL VERSION 1
          BUFFER IS CGL-BUFFER
          PAGE CONTAINS 3020 CHARACTERS
          ALIAS GLMDATA-DEMO.
       COPY GLSYSDEF-AREA AREA FROM SCHEMA NAME CGLGLOBL VERSION 1
          BUFFER IS CGL-BUFFER
          PAGE CONTAINS 3020 CHARACTERS
          ALIAS GLSYSDEF-DEMO.
       COPY GLSUMARY-AREA AREA FROM SCHEMA NAME CGLGLOBL VERSION 1
          BUFFER IS CGL-BUFFER
          PAGE CONTAINS 3020 CHARACTERS
          ALIAS GLSUMARY-DEMO.
       COPY GLJRNL-AREA AREA FROM SCHEMA NAME CGLGLOBL VERSION 1
          BUFFER IS CGL-BUFFER
          PAGE CONTAINS 3020 CHARACTERS
          ALIAS GLJRNL-DEMO.
       COPY GLPOSTRN-AREA AREA FROM SCHEMA NAME CGLGLOBL VERSION 1
          BUFFER IS CGL-BUFFER
          PAGE CONTAINS 3020 CHARACTERS
          ALIAS GLPOSTRN-DEMO.
       COPY GLINDEX-AREA AREA FROM SCHEMA NAME CGLGLOBL VERSION 1
          BUFFER IS CGL-BUFFER
          PAGE CONTAINS 3020 CHARACTERS
          ALIAS GLINDEX-DEMO.
       COPY GLMAUDIT-AREA AREA FROM SCHEMA NAME CGLGLOBL VERSION 1
          BUFFER IS CGL-BUFFER
          PAGE CONTAINS 3020 CHARACTERS
          ALIAS GLMAUDIT-DEMO.
       COPY GLSAUDIT-AREA AREA FROM SCHEMA NAME CGLGLOBL VERSION 1
          BUFFER IS CGL-BUFFER
          PAGE CONTAINS 3020 CHARACTERS
          ALIAS GLSAUDIT-DEMO.
       COPY GLBALLOC-AREA AREA FROM SCHEMA NAME CGLGLOBL VERSION 1
          BUFFER IS CGL-BUFFER
          PAGE CONTAINS 3020 CHARACTERS
```

Figure A-7 Test System Global DMCL (continued)

```
        ALIAS GLBALLOC-DEMO.
 *  DEMO AREAS                                                    00000260
      COPY EMP-DEMO-REGION AREA BUFFER GENERAL1-BUFFER            00000450
          PAGE CONTAINS 4628 CHARACTERS.                          00000460
      COPY ORG-DEMO-REGION AREA BUFFER GENERAL1-BUFFER            00000470
          PAGE CONTAINS 4628 CHARACTERS.                          00000480
      COPY INS-DEMO-REGION AREA BUFFER GENERAL1-BUFFER            00000490
          PAGE CONTAINS 4628 CHARACTERS.                          00000500
      COPY CUSTOMER-REGION AREA FROM SCHEMA NAME DEMOSCHM
          BUFFER GENERAL1-BUFFER
          PAGE CONTAINS 496  CHARACTERS.
      COPY ORDER-REGION AREA FROM SCHEMA NAME DEMOSCHM
          BUFFER GENERAL1-BUFFER
          PAGE CONTAINS 496  CHARACTERS.
      COPY PRODUCT-REGION AREA FROM SCHEMA NAME DEMOSCHM
          BUFFER GENERAL1-BUFFER
          PAGE CONTAINS 496  CHARACTERS.
      COPY SALES-REGION AREA FROM SCHEMA NAME DEMOSCHM
          BUFFER GENERAL1-BUFFER
          PAGE CONTAINS 496  CHARACTERS.

 JOURNAL SECTION.                                                 00000720
      JOURNAL BUFFER IS JRNL-BUFF.
      FILE CONTAINS 6000 BLOCKS.                                  00000740
      FILE NAME IS J1JRNL   ASSIGN TO J1JRNL                      00000750
                          DEVICE TYPE IS 3380.                    00000760
      FILE CONTAINS 6000 BLOCKS.                                  00000770
      FILE NAME IS J2JRNL   ASSIGN TO J2JRNL                      00000780
                          DEVICE TYPE IS 3380.                    00000790
      FILE CONTAINS 6000 BLOCKS.                                  00000770
      FILE NAME IS J3JRNL   ASSIGN TO J3JRNL                      00000780
                          DEVICE TYPE IS 3380.                    00000790
      ARCHIVAL JOURNAL BLOCK CONTAINS 8000 CHARACTERS.            00000800
      FILE NAME IS SYSJRNL      ASSIGN TO SYSJRNL                 00000810
                          DEVICE TYPE IS 2400.                    00000820
```

Figure A-7 Test System Global DMCL (continued)

✳ ✳ ✳

```
IDMSPARM SYSTEM=20,DMCLNAM=TESTDMCL,
         FREESTG=200,
         RMAPSIZ=25,
         PROMPT=NO
    END
```

Figure A-8 Test System #DCPARM Macro

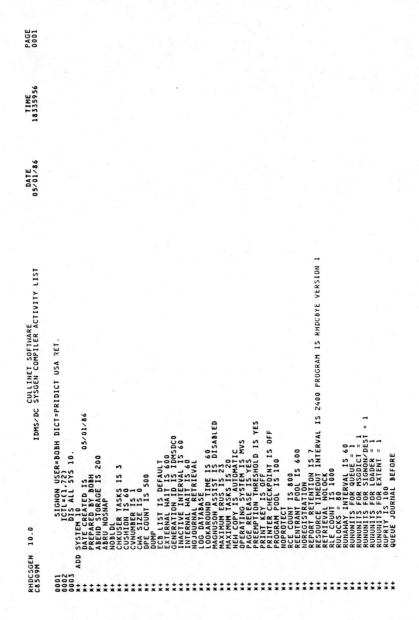

Figure A-9 Production System Generation Statements

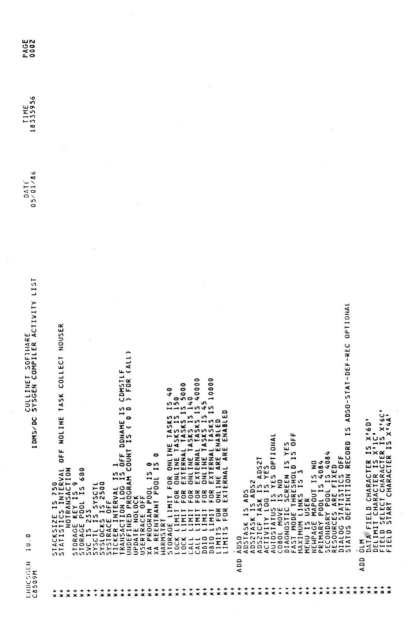

Figure A-9 Production System Generation Statements (continued)

```
RHDCSGEN  10.0          IDMS/DC CULLINET SOFTWARE        DATE        TIME      PAGE
C8509M                  SYSGEN COMPILER ACTIVITY LIST    05/01/86    18335956  0003

  *+    TRANSLATE CHARACTER IS C'2'
  *+    MODE IS STEP
  *+    NEW COPY IS YES
  *+    NUMERIC FIELD ORDER IS STANDARD
  *+    NUMERIC FIELD DECIMAL-POINT IS PERIOD
  *+    PAGE FORWARD PFKEY IS PF8
  *+    PAGE BACKWARD PFKEY IS PF7
  *+    PAGING STORAGE IS 10
  *+    QUEUE RETENTION IS 60


RHDCSGEN  10.0          IDMS/DC CULLINET SOFTWARE        DATE        TIME      PAGE
C8509M                  SYSGEN COMPILER ACTIVITY LIST    05/01/86    18335956  0004

                        ** TRANSACTION SUMMARY **

ENTITY                  ADD  MODIFY  REPLACE  DELETE  DISPLAY

SYSTEM                   0     0        0        0       1
IDMS AREA                0     0        0        0       1
IDMS BUFFER              0     0        0        0       1
IDMS PROGRAM             0     0        0        0       1
STORAGE POOL             0     0        0        0       1
XA STORAGE POOL          0     0        0        0       1
DDS                      0     0        0        0       1
DBNAME                   0     0        0        0       1
AUTOTASK                 0     0        0        0       1
KEYS                     0     0        0        0       1
ADSO                     0     0        0        0       1
OLM                      0     0        0        0       1
OLQ                      0     0        0        0       1
MAPTYPE                  0     0        0        0       1
LINE                     0     0        0        0       1
PTERM                    0     0        0        0       1
LTERM                    0     0        0        0       1
DESTINATION              0     0        0        0       1
QUEUE                    0     0        0        0       1
USER                     0     0        0        0       1
DEFAULT PERM PROGRAM     0     0        0        0       1
DEFAULT TEMP PROGRAM     0     0        0        0       1
PROGRAM                  0     0        0        0       1
TASK                     0     0        0        0       1

NO ERRORS OR WARNINGS ISSUED FOR THIS COMPILE
```

Figure A-9 Production System Generation Statements (continued)

```
REPORT NO. 19                          IDMS-DC SOURCE REPORT  C8509M              04/14/86 PAGE  1
CREPORT 019                            SYSTEM NAME: DCSYSTEM
                                       SYSTEM VERSION: 10
                                       PROGRAM DESCRIPTION

PROGRAM     TYPE        BUILDER ACTION VERSION

ADSOMAIN    PROGRAM        G      U       1
            ISA-SIZE   ERROR THRESHOLD   DUMP THRESHOLD   SECURITY CLASS CODE   OVERLAYABLE   DISABLED   PROTECT   SAVE AREA   RESIDENT   NEW COPY
               0             5                 0                  0                  YES          NO        YES        NO         YES        NO
            CONCURRENT   REUSABLE   REENTRANT    LANGUAGE
               YES         YES      REENTRANT    ASSEMBLER

ADSORUN1    PROGRAM        G      U       1
            ISA-SIZE   ERROR THRESHOLD   DUMP THRESHOLD   SECURITY CLASS CODE   OVERLAYABLE   DISABLED   PROTECT   SAVE AREA   RESIDENT   NEW COPY
               0             5                 0                  0                  YES          NO        YES        YES        YES        NO
            CONCURRENT   REUSABLE   REENTRANT    LANGUAGE
               YES         YES      REENTRANT    ASSEMBLER

IDMSCOMP    PROGRAM        G      U       1
            ISA-SIZE   ERROR THRESHOLD   DUMP THRESHOLD   SECURITY CLASS CODE   OVERLAYABLE   DISABLED   PROTECT   SAVE AREA   RESIDENT   NEW COPY
               0             5                 0                  0                  YES          NO        YES        YES        YES        NO
            CONCURRENT   REUSABLE   REENTRANT    LANGUAGE
               YES         YES      REENTRANT    ASSEMBLER

IDMSDCOM    PROGRAM        G      U       1
            ISA-SIZE   ERROR THRESHOLD   DUMP THRESHOLD   SECURITY CLASS CODE   OVERLAYABLE   DISABLED   PROTECT   SAVE AREA   RESIDENT   NEW COPY
               0             5                 0                  0                  YES          NO        YES        YES        YES        NO
            CONCURRENT   REUSABLE   REENTRANT    LANGUAGE
               YES         YES      REENTRANT    ASSEMBLER

IDMSNNKS    SUBSCHEMA      G      U       1
            ISA-SIZE   ERROR THRESHOLD   DUMP THRESHOLD   SECURITY CLASS CODE   OVERLAYABLE   DISABLED   PROTECT   SAVE AREA   RESIDENT   NEW COPY
               0             5                 0                  0                  YES          NO        NO         NO         YES        NO
            CONCURRENT   REUSABLE   REENTRANT    LANGUAGE
               YES         YES      REENTRANT    ASSEMBLER
```

Figure A-10 Production System Resident Programs

```
DEVICE-MEDIA DESCRIPTION.                                        00000010
DEVICE-MEDIA NAME IS PRODDMCL SCHEMA NAME PRODCHEM VERSION 1.    00000020
                                                                00000030
DATE.                            04/08/86.                       00000040
                                                                00000070
BUFFER SECTION.                                                  00000080
                                                                00000130
    BUFFER NAME IS DICT-BUFFER                                   00000090
        PAGE CONTAINS 3860 CHARACTERS                            00000150
        BUFFER CONTAINS 6 PAGES.                                 00000120
                                                                00000130
    BUFFER NAME IS LOAD-BUFFER                                   00000090
        PAGE CONTAINS 3860 CHARACTERS                            00000150
        BUFFER CONTAINS 10 PAGES.                                00000120
                                                                00000130
    BUFFER NAME IS LOG-BUFFER                                    00000140
        PAGE CONTAINS 3860 CHARACTERS                            00000150
        BUFFER CONTAINS 3 PAGES.                                 00000170
                                                                00000130
    BUFFER NAME IS SCRQUE-BUFFER                                 00000090
        PAGE CONTAINS 2004 CHARACTERS                            00000150
        BUFFER CONTAINS 3 PAGES.                                 00000120
                                                                00000130
    BUFFER NAME IS MSG-BUFFER                                    00000090
        PAGE CONTAINS 3860 CHARACTERS                            00000150
        BUFFER CONTAINS 3 PAGES.                                 00000120
                                                                00000130
    JOURNAL BUFFER NAME JRNL-BUFF                                00000140
        PAGE CONTAINS 7476 CHARACTERS                            00000150
        BUFFER CONTAINS 3 PAGES.                                 00000170
                                                                00000120
AREA SECTION.                                                    00000190
* IDD AREAS                                                      00000260
    COPY DDLDML AREA BUFFER DICT-BUFFER                          00000280
        PAGE CONTAINS 3860 CHARACTERS.                           00000300
    COPY DDLDCLOD AREA BUFFER LOAD-BUFFER                        00000340
        PAGE CONTAINS 3860 CHARACTERS.                           00000360
    COPY DDLDCMSG AREA BUFFER MSG-BUFFER                         00000310
        PAGE CONTAINS 3860 CHARACTERS.                           00000330
    COPY DDLDCQUE AREA BUFFER SCRQUE-BUFFER                      00000370
        PAGE CONTAINS 2004 CHARACTERS.                           00000380
    COPY DDLDCRUN AREA BUFFER SCRQUE-BUFFER                      00000370
        PAGE CONTAINS 2004 CHARACTERS.                           00000380
    COPY DDLDCSCR AREA BUFFER SCRQUE-BUFFER                      00000390
        PAGE CONTAINS 2004 CHARACTERS.                           00000400
    COPY DDLDCLOG AREA BUFFER LOG-BUFFER                         00000410
        PAGE CONTAINS 3860 CHARACTERS.                           00000420
JOURNAL SECTION.                                                 00000720
    JOURNAL BUFFER IS JRNL-BUFF.
    FILE CONTAINS 6000 BLOCKS.                                   00000740
    FILE NAME IS J1JRNL  ASSIGN TO J1JRNL                        00000750
                         DEVICE TYPE IS 3380.                    00000760
    FILE CONTAINS 6000 BLOCKS.                                   00000770
    FILE NAME IS J2JRNL  ASSIGN TO J2JRNL                        00000780
                         DEVICE TYPE IS 3380.                    00000790
    FILE CONTAINS 6000 BLOCKS.                                   00000770
    FILE NAME IS J3JRNL  ASSIGN TO J3JRNL                        00000780
                         DEVICE TYPE IS 3380.                    00000790
    ARCHIVAL JOURNAL BLOCK CONTAINS 8000 CHARACTERS.             00000800
    FILE NAME IS SYSJRNL     ASSIGN TO SYSJRNL                   00000810
                         DEVICE TYPE IS 2400.                    00000820
```

Figure A-11 Production System Global DMCL

* * *

```
IDMSPARM SYSTEM=10,DMCLNAM=PRODDMCL,
        FREESTG=200,
        RMAPSIZ=25,
        PROMPT=NO
    END
```

Figure A-12 Production System #DCPARM Macro

A.4 A SAMPLE PROCEDURE AND PROGRAMS TO AUTOMATE DECOMPILING AND RECOMPILING MAPS

Maps must be decompiled before changes can be made to records used in maps. A procedure and programs were developed to simplify the process of decompiling maps and recompiling them. Three listings are included:

- Documentation and sample OS jobstreams for the decompile and recompile procedures (Figure A-13),
- A sample program, BOBHDMAP, which identifies the maps to be decompiled and generates syntax for input to the Culli-net utilities (Figure A-14), and
- A sample program to drop duplicate syntax from the output of BOBHDMAP (Figure A-15).

by Bob Husband   3/26/85

SUBJECT: Map Decompile and Recompile Routine

A routine has been created to simplify the process of changing map owned dictionary records. The function of the routine is to read the dictionary, decompile and delete all maps associated with the records to be changed, and then recompile and regenerate the maps and regenerate any dialogs that use the records.

The routine is implemented through the use of an IDD class and attribute structure. Data Base Administration will add the attribute to the appropriate dictionary, and modify each record to be changed to include that attribute.*

Add the attribute:

> ADD ATT 121984R1 WITHIN
> CLASS 'DECOMPILE DATE'.

Link the record:

> MOD REC PFGLBL
> 'DECOMPILE DATE' IS 121984R1.

The above phrase 'DECOMPILE DATE' is a class and the '121984R1' is an attribute attached to 'DECOMPILE DATE' (the first six positions of the attribute would stand for today's month, day and year while the last two positions would represent a run number; this would be useful in the event we modify several groups of records many times in the same day).

The procedure, DECOMPM, contains a program, BOBHDMAP. This program uses the input card containing the attribute value and the dictionary name, follows the dictionary sets to obtain all maps and dialogs using the records linked to the attribute, and formats a card file. This card file is then sorted and run through a second program, BOBHDUP, which deletes duplicate cards and writes appropriate files used by the various Cullinet programs. From this point on, standard Cullinet programs decompile and delete maps. The procedure, RECOMPM, reads files created by DECOMPM, recompiles and then regenerates maps, and regenerates dialogs.

The sequence of steps are:

- Run CREPORT=256 to identify MAPs and DIALOGs that use the element(s).
- Add the date attribute.
- Modify the record with the proper attribute.
- Run DECOMPM - which will decompile and delete the maps.
- Delete/re-add or modify the record.
- Run RECOMPM - which will recompile and regenerate all the maps and regenerate all the dialogs.

The jobs DECOMPM and RECOMPM, and programs BOBHDMAP and BOBHDUP are in CM.DBIDMS.TEST.SRCLIB under those member names.

* Older dates should be purged periodically.

Figure A-13 Documentation and Jobstreams for Decompiling and Recompiling Maps

INPUT: o   Control cards and IDMS Data Dictionary.

OUTPUT: o   Listing of all the maps to be decompiled and dialogs to be regen-
             erated.

         o   Statistics showing the number of decompiled maps, and that of dia-
             logs to be regenerated.

OUTPUT DATASETS:

         o   CM.DBIDMS.TEST.DELFILE --- control cards for deleting maps.

         o   CM.DBIDMS.TEST.DECFILE --- control cards for decompiling maps.

         o   CM.DBIDMS.TEST.LODFILE --- control cards for generating maps.

         o   CM.DBIDMS.TEST.ADSBFILE --- control cards for generating dialogs.

         o   CM.DBIDMS.TEST.DCOMP --- decompiled map source code.

EXECUTION: Steps DCOMMAP, DECOMSORT and DCOMDUP are all run in IDMS local
            mode. Steps DCOMP and DELMAP run in IDMS central mode.

NOTES/COMMENTS

     This procedure assumes centralized control. The output files are not
temporary data sets or generation data groups; therefore, you cannot run multiple DECOMPM jobs on the same day without clobbering the control card files.
Additionally, RECOMPM must be run prior to any more DECOMPM runs.

RESTART

     If this job abends in any step except DELMAP, the job should be resubmit-
ted. If the DELMAP step aborts, restart the job from the DELMAP step.

ADDENDUM

     Care should be taken when making changes to any of the records which are
participating in maps. CREPORT 256 should probably be run prior to this job
to determine how many and which specific maps will be impacted. Basically,
changes involving the reordering of record elements, or changes to the picture
or usage of record elements will cause no problems. If the element names have
been changed, however, each map containing the changed names must be edited to
specify the new names. For each name, edit the data set 'CM.DBIDMS.TEST.
DCOMP', globally replacing the changed element name. CREPORT 256 will display
all maps used by the given element names. The format of the SYSIN card is:

                    CREPORT=256
                    KEYING-NAM-058 'element name1'
                    KEYING-NAM-058 'element name2'
                                   .
                                   .
                                   .

Figure A-13 Documentation and Jobstreams for Decompiling and
Recompiling Maps (continued)

PROCEDURE NAME: DECOMPM

WARNING: Please ensure that the output datasets from the previous run are no longer needed before running this proc.

JOB CONTROL LANGUAGE:

```
//STEP1   EXEC     DECOMPM
//DECOMMAP.SYSIN        DD   *
XXXXXXXXXXYYYYYYY
//DCOMSORT.SYSIN        DD   *
SORT FIELDS=(1,46,CH,A), EQUALS
//
```

where   XXXXXXXX = the dictionary attribute that will trigger this run
(example - 013084R1).
YYYYYYY = the dictionary name where the attribute and maps to be decompiled reside
(example - DEVDICT).

DESCRIPTION: This procedure is used for decompiling all maps associated with the specified dictionary records. This procedure works in combination with the RECOMPM procedure. DECOMPM consists of the following steps:

STEP NAME	PROGRAM	DESCRIPTION
DCOMMAP	BOB#DMAP	Searches the named dictionary for the attribute that will trigger this run, and evaluates all records associated with the attribute. It then finds all maps and dialogs associated with these records and formats the control cards which will be inputted to other steps. These steps will actually perform the decompile/recompile operation.
DECOMSORT	SORT	Sorts the control cards generated from step DCOMMAP.
DCOMDUP	BOB#DUP	Deletes all duplicate control cards and routes the cards to appropriate files which will be used by different steps.
DCOMP	RHDCMPUT	ILMS mapping utility which decompiles each affected map.
DELMAP	RHDCMAP1	ILMS mapping utility which deletes each affected map.

Figure A-13 Documentation and Jobstreams for Decompiling and Recompiling Maps (continued)

```
//CMDBNZP JOB (3,01700,0302),'2BWAY,21,ZURCHER',MSGCLASS=Y,                  0000100
//         MSGLEVEL=(1,1),NOTIFY=CMDBNZ,CLASS=U,COND=(0,NE)                   0000200
//*ROUTE  PRINT MLCM2BWY                                                      0001000
//DECOMPM PROC  LIB='TEST.LOADLIB',
//         LIB2='IDMS.LOADLIB',
//         LIB3='CM.DBIDMS.TEST.LOADLIB',
//         SRTLIB='SYS2.SYNCSORT.SORTLIB',
//         REG='512K'
//*****************************************************************************
//*                                                                         *
//*      DECOMPM DECOMPILES ALL MAPS ASSOCIATED WITH A GIVEN RECORD         *
//*      AS WELL AS THEIR DIALOGS (WHERE APPLICABLE)                        *
//*      AND WILL SAVE SYNTAX CARDS TO DELETE, RECOMPILE                    *
//*      AND REGENERATE THE MAPS (ASSUMABLY AFTER THE RECORD HAS            *
//*      HAS BEEN CHANGED BY SOMEONE OR SOMETHING ELSE..........),          *
//*      AND DIALOGS.                                                       *
//*                                                                         *
//*****************************************************************************
//*      SRCHES DICT FOR ATT& CLASS FINDS MAPS AN DIALOGS ASSOC W. REC
//*      FORMATS CNTL CARDS TO BE INPUTTED TO OTHER STEPS
//DECOMMAP EXEC PGM=BODHDMAP,REGION=&REG
//STEPLIB  DD   DSN=&LIB3,DISP=SHR
//         DD   DSN=&LIB2,DISP=SHR
//         DD   DSN=&LIB,DISP=SHR
//SYSLST   DD   SYSOUT=*
//SYSCTL   DD   DSN=IDMS.SYSCTL,DISP=SHR
//SYSPCH   DD   DSN=&&DECOM,DISP=(NEW,PASS,DELETE),
//         UNIT=DISK,SPACE=(1500,(10,5)),
//         DCB=(RECFM=FB,LRECL=80,BLKSIZE=1600)
//SYSIN    DD   DUMMY
//SYSOUT   DD   SYSOUT=*
//DISPLAY  DD   SYSOUT=*
//SYSUDUMP DD   SYSOUT=*
//*
//*      SORTS THE CNTL CARDS GENERATED
//DCOMSORT EXEC PGM=SORT,REGION=&REG,COND=(0,NE)
//STEPLIB  DD   DSN=&SRTLIB,DISP=SHR
//SORTLIB  DD   DSN=&SRTLIB,DISP=SHR
//SYSOUT   DD   SYSOUT=*
//SYSPRINT DD   SYSOUT=*
//SORTMSG  DD   SYSOUT=*
//SORTWK01 DD   DSN=&&WRKAWORK,UNIT=3380,
//         SPACE=(CYL,(2,1))
//SORTWK02 DD   DSN=&&WRK3WORK,UNIT=3380,
//         SPACE=(CYL,(2,1))
//SORTWK03 DD   DSN=&&WRKCWORK,UNIT=3380,
//         SPACE=(CYL,(2,1))
//SORTWK04 DD   DSN=&&WRKDWORK,UNIT=3380,
//         SPACE=(CYL,(2,1))
//SYSUDUMP DD   DUMMY
//SORTIN   DD   DSN=&&DECOM,DISP=(OLD,DELETE,DELETE)
//SORTOUT  DD   DSN=&&SRT,DISP=(NEW,PASS,DELETE),
//         UNIT=DISK,SPACE=(1600,(10,5)),
//         DCB=(RECFM=FB,LRECL=80,BLKSIZE=1600)
//SYSIN    DD   DUMMY
//*
//*      DROPS ALL DUPLICATES CNTL CARDS AND ROUTES THE CARDS TO APPRO FILE
//DCOMDUP  EXEC PGM=BODHDUP,REGION=&REG,COND=(0,NE)
//STEPLIB  DD   DSN=CM.DBIDMS.TEST.LOADLIB,DISP=SHR
//         DD   DSN=IDMS.LOADLIB,DISP=SHR
//         DD   DSN=TEST.LOADLIB,DISP=SHR
//SYSLST   DD   SYSOUT=*
//SRTFILE  DD   DSN=&&SRTD,DISP=(OLD,DELETE,DELETE)
//DELFILE  DD   DSN=CM.DBIDMS.TEST.DELFILE,DISP=SHR
//DECFILE  DD   DSN=CM.DBIDMS.TEST.DECFILE,DISP=SHR
//LODFILE  DD   DSN=CM.DBIDMS.TEST.LODFILE,DISP=SHR
//ADSBFILE DD   DSN=CM.DBIDMS.TEST.ADSBFILE,DISP=SHR
//SYSOUT   DD   SYSOUT=*
//DISPLAY  DD   SYSOUT=*
//SYSUDUMP DD   SYSOUT=*
//*
//*      DECOMPILES MAPS
//DCOMP    EXEC PGM=RHDCMPUT,REGION=&REG,PARM='DBNAME IS DEVDICT',
//         COND=(0,NE)
//STEPLIB  DD   DSN=CM.DBIDMS.TEST.LOADLIB,DISP=SHR
//         DD   DSN=IDMS.LOADLIB,DISP=SHR
//COMSLIB  DD   DSN=CM.DBIDMS.TEST.LOADLIB,DISP=SHR
//         DD   DSN=IDMS.LOADLIB,DISP=SHR
//SYSCTL   DD   DSN=IDMS.SYSCTL,DISP=SHR
//SYSLST   DD   SYSOUT=*
//SYSPCH   DD   DSN=CM.DBIDMS.TEST.DCOMP,DISP=SHR
//SYSIPT   DD   DSN=CM.DBIDMS.TEST.DECFILE,DISP=SHR
```

Figure A-13 Documentation and Jobstreams for Decompiling and
Recompiling Maps (continued)

```
//*
//*    DELETES    MAPS
//*
//DELMAP  EXEC  PGM=RHDCMAP1,REGION=GREG,PARM='DBNAME IS DEVDICT',
//        COND=(0,GE)      *** USE COND=(0,GE) TO SKIP THIS STEP
//STEPLIB DD   DSN=CM.DBIDMS.TEST.LOADLIB,DISP=SHR
//        DD   DSN=IDMS.LOADLIB,DISP=SHR
//CDMSLIB DD   DSN=CM.DBIDMS.TEST.LOADLIB,DISP=SHR
//        DD   DSN=IDMS.LOADLIB,DISP=SHR
//SYSLST  DD   SYSOUT=*
//SYSPCH  DD   DUMMY
//SYSCTL  DD   DSN=IDMS.SYSCTL,DISP=SHR
//SYSIPT  DD   DSN=CM.DBIDMS.TEST.DELFILE,DISP=SHR
//*
//        PEND
//STEP1   EXEC  DECOMPM
//DECOMMAP.SYSIN  DD  *
032685R1DEVDICT
//DCOMSORT.SYSIN  DD  *
 SORT FIELDS=(1,46,CH,4),EQUALS
//
```

Output of BOBHDMAP

```
SUCCESSFUL COMPLETION FOR BOBHDMAP: DECOMPILE DATE032685R1
# RCDATTR-081 READ          0000004
# MAPS FLAGGED              0000017
# DIALOGS FLAGGED           0000032
```

Output of BOBHDUP

```
DECOMPILED MAPS AND DIALOGS INCLUDE:
   MAP     PFAHCM
   MAP     PFAIG2M
   MAP     PFAT020M
   MAP     PFAT04M
   MAP     PFAI10M
   MAP     PFAI11M
   MAP     PFAI30M
   MAP     PFAI30MB
   MAP     PFAI30X
   MAP     PFAI31M
   MAP     PFAI31MB
   MAP     PFAI40M
   MAP     PFAI50M
   MAP     PFAI60M
   MAP     PFA211M
   MAP     PFA220M
   MAP     PFA250M
   DIALOG  BOBHO21D
   DIALOG  BOBHO21U
   DIALOG  PFAHCD
   DIALOG  PFATESTD
   DIALOG  PFAT010D
   DIALOG  PFAT02D
   DIALOG  PFAT03D
   DIALOG  PFAT04D
   DIALOG  PFAT05D
   DIALOG  PFAT07D
   DIALOG  PFA001D
   DIALOG  PFA002D
   DIALOG  PFA010D
   DIALOG  PFA110D
   DIALOG  PFA120D
   DIALOG  PFA130D
   DIALOG  PFA131D
   DIALOG  PFA140D
   DIALOG  PFA150D
   DIALOG  PFA160D
   DIALOG  PFA211D
   DIALOG  PFA212D
   DIALOG  PFA213D
   DIALOG  PFA500D
   DIALOG  PFA510D
SUCCESSFUL COMPLETION OF BOBHDUP
TOTAL RECORDS READ              0000102
TOTAL RECORDS WRITTEN           0000095
TOTAL MAPS TO BE RECOMPILED     C000017
TOTAL DIALOGS TO BE REGENERATED 0000025
```

Figure A-13 Documentation and Jobstreams for Decompiling and Recompiling Maps (continued)

PROCEDURE NAME: RECOMPM

JOB CONTROL LANGUAGE:

```
//STEP1    EXEC      RECOMPM
//ADSBGEN.SYSIPT          DD    *
SIGNON    DBNAME=DEVDICT.
//
```

DESCRIPTION: This procedure is used for recompiling all maps and dialogs as-
               sociated with the specified dictionary records. This procedure
               works in combination with the procedure, DECOMPM. RECOMPM con-
               sists of the following steps:

STEP NAME	PROGRAM	DESCRIPTION
RECOMP	RHDCMAP1	IDMS mapping utility which will recom-pile each map previously decompiled.
RELOAD	RHDCMPUT	IDMS mapping utility which will regen-erate all affected map load modules.
ADSBGEN	ADSOBGEN	IDMS dialog utility which will regen-erate all affected dialogs.

INPUT: Control card files created by the DCCMDUP step of the DECOMPM job.

OUTPUT: Listings displaying the names of maps and dialogs that have been re-
          compiled. These lists should be checked against the output of the
          DECOMPM job.

EXECUTION: All steps are run in IDMS central mode.

NOTES/COMMENTS

1)   This procedure assumes centralized control. The input files are not gen-
     eration data groups; Therefore, you cannot run multiple RECOMPM jobs con-
     currently. You must run RECOMPM in conjunction with each execution of
     DECOMPM.

2)   The utilities do not force new copies of maps or dialogs to be loaded.
     Therefore, the new copies should be brought in either by executing the
     online DCMT command or by running a UCFBTCH job.

3)   Careful note should be made of the output from step ADSBGEN (last page of
     the listing). Any errors in this utility will not cause a bad condition
     code. They will merely be flagged on the message page of the listing.

RESTART

     If this job abends in the step, RELOAD or ADSBGEN, the job should be re-
started from that step. If the job aborts during or after the step RECOMP,
rerun the last step, DELMAP, of DECOMPM before rerunning the RECOMPM job.

Figure A-13 Documentation and Jobstreams for Decompiling and
Recompiling Maps (continued)

```
//CMDBHCD   JOB (123),'2BWY,21FL,RESNICK',CLASS=U,MSGCLASS=Y,
//          NOTIFY=CMDBHC
/*ROUTE  PRINT MLCM2BWY
//RECOMPM   PROC LIB='TEST.LOADLIB',
//          LIB2='IDMS.LOADLIB',
//          LIB3='CM.DBIDMS.TEST.LOADLIB',
//          REG='512K'
//*****************************************************************
//*                                                              *
//*     BOBHDMAP DECOMPILES ALL MAPS ASSOCIATED WITH A GIVEN RECORD  *
//*     AS WELL AS THEIR DIALOGS (WHERE APPLICABLE) *
//*     - AND WILL SAVE SYNTAX CARDS TO DELETE, RECOMPILE        *
//*     AND REGENERATE THE MAPS (ASSUMABLY AFTER THE RECORD HAS  *
//*     HAS BEEN CHANGED BY SOMEONE OR SOMETHING ELSE...........),  *
//*     AND DIALOGS.                                             *
//*                                                              *
//*****************************************************************
//*
//*    RECOMPILE (ADDS TO DML) MAPS
//*
//RECOMP EXEC PGM=RHDCMAP1,REGION=&REG,PARM='DBNAME IS DEVDICT'
//STEPLIB DD   DSN=&LIB,DISP=SHR
//         DD   DSN=&LIB2,DISP=SHR
//         DD   DSN=&LIB3,DISP=SHR
//COMSLIB DD   DSN=&LIB,DISP=SHR
//         DD   DSN=&LIB2,DISP=SHR
//         DD   DSN=&LIB3,DISP=SHR
//SYSLST  DD   SYSOUT=*
//SYSPCH  DD   DUMMY
//SYSCTL  DD   DSN=IDMS.SYSCTL,DISP=SHR
//SYSIPT  DD   DSN=CM.DBIDMS.TEST.DCOMP,DISP=SHR
//*
//*    REGENERATES MAPS INTO LOAD MODULES
//*
//RELOAD EXEC PGM=RHDCMPUT,REGION=&REG,PARM='DBNAME IS DEVDICT'
//STEPLIB DD   DSN=&LIB,DISP=SHR
//         DD   DSN=&LIB2,DISP=SHR
//         DD   DSN=&LIB3,DISP=SHR
//COMSLIB DD   DSN=&LIB,DISP=SHR
//         DD   DSN=&LIB2,DISP=SHR
//         DD   DSN=&LIB3,DISP=SHR
//SYSLST  DD   SYSOUT=*
//SYSCTL  DD   DSN=IDMS.SYSCTL,DISP=SHR
//SYSPCH  DD   DUMMY
//SYSIPT  DD   DSN=CM.DBIDMS.TEST.LODFILE,DISP=SHR
//*
//*    REGENERATES ALL DIALOGS
//*
//ADSBGEN EXEC PGM=ADSOBGEN,REGION=1512K,PARM='DBNAME IS DEVDICT'
//STEPLIB DD   DSN=&LIB,DISP=SHR
//         DD   DSN=&LIB2,DISP=SHR
//         DD   DSN=&LIB3,DISP=SHR
//COMSLIB DD   DSN=&LIB,DISP=SHR
//         DD   DSN=&LIB2,DISP=SHR
//         DD   DSN=&LIB3,DISP=SHR
//SYSLST  DD   SYSOUT=*
//SYSCTL  DD   DSN=IDMS.SYSCTL,DISP=SHR
//SYSPCH  DD   DUMMY
//SYSIPT  DD   DUMMY
//         DD   DSN=CM.DBIDMS.TEST.ADSBFILE,DISP=SHR
// PEND
//STEP1   EXEC RECOMPM
//ADSBGEN.SYSIPT  DD *
SIGNON DBNAME=DEVDICT.
//
//
```

Figure A-13 Documentation and Jobstreams for Decompiling and
Recompiling Maps (continued)

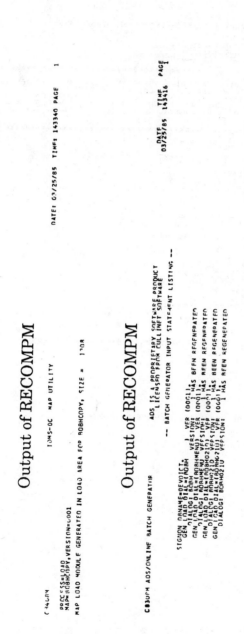

Output of RECOMPM

```
C34UBM                      IDMS-DC  MAP UTILITY                    DATE: 03/25/85  TIME: 143340 PAGE    1

 PROCESS=LOAD
 MAP=BOBHCOPY,VERSION=0001
MAP LOAD MODULE GENERATED IN LOAD AREA FOR BOBHCOPY, SIZE =   1308
```

Output of RECOMPM

```
C830PM ADS/ONLINE BATCH GENERATOR          ADS IS A PROPRIETARY SOFTWARE PRODUCT
                                             LICENSED FROM CULLINET SOFTWARE              DATE      TIME    PAGE
                                     -- BATCH GENERATOR INPUT STATEMENT LISTING --      03/25/85  143416    1

         SIGNON DBNAME=DEVDICT.
           GEN LOAD DIAL=(BOBH      )  VER (0001).
              DIALOG: BOBH        VERSION:    1 HAS BEEN REGENERATED
           GEN LOAD DIAL=(BOBHMENU)  VER (0001).
              DIALOG: BOBHMENU   VERSION:    1 HAS BEEN REGENERATED
           GEN LOAD DIAL=(BOBHO21D)  VER (0001).
              DIALOG: BOBHO21D   VERSION:    1 HAS BEEN REGENERATED
           GEN LOAD DIAL=(BOBHO21U)  VER (0001).
              DIALOG: BOBHO21U   VERSION:    1 HAS BEEN REGENERATED
```

Figure A-13 Documentation and Jobstreams for Decompiling and Recompiling Maps (continued)

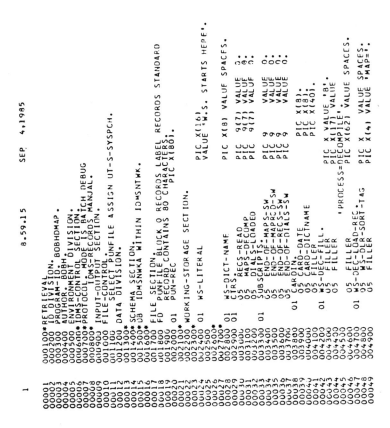

```
                                    8.59.15      SEP 4,1985

000100*RETRIEVAL.
000200 PROGRAM-ID. BOBHDMAP.
000300 AUTHOR. BOB.
000400 ENVIRONMENT DIVISION.
000500*IDMS-CONTROL SECTION.
000600* PROTOCOL. MODE IS BATCH DEBUG
000700*   IDMS-RECORDS MANUAL.
000800* IDMS-CONTROL SECTION.
000900 INPUT-OUTPUT SECTION.
001000 FILE-CONTROL.
001100 SELECT PUNFILE ASSIGN UT-S-SYSPCH.
001200 DATA DIVISION.
001300
001400 SCHEMA SECTION.
001500 DB IDMSNWKA WITHIN IDMSNTWK.
001600
001700 FILE SECTION.
001800 FD PUNFILE BLOCK 0 RECORDS LABEL RECORDS STANDARD
001900    RECORD CONTAINS 80 CHARACTERS.
002000 01 PUN-REC                    PIC X(80).
002100
002200 WORKING-STORAGE SECTION.
002300
002400 01 WS-LITERAL                 PIC X(16)
002500                               VALUE 'W.S. STARTS HERE'.
002600*
002700 01 WS-DICT-NAME               PIC X(8) VALUE SPACES.
002800 01 CTRS.
002900    05 RECS-READ               PIC 9(7) VALUE 0.
003000    05 MAPS-DECOMP             PIC 9(7) VALUE 0.
003100    05 DIALS-LOADED            PIC 9(7) VALUE 0.
003200 01 SUBSCRIPTS.
003300    05 END-OF-MAPS-SW          PIC 9 VALUE 0.
003400    05 END-OF-MAPRCD-SW        PIC 9 VALUE 0.
003500    05 END-OF-RECS-SW          PIC 9 VALUE 0.
003600    05 END-OF-DIALS-SW         PIC 9 VALUE 0.
003700
003800 01 CARDIN.
003900    05 CARD-DATE               PIC X(8).
004000    05 CARD-DICTNAME           PIC X(8).
004100    05 FILLER                  PIC X(40).
004200 01 WS-DEC-FILL.
004300    05 FILLER                  PIC X VALUE 'B'.
004400    05 FILLER                  PIC X(17) VALUE
004500                                   'PROCESS=DECOMPILE'.
004600    05 FILLER                  PIC X(62) VALUE SPACES.
004700 01 WS-DEC-LOAD-REC.
004800    05 WS-DLR-SORT-TAG         PIC X(4) VALUE SPACES.
004900    05 FILLER                  PIC X(4) VALUE 'MAP='.
```

Figure A-14 A Sample Program to Automate Decompiling Maps

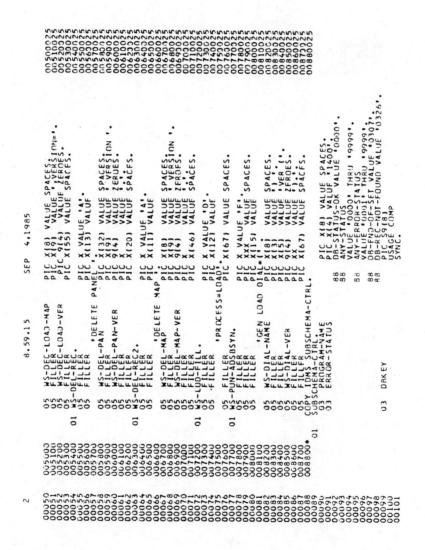

Figure A-14 A Sample Program to Automate Decompiling Maps (continued)

Figure A-14 A Sample Program to Automate Decompiling Maps (continued)

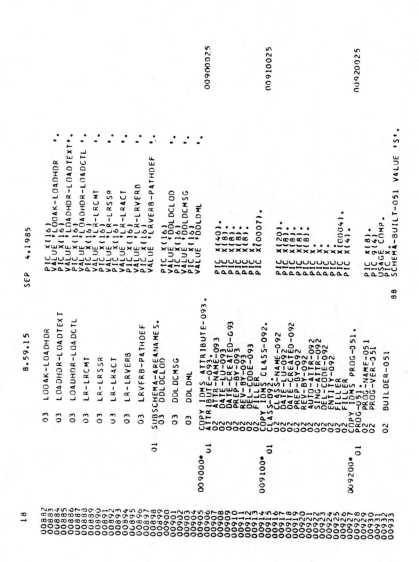

```
18                          8.59.15                SEP 4,1985

00882        03  LOOAK-LOADHDR         PIC X(16).
00883                                  VALUE 'LOOAK-LOADHDR'.
00884        03  LOADHDR-LOADTEXT      PIC X(16).
00885                                  VALUE 'LOADHDR-LOADTEXT'.
00886        03  LOADHDR-LOADCTL       PIC X(16).
00887                                  VALUE 'LOADHDR-LOADCTL'.
00888        03  LR-LRCMT              PIC X(16).
00889                                  VALUE 'LR-LRCMT'.
00890        03  LR-LRSSR              PIC X(16).
00891                                  VALUE 'LR-LRSSR'.
00892        03  LR-LRACT              PIC X(16).
00893                                  VALUE 'LR-LRACT'.
00894        03  LR-LRVERB             PIC X(16).
00895                                  VALUE 'LR-LRVERB'.
00896        03  LRVERB-PATHDEF        PIC X(16).
00897                                  VALUE 'LRVERB-PATHDEF'.
00898    01  SUBSCHEMA-AREANAMES.
00899        03  DDLDCLOD              PIC X(16).
00900                                  VALUE 'DDLDCLOD'.
00901        03  DDLDCMSG              PIC X(16).
00902                                  VALUE 'DDLDCMSG'.
00903        03  DDLDML                PIC X(16).
00904                                  VALUE 'DDLDML'.
00905
00900*   01  COPY IDMS ATTRIBUTE-093.                            00900025
00906    ATTRIBUTE-093.
00907        02  ATTR-NAME-093         PIC X(40).
00908        02  DATE-LU-093           PIC X(8).
00909        02  DATE-CREATED-G93      PIC X(8).
00910        02  PREP-BY-093           PIC X(8).
00911        02  REV-BY-093            PIC X(8).
00912        02  DEL-CODE-093          PIC X(8).
00913        02  FILLER                PIC X(0007).
00914
00910*   01  COPY IDMS CLASS-092.                                00910025
00915    CLASS-092.
00916        02  CLASS-NAME-092        PIC X(20).
00917        02  DATE-LU-092           PIC X(8).
00918        02  DATE-CREATED-092      PIC X(8).
00919        02  PREP-BY-092           PIC X(8).
00920        02  REV-BY-092            PIC X(8).
00921        02  AUTO-ATTR-092         PIC X.
00922        02  SING-ATTR-092         PIC X.
00923        02  DEL-CODE-092          PIC X.
00924        02  ENTITY-092            PIC X(0004).
00925        02  FILLER                PIC X(4).
00926        02  FILLER
00927
00920*   01  COPY IDMS PROG-051.                                 00920025
00928    PROG-051.
00929        02  PROG-NAME-051         PIC X(8).
00930        02  PROG-VER-051          PIC 9(4).
00931                                  USAGE COMP.
00932                             88   SCHEMA-BUILT-051 VALUE 'S'.
00933        02  BUILDER-051
```

Figure A-14 A Sample Program to Automate Decompiling Maps (continued)

```
8.59.15                    SEP  4,1985                                                          19

                                                                        88  DIR-BUILT-051 VALUE 'X'.
                                                                        88  SYSGEN-BUILT-051 VALUE 'G'.
                                                                        88  DML-BUILT-051 VALUE 'M'.
                                                                        88  SUBSCH-BUILT-051 VALUE 'V'.
                                                                        88  MAP-BUILT-051 VALUE 'C'.
                                                                        88  SYSGN2-BUILT-051 VALUE 'R'.
                                                                        88  DICT-BUILT-051 VALUE 'D'.
         02  ENTRY-051                                                      PIC X(4).
         02  DESCR-051                                                      PIC X(8).
         02  DATE-LU-051                                                    PIC X(8).
         02  DATE-CREATED-051                                               PIC X(8).
         02  PREP-BY-051                                                    PIC X(8).
         02  REV-BY-051                                                     PIC 9(8).
         02  PROG-DATE-051                                                  USAGE COMP.
         02  EST-LINES-051                                                  USAGE COMP.
                                                                           USAGE COMP.
         02  ISA-SIZE-051                                                   USAGE COMP.
                                                                           PIC X(0006).
         02  COUNT-051                                                      PIC X(0004).

009300*  01 02  FILLER                                                      PIC X(40).        00930025
         COPY IDMS-PROG.MAP-126.                                           PIC X(0004).
         PROG.MAP-126:                                                      PIC X(4).
009400*  01 02  FILLER                                                                       00940025
             JCT-TEXT-126
         02  FILLER
         COPY IDMS-PROGATTR-065.                                           PIC X(40).
         PROGATTR-065:                                                                        00950025
009500*  01 COPY JCT-TEXT-065
         MAPATTR-123:                                                       PIC X(40).
         COPY JCT-TEXT-123
009600*  01 02  FILLER                                                                       00960025
         COPY IDMS-RCDCOPY-063.                                            PIC X(40).
         RCDCOPY-063:                                                       PIC X(1004).
         02  FILLER                                                         PIC X(4).
             JCT-TEXT-063
009700*  01 02  FILLER                                                      PIC X(40).        00970025
         COPY IDMS-RCDATTR-081.
         RCDATTR-081:
         COPY JCT-TEXT-081
         COPY IDMS-SR-036.
009800*  01 SR-036:                                                        PIC X(32).        00980025
         02  SR-NAM-036                                                     PIC S9(8).
         02  OCCURS-036                                                     USAGE COMP.
                                                                           PIC S9(4).
         02  RCD-VERS-036                                                   USAGE COMP.

         02  DLGTH-036                                                      PIC X.

         02  BUILDER-036                                                88  SCHEMA-BUILT-036 VALUE 'S'.
```

Figure A-14   A Sample Program to Automate Decompiling Maps (continued)

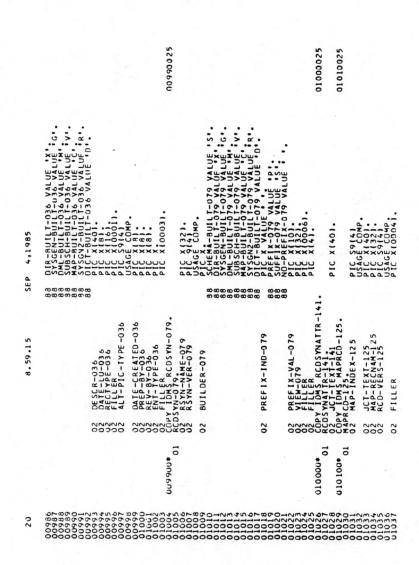

Figure A-14 A Sample Program to Automate Decompiling Maps (continued)

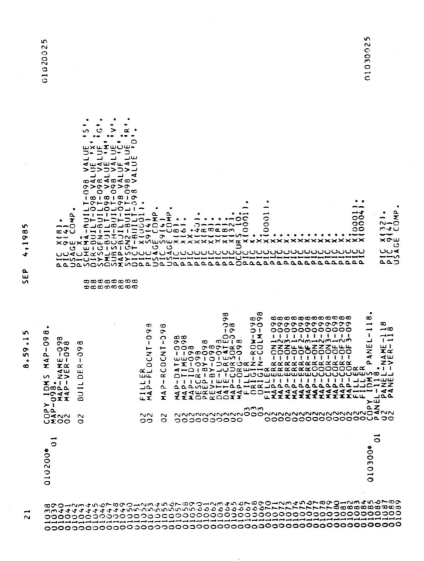

Figure A-14 A Sample Program to Automate Decompiling Maps (continued)

```
22                        8.59.15      SEP 4,1985

        02  BUILDER-118              PIC X.                                01040025
            88  SCHEMA-BUILT-118    VALUE 'S'.                             01050025
            88  DIR-BUILT-118       VALUE 'X'.                             01060025
            88  SYSGEN-BUILT-118    VALUE 'G'.                             01070025
            88  DML-BUILT-118       VALUE 'M'.                             01080025
            88  SUBSCH-BUILT-118    VALUE 'V'.                             01090025
            88  MAP-BUILT-118       VALUE 'C'.                             01100025
            88  SYSGN2-BUILT-118    VALUE 'R'.                             01110025
            88  DICT-BUILT-118      VALUE 'D'.                             01120025
        02  FILLER                   PIC X(10).                            01130025
        02  PANCREVGRPS-118          PIC X(42).                            01140025
        02  DESCRIP-DY-118           PIC X(8).                             01150025
        02  PREP-DY-118              PIC X(8).                             01160025
        02  REV-DY-118               PIC X(8).                             01170025
        02  DATE-CREATED-118         PIC X(0001).                          DMLCA001
        02  FILLER                   PIC X(00005).
        02  FILLER                   PIC X(4).
    PROCEDURE DIVISION.
*******   SORT TAGS FOR THE VARIOUS 80 BYTE RECORDS ARE SET UP
*         AS FOLLOWS:
*         B     SETS UP SYNTAX FOR DECOMPILING MAPS
*         C     SETS UP SYNTAX FOR DELETING MAPS
*         D     SETS UP SYNTAX FOR LOADING MAPS
*         E     SETS UP SYNTAX FOR GENERATING ADS DIALOGS
*******
    0010-ML-STAR.
        ACCEPT CARD-IN.
        IF CARD-DICTNAME NOT = SPACES
            MOVE CARD-DICTNAME TO WS-DICT-NAME
        BIND RUN-UNIT DBNAME WS-DICT-NAME                                 01180025
        MOVE 0001 TO DML-SEQUENCE                                         01190025
        MOVE SPACES TO SSC-NODN                                           01200025
        MOVE WS-DICT-NAME TO SSC-NODN                                     01210025
        CALL 'IDMS' USING SUBSCHEMA-CTRL                                  01220025
                          IDBMSCOM (59)                                   01230025
                          SUBSCHEMA-CTRL                                  01240025
                          SUBSCHEMA-SSNAME                                01250025
                          SUBSCHEMA-CTRL                                  01260025
                          SSC-NODN;                                       01270025

        IF ERROR-STATUS = '0000'
            NEXT SENTENCE
        ELSE
            DISPLAY 'INPUT CARD DICTNAME IS INVALID'
            MOVE 0070 TO DICTNAME
            MOVE 0070 TO RETURN-CODE
            GOBACK
        ELSE DISPLAY 'INPUT CARD DICTNAME MUST BE INPUT'
            MOVE 0070 TO RETURN-CODE
```

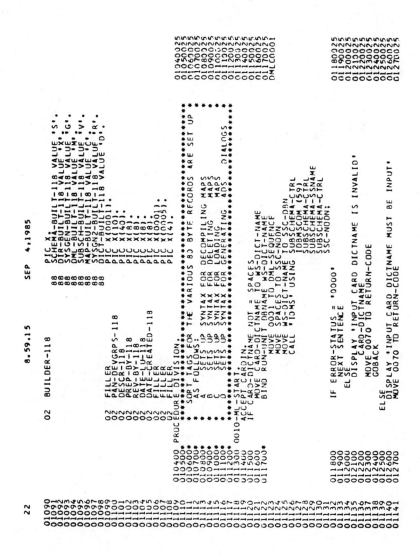

Figure A-14 A Sample Program to Automate Decompiling Maps (continued)

```
23          8.59.15   SEP  4,1985

011142   012800*   COPY GOBACK.                                          0128C025
011143   012900*   MOVE 'BOBHOMAP' TO PROGRAM-NAME                       0129C025
011144             BIND RUN-UNIT
011145        *        MOVE 0002 TO DML-SEQUENCE                         DMLC0002
011146                 CALL 'IDMS' USING SUBSCHEMA-CTRL
011147                                   IDBMSCOM (59)
011148                                   SUBSCHEMA-CTRL
011149                                   SUBSCHEMA-SSNAME;
011150
011151             BIND RCDSYNATTR-141
011152        *        MOVE 0003 TO DML-SEQUENCE                         DMLC0003
011153                 CALL 'IDMS' USING SUBSCHEMA-CTRL
011154                                   IDBMSCOM (48)
011155                                   SR141
011156                                   RCDSYNATTR-141;
011157
011158             BIND PROGMAP-126
011159        *        MOVE 0004 TO DML-SEQUENCE                         DMLC0004
011160                 CALL 'IDMS' USING SUBSCHEMA-CTRL
011161                                   IDBMSCOM (48)
011162                                   SR126
011163                                   PROGMAP-126;
011164
011165             BIND MAPRCO-125
011166        *        MOVE 0005 TO DML-SEQUENCE                         DMLC0005
011167                 CALL 'IDMS' USING SUBSCHEMA-CTRL
011168                                   IDBMSCOM (48)
011169                                   SR125
011170                                   MAPRCO-125;
011171
011172             BIND MAPATTR-123
011173        *        MOVE 0006 TO DML-SEQUENCE                         DMLC0006
011174                 CALL 'IDMS' USING SUBSCHEMA-CTRL
011175                                   IDBMSCOM (48)
011176                                   SR123
011177                                   MAPATTR-123;
011178
011179             BIND PANEL-118
011180        *        MOVE 0007 TO DML-SEQUENCE                         DMLC0007
011181                 CALL 'IDMS' USING SUBSCHEMA-CTRL
011182                                   IDBMSCOM (48)
011183                                   SR118
011184                                   PANEL-118;
011185
011186             BIND MAP-098
011187        *        MOVE 0008 TO DML-SEQUENCE                         DMLC0008
011188                 CALL 'IDMS' USING SUBSCHEMA-CTRL
011189                                   IDBMSCOM (48)
011190                                   SR98
011191                                   MAP-098;
011192
011193             BIND ATTRIBUTE-093
                   *   MOVE 0009 TO DML-SEQUENCE                         DMLC0009
                       CALL 'IDMS' USING SUBSCHEMA-CTRL
                                         IDBMSCOM (48)
                                         SR93
                                         ATTRIBUTE-093;

                   BIND CLASS-092
```

Figure A-14 A Sample Program to Automate Decompiling Maps (continued)

```
24                              8.59.15    SEP 4,1985

01194           MOVE 0010 TO DML-SEQUENCE                  DMLC0010
01195           CALL 'IDMS' USING SUBSCHEMA-CTRL
01196                            IDBMSCOM (48)
01197                       SR92
01198                       CLASS-092;
01199  *   BIND RCDATTR-081
01200           MOVE 0011 TO DML-SEQUENCE                  DMLC0011
01201           CALL 'IDMS' USING SUBSCHEMA-CTRL
01202                            IDBMSCOM (48)
01203                       SR81
01204                       RCDATTR-081;
01205  *   BIND RCDSYN-079
01206           MOVE 0012 TO DML-SEQUENCE                  DMLC0012
01207           CALL 'IDMS' USING SUBSCHEMA-CTRL
01208                            IDBMSCOM (48)
01209                       SR79
01210                       RCDSYN-079;
01211  *   BIND PROGATTR-065
01212           MOVE 0013 TO DML-SEQUENCE                  DMLC0013
01213           CALL 'IDMS' USING SUBSCHEMA-CTRL
01214                            IDBMSCOM (48)
01215                       SR6
01216                       PROGATTR-065;
01217  *   BIND RCDCOPY-063
01218           MOVE 0014 TO DML-SEQUENCE                  DMLC0014
01219           CALL 'IDMS' USING SUBSCHEMA-CTRL
01220                            IDBMSCOM (48)
01221                       SR63
01222                       RCDCOPY-063;
01223  *   BIND PROG-051
01224           MOVE 0015 TO DML-SEQUENCE                  DMLC0015
01225           CALL 'IDMS' USING SUBSCHEMA-CTRL
01226                            IDBMSCOM (48)
01227                       SR51
01228                       PROG-051;
01229  *   BIND SR-036.
01230           MOVE 0016 TO DML-SEQUENCE                  DMLC0016
01231           CALL 'IDMS' USING SUBSCHEMA-CTRL
01232                            IDBMSCOM (48)
01233                       SR36
01234  013600*  READY DDLDML USAGE-MODE RETRIEVAL.
01235           MOVE 0017 TO DML-SEQUENCE                  01300025
01236           CALL 'IDMS' USING SUBSCHEMA-CTRL           DMLC0017
01237                            IDBMSCOM (37)
01238                       DDLDML.
01239  013100   PERFORM IDMS-STATUS.                       01310025
01240  013200   OPEN OUTPUT PUNFILE.                       01330025
01241  013300 0020-ML-LOOP.                                01340025
01242  013400   MOVE CARD-DATE TO ATTR-NAME-093.           01350025
01243  013500*  FIND CALC ATTRIBUTE-093;                   DMLC0018
01244           MOVE 0018 TO DML-SEQUENCE
01245
```

Figure A-14 A Sample Program to Automate Decompiling Maps (continued)

```
25                                          8.59.15        SEP 4,1985

                     CALL 'IDMS' USING SUBSCHEMA-CTRL                      01360025
                                        SR93.                             01370025
013600     IF DB-REC-NOT-FOUND                                            01380025
013700         DISPLAY 'INPUT CARD DECOMPILE DATE INVALID'                01390019
013800         MOVE 0071 TO RETURN-CODE                                   DMLC0019
013900*        FINISH
               MOVE 0019 TO DML-SEQUENCE                                  01400025
               CALL 'IDMS' USING SUBSCHEMA-CTRL                           01410025
                           IDBMSCOM (02);                                 01420025
014000     GOBACK.                                                        01430025
014100     PERFORM IDMS-STATUS.                                           01440025
014200     WRITE PUN-REC FROM WS-DEC-FILL.                                01450025
014300     WRITE PUN-REC FROM WS-LOD-FILL.                                01460020
014400     PERFORM 0040-FIND-ALL-RECS THRU 0040-EXIT                      DMLC0020
014600*    PERFORM UNTIL END-OF-RECS-SW = 1.
           FINISH.                                                        01470025
               MOVE 0020 TO DML-SFQUENCE                                  01480025
               CALL 'IDMS' USING SUBSCHEMA-CTRL                           01490025
                           IDBMSCOM (02).                                 01500025
014700     CLOSE PUNFILE.                                                 01510025
014800     DISPLAY 'SUCCESSFUL COMPLETION FOR B0BHDMAP: DECOMPILE DATE'   01520025
014900     CARD-DATE.                        ' RECS-READ.                 01530025
015000     DISPLAY '# RCDATR-081 READ        ' MAPS-DECOMP.               01540025
015100     DISPLAY '# MAPS FLAGGED           ' DIALS-LOADED.              01550021
015200     DISPLAY '# DIALOGS FLAGGED                                     DMLC0021
015300     GOBACK.
015500* 0040-FIND-ALL-RECS.
           FIND NEXT RCDATR-081 WITHIN ATTR-JCT.
                                      SP81
                                      ATTR-JCT.
015600     IF DB-END-OF-SET                                               01560025
015700         MOVE 1 TO END-OF-RECS-SW                                   01570025
015800         GO TO 0040-EXIT.                                           01580025
015900     PERFORM IDMS-STATUS.                                          01590025
016100*    ADD 1 TO RECS-READ.                                            01600025
           FIND OWNER WITHIN SR-RCDATTR.                                  DMLC0022
               MOVE 0022 TO DML-SEQUENCE
               CALL 'IDMS' USING SUBSCHEMA-CTRL
                           IDBMSCOM (31)
                           SR-RCDATTR.
016200     PERFORM IDMS-STATUS.                                           01620025
016300*    FIND NEXT RCDSYN 079 WITHIN SR-RCDSYN.                         01630025
               MOVE 0023 TO DML-SEQUENCE                                  DMLC0023
               CALL 'IDMS' USING SUBSCHEMA-CTRL
                           IDBMSCOM (10)
                           SR79
                           SR-RCDSYN.
016400     PERFORM IDMS-STATUS.                                           01640025
```

Figure A-14 A Sample Program to Automate Decompiling Maps (continued)

```
                                        8.59.15     SEP 4,1985

016500      MOVE ZEROES TO END-OF-MAPS-SW.                              01650025
016600      PERFORM 0050-FIND-ALL-MAPS THRU 0050-EXIT                   01660025
016700          UNTIL END-OF-MAPS-SW = 1.                               01670025
016800*  ***                                                            01680025
017000*  ***   IT IS NECESSARY TO SEARCH ALL DIALOGS AS A SEPERATE      01700025
017100*  ***   ROUTINE AS WELL AS IN THESE MAP ROUTINE BECAUSE OF       01710025
017200*  ***   THE POSSIBILITY OF MAPLESS DIALOGS USING WORK RECORDS    01720025
017300*  ***   OR A WORK RECORD USED AS A NC/WORK RECORD IN A DIAL      01730025
017400*  ***   AND NOT USED IN THE MAP AT ALL - BOBH                    01740025
017500*  ***                                                            01750025
017600      PERFORM 0075-FIND-ALL-DIALS THRU 0075-EXIT                  01760025
017700          UNTIL END-OF-DIALS-SW = 1.                              01770025
017800  0040-EXIT.  EXIT.                                               01780025
017900* 0050-FIND-ALL-MAPS.                                             DMLC0024
            FIND NEXT MAPRCD-125 WITHIN RCDSYN-MAPRCD.
                MOVE 0024 TO DML-SEQUENCE.
                CALL 'IDMS' USING SUBSCHEMA-CTRL
                                  SR125
                                  RCDSYN-MAPRCD.

018000      IF DB-END-OF-SET                                            01800025
018100          MOVE 1 TO END-OF-MAPS-SW                                01810025
018200          GO TO 0050-EXIT.                                        01820025
018300      PERFORM IDMS-STATUS.                                        01830025
018400*     OBTAIN OWNER WITHIN MAP-MAPRCD.                             DMLC0025
                MOVE 0025 TO DML-SEQUENCE
                CALL 'IDMS' USING SUBSCHEMA-CTRL
                                  MAP-MAPRCD
                                  IDBMSCOM (43).

018500      PERFORM IDMS-STATUS.                                        01850025
018600*     OBTAIN OWNER WITHIN PANEL-MAP.                              DMLC0026
                MOVE 0026 TO DML-SEQUENCE
                CALL 'IDMS' USING SUBSCHEMA-CTRL
                                  PANEL-MAP
                                  IDBMSCOM (43).

018700      PERFORM IDMS-STATUS.                                        01870025
018800      PERFORM 0100-PUN-MAP THRU 0100-EXIT.                        01880025
018900*     FIND NEXT PROGMAP-126 WITHIN MAP-PROGMAP.                   DMLC0027
                MOVE 0027 TO DML-SEQUENCE
                CALL 'IDMS' USING SUBSCHEMA-CTRL
                                  SR126
                                  MAP-PROGMAP.

019000      IF DB-END-OF-SET                                            01900025
019200      PERFORM IDMS-STATUS.                                        01910025
019300*     OBTAIN OWNER WITHIN PROG-PROGMAP.                           01920025
                MOVE 0028 TO DML-SEQUENCE                               DMLC0028
                CALL 'IDMS' USING SUBSCHEMA-CTRL
                                  IDBMSCOM (31)
```

Figure A-14 A Sample Program to Automate Decompiling Maps (continued)

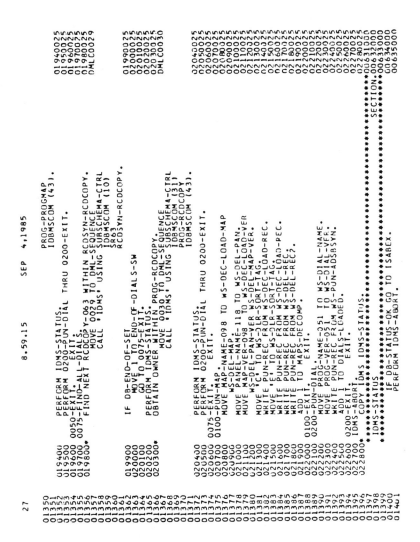

Figure A-14 A Sample Program to Automate Decompiling Maps (continued)

```
28                8.59.15      SEP  4,1985

01402   DISPLAY '***********************'                                    00636000
01403           '  ABORTING - ' PROGRAM-NAME                                 00637000
01404           '  ' ERROR-STATUS                                           00638000
01405           '  ' ERROR-RECORD                                          00639000
01407           '***** RECOVER IDMS *****'                                   00640000
01408   DISPLAY 'UPON CONSOLE.                                               00641000
01409   DISPLAY 'PROGRAM NAME - ' PROGRAM-NAME.                             00642000
01410   DISPLAY 'ERROR STATUS - ' ERROR-STATUS.                             00643000
01411   DISPLAY 'ERROR RECORD - ' ERROR-RECORD.                             00644000
01412   DISPLAY 'ERROR SET - ' ERROR-SET.                                   00645000
01413   DISPLAY 'ERROR AREA - ' ERROR-AREA.                                 00646000
01414   DISPLAY 'LAST GOOD RECORD - ' RECORD-NAME.                          00647000
01415   DISPLAY 'LAST GOOD AREA - ' AREA-NAME.                              00648000
01416   DISPLAY 'DML SEQUENCE - ' DML-SEQUENCE.                             00649000
01417   ROLLBACK.                                                           00650000
01418   MOVE 0031 TO DML-SEQUENCE                                           DMLC0031
01419   CALL 'IDMS' USING SUBSCHEMA-CTRL
01420         IDBMSCOM (67).                                                00651000

01421   ISABEX. CALL 'ABORT'.                                               00652000
        EXIT.
```

Figure A-14 A Sample Program to Automate Decompiling Maps (continued)

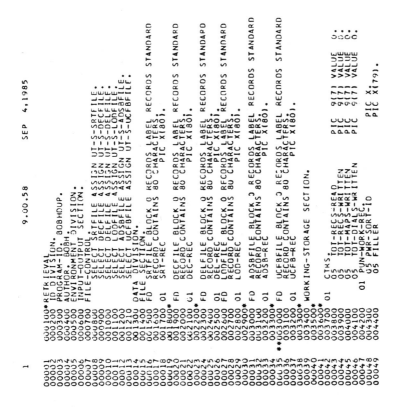

Figure A-15 A Sample Program to Delete Duplicate Syntax

```
2                          9.00.58        SEP 4,1985

004500  01  PUN-HOLD-REC.
004600      05  PHR-SORT-ID            PIC X.
004700      05  FILLER-MAPNAME         PIC X(4).
004800      05  PHR-MAPNAME            PIC X(8).
004900      05  FILLER                 PIC X(6).
005000      05  PHR-DIALNAME           PIC X(8).
005100      05  FILLER                 PIC X(53).
005200  01  UCFB-WORK-REC.
005300      05  FILLER        PIC XXX VALUE SPACES.
005400      05  UWR-PROG-NAME PIC X(12) VALUE 'DCMT V PROG '.
005500      05  FILLER        PIC X(8) VALUE SPACES.
005600      05  FILLER        PIC X(5) PIC X(8) VALUE 'N C '.
005700      05  FILLER        PIC X(6) VALUE SPACES.
005800  01  UCFB-WORK-REC2.
005900      05  FILLER        PIC XXX VALUE SPACES.
006000      05  UWR-PROG-NAME2 PIC X(12) VALUE 'DCMT VDP '.
006100      05  FILLER        PIC X VALUE SPACES.
006200      05  UWR-PROG-TYPE PIC X(4) VALUE SPACES.
006300      05  FILLER        PIC X(5) VALUE SPACES.
006400      05  FILLER        PIC X(67) VALUE SPACES.
006500  01  UCFB-WORK-FILL.
006600      05  FILLER-FILL.  PIC X(80) VALUE SPACES.
006700  PROCEDURE DIVISION.
006800  0010-START.
006900      OPEN INPUT SRTFILE.
007000      OPEN OUTPUT DELFILE.
007100      OPEN OUTPUT LODFILE.
007200      OPEN OUTPUT ADSBFILE.
007300      OPEN OUTPUT UCFBFILE.
007400      MOVE SPACES TO PUN-WORK-REC.
007500      READ SRTFILE INTO PUN-WORK-REC
007600          AT END
007700          DISPLAY 'NO RECORDS INPUTED'
007800          GOBACK.
007900      DISPLAY 'DECOMPILED MAPS AND DIALOGS INCLUDE: '
        G020-READ-SRTFILE.
            ADD 1 TO TOT-RECS-READ.
            MOVE PUN-WORK-REC TO PUN-HOLD-REC.
            PERFORM 0100-READ-SRTFILE THRU 0199-EXIT.
        0100-READ-SRTFILE.
            READ SRTFILE INTO PUN-WORK-REC
                AT END
                PERFORM 0200-WRITE-PUNREC THRU 0299-EXIT
            DISPLAY 'SUCCESSFUL COMPLETION OF ROBHDUP'.
            DISPLAY 'TOTAL RECORDS READ              ' TOT-RECS-READ
            DISPLAY 'TOTAL RECORDS WRITTEN           ' TOT-RECS-WRITTEN
            DISPLAY 'TOTAL MAPS TO BE RECOMPILED     ' TOT-MAPS-WRITTEN
            DISPLAY 'TOTAL DIALOGS TO BE REGENERATED ' TOT-DIALS-WRITTEN
            CLOSE SRTFILE DELFILE LODFILE ADSBFILE UCFBFILE
            GOBACK.
```

Figure A-15 A Sample Program to Delete Duplicate Syntax (continued)

```
3                      9.00.58        SEP  4,1985

008000       ADD 1 TO TOT-RECS-READ.                                       00800000
008100       IF PUN-WORK-REC = PUN-HOLD-REC                                00810000
008200           GO TO 0100-READ-SRTFILE                                   00820000
008300       ELSE                                                          00830000
008400           PERFORM 0200-WRITE-PUNREC THRU 0299-EXIT                  00840000
008500           MOVE PUN-WORK-REC TO PUN-HOLD-REC                         00850000
008600           GO TO 0100-READ-SRTFILE.                                  00860000
008700   0199-EXIT.      EXIT.                                             00870000
008800   0200-WRITE-PUNREC.                                                00880000
008900       PERFORM 02AA-EVAL-SORTTAG THRU 02AA-EXIT.                     00890000
009000       ADD 1 TO TOT-RECS-WRITTEN.                                    00900000
009100   0299-EXIT.      EXIT.                                             00910000
009200   02AA-EVAL-SORTTAG.                                                00920000
009300       IF PHR-SORT-ID = 'A'                                          00930000
009400           MOVE SPACES TO PHR-SORT-ID                                00940000
009500           WRITE DEL-REC FROM PUN-HOLD-REC                           00950000
009600           GO TO 02AA-EXIT.                                          00960000
009700       IF PHR-SORT-ID = 'B'                                          00970000
009800           MOVE SPACES TO PHR-SORT-ID                                00980000
009900           WRITE DEC-REC FROM PUN-HOLD-REC                           00990000
010000           GO TO 02AA-EXIT.                                          01000000
010100       IF PHR-SORT-ID = 'C'                                          01010000
010200           MOVE SPACES TO PHR-SORT-ID                                01020000
010300           WRITE DEC-REC FROM PUN-HOLD-REC                           01030000
010400           ADD 1 TO TOT-MAPS-WRITTEN                                 01040000
010500           DISPLAY '  MAP    ' PHR-MAPNAME                           01050000
                 MOVE PHR-MAPNAME TO UWR-PROG-NAME UWR-PROG-NAME2          01051001
                 MOVE 'MAP ' TO UWR-PROG-TYPE                              01051101
                 PERFORM 02BB-WRITE-UWR THRU 02BB-EXIT                     01052004
010600           GO TO 02AA-EXIT.                                          01060000
010700       IF PHR-SORT-ID = 'D'                                          01070000
010800           MOVE SPACES TO PHR-SORT-ID                                01080000
010900           WRITE LOD-REC FROM PUN-HOLD-REC                           01090000
011000           GO TO 02AA-EXIT.                                          01100000
011100       IF PHR-SORT-ID = 'E'                                          01110000
011200           MOVE SPACES TO PHR-SORT-ID                                01120000
011300           WRITE LOD-REC FROM PUN-HOLD-REC                           01130000
011400           GO TO 02AA-EXIT.                                          01140000
011500       IF PHR-SORT-ID = 'F'                                          01150000
011600           MOVE SPACES TO PHR-SORT-ID                                01160000
011700           WRITE ADSB-REC FROM PUN-HOLD-REC                          01170000
011800           ADD 1 TO TOT-DIALS-WRITTEN                                01180000
011900           DISPLAY ' DIALOG ' PHR-DIALNAME                           01190000
                 MOVE PHR-DIALNAME TO UWR-PROG-NAME UWR-PROG-NAME2         01191001
                 MOVE 'DIAL' TO UWR-PROG-TYPE                              01191101
                 PERFORM 02BB-WRITE-UWR THRU 02BB-EXIT                     01192004
012000           GO TO 02AA-EXIT.                                          01200000
012100   02AA-EXIT.      EXIT.                                             01210000
         02BB-WRITE-UWR.                                                   01220000
             WRITE UCFB-REC FROM UCFB-WORK-REC.                            01230003
             WRITE UCFB-REC FROM UCFB-WORK-FILL.                           01231003
             WRITE UCFB-REC FROM UCFB-WORK-REC2.                           01232003
             WRITE UCFB-REC FROM UCFB-WORK-FILL.                           01233003
         02BB-EXIT.      EXIT.                                             01240000
```

Figure A-15 A Sample Program to Delete Duplicate Syntax (continued)

A.5   A SAMPLE HISTOGRAM MODIFICATION

The size of collection buckets used in the system histograms can be modified using the #HSTDEF macro. Two listings are included:

- Sample #HSTDEF syntax to modify the collection buckets (Figure A-16), and
- An excerpt from shutdown statistics showing some of the modified histograms (Figure 1-17).

```
                                                              00001000
                                                              00002000

//T79A    JOB (IDMS,X2301),'IDMS',CLASS=P,
//ASMUCFB EXEC ASMFCL,REGION.LKED=800K
//ASM.SYSLIB DD
//         DD DSN=PIDMS.R10.SRCLIB,DISP=SHR
//ASM.SYSIN DD *
#HSTDEF PROGSIZE,LOW=4000,INCR=4000,BINS=40
#HSTDEF USTGSIZE,LOW=2000,INCR=2000,BINS=20
#HSTDEF GSTGSIZE,LOW=2000,INCR=4000,BINS=20
#HSTDEF PROGLOAD,LOW=2,INCR=2,BINS=5
#HSTDEF PSCRCNT,LOW=5,INCR=5,BINS=15
#HSTDEF GSCRCNT,LOW=5,INCR=5,BINS=15
#HSTDEF GQUECNT,LOW=5,INCR=5,BINS=15
#HSTDEF PQUECNT,LOW=5,INCR=5,BINS=15
#HSTDEF DBCALLS,LOW=20,INCR=20,BINS=10
#HSTDEF HISTACK,LOW=50,INCR=50,BINS=10
END
//LKED.SYSLMOD DD DSN=T79.LOADLIB.LOAD,DISP=SHR
//LKED.IN DD DSN=PIDMS.R10.LOADLIB,DISP=SHR
//LKED.OBJLIB DD DSN=PIDMS.R10.OBJLIB,DISP=SHR
//LKED.SYSIN DD *
INCLUDE IN(RHDCNTRY)
NAME RHDCHIST(R)
```

Figure A-16 Sample Histogram Modification

```
85263 17.25.34   HISTOGRAM OF TOTAL GET STORAGE SIZE
GETSTG SIZE    AMOUNT    GETSTG SIZE    AMOUNT    GETSTG SIZE    AMOUNT    GETSTG SIZE    AMOUNT
LT NEXT ENTRY  20,422    2.000          1,185     6.000          964       10.000         237
14.000         9         18.000         524       22.000         2,842     26.000         0
30.000         0         34.000         0         38.000         0         42.000         0
46.000         1         50.000         0         54.000         0         58.000         0
62.000         0         66.000         0         70.000         0         74.000         0
78.000         0         GT LAST ENTRY  0
```

```
85263 17.25.34   HISTOGRAM OF USER STORAGE SIZE
USR STG SIZE   AMOUNT    USR STG SIZE   AMOUNT    USR STG SIZE   AMOUNT    USR STG SIZE   AMOUNT
LT NEXT ENTRY  7,507     10.000         304       12.000         204       6.000          0
16.000         3         18.000         213       20.000         0         14.000         0
24.000         0         26.000         515       28.000         0         22.000         0
32.000         0         34.000         0         36.000         0         30.000         0
40.000         0         GT LAST ENTRY  0                                  38.000         0
```

```
85263 17.25.35   HISTOGRAM OF SCRATCH RECORD SIZES
SCRATCH SIZE   AMOUNT    SCRATCH SIZE   AMOUNT    SCRATCH SIZE   AMOUNT    SCRATCH SIZE   AMOUNT
LT NEXT ENTRY  0         100            0         200            0         300            0
400            0         500            0         600            0         700            0
800            0         900            0         1,000          0         GT LAST ENTRY  0
```

```
85263 17.25.35   HISTOGRAM OF QUEUE RECORD SIZES
QUEUE SIZE     AMOUNT    QUEUE SIZE     AMOUNT    QUEUE SIZE     AMOUNT    QUEUE SIZE     AMOUNT
LT NEXT ENTRY  74        100            1         200            114       300            2
400            74        500            74        600            1         700            2
800            40        900            0         1,000          0         GT LAST ENTRY  16
```

```
85263 17.25.35   HISTOGRAM OF PROGRAM SIZES
PROGRAM SIZE   AMOUNT    PROGRAM SIZE   AMOUNT    PROGRAM SIZE   AMOUNT    PROGRAM SIZE   AMOUNT
LT NEXT ENTRY  191       4.000          752       8.000          1,848     12.000         1,690
16.000         141       20.000         114       24.000         537       28.000         56
32.000         100       36.000         32        40.000         35        44.000         0
48.000         90        52.000         0         56.000         0         60.000         0
64.000         0         68.000         0         72.000         2,842     76.000         0
80.000         0         84.000         0         88.000         0         92.000         0
96.000         0         100.000        0         104.000        0         108.000        0
112.000        0         116.000        0         120.000        0         124.000        0
128.000        0         132.000        0         136.000        0         140.000        0
144.000        0         148.000        0         152.000        0         156.000        0
160.000        0         GT LAST ENTRY  0
```

```
85263 17.25.35   HISTOGRAM OF RECORD SIZES WRITTEN TO JOURNAL
JRNL SIZE      JOURNAL             JRNL SIZE      AMOUNT    JRNL SIZE      AMOUNT    JRNL SIZE      AMOUNT
               AMOUNT
LT NEXT ENTRY  0         100            0         200            0         300            0
400            0         500            0         600            0         700            0
800            0         900            0         1,000          0         GT LAST ENTRY  0
```

Figure A-17 Sample Histogram Output

Acronyms & Abbreviations

A

ABRT (Abort check point in journal)
ABRU = Aborted Run Unit
ADSA (Task code for the ADS/O application generator)
ADSG (Task code for the ADS/O dialog generator)
ADSO (System generation statement which defines ADS/O characteristics for a system)
ADS/O = Application Development System/Online
ASF = Automatic System Facility

B

BDAM = Basic Direct Access Method
BLDL (SYSTEM statement parameter)

C

CDMSIJMP (Installation utility program)
CICS = Customer Information Control System (IBM's teleprocessing monitor)
CIL = Core Image Library
CLIST (a command list)
CPU = Central Processing Unit
CTABGEN (#CTABGEN macro)
CULPRIT (Name of Cullinet's Report Generator)
CV = Central Version (Typical mode of operation for IDMS/R)
CVNUMBER (SYSTEM statement parameter)
CWA = Common Work Area (SYSTEM statement parameter)

D

DA = Data Administrator
DASD = Direct Access Storage Device
DB = Database
DBA = Database Administrator
DBIO = Database Input Output (IDMSDBIO is an IDMS/R module)
DBKEY = Database key (IDMS/R's internal identifier for database records)
DBMS = Database Management System
DBNAME (System generation statement)
DBNT = Database Name Table
DC = Data Communications (in this book, it usually means IDMS-DC)

DC/UCF = Data Communications/Universal Communications Facility

DCA = Data Communications Administrator

DCLOG (short for DDLDCLOG)

DCPARM (#DCPARM macro)

DCMT (Task code for Master Terminal commands in a DC or UCF system)

DCUF (System Task Code for various user functions)

DD = Data Dictionary

DDA = Data Dictionary Administrator

DDDL = Data Dictionary Definition Language

DDL = Data Definition Language (used to define and maintain database definitions)

DDLDCLOD (name of Data Dictionary area containing load modules)

DDLDCLOG (name of Data Dictionary area containing system log information)

DDLDCMSG (name of Data Dictionary area containing system and application messages)

DDLDCQUE (name of Data Dictionary area containing queue records)

DDLDCRUN (name of Data Dictionary area containing queue and scratch records)

DDLDCSCR (name of Data Dictionary area containing scratch records)

DDLDCTLF (name of Data Dictionary area containing transaction logging facility information)

DDLDML (name of Data Dictionary area containing basic dictionary entities, such as elements, records, users, etc.)

DDR = Dictionary/Directory Reporter

DMCL = Device Media Control Language

DML = Data Manipulation Language (statements coded in application programs to access IDMS/R databases)

DP = Data Processing

DPE COUNT (SYSTEM statement parameter)

E

ENDJ (End Job checkpoint on journal)

ERUS = External Run Units

EXTWAIT (EXTERNAL WAIT system statement parameter)

F

FBA = Fixed Block Architecture

FDR = Fast Dump Restore (a disk utility program, product of Innovation Data Processing, Inc.)

I

IBM = International Business Machines

ICMS = Information Center Management System (Cullinet Product)

IDB = Information Database, renamed ICMS (Cullinet Product)

IDD = Integrated Data Dictionary (Cullinet Product)

IDMS = Integrated Database Management System (Cullinet Product)

IDMS statement (system generation statement

IDMS-DC = Integrated Database Management System-Data Communications (Cullinet Product)

IDMS/R = Integrated Database Management System/Relational (Cullinet Product)

IDMSAJNL (Utility program to archive journal files)

IDMSBASE (Macro used to define dictionary areas, i.e., page size, file name, and device type)

IDMSDBAN (Utility program to analyze databases)

IDMSDBLU (Utility program to load databases)

IDMSDBIO (an IDMS/R module for Database Input and Output)

IDMSDDDL (Compiler for dictionary syntax)

IDMSDMLx (Data Manipulation Language Compilers, where 'x' identifies the programming language - C for COBOL, P for PL/I, etc.)

IDMSDPLX (Exit which allows duplexing of journals and databases)

IDMSDUMP (Utility program to create a copy of a database for backup)

IDMSINIT (Utility program to initialize database files)

IDMSINTC (Interface program between CICS programs and IDMS/R)

IDMSJFIX (Utility to fix some journal problems, write ABRT checkpoints, and report on journal contents)

IDMSNTWK (Schema name for data dictionary network database)

IDMSPFIX (Utility program to fix some database problems)

IDMSRBCK (Utility program to rollback database updates)

IDMSRFWD (Utility program to roll forward database updates)

IDMSRNWK (Utility program used to create dictionary network subschemas)

IDMSRSTR (Utility program to restore database contents)

IDMSRSTU (Utility program to restucture database contents)

IDMSXPAG (Utility program to expand database page size)

IDMSUNLD (Utility program to unload database contents)

IJMP (short for CDMSIJMP, the installation program)

I/O = Input/Output

IPL = Initial Program Load

J

JCL = Job Control Language

JJOB1 through JJOB5 (Names of steps in the installation jobstream)

L

LM = Local Mode

LRF = Logical Record Facility

M

MAXCVNO (parameter which defines the maximum CVNUMBER allowed, SVC parameter)

MAXERUS (System statement parameter)

MAXTASKS (System statement parameter)

O

OLE = OnLine English

OLM = OnLine Mapping

OLP = Online Log Print (task code)

OLQ = OnLine Query

P

PC = Personal Computer, i.e., microcomputer

PDE = Program Definition Element (an entry in the program definition table)

PSW = Program Status Word

PTERM (Physical Terminal, a system generation statement)

PTF = Program Temporary Fix

Q

QA = Quality Assurance

QA/AT = Quality Assurance/Acceptance Testing

QFILE (A group of OLQ commands stored in the data dictionary which may be executed by name)

R

RBB = Record Buffer Block

RCE COUNT (SYSTEM statement parameter)

RHDCPRLG (Utility program to print and clear the log area of the DD)

RHDCRUAL (System initiated run units used during dictionary access)

RHDCSGEN (System generation compiler under Release 10)

RHDCSGN1 (System generation compiler under Release 5.7)

RHDCSGN2 (System generation compiler under Release 5.7)

RLE COUNT (SYSTEM statement parameter)

RULOCKS (SYSTEM statement parameter)

S

SMP = Space Management Page
SOS = Short on Storage
SSC (task code for the online subschema compiler)
SVC = Supervisor Call
SYSLOCKS (SYSTEM statement parameter)
SYSGEN (Short for system generation)
SYSTRACE (SYSTEM statement parameter)

T

TCAM = Telecommunications Access Method
TP = Teleprocessing
TSIS = Technical Support Information System

U

UCF = Universal Communications Facility (Cullinet product)
USERTRACE (SYSTEM statement parameter)

V

VSAM = Virtual Sequential Access Method
VTAM = Virtual Telecommunications Access Method

W

WTOEXIT (Write To Operator Exit, a Cullinet-supplied exit which
    traps log and journal status messages written to the operator and
    automatically initiates log and journal archiving jobs)
WTOR = Write To Operator Request

Glossary

A

Abend: Abnormal ending of a program's processing

Area: IDMS/R databases are composed of areas. An area may contain one or more types of records. All occurrences of a given type of record are stored in the same area.

B

Backup: To create a copy of a database, file, or area for use if the primary database, file, or area becomes corrupted.

C

Central Version (CV): The mode of IDMS/R operation which permits multiple concurrent update access to database areas. Central Version operation is the most common mode of operation.

Checkpoint: A processing boundary marked on the journal file. BIND RUN UNIT, COMMIT, FINISH, and ROLLBACK statements cause a checkpoint to be written to the journal. If a run unit abends, IDMS/R rolls back all updates made by the run unit since the previous checkpoint and writes an abort checkpoint to the journal.

COMMIT or COMMIT ALL: DML statements that cause a checkpoint to be written to the journal file, signaling the end of one recovery unit and the beginning of another. In addition, COMMIT causes explicit and exclusive record locks to be released; COMMIT ALL causes all locks to be released.

Compile: The process of creating object code from source code

Currency: A run unit's 'position' in a database, i.e., a table where IDMS/R keeps track of the DBKEY for the last record accessed, and the last record accessed for each type of record, set, and area in the run unit's subschema.

D

Data portion of a database record: IDMS/R database records are composed of two parts, a data portion and a prefix portion. The data portion contains the application-supplied field values for the elements of the record. The prefix portion contains IDMS/R-supplied database keys of related records which are used as internal pointers by IDMS/R.

Database (DB): An IDMS/R database is a data structure grouping elements into records, relating records to each other in set relationships, grouping records into areas, and relating areas to database files. An IDMS/R database is defined in a schema. Access to the database is further refined through subschemas and Device Media Control Language, DMCL's.

Database key (DBKEY): The unique logical address of a database record. It is translated by IDMS/R to a physical disk address during database access.

Database load: The process of storing a large number of records in the database, typically an initial database load taking place just after a new database structure has been defined.

Data Definition Language (DDL): Syntax used to define and maintain database definitions

Data Dictionary Definition Language (DDDL): Syntax used to maintain information in data dictionary

Data Manipulation Language (DML): Statements coded in application programs to access IDMS/R databases

Device Media Control Language (DMCL): Statements input to the DMCL compiler naming database files, journal files, and file input/output buffer pools. The object module created after running the DMCL compiler is also called a DMCL.

Dialog: An ADS/O "program" is called a dialog.

E

Entity occurrence: A specific case of an entity type. For example, the CUSTOMER record is an occurrence of the RECORD entity type. There may be any number of occurrences of each entity type.

Entity type: A named component of the data processing environment about which data will be stored in the Data Dictionary. USER, RECORD, PROGRAM, etc., are examples of types of entities.

External Run Unit: Any requester of IDMS/R services that is executing in a different partition/region. This includes Batch programs (user programs and system utilities/compilers that run in batch) and native TP programs which contain embedded DML statements.

External teleprocessing monitor: A teleprocessing monitor, such as CICS, executing in a different partition/region than IDMS/R, yet handling communications with online terminals accessing IDMS/R databases.

F

File, database: A file which contains database records, i.e., a BDAM or VSAM file which has been defined in a schema and DMCL to contain database records, initialized by the IDMSINIT utility, and which programs access only through IDMS/R. Relationships between database records are easily maintained.

File, conventional or 'flat': A file accessed either randomly or sequentially using standard operating system access methods. Unlike databases, conventional files do not maintain data relationships.

G

Generation: The process of creating a load module based upon operator input, generating a dialog or map load module for example.

I

INFLIGHT: Run units which were in the midst of processing when the system abended.

Integrated Database Management System-Data Communications (IDMS-DC): The combination of database manager with full IDMS Data Communications facilities using either BTAM, VTAM, or TCAM access method to communicate with online terminals a Cullinet Product.

Internal run unit/task: Any user or system program that is executing in the same partition/region as the IDMS/R system. This includes DC programs, online system software such as Online mapping, Online IDD, etc., and ADS/O dialogs.

J

Journal: A file used by IDMS/R for storage of before and after images of updated records. Journal information is used to recover the database(s) from run unit abends, system failure, and disk errors.

L

Local mode: The mode of IDMS/R operation in which a single batch program uses a dedicated copy of IDMS/R database access logic, subschema, and DMCL modules.

Locks: Record and area locks are facilities of IDMS/R for prevention of concurrent update of records and/or areas.

Lock, Area: A flag set on the first space management page of an area, indicating that the area is unavailable for update by any IDMS/R program other that the IDMS/R program which set the lock. During normal startup processing, IDMS-CV locks all areas which will be updated during the run to prevent concurrent update of the areas by another CV or Local Mode IDMS. Only those run units running under the CV or Local Mode which set the area lock may update records in the area.

Lock, Record: IDMS-CV maintains run unit lock tables to keep track of the database keys of records locked by each run unit. A record which has been locked by one run unit is unavailable for update by another run unit; depending on the type of lock, the

record may also be unavailable for retrieval by another run
unit. Locks are either exclusive locks or shared locks. Locks
may be established implicitly or explicitly.

Lock, Explicit: A record lock set by a program or dialog explicitly
coding KEEP or KEEP EXCLUSIVE. KEEP requests an explicit
shared lock on the record. KEEP EXCLUSIVE requests an
explicit exclusive lock on the record.

Lock, Exclusive: An exclusive lock on a record prevents other run
units operating in UPDATE usage mode from retrieving or updating the record. Only the run unit which has exclusively
locked the record may update it. An exclusive lock is sometimes called a write lock.

Lock, Shared: A shared lock on a record prevents other run units
from updating the record. Many run units can have a shared
lock on the same record concurrently. A shared lock is sometimes called a read lock.

Lock, Implicit: Implicit locks are record locks set by IDMS-CV automatically during the normal processing of a run unit. CV
automatically maintains exclusive locks on all records updated
by a run unit, and shared locks on all records on which the run
unit has currency.

Log file: An ongoing record of system activity.

M

Multi-threaded: Capable of concurrent use by multiple tasks, run
units, programs, etc.

O

Occurrence: A specific case, for example, the XYZ Company customer record is an occurrence of the CUSTOMER record type.

P

Prefix portion of a database record: IDMS/R database records are
composed of two parts, a data portion and a prefix portion. The
data portion contains the field values for the elements of the
record. The prefix portion contains database keys of related
records which are used as internal pointers, i.e., logical
addresses, by IDMS/R.

Program: A module that can be loaded into main storage. This includes batch programs, native TP application programs, DC
programs, ADS/O dialogs, tables, subschema tables, database
procedures, user exits, etc.

Program, Native TP: Online programs that execute under an external TP monitor, typically CICS. If they contain embedded
DML statements, i.e., are coded with BIND, READY, access,
and FINISH statements to access records from an IDMS/R
database, then they are external run units.

Program, Nonreentrant: A user program that contains dynamically-modified code. One copy of the program may be used by only one task at a time. Nonresident, nonreentrant programs are loaded into the program pool.

Program, Nonresident: Any program that is loaded into IDMS/R main storage as needed, and overlaid in main storage when it is not in use and the storage is needed for some other program. This is the default treatment for user programs, dialogs, subschemas, etc. Response time for nonresident program execution often includes the time it takes to load the program, unless the program still happened to be in main storage from a previous execution.

Program, Reentrant: A user or system program that contains no dynamically-modified code, i.e., the processing of the program does not make any changes to the program itself. This means that a single copy of the program can be shared by several tasks, so that one copy of a program is executing concurrently for multiple terminal operators. All system programs are reentrant. Some user programs are reentrant, including dialogs, maps, tables, subschemas, and any fully reentrant assembly language DC programs.

Program, Resident: A user program loaded during startup processing into a portion of main storage and remains there for the duration of the run. Programs are declared resident by coding a sysgen PROGRAM statement for the program which specifies the parameter RESIDENT.

Pseudo-conversational: The technique of displaying a map, specifying the next program to process, and returning control to the telecommunications monitor, thus releasing resources during the pseudo-converse. When the operator responds, the next program begins processing.

Pseudo-converse: The time between display of a map and the operator's subsequent response.

Punch: Using the PUNCH statement to generate card image output from the IDMSDDDL or system generation compilers

Q

Quiesce point, level zero: A time when no run units are processing, i.e., just after a run unit ends processing, when that run unit was the only active run unit.

R

Recovery unit: All IDMS/R-related processing between journal checkpoints by a run unit. The recovery unit defines the data to be restored if the run unit abends.

Restore: The process of restoring the contents of a database, area, or file to a previous condition, involving backup copies and/or journal information.

Run unit: All IDMS/R-related processing of a program or dialog from its first call to IDMS/R, either a BIND RUN UNIT statement or a READY statement, to termination of IDMS/R processing, either a FINISH or ROLLBACK statement or a program abend.

S

Schema: A schema is the source definition of an IDMS/R database, grouping elements into records, grouping records into areas, relating records to other records in set relationships, and relating areas to database files. The schema defines the entire database, including all elements, records, sets, areas, and files.

Single-threaded: Capable of use by only one program, run unit, etc., at a time.

Space management page (SMP): The first page of each database area. Large areas may have additional space management pages. IDMS/R uses space management pages to keep track of the free space available for storage of records in the database area. In addition, area locks are maintained on the first space management page of each area.

Subschema: A subschema includes the elements, records, sets, and areas which programs, dialogs, or users (through OLQ for example) will be allowed to access. A subschema also may limit the permissible functions by prohibiting certain verbs, such as ERASE, or using the Logical Record Facility. Unlike the schema, a subschema provides a limited view of the database, including only those elements, records, sets, and areas needed for particular processing.

Synonym: Alternate name for an element, record, etc., which may be documented in the data dictionary.

T

Type: A general category, for example, CUSTOMER is a type of record defined in a database schema. The records for ZYX Company, DEF Company, etc., are occurrences of the CUSTOMER record type.

U

User: An online terminal operator, typically end-users in a production system and application developers in a test system.

Utility: Special purpose programs for database maintenance, reporting, backup, and recovery.

W

Warmstart: The recovery processing the system goes through when it is brought back up after a crash.

Index